Religion and Politics

The International Library of Politics and Comparative Government

General Editor: David Arter
Associate Editor: Gordon Smith

Titles in the Series

France
David S. Bell

**Constitutions and Constitutionalism –
Practice**
Richard Bellamy and Dario Castiglione

The United Nations, Volumes I and II
Sam Daws and Paul Taylor

Italy, Volumes I and II
Mark Donovan

Australia and New Zealand
Hugh V. Emy

Germany, Volumes I and II
Klaus H. Goetz

Revolution and Political Change
Alexander J. Groth

China, Volumes I, II and III
Lin Chun

Feminism and Politics, Volumes I and II
Joni Lovenduski

Religion and Politics
John T.S. Madeley

Israel
Gregory S. Mahler

**Comparative Public Administration
Volumes I and II**
Moshe Maor and Jan-Erik Lane

New Politics
*Ferdinand Müller-Rommel
and Thomas Poguntke*

Elections and Voting Behaviour
Pippa Norris

Legislatures and Legislators
Philip Norton

The European Union, Volumes I and II
Neill Nugent

Transitions to Democracy
Geoffrey Pridham

United Kingdom, Volumes I and II
R.A.W. Rhodes

European Security Organisations
Trevor Salmon

**The Media, Journalism and
Democracy**
Margaret Scammell and Holli Semetko

National and International Security
Michael Sheehan

The United States, Volumes I, II and III
Alan Ware

**The Politics of the Postcommunist
World, Volumes I and II**
Stephen White and Daniel N. Nelson

Party Systems
Steven B. Wolinetz

Political Parties
Steven B. Wolinetz

Religion and Politics

Edited by

John T.S. Madeley

The London School of Economics and Political Science, London, UK

ASHGATE
DARTMOUTH

Published by
Dartmouth Publishing Company
Ashgate Publishing Limited
Gower House
Croft Road
Aldershot
Hants GU11 3HR
England

Ashgate Publishing Company
Suite 420
101 Cherry Street
Burlington, VT 05401-4405
USA

Ashgate website: http://www.ashgate.com

British Library Cataloguing in Publication Data
Religion and politics. – (The international library of
   politics and comparative government)
   1. Religion and politics 2. Comparative government 3. Church
   and state
   I. Madeley, John T. S.
   322.1

Library of Congress Control Number: 2002113031

ISBN 1 85521 906 9

Printed in Great Britain by The Cromwell Press, Trowbridge, Wiltshire

Contents

PART III   RELIGION AND ELECTORAL POLITICS

PART IV   RELIGION, PUBLIC POLICY AND THE POLITICS OF IDENTITY

Acknowledgements

The editor and publishers wish to thank the following for permission to use copyright material.

American Political Science Association for the essay: Arend Lijphart (1979), 'Religious vs. Linguistic vs. Class Voting: The "Crucial Experiment" of Comparing Belgium, Canada, South Africa, and Switzerland', *The American Political Science Review*, **73**, pp. 442–58.

Baylor University for the essay: John G. Francis (1992), 'The Evolving Regulatory Structure of European Church–State Relationships', *Journal of Church and State*, **34**, pp. 775–804.

Blackwell Publishers Ltd for the essays: Howard Caygill and Alan Scott (1996), 'The Basic Law versus the Basic Norm? The Case of the Bavarian Crucifix Order', *Political Studies*, **44**, (Special Issue), pp. 505–16. Copyright © 1996 Political Studies Association; Brian Girvin (1986), 'Social Change and Moral Politics: The Irish Constitutional Referendum 1983', *Political Studies*, **34**, pp. 61–81; Lauri Karvonen (1993), 'In From the Cold? Christian Parties in Scandinavia', *Scandinavian Political Studies*, **16**, pp. 25–48; John McGarry and Brendan O'Leary (1995), 'Warring Gods? Theological Tales', in John McGarry and Brendan O'Leary, *Explaining Northern Ireland: Broken Images*, Oxford: Blackwells, pp. 171–213, 463–71; Geoffrey C. Layman and Edward G. Carmines (1997), 'Culture Conflict in American Politics: Religious Traditionalism, Postmaterialism, and U.S. Political Behavior', *The Journal of Politics*, **59**, pp. 751–77.

Cambridge University Press for the essay: Kees Van Kersbergen and Uwe Becker (1988), 'The Netherlands: A Passive Social Democratic Welfare State in a Christian Democratic Ruled Society', *Journal of Social Policy*, **17**, pp. 477–99. Copyright © 1988 Cambridge University Press.

Comparative Politics for the essays: Daniel H. Levine (1986), 'Religion and Politics in Comparative and Historical Perspective', *Comparative Politics*, **19**, pp. 95–122; Mark Juergensmeyer (1995), 'The New Religious State', *Comparative Politics*, **27**, pp. 379–91.

Dædalus, Journal of the American Academy of Arts and Sciences for the essays: N.J. Demerath III (1991), 'Religious Capital and Capital Religions: Cross-Cultural and Non-Legal Factors in the Separation of Church and State', *Dædalus*, **120**, pp. 21–40; Juan J. Linz (1991), 'Church and State in Spain from the Civil War to the Return of Democracy', *Dædalus*, **120**, pp. 159–78.

Elsevier Science for the essay: Sarath Amunugama (1991), 'Buddhaputra and Bhumiputra? Dilemmas of Modern Sinhala Buddhist Monks in Relation to Ethnic and Political Conflict', *Religion*, **21**, pp. 115–39.

Frank Cass Publishers for the essays: Eliezer Don-Yehiya (1987), 'Jewish Messianism, Religious Zionism and Israeli Politics: The Impact and Origins of Gush Emunim', *Middle Eastern Studies*, **24**, pp. 215–34; John Madeley (1982), 'Politics and the Pulpit: The Case of Protestant Europe', *Religion in West European Politics*, **5**, pp. 149–71.

Series Preface

The International Library of Politics and Comparative Government brings together in one series the most significant journal articles to appear in the field of comparative politics in the last twenty-five years or so. The aim is to render readily accessible to teachers, researchers and students an extensive range of essays which, together, provide an indispensable basis for understanding both the established conceptual terrain and the new ground being broken in the fast changing field of comparative political analysis.

The series is divided into three major sections: *Institutional Studies, Thematic Studies* and *Country Studies*. The *Institutional* volumes focus on the comparative investigation of the basic processes and components of the modern pluralist polity, including electoral behaviour, parties and party systems, interest groups, constitutions, legislatures and executives. There are also collections dealing with such major international actors as the European Union and United Nations.

The *Thematic* volumes address those contemporary problems, processes and issues which have assumed a particular salience for politics and policy-making in the late twentieth century. Such themes include: democratization, revolution and political change, 'New Politics', nationalism, terrorism, the military, the media, human rights, consociationalism and the challenges to mainstream party political ideologies.

The *Country* volumes are particularly innovative in applying a comparative perspective to a consideration of the political science tradition in individual states, both large and small. The distinctive features of the national literature are highlighted and the wider significance of developments is evaluated.

A number of acknowledged experts have been invited to act as editors for the series; they preface each volume with an introductory essay in which they review the basis for the selection of articles, and suggest future directions of research and investigation in the subject area.

The series is an invaluable resource for all those working in the field of comparative government and politics.

DAVID ARTER
Professor of Nordic Politics
University of Aberdeen

GORDON SMITH
Emeritus Professor of Government
London School of Economics and Political Science

Introduction

This volume more than any of the others in the International Library of Politics and Comparative Government series is devoted to a subject area which cross-cuts conventional sub-disciplinary boundaries in the study of comparative politics. A good claim can even be made that significant connections between religion and politics can be identified in all of the thematic areas mentioned in the Series Preface: democratization, revolution and political change, 'New Politics', nationalism, terrorism, the military, the media, human rights, consociationalism and the challenges to mainstream political ideologies.[1] Nor is this any longer an observation which only one-eyed enthusiasts with (more often than not) an unusual religious background can be expected to make. Over the past twenty-five years the study of religion and politics – and especially of the impact of the first on the second – has witnessed a veritable renaissance. Political philosophers and historians of political thought have always remained aware of the importance of religious ideas and motifs in political philosophy in certain periods – and the revival from the early 1970s of normative debates between liberals, communitarians and others has occasioned a return to some of the foundational issues regarding the ethical dimensions of the state in which the place of religion has again become controverted.[2] More empirically-oriented political scientists on the other hand have until recently tended to treat 'the religious factor' in politics as little more than a curiosity, a survival, the traces of which could shortly be expected to disappear. In this they shared – and many still share – the core assumption of most mainstream social scientists of the last century that, whether for good or ill, modernization entails secularization, that is, the progressive decline and probable, eventual extinction of religion as a social and political force. The plausibility or cogency of this assumption has been placed in doubt, however, by political events of recent decades which appear to indicate that religion, with its related issues and concerns, has unexpected staying power. For some 25 years – the period from which the essays in this volume were selected – commentators and scholars have claimed that there has been an ongoing 'resurgence of religion', whether as religion itself, or as a factor in politics.[3]

By common account 1979 was the symbolic year in which secularization assumptions were most comprehensively confounded, if not destroyed. This was the year of Jonestown, Guyana, with the mass suicide and/or killing of 914 persons, of the mobilization of the American Christian Right in preparation for the 1980 US presidential campaign, and of Pope John Paul II's visits to both the Puebla Conference of Latin American Bishops in Mexico and his Polish homeland with its momentous consequences over the following decade. It was also of course the year which started with the Ayatollah Khomeini's return to Iran to erect the first new clerical state of the modern era, and ended with an attack by Islamist militants on the Great Mosque in Mecca. If 1979 was something of a climacteric it was preceded by a number of auguries which can be identified in retrospect; thus, Kepel identifies 1975 as the central date of what he calls 'the great reversal of the 1970s' while others have pointed to the recrudescence of conflict in Northern Ireland in the late 1960s.[4] Contemporary comment on the latter event illustrates one of the features of most of the dramatic occurrences, which are often taken to exemplify religious 'resurgence': a profusion of instant scholarship often focusing on religion as the key variable in the most diverse and complex conflicts. Thus in 1969, the year the dormant conflict erupted again into major violence, the journalist Andrew Boyd published the pot-boiling 'Holy War in Belfast'.[5] Even Richard Rose in his much more considered and scholarly analysis published two years later presented Northern Ireland as a bi-confessional society riven by unbargainable conflicts rooted in religion, the effects of which gravely undermined claims to political legitimacy.[6] And in his review of the vast range of writing and research on the conflict which had already accumulated by 1990, John Whyte found that the one thread in terms of which it was possible to relate most of the items to each other was their assessment of the place of religion in the conflict.[7]

As the first essay reprinted here points out, writing and publishing on religion and politics became 'something of a growth industry' after 1979, the products of which have been very uneven in quality; some of the 'instant scholarship' generated even attributed 'to religion all the decisive impact once reserved for Marxism or modernization', while the ten works reviewed in the essay also indicated that sound scholarship of theoretical significance was to be found across a wide range of topics.[8] Since then a great deal of good work has been done on a great number of issues dispersed over large expanses of both space and time. The essays assembled here indicate some of the richness of the field or, rather, of the *thematic interconnection* between religion and politics, since it is not clear that one can speak of an 'established conceptual terrain' such as can be said to characterize, for example, the study of nationalism or 'New Politics' with their core debates, approaches and schools.[9] Even the division of the selected essays into four sections can be said to be speculative; certainly, some essays could have appeared in more than one section. The selection has been made in part with an eye precisely to indicating the richness and diversity of approaches, objects and styles of analysis, as well as the range of topics. Some items are included because they span widely and facilitate the development of comparative perspectives even where their actual conclusions might be open to serious question. Others are included on the basis that they illustrate distinct approaches to the chosen subject matter or that they deal with very particular objects of study. Yet others provide a critical conspectus of some core debates in the literature.

Religion and Regime

The first section brings together essays which in one way or another address the question of how and why different religions relate differently to questions affecting the structure and legitimacy of political regimes. Collectively they span most of the continents and several of the world's principal religious traditions, particularly over the modern period. As required by the nature of the subject matter however, all, in addition, make significant reference to historical continuities and discontinuities, so extending still further the generic scope.[10] Modernist views tend to discount the importance of such 'carry-overs', stressing for example the claim that the template of the modern state, which emerged in Europe in the sixteenth and seventeenth centuries, was designed precisely to exorcize the threat of religious conflict; alternatively, that since the French Revolution the emergence of other political, economic and cultural forces has been such as to consign institutional religion to irrelevance or, at least, marginality.

Recent study has led to a re-evaluation of this perspective however and provided a wealth of evidence, which supports the view that the relevance of religion to politics in the modern world is not only long-standing but also remarkably persistent, at least in some settings.

In the course of reviewing ten studies of the mutual interaction of religion and politics in different time periods and cultural contexts Levine's essay (Chapter 1) provides a comparative historical perspective, which illustrates the breadth and variety of the field while identifying some of the common theoretical challenges. On this basis he argues that '[r]eligious ideas, structures, and practices have a logic of their own' and that it is impossible to understand the way politics and religion interact unless this logic is understood and appreciated. Nor is the logic the same for all systems of religious ideas and interests; as the four studies of millenarianism he reviews illustrate, for example, the idea that religion invariably aligns itself with political conservatism or reaction is palpably false. The discussion of covenantal religion in early North America, liberation theology in 1970s Latin America, and of Iranian Shi'ism over the centuries further underlines the point. Halliday's essay (Chapter 2, an extended and revised version of an essay which first appeared in 1983) approaches the almost iconic case of the Iranian revolution from a very different perspective however. While Levine (and Arjomond, one of the authors Levine reviews) tend to view the impact of religion in politics as demonstrating 'the creative power of ideas and their ability to move individuals, groups, and large collectivities in new and unexpected ways', Halliday sees in the Iranian Revolution a challenge to show 'how an apparently religious event was the result of other, more mundane, processes'. He confronts the paradox of how it could at one and the same time be 'the first ever "modern" revolution' and the first contemporary revolution to be religious in orientation: 'For the first time in modern history (that is, since 1789), a revolution took place in which the dominant ideology, forms of organization, leading personnel and proclaimed goal were all religious in appearance and inspiration.' He points out that some of the less remarked ideological features of the revolution also owed much to its religious inspiration; its rejection of ideas of historical progress, material improvement, national assertion, historical legitimation, and democratic sovereignty were both patently anti-modern and rooted in a particular understanding of Shi'ite Islam. In his view this was 'a comprehensively reactionary revolution' which nonetheless graphically illustrated the 'ideological ductility' of Islam and the related notion that there is not one Islam but many, each with its local colouration.

While the Iranian revolution and its consequences may be taken as a spectacular illustration of the reactionary uses and tendencies of religion in certain circumstances, Gill's essay (Chapter 3) serves as a reminder of how and under what circumstances a once-reactionary religious tradition can shift in progressive directions. Latin American Catholicism in the 1950s (and in some cases up into the 1970s) appeared to present a copybook demonstration of how institutional religion seemed to have an 'elective affinity' for repressive authoritarian regimes. The analysis indicates however that in some parts of the region, but not others, Catholicism moved into opposition against dictatorial rule and suggests that the explanation for these countervailing shifts can be found in the contrasting conditions facing the church in different countries. Where the church was challenged by the growth of Protestantism, it shifted to a 'membership retention strategy' which required a greater sensitivity to the needs and interests of the membership, which led in turn to a regime-critical stance. Gill's essay is a notable example of the uses to which rational choice theory and approaches can be put in the fields of study of both religion itself and religion-and-politics.[11]

The recrudescence in the late 1960s of the Northern Ireland conflict, which on the face of it pits Catholics against Protestants, as in the days of Europe's wars of religion, has also presented a challenge of explanation to political scientists. McGarry and O'Leary (Chapter 4) approached the question of what role religion has played in the Northern Ireland conflict by means of a critical review and analysis of secondary treatments which purport to explain the conflict. They identify and present four different types of religious explanation, rejecting each in turn. They even reject the fourth (that religion matters in maintaining and reinforcing social boundaries between Catholics and Protestants) despite accepting 'the salience of religion as an ethnic marker', arguing that 'ethnic divisions cannot be reduced to religion, or church policy on education, or mixed marriages'. They state, uncontroversially, that while Protestants and Catholics are divided by religion, they are also divided by differences in economic and political power, by historical experience, and, most intensely, by national political identity, but do not address the argument that these differences themselves might only exist on the basis of four hundred years of state-directed religious discrimination. More controversially they state: 'Although we share the liberal prejudice that religious fanaticism and dogma are likely to be productive of violence, we are not persuaded that they are the keys to understanding violence in Northern Ireland. If one wants to argue that there is an important religious dimension to the conflict it is more prudent [sic] to argue that there exists a conflict between "civil religions" or "secular religions" i.e. to maintain that each community worships its own nation and does so in an exclusivist manner'.[12]

Amunugamar (Chapter 5) and Vrcan (Chapter 6) also examine bitter ethnic conflicts in which religious identities ostensibly play an important part in defining the conflict situation in, respectively, Sri Lanka and former Yugoslavia. In both cases a tension is observed between universalistic religious principles and the particularist interests of communities of adherents which tend to subvert them. In Sri Lanka the means by which a seemingly pacific religious tradition (Therevada Buddhism) became associated with rising violence from the early 1980s is explained in terms of the notion of Sinhalese 'custodianship' of Buddhism being so strong that monks were willing to rationalize the use of violence, even though it contradicted the tenets of Buddhism. In Yugoslavia the idea that the armed conflicts of the early 1990s should be seen as religious wars concerned to protect the religious integrity and authenticity of particular 'faith communities' is quickly dismissed, but the many subsidiary ways in which religion has been actively engaged and implicated in the conflicts are briefly reviewed. Finally, Kalyvas (Chapter 7) examines the case of Belgium where a vigorous religious conflict in the late nineteenth century eventuated in an accommodation between what is presented as a distinctively 'a-liberal' Roman Catholicism and the liberal-democratic state. The argument is made that this paradoxical outcome can only be explained if attention is paid to the Catholic church's interests rather than to normative religious principles. Kalyvas refers to the distinction developed by some Catholic theologians between the ideal 'thesis' and the actual 'hypothesis' which emerges in particular conjunctures, the former representing a religiously ideal outcome, the latter all that can be attained under given circumstances.

The Politics of Church–State Relations

What is conventionally called 'church–state relations' is potentially an extraordinarily rich field for comparative political analysis but it is one which has been as much neglected in recent decades as it was once intensively cultivated by political philosophers and theologians in the early-modern period in Europe.[13] There is an enormous body of American legal scholarship which deals with church–state relations in the USA; much of it refers to the political circumstances surrounding the adoption of the first amendment with its guarantee of free exercise and its ban on church establishment, the judicial politics of its interpretation and implementation, and other complex matters with a more or less direct connection to the concerns of comparative politics.[14] The sophisticated conceptual apparatus, which has been produced by this long and strong tradition, developing as it has in the very particular circumstances of the USA, has however been little used by political scientists. Demerath (Chapter 8) argues that, despite impressions to the contrary, American experience in this field is not in fact so completely idiosyncratic relative to that of other culturally quite different contexts such as in Pakistan, Thailand, Indonesia and Sweden; he argues in particular that although these countries can (or could) be classified as 'religious states' with officially recognized religions, they each in fact display a functional separation of religion and government, similar to that characteristic of the USA. Most of the other contributions, however, illustrate the contrasts rather than the similarities which exist in this field. Keddie's essay (Chapter 9) on secularism in Turkey deals with a case where secularization is better understood as a (political) project than a (sociological) process, a project moreover to which the military–political elite of that country has been devoted for most of the last century but which since the 1970s Islamist campaigners (or 'fundamentalists') have increasingly challenged. Instead of the overused and frequently misused terms 'fundamentalism' and 'fundamentalists', Juergensmeyer (Chapter 10) prefers to use the term 'religious nationalists' on grounds that their motivations are as political as they are religious. In so doing he avoids the option of 'reducing' religion to nationalism, implying instead that religious nationalists are committed to a struggle for new forms of national order based on religious values, so challenging central liberal democratic assumptions at a time of liberal democracy's seeming ascendancy after the collapse of communism.

Comparative politics, especially in this field, has to address comparisons across time as well as space and the Burns essay (Chapter 11) reviews the processes of ideological change which occurred in the papacy over the century up to Vatican II and led it to moderate its integralist political ambitions in favour of a narrower concentration on matters of faith and morals. The Catholic church's complete reversal in the mid-1960s on the matter of its role in temporal government constitutes an interesting case of religious change responding to structural constraints and opportunities, which illuminates some of the more recent shifts in religious–political alignments. Within the narrower confines of Israeli politics the rise of Gush Emunim in the 1970s, with its commitment to settlement in the occupied territories as the fulfilment of a divine mandate, is concerned with the countervailing tendency towards *greater* political involvement, not least by means of direct action. Don-Yehiya's essay (Chapter 12) stresses the influence on the followers of the movement of one particular religious leader, Rav Zvi Yehuda, with his particularistic version of religious Zionism emphasizing the territorial–political dimension of Jewish redemption. Despite its relatively short half-life the impact of the movement has been enormous not least by acting as a fulcrum around which the politics of Israel have been 're-Judaized' and, partly as a consequence, the security predicament in the whole Middle East rendered even more intractable in recent years. In this context the anodyne term 'church–state relations' seems doubly ill-suited to the ideological 'Sturm und Drang' which has centred on the religious–political character of the state of Israel; it serves nonetheless to illustrate both the variability and the potential importance of these relationships.

Francis's essay (Chapter 13) on the regulatory structure of church–state relations in Europe addresses a much broader canvas and provides a useful taxonomy of patterns and mechanisms. As he points out no European state has ever fully adopted the liberal tradition of the religious neutrality of the state as this is understood in the USA, even though a clear trend can be identified in the direction of decreasing state 'interference' in the internal affairs of the main churches. The continuing action of churches as 'successfully incorporated interest groups' means, however, that they continue, directly or indirectly, to wield a degree of influence over important areas of policy within the domain of the state. Linz's essay (Chapter 14) surveys the dramatic shifts over the last century of the Catholic church in Spain. As a wholly Catholic state which came into existence on the back of an anti-Islamic crusade of reconquest and the site of the last of Europe's religious wars (in the 1930s), Spain saw the establishment between 1945 and 1957 of full-blown clericalism under the aegis of Franco's authoritarian version of 'national Catholicism'. Progressive shifts from 1957 on, however, have led to a situation whereby after the introduction of the 1978 constitution the country can be held up as a 'model of a friendly or at least nonantagonistic separation of church and state'. It is interesting to note that the model so recently adopted differs significantly from the American separation model insofar as it allows for a continuing cooperation between church and state. In this respect it is closer to the 'positive neutrality' which many American commentators of a conservative stripe are now pressing for.[15]

Religion and Electoral Politics

One of the areas where the impact of the religious factor on politics has been most frequently remarked is in that of competitive mass politics, as it has been subjected to both extensive and intensive analysis since the diffusion of survey and other quantitative data and techniques after 1945. For long it was the impact of social class, which understandably received most attention to the extent that in 1960 Seymour Martin Lipset could portray electoral competition in the liberal democracies as more than anything an 'expression of the democratic class struggle'.[16] Seven years later Lipset co-authored with Stein Rokkan a seminal essay on party systems and voter alignments which presented a much more nuanced picture, however, in which the role of religious cleavages in the formation and operation of Europe's party systems received a prominent place.[17] Janda's essay (Chapter 15) confirms that the prevalence of politically relevant religious cleavages is not confined to Europe; in an analysis spanning 150 parties in 53 nations he confirms that although the influence of religion on party support is less pervasive than region, it is much more salient or critical where it does occur. Lijphart's complementary analysis (Chapter 16) also confirms the strength of the impact of religious (relative to class and linguistic) cleavages, if by a different route. He runs what he calls a 'crucial experiment', which involves comparing the four countries with competitive party systems where all three cleavage bases coexist and concludes that in the contest between the three determinants of party choice, religion emerges as the victor with language a strong runner-up and class a distant third. In this context Lijphart identifies what he calls a paradox of religious voting, which raises the question why it seems to persist even where religious issues cannot be said to be particularly salient in public political debate.

As a quick overview of all the essays just referred to makes clear, the strength of religious cleavages in long-established liberal democracies is particularly noteworthy where Catholicism is strongly represented, whether as a historically hegemonic creed or as a strong minority presence. The Madeley essay (Chapter 17) lays this point out most clearly through a reanalysis of data from seventeen different West European countries. It also shows, however, that the correlation between the proportion of the population of Catholic adherence and the strength of the religious factor is not linear; rather, the countries of mixed religious adherence are, on the measure used, just as much subject to the impact of the religious factor in politics as are the overwhelmingly Catholic ones. Its relative weakness and marginality in the overwhelmingly Protestant countries of northern Europe on the other hand calls for some explanation which goes beyond mere confessional labelling and this is addressed in both the Madeley and Karvonen essays. Karvonen (Chapter 18) examines the record of the Christian parties in Scandinavia and finds them to represent distinctive traditions of religious revivalism (in the otherwise monochrome Lutheran settings) whose electoral vicissitudes are to be explained by their capacity to act as channels for protest voting. The conclusion emerges that the explanation for the differential incidence of religious parties and religious voting is to be sought partly in the structure of church–state relations, which critically affects patterns of interest, and partly in the nature of religious cleavage patterns which in 'Protestant Europe' is related to religious differences both internal and external to the historically dominant churches.

The essays by Bruce (Chapter 19) and Layman and Carmines (Chapter 20) address the paradoxical case of the USA, historically a predominantly Protestant immigrant society, where the last two decades have witnessed a return to political prominence of conservative religious forces, which had last featured strongly in the 1920s.[18] Layman and Carmines argue on the basis of a principal components analysis that it is contrasting cultural orientations, involving on one side religious traditionalism (or, more popularly, 'religious fundamentalism'), which underlie this phenomenon rather than the distinction between materialist and post-materialist orientations which have been the subject of so much recent attention by Ronald Inglehart and his co-researchers. They conclude that when citizens are concerned about cultural matters such as abortion, homosexual rights, the use of prayer in the public schools, and so on, it is their inherited religious orientations, rather than the degree to which they might subscribe to postmaterialist values, which informs their political response. Bruce reviews the history of the new Christian Right in America including what at the time of the essay (1990) was seen as its relative failure and adduces reasons why, because of the highly pluralistic structure of American religion, it can probably never succeed in becoming anything more than an active pressure group for the views of a religious minority. This conclusion supports and illustrates Bruce's continued endorsement of the orthodox model of secularization.

In the other superpower of the cold war era, Russia, secularizing trends in recent years seemed to have been decisively reversed as traditional religion – in this case Russian Orthodoxy – seemed to be making a comeback with the end of communism. A number of dramatic moves were made to reconnect with the country's religious past in continuation of the rapprochement which actually predated the end of the Soviet Union and is probably best symbolized by the celebrations of the church's millennium in 1988. Since then the church's profile has been transformed from what it was under the Soviet regime, although as the essay by Stephen White *et al.* (Chapter 21) makes clear its political impact has remained modest. There appears to be ample evidence for the strength of conservative social values amongst religious believers but little prospect on this analysis for the likely emergence of a religious–political movement similar to that found in the only remaining superpower. Meantime the leadership of the Russian Orthodox church continues to promote its interests, not least by calling for restrictions on the proliferation of non-traditional sects and cults, which has occurred in the context of the new religious freedoms introduced in 1990.

Religion, Public Policy and the Politics of Identity

This group of essays introduces work done in two relatively new growth areas in political science: policy studies and the study of cultural conflict in both of which the role of religion has given rise to much discussion. In a manner reminiscent of the 'rediscovery' of the importance of religion in electoral competition, Castles (Chapter 22) argues that the religious factor is as relevant to understanding cross-national variance in a wide range of public policy outcomes as is the impact of socio-economic and political factors. The range spans much more widely than, for example, the education and narrowly-defined 'politics of morality' issues, which have been of perennial concern to many churches, and includes broad welfare-state and labour-market issues especially, Castles argues, where gender-related outcomes are at issue. The existence of a Catholic 'family of nations' with significant family resemblances is outlined, although parts of this argument have been vigorously contested.[19] Van Kersbergen and Becker (Chapter 23) also argue for the relevance of the religious factor in the construction of distinctive patterns of welfare-state provision in their analysis of the Netherlands where Christian, rather than Social, democracy was the leading political force in the relevant period of welfare-state extension and expansion. The Dutch pattern is presented, not so much as a weaker form of the social democratic pattern which prevails, for example, in Scandinavia, but as a distinctive form which reflects the influence of a particular set of doctrines and preferences peculiar to Dutch religious groups, both Catholic and Protestant.

While broader public policy issue areas have been scrutinized for the impact of the religious factor, other more traditional issues relating to religious freedom continue to arise. Thus, the issue of the recognition of Scientology as a religious body – thereby receiving the protection, even privileges, proper to religious bodies – has arisen in many jurisdictions, while in France the issue of whether Islamic girls should be allowed to wear the *foulard* headdress (as required by some traditional Muslims) in public schools became a major symbolic issue in the late 1980s. Caygill and Scott (Chapter 24) analyse another of the symptomatic issues of this sort, which highlights controversial aspects of church–state relations and their wider implications, in Germany. In the case examined, that of the Bavarian Crucifix Order, which was finally determined by a judgement of the German constitutional court in 1995, the underlying issue is argued to revolve around the question of the cultural identity of a local community and what rights such communities can rightfully claim.

The Cooper essay (Chapter 25) addresses questions posed by the contrasting treatment of 'peace' issues as between Protestants and Catholics in West Germany. In the context of a broad presentation of the handling of these issues from the 1940s to the 1980s, she argues that the contrast can only be explained by differences between the two traditions in doctrine and organizational structure. The analysis also carries forward in time the discussion of the changing relationship between Catholicism and liberal democracy addressed in the Burns essay and suggests that the practical implications of the reforms instituted at Vatican II took a long time to register in certain parts of the Catholic world. Girvin's essay (Chapter 26) on the 1983 Irish constitutional referendum on abortion also illustrates the variability between different contexts in the operation of the religious factor in politics; although it is not *de jure* established, the Catholic Church in Ireland has *de facto* been a very powerful institution for most of the twentieth century. The 1983 referendum serves both as a latter-day reminder of how churches, in the past and still on occasion, can exert their influence, and as a demonstration of the increasingly obvious limits to such power. Issues related to Catholic social doctrine have continued periodically to rack the politics of the Irish republic; most recently, in March 2002, a third constitutional referendum on abortion failed to tighten the ban in a manner approved by the church. As Girvin points out, conflicts around matters of this sort have had the effect, novel in Ireland, of exposing – or even creating – political division along lines of religious cleavage internal to Irish Catholicism.

Asad's essay (Chapter 27) on the broader implications of the Rushdie affair in Britain serves to link it with the more generic problems arising from the fact of multiculturalism. Questions about the politics of difference or identity have become ever more prominent in the decade since the essay was published, in particular under the impact of events following the terror attacks in New York and Washington in September 2001. The polemical tone reflects the sensitivity of the issue and its ability to generate (or at least attract) heated comment; the politicization of religious traditions by or on behalf of Muslim minority groups, with its potentially profound implications for politics, has been partially realized not least in dialectical response to the advances made by organizations on the radical right in many parts of the world. Prodromou (Chapter 28) also makes a provocative case in respect of the way the world of Eastern Orthodoxy has often been, and continues to be, presented in Western political science and commentary. She claims that Huntington's typification of Orthodoxy in his highly controversial 1993 essay on a coming 'clash of civilizations' unfairly stigmatizes it, along with other religious traditions (in particular the Islamic), as inherently authoritarian, reactionary and undemocratic.[20] A number of other works are also taken as evidence that an emergent neo-modernization perspective obscures understanding of unfamiliar religious and other cultural traditions, which should, following Weber, be interpreted and understood first in their own terms. In the case of Orthodoxy in particular a thorough and unprejudiced analysis of church–state relations over time would, she argues, undermine the stereotyped thinking evident in much Western commentary and analysis.

The Research Agenda

No volume of readings can hope to do justice to the great variety and richness of recent scholarship on the interconnection of religion and politics in any one part of the world, let alone across it. Even restricting the scope to questions of particular interest to empirically-minded political scientists with an interest in comparative politics does not help greatly; scholars of many disciplines and approaches specializing in the study of widely dispersed areas of the world in different time periods have produced work which would qualify under that heading.[21] The selection made here is intended to reflect this variety and richness while also serving to point up areas where the need for further research is indicated.

As a field of study where different disciplines meet and intermingle, it is not surprising that some basic methodological issues should often come to the fore. In his introduction to a 1992 volume of essays on religion and politics, the sociologist Robert Wuthnow argued that then-contemporary theories of religion and politics such as those provided by modernization, critical and world-systems theory needed to be 'revised, synthesized, or abandoned altogether'.[22] In a more positive vein he called for an 'interpretive' approach to theory directed towards providing interpretative frameworks which make it possible to grasp the meaning of events. This would seem to be close to Levine's view quoted above to the effect that religious–political interconnections can only be properly understood if it is appreciated that religious ideas, structures and practices have a logic of their own. Conventional social science approaches tend by contrast to emphasize explanation and control, instead of interpretation and understanding, and the more recent developments in political science approaches, such as rational choice modelling and 'the new institutionalism', continue to maintain this emphasis. The study of religion and politics presents a classic field where the rival claims of these approaches can be tested out and their mutual compatibility, even perhaps their complementarity, investigated.

Prodromou's suggestion about studying church–state relations as a way to getting beyond stereotyped thinking about Eastern Orthodoxy's 'caesaropapist' image suggests a direction for future research which is already beginning to bear fruit.[23] As already noted above, the political opening up of central and eastern Europe after the fall of communism presents a series of new challenges in which the place of the churches and religion is at the forefront of controversy. Recent developments in both the 'new institutionalism' and the study of regulation in political science should help to strengthen the theoretical grounding of research in this area, in addition to work done on the aetiology of religious–political groups and organizations as they develop. The ongoing trend towards applying rational choice approaches to the study of religion and politics can also enrich the field by revisiting and reanalysing historical conjunctures as well as those of the present, if only to demonstrate with clarity the limits to which such explanatory approaches can successfully be pressed.[24]

Two cross-disciplinary areas of research, which will doubtless continue to be of interest to students of comparative politics arise in connection with nationalism and fundamentalism studies, where rival approaches continue to contest the territory.[25] In the new turbulence of the world post September 2001, both internally to nation states and globally, the role of religion in politics will continue to draw attention to the incendiary possibilities of conflicts based in part on mutual incomprehension and antipathy as well as, in part, on conflicting interests. Liberal–democratic theorists' insistence on the religious neutrality of the state and, more heroically, of an emergent new world order will in all probability be contested by religionists, both moderate and radical, so that the study of possible alternative systems of amicable accommodation, mutual adjustment and conflict-resolution will continue to be an urgent political priority, as well as a standing challenge to political science.

Notes

1   See Series Preface, above p. xi.
2   See, for example, the contributions to R.B. Douglass, G.M. Mara and H.S. Richardson (eds) (1990), *Liberalism and the Good*, London: Routledge.

3   See, for example, the recurrence of the term resurgence in the titles of: R. Antoun and M. Hegland
    (eds) (1987), *Religious Resurgence: Contemporary Cases in Islam, Christianity and Judaism*,
    Syracuse: Syracuse UP; E. Sahliyeh (ed.) (1990), *Religious Resurgence and Politics in the Modern
    World*, Albany: State University of New York Press; G. Kepel (1994), *The Revenge of God: The
    Resurgence of Islam, Christianity and Judaism in the Modern World*, Cambridge: Polity Press;
    D. Westerlund (ed.) (1996), *Questioning the Secular State: The Worldwide Resurgence of Religion
    in Politics*, London: Hurst & Co.

4   Kepel, *The Revenge of God*, pp. 2–12. A. Shupe (1990), 'The Stubborn Resistance of Religion in the
    Global Arena', in Sahliyeh, *Religious Resurgence*, p. 20.

5   A. Boyd (1969), *Holy War in Belfast*, Tralee: Anvil Books.

6   R. Rose (1971), *Governing without Consensus: An Irish Perspective*, London: Faber and Faber.

7   J. Whyte (1990), *Interpreting Northern Ireland*, Oxford: Clarendon Press.

8   Jose Casanova, certainly one of the sounder scholars, went so far in 1994 as to claim that '[d]uring
    the entire decade of the 1980s it was hard to find any serious political conflict anywhere in the world
    that did not show behind it the not-so-hidden hand of religion'. J. Casanova (1994), *Public Religions
    in the Modern World*, London: University of Chicago Press, p. 3.

9   The phrase is used in the Series Preface printed on p. xi above.

10 'In no other sector of social activity has the weight of the past, which is always important, been so
    determinant as in religion and its relations with society.' R. Remond (1999), *Religion and Society in
    Modern Europe*, Oxford: Blackwell, p. 17.

11 The core analogy of religious markets with all the paraphernalia of regulation, consumers and
    producers, barriers to entry etc., is argued to illuminate important questions such as the relative
    vibrancy or dormancy of religious life in, respectively, open religious-market societies, such as the
    USA, and more religiously monopolistic (non-market) societies, such as are found hypothetically in
    Scandinavia with its state churches. See L. Young (ed.) (1997), *Religion and Rational Choice*, London:
    Routledge; and M. Chaves and D. Cann (1992), 'Regulation, Pluralism and Religious Market
    Structure', *Rationality and Society*, **4** (3), pp. 272–90. For a vigorous critique of this approach see
    S. Bruce (1999), *Choice and Religion: A Critique of Rational Choice Theory*, Oxford: Oxford
    University Press.

12 See McGarry and O'Leary, below, [p. 212].

13 As Demerath points out the phrase is 'Christocentric' since the term 'church' only has an exact
    referent in the Christian tradition(s). It is also potentially if not actually in practice 'ecclesio-centric',
    ostensibly directing attention only to churches of whatever faith, while denominations, sects, cults
    and other forms of religious association familiar to sociologists of religion are not included.

14 See J. Witte (2000), *Religion and the American Constitutional Experiment*, Boulder: Westview, for
    an excellent recent review of the field.

15 See, for example, S.V. Monsma and J.C. Soper (1997), *The Challenge of Pluralism: Church and
    State in Five Democracies*, Oxford: Rowman and Littlefield. See also J. Madeley and Z. Enyedi
    (eds) (2003), *Church and State in Contemporary Europe: The Chimera of Neutrality*, London:
    Cass.

16 S.M. Lipset (1960), *Political Man*, Garden City NY: Doubleday.

17 S.M. Lipset and S. Rokkan (1967), 'Cleavage Structures, Party Systems, and Voter Alignments: An
    Introduction', in S.M. Lipset and S. Rokkan (eds), *Voter Systems and Party Alignments*, New York:
    The Free Press.

18 The impact of the religious factor in US politics is not however to be reduced to the headline-
    grabbing developments of recent times. Already in 1974, on the basis of a review of historical work
    on the impact of 'religious animosities' on partisan differentiation in the USA, Philip Converse
    concluded that it could 'be argued convincingly that as a sort of "hidden agenda" they have affected
    the main trends in party alignments more deeply and persistently than any other types of social
    differentation'. P. Converse (1974), 'Some Priority Variables in Comparative Research', in R. Rose
    (ed.), *Electoral Behavior: A Comparative Handbook*, London: Collier Macmillan, p. 733.

19 See, for example, G. Therborn (1994), 'Another Way of Taking Religion Seriously: Comment on
    Francis G. Castles', *European Journal of Political Research*, pp. 103–10.

20 S.P. Huntington (1993), 'The Clash of Civilizations?', *Foreign Affairs*, **72** (3), pp. 22–49.

21 Those with an interest in the place of religion in international relations will find little of direct interest here. For a number of essays on this area of research see D. Johnston and C. Sampson (eds) (1994), *Religion: the Missing Element in Statecraft*, New York: Oxford University Press.

22 R. Wuthnow (1991), 'Understanding Religion and Politics', *Religion and Politics*, **120** (3), Proceedings of the American Academy of Arts and Sciences, p. 11.

23 For recent publications of the structure and dynamics of church–state relationships in Europe, see G. Robbers (1996), *Church and State in the European Union*, Baden-Baden: Nomos Verlagsgesellschaft; J. Madeley and Z. Enyedi (eds) (2003), *Church and State in Contemporary Europe: The Chimera of Neutrality*, London: Cass.

24 An impressive demonstration of how such an approach can be used to make sense of a peculiarly complex historical record is provided by S. Kalyvas (1996), *The Rise of Christian Democracy in Europe*, London: Cornell University Press.

25 On fundamentalism the largest and best collection of comparative scholarship is to be found in: M. Marty and R. Appleby (eds), *The Fundamentalism Project: Fundamentalisms Observed* (1991), *Fundamentalisms and Society* (1993), *Fundamentalisms and the State* (1993), *Accounting for Fundamentalisms* (1994), *Fundamentalisms Comprehended* (1995), Chicago Ill.: University of Chicago Press.

Part I
Religion and Regime

[1]

Religion and Politics in Comparative and Historical Perspective

Daniel H. Levine

Said Amir Arjomond, *The Shadow of God and the Hidden Imam: Religion, Political Order, and Societal Change in Shi'ite Iran from the Beginning to 1890*, Chicago, University of Chicago Press, 1984.

Jean Comaroff, *Body of Power, Spirit of Resistance: The Culture and History of a South African People*, Chicago, University of Chicago Press, 1985.

Karen Fields, *Revival and Rebellion in Colonial Central Africa*, Princeton, Princeton University Press, 1985.

Michael Gilsenan, *Recognizing Islam: Religion and Society in the Modern Arab World*, New York, Pantheon Books, 1982.

James Davison Hunter, *American Evangelicalism: Conservative Religion and the Quandary of Modernity*, New Brunswick, Rutgers University Press, 1983.

Reynaldo Clemena Ileto, *Pasyon and Revolution: Popular Movements in the Philippines, 1840–1910*, Quezon City, Ateneo de Manila University Press, 1979.

Thomas Kselman, *Miracles and Prophecies in Nineteenth Century France*, New Brunswick, Rutgers University Press, 1983.

Hue-Tam Ho Tai, *Millenarianism and Peasant Politics in Vietnam*, Cambridge, Harvard University Press, 1983.

Nicholas Wolterstorff, *Until Justice and Peace Embrace*, Grand Rapids, William B. Eerdmans Publishing Company, 1983.

David Zaret, *The Heavenly Contract: Ideology and Organization in Pre-Revolutionary Puritanism*, Chicago, University of Chicago Press, 1985.

Writing on religion and politics has become something of a growth industry in recent years. The renewed salience of religion in the politics of cases otherwise as distinct as Iran, Central America, southern Africa, Poland, and the United States has spurred an urgent search for information and understanding. Even setting aside the obvious shortcomings of much instant scholarship, which now attributes to religion all the decisive impact once reserved for Marxism or modernization, we still find a noteworthy body of empirically grounded, theoretically significant research on religion and politics. The books reviewed here provide a fair sample of recent scholarly work. They have something important to say about key issues in the everyday practice of religion and politics, and also about how best to explain

95

their relationship and mutual impact now as in the past. Further, they shed light on basic social science concerns and help lay to rest, once and for all, a number of long dominant assumptions about the nature of social and political change and the role religion plays in these processes.

The research under review here is not just a reaction to current events. Most of this work was in progress long before the rush of public and official interest in religion and politics. Moreover, with rare exceptions those working on Latin America, Asia, Africa, and Europe, on Catholicism, Islam, and Buddhism, conceived and carried out their studies innocent of the fact that scholars with similar interests were at work elsewhere. But despite barriers of discipline, regional concentration, and concern with specific cultural and religious traditions, the central questions turn out to be remarkably similar.[1] The following points, among others, help to make this a coherent literature: first, a stance which sees change in religion as normal and continuous; second, from this, a common attempt to grasp its impact on politics not as aberrant or irrational, but rather as a logical outgrowth of central religious themes and structures; third, a shared concern to reassess "popular religion," placing it in the context of on-going links to dominant institutions of power and meaning; and finally, a commitment to reread history "from below" and thus to see the links between everyday life and the high politics of "state and church" (however defined in a particular society) in a radically new light.

At a general theoretical level, these themes reveal a shared focus on the sources of change in ideas and on their links to class, context, and institutional transformations. They also point to reassessment of religion's role in social and political change. Why this concern with religion and politics, and why in these particular ways? Much of the answer lies in a reaction to long prevailing assumptions in the social sciences, which made religion secondary to supposedly more immediate, "real," or rational social, economic, and political forces. Three assumptions are critical here. The first makes religion epiphenomenal; the second takes religious motives or groups as less evolved alternatives to politics, at best "prepolitical" way stations; the third awaits an inevitable secularization—here, religion appears mostly as a survivor from the past, doomed to privatization and disappearance. Much early work on "modernization" took these premises for granted. In contrast, the studies reviewed here stress the long-term character of religious movements and their continuing creative link to politics at all levels. From this vantage point, at issue in the link of religion to politics is less secularization (growth or decline in gross terms) than restructuring.

Assumptions of this kind hinder understanding by obscuring the sources and dynamics of change within religion. Religious ideas, structures, and practices have a logic of their own. Individual and group action may thus be governed as much by that logic as by adherence to related social or political agendas. Analysis which stays within the contours of conventionally defined political events is likely to misread the process. By focusing on immediate concerns, and then projecting current configurations into the past, it reifies a particular form of religious-political convergence, without regard for understanding how the issues came to take on their present character and structure. Moreover, an exclusive concern with outcomes (who wins or loses on a national scale) also makes it hard to identify and grasp the sources and long-term dynamics of motivation which empower popular groups in repeated efforts at organization and action, often against what seem to be impossible odds.

Daniel H. Levine

Consider the case of millenarian movements, which as a matter of fact most often "fail." To say they fail means, in common usage, that they do not "take power," that they are defeated militarily and scattered politically. This is generally correct. But suppose that to this judgment we counter that of a peasant organizer quoted by Reynaldo Ileto to the effect, "No uprising fails. Each one is a step in the right direction" (p. 7). The judgment cannot be lightly dismissed, nor should it be incorporated without a further reflection into a neo-Marxist framework of "inevitable revolution." To say that no insurrection fails means that each contributes to nurturing an independent popular consciousness, thus making continued struggle possible. Moreover, as we shall see, Ileto shows how rereading Filipino history from below uncovers a stock of ideas, symbols, and forms of action derived from popular passion plays, the *pasyon* of his title. These undergird popular uprisings throughout the nineteenth and early twentieth centuries. Ileto establishes that analysis which rescues the centrality of religious themes and motives adds significantly to the understanding of change and conflict in the Philippines.

Like most of the authors considered here, Ileto denies that popular groups are mere clay, passive reflectors of the dominant culture. Instead, he details how they take images and messages from dominant institutions and rework these in accord with their own understanding of history and tradition, with a calculation of possibilities, and with an eye to what they see as urgent and immediate needs. The case of millenarian movements suggests that, when students of religion and politics abandon the confines of formal institutions and go beyond the relatively clear lines of systematic theology, doctrine, and law to the analysis of popular experience, they must be careful not to carry elite-focused categories with them. Popular groups may use other criteria of significance and put event, structure, and meaning together in different ways.

Careful attention to the dynamics of popular-institutional linkage is important, but there is a prior question. Why religion? Why should religion be a perennial source of political meaning and action? What conditions make for change in religion and combine to give religious ideas a ready audience at any given historical moment? Much analysis is content to follow Max Weber, noting the "elective affinities" between religious and political ideas, institutional forms, and practices. This perspective is enormously fruitful, but concern with elective affinities can hinder understanding by accepting conjuncture as an explanation in itself. Moreover, showing how particular ethical norms or organizational forms "fit" the life pattern of different groups is important, but it is too passive and gives too little place to the sources and pathways of change. By stressing conjuncture and fit so much, an unreconstructed Weberian analysis gives too much weight (albeit unwittingly) to equilibrium and homeostatic balance and not enough to dimensions of power, conflict, and change within religion and between religion and politics. It also ignores Weber's own repeated concern to specify the conditions (especially the character of "crisis") when religion changes and acquires special salience.[2] Finally, it fails to acknowledge religion's tremendous *consolidating* power. I refer to the peculiar ability of religious metaphors, places, and rituals to sum up and intensify experience. They do this by joining everyday events to a sense of supernatural intervention and by reinforcing religious ideas with material resources and a net of repeated human interactions. This is what religious organizations and rituals *do*, and this is why they are so powerful at unifying behavior across social levels and in different arenas and walks of life.

Comparative Politics   October 1986

How best to think about religion and politics and to find order in the variation of historical and contemporary experience? The main body of this essay addresses these questions as follows. An initial discussion of required theoretical reorientations is followed by a close look at the works under review, grouped for purposes of exposition by focus and region. I start with Ileto, Fields, Comaroff, and Tai, who share an interest in millenarian movements and in different ways address the significance (and the problem) of writing history from below. The next section looks at Zaret and Kselman, whose work on the Puritans and on nineteenth-century France sheds much light on the genesis and development of popular-institutional ties. The following three sections examine studies on Islam (Gilsenan and Arjomond), American fundamentalism (Hunter), and the implications of liberation theology (Wolterstorff). These four books share a concern with ideological and institutional change and with the way transformations in religion mediate and give special character to the links of everyday life with the high politics of culture and power. I close with a brief sketch of an agenda for future research.

A good place to begin theoretical reconstruction is with specification of some of the problems recent scholarship addresses and in large measure overcomes. Three in particular underlie the deficiencies of much conventional analysis: narrow definitions and inadequate concepts, overly intellectualized and elite-focused agendas, and disciplinary and regional parochialism.

Conventional concepts have confined our sense of the issues within unduly narrow limits. Scholarly attention has focused too much on explicitly political ideas or vehicles (parties, elections, and direct manipulation of religious events). Research thus latches on to the apparent political *result* of religious action, with little sense of how or why religion may have stimulated or sustained action in the first place. Of course, explicitly political vehicles are important: politicians and public officials often use religion for their own purposes. But if analysis starts here, a great deal is missed. Much of the theoretical and practical import of religion and politics lies less in conventional outcomes of this kind as in the way changes within religion are associated at once with new kinds of social organization and with the legitimation of new ideas about activism, power, and governance in ordinary life. This is what lays down a cultural foundation for authority (or for resistance to its claims). It is here that the human solidarities which make any action endure are built. From this perspective, explicitly political events appear as the end of a long chain of events, not its beginning.

These reflections suggest a need to reformulate common questions about the ideological direction of "politicized religion." Instead of asking if religion is "revolutionary," "moderate," or "conservative," one might more profitably look at structural issues, especially those affecting the way popular and institutional levels are linked to one another. Research would then consider how religious change provides a medium for the crystallization, organized expression, and occasionally enhancement of popular culture and action. Ideological direction of course will vary with the specifics of tradition, context, and circumstances, but the contrast between social and cultural "levels" remains. Jean Comaroff puts it this way: "if we confine our scrutiny to the zero-sum heroics of revolution successfully achieved, we discount the vast proportion of human social action which is played out, perforce, on a more humble scale. We also evade, by teleological reasoning, the real questions that remain as to what *are* the transformative motors of history" (p. 261).

Daniel H. Levine

The point is simultaneously theoretical and methodological. To understand how religion and politics interact and change together, analysis must accept the logic of religious belief and practice. This requires a conscious effort to hear it as expressed, to see it as practiced, and to construct or reconstruct the context in which these religious ideas resonate. Only then is it possible to see how and why religion helps people to make sense of the world and to organize themselves and others to deal with it. All this adds up to the need for scholarship to begin with what religious groups and people *actually do*, and not with an account of why they do not do things of interest to social scientists, such as engaging in explicitly political activities.

The perspective outlined here requires a systematic effort to go beyond intellectualized and elite-focused categories. Consider the question of doctrine and ideology. How do average people perceive and act upon the formal ideas of religion and politics? Clearly, no simple deduction from doctrine to motivation and practice is possible. The links are not direct, but mediated in all instances by context and class. The case of Latin American liberation theology may serve to illustrate the point. A great deal has been written on liberation theology, and I consider the issues in some detail below. Here, I wish only to note that, in the vast scholarly and polemical literature on the subject, most attention has gone to clarify and characterize this theology *as a system of ideas*. But the theologians themselves stress the wisdom of the people. They take theology less as a tightly drawn set of ideas than as a group of reflections made about, and from within, a world of injustice and oppression. Their whole position thus enhances the value of popular insight.[3] This is not to suggest that the ideas themselves lack importance: they have legitimized new goals and new kinds of organization with great and enduring impact. But the process does not operate in a neat, deductive fashion. Rather, throughout Latin America popular groups have taken these ideas and reworked them in the context of urgent everyday needs and conflicts. In the process, they transform a limited religious agenda into something much broader, moving themselves and their groups to the center of political conflict. Along the way, religious symbols, ideas, and celebrations acquire new meaning, spurring and underscoring a changed appreciation of the proper bases of society and politics while at the same time empowering new commitments for change.[4]

Thinking about ideology in this way helps to clarify the issues of linkage, leadership, and legitimacy. As to linkages, it is clear that whatever linkage exists, however it may be organized and mediated, traffic along its pathways is never one way only. Institutions reach out to popular groups; popular groups select and rework. All this is unobjectionable, but the reader will note that attention to linkage conceals much ambiguity as to just *what* (or who) is "linked." In what follows, I take linkage primarily in structural and class terms. Thus, linkage "joins" popular groups with elites and the institutions they control and operate. It also knits everyday life and local grass-roots contexts with formally organized expressions of culture and power. The predominant pattern of social structure and cultural formation in the modern world, which leaves most people poor and unlettered, means that for all practical purposes these are one and the same.

Legitimations and leadership are related. Much of the struggle around religion and politics centers in some way on legitimation. Legitimation is contested at many levels, in struggles to claim the moral authority of religion and divine will (however defined) for different sorts of group practice and commitment and for alternative structures of power. Legitimation thus

99

Comparative Politics   October 1986

involves setting religion *as a unit* ("Church," *'ulema*, etc.) for or against some structure of power and authority. It also denotes the emergence and possible promotion *within* religion of alternative legitimations of authority. These provide a basis for common action and also a set of "spaces" (literally groups, buildings, practices, rituals) in which such new ideas can be worked out, shared, and reinforced.

As to leadership, the central issue is less *which* leader is endorsed or promoted than a struggle to determine what makes any leader legitimate in the first place. One tradition looks for traits of inherited power, authority of office, or some special "gift" of divine inspiration. But these Weberian categories (traditional, legal-rational, charismatic) are not especially helpful. They fail to address how religious change at once legitimates new kinds of leaders while eliciting potential leadership cadres from hitherto passive or suppressed groups. New religiously inspired theories and structures enhance the value of participation while providing experience in participation and self-governance. Once underway, the process can become self-sustaining. This was notable among the Puritans, whose leaders were a new class in seventeenth-century England. It appeared in colonial Vietnam and Central Africa early in this century, has long been visible in the Philippines, and can now be seen in southern Africa and Central America. Hunter's study of the American evangelicals suggests that much the same thing is going on in the United States today.[5]

While analysis must go beyond the formal limits of institutions, their continued impact cannot be ignored. Institutions are more than just machines for grinding out documents or allocating roles and statuses in a formalized way. They are vital, changing structures which help to form the contexts in which experience is lived and judged. They provide identity, continuity, and nets of solidarity much valued by members, despite possible rejection of specific institutional leaders or positions. The fact of membership binds individual or group action to a broader moral horizon and to a shared tradition. This is not to make popular groups mere clay in the hands of elites, but simply to note that links between them are of mutual interest, ties that neither side is quick to abandon. Analysis which forgets the binding quality of religious institutions and looks only to gross concepts like "elite manipulation" or "popular struggle" misses much of the reason why people join religious groups in the first place. It thus fails to see how *religious* motives and values undergird other aspects of group life and keep them going in the face of possible adversity.[6]

Is religion reactionary, revolutionary, neutral, or what? As asked the question cannot be answered. But if we look at cases, ground theory in empirical analysis, and begin to draw systematic parallels and comparisons, some understandable configurations emerge. One visible line of change detaches religious from political institutions, putting the *direction* of religion's political legitimations up for grabs. A second hinges on struggles within religion to define the proper status and role of popular groups, and thus to control access to sacred power and to power in general. A third builds on these and is worked out through conflict within religion and politics to create enduring popular support. The process is complex and multifaceted, but not chaotic. Order can be found in all this variation if we begin by listening to what people say and searching for the way their voices are structured and linked to one another and to patterns of domination in culture, economy, and politics.

A final point for general reflection concerns regional and disciplinary parochialism. The current salience of religion in politics clearly shares many common features in cases otherwise as distinct as Latin America, Iran, southern Africa, the Philippines, and the

Daniel H. Levine

United States. Of course, the *resolution* of the issues differs from case to case. But in all instances, religion appears as a source of enormous creative political energies, changing expectations, challenging accepted notions of legitimacy, and refocusing action on new areas and issues of conflict. The pattern cannot be dismissed as either the result of temporary aberrations or the end product of contamination by "outside" interests. It is too familiar from past history and too common now to make such arguments even minimally acceptable. In any case, the ideological directions salient in one case cannot be transferred *tout court* to another. Religious change is associated with all kinds of political orientations; no single stance is true by definition.

Disciplinary parochialism carries its own hazards, especially a tendency to focus either on institutions or mass phenomena, formal or informal protest, ideas or structures. Sociologists and political scientists have generally fallen on the first half of this divide, with anthropologists sinning on the popular side of the equation. But the dichotomy and the separation it engenders are both false and misleading. Institutions constantly strive to organize popular sectors; there are no institutions without members, at least not for very long. In turn, popular religion is no "natural," spontaneous product. It emerges through the long-term encounter of popular groups with larger structures of domination. Institutional and popular dimensions must be seen together, and it is a particular virtue of the studies collected here that the authors undertake this double enterprise in systematic yet diverse ways. It is time to turn to the books themselves.

Ileto, Fields, and Comaroff all strive to explain the origins and political import of popular religious movements. They stress the need to reconstruct history from below. In their view, rescuing the autonomous logic and structure of popular movements is a prerequisite to full understanding of their political significance. Ileto and Fields in particular underscore the links of millenarian movements to dominant institutions but strongly reject the bias of conventional accounts towards a preoccupation with their weird, exotic, and supposedly prepolitical character. Comaroff is less concerned with the millenarian character of groups than with how they provide a language and a structure for resistance in everyday life.

Pasyon and Revolution, published in 1979, is the oldest of the works reviewed in this essay. Because it came out in Manila, the book has taken longer to get the general scholarly attention it deserves. The author rereads the historical record to show how popular movements drew on a pervasive tradition of passion plays for models of leadership and action and for an explanation of conflict and change. In this tradition, they also found values with which to justify resistance to domination and to empower repeated insurrectionary efforts. Such reanalysis of the historical record rests on a premise which is at once methodological and theoretical. The methodological case turns on *decoding* the meaning of peasant action to peasants. This is done through a careful look at the language they used to describe events and actions. The theoretical argument follows closely from the choice of methods and data. Ileto rejects elite-biased sources which stress the irrationality of popular movements. He also denies the validity of social science concepts that paint popular movements as simply blind reactions to change.

These arguments are elaborated in the first chapter, "Towards a History From Below." Ileto shows that the language and typical structure of passion plays and related Holy Week celebrations shaped the general style and concerns of peasant brotherhoods and uprisings

Comparative Politics   October 1986

throughout the late Spanish and early American colonial periods. The author's history from below is filled out with a rich array of popular songs, poems, confessions, prayers, and proverbs. Ileto also uses, perforce, Spanish and English sources (such as trial transcripts and police records) but is always careful to decode the popular meaning hidden in the official written record. For example, when popular movements engage in repeated "errors," when otherwise inexplicable behaviors like weeping or repeated instances of "useless" sacrifice occur, Ileto sees these not as aberrations, but rather as markers setting off the contours of popular consciousness.

At one level, the typical *pasyon* stresses resignation, sacrifice, and suffering. But Ileto brings out an alternative text that gave popular classes a model of leadership and an explanation for the pattern of events.

> In its narrative of Christ's suffering, death and resurrection, and of the Day of Judgement, it provides powerful images of transition from one state or era to another, e.g. darkness to light, despair to hope, misery to salvation, death to life, ignorance to knowledge, dishonor to purity, and so forth. During the Spanish and American colonial eras, these images nurtured an undercurrent of millenial beliefs which in times of economic and political crisis enabled the peasantry to take action under the leadership of individuals or groups promising deliverance from oppression (pp. 18–19).

Why was the *pasyon* so central? Ileto's answer combines attention to the consolidating power of religious belief and practice, stress on the familiarity and constant availability of passion plays as a medium, and analysis of how "crisis" (decline of Spanish rule, failed struggle for independence, and imposition of American domination) made the messages immediate and real. The plays were used widely throughout the year. There were reading sessions in homes with individuals singing the stanzas and regular performances with costumes and processions. In an illiterate society, the *pasyon* provided a language and a set of concepts for expressing resistance. They also presented a powerful central figure in Christ, portrayed in the plays as a subversive. Christ is fully identified with the poor and humble, and he breaks the conventional bonds of family and authority to create a new brotherhood and a new era ("follow me . . . "). Ileto underscores the complex impact of the model of Christ, combining stress on conversion to a serene and pure inner self, breaking with the past in order to travel, preach, and found new communities, with compassion over suffering and confidence in rebirth.[7] Why did rebels fight to the end against overwhelming odds? They were sure that "salvation was contingent on being prepared to die" (p. 77).

The main body of *Pasyon and Revolution* (chapters 2–6) details seventy years of popular uprisings. Ileto argues that if we can identify the sources and properly read the discourse of popular groups, we can achieve a fuller and more reliable understanding of their motives and actions. He establishes clear continuities among the movements and on this basis outlines an underlying popular consciousness which explains the durability of opposition and the repeated appeal of certain kinds of revolutionary leaders. To argue this way is not to say that Filipino peasants are really playing out the *pasyon* in their uprisings. Rather, the *pasyon* offers a stock of symbols and solidarities which together structure the ground for action.

> Through the text and associated rituals, people were made aware of a pattern of universal history. They also became aware of ideal forms of behavior and social relationships, and a way

Daniel H. Levine

to attain these through suffering, death, and rebirth. And so in times of crisis—economic, political, real or imagined—there was available a set of ideas and images with which even the rural masses could make sense out of their condition. Popular movements and revolts were far from being blind reactions to oppression. They became popular precisely because leaders were able to tap existing notions of change; the *pasyon* was freed from its officially sanctioned mooring in Holy Week and allowed to give form and meaning to the people's struggles for liberation (p. 316).

Pasyon and Revolution is an impassioned piece of engaged scholarship. In his search for understanding, Ileto reaches for new kinds of theory and data and in the process strives to give popular groups the dignity and recognition long denied them by those who create history from above, which we find in the written record. Thus, "the subjects of this book have at one time or another been called bandits, ignoramuses, heretics, lunatics, fanatics, and in particular, failures. Not only has this been a way in which the 'better classes' keep these people in oblivion; worse, this signifies a failure or a refusal to view them in the light of *their* world. Oddly enough, such epithets are found in the *pasyon*; popular culture itself anticipates such attitudes on the part of the elite. But as we move forward on the path to *kalayaan* [independence], we can hardly ignore the voices from below" (p. 319).

In *Revival and Rebellion in Colonial Central Africa*, Karen Fields takes up a similar agenda. In empirical terms, she combines analysis of the ideology and structure of British indirect rule with attention to the sources, nature, and political import of the Watchtower movement. In theoretical terms, she confronts and demolishes several generations of social science work (above all in British social anthropology) which was of great influence in shaping both scholarly and popular understanding of change in Africa. Fields shows that the discourses of colonial authorities, missionaries, and anthropologists were mutually dependent. Together, they misread African society, gutting it of power and of the capacity for internally generated change. Their vision rested so heavily on a crystallized concept of custom and ritual that in effect they denied that any African could see beyond the rites and ceremonies to imagine a new or different order of existence. From this perspective, any movement for change (above all one cloaked in religious language) was reduced to the level of irrational reactions to "stress and strain." Fields rejects all this with great force (e.g., p. 282) and shows that the millenarians (Watchtower) imagined a new order and worked rationally and methodically to bring it about.

Her theoretical critique leads Fields to important methodological points. In particular, she challenges the assumptions built into conventional anthropological method which stress close analysis of a self-contained field of custom (in "my village"). She stresses how much these villages, the "African society" portrayed by classic ethnographies (and indeed the whole structure of indirect rule), were contingent on the concentration of power in British hands. To focus attention only within the subordinate unit, with no specification of linkages to power, is to miss what makes the whole system go. The basic fact is that political power was reserved to the British, and sacred power to the missionaries. The available field of action within African society was thus radically circumscribed. The point is important, because any adequate understanding of millenarian movements requires reconstruction of the context which gave millenarian ideas meaning, appeal, and impact in the first place. A false or frozen history makes this impossible.

103

As an alternative, Fields works to reconstruct the horizon within which the millenarians acted and thought, rooting their ideas and conflicts in the context of ordinary social life. "If we do this, then we need not try to explain why individuals should have been impelled out of ordinary circumstances toward extraordinary belief. Rather, since belief would then come into view as routine common sense, we would try to see how the supernatural was embedded in mundane social relations" (p. 21).

Revival and Rebellion begins, in the introduction, with a brilliant discussion of how to study millenarian movements. Part I analyzes the "Problem of Political Order" and establishes a clear line for understanding colonial rule and its impact on African societies. Part II considers the "Political Problem of Evil," exploring the genesis and particular manifestations of Watchtower and showing why this *religious* movement was inevitably and tremendously political. Finally, Part III, on "Elementary Norms of the Religious Life," considers the routine of religious belief and practice as organized contrastingly by colonial authorities, missionaries, and Watchtower. Throughout, the author explicitly joins the reunderstanding of millenarian movements to reanalysis of the general structure of power and domination. Watchtower made sense in colonial Central Africa because it used images, models, and mediations familiar in ordinary experience. It was therefore religious and political at one and the same time—a fact fully recognized by participants and also by colonial authorities, whose police covered the movement's activities in detail, describing them at one point as "ecclesiastical bolshevism" (p. 238). Fields stresses that when Watchtower came to Africa from America, it found ready adherents and a structure of opportunity which intensified the appeal of many of the movement's basic features: belief in the return of the dead, expectation of a worldly paradise to come, insistence on preaching and on fulfilling one's biblically derived duty in every walk of life (pp. 96–97).

The chapters of Part II describe Watchtower in three charismatic outbursts in 1908, 1917, and the dramatic witch cleansing of 1925. In each case, Fields shows how the movement drew on local experience for themes and followers and why it was so threatening to colonial authorities. Conflict typically hinged on power: control of access to sacred power, control of the links of sacred power to politics, and control of critical points in the process, such as baptism and ritual purification. Access to sacred power had very concrete meaning in the colonial system, where the missions controlled and restricted authority within the churches, keeping native Africans in permanent apprenticeship. In such a context, the assertion of autonomous spiritual power (e.g., in preaching or baptism) was an act of political independence. Like the Puritans centuries earlier, Watchtower preachers were thoroughly versed in the Bible and made their own interpretations. They loved to debate and stood their ground against mission authority. Hence the charges of heresy and "ecclesiastical bolshevism" which reflect the authorities' tendency to take only some kind of preaching and practice as religiously acceptable.

Baptism itself had critical religious and political implications. The struggle over Watchtower baptism galvanized groups and served as a catalyst for large-scale mobilization (pp. 268–69). Religion and politics were inseparable here because the whole symbolic and material structure of religion was directly bound up with power and authority. Withdrawal from the ambit of the missions challenged a central pillar of colonial rule. Refusal to continue "traditional" religious observances (for example to chiefs or ancestors, regarded

Daniel H. Levine

by Watchtower as pagan) in effect denied the legitimacy of chiefly authority and thus undercut the whole of indirect rule (pp. 135, 152).

Fields notes the great force and appeal of charismatic practices in Watchtower. She argues that ecstatic practices, trances, prophecies, speaking in tongues, and the like are best seen as a thorough break with convention. In her view, popular groups are especially open to charismatic power, whose expression models their own sense of disorder in the order the world provides. Moreover, the message of the Bible made sense to Africans in a way long forgotten by their missionary teachers.

> Evangelization in Africa did not require argument as to whether extraordinary power existed, as it must have in much of contemporary Britain. Less for African hearers than for their mission mentors did the point need emphasizing that supernatural forces could transform one's life for good or ill. Missionaries, after all, were products of what Weber called a "disenchanted" world. I imagine that it was with a certain double-mindedness that they taught as the real truth Paul's proclamation about transcending the world: "Behold I shew you a mystery. We shall not all sleep, but we shall be changed." [1 Cor 15:51] (p. 157).

Fields thus joins Ileto in making the rescue and reconstruction of popular religion a basic theoretical and methodological task. The enterprise requires a fresh reading of the "official" record, along with a systematic effort to criticize and transcend the expectations bequeathed to us by generations of social science forebears. Jean Comaroff's study of the Tshidi in southern Africa takes a similar tack. Her reconstruction of popular religion marries the richness of traditional ethnography with an explicit concern to go beyond its bounds, linking ethnographic detail to the understanding of power and institutions. She focuses deliberately on less dramatic, more everyday events. Much of the substance of this book is thus less conventionally "political" than the events presented by Ileto or Fields. But this is precisely the point Comaroff wishes to drive home. Throughout *Body of Power, Spirit of Resistance*, the author consistently and successfully links details of daily life to larger institutional patterns: households, rituals (e.g. of healing or initiation), and particulars of dress or the use of space to political economies. She argues that each level nourishes and promotes the other, and together they build new meanings into the routines of daily life.

Comaroff sees religious ideas and practices as cradles of identity, moral dissent, and solidarity. They provide ways of responding to domination, finding self-worth and meaning in resistance to oppression without full-blown, direct confrontation. From this vantage point, religion is both a theory and a practical consciousness linking ordinary experience to the larger world.

> The *Realpolitik* of oppression dictates that resistance be expressed in domains seemingly apolitical, and the dynamics of resistance among oppressed people elsewhere have shown that the connection between seemingly unworldly powers and movements and the politics of liberation is subtle and various, denying dichotomization in terms of resistance or compliance (pp. 261–62).

The author gives special attention to how indigenous peoples borrow and transform the cultural products of western domination. The latter part of her book examines the growth and meaning of the Church of Zion among the Tshidi. This movement began as a messianic sect near Chicago in the late nineteenth century. But like Watchtower, Zionism took on new force and character in Africa (p. 213). Comaroff sees this sort of transfer and reworking as part of the unwritten history of colonialism (p. 254), an instance of the general *bricolage* through which a second global culture is created in the shadow of the first. Peripheral peoples work with the tools at hand.

> When expressions of dissent are prevented from attaining the level of open discourse, a subtle but systematic breach of authoritative cultural codes might make a statement of protest which, by virtue of being rooted in a shared structural predicament and experience of dispossession, conveys an unambiguous message. In such contexts, ritual provides an appropriate medium through which the values and structures of a contradictory world may be addressed and manipulated. And it is in this capacity that the sociocultural forms of Zionism have been pressed into service (p. 196).

Body of Power, Spirit of Resistance begins with a historical ethnography that lays the basis for detailing the "structure of the conjuncture" between the Tshidi and their European conquerors. Part II, on "Culture, Consciousness, and Structural Transformations," explores the articulations between Tshidi society and culture and the white world, up to and including apartheid. Part III on "Zion," along with the conclusion, presents a contemporary account of the Tshidi, with special attention to two churches, the Full Witness Apostolic Church of Zion and the larger Zion Christian Church.

Comaroff's study of the "structure of the conjuncture" lays a foundation for rereading history from below. She identifies enduring themes in Tshidi culture, above all concerns about the body, health and healing, production, and the meaning of space. She then shows how these are expressed in different ways over time. Throughout, rituals and symbolic usages are explicitly linked to issues of power and to a sense of control over the environment as over material forces generally. Like Fields, Comaroff demonstrates how the missions perforce played out an imperial logic. In such a context, independent forms of Christianity served as a medium for disengagement from the colonial project and underwrote a new social construction for the personal and natural world (pp. 171, 213).

Ileto, Fields, and Comaroff together expand the search for political meaning into analysis of the ordinary language, routine, and structure of religion. They underscore the transformative and mobilizing potential of "popular religion," so long considered synonymous with passivity and resignation. Comaroff goes furthest in this regard, focusing almost exclusively on informal politics and everyday resistance. At this point a reader may well ask, "so what?" What does it all matter if, in the end, there is no shift in outcomes or in the structure of power? First, the process clearly matters to those involved. Even if enduring collective action never develops, the search for meaning and control goes on in the spaces available in daily life. The powerless work with the tools at their command. Second, all the authors show how religion can nurture dissent, delegitimize established orders, and provide a seedbed for new kinds of leadership and solidarities which can be put to any purpose, given appropriate circumstances.

Hue-Tam Ho Tai's analysis of *Millenarianism and Peasant Politics in Vietnam* takes a more conventional approach. Tai details the origins and growth of the Hoa Hao in the Mekong delta region of Vietnam. She sketches the context from which Hoa Hao emerged, describes its structure, message, and appeal, and gives special attention to competition

Daniel H. Levine

between Hoa Hao militants and Viet Minh cadres for control of peasant mobilization.[8] The Hoa Hao is an exceptionally interesting example of the creation of a religion and of the process by which it became a central ideological and organizational force. After the appearance of its charismatic leader and prophet, Huynh Phu So, the new religion grew in very little time to control millions of adherents, important administrative and welfare structures, and a significant armed force. But Tai's analysis is disappointing. In theoretical terms, the author works from neoevolutionary premises which paint millenarian movements as ''prepolitical.'' The whole argument of the book is thus pitched to show why the Hoa Hao were destined to be absorbed and replaced by the Viet Minh. The movement's success is attributed in functionalist terms to a fortuitous ''filling of the gap'' left between the decline of traditional society and the consolidation of a revolutionary project.

Tai provides fascinating data on Hoa Hao ideology and structure. Religious and political themes were fused here in a xenophobic and antielitist rejection of cities and foreigners. Huynh Phu So praised the pure and simple life and stripped religious practice down to the minimum. Like the Hebrew prophets, he despised the ''feasts and solemn assemblies'' of established religion (pp. 146–47). Hoa Hao's decentralized structure is relevant here, for in effect it put the burden of organization and growth on peasant communities themselves (p. 126). One only wishes Tai had given more play to these dimensions, and thus to the meaning of politics and the way religion empowered political/religious action, than to competition with the Viet Minh. By stressing the end point so heavily and reading back from outcomes to the process itself, the author misses a chance for fuller understanding of the sources and pathways of this powerful new religion.

Successful treatment of the issues raised to this point calls for historical study. Each of the authors discussed thus far makes reconstruction of popular history a central task. They go about it in different ways, but let us consider for the moment the implications of this common stress on ''history from below.'' Croce wrote somewhere that ''each true history is contemporary history.''[9] The implication is subtly double: first, that each generation reads its own concerns into the past; second, that all good history must be founded on an imaginative reconstruction of the past as experienced then. I have suggested here that the focus of much recent work on religion grows in large measure from dissatisfaction with prevailing assumptions and conventional explanations in the social sciences. But what makes for a valid reconstruction of the past? If we accept the basic idea of a gap between levels (elite-mass, institutional-popular, great and little traditions), a first step holds that a ''good'' reconstruction is one which makes sense now, which creates a comprehensible, expandable pattern out of what we know of the past, and which throws new light on the links between historical periods.

I do not propose a false or reified ontology, whereby ''Christianity,'' ''Islam,'' ''Buddhism,'' or even ''religion'' mean the same things once and forever, equal in all places and circumstances. My goal is more modest—to stress that an attempt to grasp the dynamics of past experience, as lived and understood by competing social groups, can illuminate present conditions. I also suggest that well-known methodological problems, such as what to count as sources or how to weigh the written record against the data of popular culture, are more than matters of technique. At issue are theoretical judgments about how to specify valid criteria for identifying any evidence as authentic and relevant.[10]

107

Even more notable than the historical focus of recent research is the surge of fine studies reassessing the links between religion, society, and politics in the past. They shed light on the origins of what we loosely call "tradition."[11] They also underscore how much contemporary concerns are not unique, but rather pop up repeatedly in human history. No neoevolutionary framework can deal adequately with this experience. From a wealth of outstanding historical studies, I have taken two for comment here: David Zaret's account of early Puritanism, *The Heavenly Contract*, and Thomas Kselman's analysis of *Miracles and Prophecies in Nineteenth Century France.*

Much has been written in recent years about the Puritan Revolution, one of the earliest and most spectacular instances of religiously infused revolutionary movements in the modern period. Parallels are often drawn to current events in Latin America, especially given the salience of independent religious organization and access to be Bible there.[12] Nineteenth-century France is often taken as a classic instance of long-term secularization, but on reconsideration the case appears more complex and ambiguous. Kselman shows a permanent struggle between church and state, a contest whose ground shifted slowly as both religion and politics developed new mediations. Moreover, the political salience of miracles, shrines, and prophecies pointed up by Kselman is not of antiquarian interest alone. Shrines and holy men played a key role in the Iranian revolution and have long been salient in many other religious traditions.

The significance of the Puritan Revolution in our own culture makes it appropriate to start with *The Heavenly Contract*, a work of historical sociology at its best. Zaret shows how change and conflict in religion and politics were linked to contemporary social, economic, and cultural transformations. These created and enhanced new forms of independence and lay initiative throughout the social order. He finds that when the Puritan clerics sought to convince their followers, they were forced to adapt the original messages and organizational forms to fit popular demands and expectations. In the long run, this undermined clerical authority, while magnifying the status and role of average people in all walks of life.

As Puritan clerics developed metaphors and models through which to present their message to believers, they turned to notions of contract. Ideas about contract were generally familiar, made sense to the laity, and confirmed for them how God's will worked in the same way throughout human experience. The underlying equality in the very notion of contract further established a basis for the regulation of behavior not so much by clerical supervision and authoritative control as through a rigorous, methodical, and independent adherence to ethical standards. The well-known result was to forge a body of motivated, confident, self-reliant, and exceptionally determined believers.[13]

Zaret argues convincingly that the foundations of religious and political revolution were laid down over more than a century, in a process whereby growing dissent and popular reformation democratized criticism and enshrined the value of reason, skepticism, and independent judgment. This "charisma of reason" (p. 26) was grounded in the spread of literacy, itself spurred by independent access to the Bible, and by the general expansion of commerce, trade, and industry. Early Puritanism drew these elements together in a stress on rationalization and preaching. Zaret distinguishes rationalization from secularization (p. 40) and shows how central rationalization was to Puritan experience. Ritual, magic, and the authoritative role of the clergy were all rejected by a laity which could read the Bible for itself and sought edification more than ritual in their religious practice. Zaret presents a

Daniel H. Levine

wealth of examples from sermons and pamphlets which document this stress on independent judgment (e.g. p. 56).

Oponents of the Puritans feared the consequences of independent learning and judgment by believers. They complained of too much reading and discussion and were especially troubled by ''gadding behavior.'' Many Puritans felt free to leave their home parishes and ''gad about,'' looking for churches where preaching and edification were prominent (pp. 116–118). This undercut the whole structure of local authority, including compulsory church attendance. Zaret notes many disputes between Puritan masses and their clerics hinging on popular rejection of baptism, special clothing, and external signs such as kneeling and making a cross in the air. Such conflicts caught clerics between an independent and demanding clientele and the aristocratic patrons who ''held the living.'' One harsh critic of the time put the dilemma strongly, noting that he desired that

> all would not preach who can speak; because St Paul calls every family a church, would not turn every table's end into a pulpit; that the feet in this body should not presume to see nor the hands to speak; that the clue of predestination might not be sealed up at the spindle nor the decrees of God unravelled at the loom; that our lay divines would see themselves as well as the clergy leaving . . . the disputes of religion to the decision of the church (p. 93).

The author elaborates on the significance of ideas about contract, placing them in the context of the history of covenant theory and its transformation in England. He then specifies how religious lessons were drawn from contractarian language. Zaret argues that the idea of a ''heavenly contract'' framed Calvinist notions of election, predestination, faith, and grace in ways which made them more meaningful and immediate to believers (p. 153). The worldly lessons drawn from contract were basic to the general Puritan view of the proper conduct of affairs. Contracts require mutual informed consent, joint fulfillment of conditions, and a formal equality among contracting parties. Working with contractual notions, the Puritans elaborated a ''possessive individualism'' whereby believers owned themselves and their spiritual properties. They then contracted with God, paying the debt of sin with faith. The notion of property in self reinforced a broad opposition to unlimited claims for authority (as from the king, p. 188) and further resonated with Puritan resistance to controls over economic life, as enshrined for example in traditional ideas about stewardship (p. 189).

The long-term impact on social policy was equally notable. Consider the case of welfare. Puritan standards for the *use* of property abandoned the idea of terms set by authoritative spiritual mediators (e.g. the ''fair price'' of traditional church doctrine) for an inner test: was the person one of the elect, and hence acting within the grace of God? The Puritans went further, building an analogy between accumulation of property and the need for rationalized business methods, on the one hand, and a process of spiritual accumulation, methodical spiritual diligence, and the reckoning of spiritual accounts, on the other. Such metaphors were central to later debates over social welfare and the poor and remain deeply embedded in contemporary Protestant views of self and society.

In form and language, *Miracles and Prophecies in Nineteenth Century France* is a more conventional and less self-consciously theoretical work than *The Heavenly Contract*. But this is not to downgrade the result. Kselman is sympathetic to popular religion and thus

109

willing to take beliefs (e.g. in miraculous cures, apparitions, and shrines) at face value and not dismiss them or explain them away. This intellectual openness, added to a sure sense of institutional change and of the texture of the developing national arena for culture and politics in nineteenth-century France, helps the author to craft an illuminating account of how and why key aspects of popular religion were so tightly woven into the political discourse of the period.

Kselman focuses on the upsurge of miracles, shrines, and prophetic movements in France during the last century. He details popular beliefs about God, Christ, the church, and the saints and describes the rise of Marian devotion. These aspects of popular belief and practice were deliberately taken up by the church. Church leaders did more than accept what came their way; they selected, promoted, and gave favored elements new and enduring structure. Parallels were repeatedly drawn between religious suffering, cure, and redemption and the generally low state of French society at the time. Moreover, individual miracles and shrines were sanctioned (for urban, rural, and new national clienteles), and national organizations developed to manage pilgrimages (pp. 197, 199).

This general process is central to Kselman's analysis of "The Institutionalization of the Miraculous" (chapter 6). He shows how the church cultivated miracles as a matter of policy, part of its general plan for responding to rifts with the state and to the resulting loss of official support. Through instruction, mission, and sponsorship of miracles France's Catholic hierarchy strove to create a fervent citizenry, whose piety would be "managed" through organizations centered on the shrines. Three well-known instances were the promotion of miraculous medals and the development of shrines around LaSalette and Lourdes. All this had specific political meaning at the time.

> Perhaps the key issue confronting the European prophetic movement was political legitimacy. The French Revolution had shown that both geographic boundaries and political constitutions were mutable, thus raising the question of what should serve as the basis of the state. Romanticism proposed racial and linguistic solidarity and a sense of a common past as the constitutive principles. At the same time, romanticism looked favorably on mystical intuition and religious faith as ways of knowing superior to rational inquiry and analysis. Popular belief in prophecies, suspect during the Enlightenment, was therefore regarded favorably by nineteenth-century intellectuals. The prophetic tradition was able to serve as a link between the intellectual elite and the common people in shaping attitudes toward existing and emerging states (p. 83).

The political character of efforts to institutionalize the miraculous is multifaceted. Untrammeled charismatic energies are very threatening, and as a rule institutions strive for control, distrusting exuberant and unbridled popular devotions. Such fear is both a practical matter of crowd control ("public order") and more generally reflects leadership desire to retain the ability to shape popular consciousness, choosing *which* miracles to sanction. We can assume that potentially miraculous events happen all the time. It is the recognition of miracles and the organization of their social, cultural, and political salience which varies with time and setting. Questions of sacred and political power set the outcome here, and yesterday's madman is today's saint, or *vice versa*. While the church cannot completely control eruptions of charismatic power, it can try to shape and regulate them once they occur. In this case, as with the Puritans, church leaders were drawn closer to popular

Daniel H. Levine

culture, partly from conviction but mostly out of calculation of the value of a strategy with mass appeal.

Kselman clarifies the conditions under which certain religious themes (e.g. miracles, healing, and the redemptive value of suffering) can acquire political salience. He also shows how attention to the dynamics of change within religion can make sense of political alliances. For example, it is generally agreed that the end result of the process Kselman studies was a combination of royalism, conservative politics, and anti-Semitism. Begin with the religious and cultural underpinnings of the process, and the results come into sharper focus: "these climactic expressions were possible in part because nationalism had been a well-established theme in the devotional and prophetic literature that had circulated throughout the century" (p. 197). But atavism is not all there is to the process.

> While miracle cults evoked nostalgic memories of a mythic past of uniform belief, they also offered an alternative to it. The community of belief was no longer to be the neighborhood or the village: it was expanded to include all of France, or at least all those of France who shared similar religious convictions. National confraternities, organized pilgrimages, and the diffusion of mass-produced images and literature were an attempt to use miracles to help create a sense of loyalty to French Catholicism, and beyond that, to the universal Church (p. 199).

The general themes Kselman examines can of course be found in most religious traditions, especially those where ideas about salvation play a central role. Many cases, historical and contemporary, demonstrate the impact of those extraordinary interventions of the supernatural into daily life which move great numbers of people and which we conventionally call "miraculous." This is a power *concentrated* in particular leaders and places, in prophets, holy men, and shrines, and brought to daily life through regular, organized rituals. As it finds expression, political and religious symbols, mediations, and discourses fuse.

This process was critical in the Iranian revolution and undergirds much of the upsurge of "fundamentalist" activism in the Islamic world. If studies of religion and politics are a growth industry, writing about "Islamic fundamentalism" is surely an off-shore export platform! But like instant scholarship generally, most of these studies are disappointing. They draw their research agenda from strategic and narrowly political needs, and hence lack empathy with the movements they consider.[14] It is not surprising, then, that they fail to address religion's autonomous role as source and agent of change in any serious way. These comments notwithstanding, there is some very good work on Islam, two examples of which are considered in the next section: Michael Gilsenan's *Recognizing Islam* and Said Arjomond's theoretically rich history of Iranian Shi'ism.

Gilsenan begins by noting that "Islam" has contrasting meanings for different groups at the same time. It is thus false to discuss "Islam and politics" as if the phenomenon were everywhere and at all times the same. It is also misleading to isolate any single facet, such as "Islamic fundamentalism," without specifying relevant classes and groups and the circumstances of its appeal. These cautionary notes do not mean that no generalization is possible. They simply point up the need to know specific conditions and the importance of being aware that much of the conflict now swirling around Islam is in fact a struggle to define and control what islam itself means and requires of true believers.

111

Comparative Politics   October 1986

The major contributions of *Recognizing Islam* come in two areas: the systematic relation of religion (and especially "tradition") to class and political change, and the analysis of why, to whom, and with what implications certain religious ideas (especially grace or *baraka*) have appeal. Gilsenan shows that in cases ranging from Ottoman Turkey to Egypt and Iran the growing "modernization and secularization" of the state had a paradoxical impact. The formally Islamic character of political institutions was diluted or eliminated completely, while the effective Islamic character of society and culture was magnified, above all for marginal groups. This unintended outcome grew from the dynamics of class formation and class relationships and the way these were mediated by religion and ideology. All across the Islamic world, ruling groups adopted "rationalist and technocratic" ideologies and justifications of their regimes. They pushed religion to the side, treating it as an irritant: at best a concern of the lower orders, tolerated, but taken mostly as an inevitable holdover from the past. The class gap was thus reinforced by a cultural and ideological break. In the process religion came more and more to crystallize and define the identity of poor and marginal classes and also of aspiring lower or middle class groups excluded from the new power arrangements. Elite strategies and justifications thus unwittingly enhanced the power of religion, drove new adherents to it, and gave religious leadership (jurists and holy men, *'ulema* and *sheiks*) a new cultural status, free from the traditional role of legitimizing state power.

> Every attack, therefore, did not necessarily diminish religion but helped to increase that polarization and antagonism of social groups that was being produced by economic change, the growth of the modern state, and European power. The latter used its law as instrument and ideology and displaced the previous, local framework and its guardians (the 'ulema). The displacement did *not* mean the secularization of society. It meant, rather, the shift in the social signification of religion and the nature of the strata who would begin to regard themselves as "the true believers" (p. 44).

A central outcome of this process was to distinguish religion *as such* from other views of the world and patterns of experience. Something identified as "tradition" emerges. As Gilsenan shows, the idea of Islam as "tradition" is a very recent crystallization from the ideologies of class and status. The end result was to separate religion from the state, give it independent status as "ideology," and thus set up a series of potential religious-political conflicts.

Two related dimensions undergird the whole process. First, religion becomes an index of cultural authenticity in opposition to foreigners and a foreign-oriented elite. Second, Gilsenan (much like Fields or Kselman) stresses that a pervasive emphasis on miracles, suffering, and holy men highlights aspects of daily life (instability, suffering, perceived irregularity) with special meaning for the religious masses. His account of "Miracles and Holy Men" (chapters 4 and 5) is placed in the context of a general discussion of Sufism, a variant of Islam stressing mysticism and ecstatic practices. In practical terms, Sufism has long promoted militant brotherhoods and given enhanced status and role to holy men and shrines. All this has considerable political import, for these leaders (and their lineages) carry enormous authority in some areas, such as the communities of South Lebanon, Morocco, and Egypt that Gilsenan discusses.

Gilsenan sets out to explain who and why *baraka* is experienced and with what impact.

Daniel H. Levine

Sufi followers have generally been marginal to the institutions of orthodox Islam (*'ulema*, jurists, schools). Popular Sufism stresses open participation, ecstasy, surprise, and change. Irregularity is the norm, and manifestations of grace find an audience and feel true precisely because they are disruptive (p. 89). *Baraka* mediates the supernatural into ordinary life and thus fits our common notions of "religion." But as Gilsenan points out (p. 114), the label is not too helpful. It carries undue overtones of order and structure, derived from the domesticated and routinized grace western tradition makes us expect. In contrast, Gilsenan underscores *baraka's* irregularity and its disruptive potential when projected onto shaky structures and conventions. *Baraka* is also in some sense quite predictable: specialized elites produce and project it, and masses take it as a foundation for meaning in an alienating world.

> Baraka is therefore a vital part of the religious *bricolage* of the poor, part of a cobbling together of all kinds of different events, relations, and persons into a single form that contains objects of many different colors, shapes, and sizes. . . . . It can be the language of domination or of the dominated, but in completely contrasted forms and with very different significance (p. 115).

Toward the end of his book, Gilsenan returns to the theme of order and variation in Islam. He again stresses the need to specify context and conditions, especially in discussions of the so-called Islamic revival. (p. 228). While certain core elements of Islam as a religion (institutions, schools, laws, even *baraka*) can be identified and traced across cases, it is wrong to reify religion as somehow "a transcendent power both outside and within time, untainted by history, yet lying beyond it and able to determine it, transforming yet even the same" (p. 254). The problem is to specify just what constitutes "Islam" for whom, when, and with what consequences.

Gilsenan helps by noting the different senses given to "tradition" and to "popular religion" in contemporary Islamic discourse. He avoids over-stress on continuity or misleading presumptions of sociocultural homogeneity. Instead, he highlights the convergence of class marginality with rapid, discontinuous change. An available clientele is created which brings urgent needs to its encounter with "religion." The needs in question are at once economic, social, cultural, and political, personal and collective.

> A rhetoric of liberty and independence breaks on the barren shores of food scarcity, or low-paid and dead-end government jobs, or a "guest worker" hostel in Europe, or the crowded and expensive flats of a city that assumes far too much income to allow for the costs of a marriage for an individual from these strata until perhaps the middle or late 20s. Out of the instability, unease, and immobility comes the call for a transformation of society through the application of the Quran and the Holy Law to the whole of social life. It is, on the one hand, practical and organized around specific projects, and on the other hand, utopian and repressive, excluding those who do not follow the regulations and tracks defined by the group (p. 263).

Recognizing Islam rests on a particular vision of how religion is institutionalized in the Islamic world. Arjomond's work on Iranian Shi'ism deepens understanding of institutional change in what has become a critical case of "religion and politics" in the contemporary world. Arjomond is interested in how the rationalization of doctrine, law, and structures affects political organization and action. He stresses the development of a *political ethos*

113

which sanctions certain kinds of authority relations and makes them normal and expected. The emergence of a separate structure of religious authority (a hierocracy) is critical. Its establishment laid the foundations upon which Shi'ism could assume any one of a number of political positions. The key point is not to identify any single stance with Shi'ism, as if the alternatives were frozen once and for ever. Rather, it is to understand how the impact of any position rests on the independent authority of religious specialists to specify the ethics of sacred law as they apply to power and practice. Following Weber, Arjomond puts this in terms of the world accepting and world rejecting principles of Shi'ism, both of which have been prominent in Iranian history (pp. 18, 19).

The author traces the development of these issues over 500 years in Iran. A few themes are juxtaposed throughout: the intellectual and legal development of Shi'ism; the spread of popular Sufism, with characteristic intense devotion to the Imam; and the gradual consolidation of a hierocracy from what began as a loose collection of religious notables. Religious themes are systematically set against long-term patterns of rulership in Iran, above all the prevailing ethos of kings as deputies of God. A basic contrast and potential opposition is thus established between the Hidden Imam (an expected religious leader, source of guidance and justice) and the Shadow of God on Earth, a patrimonial king with religious properties. Hence the title of the book.

Unlike many recent students of Iran, Arjomond is not directly concerned with methods of mobilization, with the symbology of suffering and redemption, or with the role of passion plays as political exemplars.[15] He clarifies these topics but focuses instead on the long-term evolution of authority relations. He shows how Shi'ism came to the present, why it took the particular form it did, and what implications it has had for politics. Three elements converge to give characteristic value to authority in Shi'ism: the concept of religious leadership, or Imamate; the "Mahdist tenet," according to which the Twelfth, or Hidden, Imam will return as messianic leader and redeemer; and the extensive juristic authority of religious specialists, including their ability to reinterpret the canons of Muslim belief and practice (pp. 13–15).

In the aftermath of the Safavid dynasty, which made Shi'ism the state religion early in the sixteenth century, religious and political authorities were decisively split. Safavid claims to sacred power gave way in later dynasties to an institutionalized division. This shielded the emerging hierocracy from political control (p. 233), giving it an independent basis for criticism and action. As noted, Arjomond's focus on authority makes issues like political mobilization and the revolutionary use of religious symbols and rituals less central to the analysis. But his historical account deepens the understanding of contemporary Iran. For example, he shows that it is precisely in the altered institutional context of nineteenth-century Iran that the mounting, production, and diffusion of passion plays (*ta'zieh*) becomes a central religious and political enterprise. Throughout this period, theaters were built and performances undertaken in growing numbers. Moreover, a conscious attempt was made to use these and other religious vehicles for mass mobilization. An early expression came with patriotic opposition to the Russians. Later manifestations were directed at the British and most recently at the late Shah and the United States. By showing how recent such "traditional" vehicles are in Iran, the author clarifies how religion can take on overt political significance, moving in this instance from a long heritage of quietism to justify and spur activism of all kinds.

114

Daniel H. Levine

Although Arjomond's formal historical account ends in 1890, his conclusions are relevant to later events, including the overthrow of the Shah and the setting up of the Islamic Republic. He clarifies the peculiarly Iranian fusion of religion and politics at work in these events and the special role of the hierocracy as an autonomous structure of power. The Shah may have been king by the grace of God, but in Iran the religious jurists were able to dispute his legitimacy in times of crisis. Their own status as carriers of an authentic national identity was enhanced by the corruption and cultural alienation of the Pahlavi regime. Economic and political crisis served as triggers in Iran, and the accumulated effect of change gave the hierocracy a catalytic role. Thus, it was able to win in 1979 what had been lost earlier in this century and rarely claimed in any direct way in the past.

Together, Gilsenan and Arjomond clarify the kinds of questions which need to be asked about phenomena like "Islamic fundamentalism." Understanding the political character of Islam and more specifically of "Islamic fundamentalism" requires systematic attention to the evolution of Islamic formulations and to the way they are carried by formal structures, picked up and transformed by changing social groups. At this point, I want to take the discussion home and consider American fundamentalism, so visible in the news over the last decade.

James Davison Hunter's *American Evangelicalism* helps us to understand the origins, beliefs, practices, and likely sociopolitical projection of American fundamentalist churches. Hunter challenges the secularization model as classically formulated. He stresses instead a process of adaptation and resistance which changes religion as religion itself alters the cultural and political landscape. In his view, American evangelicalism is caught in a long-term struggle with predominant American norms of cultural pluralism. Part of the response has come through adaptation, especially greater tolerance, civility, and incorporation of a therapeutic language into religious discourse. Resistance appeared first as withdrawal and self-enclosure in a net of reinforcing affiliations and institutions, but more recently in a vigorous, explicitly political challenge to prevailing norms.

Hunter begins with a fine account of the origins of American fundamentalism. As a separate entity, fundamentalism emerged in reaction to the cultural disestablishment of American Protestantism early in this century. From the beginning fundamentalists set themselves off from "main line" Protestantism through their belief in biblical inerrancy and their literalist interpretation of the Bible. These differences were magnified by characteristic fundamentalist stress on Bible reading and public testimony, overwhelming concern for personal salvation, and the systematic organization of life to this end. Hunter stresses the methodical quality of fundamentalist spirituality and the way it rationalizes the achievement of salvation. A notable result of this process has been the production of a number of multistage guidebooks for believers and a general concern with effective packaging of the message (p. 76).

Hunter provides a useful "demographic profile" of fundamentalism (charter 4) and establishes that evangelicals have a very high "index of belonging" (p. 56). Evangelicals appear much more likely to complement church attendance with organizational membership than do other kinds of Christians. This is the result of a deliberate strategy, which since the 1920s has channeled evangelical energies into building a large, stable, and mutually reinforcing infrastructure of churches, schools, and the like. Facing broad cultural pressures

115

for pluralism, tolerance, and privatization of religion, fundamentalists also responded by repackaging their message to cut down the exclusiveness of earlier stress on predestination and the salvation of the elect. Hunter suggests that civility may have been purchased at too high a price: today's God is no longer the unknowable, literally awful presence we find in the Bible. He is more friend and guidance counselor than Lord or Judge. As spiritual experience has been repackaged, it has also been domesticated and focused more sharply on therapeutic concerns like individual happiness, fulfillment, and personal balance (pp. 86–90).

This analysis sets the main lines of evangelical thinking and clarifies the likely character of any political action today's fundamentalist churches may undertake. Hunter prepares one for a curious mix of tolerance and rigidity, civility and pressures for public piety. The concern with attractive religio-political packaging is born of a heritage of running against the grain, and thus seeking to fit the dominant pattern but with a different message. The author shows that despite the intrusion of therapeutic terms and goals (with their characteristic preoccupation with the self),[16] evangelicalism at the same time has vigorously resisted privatization in favor of a bold political project.

The specific character of evangelical political action grows from its characteristic message and structure. Evangelicals take material and spiritual reality as joined and on these grounds contest the deinstitutionalization of piety and morality. Moral and political threats are thus inseparable. "Politics" here refers both to the organization of American society and to the danger posed for American society as a whole by the external, Communist threat. The drive to reestablish moral rules in and through politics is grounded in the notion of God's contract or covenant with his people. Thus, "deinstitutionalization of Christian morality is perceived as an assault on the covenant relationship. America as a nation is disobedient to God's will" (p. 113). From this vantage point, the nation's inner decay and international difficulties are best countered by Christian mobilization, effected through congregational organization and conventional political activism.

Hunter believes that the recent political salience of evangelicals is probably just a bubble, concealing long-term weaknesses and contradictions. He sees evangelicals as fighting a losing battle. It is hard to advance a complaint which runs so very counter to the main trends of American social and cultural life. In any case, the effort requires so much repackaging that in the end core evangelical beliefs are gutted (pp. 122, 125). For Hunter, the survival of a distinct evangelical world-view depends above all on the maintenance of separate, reinforcing sociocultural institutions which "acting as plausibility structures would be capable of reimposing their objectified meanings on a laity perplexed by contrary realities of day to day life, of reassuring the doubters that things are all right after all" (p. 132). This suggests that innovations in publication, national organization, and the use of mass media are of particular salience for the future.

Hunter offers a compelling portrait of the evangelicals in contemporary America. His analysis of the inner dynamics of religious change illuminates the likely implications of any individual or collective "political action" fundamentalists may undertake. A similar strategy, working from religion to politics and back, is appropriate for the study of liberation theology. I noted earlier that liberation theology has lately become the subject of considerable controversy. The next section puts liberation theology in historical perspective,

Daniel H. Levine

as one recent attempt to reformulate religion's meaning and implications in ways which highlight themes of justice, action, commitment, and "politics."

Nicholas Wolterstorff's *Until Justice and Peace Embrace* contains the 1981 Kuyper lectures at the Free University of Amsterdam. In these lectures, the author compares liberation theology to neo-Calvinist reform movements in nineteenth-century Holland. He sees both as instances of "world-formative Christianity" which elaborates a vision and justification of social reform and political action rooted in an understanding of God's active presence in the world. Each emerges in a context of extreme poverty and injustice, where an old social system is decaying and the shape of the future is being fought over. Like Zaret's Puritans, adherents of both stress independent access to the Bible and root action firmly in biblical teachings.

Being "rooted" in the Bible suggests constant reference to biblical metaphors, images, and examples. Moreover, not all biblical passages will do: Wolterstorff shows that both schools stress the Hebrew prophets, men who by argument and example stressed God's active presence in the world and His desire for justice. Being rooted in the Bible also means that reading, commenting on, and discussing biblical texts is a central activity, a unifying point for organization and action. This was true for the Puritans and the neo-Calvinists and is central to grass-roots groups in Latin America now. Religious groups with an initial agenda of Bible study have been founded in large numbers all across the region. Bible study has remained central to their practice, even as the groups have taken on critical roles in organizing and legitimizing popular political action.[17]

Liberation theology emerged in Latin America in response to the broad changes in Catholicism since the Second Vatican Council. Writers in this school share a concern with historical change, insist on the necessity and legitimacy of action to promote justice, and give place of preference to everyday experience as a source of religiously valid values. From these foundations, liberation theology has stimulated new kinds of collective organization and undergirded a new kind of clerical populism throughout the region, whereby sympathetic priests, sisters, and pastoral agents "go to the people." Their notion of religious service enhances values of solidarity and shared experience and identifies strongly with people whose lives are deformed by oppressive structures. In all these ways, liberation theology has created a new agenda in both church and politics, with great stress on democratization and equality in the structures each provides. The result has been pervasive, often bitter conflict in both churches and political systems.[18]

All this has been so much in the news lately that it is instructive to step back from the contemporary scene and consider liberation theology in light of Wolterstorff's comparison. Chapter three draws a few explicit parallels between liberation theology and neo-Calvinism. Both are concerned with victims; both stress the need for structural transformation over charity; and both locate the center of human action in change in this world. Both also stress the long-term process of human self-transformation through history as a central part of God's plan, a constituent element in the coming of the Kingdom. Human potential is thus never set once and for all. Economic, social, and political structures are vital to each school, for they shape the way this potential develops and thus affect the unfolding of divine will through human action.

There are also important differences which give a distinct tone to each school's social and

117

Comparative Politics   October 1986

political analysis. Two are especially noteworthy: the perspective on social conflict and the way in which average experience is valued and used. Each theology sees conflict as the result of injustice. But for neo-Calvinism the root of the problem is idolatry, specifically exaggerated faith in *growth*. In contrast, for liberation theology conflict arises from the domination of some groups by others. Domination itself is explained in terms of class and class conflict, Marxist categories which acquire religious sense through incorporation into expanded notions of sin. Liberation theology stretches ideas about sin beyond conventional limits of individual misdeeds to characterize entire social systems whose structural sin thwarts God's plan by sustaining injustice (p. 66).

Neo-Calvinists and liberation theologians take different perspectives on the religious value of ordinary experience. Wolterstorff points to the characteristic Calvinist emphasis on mastery and responsible action in a calling. These give place of preference to those who work—who create and shape things, events, and processes. From this perspective, average people are central sources of insight and guidance, and the authoritative, mystical quality of the clergy is undercut.[19] The issue is more ambiguous for liberation theology, and a number of contradictions and problems appear. Liberation theology does stress informed participation, lay autonomy, and the value of everyday experience. But the stress on the poor (class-defined) as source and object of religiously valid action, with its implications for group autonomy and governance, clashes directly with the hierarchical structures, authority patterns, and canons of legitimacy on which Catholicism is founded.

Wolterstorff argues that liturgy, ritual, and worship are central to a proper understanding of religion. They lie at the core of any adequate definition of "participation" in religion and give concrete meaning to the sense of identity, authenticity, and belonging religion can provide. The everyday experience of religion they provide undergirds the solidarities which make any action possible. This is what binds members together apart from commitment to any particular social or political agenda the group may develop. But liturgy and worship are often ignored in the rush to look at practical concerns and immediate events. Even within the churches, ritual and worship are seen in instrumental terms, not important in themselves but simply energizers for the primary task of "relevant" social action (p. 148). To Wolterstorff, this perspective cuts the heart from religion. It clouds understanding of what people got out of religion in the first place and obscures the sources of religion's repeated and enduring power to move human action.

The issue is relevant today. Go to the field almost anywhere in Latin America, and take a range of grass-roots groups commonly identified as "activist" or "politicized." Almost without exception, they are religious in origin and remain religious at the core. This means that members value religious practice and make liturgies, processions, prayers, and the like central to group experience. They demand these services from priests and sisters who are often reluctant, anxious instead to move on to the "more urgent" business of social or political reconstruction. The matter has become especially salient as the new grass-roots groups noted earlier have turned into key arenas for political and religious conflict. In the struggle to control and orient such groups, the centrality of religious practice in group life has become a major issue between "conservatives" and "progressives." They also contest the nature of authority relations and the determination of what constitutes a legitimate agenda for reflection and action.[20]

Struggle on these dimensions lies at the heart of what appears as "religion and politics"

Daniel H. Levine

in Latin America today. It is more basic than "Marxist-Christian conflict," for example, because it joins the definition of relations within the church to a contest over the institution's proper social and political projection. The process is political in two related senses. Politics appears in one guise through the challenge group autonomy poses to established lines of power and authority in the churches. Politics also appears because the ordinary practice of these groups makes collective action seem possible and legitimate to average people. At the same time, the substance of everyday group discourse (rooted in Bible study, especially the Hebrew prophets and a new vision of Christ) advances themes of equality and justice which are viewed with deep suspicion by civil and military authorities. In case after case, the result has been to make grass-roots groups, clergy, sisters, and "pastoral agents" generally into primary targets for repression. Central America provided especially telling instances of this process in recent years.[21]

Limitations of space make extended commentary on these issues impossible here. But religion's centrality to political values and action in Central America, as in other cases noted here, makes one question imperative. Given the obvious dangers, why do people participate in such groups at all? What is their appeal? Why did members not simply revert to the passivity and fatalism supposedly characteristic of popular religion? The answer is complex but ultimately rests on understanding how change in the structure of popular life intersected with new religious messages and organizational forms. Already poor, Central American peasants have been notably impoverished and proletarianized over the last twenty-five years. With the surge of the agroexport sector in the 1960s, the economic basis of traditional rural life was undercut, and peasants were converted *en masse* into seasonal laborers. They are worse off, but at the same time available in new ways. These social and economic changes occurred just as major ideological and organizational innovations got under way in the churches. The convergence was decisive. It was also explosive, for when religious innovation promoted ideas about justice (e.g. through liberation theology) and placed these ideas in the context of Bible study and the creation of reinforcing group structures an audience was ready. New groups were already established, and peasants were active as members, absorbing ideas and creating new bonds of friendship and community when repression escalated sharply in the mid and late 1970s. At that point, the moral sanction of the churches, along with solidarity and mutual support in the groups, helped sustain membership and its commitments as both possible and correct. Groups were thus radicalized, and not simply cowed by increased repression.

How best to understand the mutual impact of religion and politics? The first step to greater knowledge is to see that influence runs both ways. Political action and commitment grow from religious motives and structures; politics gives models and provides pressures which spur reflection, organization, and action. The whole process spills over formal ideological and institutional limits, shaping and drawing strength from the everyday experience of meaning and power. A second step comes with realization that all this operates not only through the pursuit of short-term goals, but also through building languages, universes of discourse, and expectations. These create "spaces" which in the long run can be filled with different ideological contents. Analysis must begin with these basic changes and explore how they are worked out at different levels. Only then will it become clear why they emerge

119

linked to each other in recognizable configurations which appear repeatedly across time, space, and cultural boundaries.

What does all this suggest for the future? How should new research be organized and focused? Agendas for future work can be put together in several ways. The easiest is to compile lists of empirical research questions. In all probability, we will never have complete coverge of contemporary, let alone historical, aspects of religion and politics: parties, leaders, symbols, ideologies, shrines, movements, etc. But this building-block approach is likely to be disappointing. The problem is not simply to get "all the facts." We must first establish what the relevant facts are, and this task calls for theoretical clarification.

In the study of religion and politics, the very definition of the field, and hence of key questions for research, is very much up for grabs; little is truly settled. Therefore, construction of an agenda for the future must start with reflection on the proper lines of research. What are the kinds of acts we need to study? Which questions can and should be asked? A close reading of the books reviewed here uncovers the outlines of an emerging agenda, which can be boiled down to the following related areas of concern.

First, research needs to focus on the sources of transformation in religious ideas. This involves debates within organized religion, the creation of new religions like Hoa Hao, and the kind of religious *bricolage* now so common along the world's periphery. Second, the appeal of these ideas to concrete groups must be specified. How do new ideas "fit" the needs and practices of emergent or already existing social groups? What sorts of structural changes make some kinds of ideas more or less appealing? The impact of contractarian notions among the Puritans, the meaningfulness of ideas about religious leadership worked through metaphors of sacrifice and suffering, and the spread of democratic forms in grass-roots Catholicism today are all cases in point. Third, competing attempts to shape religion must be specified and each associated with an identifiable power base and organizational net. It makes a difference who defines group agendas and what sort of structures mediates action. Are we dealing with sheikhs and mullahs, Watchtower preachers, bishops, Jesuits, or independent peasant activists? Fourth, attention to change must not obscure continuities. These rest in part on the staying power of institutions but in a more basic sense arise from the conjunction of everyday needs with the structure of opportunity. In his work on religion, Weber drew a broad distinction between normal times and times of crisis. Normal times are not hospitable to charismatic power; prophets and religious innovation generally find a more ready audience in moments of crisis.

Much of the task of understanding religion and politics, then, is to identify the structural conditions which make religion salient and to figure out why it makes sense to speak of Watchtower, Catholicism, Islam, Hoa Hao, and the Puritans in the same breath. At a minimum, these conditions include the decay of some older system, the delegitimation of its characteristic symbols and mediations (leaders, organizations, rituals), and a further process which changes the routines of average people to bring them together in new ways, make them more available for organization, and enhance popular imagery and solidarity in the process. The expansion and transformation of commerce and the growth of literacy in seventeenth-century England, the proletarianization of Central American or Vietnamese peasants, and the broad cultural, political, and organizational impact of colonialism in Africa or Asia are cases in point.

This research agenda takes off from ideas and works outward to social class, structures,

Daniel H. Levine

and institutions and then back again through ideas to action. Obviously, comparable agendas could be built on other bases, class for example. But a peculiar value of studying religion is that it reinforces our sense of the creative power of ideas and their ability to move individuals, groups, and large collectivities in new and unexpected ways. In the final analysis, the way we think about things organizes how we act, what we seek, and how we see and interpret events. Of course, this is not a matter of ideas alone, as if ideas were disembodied, ethereal manifestations, just "in the air" in some vague way. Ideas are closely linked to structures: they are carried by institutions and worked out in the daily routines and expectations of all sorts of groups. Moreover, it is not all the same even within what we conventionally define as a single "society" or "culture." These are matters of conflict and struggle.

The key point for analysis is thus not to reify a particular unit or orientation at any point in time. Islam, Catholicism, Buddhism, or even "religion and politics" should not be frozen in a single form. The orientation of a given class, group, or institution cannot be assumed to hold now or in the future as in the past, here as there. Instead, research must address the formation of "packages," clusters of elements and legitimations. Studies could then specify how such configurations are put together, by whom, and under what circumstances. How are "packages" related to one another in a given social order, what makes for success or failure, why the appeal to specific groups? The result of all this would be work focused less on "Catholic radicalism," "Islamic fundamentalism," millenarian movements, and the like, as on the clustering of ideas, leadership, followers, resources, and opportunities which make these emerge and give them enduring impact. Within this general field of topics, as I have suggested, particular attention should go to linkages, especially those binding masses and elites, popular and institutional discourses, and levels of reality.

NOTES

1. The study of religion and politics is thus an example of how theoretical reassessment and empirical change can go hand in hand. The phenomenon is not new. When Tocqueville looked at religion in America, he knew the subject was unfashionable but saw how central religion was to American culture and politics. Tocqueville had this to say: "Eighteenth century philosophers had a very simple explanation for the general weakening of beliefs. Religious zeal, they said, was bound to die down as enlightenment and freedom spread. It is tiresome that the facts do not fit this theory at all." Alexis de Tocqueville, *Democracy in America*, vol. I (New York: Anchor Books, 1969), p. 295.

2. For the most complete statement of Weber's views, see Max Weber, *Economy and Society*, vol. 1, G. Roth and C. Wittich, eds. (Berkeley: University of California Press, 1978), esp. ch. 6.

3. I discuss the vast and ever-growing literature on liberation theology in Daniel H. Levine, "Religion, Society, and Politics: States of the Art," *Latin American Research Review*, 16 (1981), 185–209, and also "Religion and Politics: Drawing Lines, Understanding Change," *Latin American Research Review*, 20 (1985), 185–202. Recent noteworthy additions to this literature include J. L. Segundo, *Theology and the Church: A Response to Cardinal Ratzinger and a Warning to the Whole Church* (Minneapolis: Winston Press, 1985), and J. Sobrino and J. Hernandez Pico, *Theology of Christian Solidarity* (Maryknoll: Orbis Books, 1985).

4. In Phillip Berryman's terms there was a movement "from evangelization to insurrection." See Phillip Berryman, "El Salvador: From Evangelization to Insurrection," in D. Levine, ed., *Religion and Political Conflict in Latin America* (Chapel Hill: University of North Carolina Press, 1986), pp. 58–78. The overall process has been described in various recent works. On Central America, see above all P. Berryman, *The Religious Roots of Rebellion: Christians in the Central American Revolutions* (Maryknoll: Orbis Books, 1984); on Brazil, see S. Mainwaring, *The Catholic Church and Politics in Brazil, 1916–1985* (Stanford: Stanford University Press, 1985). Of course, not all cases have radical outcomes. For a comparative perspective, contrasting "progressive" Brazil with "conservative" Colombia, see D. Levine and S. Mainwaring, "Religion and the Nature of Popular Protest in Latin America," forthcoming in S. Eckstein, ed., *Protest and Resistance in Latin America*.

Comparative Politics   October 1986

5. The range of cases noted here suggests that thē process has no set ideological direction or outcome. A South African case quite different in tone from those cited in the text is T. Dunbar Moodie's *The Rise of Afrikanerdom: Power, Apartheid, and the Afrikaner Civil Religion* (Berkeley: University of California Press, 1975).

6. My experience in Latin America suggests that Catholic radicals ignore this at their peril. Attempts to condemn the Pope or local bishops as "reactionary" often end up in their losing popular allies, whose respect for these figures cuts through any possible commitment to actions the Pope or bishops might not favor.

7. Latin American reflections of this phenomenon may be seen, for example, in J. Sobrino, *Christology at the Crossroads* (Maryknoll: Orbis Books, 1978), and L. Boff, *Jesus Christ Liberator* (Maryknoll: Orbis Books, 1978).

8. For further details on Hoa Hao and other religious movements in Vietnam, see J. S. Werner, *Peasant Politics and Religious Sectarianism: Peasant and Priest in the Cao Dai in Vietnam* (New Haven: Yale University Southeast Asia Studies Monograph Series No. 23, 1981), and S. Popkin, *The Rational Peasant: The Political Economy of Rural Society in Vietnam* (Berkeley: University of California Press, 1979), esp. chs. 3 and 5.

9. Cited in H. S. Hughes, *Consciousness and Society* (New York: Vintage, 1961), p. 211.

10. On the historical study of popular religion, see above all N. Davis, "Some Tasks and Some Themes in the Study of Popular Religion," in C. Trinkaus and H. Obermann, eds., *The Pursuit of Holiness in Late Medieval and Renaissance Religion* (Leiden: E. J. Brill, 1974), pp. 307–36. A useful recent discussion is T. Kselman, "Ambiguity and Assumption in the Study of Popular Religion," in Levine, ed., *Religion and Political Conflict*, pp. 24–41.

11. Cf. T. Ranger and E. J. Hobsbawm, eds., *The Invention of Tradition* (Cambridge: Cambridge University Press, 1983).

12. For example, M. Dodson, "Nicaragua: The Struggle for the Church," in Levine, ed., *Religion and Political Conflict*, pp. 79–105.

13. The stress on spiritual self-possession, self-control, and congregational independence had far-reaching consequences. In Christopher Hill's words, "If there is a spark of the divine in all men, preaching should not be a clerical monopoly. No spoken or printed word should be suppressed, lest God's trust be lost. If all men were equal before Christ, should they not also be equal before the law?" *The Century of Revolution* (New York: W. W. Norton, 1982), p. 147. See also Hill's illuminating *God's Englishman: Oliver Cromwell and the English Revolution* (New York: Harper & Row, 1970).

14. Among recent works on Islam which are disappointing are D. Pipes, *In the Path of God: Islam and Political Power* (New York: Basic Books, 1983), and R. Wright, *Sacred Rage* (New York: Simon & Schuster, 1985). Cf. the recent collections edited by J. L. Esposito, *Voices of Resurgent Islam* (New York: Oxford University Press, 1983), and S. A. Arjomond, *From Nationalism to Revolutionary Islam* (Albany: SUNY Press, 1984). A highly critical account of this literature is J. Green, "Islam, Religiopolitics, and Social Change," *Comparative Studies in Society and History*, 27 (April 1985), 312–22. See also D. Laitin, "Religion, Political Culture, and the Weberian Tradition," *World Politics*, 30 (July 1978), 563–92.

15. For example, M. M. J. Fischer, *Iran from Religious Dispute to Revolution* (Cambridge, Mass.: Harvard University Press, 1980).

16. On therapeutic metaphors in American culture, see R. Bellah et al., *Habits of the Heart: Individualism and Commitment in American Life* (Berkeley: University of California Press, 1985), esp. part 1.

17. These groups are known in Latin America as base communities or CEBs (from the Spanish *comunidades eclesiales de base*, base ecclesial communities). For further details on CEBs, see Daniel H. Levine, "Religion and Politics: Dimensions of Renewal," *Thought*, 59 (June 1984), 117–142, and "Religion, Politics and the Poor in Latin America Today," in Levine, ed., *Religion and Political Conflict*, pp. 3–23.

18. Witness the controversies surrounding Pope John Paul II's visits to Latin America and the intense debate over such issues before and during the Extraordinary Synod of Bishops held in Rome in late 1985. On the synod, see P. Hebblethwaite, *Synod Extraordinary* (London: Darton, Longman & Todd, 1986).

19. This suggests that Calvinism's relation to secularization is ambiguous. Calvinist ideas help to constitute secular society by making it legitimate to turn individual and collective energies to activity in this world. But they also sacralize the world, placing events and actions in the context of God's creation. A covenant model underlies all human action, stamping the whole package with a legitimacy derived from the sense of doing God's will.

20. A notable fight for power and control is now underway in Latin American Catholicism. At issue is how to define the relevant "people" for the church and how to organize their ties to ecclesiastical institutions. Who will set the agenda for popular groups? Should they stress spiritual issues, social and political concerns, or some as yet undetermined mix? Who will staff and direct training programs, run mimeograph machines, record and distribute cassettes, and found, monitor, and nurture new religiously inspired groups? On these issues, see Daniel H. Levine, "Colombia: The Institutional Church and the Popular," in Levine, ed., *Religion and Political Conflict*, and also Levine and Mainwarning, "Religion and the Nature of Popular Protest in Latin America."

21. The best general account of the process in Central America is Berryman's *Religious Roots*. I discuss this book in "Religion and Politics: Drawing Lines, Understanding Change." Also notable is A. Carrigan's *Salvador Witness: The Life and Calling of Jean Donovan* (New York: Simon & Schuster, 1985). For more detailed comment on *Salvador Witness*, see Daniel H. Levine, "Whose Heart Could Be So Staunch?," *Christianity and Crisis*, July, 22, 1985.

[2]

The Iranian Revolution in Comparative Perspective

Fred Halliday

The preceding chapter has argued, in a broad overview of modern Middle Eastern history, that the development of the region's politics cannot be explained by reference to a set of religious doctrines, or to some fixed social and political entity called 'Islam'. The purpose of this chapter is to test that argument against the key event in modern Middle Eastern history which appears more than any other to show the importance of Islam. The Iranian revolution of 1978–79 was made in the name of religion and its call for a resurgent Islam resonated through the Middle East and beyond. Nowhere in the modern period has the challenge of explanation, of showing how an apparently religious event was the result of other, more mundane, processes, been so sharply posed.

The Iranian revolution was indeed one of the epic events of postwar history, involving a remarkable level of political mobilization, crisis on an international scale and political brutality. Contrary to the expectations of many, the apparently stable regime of the Shah was overthrown in 1978–79 and a new post-revolutionary system successfully established and maintained. Yet beyond its importance for the history of modern Iran and of the world as a whole, the revolution has posed complex analytic questions both for those who seek to relate it to the overall course of modern Iranian history, and for those who want to compare it to other modern revolutions. It can also serve as an important case-study of how far Islam as a religion can explain the course of political events in a late twentieth-century context. If the Iranian upheaval deserves the name 'revolution' – defined in terms of a high level of mass mobilization, destruction of an existing political and social order and the establishment of a distinctly new order – then it would seem to be a quite unusual variant, a development as atypical as it was unexpected.

It is, however, worth remembering that all revolutions exhibit characteristics that are unexpected, that they can upset the schemata of social analysis as much as they overthrow established systems of power. The French revolution challenged many of the rationalist assumptions of the Enlightenment. Antonio Gramsci, himself a communist leader in Italy, called the Russian revolution 'the revolt against *Das Kapital*' because of the way it appeared to defy the economic determinism that underlay earlier Marxist thinking. The Iranian revolution was certainly an original event, but it is advisable to be more than a little cautious about specifying just where this originality lies.

A tentative discussion of this revolution's originality can therefore serve three functions: to prevent facile locking of the Iranian case into preconceived patterns of Iranian history or the sociology of revolutions; to counter claims that the Iranian revolution represents a wholly original process, a *sui generis* event to which available concepts of historical analysis and rational explanation cannot be applied; and to match general conceptions of how 'Islam' affects politics and society against a particular case, and one in which an Islamic regime has been established and maintained. A proper emphasis upon the novelty of the Iranian revolution and of its Islamic character can be balanced by some comparative caution, by suggesting that not all that has occurred in Iran is either unique, or as resistant to external comprehension as many would suggest.

The novelty of the Iranian revolution can be said to reside, in the first instance, in the role played within it by religion and in particular by what is loosely termed 'religious fundamentalism'. For the first time in modern history (that is, since 1789), a revolution took place in which the dominant ideology, forms of organization, leading personnel and proclaimed goal were all religious in appearance and inspiration. This in itself distinguishes the Iranian from other revolutions of the modern era. Given the manner in which Islam seeks to legislate for many areas of social activity, this religious imprint has involved an attempt to transform law, culture, polity and social practices in Iran in line with a model supposedly elaborated in the seventh century AD.

A consideration of various other features of the ideology of the Iranian revolution, often overlooked in the too generalized emphasis on religion, serves to show that paradoxically they too have a religious derivation and also distinguish the Iranian case. The first of these ideological features is the rejection of ideas of historical progress: Ayatollah Khomeini explicitly proposed a return to an earlier model of social and political practice and a rejection of many aspects of modernity. Such historical and ideological throwbacks have been seen in other revolutions and nationalist movements: the past can always be used to provide convenient legitimation. But the Iranian case went much further, because such a regression was the basis of the whole revolutionary programme. In the proper sense of the word, what happened in Iran was a comprehensively *reactionary* revolution, restoring to the term its original, astronomical, meaning of *return* to a previous order. A second consequence follows from this. While economic and material factors and aspirations played a part in the Iranian revolution, the leadership was reluctant to recognize the fact and tended rather to reject the idea of material improvement. Khomeini attempted to lower the material aspirations of the population by inculcating his ideal of generalized austerity, in which Western consumer goods were rejected and the faithful could live in a state most conducive to religious devotion.[1] Khomeini on one occasion declared that the goal of revolution was not to provide the people with cheap melons. On another, he told President Bani-Sadr that the American embargo during the hostage crisis would not be detrimental to the population for 'In the time of the Prophet, they ate only one date a day.'[2] Thirdly, while nationalist themes of assertion and rejection were articulated, the Iranian revolution was undertaken in the name of universalistic religion, and comparatively little stress was placed on Iran as a national entity. Its universalism was more pronounced than that of the French or Russian revolutions. This was evident both in the cultural shift that accompanied the revolution, which saw the rejection of many features of indigenous Iranian culture as well as values that were regarded as Western, and in the projection of Iran's revolution as the first episode by an insurgent Muslim world in the overthrow of its oppressors.[3]

A fourth ideological peculiarity, the rejection of history, followed from this. Far from vaunting the heroes and strugglers of earlier generations, as other revolutionary and nationalist movements have tended to do,[4] Khomeini appeared to regard almost all the earlier leaders of Iranian opposition movements, both secular and religious, as obstacles to his legitimacy, which he derived from the Islamic leaders of the seventh century, the Prophet Muhammad, and the founders of Shi'ite Islam. Khomeini's symbolic recourse to doctrine to secure legitimacy accounts for the fifth ideological quirk of the Iranian revolution, namely the fact that while it was a mass uprising, it cannot even theoretically be considered a democratic revolution.[5] Khomeini's writings and the constitution of the Islamic Republic made clear that ultimate power rests with the divinely inspired religious authority, the *faqih*, who can override all elected bodies and can dictate his views to the faithful. Khomeini tended to suggest that this presented no problem since there could be no contradiction between the faithful and the *faqih*; but were such an unexpected event to occur then he was in no doubt that the will of the *faqih* held sway. The reality of the Iranian revolution therefore contrasted markedly with the conception of revolution that had prevailed since the late eighteenth century: it rejected historical progress, material improvement, national assertion, historical legitimation, and democratic sovereignty – five themes which, however violated in practice, were at least invoked formally by modern revolutions from 1789 onward.

Yet this wholesale religious character is not, even in its appearance, as all-encompassing as might be assumed. Khomeini's ideas were fundamentalist in their claim to derive everything from sacred texts, but they were not fundamentalist or traditional in the sense that these terms imply inheritance from the past. Both the ideas themselves, and even more the political and social effect they had, were novel, dependent upon modern social conditions and modern political debates on which they drew quite freely, though without attribution.[6] Furthermore, it is possible to pose the same questions of Khomeini's ideas as one would of any set of radical ideas that find a mass following and make an impact on history. Which social groups supported these ideas, and why? What were the determining

factors in the history of the country concerned which enabled
such a movement to gather force at the time it did? Why was it
possible for this opposition to defeat the established state? What
kinds of social and political change have accompanied its triumph?
The Islamic revolutionaries have their own answers to these
questions which usually involve divine agency. Others may be
hesitant about accepting these answers, even while viewing them
with interest for what they tell us about the intentions and ideology of those who directed the revolution itself. Different responses
may, therefore, be suggested.

If we depart for a moment from its religious character, the
Iranian revolution appears more familiar. It was made by a wide-
ranging alliance of social groups, drawing its support from dissident sections of the civil service and trading communities, and
from much of the poor urban population. These forces were
mobilized against a dictatorial political regime by a charismatic
leader and by an ideology of revolutionary legitimacy.[7] In other
words, the Iranian revolution developed in the context in which
populist movements have arisen in many other Third World
societies. Even the religious character of the revolution is, in
historical perspective, not so unique. History is replete with
instances of rebel movements challenging temporal rulers in the
name of God, and of clerical leaders organizing such movements.
The aspiration to create a sanctified order on earth runs through
much of the history of medieval Europe and the Middle East and
through that of nineteenth-century China. Newly urbanized populations in other countries have been known to turn to religion as
a means of responding to the tensions of their new environment.
In Iran itself, the mullahs were at the forefront of other protests
in modern times, specifically the 1891 Tobacco Protest and the
Constitutional Revolution of 1906.[8] What is unique about the role
of religion in the Iranian revolution is that it became prominent
in the latter half of the 1970s and, in particular, that it succeeded
in overthrowing the established regime.

However, the originality of the Iranian revolution does not lie
only in its religious character. If Iran's upheaval was unique in the
prominence occupied by this 'traditional' theme, it was unique
too for its very 'modern' features. The first contemporary revolution to be religious in orientation, the Iranian revolution was also

the first ever 'modern' revolution.[9] This 'modernity' is evident in four respects. First of all, the revolution took place in a society far more socio-economically developed, in major respects, than was Russia in 1917 or China in 1949. Half of the population lived in urban areas, per capita income was over $2,000 and, however unevenly this was distributed, it meant that most Iranians living in the cities were materially better off than a decade before. It was not the *sans-culottes* who made the revolution, but people who had benefited materially from a process of rapid capitalist modernization.[10] Second, in contrast to all other Third World revolutions, the Iranian revolution happened in the cities. Many of those who took part in it may have been peasants (that is, of rural origin), but it was an urban event, produced by the conditions of the major cities in the 1970s. The contrast with China, Vietnam and Cuba is evident. Third, and again in contrast with other Third World revolutions, the Iranian upheaval was carried out through political confrontation rather than armed conflict. Thousands of people died in the last months of the Shah's regime, but they were mainly unarmed demonstrators, not guerrillas. Only in the last days of the Shah's regime did armed confrontation become the dominant form of resistance: the preceding months had been dominated by the street demonstration and the political general strike, forms of opposition associated with the schemata of revolution in the most advanced Western countries.[11] Finally, the fall of the *ancien régime* happened without it having been weakened through confrontation with any external force, as is normally believed necessary for the removal of an authoritarian regime. Neither defeat in war nor serious international economic pressure assisted the advance of the Islamic revolutionaries, and they themselves received no significant help from abroad.

From the perspective of twentieth-century revolutions, these 'modern' features are as original as the Islamic character of the Iranian case. It can therefore be said that the originality of the Iranian revolution resided neither in its 'traditional', nor in its 'modern' character but in the interaction of the two.[12] It is this combination which accounts for both the success and the peculiarity of the revolution in its initial stages, but it was also the increasing disassociation of the two which complicated the establishment of a post-revolutionary order.

48 *Islam and the Myth of Confrontation*

The course of the revolution

The events that led directly to the fall of the Shah spanned a period of little more than one year. Mohammad Reza Pahlavi had been on the throne since 1941 and had been an autocratic ruler since 1953 when, with the assistance of the United States and Britain, a military coup had overthrown the nationalist government of Mohammad Mosaddeq. Since that time there had been only sporadic open opposition to the regime; the period 1960–63, when nationalist politicians and a section of the clergy led by Ayatollah Khomeini had protested against the Shah's control of political life and against the reforms he was instituting, was the notable exception. After over a decade of apparent calm, marked only by minor urban guerrilla activities, the opposition became more active in 1977, circulating critical statements and holding protest meetings. In January 1978 street protests began, organized by religious students in the city of Qom protesting at a newspaper article which insulted the exiled Khomeini. For the next few months there were successive protests and strikes in the main urban centres of Iran, in which the local clergy usually played an important organizing role and in which the bazaars, the historical centres of trade and finance, gave support by going on strike.

The regime did not appear to be in mortal danger, however, until September 1978 when, at the end of the fasting month of Ramadan, the traditional religious processions rallied over one million people in Tehran for what became political protests. The imposition of martial law on 8 September, followed by the shooting of demonstrators, only temporarily stemmed the protest movement, and in October a wave of strikes began. Although at first organized to make economic demands or as protests at press censorship, these strikes set in motion a process which led to a nationwide political general strike in late November and December. The first victims were the oilfields, whose standstill effectively blocked off Iran's export earnings and deprived the armed forces of diesel fuel. On 5 November, under pressure from a restive military leadership, the Shah appointed a military government. Lacking political cohesion, the new government was in any case unable to end the strikes and in early December found itself forced to permit a new round of street demonstrations to mark the

traditional Shi'ite festival of Ashura. This provided the opportunity for the demand to be made more clearly than ever before
that the Shah must depart. By this time, Khomeini had become
not only a symbol of opposition but also an increasingly active
leader; from his base in Paris he insisted on no compromise with
the Shah or those in any way associated with him.

On 15 January 1979 the Shah left Iran, leaving behind a de-
moralized and divided army, and a government headed by former
opposition leader Shahpour Bakhtiar. A committed secularist and
courageous individual, Bakhtiar overestimated both his own
political resources and the loyalty of the army. He also under-
estimated the degree to which he had discredited himself by being
seen to accept his office from the Shah. Khomeini refused to
negotiate with the Bakhtiar government and, after returning to
Iran on 1 February, he pronounced Mehdi Bazargan head of a
rival government. For ten days Iran had two governments; but on
10 and 11 February, following pro-Khomeini mutinies in the
garrisons of Tehran, groups of armed civilians seized control of
government buildings and military camps. The army command
declared itself neutral in the conflict between Khomeini and
Bakhtiar; the latter and his associates, together with remnants of
the royalist court, either fled or were arrested.

The new Bazargan government then proceeded to institutionalize the post-revolutionary regime. On 30 March a referendum
proclaimed Iran an Islamic Republic. In November 1979 a new
Islamic constitution was similarly passed by referendum, and
Khomeini was officially accepted as the *faqih* or supreme judicial
authority with extensive powers. In January 1980 Abol-Hasan
Bani-Sadr was elected president and, following its election, the
Majlis or parliament, dominated by the Islamic Republican Party,
selected as prime minister Mohammad Ali Rajai, an opponent of
Bani-Sadr. These institutional developments were, however, over-
shadowed by other processes and crises: the virtually undisputed
dominance of Khomeini as leader of the new republic weakened
any other political forces and encouraged factionalism among
those eager for his support. Meanwhile, the deterioration of the
social and economic structures of the country, combined with
increasingly antagonistic international relations, impeded attempts
to create a new and viable post-revolutionary order.[13]

Beyond those traditional and modern aspects that gave this revolution its unique and paradoxical character there were other remarkable features. One was the suddenness of the event. Despite the underground opposition of the 1960s and 1970s, and despite the socio-economic tensions associated with uneven and rapid economic expansion, the years prior to the revolution were not marked by major political or social unrest. Neither was the upheaval preceded by a significant economic crisis such as a recession affecting substantial parts of the population. Nor did this crisis develop inside Iran as a result of conflict with other states: the frequently observed pattern of revolution following war or comparable international challenges to the power of a state could not be applied to Iran. Few people, whether observers or participants, were conscious even six months before the Shah fell that the regime was in serious trouble, and even the pronouncements of the Ayatollah Khomeini indicate that his growing sense of confidence, reflected in his more and more militant demands, developed in response to the course of events in Iran itself. Yet the revolution was not a chance event: it defeated not a decayed autocracy but a state that had appeared to be one of the stronger and more decisive of Third World regimes, and one, moreover, that had enjoyed considerable support from abroad. Although it is necessary, in the light of subsequent events, to revise the picture of the Shah's regime as one at the zenith of its power, it would be a mistake to underestimate the combined force of the revolutionary pressures which were necessary to overthrow the established Iranian state. In a condensed and schematic form, there are five central areas in which the causes of the revolution may be discerned.

Rapid and uneven economic development

In the two decades prior to the revolution Iran had undergone substantial socio-economic transformation and had made considerable advances towards becoming an industrialized capitalist society.[14] Yet in previous decades Iran had undergone relatively little transformation, and the accelerated changes of the 1960s and 1970s both produced exceptional tensions within the society and sustained certain pre-capitalist or pre-industrial sectors that were to facilitate the upsurge of 1978.

The main reason why the revolution occurred was that conflicts generated in capitalist development intersected with resilient institutions and popular attitudes which resisted the transformation process.

The impetus for economic expansion came from Iran's oil industry, whose revenues rose from $45 million in 1950 to $1.1 billion in 1970 and, following the multiplication of prices by OPEC, to $20.5 billion in 1976. By the late 1970s, per capita income in Iran was over $2,000, industrial output was growing at over 15 per cent a year, and up to half the population was living in the towns. Urban Iran appeared to be enjoying widespread prosperity, and virtually no social groups in the cities suffered a net fall in income. But the very process of transformation, mistermed 'modernization', was itself contradictory.

This oil-fuelled growth generated its own problems. First, the availability of oil revenues subsidized many areas of the economy and so enabled them to remain uncompetitive and unproductive. Oil assisted economic changes, but it also subsidized inefficient sectors, fostered a large service sector and state apparatus, and gave the Iranian government the illusion that it could dispense with the disciplines that developing societies without oil had to respect. Although much of the economic change was real, there was also much that was illusory. Even in its own terms, however, the oil boom could not last, and the period 1977–78 saw a relative slowing down. GNP stagnated in these years; inflation increased, particularly in rents; certain commodities grew scarce; and power cuts occurred, angering urban-dwellers. There was no widespread hardship, but the slowing down had political effects as entrepreneurs lost confidence and as the government enforced price controls on merchants to combat inflation. The decision of the cost-cutting Amuzegar government to suspend state subsidies to the clergy in 1977 must also have had its consequences.

More important for the mass of urban poor, however, were the inequalities and tensions associated with the boom itself: while the gap between rural and urban incomes began growing in the late 1960s, inequalities in the urban areas themselves began to be increasingly pronounced. By the mid-1970s it was calculated that the top 10 per cent of the population accounted for 40 per cent of expenditure; in addition, the urban poor suffered from the housing shortage, with the result that some had to spend up to 70 per cent of their income on rents. The population of some cities doubled in a decade, and while the migrants may have benefited from higher incomes there, they suffered the loss of the support systems of village society. To make matters worse, there was widespread corruption, involving members of the royal family. Beyond the unevenness of the economic expansion lay the unevenness of the transformation itself: the fact that despite industrialization and partial modernization, the transition was not taking effect. In agriculture the land reforms of the 1960s produced a cash-crop sector tied to the urban economy, but far more of the land was cultivated in family-sized units relatively isolated from the rest of the economy. The towns had a long tradition of commercial and religious institutions grouped around the bazaars which, in the face of the changes from above, adapted but retained their independence and their hostility to the Shah's state. There was a high degree of industrialization, with two and a half million people employed in manufacturing of some kind – a very high figure by Third World standards, representing about a quarter of the total labour force. Yet the great majority were employed in small artisanal units, retaining the production processes and cultural values of an earlier epoch.

Comparable dichotomies could be observed in the fields of distribution and finance. Despite the emergence of a modern banking system and of modern retail outlets, a good deal of financial and commercial activity remained under the control of the bazaar which had in the past fully controlled these sectors. The bazaar merchants resented their relative demotion by banks and new retail systems, yet their absolute position improved greatly with the expansion of economic activity in the country, so that the two-thirds of retail trade they retained enabled them to lend to those whom the banks regarded as unacceptable. It was also the bazaar that had traditionally financed the religious institutions, the mosques, shrines and religious schools.[15] This was, then, a sector that combined considerable influence in the country with deep antagonism to the new economic structures and to a regime which posed a direct threat to its influence by attempting to restrict the area in which the bazaar merchants could manoeuvre. Those merchants were one component in an explosive triangular partnership that also incorporated the clergy and the urban poor, the latter retaining the values of the pre-industrial society. The transformation of Iranian society therefore preserved and even promoted institutions of economic and social activity that acquired new potential for opposition within the altered context created by this transformation.

The political weakness of the monarchy

The Shah's personality helped weaken not only the army but also the state. The role of the individual in history is not only that of instigator and agent, but also of being a weak link in a system of political power. This factor alone cannot explain the Iranian revolution, any more than the characters of Louis XVI and Nicholas II can explain the fall of the Bourbons and Romanovs. But the Shah's grandiose distance from the realities of Iran helped introduce those development programmes which created the socioeconomic context of the revolution; his ignorance of conditions in the country, together with his tendency to withdraw into silent meditation and his paralysis of will, were ill-suited to his coping with the crisis of 1978.[16] He seems to have known from about 1974 that he had cancer, and this may account both for the recklessness of some of his projects and for the fatalism he displayed in his final months of power. If such speculation is permissible, one could argue that no monarch could have saved the regime in the last few months of its existence, but that an autocrat of a different stamp might have been able to prolong its existence or take effective corrective measures early in 1978. Whatever the importance of this personal factor, it certainly seems to have contributed to the unexpectedly rapid disintegration of the regime.

In certain respects, the Pahlavi regime never enjoyed widespread legitimacy. Both the Shah and his father had come to power through military coups, and both ruled through political dictatorship. By the time of his fall, the Shah had had many thousands imprisoned and tortured. Khomeini's designation of the Shah and his father as 'usurpers' therefore struck a chord in Iranian political life, although the precise interpretation of this term may have varied, depending on whether it was alternative secular forces that were seen as having been displaced (in the cases of the 1906 Constitution and the coup that removed Mosaddeq) or rather the legitimate leading role of the clergy. Both Pahlavis were also seen as illegitimate rulers because of their reliance on foreign support. Certainly the attempts by the Shah to generate intermediate institutions of legitimation in the post-1960 period were a failure; the *Majlis* and the parties in it were phantoms, and neither Pahlavism as a national ideology stressing the pre-Islamic past, nor authoritarian concepts of *farmandari* or 'commandism', were widely accepted.

Yet the quality of the Shah's political illegitimacy was not constant: the dictatorship of the 1950s, and the prospects of economic improvement of the 1960s and early 1970s, seem to have produced at least some tacit acceptance. But the ironic consequence of the boom of the mid-1970s was to undermine this tacit acceptance by highlighting the inequalities and corruption inherent in the regime. Nor did this concern only the urban poor and the bazaar merchants: it also exposed one of the fatal weaknesses of the regime, namely the alienation of large sectors of the middle class. Despite the fact that this class benefited from the regime and could have had little expectation of improvement without the Shah, they failed actively to support his government. Their alienation cannot be attributed solely to the fact that the regime was a dictatorship which denied the rich and educated a voice in the affairs of a government which simply reflected the specific factions at court and the skewed distribution of oil wealth. Here Iran differed from Franco's Spain and Pinochet's Chile: while the material improvement offered to the middle classes was far greater in Iran, so too was the separation of those in power from the middle class. The result was that the Shah failed to mobilize an active social constituency in his period of success and was thus left isolated throughout the course of the revolution.

This fissure helps explain another important feature of the revolution, the demoralization of the army. One cause was the form that the confrontations of the revolution took. Huge unarmed crowds assembled, backed by the disconcerting and potentially hegemonic ideology of Islam. This was a threat any army would have had difficulty resisting in the absence of an occasion to take the offensive. The structure of the army, with its corrupt top officer corps and mass of conscripts beneath, also made it more liable to political demoralization. Khomeini himself devoted considerable attention to this issue, making appeals that would be most likely to undermine the army while at the same time seeking to avoid bloody confrontations. Another important factor was the conduct of the Shah himself and his failure to give strong leadership in the final months. When he left the country in January 1979 the army leadership was divided. The crisis of the final days was settled because, in the face of Khomeini's movement, the top army leadership signed a secret agreement with the opposition.[17] Yet beyond all these factors lies the fact that the army was, from the beginning, isolated in Iranian society: it was the instrument of the Shah. It had never fought a successful war and lacked any martial legitimacy. The gap between the majority of the middle class and the regime meant that in Iran, in contrast with other countries where armies have seized power to pre-empt revolutions, the military lacked the political and social support which an active political constituency can provide.

The broad coalition of opposition forces

Theda Skocpol's study of the French, Russian and Chinese revolutions forcefully contests the idea that revolutions are purposive activities in which a group of people consciously organize to overthrow a regime.[18] She points out that revolutions arise in situations of structural crisis for the society in question, and that those who initiate revolutions are not necessarily those who ultimately wield power in the post-revolutionary order. All revolutions produce groups who say the cause has been 'betrayed'. In Iran, the liberals and guerrillas who were openly contesting the regime in 1976 and 1977 were displaced in January 1978 by the clerical and bazaar forces; indeed, even within the Islamic forces the leadership gradually passed from cautious clergy like Shariat-Madari and from reformist Muslim militants like Bazargan and Bani-Sadr to the more hardline clergy of the Khomeini–Beheshti variety. At the same time, the revolution was not carried out by a political party. One of the proudest claims of the Islamic militant was: 'Our greatest strength is our lack of organization.'[19]

The broad and rapidly congealed coalition of forces that overthrew the Shah was strong precisely because of its diverse and spontaneous character; it was also one of the causes of the factionalism and paralysis of the post-revolution period. On the other hand, political organization did play its part in the Iranian revolution. The secular political parties were small and played only a secondary or even marginal role in the events of 1978–79; even when they participated they were forced to join the dominant Islamic trends. Far more important was the organization of the clergy; based in each locality of the city and with centres in the mosques and shrines, they were able to use religious networks to mobilize the population. These networks may have been decentralized and, initially, not designed for political purposes, but they acquired a leading organizational role in the crisis of 1978 and had, by the latter half of the year, acquired in Khomeini a determined and appealing leader. Behind the clergy there also lay the underground *Fedayin-i Islam* grouping, a militant sect founded in the 1950s. There is reason to doubt whether Khomeini himself was a member, but some of the leading clerical figures were, and they had been determined for over two decades to wrest power from the Shah. The case of the Iranian revolution demonstrates the possibility of purposive action in a revolutionary situation: it was the clergy who directed the struggle throughout.

The social forces that responded to the movement varied. In the first clashes of 1978 the main components were theology students and bazaar merchants, but these groups, far more in touch with the population than the secular parties, were able to call on the urban poor who became the foot-soldiers of the major demonstrations in the latter part of the year. Parallel to these protests, the students and parties continued their actions, and in the final weeks of the regime it appears that significant numbers of middle-class people also joined in the demonstrations. The slogan raised in the final weeks was simple enough: 'Independence, Freedom, Islamic Republic'. The one commanding aim was to oust the Shah: many who doubted the suitability of Khomeini none the less supported the movement in the hope that it could achieve the desired aim. Among the secular and middle-class forces many hoped that once the Shah had gone they could deflect the movement away from its clerical patrons. This enabled such people to support the movement with appropriate optimism, but it represented an underestimation of the strength of the religious forces.

The resulting relationship between social classes and political leadership was an example of the combination of traditional and modern forces in the Iranian revolution, which mobilized large numbers of people representing various social groups. Without such numbers, and the arousing of insurrectionary consciousness in these groups, the revolution would not have succeeded. The strikes that paralysed the country from October 1978 on became a great and unified exertion of social power by different classes in pursuit of a defined political goal. Yet these classes acted in the name of, and under the leadership of, an Islamic force that denied the relevance of class forces and class goals. The post-revolutionary period showed that the workers and merchants, despite the power they had demonstrated in the revolution, were unable to wield their power independently of the religious authorities, let alone in opposition to them. Subsequent accounts would argue either one side of this process or the other – that this was an Islamic revolution brought about by the exertions of an undifferentiated body of believers, or that the revolution was a proletarian upheaval later betrayed and crushed by a usurping and counter-revolutionary clergy. Neither account appears to be sufficient. The strength, as well as much of the tragedy, of the revolution lay in the manner in which both aspects were combined.

The mobilizing role of the Islamic religion

In the Iranian revolution several factors together produced the unique result of a twentieth-century state run by the clergy along lines derived from the Quran and Islamic law, in which the major influence lies in the hands of a personage constitutionally designated as the interpreter of holy texts. One negative factor which played its part in giving prominence to Islam as an ideology of opposition was the systematic destruction by the Shah and his father of the *secular* opposition forces that had mobilized protest movements in earlier decades.[20] Even the guerrilla groups, the

Fedayin and *Mujahidin*, were at a low ebb by the mid-1970s. The result was that, as in other societies where secular forms of protest are blocked off, religion in Iran became a symbol and an organizing centre for a protest that might otherwise have taken a more conventional secular form. Had Mosaddeq not been kept inside Iran and subsequently died, he might have developed some of the allure of the Ayatollah Khomeini.

This 'vacuum' theory is not, however, sufficient. Several other factors have to be taken into account. First, in all its forms Islam claims to be able to legislate for the whole of human activity. In Islam there is no formal distinction between church and state (though in practice the clergy has through history tended *not* to challenge *fundamentally* the legitimacy of a state governed by a monarch or other ruler who is not a cleric). The very concept of the secular is theoretically excluded, and all social ideas must be legitimated by derivation from the holy texts. In terms of political theory this assertion finds its expression in the attempt to define an 'Islamic' concept of government. In social activity, Islam prescribes modes of behaviour for everyday life and human relations. Like Judaism and Hinduism (though not Christianity), it has concepts of clean and unclean and stipulates ritual activities for each day: in the language of anthropologists, it enjoins *orthopraxy* as well as *orthodoxy*. As a result, the call for an Islamic society or Islamic polity is far more deeply rooted in the basic doctrine of Islam and in the historical consciousness of Muslim societies than comparable Christian claims. Islamic countries have in practice often exhibited a wide gap between the religious and secular domains, but this has not altered the theoretical overlap of the two upon which Islamic thinkers can draw.

A second factor is the ideological ductility of Islam in general, and of Shi'ite Islam in particular.[21] While considerable energy is expended by believers and non-believers alike in arguing which political principles can be derived from Islam, both the evidence of interpretation and the fluid formulations of the Quran itself suggest that Islamic theory allows a wide range of derivations. According to the external circumstances of the time and the concerns of individual interpreters, different principles may be derived with equal authority from the holy texts. The doctrine does not enjoin a specific course of action but provides themes that can justify a variety of courses. One possible line of interpretation is what one may term the *demotic* (as opposed to *democratic*). Islam does not have a religious hierarchy and the position of its clergy depends to a considerable extent upon popular assent. At the same time some of the themes of Islam, such as emphasis on the common concerns of the community of believers, opposition to tyrants and support for struggle, can serve the cause of popular mobilization.[22] The very plainness of Islamic prayer meetings, in contrast with the ceremonials of Christianity, confirms this demotic tendency. Because all such policies claim to be derived from the word of God and are interpreted by those with authority, they are not at all democratic, but can still serve the purposes of political mobilization.

In Shi'ite Islam there are further dimensions to this demotic and undemocratic potential. Traditionally, in Sunni Islam the caliph or his equivalent was the head of state. The caliphs were direct descendants of the Prophet, and since they embodied temporal and religious power, in theory at least, there was no problem of ensuring legitimate government. Born of a division in the Islamic movement, Iranian Shi'ism holds that the Twelfth Imam went into hiding, and believes in the occultation or *gheiba* of this Imam, God's representative on earth. Great stress is also laid on the sufferings of Shi'ites at the hands of unjust rulers, and upon the cult of the Shi'ite martyrs, Ali and his sons, Hasan and Husein. Both these factors combine to *permit* the idea that Shi'ism is an ideology which rejects temporal order, a permanent dissidence *vis-à-vis* both orthodox Sunni Islam and established state authorities. (At the time of the revolution some – Western-educated – advisers to Khomeini liked to say: 'We are the Trotskyites of Islam.') Other interpretations are, of course, possible. Conservatism and political quietism are just as reconcilable with Shi'ism because Shi'ism is neither inherently radical nor inherently compliant. For over a century after Iran became an officially Shi'ite state in 1501 the clergy was properly integrated into the state structure. Shi'ism in sixteenth-century Iran served the function of Protestantism in Elizabethan England – as a state religion designed to distinguish the monarch's realm from other states, in Iran's case from Ottoman Turkey. But this arrangement broke down in the eighteenth century, and from then on there has tended to be opposition

60   *Islam and the Myth of Confrontation*

between state and at least some *ulema*, a clash that broke out at the turn of the twentieth century.[23]

Within the many variant and contingent consequences of original Shi'ite theory, two have had particular political pertinence – one institutional, the other ideological. The institutional consequence concerns the financial bases of the clergy. In Sunni Islam where the state is legitimate the faithful pay their *zakat* and a further levy known as the *khoms* (fifth) is paid directly to the clergy. This means that the clergy are independent of the state in a manner unique in the Muslim world, and that the populace is able to make the religious personnel responsive to their demands. In Iran in the 1960s and 70s there existed a religious establishment of several thousand mosques and shrines, several tens of thousands of *mullahs*, and a network of *madrases* (religious schools). Mainly funded by *bazaaris*, these were independent of the Shah's control.[24] Ideologically, this link with the people meant that the clergy had little room for improvisation or change. Reflecting the concerns of a conservative constituency, the Iranian *mullahs* were far less concerned to face the intellectual challenges of the modern world than their more autonomous counterparts in the Arab Sunni countries.[25] One of the central Shi'ite debates concerned the status of authority in the period of the *gheiba*: while one school accepted temporal authority or advised a process of patient dissimulation or *taqiye*, others advocated a political role for the clergy and derived this course of action from certain Quranic principles. It was this latter option that Khomeini was to embrace. In popular Shi'ism, there also lay ideological themes that could be used for political advantage. One was the theme of martyrdom and sacrifice, celebrated every year in the passion plays commemorating the death of the Shi'ite leader Husein in the seventh century. The other was the belief in a future golden age, a time when the Twelfth Imam would come out of occultation to create a just society upon earth. If the former was conducive to extremes of political militancy in a revolutionary period, the latter provided a theological goal that enabled many to hope that an Islamic Revolution would indeed create a new and better society on earth. By failing to specify the characteristics of such a society, Khomeini maintained the support of a wide range of social groups.

Revolutions require organization and ideology, and both were provided in some measure by Shi'ism in its institutionalized Iranian form. But revolutions also require leaders, and in Ayatollah Ruhollah Khomeini the Islamic movement found such a person. Khomeini had a history and a personality appropriate to his role. He had opposed the Shah in the early 1960s and had been exiled in 1964. He was known to be honest and courageous; he spoke in a clear, uncompromising, and often cruel tone. He also exhibited shrewd political judgement: he saw that his greatest asset was to have nothing to do with the Shah's regime, and he kept his intentions for the future regime as vague as possible in order to maximize political support. He also found the proper moment to strike – mobilizing his supporters for the final push in late 1978, skilfully weakening the army, and returning to seize decisive control of the Iranian state. As a revolutionary leader Khomeini had luck, but he also had skill.

Khomeini was in many respects the epitome of a charismatic leader. He came to the fore during a time of rapid social change and tension, and appeared to be exempt from the sinful and compromising world around him. He also appropriated the religious title of Imam, which gave some suggestion that his role was analogous to that of the returning Twelfth Imam. Another reason for his assuming this title was that it circumvented the problem of his not being the senior ayatollah while investing him with a (higher) religious authority. There are certainly many who seem to have believed not that he was the Twelfth Imam, but that he would none the less introduce a just society as promised in the Shi'ite dramas.[26] He himself never claimed to have the specific attributes of the Imam in Shi'ite doctrine – the ability to transmit the word of God as conveyed by angels, the power to effect miracles, and the quality of being *ma'sum* (immune from sin). But the position of *faqih*, or supreme interpreter of the law, where both interpretation and law are invested with religious authority, certainly raised him well above other mortals and members of the Shi'ite clergy. Assuming this religious legitimacy had been established *before* the revolution, the very success of the events of 1978–79 appeared to strengthen Khomeini's authority and the aura of God-given power he sought to cultivate.[27]

It is in this context that the thought of Khomeini became

particularly influential. Khomeini belonged to that minority faction within Iranian Shi'ism who held to the activist interpretation of the Shi'ite dilemma: he criticized monarchy and thought the clergy should play a leading role in government. Yet the logical development of this thesis came only in response to the potential effect it might have. While his early writings of the 1940s were critical of monarchy, they did not go as far as to condemn it outright; and even in the 1960s Khomeini accepted the legitimacy of the 1906 Constitution. However, his lectures on Islamic government published in 1971 reject monarchy and advocate the concept of *velayat-i faqih* (*velayat* means government or legal authority, here combined with *faqih*, the standard Islamic term for someone who interprets the law). The concept of *velayat-i faqih* as elaborated by Khomeini is 'therefore a forthright attempt to legitimize governance by Shi'ite clergy in the temporal as well as the spiritual realm. In 1978, however, he went further and openly rejected the 1906 Constitution, instead introducing the concept of Islamic Republic, his idea of the society Muslims should try to recreate on earth.

For all its invocation of a return to the past, however, the concept of the Islamic Republic was, like many of Khomeini's other ideas, a skilful fusion of Quranic and modern themes with the Shi'ite aspiration of one day seeing a just society on earth created by the returning Imam. Khomeini divided societies into two categories of people – the *mostazafin* and *mostakbarin* (literally, those made weak and those made big) – two Quranic terms which began to be used in the populist sense of 'oppressed' and 'oppressor'.[28] His attacks on *fesad* or corruption certainly had a Quranic moralism about them: the main charge on which many of the Shah's supporters were executed was of 'spreading corruption upon the earth'.[29] Yet the term corruption would, in the eyes of many poorer Iranians, include more secular derelictions as well. Even Khomeini's relation to nationalism was ambiguous, because in the first period of his rule he virtually never mentioned the word Iran at all, laying stress instead on Islam and on the need to recreate the Islamic 'Universal State'. Yet much of his diatribe against the West and Western values had an unmistakeably nationalist ring, and followed what some secular Iranian intellectuals had been saying for a long time.[30] It picked up on the influence of Frantz Fanon mediated to Iran via the thought of Ali

Shariati, the lay Muslim philosopher whose writings had a great impact upon the younger generation.[31] The war with Iraq that began in September 1980 forced Khomeini to lay greater explicit stress on nationalist themes: just as Stalin was forced by the German invasion of 1941 to evoke the greatness of Mother Russia, so Khomeini turned to mobilizing support in the name of Iranian patriotism. In this sense even the *faqih* and the role of the Imam could epitomize standard populist–nationalist leadership themes.[32]

However, as his attitude towards modernity shows, Khomeini did not accommodate secular forces. In contrast to some earlier Islamic thinkers such as al-Afghani, who did emphasize the need for Islam to come to terms with science and democracy, and who openly acknowledged the ductility of Islamic thinking, Khomeini reasserted the hostility of Islam to modern ideas and the need to re-establish authoritative doctrinal purity in all matters.[33] Yet even this misleading traditionalism was not, as we have seen, simply based on an extrapolation from doctrine, but was rather an accommodation to the popular mood in Iran itself, at least as the clergy perceived it. Indeed, both the political strength of the Islamic movement in Iran and the particular theological interpretations that emerged in the 1970s were made possible only by the new socio-economic conjuncture in which the clergy found themselves. In sum, the transformation of Iran, with the unevenness and transitional features already discussed, provided the context for the fusion of a discontented urban coalition with the opposition current within the clergy. What might otherwise have been a more recognizable populism, a movement of the oppressed against the oppressor and in search of a perfect society, was shaped and was given the necessary organization and ideological confidence with which to prevail by the clerical forces led by Khomeini.

The ambivalent international context

At first glance international factors seem to have played an atypically minor part in the course of the revolution itself. The Iranian state had not been weakened by any foreign military defeat or comparable external challenge to its prestige and capacity to govern.[34] Neither the opposition movement nor the Shah enjoyed active foreign support in the final months of the contest. Indeed the absence of any financial or other material backing for the opposition, and the failure of the United States more actively to intervene on the Shah's behalf, are among the most striking characteristics of the whole process.

The Iranian revolution was nonetheless in a definite sense international. It had deeply unsettling effects on the West Asian region, appearing to challenge the rulers of Iraq and the Arabian Peninsula and to stimulate Shi'ites in Lebanon, and to encourage the Islamic forces fighting the revolutionary Afghan government which had come to power in April 1978. After the revolution, Iran extricated itself from the alliance system that the United States had created in the region and became embroiled in two major international conflicts: the fifteen-month dispute over the American hostages and the war with Iraq that began in September 1980. If the Iran crisis of 1946 was (together with Poland) one of the two issues which started the Cold War, the rejection thirty-five years later of the arrangements of 1946–47 by the populations of the two countries introduced a major element of international uncertainty in the 1980s.

Yet the revolution was international in another overt sense, namely in the manner in which Iranians perceived it. Despite the revolutionary universalism posed by Islam, it was felt to be a nationalist movement against the political, economic and cultural influence of the West, and of the United States in particular. This perception was reinforced by one of the most enduring features of Iranian political culture, the belief that political events are determined by a foreign hand. This is as true of the Shah and his supporters, who blamed the revolution on a Western conspiracy to bring Khomeini to power, as it was of Khomeini and the forces associated with him, who regarded the Shah as *sag-i Carter* ('Carter's dog') and continued after the Shah's departure to uncover foreign conspiracies at every turn of events. There was a considerable degree of foreign influence in Iran prior to the revolution, and in this sense the perspective of the revolutionaries had some justification; but the real extent of external interference was far less than was supposed and pointed to the prevalence of that collective paranoia which is such a strong feature of Iranian political life. It fosters such a debilitating atmosphere of helplessness that, far from enabling Iranians to emancipate themselves from foreign domination, it all too often incapacitates them.

Although such conspiracy theories are common in many societies, it can be argued that their particular virulence in Iran owes much to the pattern of foreign policy domination in earlier decades. Never a formal colony of any European power, Iran did not therefore pass through the clear break with foreign authority that independence involves. Moreover the patterns of semi-colonial control used by Britain, Tsarist Russia and later the US – influencing ministers, fostering dissension in the provinces and suborning the military – were precisely those most likely to engender a conspiracy mentality among Iranians.[35] Once this was coupled with the intense exposure to foreign influences at an everyday level in the 1960s and 1970s, and to the fact that the Shah himself *had* been brought back by American covert assistance in 1953, it was less surprising that a simplified picture of foreign control should persist and should substitute for more accurate and intellectually more demanding analyses.

Essentially, foreign forces shaped the revolution in at least three respects. First, the whole context in which the upheaval occurred was one of socio-economic transformation under which Iran was increasingly integrated into the world market and exposed to the economic, social and cultural influences of the West. The rate of Iran's oil output – over 6 million barrels a day – was dictated not by a rational calculation of what revenues Iran could most effectively absorb but by the demands of other countries for greater supply. The political and military build-up of the Shah's regime came about as a result of strategic decisions made in Washington. The cultural gap between the Westernized middle class and the class of new migrants in the major towns was one of the underlying tensions that helped ignite the revolution. Above all, oil introduced external revenue into the society without any comparable transformation of its socio-economic and productive structures.[36] Unregulated oil revenues progressively dislocated the regime from its social context and thereby rendered Iran more vulnerable to a sudden upsurge from below.[37]

A second international factor was the Shah's reliance on foreign support in 1953 and his visible friendship with the United States, together with his quiet but overt sympathy for Israel. This support

66   *Islam and the Myth of Confrontation*

certainly facilitated his control of Iran in the 1950s and 1960s, but in the longer run, like the oil revenues, it undermined his internal bases of support and encouraged his belief that a loyal domestic following could be dispensed with. For this reason, the United States was unable to intervene to save him. The pattern of such interventions, from Vietnam to Iran in 1953, shows that in order to succeed, an action of this kind requires that certain internal conditions prevail. These conditions, which would include a sympathetic middle class or a motivated, repressive army, were absent in Iran by the time the full dimensions of the crisis had become clear in the late 1970s.

The third aspect was US policy in the 1977–79 period. Certainly, it would be a mistake wholly to exclude those factors to which the Shah himself, in his memoirs, draws attention: the Carter human rights policy and the confusions of US policy-making in the final weeks.[38] Yet these were not the determinant factors. Those issues upon which US critics focused attention – human rights violations and the high level of arms sales – were not those most prominent in the complaints of Khomeini and his followers; the subsequent vicissitudes of Islamic justice do not suggest that a desire for due process or improved prison conditions was paramount in the minds of those who flocked to the December 1978 Ashura demonstrations. What can be said is that the Carter policy on human rights reinforced the internal process of political decompression in Iran in 1977 that the problems of the 1974–76 boom had created, and through which certain liberal politicians were able to begin some public activity. It was the example of these secular forces that contributed to the feeling among the *bazaaris* and *mullahs* that they too could now be somewhat bolder.

The events of 1978–79 themselves show little signs of having been influenced by Washington. Until early November 1978 the American government did not recognize that Iran was undergoing a revolution, and by that time no course of action, except the dispatch of substantial numbers of troops, would have staved off defeat. The USA was constrained by domestic considerations such as the post-Vietnam reluctance to engage in foreign wars, and also by Iran's strategic position. US intervention, as Brezhnev warned in November 1978, would have run the risk of triggering Soviet intervention in accordance with the Soviet interpretation of their 1921 treaty with Iran. But, beyond such considerations the overriding explanation of why such a course of action was impossible lay in the crumbling of the Shah's own regime and of his own sense of determination. There remains the question of whether, in the final days, the United States could have achieved some compromise between Khomeini and the army commanders which would have stemmed the full tide of insurrection that followed.[39] This too is an unlikely scenario, since there was little incentive for Khomeini to accept it and, once in power, Khomeini failed even to respect the agreement on immunity of top commanders which he had signed in early February. Therefore, despite the fact that the revolution was affected by both the realities and the myths of Iran's international context, the actual course of events did not entail the involvement of foreign states.

Islamism in power: the record of the Khomeini decade

The analysis so far has focused on the period of the revolution itself and on its immediate aftermath. The passage of time enables us, however, to look at this revolution with a measure of hindsight: not least among the issues which it is possible to consider in retrospect is the way in which 'Islam' was shaped by political requirements, and the needs of those in power. The death of Ayatollah Khomeini on 3 June 1989 brought to an end the first decade in the life of the Islamic Republic of Iran and provides one point from which to assess the character and consequences of Iran's revolution. The consolidation of the regime after 1979 and its continuation after Khomeini's death provide much material for analysis of what the practice of Islamism means in terms of political and social control. It also illustrates the greatest failing of Islamist movements in general: namely, their lack of an economic programme.

Khomeini's achievement in his ten years in power was considerable – in making the revolution, in remaining in power and, not least, in ensuring a smooth transition after his death. Two factors aided that transition. One was that his regime had been run by a group of clergy who had been his students years before and who constituted a loose but effective revolutionary cadre around him.

It was these people who maintained sufficient unity after 3 June 1989 to ensure that Ali Akbar Hashemi-Rafsanjani, already the most influential government personality after Khomeini, was able to assume power and be elected to the new chief executive position of president. The other factor, evident in the popular response to Khomeini's death, was the immense authority which the revolution and the Ayatollah in particular retained among the population, despite all the difficulties of the post-revolutionary period. The revolution and eight-year war with Iraq had brought immense privations to Iran, and sections of the population had been alienated by repression. But there can be no doubt that, ten years after Khomeini came to power, the Islamic Republic enjoyed considerable legitimacy within Iran: it was this support that made it more possible for Khomeini's associates to organize a smooth transition.

Khomeini's last years were, however, marked by great difficulties for Iran: these followed, to a considerable extent, from uncertainty within the ideology of the revolution itself. The first uncertainty lay in the precise role of the state in the new post-revolutionary situation, and the relationship between government and Islam itself. In the early period of the Islamic Republic, greatest emphasis was laid on the question of how Islamic thinking could influence state policy. Thus the constitution was rewritten to include the concept of the *velayat-i faqih*, the vice-regency of the jurisconsult; economic policy was altered to preclude the taking or granting of interest-bearing loans; education was transformed to reflect Islamic thinking, as was the law; women were forced to wear the *hijab*. However, this Islamization of the state went together with another debate on how far the precepts of Islam could act as a constraint upon the actions of government. This was a debate opened in the first instance by religious opponents of the Khomeini regime, who argued on Islamic grounds for a limitation of the new republican regime's power; but the argument soon came to be prevalent within the state itself, in discussion of such issues as government control of trade and finance, and intervention in the economy in the name of planning. Those within the government who adopted a more conservative attitude to economic policy, opposing state intervention, used this Islamic argument to block reform measures.

It was in this context that Khomeini, in January 1988, made one of his most important political pronouncements, in the form

of a letter to the then president, Ayatollah Khamene'i. Khamene'i
had apparently argued that the government could exercise power
only within the bounds of divine statutes. But Khomeini disagreed,
stating that government was 'a supreme vice-regency bestowed by
God upon the Holy Prophet and that it is among the most important of divine laws and has priority over all peripheral divine
orders'. He itemized a set of issues on which, if this view was not
valid, the government would not be able to take action. These
included:

> Conscription, compulsory despatch to the fronts, prevention of the
> entry or exodus of any commodity, the ban on hoarding except in two
> or three cases, customs duty, taxes, prevention of profiteering, price-
> fixing, prevention of the distribution of narcotics, ban on addiction of
> any kind except in the case of alcoholic drinks, the carrying of all
> kinds of weapons.

Khomeini continued:

> I should state that the government which is part of the absolute vice-
> regency of the Prophet of God is one of the primary injunctions of
> Islam and has priority over all other secondary injunctions, even
> prayers, fasting, and *hajj*. The ruler is authorized to demolish a mosque
> or a house which is in the path of a road and to compensate the owner
> for his house. The ruler can close down mosques if need be, or can
> even demolish a mosque which is a source of harm ... The govern-
> ment is empowered to unilaterally revoke any Shari'a (Islamic law)
> agreements which it has concluded with the people when those agree-
> ments are contrary to the interest of the country or to Islam. It can
> also prevent any devotional or non-devotional affair if it is opposed to
> the interests of Islam and for as long as it is so.[40]

This explicit statement was not just a legitimation of what
already existed in Iran, namely a clerical dictatorship. The
concept of the 'absolute vice-regency' (*velayat-i mutlaq*) was a major
new formulation of Islamist politics in the context where an
Islamic state had already been created. Yet like all such legitimations (for example, the dictatorship of the proletariat) it contained its own internal contradiction: for the legitimation of the
state and of the *faqih* lay in their fidelity to Islamic precepts, and
yet these two authorities, derived from Islam, were now being
used to justify overriding whatever Islam enjoined. The key to

this new legitimation was given by the concept, invoked in the quotation above, of *maslahat* or the 'interest' of the Muslim people. It was in the name of this interest, which the *faqih* alone could identify, that the specific injunctions of Islam could be overridden. Conservative opposition had been based in the Council of Guardians, a clerical body designed to see whether parliamentary decisions contradicted Islamic precepts. Khomeini broke this deadlock by creating a new committee, for the 'Discernment of the Interest of the Islamic Order' (*Tashkhis-i maslahat-i nizam-i Islami*), which now had overall power. Never were the underlying political priorities of Islamism clearer: the tactical concern of Khomeini was to use the concept of 'interest' and of the absolute authority of the jurisconsult to override conservative opposition within the regime; the overall goal was to invert Islamic authority so as to free the actions of the state from any Islamic restrictions, particularly in regard to property.

A similar political determination could be seen in the manner in which Khomeini handled another difficult area of state policy, that of the export of revolution. In common with all revolutions, Iran's was presented as a model which could be promoted and reproduced elsewhere. The concept 'export of revolution' (*sudur-i inqilab*) was commonly used by Iranian officials. It included the conventional means of exporting political radicalism – arms, financial support, training, international congresses, propaganda and radio programmes. Islamic tradition also provided specific elements that could be added to this process. Thus, at the ideological level, Khomeini could claim that the Islamic peoples were all one and that in Islam there were no frontiers. In organizational terms, the already established links between different religious communities across the Muslim world provided a network for building revolutionary links. Until the clashes of 1987 when around 400 Iranians were killed, the *hajj*, the annual Pilgrimage to Mecca, acted as a means for propagating Iran's revolutionary ideas.[41]

The most important component of this militant policy was the attempt to export Islamic revolution to Iraq. Iran had called for this before the Iraqi invasion of September 1980, and it became Khomeini's rationale for continuing the war after July 1982 when the Iraqis were driven out of Iranian territory. In the end, of course, it failed: the Iraqi population did not rise up, and the Baghdad regime did not collapse. In August 1988 Iran was forced to accept a ceasefire. In his speech calling for a ceasefire, Khomeini stated that for him this was worse than drinking poison, but that he was forced by political and strategic necessity to do it. This enormous setback in the promotion of revolution abroad did not, however, lead to an acceptance that promotion of Islamic radicalism abroad was impossible. Iran continued to play a role in arming and guiding Shi'ite guerrillas in two countries, Lebanon and Afghanistan, and in the bitter aftermath of the war it maintained a steady criticism of Saudi Arabia, whose 'corrupt' rulers it saw as enemies of Islam.

The proclamation of Iran's continuing role as leader of the oppressed across the world was important not just for external reasons, promoting the image and prestige of Iran, but also internally as a means of sustaining the morale of the population, distracting from domestic economic crisis, and preventing an emergence of 'liberalism', a spirit of compromise or accommodation with the outside world. After the August 1988 ceasefire, Khomeini felt there was a danger that the Iranian revolution would falter and would lose its revolutionary orientation. It was in this context that he reasserted his view that Iran should remain independent of international economic forces, even at the cost of austerity.[42] But he also used an issue that gave him the opportunity to provoke a major crisis with the non-Islamic world and at the same time to present Iran as the leader of the Islamic cause. Khomeini's call for the death of Salman Rushdie, the author of *The Satanic Verses*, was a means of meeting his two main policy goals – mobilization at home, confrontation internationally.[43]

Both of these policies reflected Khomeini's political thinking: the way in which priorities of power and the maintenance of state control determined his use of Islamic concepts and interpretation of 'tradition'. Ultimately, the political assessment of Khomeini's legacy will depend on the extent to which the Islamic Republic endures and whether the regime can resolve the most pressing problem it faces, namely that of revitalizing an economy in collapse. Whether or not it succeeds, however, the measure of Khomeini's achievement should not be understated.

Conclusions

Three general conclusions seem relevant to the overall issue of the relationship between religion and politics, and the extent to which the Iranian revolution exemplifies the course of other upheavals in the contemporary world.

The unique combination of modern and traditional in the Iranian revolution had both institutional and ideological features. The modernity of the revolution was above all accounted for by the transformation of Iranian society in the 1960s and 1970s, the rapid urbanization and industrialization, and the demographic and social tensions this produced. Without this transformation, the Islamic movement could have arisen again, as it had in the 1890s, in the 1900s, and in the early 1960s, but it would have been much less likely to succeed. The destruction of the monarchical regime and the neutralization of its foreign support were made possible by the great force with which the urban movement erupted, a force derived from this process of profound social transformation. Even in ideological terms, the movement reflected the contemporary world environment, both in the themes it invoked and in the manner in which the enemy was viewed. At the same time, the movement drew on traditional forces which had survived and even flourished in the years of transformation. In the cities, the bazaars (and the link of bazaar and mosque) gave the opposition a rallying point and an organizational backbone. The clergy provided an ideology of resistance and the principles for an alternative society. The political culture of the mass of the urban population continued to be characterized by religious beliefs and an acceptance of the role of the clergy in political life.

The Iranian revolution was only to some extent a religious revolution. The values, personnel and goals were all defined in religious terms, the society which has subsequently been created is one which its creators would argue is modelled on the Quran and on Islamic law, and undoubtedly religious beliefs and the specific interests of the clergy made indispensable contributions. Yet the image of an 'Islamic revolution' is too simple. First of all, the concept of religion is itself variable. In Islam it encompasses far more than in Christianity, where the principle of a division between church and state has existed for some centuries.

The Iranian Revolution in Comparative Perspective   73

Doctrinally, Islam does not admit the secular. Though a separation of the secular and the religious has come to prevail over the centuries, it has been far easier for those who wish to reassert the comprehensive claims of Islam over all areas of social and political life to do so than it would be in the case of Christianity. Second, the factors enabling the clergy to challenge and over-throw the Shah were eminently secular ones. Thus the Iranian revolution has more in common with revolutions in other societies than the specifically religious dimension will permit. Material living conditions, opposition to royal dictatorship, and hostility to foreign influence all played important roles in preparing the Shah's downfall. Third, even the very ideology and programme of the revolutionaries contained many themes common to other revolutionary situations: re-establishment of national independence, expropriation of the rich, punishment of the guilty and corrupt, and redistribution of wealth. The decisive manner in which Khomeini's forces took control of the state and consolidated their hold by the creation of a set of new revolutionary institutions was eminently intelligible to anyone aware of what is involved in the establishment of a new state power.

The paradoxical unity of the 'modern' and the 'traditional' in the Iranian revolution accounted for the success of the Shah's opponents, but this unity did not long survive the monarch's fall. The history of post-revolutionary Iran is to a considerable extent that of a growing dislocation of these two components. The attempt to create a clergy-dominated or hierocratic society based on allegedly seventh-century principles in the last quarter of the twentieth century has encountered many problems that permit no easy resolution. The impact of the revolution and its aftermath on the economy has been to lower living standards throughout urban society and to provoke considerable unemployment and inflation. The defiance of all outside powers, together with Iran's call for the spread of Islamic revolution, led the regime into a full-scale war with Iraq, with enormous loss of life and catastrophic consequences for the economy. The imposition of a new form of centralized rule, dominated by the clergy, generated widespread opposition from political forces who supported the overthrow of the Shah but did not support the establishment of an Islamic Republic ruled by the *faqih*. These three dimensions, economic, international and political, therefore presented very real limits to the plan of creating an Islamic Republic.

The Iranian revolution achieved great levels of mobilization and political impact in the struggle against the Shah and in the immediate post-revolutionary aftermath. Once difficulties arose, and the broad united front that had toppled the Shah broke up, Khomeini was able to establish a regime built in his own image and successfully to crush the various opposition forces he faced. The success of the revolution lay not only in the destruction of an old regime, but in the successful establishment of a new one, different in many significant respects from that which it had replaced. If it shared more than it admitted with the Pahlavi regime, it was none the less built on very different systems of power, social support and values. Yet, while this regime survived its first sixteen years, the prospects for its long-term stability remain uncertain.

The hopes raised by the Iranian revolution were extremely high, and it is not the only revolution to have disappointed its original supporters, let alone to have failed to create a perfect society on earth. The post-revolutionary history of Iran has not only highlighted the limitations of the solutions offered by the Islamic clergy, but also soon after his accession to power led Khomeini to stress an archaism inherent in his thought in appealing to blood and sacrifice, the persecution of enemies and former allies, the brutal imposition of discriminatory Islamic codes of behaviour for women, the callous neglect of human life in the war with Iraq, and the incitement to persecute sexual and religious deviants. All these and more are the themes and policies to which the Imam resorted in order to implement his programme.

Through the revolution Iran became the site of a competition between the theological and the material, the clerical and the secular. The first round certainly went to the theological and the clerical. But how far these forces could sustain their advance in the face of material problems and an inability to meet many of the basic needs of the population remained an open question. As time passed, the impact of the material, and of a broad popular aspiration for economic improvement, became more evident.[44] The regime itself began to lay stress on its economic achievements, and to justify the revolution in terms of what it had provided in this domain.[45] Yet, by all accounts, this appeared to be too little, and too late. It was an ironic comment on the fate of the revolution, and of its Islamic aspirations, that by the early 1990s the story was circulating in Tehran that there was now only one authoritative Ayatollah left in the country: his name was 'Ayatollah Dollar'. Itself a product of social and material conditions to an extent that it was reluctant to admit, by the mid-1990s the Islamic Republic of Iran appeared to be in danger of foundering on the very worldly considerations it had sought, sixteen years before, to deny.

1. Karl Griewank, *Der neuzeitliche Revolutionsbegriff* (Weimar: Herman Böhlaus Nachfolger, 1955), ch. 1.

2. Author's conversation with Abol-Hasan Bani-Sadr, Auvers-sur-Oise, France, August 1981.

3. Thus Radio Ahvaz, broadcasting in Arabic on 1 September 1980: 'This awaiting universal Islamic state will demolish all tyrannical thrones built on the corpses of the oppressed. The sword of justice will claim all charlatans, agents, and traitors.' See my 'Iranian Foreign Policy Since 1979: Internationalism and Nationalism in the Islamic Revolution', in Juan Cole and Nikki Keddie (ed.), *Shi'ism and Social Protest* (London: Yale University Press, 1986).

4. One exception is the nineteenth-century Shi'ite writer Mullah Ahmad Naraqi, an exponent of the *Usuli* school, which did emphasize the powers of juridical authorities in Islam. But Naraqi did not extend this to include full political power, as Khomeini was later to do (Said Amir Arjomand, 'The State and Khomeini's Islamic Order', *Iranian Studies*, vol. XIII, nos 1–4 (1980), p. 154). What is striking is that Khomeini does not invoke the precedent of those conservative writers who opposed the secular constitution of 1906. Indeed, while he exhibited an initial tolerance of the 1906 Constitution, he seems later to have regarded the whole period of the Constitutional Revolution as an embarrassment.

5. This point has been well made by Mohammad Ja'far and Azar Tabari, 'Iran: and the Struggle for Socialism', *Khamsin*, no. 8, 1981.

6. Sami Zubaida, *Islam, the People and the State* (London: Routledge, 1989).

7. Ervand Abrahamian, *Iran Between Two Revolutions* (Princeton: Princeton University Press, 1982), pp. 530–7.

8. For a guide to the earlier role of the clergy in Iran, see Nikki Keddie, *Iran: Religion, Politics and Society* (London: Frank Cass, 1980), and her *Religion and Rebellion in Iran: The Iranian Tobacco Protest of 1891–92* (London: Frank Cass, 1966). Strictly speaking Islam does not have a clergy in the sense of an ordained body of men, but in this text I have used the term 'clergy' interchangeably with the word *ulema*, literally 'those who know', the standard Arabic Muslim term, and the word *mullah*, the word normally applied to Shi'ite clergy in Iran. Iranians themselves tend not to use the word *mullah*, but to talk of the *akhund*, a slightly derogatory term for an ordinary clergyman, or of the *ruhaniyat*, the body of religious personnel. Higher-ranking clerics are called *mujtahids*, meaning that they have the authority of *ijtihad*, independent judgement on holy matters, whilst the highest ranking are called *ayatollah*, literally 'sign of God'. For a general discussion of Iranian terms for the clergy, see Roy Mottahedeh, *The Mantle of the Prophet* (London: Chatto & Windus, 1986), pp. 231–2. Given the absence of any established hierarchy, the designation *ayatollah* is a result of promotion and reputation within the Islamic institutions. Prior to the revolution it was a term confined to a small number of clergymen, of whom Khomeini was neither the senior nor the most learned. The term *Imam*, applied to Khomeini, represents a verbal inflation, but is an honorary title

and, at least officially, does not indicate any claim to his being one of the line of Twelve Imams who the Shi'ites believe are the true followers of Mohammad.

9. The Iranian revolution has generated a widespread analytic literature. See, *inter alia*, Nikki Keddie, *Iran and the Muslim World, Resistance and Revolution* (London: Macmillan, 1995); Farideh Farhi, *States and Urban-based Revolutions* (Urbana: University of Illinois Press, 1990); Mohsen Milani, *Iran's Islamic Revolution: From Monarchy to Islamic Republic* (Boulder, Colorado: Westview Press, 1988); Mansoor Moaddel, *Class, Politics and Ideology in the Iranian Revolution* (Oxford: Columbia University Press, 1993); Misagh Parsa, *Social Origins of the Iranian Revolution* (New Brunswick: Rutgers University Press, 1989).

10. We do not yet have the detailed information necessary to establish who were 'the faces in the crowd' that made the Iranian revolution, that is, a precise evaluation of the social forces behind the revolution. While it appears, from the very size and superficial appearance of the demonstrators, that members of all social groups participated, it is much less clear what the proportions were. Some initial indications are given in Farhad Kazemi, *Poverty and Revolution in Iran* (London: New York University Press, 1980). He suggests that it was second-generation migrant industrial workers, not the poorest inhabitants of shanty towns, who participated most in the revolutionary protests. The poorest sections were still outside the social networks that would have drawn them into the demonstrations of late 1978. For an important, earlier study of this issue, see Ervand Abrahamian, 'The Crowd in Iranian Politics, 1905–53', in Haleh Afshar (ed.), *Iran: A Revolution in Turmoil* (London: Macmillan, 1985).

11. The demonstrations in the last months of the Shah's regime, involving up to 2 million people in Tehran, and several million more in provincial towns, were the largest protest demonstrations in human history. States have mobilized larger numbers in supportive marches – as in China's Tien An Men Square – but such crowds have never before been seen in an oppositional context.

12. The terms 'modern' and 'traditional' have been subject to considerable criticism. Their use here does not denote acceptance of a more general picture of social development as being conceivable in terms of a unilinear progression from one to the other. They are used here in a more figurative sense, to distinguish characteristics of Iranian society associated with its past from those resulting from the changes of the last decade.

13. No full account of the revolution has yet been written, but surveys are included in Abrahamian, and in Nikki Keddie, *Roots of Revolution* (London: Yale University Press, 1981). Also of interest are Robert Graham, *Iran: the Illusion of Power*, second edn (London: Croom Helm, 1979), Mohammed Heikal, *The Return of the Ayatollah* (London: André Deutsch, 1981), and L. P. Elwell-Sutton, 'The Iranian Revolution: Triumph or Tragedy', in Hossein Amirsadeghi (ed.), *The Security of the Persian Gulf* (London: Croom Helm, 1981). The best eyewitness account is Paul Balta and Claudine Rulleau, *L'Iran Insurgé* (Paris: Sindbad, 1979). On post-revolutionary developments the outstanding study is Shaul Bakhash, *The Reign of the Ayatollahs* (London: I.B. Tauris, 1984).

Notes

Bakhtiar's own account is given in his *Ma Fidelité* (Paris: Albin Michel, 1982). See also my interview with him in *MERIP Reports*, no. 104, March–April 1982.

14. Robert Graham provides invaluable analysis of many aspects of the economic change; see also my *Iran: Dictatorship and Development* (London: Penguin, 1979), and the references contained therein. On rural conditions, see Eric Hooglund, *Land and Revolution in Iran, 1960–1980* (Austin: University of Texas, 1982). A general economic overview is given by M. H. Pesaran, 'Economic Development and Revolutionary Upheavals in Iran', in Haleh Afshar (ed.), *Iran: A Revolution in Turmoil*.

15. The merchants of the Tehran bazaar were particularly incensed in 1976 when the municipal authorities proposed to build a new urban highway that would have passed through the middle of the bazaar area.

16. American Ambassador William Sullivan complained bitterly of the Shah's indecisiveness, a characteristic foreign observers had noted during the crisis of the early 1950s. Roger Cooper, a British journalist who met the Shah in September 1978, reported that the monarch flatly refused to believe there were any slums in Tehran, a fact evident to the most casual observer. Some pertinent observations are given in Fereydoun Hoveida, *The Fall of the Shah* (London: Weidenfeld & Nicolson, 1980).

17. The army chief-of-staff, General Qarabaghi, was allowed to retire to his home and later went into exile. More mysterious was General Fardust, the former chief of the Shah's private intelligence service, who reportedly became head of SAVAMA, a new state security organization.

18. Theda Skocpol, *States and Social Revolutions* (Cambridge: Cambridge University Press, 1979), pp. 14–18. Skocpol's own reflections on the Iranian revolution are in 'Rentier State and Shi'a Islam in the Iranian Revolution' in *Theory and Society*, May 1982, reprinted in Theda Skocpol (ed.), *Social Revolutions in the Modern World* (Cambridge: Cambridge University Press, 1994). She points to the sociological weakness of rentier states and the mobilizing potential of Shi'a Islam as special factors enabling the Iranian revolution.

19. Ibrahim Yazdi, Foreign Minister of the Islamic Republic, in interview with the author, Tehran, August 1979.

20. An important comparative perspective on the 1979 revolution is given by the Mosaddeq period, when secular nationalism and a mass communist movement predominated: see Richard Cottam, *Nationalism in Iran* (Pittsburgh: University of Pittsburgh Press, 1964). The clergy at that time gave some support to Mosaddeq, but turned against him in 1952 and did not oppose the 1953 coup. Khomeini never mentioned Mosaddeq's name in a positive light and argued that his fall was a result of his abandoning Islam.

21. For discussion of this issue see Said Amir Arjomand, 'Shi'ite Islam and Revolution in Iran', *Government and Opposition*, vol. 16, no. 3 (summer 1981), Edward Mortimer, *Faith and Power* (London: Faber, 1982), ch. 9, and Hamid Algar, 'The Oppositional Role of the Ulema in Twentieth Century Iran', in Nikki Keddie (ed.), *Scholars, Saints and Sufis* (Berkeley: University of California Press, 1972). Also indispensable is the work of Akhavi, cited in n. 23 below.

22. Muslim radicals find confirmation in certain verses of the Quran which

224   *Islam and the Myth of Confrontation*

are supposed to reinforce their orientation: for example, 'We willed that those who are being oppressed would become the leaders and the rightful inheritors of the world' (sura 28, verse 5); and other verses promising a speedy punishment for those who oppress. Khomeini's word for 'oppression', *zulm*, is the conventional Islamic word for tyranny.

23. An extremely shrewd and careful discussion of these points is contained in Shahrough Akhavi, *Religion and Politics in Contemporary Iran* (Albany, NY: State University of New York, 1980). Akhavi demonstrates the contingency of Islamic thought and hence the availability of a wide range of equally valid 'interpretations'. On Islam as a state religion under the Safavids, see I.B. Petrushevsky, *Islam in Iran* (London: Athlone Press, 1985), ch. 13.

24. A careful study of the organization and curricula of the Qom *madrases* in the mid-1970s is given by Michael Fischer in *Iran: From Religious Dispute to Revolution* (Cambridge, Mass.: Harvard University Press, 1980).

25. Akhavi, *Religion and Politics*, pp. 126–7. He quotes one reforming *mullah* who denounced *avam zadigi*, the effects of mass mindlessness, and said it was better to be affected by 'floods, earthquakes, snakes, and scorpions' than to be subject to the will of the masses on matters of reform.

26. Some of the theorists of Islamic revolution have developed a concept of a just or unitary society, based on the Islamic concept of *touhid*, or unity of God and man. These writers include the lay theoretician Ali Shariati and former President Abol-Hasan Bani-Sadr. But it does not seem that Khomeini ever accepted this concept, and he laid much greater stress on the need to implement the rules of Islamic jurisprudence.

27. In the post-revolutionary period Khomeini was officially described by three titles: Imam, Leader of the Revolution, and Founder of the Islamic Republic. These three sources of his legitimacy represented religious authority, the aura of success, and the programme he sought to implement. His frequent designation as 'Imam of the Islamic Nation', where 'nation' is a translation of the word *umma*, illustrates the ambiguous character of the constituency he was meant to represent: Iran or a wider Islamic world?

28. Khomeini's main writings are contained in *Islam and Revolution*, translated and annotated by Hamid Algar (Berkeley: Mizan Press, 1981).

29. The charge of being a *mofsid fi'l arz* ('spreader of corruption on earth') is one common charge in such cases. The other is that of being *mohareb be khoda* ('declaring war on God'). If concepts of legitimacy are essential in mobilizing populist coalitions, so too are concepts of denying legitimacy to the other side. Khomeini's favourite term for the Shah was *taghut*, a term usually derived from an Arabic root meaning to tyrannize. In fact, *taghut* has a different root, meaning idol or a false god. In later terminology Khomeini was referred to as the *bot shekan*, the 'Idol Smasher', with the Shah as the first idol to be broken, Carter the second, Bani-Sadr the third, and, it was hoped, Iraqi leader Saddam Hussein the fourth. *Bot* is a Persian language equivalent of *taghut*. His use of other sources is well illustrated by another term of abuse: *kravati* (someone who wears a tie).

30. In particular, the writer Al-i Ahmad, whose work *Gharbzadegi* ('intoxica-

tion with the West') was very popular among university students in the 1970s. Although the son of a *mullah*, Al-i Ahmad himself was rather anti-clerical in his writings. For an account of his ideas, see Mottahedeh, *The Mantle of the Prophet*, pp. 287–315.

31. On Ali Shariati see Fischer, *Iran*, Keddie, *Roots of Revolution*, and Mangol Bayat-Phillip, 'Shiism in Contemporary Iranian Politics: The Case of Ali Shariati', in Elie Kedourie and Sylvia Haim (ed.), *Towards a Modern Iran* (London: Frank Cass, 1980). Shariati too was quite anti-clerical, and is regarded by most religious authorities as an unlettered upstart. His writings fall into the mainstream of Third World cultural and nationalist writings of the 1970s. He died in London in 1977. See his *On the Sociology of Islam* (Berkeley: Mizan Press, 1979).

32. One exceptional element in Khomeini's populism was his use of irate paternalism, as he threatens to chastise and punish his followers. This is of course partly a note of Quranic punitiveness which will be familiar to his audience, but contrasts with the rhetoric of other secular populists. In a speech in August 1979 he declared: 'When we broke down the corrupt regime and destroyed this very corrupt dam; had we acted in a revolutionary manner from the beginning, had we closed down this hired press, these corrupt magazines, these corrupt parties and punished their leaders, had we erected scaffoldings for the hanging in all the major squares, and had we chopped off all the corrupters and the corrupted, we would not have had these troubles today.' But he goes on: 'I beg forgiveness from almighty God and my dear people.'

33. See Keddie, *Religion and Rebellion*, pp. 27–8, where the Muslim reformer Malkam Khan discusses how to justify modern principles in Quranic terms.

34. Skocpol, *State and Social Revolution*, pp. 19–24, outlines a theory of the international dimension of revolutions on which I have drawn here.

35. For the earlier decades of the century see the classic E. Brown, *The Persian Revolution* (London, 1909; reprinted London: Frank Cass, 1966); for the early 1950s see Kermit Roosevelt, *Countercoup* (New York: McGraw Hill, 1979), a vivid account of the American and British roles in preparing the 1953 coup that reinstalled the Shah.

36. Hossein Mahdavy, 'Patterns and Problems of Economic Development in Rentier States: the Case of Iran', in M. A. Cook (ed.), *Studies in the Economic History of the Middle East* (London: Oxford University Press, 1970), and Homa Katouzian, *The Political Economy of Modern Iran, 1926–1979* (London: Macmillan, 1981).

37. Skocpol stresses the growing autonomy of the state as another central feature of the revolutions she describes. While in my view she overstates the disassociation of ruling class and state apparatus, she none the less indicates a feature of revolutionary situations which contributes to explaining why, at a particular time, an existing state is overthrown. See n. 18 for her application of this thesis to Iran.

38. According to his post-revolution memoirs, the Shah ignored the growing crisis in his country and focused uniquely on the role of the US mission to

226   *Islam and the Myth of Confrontation*

Iran in the last days of his reign: Mohammad Reza Pahlavi, *The Shah's Story* (London: Michael Joseph, 1980).

39. William Sullivan argues that some accommodation with Khomeini might have been possible in early 1979, but that this was excluded by an unrealistic 'hard line' being pursued by Brzezinski, the President's National Security Adviser, in 'Dateline Iran: the Road Not Taken', *Foreign Policy*, Washington, no. 40 (Fall 1980), and his *Mission to Iran* (New York: Norton, 1981). The best accounts of US–Iranian relations are in Barry Rubin, *Paved with Good Intentions: The American Experience in Iran* (New York: Oxford University Press, 1980), and Gary Sick, *All Fall Down, America's Tragic Encounter with Iran* (London: I.B. Tauris, 1985). See also my discussion of variant US accounts in *MERIP Reports*, no. 140, May–June 1986.

40. Text of Khomeini's letter to Khamene'i in *BBC Summary of World Broadcasts* part 4, 8 January 1988. For analysis see: J. Reissner, 'Der Imam und die Verfassung', *Orient*, 29, 2, June 1988. Khomeini's theorization of how an Islamic state can, for reasons of state interest, override religious precepts has an ironic relevance to the Rushdie affair: Iranian and other defenders of the death sentence on Rushdie claim that Khomeini's condemnation of Rushdie to death cannot be overridden because it is necessitated by religious principle. Application of Khomeini's *maslahat* principle would suggest that, if Iranian political leaders thought it was in their interests to do so, they could cancel the death sentence. That they do not do so is not because of some religious compulsion but because, within the politics of the Islamic world, it is still profitable for them to maintain their stance.

41. On Iranian foreign policy since 1979 and the place within it of Islamic themes, see my 'Iranian Foreign Policy Since 1979' in J. Cole and N. Keddie (ed.).

42. The concept of *zuhd* or austerity, often associated with forms of mysticism, was important in Khomeini's rhetoric and welded conveniently with the anti-consumerism of Third World populist and revolutionary ideology. In some ways Khomeini's use of anti-imperialist *zuhd* was analogous to the usage of the concept by the Imam of Yemen who in the 1950s declared that Yemen would prefer to be poor and independent than rich and dependent. How far the Iranian, or Yemeni, people were committed to such austerity was, and is, another matter.

43. On the broader politics of the *Satanic Verses* affair, see ch. 4, pp. 125–27 below. In addition to any general religious concerns, the Iranian authorities may have taken offence at the novel's account of the Imam in exile in London, all too recognizable as a fictional portrayal of Khomeini's stay in Paris in late 1978 and early 1979 prior to his return to Tehran. 'The curtains, thick golden velvet, are kept shut all day, because otherwise the evil thing might creep into the apartment: foreignness, Abroad, the alien nation. The harsh fact that he is here and not There, upon which all his thoughts are fixed ... In exile no food is ever cooked: the dark-spectacled bodyguards go out for take-away. In exile all attempts to put down roots look like treason; they are admissions of defeat.' – Salman Rushdie, *The Satanic Verses* (London: Viking, 1988), pp. 206, 208.

Notes   227

44. On later developments, see Anoushiravan Ehteshami, *After Khomeini: the Iranian Second Republic* (London: Routledge, 1994). Some have queried the validity of the term 'second republic' on the grounds that it overstates the discontinuity between the Khomeini and post-Khomeini periods; but the case for using the term is certainly defensible, given the important constitutional changes that followed Khomeini's death with the formation of a presidential system.

45. In a speech on the tenth anniversary of the revolution Chief Justice Musavi-Ardebili listed eleven achievements of the revolution: in addition to fostering revolution and Islamizing laws, these included Iran's independence, improving conditions in the villages, safeguarding the national economy, developing self-reliance in industry, promoting agricultural production ('Iranian Chief Justice outlines Islamic Revolution's Achievements since 1979', *BBC Summary of World Broadcasts*, ME/0075/A/4–6, 15 February 1988).

[3]

Rendering unto Caesar? Religious Competition and Catholic Political Strategy in Latin America, 1962–79*

Anthony J. Gill, *University of California, Los Angeles*

Since the late 1950s, the Latin American Church has undergone radical changes in terms of theology and pastoral organization. Innovations such as liberation theology and *comunidades eclesiales de bases* (CEBs) have tended to reinvigorate the political role the Church plays in society. Moreover, in several authoritarian regimes, the Roman Catholic Church has been the sole source of opposition. Nevertheless, this change has not been uniform across Latin America. Several national episcopates supported authoritarian rule in the 1960s and 1970s. This study examines the role of religious competition (between Catholics and non-Catholics) in determining whether the national Church hierarchy endorses or opposes dictatorial rule. I argue that the increasing presence of Protestantism in some countries has forced the episcopate to adopt membership retention strategies that are antithetical to the military's goal of suppressing subversive organizations. Application of nonlinear regression techniques to preliminary data provides a test of this hypothesis.

Introduction

During a 12-day tour of Brazil in 1991, Pope John Paul II issued "a warning to priests against deep political involvement."[1] Such counsel was not new: the Brazilian Catholic Church has epitomized the new "progressive" stance of Catholicism in Latin America. Once considered a static, authoritarian institution tied to the dominant classes and incapable of promoting democratic values, the current Catholic Church has often served as the sole voice of opposition to dictatorship. Much of this change can be traced to the institutional liberalization of Vatican Council II and the regional conferences that translated these reforms into a "preferential option for the poor." However, change in the Latin American Church has not been uniform. While several national episcopacies have officially opposed authoritarianism, others have supported dictatorial rule—either

*Comments on earlier versions of this paper were gratefully accepted from Glen Biglaiser, David Brown, Gretchen Casper, Mark Chaves, Cornelia Butler Flora, Jeff Frieden, Barbara Geddes, Laurence Iannaccone, Carlos Juarez, David Lopez, Daniel O'Neil, and Laura Nuzzi O'Shaughnessy. John Zaller aided in the statistical applications. As always, any mistakes herein are mine alone. Finally, I extend my appreciation to my wife, Becky, for her continuing support during this ongoing project.

[1]"Pope Warns Priests to Avoid Deep Involvement in Politics," *Los Angeles Times*, 26 October 1992, F16.

American Journal of Political Science, Vol. 38, No. 2, May 1994, Pp. 403–25
© 1994 by the University of Texas Press, P.O. Box 7819, Austin, TX 78713-7819

Anthony J. Gill

actively or passively. This paper examines the country-by-country variation in the Catholic Church's official position toward authoritarian regimes from 1962 to 1979.[2]

Much of the recent scholarship on Latin American Catholicism favors the single-case study approach and emphasizes the role of increasing
poverty and repression in the region. While greatly contributing to our
empirical understanding of progressive Catholics in these areas, single-
case studies are limited theoretically by their lack of variation on the
dependent variable. Therefore, the continued presence of conservative
churches in other impoverished and repressive countries cannot be adequately explained.

Using a comparative methodology, I examine both progressive and
conservative churches in an attempt to develop testable propositions of
Church behavior in Latin America. Obviously, much of the detailed richness unique to individual case studies will be lost by this approach. However, I believe the theoretical gains from broad comparisons adequately
balance such costs. This study differs from previous work in two additional respects: (1) the unit of analysis—the Church hierarchy; and
(2) the importance placed on religious competition and deregulation (i.e.,
"supply-side" religion vs. the predominant "demand-side" orientation).

To explain the variation in *official* Church policy toward military
regimes, I focus upon the role of the episcopacy. Bishops represent a
vital intersection between the Church's pastoral agents (e.g., parish
priests) and the state. They must pursue the often contradictory goals of
supporting progressive pastoral agents, while simultaneously promoting
the institutional interests of the Church in the political sphere. If, and
when, the Church's pastoral interests conflict with the ambitions of the
political elite, the episcopacy must make a strategic choice between
carrying out their evangelical mission or maintaining an alliance with the
ruling class. This conflict is most apparent under right-wing authoritarianism, since pastoral efforts among the poor threaten the internal security
of the regime.

Additionally, rather than viewing Catholic progressivism from the
"demand-side" (i.e., increased desire for social justice and spiritual guidance), I hypothesize that the Church's new stance is a strategic response
to an increasing *supply* of religious and ideological alternatives—
Protestants, Spiritists, and Marxists. Given the long history of political

---

[2]This period covers the significant growth of Protestant missionary activity and indigenous religions (e.g., spiritism and Pentecostalism), which began during the 1930s. The year
1979 saw a scaling back of sanctioned Catholic political activity, due largely to orders from
Pope John Paul II, and the gradual return to democracy in the region.

and economic repression in Latin America, there has always been a relatively high demand for justice; the Catholic Church has had over four centuries to address this problem but has chosen to do so only in the last three decades. For this reason, the explanatory power of demand-side theories is brought into question.

What has recently changed, though, is the supply of religious "goods and services." To prevent nominal Catholics from choosing competitors, the episcopacy has advocated (or at least tolerated) innovative reforms that better serve these individuals. Fierce competition will most likely exist where official state support for Catholicism is minimal. Nevertheless, separation of Church and state (in the absence of competition) is not a sufficient condition for explaining Church opposition. Even under conditions of separation, the episcopacy will still desire friendly relations with the regime so as to influence policy decisions and obtain the highest possible amount of state subsidies.

I argue that the presence of religious/ideological competition increases the importance of obtaining active followers among nominal Catholics, predominantly the rural and urban poor. The Church may choose to do this by some mix of direct pastoral organization (e.g., base communities) and state assistance (e.g., subsidized Catholic education). If legal separation exists between the Church and state, the probability of obtaining favorable policies is reduced and the Church will favor pastoral organization. Because authoritarian regimes oppose organization among the lower classes, pastoral efforts among the poor will be viewed by them as potentially threatening. Church opposition to dictatorship manifests itself after the military represses such efforts and prevents the Church from fulfilling its proselytizing mission. In summary, competition forces the Catholic Church to adopt membership retention strategies that often contradict the internal security concerns of authoritarian states.

The Political Economy of Religion

Prior to examining the Latin American cases, it is important to understand the nature and effects of the religious economy. Like business firms, religions are producers. But they produce a rather uncommon set of goods and services (i.e., answers to the fundamental questions of life and death). Stark and Bainbridge capture the economic exchange aspect of religion by observing that ". . . humans would prefer not to die. Lacking scientific means to achieve immortality, they can at best settle for compensators in the form of hopes for the life to come" (1987, 38). Religions serve as the unique providers of supernatural compensators.

There are two basic difficulties with the production of religious goods. First, spiritual goods are highly intangible: payoffs to consumers (e.g., salvation) may never be received. Thus, the products must be accepted on faith (Stark and Bainbridge 1987, 37). Second, religious goods, as expressions of faith, are useful only to the extent that they go unquestioned. If religious consumers begin sincerely doubting the provision of a reward, it is unlikely they will expend the time and resources necessary to remain loyal. Given a high degree of intangibility, competing religions with different messages should have the effect of casting doubt upon all religion. Under such pluralistic environments, one would expect high rates of religious defection and a general trend toward "secularization."

If this hypothesis is correct, and religious pluralism is deleterious to the religiosity of society, it is reasonable to assume that monopoly will be valued highly among religious producers. After all, there can be only one "Absolute Truth." Thus, unlike other economic firms, *it would appear* that religious production is most efficient (i.e., producing the greatest amount of spirituality at the lowest cost) under monopoly.

However, classical economics points to a contrary conclusion. Adam Smith, in a much overlooked passage in *The Wealth of Nations,* addresses the inherent problems of religious monopoly:

> . . . The clergy, reposing themselves upon their benefices, had neglected to keep up the fervour of faith and devotion in the great body of the people; and having given themselves up to indolence, were becoming altogether incapable of making any vigorous exertion in defence even of their own establishment. The clergy of an established and well-endowed religion frequently become men of learning and elegance, who possess all the virtues of gentlemen . . . but they are apt gradually to lose the qualities, both good and bad, which gave them authority and influence with the inferior ranks of people. . . . Such a clergy . . . have commonly no other resource than to call upon the civil magistrate to persecute, destroy, or drive out their adversaries, as disturbers of the public peace. It was thus that the Roman catholic clergy called upon the civil magistrate to persecute the protestants.   (Smith 1986, 307–08)[3]

Leaders of a religious monopoly are under no pressure to conform their product to the desire of their constituents, since those constituents cannot obtain spirituality elsewhere. If barriers to entry into the religious market are high (e.g., state-regulated religion), parishioners have only the option to "believe" or withhold participation. And with poor product offering, the latter is more likely. Thus, according to Smith's logic, *"religiosity"*

---

[3]This observation is hardly unique to Adam Smith. Almost three centuries earlier, under Catholic hegemony, Machiavelli observed: "If the Christian religion had from the beginning been maintained according to the principles of its founder, the Christian states and republics would have been much more united and happy than what they are. Nor can there be a greater proof of its decadence than to witness the fact that *the nearer people are to the Church of Rome, which is the head of our religion, the less religious are they.* . . . We Italians then owe to the Church of Rome and to her priests our having become irreligious and bad" (Machiavelli 1950, 151; emphasis added).

should be most fervent in areas that allow various sects to compete for members.

Recent studies of Western democracies confirm that religiosity flourishes in areas where religious pluralism is high. Using data on religious participation and beliefs in Europe, Laurence Iannaccone discovered that "among Protestants . . . church attendance and religious belief both are greater in countries with numerous competing churches than in countries dominated by a single church" (1991, 157). After accounting for state regulation of religion, Chaves and Cann (1992) found similar evidence supporting the positive relationship between competition and religiosity. Such findings are consistent with earlier work done on Catholicism in the United States: religious activity was most intense in cities with high levels of religious competition (Stark and McCann 1989).

Despite the beneficial "spiritual" effects derived from competitive religious markets, religious monopoly often arises, generally with the aid of the state. It is not surprising that producers generally prefer monopoly over competition and will devote considerable effort to achieving such status. However, such monopolies are rarely permanent: anticlerical revolutions and the rise of secular governing ideologies have eroded the popularity of the theocratic state.

From the vantage point of this inquiry, the critical question for examination is, How do monopoly churches react when faced with increasing competition? Assuming "intangibles" are difficult goods with which to retain customer loyalty, competing religions will attempt to provide members with tangible rewards as incentives for remaining faithful (Stark and Bainbridge 1987, 37). Relative to other available faiths, religions that excel in providing desired tangible goods will be successful in both attracting and retaining members. With this in mind, it is not surprising to see competing denominations arrange community service projects and social events. Faced with competition, monopoly religions will also find it in their interest to do the same.

Historical Overview of the Latin American Religious Economy

Is the weakness of monopoly faith apparent in Latin America? The general consensus of scholars investigating Latin American Catholicism is that, while an overwhelming majority of Latin Americans claim to be Catholic, few actively participate (Maryknoll Fathers 1954; Willems 1967; Vallier 1970; Nuñez and Taylor 1989; Stoll 1990). Interestingly, Latin America contains the world's largest population of Catholics but continually suffers from an extreme shortage of priests (Einaudi et al. 1969). Table 1 exposes this weakness. The number of priests per 10,000 Catholics in the United States and Great Britain—two minority Catholic

Table 1. Penetration of Religious Personnel
(Latin America and Selected Countries)

Country	Year	Catholic Clergy per 10,000 Catholics[a]	Population Catholic %	Clergy Indigenous %
Argentina	1971	2.0	95.8	59
Bolivia	1973	1.8	93.2	30
Brazil	1970	1.5	90.2	58
Chile	1971	3.0	84.3	45
Ecuador	1972	2.7	96.7	76
El Salvador	1970	1.1	96.8	61
Guatemala	1970	1.2	95.0	13
Honduras	1972	0.9	96.3	21
Nicaragua	1970	1.4	95.5	NA
Uruguay	1970	3.8	61.0	64
Australia	1972	10.8	28.6	90
France	1973	2.0	80.3	94
Great Britain	1972	10.5	13.0	90
India	1974	11.9	1.2	88
Poland	1976	6.7	82.1	100
South Korea	1976	8.0	3.6	71
Spain	1972	4.4	97.6	99
Sweden	1970	10.4	1.2	NA
Switzerland	1970	8.3	49.6	90
United States	1975	9.8	28.1	95
West Germany	1971	4.9	48.5	96
		$r = -0.91$		

[a]Aggregation of diocesan priests and "other" religious.

Source: Barrett (1982).

countries—is nearly five times as great as most Latin American countries measured. Whereas the typical Latin American country has approximately 1.9 priests per 10,000 Catholics, the numbers are 9.8 and 10.5 for the United States and Great Britain, respectively. This finding is significant for two reasons. First, the number of parishioners that the Catholic Church can reach in Latin America is severely limited. Rural villages receive only periodic visits from priests.

Second, the low priest/parishioner ratio reveals an inability to recruit clergy. In fact, recruitment has been so meager in some countries that the majority of priests are foreigners. This is somewhat unexpected considering the rampant poverty in the region; the priesthood provides low-cost education, guaranteed work, and a reliable (albeit sometimes small) salary.

The trend in the 1960s and 1970s showed little sign of improvement. In only five countries—Costa Rica, Cuba, Panama, Mexico, and Colombia—were new ordinations adequate to maintain a constant supply of clergy. All other countries witnessed a decreasing number of indigenous clergy (Einaudi et al. 1969, 20; Barrett 1982, passim). Thus, Catholicism's most populous region contains a Church incapable of attracting a sufficient supply of local clergy to adequately serve its parishioners.

From a theoretical standpoint, Table 1 bolsters Adam Smith's observation that religious monopolies are weak. The correlation between percentage of Catholics in the population and the priest/parishioner ratio is −0.91. It is interesting to note that France and Spain, the only noncommunist "Catholic" European countries[4] examined here, have low priest/parishioner ratios. Similarly, the least "Catholic" nation in Latin America, Uruguay, has the region's highest priest/parishioner ratio.

Given the relative lack of Catholic penetration into society, the region has been fertile ground for alternative religious movements, from mainline Protestants to spiritist groups. In terms of Protestant evangelical missions alone, several areas of Latin America have seen highly visible growth since the 1930s. This growth has occurred primarily for three reasons: (1) Liberal political victories; (2) renewed focus on Latin America by North American evangelicals;[5] and (3) the tangible benefits provided by these competitive denominations, making conversion an attractive alternative for many nominal Catholics.

During the first century following independence from Spain and Portugal, battles were waged between forces seeking to preserve much of the colonial structure of Latin America (Conservatives) and those who

---

[4]While the majority of Poland's population is Catholic, the Church faces relatively fierce competition in the form of the regime's atheistic ideology. Therefore, it does not enjoy the same monopoly privileges as the Churches in France and Spain do. Not surprisingly, under such circumstances Catholicism provides an attractive alternative to the dominant ideology.

[5]Evangelicals refer to specific denominations and nonaffiliated organizations (e.g., Campus Crusade for Christ) that actively promote conversion to their faith. David Stoll has defined an evangelical as someone who adheres to three criteria: "(1) the complete reliability and final authority of the Bible, (2) the need to be saved through a personal relation with Jesus Christ, often experienced in terms of being 'born again,' and (3) the importance of spreading this message of salvation to every nation and person" (1990, 3). Not all Protestants are evangelicals. However, a large majority of Latin American missionaries are evangelicals.

wished to modernize their respective countries (Liberals). The Church often served as a focal point of this conflict (Mecham 1966, 38–87). Liberals saw the Church as a colonial remnant that kept Latin America in a subservient position to foreign powers. Their leaders sought to weaken the power of the Church by instituting laws ensuring freedom of worship. In most countries, anticlerical modernizers won this struggle, and the doors were opened to other religions (Mecham 1966, passim).

Liberal victories were not the only reason for Protestant expansion in the nineteenth century. In some countries where the Catholic Church remained dominant (e.g., Argentina and Paraguay), the need to attract foreign skilled workers prevented the total exclusion of mainline Protestants (e.g., Lutherans, Anglicans). These denominations were acceptable to Catholic officials, since they typically avoided proselytizing. In general, the dispute between Church and state was resolved prior to the 1940s (Dussel 1981, 101–04), and most countries permitted at least a minimal degree of religious freedom.

Despite laws guaranteeing religious freedom in the early twentieth century, the heyday of Protestantism was delayed because of the focus of evangelical missionaries. Prior to the 1930s, missionary activity centered on the non-Christian world—Africa, Asia, and the Pacific (Montgomery 1979, 89). With increasing political turmoil in these regions, many North American evangelicals turned attention toward their southern neighbors beginning in the mid-1930s. Expansion came rapidly: whereas the number of Protestants in Latin America increased by 271% between 1916 and 1938, the following 19 years (1938–57) witnessed the Protestant population jump approximately 569% (Dussel 1981, 359).

These missionary movements were successful both in attracting parishioners and in recruiting indigenous ministers, a skill the Catholic Church lacked. Thus, the strategy of post–World War II evangelicals was not only to expand broadly in the region but to obtain depth of commitment by tying indigenous participants to their churches via organizational incorporation.

Finally, the evangelical missions that entered Latin America after 1930 provided converts with many benefits that the Catholic Church did not. These benefits often came in the form of medical clinics, literacy campaigns, community improvement projects, and the ability to participate actively in religious services. Thus, whereas the Catholic Church traditionally ignored—for lack of resources and enthusiasm—the rural and urban poor, Protestant missionaries found it relatively easy to win converts by providing opportunities for self-improvement. The demand for alternative forms of worship always existed in Latin America but did not become evident until new suppliers were allowed to move in.

In the face of rapidly encroaching competition, it is reasonable to expect the Catholic Church to initiate programs aimed at retaining nominal parishioners. Given the immense institutional size of the Catholic Church in Latin America, such a change in strategy—from apathetic monopoly to active competitor—is bound to have some sociopolitical ramifications, especially with regard to the traditional relationship of "cross and sword." It is to this subject that we now turn.

Political Effects of Religious Competition: A Hypothesis

In attempting to explain the variation in official Catholic responses to authoritarianism, I argued earlier that the presence of religious competition should raise the value of obtaining active parishioners in marginally Catholic areas, since all religions wish to maintain maximum influence over their flock. The Church may choose to do this by combining direct organization among marginal participants and state assistance (e.g., banning competition).[6] If Church and state are "legally separated,"[7] the probability of obtaining state assistance is greatly reduced, and bishops will favor pastoral organization, typically among the poor.

Given that the ultimate products of religion are intangible (e.g., salvation), the Church will find it necessary to provide visible benefits to attract constituents, provided the competition is doing the same. Christian base communities, which stress lay community organization, have been a popular method of reinvigorating Catholic participation. Furthermore, the religious message presented by many base communities often emphasizes the need visibly to change exploitative relationships—an idea popular among the lower classes. Both the empowerment of the poor via autonomous organization and the spiritual message invoked appear revolutionary and threaten the security of the military state. Subsequent attacks against Catholic pastoral missions will generally be seen as a

---

[6]Use of the state to prohibit religious competitors has not been uncommon in Latin America. As part of negotiations between the United States and Brazil over the latter's participation in World War II, President Vargas requested that the United States stop sending Protestant missionaries to his country (Pierson 1974, 177). Pressure for this request came directly from Cardinal Sebastião Dom Leme and several other bishops. The influence they exerted over Vargas on matters of important diplomacy challenges the "stylized fact" that the Church, when aligned with the state, is merely a puppet.

[7]As noted earlier, "separation" of Church and state (if it existed) occurred prior to the onset of authoritarianism. No military regime—to my knowledge—reversed this policy during its tenure. However, of greater importance for this study is the degree of religious freedom existing in each country. In all the cases examined here, religious toleration was legally mandated, thus evangelicals and spiritists could theoretically practice their faith without fear of prosecution. In reality, persecution did exist, but was generally not initiated by the state—private citizens would harass Protestants while the state looked askance.

challenge to the institutional autonomy of the Church, leading Catholic officials to denounce the regime (Smith 1980).

Where competition for latent membership is present, but no formal separation of Church and state exists, the Church will attempt to use its access to state resources to attract latent members and/or suppress the competition. Prohibiting competition is more cost effective than actually competing. From this standpoint, it is logical to assume that maintaining friendly relations with the state is in the interests of the Church.

Finally, if no significant competition exists, the Church will seek friendly relations with the current regime, regardless of legal separation between church and state; since the government controls precious resources, there is a constant incentive for the institutional Church to maintain amicable relations with the current regime. Such a strategy preserves all possible options of parishioner service.

Lacking effective competition, the Catholic Church has little incentive to conform its "product" to the needs of the poor. Pandering to the economic and political elite is strategically beneficial because the rich and powerful control resources the Church desires. Moreover, the poor, having little to give the Church in a material sense, cannot obtain spirituality elsewhere—they are "captive Catholics." Competitors seeking to enter the religious market and gain parishioners can easily do so by providing for the needs of the neglected lower classes. Without a meaningful connection to Catholicism, and enticed by material benefits and socioeconomic opportunities provided by competitors, the poor make easy targets.

Membership loss forebodes declining sociopolitical influence for the institutional Church in that it can no longer control its parishioners. To rectify the problem, prelates must initiate pastoral reforms aimed at winning back the poor. In societies organized around class, such a shift could be construed as a betrayal of the traditional "cross and sword" alliance, thereby paving the way for future antagonism. Authoritarianism, which seeks to suppress exactly what the Church must do to maintain members (i.e., organize the poor), makes the conflict manifest.

To test the religious competition hypothesis, we need answers to three questions. First, was the Catholic Church threatened by competitive advances in the hemisphere? Second, does a positive relationship exist between increasing competition and the rise of a "progressive" Catholic episcopacy? And third, what is the direction of causality: did evangelical Protestantism develop as a response to liberation theology, or did Catholic pastoral activity respond to evangelicalism and other threats?

Twelve cases are examined. Countries with predominantly proauthoritarian or neutral episcopacies include Argentina, Bolivia, Guatemala, Honduras, Paraguay, and Uruguay. Brazil, Chile, Ecuador, El Salvador, pre-1979 Nicaragua, and Panama compose the antiauthoritarian cases.[8] The principal selection criterion was the presence of right-wing authoritarian rule after 1962. This year was chosen as a starting point to control for the effects of Vatican Council II. Since all bishops were exposed to the liberalizing reforms of Vatican II after 1962, it is possible to eliminate this as a principal cause.

Analysis focuses primarily on competitive pressures from evangelical Protestants and spiritist groups. The role of communism as an ideological competitor to Catholicism is not extensively analyzed because most military regimes during the 1960s and 1970s were devoutly anticommunist, and thus the Church had a natural ally against its Marxist competitors. From the Church's vantage point, if the junta promises to eliminate the competition, less pastoral energy needs to be expended on combating this threat. Indeed, despite accommodation with the Allende regime in Chile, several progressive bishops initially supported Pinochet's coup as a means of returning social stability to a country upset by ideological conflict (Smith 1982, 287–94).

From the vantage point of the state, Protestants posed little threat to national security.[9] There was no compelling need to eradicate them,

---

[8]Categorization of these national episcopates as either proauthoritarian or antiauthoritarian is derived from general remarks throughout the literature on the Catholic Church, especially Mainwaring and Wilde (1989). Although bishops in all 12 countries have been critical of flagrant military abuses at various times, Mainwaring and Wilde note that "Argentina is only the most dramatic example among many countries where, in the face of dictatorship and violence, the Church did not assume such a political role; *the Churches of Guatemala, Paraguay, and Uruguay also supported, more than they denounced, military rule. In these countries, progressive Church sectors criticized authoritarian rule, but they failed to move the ecclesiastical institution as a whole.* Far from catalyzing a protective response by the hierarchy, state repression annihilated the radical Catholics" (1989, 14; emphasis added). Confirming evidence was found in Barrett (1982), Martin (1990), Mignone (1988), Levine (1984), and Department of the U.S. Army *Area Handbook Series* (various years and countries).

The unit of analysis here is the national episcopacy—the makers of official Church policy. While it is recognized that not all bishops will agree with one another, the national hierarchies have generally acted in unison on important political questions. This analytical aggregation is similar to studies examining political parties: even though not all party members agree on every issue, a general consensus still exists upon which to observe and predict behavior.

[9]Contrary to popular wisdom, not all evangelical Protestants are fervent right-wingers. In fact, a substantial number of evangelicals were privately critical of militarism (Montgomery 1979). A number of Protestant missionaries that I have interviewed hold rather liberal viewpoints. However, being "strangers in a strange land" often meant that silence was the best means of survival.

414   *Anthony J. Gill*

and therefore, policing resources could be spent elsewhere. Mild pressure from the United States to maintain religious freedom, coupled with the need to appease skilled immigrant labor, also reduced the government's incentive to purge their countries of non-Catholics. This meant the Church was basically left to its own devices when dealing with proselytizing denominations. There were, of course, exceptions. Bishops in both Paraguay and Argentina were instrumental in convincing the government to expel the Jehovah's Witnesses (FBIS 1978; FBIS 1979).

Results

Considering that during the middle of the twentieth century, Catholics constituted more than 95% of the Latin American population, it would seem unlikely that Protestant missionaries could pose a severe threat. However, beginning in the early 1950s, key policymaking sectors of the Catholic Church worried about competitive pressures. In his discussion of the 1953 Chimbote (Peru) Conference—sponsored for Inter-American Catholic Action Week—Hellmut Gnadt Vitalis notes, "The Church cannot remain indifferent to the loss of no fewer than 1,000 adult Christians per day, who are separated from the mystical body of Christ. Often they are deceived by the offers made by those who are preaching a mutilated and deformed Christianity" (1969, sec. 8, 15). Even the Maryknoll Fathers, during a 1954 conference in Peru, rallied Catholics to resist Protestant encroachment, declaring as one of their primary goals the "winning of the non-Catholic Christian which means the Protestant and other Christian groups separated from the Church" (Maryknoll Fathers 1954, 290).

Similar concerns were echoed among the most prominent Church officials, and methods to address the problem became a priority.

> Pope Pius XII, in his second speech at the World Congress of the Secular Apostolate [c. 1955], mentioned four mortal dangers for the Catholic Church in Latin America: Protestantism, laicism, marxism and spiritism. He said that in order to overcome these necessities and dangers, it is necessary to provide able priests in sufficient numbers. . . . As the lack of native or local clergy cannot be solved in a short term, the pontifical documents asked for the help of clergy from other nations. Even this cannot solve the problem of Latin America in a quick and definitive way; therefore a call is made to the laymen. Further, these documents do not refer only to the persons who may help, but also mention the necessity of finding new methods which may be adequate for the peculiar conditions of this time, the best use of technical means, methods, and forms as instruments to help achieve better the virtue and diffusion of truth.   (Vitalis 1969, sec. 3, p. 1).

Sanctioned by the pontiff himself, maintaining the faithful became a prime concern among numerous theologians and episcopal advisors. Notice that in association with the warnings of competition, a call was made to activate members of the previously ignored laity.

Although ecumenical movements encouraging cooperation between Catholics and Protestants have gained some popularity since the late 1960s, the Church has generally remained firm in its opposition to Protestantism. Even today, Nuñez and Taylor note, "The pope's [John Paul II] attitude toward evangelical growth in Latin America has led his church toward a harder line, calling for a reconversion of former Catholics, calling for national and continental 'evangelism crusades,' inviting evangelicals to return and embrace the only mother church" (1989, 145). Such "crusades" have had the effect of turning the Church's attention toward its most nominal members where competition is most fierce—the rural and urban poor.

At first, action was directed outward against Protestants, frequently leading to violence. In the 1930s and 1940s, it was not uncommon for evangelicals to be physically attacked by Catholic mobs or have their churches burned down (Stoll 1990, 18–19, 26; Nuñez and Taylor 1989, 144–46; Bialek 1963, 93–97). After it became apparent that violence could not stop Protestantism, a new strategy was developed—listen and respond to the needs of nominal Catholics. Ivan Vallier notes that ". . . as the Church loses its capacity to command obedience and passes into a phase where it must rely on voluntary compliance, the feelings of the rank and file assume a new importance" (1970, 110). Competition revealed the Church's incapacity to "command obedience": When relatively large numbers of supposed Catholics began defecting, the hierarchy realized that it had a problem and took remedial action.

One method of responding to the growing membership crisis was Catholic Action. Originally a European lay movement meant to bring Catholic social teaching closer to parishioners, the application of Catholic Action in several Latin American countries during the late 1950s served to compensate for the lack of clergy. Unfortunately, Catholic Action did not spread rapidly due to its focus on activating the middle class and university students—groups traditionally tied to the Church (Turner 1971, 50).

Efforts to reach out among the poorest sections of society relied upon a new indigenous innovation—*comunidades eclesiales de bases* (CEBs). In addition to their religious functions, CEBs also provide social and economic benefits to the communities they serve, including literacy campaigns (Van Vugt 1991), job training for dislocated workers, medical and financial assistance to the needy, agrarian projects, and self-help groups aimed at promoting human capital development (Vallier 1970; Bruneau 1980). These groups are numerically prominent where religious competition is fierce—Brazil, Chile, El Salvador, and Nicaragua.

Ironically, the methods employed by Catholic Action, the CEBs, and other lay-based Catholic organizations were inspired by, and modeled

Religion and Politics

Anthony J. Gill

after, their competition. Involvement of the laity, weekly Bible discussions, and community service projects are tactics that have been favored by Latin American evangelicals since the early twentieth century (Stoll 1990). Early on, some Catholics recognized "the ability of the Protestants to conduct schools and hospitals, with a very small amount of foreign personnel by using a great many national workers in their schools and hospitals. . . . We [Catholics] don't seem to have developed that technique well" (Maryknoll Fathers 1954, 287). The techniques of Protestants were eventually adopted as Paul Turner's study of Oxchuc, Mexico, shows: "In reaction to the success of Protestantism, some priests started a counteraction using similar methods to those employed by the missionaries. . . . The reason why the . . . Catholics are making comparable gains is because they have been influenced by Protestantism" (Turner 1979, 259). Protestantism has been a source of both competition and inspiration for the Roman Catholic Church.

Once established, CEBs often became a center for progressive political action. Under authoritarian regimes, such activity acted as a lightning rod for military repression. In one incident among many, base communities in Nicaragua demanded lower utility rates and improved public transportation for impoverished neighborhoods, prompting a violent reaction by Somoza's National Guard (Lernoux 1980, 91–94). Not only did increased demands for social justice annoy dictators who considered such claims revolutionary, but the Church's action among the lower classes isolated traditional Catholic supporters among the economic and political elite. Thus, at the same time prelates saw their pastoral workers harassed, tortured, and killed, they were losing support among traditional allies. These two factors pressured several national episcopacies into opposing the political and economic system that was at odds with their most critical institutional interest—retaining parishioners. Not surprisingly, in countries where membership loss was not a major problem (e.g., Uruguay, Argentina), bishops were less likely to support pastoral strategies that alienated the ruling elite.[10]

Having established reasonable evidence supporting the claim that Catholic officials considered Protestants a credible threat, and seeing that the threat preceded and inspired a Catholic "Counter-Reformation," it becomes necessary to ask if a correlation exists between Protestant growth and antiauthoritarian episcopacies. In addition to the religious

---

[10]This does not mean that progressive activity did not exist in these countries. Rather, grassroots efforts to reach the poor by some clergy were not officially sanctioned. As I am primarily concerned with the position of the institutional Church, the existence of small progressive movements in countries with proauthoritarian hierarchies is not problematic.

competition hypothesis, two alternative causes for the rise of progressive Catholicism are considered: poverty and repression.[11]

The most common explanation for the rise of Catholic progressivism (and antiauthoritarianism) has been a religious awakening to the poverty and repression associated with dependent development (Berryman 1984; Gutiérrez 1973; Lernoux 1980). This hypothesis assumes that most Latin American governments exist to serve the interests of the dominant classes, while Catholicism's inherent mission is to serve the poor. As the disparity between rich and poor increased dramatically under military regimes during the 1960s and 1970s, it is argued that the structural causes of poverty became more apparent. Catholic bishops turned their attention away from treating the symptoms of poverty and began attacking what they considered to be the root of the problem: capitalism and authoritarianism (Gutiérrez 1973, 106–07). From this thesis, we would anticipate progressive episcopacies in countries with low standards of living and an increasingly unequal distribution of wealth.

To test the competition, poverty, and repression hypotheses, cases were dichotomously categorized as to each episcopacy's stance toward dictatorship (oppose = 1; support = 0). Measurement of competition consisted of the percentage increase of non-Catholic proselytizing faiths (e.g., evangelicals, marginal Christian sects, spiritist/indigenous groups) from 1900 to 1970 (Barrett 1982). Only proselytizing denominations were considered; "ethnic" Protestants were excluded, since they do not actively seek to convert Catholics to their faith. A physical quality of life index (PQLI) for the mid-1970s, the height of Latin American authoritarianism, measured relative poverty. Finally, the Freedom House index of civil rights served as a proxy for repression, calculating the average score (1 = most free, 7 = most unfree) for each country's authoritarian period until 1979.

Looking at the raw data (see Table 2), 10 of the 12 cases appear to support the religious competition hypothesis. Within-Group averages of the level of competition show a moderately strong positive relationship between religious competition and an antiauthoritarian stance. On close examination, in five of the six antiauthoritarian cases—Brazil, Chile, El Salvador, Nicaragua, and Panama—relatively high religious competition

---

[11]In the literature on the progressive Church, which often relies heavily upon dependency theory, these two variables are generally considered to be highly correlated. State repression is supposedly used to subordinate the interests of rural and urban workers in order to divert capital to the upper classes. See Lernoux (1980) and Berryman (1984) for typical examples of this approach. In the analysis below, I separate poverty and repression for analytical simplicity.

Table 2. Data on Religious Competition, Quality of Life, and Repression

Country	Competition %	PQLI	Repression
Proauthoritarian:			
Argentina	2.7	85	5.3
Bolivia	4.1	39	4.3
Guatemala	6.3	54	3.5
Honduras	3.1	53	3.0
Paraguay	2.1	75	5.2
Uruguay	1.2	86	4.7
Average	3.3	65	4.3
Antiauthoritarian:			
Brazil	12.0	66	4.8
Chile	15.5	79	5.0
Ecuador	2.9	69	3.7
El Salvador	5.5	64	4.4
Nicaragua	5.6	55	4.3
Panama	4.4	79	5.7
Average	7.7	69	4.7

Competition: Percentage increase of "competitive religious groups," 1900–70 (Barrett 1982).

PQLI: Physical quality of life index, mid-1970s. Calculated from the mean of three equally weighted items: life expectancy at age one, infant mortality, and literacy at age 15+ (Wilkie and Reich 1980, 4). High = higher living standards.

Repression: Average civil rights score for authoritarian period until 1979 (Gastil, various years). High = most repressive.

(i.e., above the median level of 4.25%) preceded and inspired a progressive Church that suffered greatly at the hands of the military. Likewise, five of the neutral or proauthoritarian Churches—Argentina, Bolivia, Honduras, Paraguay, and Uruguay—faced comparatively little competition, did not pursue pastoral strategies on an extensive basis, and were not systematically harassed by the government. Although small progressive sectors were attacked in these countries, pastoral agents received little support from the Catholic hierarchy (Mainwaring and Wilde 1989, 14). The within-group averages for the PQLI and repression provide little evidence of a systematic relationship between these variables and a national episcopacy's position toward authoritarianism.

Multivariate analysis was employed to test further the strength of

Table 3. Probit Analysis

Variable	Model 1	Model 2	Model 3	Model 4
Constant	−5.152	−1.587	−5.707	−3.588
	(4.282)	(2.332)	(4.201)	(3.109)
Competition	0.622*		0.612*	0.425*
	(0.383)		(0.369)	(0.286)
PQL index	0.050	−0.003	0.046	
	(0.062)	(0.034)	(0.045)	
Repression	−0.086	0.401		0.382
	(0.833)	(0.660)		(0.586)
$N = 12$				
Percentage correctly predicted	83.3	41.7	83.3	83.3

Note: Dependent variable = opposition.

Standard errors are in parentheses.

See Table 2 for descriptions of variables.

*Significant at the 10% level.

the relationship between hypothesized variables. Given the dichotomous nature of the dependent variable (opposition or support), probit was chosen as the appropriate statistical technique. The following relationships are anticipated:

Competition	Positive (+)
Poverty (PQLI)	Negative (−)
Repression	Positive (+)

Initial results show mild statistical significance supporting the religious competition hypothesis (see Table 3). All three models that included the competition variable resulted in statistical significance at the 10% level. Given that the *t*-test is highly dependent on sample size, the small number of case studies ($N = 12$) may account for the weak significance. Neither the repression nor the poverty variables were statistically significant. Furthermore, in two of the models (1 and 3), the PQLI variable did not have the anticipated sign. Similarly, counterintuitive results for the repression variable appeared in model 1.

Probit coefficients can be used to calculate the relative probability of obtaining a result on the dependent variable for various values of the independent variables. So as to include both the poverty (PQLI) and repression variables, model 1 is used as the basis for calculation. Assuming median values for PQLI (67.5) and repression (4.55), a cumulative probability function is calculated for the range of values associated with religious competition, 1% to 16% (see Figure 1). From this distribution, we can estimate that the probability a Church hierarchy will be antiauthoritarian when faced with only a 1% level of competitive pressure will be roughly 6%. There is a 50% chance an episcopacy will be antiauthoritarian at a competition level of 3.49%, ceteris paribus. Substantively, these results suggest a relatively modest increase in religious competition (4% to 6%) is needed to push the Church into a "preferential option for the poor" and the antiauthoritarian stance associated with the exercise of that option.

Although measures of fit are somewhat ambiguous for probit models, results indicate that 10 of the 12 cases (83%) examined were predicted correctly. When we look back at the raw data (Table 2), we notice that Guatemala and Ecuador appear to cause difficulties for this analysis. (Coupled with the small sample size, the presence of these "outliers" may help to explain the observed level of statistical significance.) The former had one of the highest Protestant growth rates in Latin America beginning in the 1940s and was even governed by an evangelical dictator—General Efraín Ríos Montt—whose short-lived government in 1982 was viewed as a directive from God (Stoll 1990, 180–217). On the other hand, Protestant influence across Ecuador was the lowest of the 10 countries studied here. Despite this seeming lack of competition, the Ecuadoran episcopacy was quite adamant in opposing the military after 1976. Brief explanations of these cases are warranted here.

At initial glance, the Guatemalan case contradicts the religious competition hypothesis. Throughout the 1970s, both Protestants and communist guerrillas successfully recruited the indigenous population living in Guatemala's highlands (Stoll 1990, 202–03). Despite the mass slaughter of Indians, the archbishop of Guatemala City, Cardinal Casariego, accommodated the various military governments that came to power. In part, this reluctance to criticize the military may have resulted from the Church's participation in the 1954 coup that ousted the democratically elected president, Jacobo Guzmán Arbenz (Schlesinger and Kinzer 1982, 154). Arbenz had encouraged the growth of Protestantism to undermine conservative opposition to his presidency. In essence, certain Church officials placed their faith in the military to ensure that anticlerical politicians would not return to power.

Not all bishops held such a conservative position, however. Catholic officials working in rural areas were highly critical of these brutal dictatorships. One bishop, Juan Gerardi, fled the country in 1980 after being targeted for assassination for his progressive stance (Berryman 1984,

421

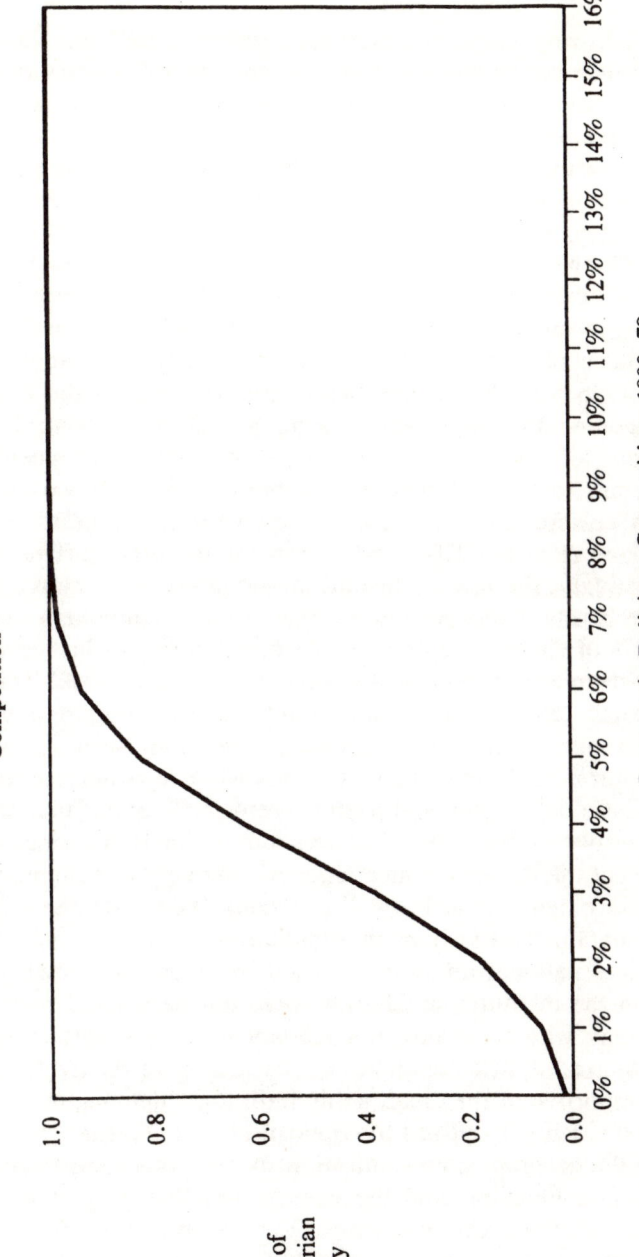

Figure 1. Cumulative Probability Function for Various Levels of Religious Competition

Probability of Antiauthoritarian Episcopacy

Increase in Religious Competition, 1900–79

Note: Assuming PQLI = 67.5 and repression = 4.55.

204–06). Following Cardinal Casariego's death in 1985, the Guatemalan hierarchy began taking a more critical stance toward military rule and its associated abuses. In this case, it appears as if one strategically situated cardinal controlled the Church's agenda and effectively blocked a growing progressive movement within the Church. The probabilistic nature of the religious competition model predicts that such an outcome is unlikely, though not impossible.

Ecuador provides an interesting contrast. As with Guatemala, the Ecuadoran Church allied with Conservatives in order to protect its prerogatives from modernizing Liberals (Bialek 1963). Unlike Guatemala, however, this conflict resolved itself relatively early in Ecuador's history, and since 1906 the Church has begrudgingly accepted the freedom of worship decreed by the Liberals (Aguilar-Monsalve 1984). Ironically, with religious toleration ensured by law, Protestants, until recently, have been reluctant to target Ecuador as a mission field. Nevertheless, the Ecuadoran episcopacy has become known for its progressive policies regarding land reform, CEBs, and opposition to authoritarianism.

Interestingly, the few Protestant missionaries who entered Ecuador have been highly concentrated in one area, Chimborazo. By 1976, roughly 10% of Chimborazo's Quichua population was Protestant (Stoll 1990, 273) despite a countrywide population of about 3%. This region also happened to be home to the country's most progressive bishop, Leonidas Proaño. Facing such intense competition, Msgr. Proaño organized a pastoral conference in 1976 in his Riobamba diocese to discuss efforts at Catholic renewal and pastoral reform. In attendance were several progressive Chilean and U.S. religious officials. Fearing that "the participants at the Riobamba meeting were 'subversive communists plotting the government's overthrow'" (Lernoux 1980, 141), the military arrested and detained all bishops in attendance.

With international attention focused on Riobamba, such a blatant attack upon the institutional Church could not be ignored by the Ecuadoran bishops who were not in attendance. Interestingly, these other bishops, who faced little competitive pressure, were relatively conservative and supportive of the dictatorship until this "defining moment": the Riobamba incident galvanized the opposition to militarism.

Given the geographic concentrations of religious competitors in both Guatemala and Ecuador, and the observation that progressive bishops were located in the areas of greatest competition, it becomes apparent that an examination of the Church in Latin America could be improved upon by employing the dioceses as the primary unit of analysis. Unfortunately, Protestant data do not conform to Catholic definitions of parishioner organization (and any attempt to convince Protestant record-keepers to do so would be the methodological equivalent of the Counter-Reformation). Given current data restrictions, analysis of the episcopacy as a national unit is the best available test of the competition hypothesis. One final qualitative consideration should be noted here. The Catholic Church is an international institution and cross-national transfers of information are relatively easy. Problems and solutions to competition in one country can teach other national episcopacies to take preventive measures before their problem grows too large. Thus, countries that do not appear to have much to worry about may nonetheless engage in pastoral reforms after observing other countries. In other words, the competitive threshold for pastoral reform should decrease as time progresses. Chile and Brazil, arguably two of the most progressive Churches in Latin America, were the first to face intense competitive pressures and were also the first to initiate progressive reforms. Today, almost all episcopacies support some degree of pastoral reform. Even Bolivia, with a traditionally conservative hierarchy, recently published a manuscript calling for pastoral action among the poor to deal with *"el desafío de las sectas"* (Damen 1988).

Conclusion

As Latin America increasingly opens itself to a wide array of religious faiths, we should expect to see the Catholic Church adjusting its traditional role to compete with and accommodate Protestant sects. Base communities and the Church's "preferential option for the poor" can be seen as a response to Protestant growth in the region. Such changes, as we have seen, are bound to have political impacts. If anything, the liberalization within the Church itself, as it seeks to widen its appeal among nominal Catholics, should help lay the groundwork for democratic institutions at the grassroots level. This paper has demonstrated that when such liberalization occurs under authoritarian regimes, the traditional alliance between Church and state is severed and the Church will likely end up in opposition to the military ruling elite. Under democratic regimes, we may anticipate the Church playing a large role in solidifying democratic norms throughout Latin American society. This in no way assures the success of democracy in the region, but it does enhance its prospects.

Finally, a theory of religious competition, as applied in this paper, would add a new twist to the previously discredited cultural theories of political development. An integral part of these cultural theories was that Latin America could not develop political democracy because the dominant religion, Catholicism, stressed paternalism and strict obedience to authority. Rather than these values being intrinsic to the Catholic faith,

424   *Anthony J. Gill*

I argue that they are a function of religious monopoly. Lacking competitive pressures, the Catholic clergy had no incentive to activate the majority of its constituents in its faith. Faced with competition, the Church
appears to be discovering the value of democratic practices.

Manuscript submitted 1 Feb 1993
Final manuscript received 24 May 1993

REFERENCES

Aguilar-Monsalve, Luis. 1984. "The Separation of Church and State: The Ecuadorian
    Case." *Thought* 59:205–18.
Barrett, David B., ed. 1982. *World Christian Encyclopedia*. Nairobi: Oxford University
    Press.
Berryman, Phillip. 1984. *The Religious Roots of Rebellion: Christians in Central American
    Revolutions*. Maryknoll, NY: Orbis Books.
Bialek, Robert W. 1963. *Catholic Politics: A History Based on Ecuador*. New York: Van-
    tage Press.
Bruneau, Thomas. 1980. "Base Christian Communities in Latin America: Their Nature and
    Significance (Especially in Brazil)." In *Churches and Politics in Latin America,* ed.
    Daniel Levine. Beverly Hills: Sage.
Chaves, Mark, and David E. Cann. 1992. "Regulation, Pluralism, and Religious Market
    Structure." *Rationality and Society* 4:272–90.
Damen, Franz. 1988. *El desafío de las sectas*. Series Fe y Compromiso 5. La Paz, Bolivia:
    Secretario Nacional de Ecumenismo.
Dussel, Enrique. 1981. *A History of the Church in Latin America: Colonialism to Liberation
    (1492–1979)*, trans. Alan Neely. Grand Rapids: Eerdmans.
Einaudi, Luigi, Richard Maullin, Alfred Stepan, and Michael Fleet, eds. 1969. *Latin Ameri-
    can Institutional Development: The Changing Catholic Church*. Santa Monica, CA:
    Rand.
Foreign Broadcast Information Service (FBIS). 1978. "Jehovah's Witnesses Banned." 16
    February 1978, B3.
———. 1979. "La Tribuna Discusses Banning of Jehovah's Witnesses." 9 January 1979,
    H1.
Gastil, Raymond. Various years. *Freedom at Issue*. New York: Freedom House.
Gutiérrez, Gustavo. 1973. *A Theology of Liberation: History, Politics, and Salvation*, trans.
    Sister Caridad Inda and John Eagleson. Maryknoll, NY: Orbis Books.
Iannaccone, Laurence R. 1991. "The Consequences of Religious Market Structure: Adam
    Smith and the Economics of Religion." *Rationality and Society* 3:156–77.
Lernoux, Penny. 1980. *Cry of the People: The Struggle for Human Rights in Latin
    America—the Catholic Church in Conflict with U.S. Policy*. New York: Penguin.
Levine, Daniel H. 1984. "Religion and Politics: Dimensions of Renewal." *Thought* 59:
    117–35.
Machiavelli, Niccolo. 1950. *The Prince and the Discourses*. New York: Modern Library.
Mainwaring, Scott, and Alexander Wilde, eds. 1989. *The Progressive Church in Latin
    America*. Notre Dame: University of Notre Dame Press.
Martin, David. 1990. *Tongues of Fire: The Explosion of Protestantism in Latin America*.
    Cambridge, MA: Basil Blackwell.

Maryknoll Fathers. 1954. *Proceedings of the Lima Methods Conference of the Maryknoll Fathers*. Lima, Peru: Maryknoll House.

Mecham, J. Lloyd. 1966. *Church and State in Latin America: A History of Politico-Ecclesiastical Relations*. Chapel Hill: University of North Carolina Press.

Mignone, Emilio F. 1988. *Witness to the Truth: The Complicity of Church and Dictatorship in Argentina, 1976–1983*, trans. Phillip Berryman. Maryknoll, NY: Orbis Books.

Montgomery, T. S. 1980. "Latin American Evangelicals: Oaxtepec and Beyond." In *Churches and Politics in Latin America*, ed. Daniel Levine. Beverly Hills: Sage.

Nuñez, Emilio A., and William D. Taylor. 1989. *Crisis in Latin America: An Evangelical Perspective*. Chicago: Moody Press.

Pierson, Paul Everett. 1974. *A Younger Church in Search of Maturity: Presbyterianism in Brazil from 1910 to 1959*. San Antonio: Trinity University Press.

Schlesinger, Stephen, and Stephen Kinzer, eds. 1982. *Bitter Fruit: The Untold Story of the American Coup in Guatemala*. Garden City, NY: Anchor Books.

Smith, Adam. [1776] 1986. *The Essential Adam Smith*, ed. Robert L. Heilbroner with the assistance of Laurence J. Malone. New York: Norton.

Smith, Brian H. 1980. *Old Allies, New Opponents: The Church and the Military in Chile, 1973–1979*. Washington, DC: Wilson Center.

——. 1982. *The Church and Politics in Chile: Challenges to Modern Catholicism*. Princeton: Princeton University Press.

Stark, Rodney, and William Sims Bainbridge. 1987. *A Theory of Religion*. New York: Peter Lange Publishing.

Stark, Rodney, and James C. McCann. 1989. *The Weakness of Monopoly Faiths: Market Forces and Catholic Commitment*. Presented at the meeting of the American Sociological Association, San Francisco.

Stoll, David. 1990. *Is Latin America Protestant? The Politics of Evangelical Growth*. Berkeley: University of California Press.

Turner, Frederick C. 1971. *Catholicism and Political Development in Latin America*. Chapel Hill: University of North Carolina Press.

Turner, Paul R. 1979. "Religious Conversion and Community Development." *Journal for the Scientific Study of Religion* 18:252–60.

U.S. Army, Department of. Various years. *Area Handbook Series*. Washington, DC: Government Printing Office.

Vallier, Ivan. 1967. "Religious Elites: Differentiations and Developments in Roman Catholicism." In *Elites in Latin America*, ed. Seymour Martin Lipset and Aldo Solari. New York: Oxford University Press.

——. 1970. *Catholicism, Social Control, and Modernization in Latin America*. Englewood Cliffs, NJ: Prentice-Hall.

Van Vugt, Johannes P. 1991. *Democratic Organization for Social Change: Latin America Christian Base Communities and Literacy Campaigns*. New York: Bergin and Garvey.

Vitalis, Hellmut Gnadt. 1969. *The Significance of Changes in Latin America Catholicism since Chimbote 1953*. Cuernavaca, Mexico: Centro Intercultural de Documentacion.

Wilkie, James W., and Peter Reich. 1980. *Statistical Abstract of Latin America*. Vol. 20. Los Angeles: UCLA Latin American Center.

Willems, Emilio. 1967. *Followers of the New Faith: Cultural Change and the Rise of Protestantism in Brazil and Chile*. Nashville: Vanderbilt University Press.

[4]

Warring Gods?
Theological Tales

John McGarry and Brendan O'Leary

Foreign journalist: Who is King Billy?
Ulster Protestant: Ach away man, and read your Bible!'
Apocryphal Belfast story

'Religion' one student said 'is a red herring'. I said if so it was a red herring about the size of a whale.
Conor Cruise O'Brien, Irish agnostic, literary critic, politician, and journalist[1]

Northern Ireland is best-considered a bi-confessional society.
Richard Rose, American political scientist[2]

The trouble with Christianity [in Northern Ireland] is not that it has been tried and found wanting, but that it has been wanted yet never tried.
Simon Lee, English Catholic and law professor[3]

In [Ulster] . . . the scriptures have been the single most compelling determinant of the way people have thought about their world.
Donald Akenson, American historian[4]

Modernization is supposed to mean secularization, declining religiosity, and preoccupation with 'this-worldly' or material matters. Northern Ireland is located in the UK, the birthplace of modernity according to the ancestors of social science. Yet significant numbers of journalists, historians and social scientists place religion at the heart of the conflict: and Brian Gable's cartoon captures their feelings (see figure 5.1). Much of the British public shares this verdict. If they are right important implications follow. Socio-economic inequalities, cultural or

172   *Internal Explanations*

Figure 5.1 Brian Gable's view of theological sentiments in
Northern Ireland (*Globe & Mail*, 2 November 1993)

national differences, inter-state relations, and political institutions must be of secondary or no importance. The conflict
must be pre-modern, with essentially endogenous roots.[5]
Policy-implications also follow: 'religious' solutions have to
be canvassed such as secularization, ecumenism, or integrated
education. Alternatively despair may be encouraged, because
the devout are not famous for tolerance.

We will argue that those who think the conflict is fundamentally or primarily based on religion are wrong. Conflict
is indeed waged between two communities whose members
are religiously differentiated, but they are also divided by
broader cultural differences, national allegiances, histories of
antagonistic encounters, and marked differences in economic
and political power.

Their sense of different and shared kinship, although marked
by religion, is not reducible to religion. These divisions are
multiple and reinforcing, and, to the extent that they can be
separated, of varying importance to different individuals. With
some exceptions those who are strongly religiously motivated
are not the major causes of antagonism, stalemate, or political
violence. Nevertheless the views of those with whom we
disagree must be fairly considered, so we first present the

available religious explanations in their clearest and most persuasive articulations.

Four generic types of religious explanation of Northern Ireland can be found, and shall be considered in turn:

- religion matters equally to Protestants and Catholics,[6] and is the cause of antagonism;
- religion matters most to Protestants, and Protestantism is at the root of the conflict;
- religion matters most to Catholics, and Catholicism is at the source of the conflict; and
- religion matters in maintaining and reinforcing social boundaries between Catholics and Protestants, i.e. it matters socially rather than theologically.

Northern Ireland as a Conflict between Catholics and Protestants

Religious devotion is extremely high in Northern Ireland: 1,280 of 1,291 respondents to Rose's Loyalty Survey, conducted in 1968, gave a denominational identification when asked their religion; 95 per cent of Catholics reported going to mass at least once a week, a rate about three times as high as nominal Catholics in France or Austria; 46 per cent of Protestants attended church at least once a week, a rate over twice as high as that of Protestants in Great Britain; and Northern Ireland rated second among Western polities in church attendance, beaten only by the Republic of Ireland.[7] The Policy Studies Institute's Survey revealed that in the 1980s 70 per cent of adults in Northern Ireland went to church at least once a month, compared with 21 per cent in Great Britain.[8] Other indicators of religiosity establish a similar picture of formally devout peoples, as do recent surveys.[9] Although table 5.1 suggests declining religiosity, in so far as church attendance measures religiosity, the region still 'deserves its reputation as a religious society'.[10] The proportion of the population which professes no religion (12 per cent) is considerably less

174   *Internal Explanations*

Table 5.1 Church attendance in Northern Ireland, 1968–89

Year of Survey (high and low attendance rates)	All	Roman Catholics	Protestants
1968			
Once a week or more	66	95	46
Never	4	1	5
1978			
Once a week or more	53	90	39
Never	10	3	10
1989			
Once a week or more	54	86	44
Never	16	3	15

Sources: R. Rose, *Governing without Consensus: An Irish Perspective* (London: Faber, 1971); E. Moxon-Browne, *Nation, Class and Creed in Northern Ireland* (Aldershot: Gower, 1983); and J. Curtice and T. Gallagher, 'The Northern Irish Dimension', in R. Jowell, S. Witherspoon, and L. Brook (eds), *British Social Attitudes: the 7th Report* (Aldershot: Gower, 1990).

than that in Great Britain (34 per cent) and we can testify to the pressures to conform to religious norms encountered by young non-believers.

Observers describe the groups in conflict as Catholics and Protestants, or use Catholic/Protestant and nationalist/unionist as interchangeable sets of antonyms.[11] This careless terminology derives from undeniable facts: nationalist parties and republican paramilitaries derive their support almost exclusively from Catholics, while unionist parties and loyalist paramilitaries are overwhelmingly supported by Protestants. The correlation between political partisanship and religion is very high. In one 'index of religious voting' Northern Ireland's score was 81 – in a possible range from 0 to 100.[12] Compared with other countries with Protestants and Catholics, Northern Ireland registered an 'unprecedented magnitude': Great Britain measured 7, the USA 16, Australia 14, and Canada 14. Even West Germany and the Netherlands, which have had major historical confrontations between Catholics and Protestants, had scores of 29 and 50 respectively.[13] In a more recent comparative evaluation of the association between religious affiliation and party political support Northern Ireland had the strongest association – way ahead of the Netherlands, Norway,

Italy, West Germany, the USA, Hungary, East Germany, Great Britain and New Zealand.[14] The 'index of dissimilarity' between 'regular' Protestants and Catholics, i.e., regular church-goers, was 77 points – 77 per cent of the sample would have had to change political preferences for the two distributions to become identical. The index of dissimilarity between 'irregular' Protestants and Catholics was not much lower, at 67 points.

Such evidence produces an understandable but superficial reaction: the conflict must be religious if the groups engaged in electoral competition and paramilitary struggle are religiously defined.[15] This reading is strengthened by the highly visible political role of Protestant clergy. Three of the thirteen unionist members of the Westminster parliament elected in 1992 are Protestant ministers: the Reverend Dr Ian Paisley of the DUP, who is also one of Northern Ireland's three members of the European Parliament, the Reverend Martin Smyth of the UUP, who is also the head of the explicitly anti-Catholic Orange Order, and the Reverend William McCrea, whose profitable country-and-western singing mimics the Protestant fundamentalism of the deep South of the USA. Paisley, a graduate of Bob Jones University, also located in the deep South of the USA, is probably Northern Ireland's best known and most (locally) popular politician. He began his public life as an incessant scourge of ecumenism, and by encouraging a celebrant of black masses. His protests against the Catholic Archbishop of Westminster's invitation to a Royal wedding,[16] the Pope's visit to Britain, diplomatic relations between the UK and the Vatican, and the Pope's address to the European Parliament, reinforce the perception of Northern Ireland as a site of theological war.

Secular people find it difficult to understand how a religious conflict could be fought in Western Europe in the late twentieth century; so, having persuaded themselves that they have found one, they attribute it to the peculiar, atavistic and anachronistic devoutness of Irish Catholics and Protestants. The condescension with which the English often regard the Irish is reinforced by their perception that the latter are culturally retarded, still engaged in struggles which modern nations (like England) have resolved. As one English journalist comments: 'The passions

176   *Internal Explanations*

which are shared by Mass-going Gael and Calvinist planter, which sustain them indeed in the fashion of two drunks tilted out of the horizontal into a triumphal arch, are nothing to us.'[17]

Local atheists share these prejudices, blaming the conflict on their superstitious neighbours. Thus the Ulster Humanist Association attributes Northern Irish politics to the dogmatic and uncompromising nature of the religious beliefs which 'provide meaning to the lives of most people'.[18]

The secular view that *the* problem is one of conflicting religions is shared by the ecumenical movement, inside and outside Northern Ireland. Ecumenists attribute the conflict to Christian churches stressing their differences, rather than their similarities: it is no 'Holy War'[19] in their eyes; it is profane. The rival churches are condemned as sectarian apologists for the political movements in their communities.[20] This perspective was illustrated by one of McGarry's colleagues. Seeing him with Gallagher and Worrall's ecumenical *Christians in Ulster* under his arm, she looked quizzically at the title before remarking that she didn't think there were any Christians in Ulster.

Catholicism and Protestantism are widely blamed for violence, for replaying the clash between reformation and counter-reformation forces in the seventeenth century,[21] and for conducting a religious war otherwise allegedly confined to the Middle East.[22] Some hold the churches responsible for violence because they create a sectarian environment and selectively condemn atrocities:[23] Protestant churches are criticized for condemning republican violence and condoning the excesses of the security forces, while the Catholic church is criticized for alleged ambivalence towards republicanism and for condemning the 'security' forces.

There is a widespread assumption amongst liberals that religious beliefs make people more rather than less disposed to engage in violence; 'sacred violence' absolutizes politics. The corollary, that a more secular Northern Ireland would be less violent, is rarely openly argued – although it is assumed. A direct connection between religion and political violence has been advanced forcefully by the political scientist David Rapoport,[24] who maintains that religions have both violence-reducing and violence-producing dimensions. They inspire total loyalties; are used to justify wars; and wars of religion are amongst the most ferocious of all. No major religion 'eschews violence under all conditions'.[25] Christianity is the most warlike of the world-religions. 'The foremost authority on genocide, Leo Kuper, has concluded that in virtually every case of genocide religious differences were an element.'[26] The discourses of religions are ambiguous, suffused with violence as well as critiques of violence.[27] Religion may be used to tame violence, especially domestic violence, but it can also be marshalled negatively, to sanction violence against outside communities. Northern Ireland is tailor-made for this perspective, which makes it comprehensible why people fight and kill one another. Brian Walker, Chairman of the New Ulster Movement, holds this view.[28] Richard Rose writes:

> Religion, by contrast [with class], often raises issues based upon a non-bargainable absolute value . . . The history of the Roman Catholic Church and of various Protestant denominations illustrates the impossibility of compromise when transcendental and worldly values are in conflict.[29]

Another commentator attributes some of the violence of Catholic and Protestant paramilitaries to the social doctrines of both theologies – the Catholic doctrine of a 'just war' and the Protestant 'Covenant theology'.[30]

Ecumenists and secular humanists differ in their prognoses and prescriptions. Ecumenists see salvation in common Christian values.[31] They commend Dietrich Bonhoeffer's suggestion for peace through a 'religionless Christianity' which transcends sectarianism.[32] Humanists, by contrast, regard secularization as the best hope for peace. A 'critical mass' of unbelievers will lead to normal politics – negotiable disputes over the allocation of economic resources and manageable ideological conflict between conservatives, liberals and socialists.

178   *Internal Explanations*

Protestantism is at the Root of the Conflict

Some claim the Protestant religion is central to understanding
Northern Ireland, even though, as table 5.1. suggests, Protestants display, statistically, less overt religiosity than Catholics.
The idea is that the intractability of the conflict stems from
the distinctive Protestantism found in Northern Ireland. This
perception partly accounts for the unpopularity of the unionist
cause in international circles. Protestants are portrayed as 'a
bitter and bigoted clan of power-hungry, religious fanatics'.[33]
The *Oxford Children's History* describes Ulster Protestants
as extremists who are not 'like our Church of England
people ... They just hate Catholics in a way that we find
difficult to understand'.[34] And many Irish Catholics agree that
the religious zealotry of Protestants is more culpable than any
failings in their own religion.

Numerous analysts claim that Protestantism is central to
unionism while maintaining that Irish nationalism, by comparison, is a largely secular phenomenon. An historian of the
home rule controversies writes that 'For Catholics the problem was largely political; for Protestants largely religious';[35]
a psychologist maintains that 'For Protestants, their differences
with Catholics are primarily religious ... Catholics' objection
to Protestants concern not their religion, but their political
outlook ... ';[36] a political scientist believes that 'The Protestant perspective, is ... essentially religious';[37] and an agnostic
literary critic argues that whereas 'Ulster Protestants do fear
Catholicism, Ulster Catholics do not fear Protestantism'. The
typical Catholic 'may fear the material power of Protestants,
but he has no fear whatever of Protestantism. He knows little
and thinks little about it; there is simply no equivalent on his
side to the Protestant brooding on the Pope of Rome.'[38] This
verdict is shared by Richard Rose:

> Protestants tend to see their regime as a bulwark of religious
> faith against Catholics within the six counties, against the
> mere Catholic Irish outside their provincial pale, and against
> the forces of error and darkness everywhere growing stron-
> ger in a threatening and increasingly ecumenical world.[39]

Warring Gods?   **179**

Table 5.2 Religious denominations in Northern Ireland, 1961–91

Denomination	1961	1971	1981	1991
Roman Catholic	35	31	29	38
Presbyterian	29	28	24	21
Church of Ireland (Anglican)	24	23	20	18
Methodist	5	5	4	4
Baptist	1	1	1	1
Brethren	1	1	1	1
Congregationalist	1	1	1	1
Free Presbyterian	0	0	1	1
Other Protestant denominations	1	2	3	4
Not stated	2	9	20	8
Atheists/Agnostics/None	n/a	n/a	0	4

Notes:
1. The figures are expressed as a (rounded) percentage of the total respondents to the census.
2. In 1971, 142,511 people refused to answer the religious question. In 1981, 274,584 people refused, and many thousands refused to be enumerated. In 1991, 114,827 people did not state an answer to the question on religion.
Sources: Northern Ireland Census of Population (1961, 1971, 1981, 1991).

This school of interpretation believes that Catholics are confident about their religion and have no fear of Protestant proselytism.[40] Roman Catholics are the largest single denomination in Northern Ireland, part of a large majority on the island, and members of a church with a highly visible international organization. Moreover, the disrupted censuses of 1971 and 1981 masked the fact that Catholics make up a growing percentage of Northern Ireland's population, as table 5.2 suggests.[41] Therefore, it is said, Catholic fears about Protestant evangelicalism cannot have rational foundations and cannot explain the conflict; Catholics separate their faith from their politics; Catholics see the conflict as one over political power, national identity and economic inequality; moderates seek economic and political equality whereas militants want a secular united Ireland; northern nationalism is liberal or socialist; and Catholics have no difficulty supporting nationalist Protestants, whether they be Wolfe Tone, Charles Stewart Parnell, or Ivan Cooper, the civil rights leader elected to Stormont in 1969.[42]

However, so the argument goes, Protestants fear the resourcefulness and power of the Roman Catholic church,[43]

180   *Internal Explanations*

though they despise the Catholic community's lack of material power. Unlike Catholics, Protestants are uncertain about their national identity, and fall back upon their religion for symbolic solace.[44] There is no Protestant equivalent to the Catholic tradition of following leaders from the other community. Catholics did not stand as unionist candidates during the Stormont regime, and the Orange Order opposed Catholic participation in the UUP. Even today the explicitly sectarian Orange Order remains integrally linked to the Ulster Unionist Party.

The most complete statement of the view that Protestantism is central to the conflict has been advanced by the sociologist of religion Steve Bruce:[45] 'The Northern Ireland conflict is a religious conflict. Economic and social differences are also crucial, but it was the fact that the competing populations in Ireland adhered and still adhere to competing religious traditions which has given the conflict its enduring and intractable quality.'[46] The Ulster plantation introduced a devoutly Protestant people into counter-reformation territory. The Calvinist doctrine of predestination and the Westminster Confession of Faith encouraged exclusivist attitudes towards Catholics. Communal conflict was religiously based and eventually organized by the Orange Order, which insisted on pan-Protestant religious supremacy and apartheid. Partition and devolution after 1920 gave rise to a 'Protestant parliament for a Protestant people', in which Protestant privileges were protected. The collapse of Stormont was precipitated because Terence O'Neill adopted secular liberalism, compounding Protestant insecurities flowing from the ecumenical movement prompted by the second Vatican Council (1962–5).

Ulster Protestants, according to Bruce, are an ethnic group defined by their religion. Non-religious collective identifications have been rejected because secular socialism and liberalism do not erect barriers between Protestants and Catholics. The fact that many Protestants do not practise their religion is very conveniently explained: 'Protestantism' is a form of ethnic identity with crucial religious content – secular Protestants 'are not far removed from an evangelical religious commitment' and 'find something appealing about evangelicalism'.[47] They

Warring Gods? 181

have been raised by practising Protestants, attended Sunday schools, and retain sufficient commitment to persuade their wives (sic!) and children to attend Church![48] According to Bruce four features of unionist politics have religious roots:

(i) *their unwillingness to accommodate Catholics.* No unionist politician can accommodate Catholics and retain substantial trust amongst Protestants.[49]

(ii) *their unwillingness to entertain a united Ireland.* Fears about the power of the Catholic church in a united Ireland provide the 'main' reason why Protestants object to a united Ireland.[50]

(iii) *their desire to maintain the Union.* The Union protects their Protestant way of life, including their civil and religious liberties, which are far more important than their national identity. Protestant loyalty to the Union is conditional on Britain upholding the Protestant Constitution of 1688 and protecting them from a Catholic Republic. Opinion polls, in Bruce's view, record a significant reluctance amongst Ulster Protestants to embrace Britishness,[51] because Great Britain is secular and offends the 'religious and ethical sensibilities' of Ulster Protestants, who believe it is progressively abandoning the Protestant Constitution.[52] These considerations allegedly explain the lack of support for integration among Protestants.[53]

(iv) *Unionists' support for Paisley and the DUP.* The huge electoral support for Paisley, who wears his religion on his sleeve, and for the DUP, a party distinguished by its evangelicalism, confirms the salience of religion.[54] In elections to the European parliament Ian Paisley easily out-polls competition from non-evangelical unionists.

In a comparative study, Don Akenson pursues a similar argument to Bruce, but an historically more precise one. He argues that Ulster Protestants, Afrikaners and Israeli Jews all saw themselves as 'chosen people', people with an Old Testament biblical covenant with God.[55] The Ulster Protestants' belief that they were a chosen people explains their sense of superiority to Catholics, their willingness to discriminate, their

182   *Internal Explanations*

endorsement of endogamy, their cohesiveness, their unwillingness to compromise, their rejection of religious pluralism, the
strangeness of their political language to outside observers,
and their attachment to Ulster, which they saw as a promised
land.[56]

Catholics, by contrast, are politically motivated by secular
nationalism: republicans adopt political positions hostile to
the Catholic hierarchy of Ireland and of Rome, who can do
nothing to stop IRA violence.[57] Bruce's argument, written
from a perspective which claims to be empathetic – if not
sympathetic – to evangelical Protestants, in fact reproduces
that of many nationalists who agree that Protestants lack a
real British identity, and that they would fully embrace an
Irish national identity and be content in a united Ireland if
it respected their religious sensibilities and freedoms.[58]

Catholicism is at the Root of the Conflict

By contrast, many believe that the Roman Catholic church
plays a greater role in promoting conflict than Protestantism.
A minority of Protestants, mainly evangelicals and fundamentalists, think that the Irish nationalist movement is under the
control of the Vatican, pursuing the extirpation of Protestantism. Rome is held responsible for 'religious genocide' in the
Republic, where the Protestant minority declined from 10 per
cent of the population in 1911 to 4.1 per cent in 1971 (see table
5.3).[59] The decline is attributed to Papal laws on intermarriage,
which once obliged the Catholic *and* the Protestant partner to
bring up their offspring as Catholics. The Catholic church's policy towards the offspring of mixed marriages is held responsible
for the 'genocide',[60] and for tipping the increasingly delicate
demographic balance in Northern Ireland. More generally,
the atmosphere created by the hierarchy's insistence that
Catholic morality be enforced in public policy is held to have
prompted Protestant emigration from the Republic,[61] though
no systematic evidence is cited in support of this thesis. Liberal
unionists accuse the Catholic hierarchy of teaching nationalist
doctrines in school; of refusing to accept the legitimacy of

Warring Gods? **183**

Table 5.3 Religious denominations in independent Ireland

Religious denomination	1926	1936	1946	1961	1971	1981	1991
Roman Catholic	92.6	93.4	94.3	94.9	93.9	93	91.6
Church of Ireland	5.5	4.9	4.2	3.7	3.3	2.7	2.5
Presbyterian	1.1	0.9	0.8	0.7	0.5	0.4	0.4
Methodist	0.4	0.3	0.3	0.2	0.2	0.2	
Jewish	0.1	0.1	0.1	0.1	0.1	0.1	0.04
Other religion	0.3	0.2	0.3	0.4	0.2	0.3	1
No religion	–	–	–	–	0.3	1.2	1.9
Not stated	–	–	–	–	1.6	2.1	2.4

Notes:
(i) Figures expressed as a percentage, and rounded to one decimal place.
(ii) The 1951, 1956, 1966 and 1979 censuses did not include religious questions.
(iii) From 1911 until 1961 'No religion' and 'Not stated' were included in 'Other'.
(iv) Until 1991 'Protestants' without specific denomination were classed as Church of Ireland, so we have treated this as one category.
Sources: Census of Ireland (1926, 1936, 1946, 1961, 1971, 1981, 1991).

the Union, the Stormont parliament, and the security forces; and of conspicuously refusing to excommunicate members of the IRA – as it did during the Irish civil war of 1922–3.[62] Their sympathizers, like Conor Cruise O'Brien, maintain that 'Irish nationalist ideology, Irish Republicanism . . . beneath an increasingly perfunctory pseudo secular cover, is Irish Catholic holy nationalist.'[63]

For some unionists the 'unfinished business' of Irish nationalism is Catholicization and the eradication of the Protestant religion:[64] the 'Roman Catholic IRA', the full title given to the IRA by Paisleyites, is the Vatican's storm-troopers, and its killing of Protestants is merely a more direct form of genocide than that practised by its co-religionists across the border.[65] In a submission to the inter-party talks held at Stormont in June 1991, Ian Paisley declared 'These talks cannot and will not stop the Roman Catholic IRA nor will it stop acts of terror by those who claim the name Protestant.'[66] In this perspective republican paramilitaries *are* Catholics, loyalist paramilitaries are not *real* Protestants. Since Catholics are bent on eradicating Protestantism, accommodation must be resisted. Paisley and his supporters point to the explicit support for a united Ireland expressed by the former Catholic Primate of all Ireland, Cardinal O'Fiaich, and other members of the hierarchy. They

184   *Internal Explanations*

highlight the refusal of the Catholic church to condemn the
1981 hunger-strikers,[67] the willingness of the church to bury
hunger-strikers and IRA dead in consecrated ground, and
the finding of IRA arms on Catholic church grounds.[68] The
alleged participation of priests like Father Ryan in the IRA's
activities, and the massacre of Protestant evangelicals at prayer
by republican militants in 1983, are presented as proof of the
indissoluble alliance of Irish nationalism and Catholicism. As
Jim Allister of the DUP declared:

> It is this insoluble (sic!) marriage of Roman Catholicism to
> militant Irish republicanism, where the latter is seen as the
> 'political' expression and promoter of the former, which makes
> [impossible] what should otherwise be possible, namely the
> co-existence of the political expressions of Protestantism and
> Roman Catholicism in Ireland.[69]

Liberal and socialist unionists also emphasize the link between Roman Catholicism and Irish nationalism.[70] They agree
with the fundamentalist Protestant critique of the Republic,
but attack the Roman Catholic church's influence from a
perspective formally critical of fundamentalism. They reject
the view that Protestantism defines unionism, and maintain
that the false juxtaposition of secular Irish nationalism with
a religiously exclusive unionism alienates the British on whom
the unionists depend, and plays into the hands of republican
intellectuals.[71] The international unpopularity of unionism
and the external sympathy for Irish nationalism, even in
Britain, are attributed to the high profile of Protestant
fundamentalists with Cathophobic views.[72] Liberal unionists
therefore stress a competing tradition in Ulster unionism.[73]
Religious exclusivism, they claim, triumphed over liberalism,
not because Protestantism was fundamental to unionism but
in reaction to strident Catholic nationalism. Only when
Catholicism and nationalism became 'indissolubly linked' did
the divisions between fundamentalist and liberal unionism
disappear.[74]. Exclusivist unionism became ascendant after
1920 because Britain foisted devolution on the unionists,
cutting them from the British liberal mainstream.[75] In this

perspective, unionists have no intrinsic desire to dominate or exclude Catholics. In fact, some Catholics are unionists, which Bruce's analysis cannot explain. The UK is defended as a pluralist, tolerant and diverse state, not because of the sectarian Williamite settlement and the desire to lord it over Catholics; and the Republic is seen as its Manichean opposite, a sectarian, intolerant and homogenizing state. They think that recent constitutional travails over divorce, contraception and abortion have shown how distinctive the Republic wants to remain – at a time when there was every incentive to prove its liberality and when this appeared to be the official strategy of successive governments.[76] Thus the tables are turned. Unionists are not anachronistic religious fanatics; and the real axis of conflict is between unionists who want a tolerant UK, and nationalists who want to follow principles of 'national homogeneity and religious authority'.[77]

Religion Maintains and Reinforces the Social Boundary

Social scientists, especially anthropologists, agree that Northern Ireland is a segmented society with a clear social boundary between two major communities,[78] cemented by endogamy and educational and residential segregation. These boundaries make social interaction difficult and, especially in working-class districts, facilitate communal ghettos which promote group solidarity, myths, mutual ignorance, intolerance, prejudice, and stereotyping. Many social scientists and secular intellectuals (overlapping categories) hold the churches directly and indirectly responsible for maintaining this social frontier.

Churches provide a meeting place for members of their flock. Attendance at religious services spills over into other religiously driven activities. The Catholic church organizes associations like the St Vincent de Paul Society, the Pioneer Association of the Sacred Heart, and the Legion of Mary, as well as various youth organizations. Protestant churches have Sunday schools, Bible study groups, Boys Brigades and

186   *Internal Explanations*

Girl Guides.[79] In addition, the Orange Order preaches and practises religious apartheid and condemnation of Romanist 'idolatry'. Most adverse commentary centres, however, on the churches' role in maintaining and reinforcing social division through their attitudes to endogamy and segregated education. This 'is the most significant aspect of the role of religion in the divisions and conflicts in Ireland and goes to the heart of the matter'.[80]

Endogamy. In 1968 96 per cent of respondents to Rose's Loyalty Survey had parents of the same religion.[81] Research suggests that mixed marriages formed 6 per cent of the total in Northern Ireland during the four decades 1943–82, which compares strikingly with marriage patterns in England and Wales, where 67 per cent of marriages involving Roman Catholics are mixed.[82] Given the importance of parents in transmitting values to children, this high level of endogamy, even though it may have fallen in recent years, is extremely important in maintaining group boundaries.[83] Blame has often been pinned on the Catholic church's animosity towards intermarriage and on its insistence in the papal *Ne Temere* decree of 1908 that *both* partners in a mixed marriage had to agree to raise their children as Catholics. This decree has been relaxed since the apostolic letter *Matrimonia Mixta* of 1970 – only the Catholic partner is now required to give this undertaking. Though the Protestant churches do not have the same explicit barriers to intermarriage, they do not encourage it.[84] The Orange Order prohibits members participating in any Roman Catholic religious ceremony, including marriages and funerals.

Segregated education. Northern Ireland's education system is almost totally segregated into Catholic and state schools at the primary and secondary levels – less than 2 per cent attend integrated schools. The two universities are formally integrated, although one study of Queen's University Belfast showed that it is no haven of liberal integration in a sectarian sea,[85] while third-level teacher-training colleges are explicitly segregated.[86] The Catholic hierarchy promotes separate Catholic education because it believes it is the best way to reproduce Catholic values.[87] Less kindly, the Roman Catholic church's motives are defined as ethnocentric and reactionary, based on its historic campaign against proselytism and its contemporary battle against secularism.[88] However, the segregated system is broadly supported by the Protestant churches because the state schools are in effect Protestant – biblical readings are normal in such schools. Despite the idea prevalent amongst academic foreigners that segregated education is a product of the Catholic church,[89] Protestant churches helped build the present system and vigorously opposed past attempts at integration.[90] The scale of educational segregation is such that less than 2 per cent of children attend integrated schools.

Numerous commentators believe segregated education fosters conflict; it promotes bloc solidarity; strengthens sectarianism; and encourages ignorance of the other community. The two school systems teach a culturally biased curriculum, not just in religious instruction, but in potentially divisive subjects like history and language. They encourage different games: Catholic schools promote Gaelic sports, like hurling, camogie and handball; state/Protestant schools encourage sports associated with the British Empire, like rugby or cricket.[91] The divided schools exacerbate socio-economic differences between Catholics and Protestants: Catholic schools allegedly encourage the arts while Protestant schools put greater emphasis on science and mathematics, which some claim differentially affects pupils' prospects in the labour market.[92] Similarly, one observer claims that Catholic under-representation in public service can be explained by a self-fulfilling prophecy – Catholic teachers tell their students they will not be hired in governmental institutions, so they do not apply![93] Less controversially, segregated education has undoubtedly contributed to religiously based teaching unions, erecting obstacles to cross-cutting cleavages based on employee solidarity.[94] The location of schools also reinforces residential segregation.

For many it follows that integrated education would be a positive development, promoting understanding and reconciliation.[95] Some claim it would be 'the single potentially most helpful step'.[96] Supporters of integrated education have included lobby movements like *All Children Together*; Lord Londonderry (Northern Ireland's first minister of education);

188   *Internal Explanations*

Table 5.4 Public opinion on what the government should do
on mixed schooling

	Protestants	Catholics
Encourage it	57	67
Discourage it	9	5
Leave things as they are	33	28

Source: A. M. Gallagher and S. Dunn, 'Community Relations in Northern
Ireland: Attitudes to Contact and Integration', in Peter Stringer and Gillian
Robinson (eds), *Social Attitudes in Northern Ireland, 1990–91 Edition* (Belfast:
Blackstaff Press, 1991), 16.

Sir James Craig, *before* he became Northern Ireland's first
prime minister; Terence O'Neill;[97] as well as several academics.[98] More surprisingly, perhaps, the harmful effects of
segregated education have been noted by a leading Catholic
journal;[99] by Jesuits and professors at Maynooth, the Republic's
leading seminary; and by at least one Catholic bishop.[100] A
1986 survey of Northern Irish Catholic priests found that
33 per cent agreed that 'integrated education would reduce
some of the problems in Northern Ireland' while 41 per
cent did not oppose it 'in principle'.[101] Integrated education
received some support from the education minister in the brief
power-sharing executive which sat during early 1974, from the
Labour government during 1974–9 and, most recently, from
the Conservative government which in 1990 made more funds
available for integrated education. The Education Reform
(Northern Ireland) Order 1989, which became law on 19
February 1990, temporarily created a privileged new category
of school, 'grant-maintained integrated' (GMI) schools, which
had all of their recurrent and capital expenditure met by the
Department of Education – unlike Catholic schools before
1992. Indeed from 1988 until 1992 it appeared that the government intended to support integrated schools at the expense
of mono-religious state schools.

Opponents of segregated education muster survey evidence
in support of their cause. A 1968 survey, for example, showed
that 64 per cent of adults favoured integrated education.[102]
A survey in 1978 found that 81 per cent of Protestants and
84 per cent of Catholics disagreed with the statement 'It is a

bad idea to mix Protestant and Catholic children in the same schools.'[103] The 1989 Social Attitudes Survey produced the responses displayed in table 5.4. These figures suggest that a 'positive climate' exists for integrated schools – even though significant minorities of Protestants (42 per cent) and Catholics (33 per cent) do not want the government to encourage mixed schooling.[104] They also suggest that segregated education is something which majorities in both communities regard as amenable to change.

The Limits to Religious Explanations: Two Religions in Conflict?

The foregoing accounts attach fundamental or primary importance to religion in explaining political antagonism, political violence and political stalemate. However, as the following arguments suggest, there are major flaws in these analyses.

Measurable levels of religiosity, such as church attendance, are remarkably high in Northern Ireland when compared with elsewhere in western Europe,[105] but the fact is that conflict started, escalated, and has continued while these levels have been declining. Other measures of religious irregularity – of divorces or of children born outside marriage – indicate that Northern Ireland is becoming more secular. Since 1981, the divorce rate, while lower absolutely, has been increasing at about the same rate as in Great Britain. Between 1981 and 1987 the rate of births outside marriage more than doubled, compared with an increase of 83 per cent in the whole of the UK. By 1987 the illegitimate birth-rate level had reached the UK rate for 1981, so on this 'index' Northern Ireland is a mere six years behind the UK.[106] Such 'secularization' has not affected the continuing high levels of support for nationalist and unionist political parties, so it is at least questionable whether more of the same will make a significant difference.

Significantly, there is no noticeable correlation between those areas most affected by the conflict and the intensity of the religious convictions of the inhabitants. Rural areas

190 *Internal Explanations*

around Ballymena, heartlands of support for Paisley, are tranquil and generally free of political violence. Nationalist towns like Crossmaglen may be devoutly religious but it is more difficult to make this argument about West Belfast, where there have been noticeable declines in church attendance in both blocs.[107] John Darby reported in 1986 that church attendance was estimated by local clergy in one Catholic area of Belfast at 33 per cent.[108] One study of the Shankill, where Protestant paramilitaries and the DUP have significant support, indicated that Protestant church attendance had dropped to about 15 per cent in the late 1970s.[109] Another detailed analysis of the Protestant working class in Belfast depicts them as distinctly secular, like the working class in industrial cities elsewhere:[110] the Reverend Martin Smyth's pious observation that Shankill working-class Protestants 'are bible-lovers if not bible-readers' is scarcely compelling evidence of religious consciousness.[111] The spatial and per capita distribution of violence is highly concentrated in urban sites, which are, as elsewhere in the world, less religious than rural zones.[112] Indeed one can go further and suggest that urban paramilitaries become religious, or more religious, *after* they have been incarcerated!

Relations between the churches were improving when conflict erupted in the late 1960s. The second Vatican Council had formally abandoned the Roman Catholic claim that 'outside the Church there is no salvation', paving the way for ecumenism. Even if we concede, for the sake of argument, the Paisleyite claim that this step marked religious imperialism in a new tactical guise, it is difficult to understand why ecumenism should have been more successful in promoting Catholic violence, or Protestant counter-violence, than Rome's previous and blunter claim that all Protestants were heretics. Since the conflict erupted in the late 1960s there has been a fair amount of ecumenical activity and inter-church co-operation,[113] and the present co-operation of the churches is very different from what occurred in earlier crises: for example, during the home rule controversies the Protestant churches played leading roles in promoting the Ulster Covenant. The churches have not always taken a united position on excesses by the security forces, paramilitary violence, or political proposals, but this behaviour

Warring Gods?   **191**

often indicates that they are following their flocks, rather than leading them. To expect a consensus from pastoral churches in divided communities is wishful thinking. In any case, claims that partisan statements by church leaders are responsible for the violence are exaggerated, and no more plausible than the view that religious statements against violence have kept it at lower rates than would otherwise have been the case.

Significantly, political activists in Northern Ireland seek to avoid religious labels. The organizations of the minority embrace secular political values in their titles: 'nationalism' or 'republicanism', 'social democracy', and 'socialism' provide their vocabularies. No minority party or paramilitary group describes itself religiously – only Paisleyites describe the IRA as the 'Roman Catholic IRA'. Politically they refer to 'their community' as 'the northern nationalist community'. Nationalists boast proudly of a famous tradition of Protestant nationalists – though as one revisionist historian has observed, they are important as 'deviants, not as representatives of a latent syndrome'.[114]

Politicians who are Catholics have been and are lay people with differing religious commitments – by contrast with Latin America, no Catholic clergy have stood for political office. The old Nationalist Party had close links with the Catholic church, but the civil-rights movement of the late 1960s was led by lay Catholics, and at present neither of the two major northern nationalist parties enjoys a particularly close relationship with the church, although the SDLP has much greater standing and respectability with the hierarchy than Sinn Féin. Republican paramilitaries include practising and non-practising Catholics, and there is little or no correlation between the intensity of Catholic (or Protestant) religious views and fighting-commitment.[115] Catholic voters have shown willingness on many occasions to support individuals who enjoyed a closer relationship with Trotsky and Marx than with the Pope, returning one 'cradle Catholic', Bernadette Devlin, to the Westminster parliament in 1969. One of her opinions was that[116] 'Among the best traitors Ireland has ever had, Mother Church ranks at the very top, a massive obstacle in the path to equality and freedom.'[117] In 1981 Catholic voters

192   *Internal Explanations*

in Fermanagh and South Tyrone elected another MP, Bobby
Sands, a convicted IRA man, whose distinctly untheological
qualification was that he was starving himself to death in British
custody.

Nationalist politicians propose secular not theological policies. Their micro-proposals are for economic reforms or
changes to the policing and judicial systems. Campaigning
on religious issues, like full-funding for segregated education,
was left to the Catholic church by the SDLP to an extent
unimaginable during the era of the Nationalist Party – although
the SDLP has been equivocal and divided on public policy on
contraception and Brook clinics, and its members generally
oppose legalizing abortion, whereas Sinn Féin supporters are
more liberal on these matters. The key macro-policy of nationalist politicians and militants is an agreed or united Ireland
which would transcend sectarianism, rather than the construction of a Catholic state. The formal targets of republican paramilitaries between 1969 and 1994 were those who defended
the Union, not those who defend Protestantism. Republican
paramilitaries generally avoided targeting Protestant religious
personnel and institutions. Only one Protestant cleric was
killed by republicans between 1969 and 1994, the Reverend
Robert Bradford, and he was a hard-line UUP MP with out-
spoken views on how to deal with the IRA hunger-strikers.
The isolated incident at Darkley in 1983 when republican
gunmen – probably from the INLA – killed three Protestant
evangelicals during a religious service, may provide proof
enough of republicans' religious agenda for Free Presbyterians,
but it will not do for social scientists.

IRA violence cannot be convincingly explained, as Fulton
believes,[118] by the argument that its activists have been motivated by the Catholic doctrine of a 'just war'. The Catholic
hierarchy pronounced that the situation in Northern Ireland
did not meet the criteria necessary for a just war,[119] and what,
in any case, is intrinsically 'religious', never mind 'Catholic', about taking up arms against a perceived aggressor or
oppressor?[120] Few religions, or for that matter value-systems,
reject armed retaliation against tyranny. Franz Fanon, no
theist, thought that violence was the only way to cleanse a

Warring Gods? **193**

people of oppression, and his French admirer, atheist Jean-Paul Sartre, declared that violence was like Achilles' lance – it healed the wounds it made.[121] These masculine and romantic justifications of violence resemble those articulated by many republicans; they did not need, and did not receive Papal endorsement. And even if Catholic 'just war' doctrine had justified IRA violence, it would not have followed that religion had been 'causing' the violence. Its root causes are better undertood against the background of institutions which provoked people into declaring a just war in the first place and in the opportunities and perceived benefits from violent collective action. It is possible to explain – though not justify – republican violence strictly through reference to nationalist ideology, the suppression of economic, cultural and political rights, and the historically widely dispersed lesson that 'force can work'. When interviewed, these arguments pour naturally from the lips of former IRA activists and supporters of Sinn Féin. There is no need to invent ingenious religious agendas to account for militant republican paramilitarism.

On the unionist side, political organizations define themselves as 'loyalist' or 'unionist'. There is one interesting example since 1969 of a unionist party describing itself religiously, Paisley's Protestant Unionist Party. However, it changed its name to the Democratic Unionist Party in 1971 because of the limited attractiveness of the explicitly religious label – and it was some time before the party attracted significant support. Loyalist paramilitaries also generally shun religious appellations – with the exception of the Protestant Action Force. The absence of denominational titles in political and paramilitary organizations is all the more remarkable given their existence in other countries which are not racked by conflict, religious or otherwise. The Ulster Unionist Party, the Democratic Unionist Party, the Social Democratic and Labour Party of Northern Ireland, and Sinn Féin are not religiously labelled, even if their support-bases are religiously differentiated. The objectives of these parties, with the possible exception of the DUP, are secular. The IRA, the INLA, the IPLO, the UDA, and the UVF are not religious bodies. Finally, we can make our point counterfactually. Imagine that

194   *Internal Explanations*

Northern Ireland's two major political parties, the UUP and
the SDLP, had denominational titles – say the Protestant
Popular Party of Ulster and the National Catholic Democratic
Action Party. These labels would not necessarily signify a
religious conflict, since they might just serve as markers for two
ethnic blocs, defined by religion, but whose members did not
practise their ancestral beliefs. As we have seen, the political
language of both protagonists appeals to the discourses of
nationalism, the principles of self-determination and democratic majoritarianism, ideas which are, in principle, and in
practice, detached from religious world-views. Moreover, the
sectarian interest-associations, like the Orange Order and the
Ancient Order of Hibernians (AOH), are far less significant
than they were seven decades ago. The AOH is now better
supported on St Patrick's Day in the USA than in any part of
Ireland. The Orange Order was by-passed as a vehicle of ethnic
organization, both in 1974, when the Ulster Workers Council
organized a loyalist strike against the power-sharing Executive,
and after the Anglo-Irish Agreement of 1985, when the newly
formed Ulster Clubs organized pan-unionist opposition.

The principal unionist parties and the loyalist paramilitaries
are exclusively Protestant, but many of their supporters do
not practise any faith. The high profile of Protestant clerics
notwithstanding, the overwhelming majority of unionist politicians are lay people. They address themselves to secular issues,
calling for a strengthening of the Union and for stronger
security policies. They do not call for a Protestant theocracy
– although one could read the 1688 British Constitution in that
light! Of course, national preferences might be dictated partly
by religious motivations – a united Ireland, after all, would
be overwhelmingly Catholic while the UK is overwhelmingly
Protestant or secular – but if these political agents are primarily
interested in these religious agendas, they have done a good
job of concealing it, from their followers as well as others.
Loyalist paramilitaries generally shun overtly religious targets.
Catholic churches have remained relatively inviolate, and not
one Catholic priest has been killed by loyalist gunmen – though
one, Father Fitzpatrick, was killed by an army sniper as he was
administering the last rites.[122] It must be perplexing for those

Warring Gods?   **195**

Table 5.5 Perceived causes of 'The Troubles', by religion

	Protestants	Catholics
1 Political, constitutional	35	32
2 Discrimination, rights	21	27
3 Violence, terrorism	16	7
4 Attitudes	15	15
5 Religion	13	12
6 Social, economic	11	15
7 Segregation	5	4
8 Others	18	15

Source: D. Smith and G. Chambers, *Inequality in Northern Ireland* (Oxford: Clarendon Press, 1991), 68.

who believe that the paramilitaries are involved in a *jihad* that 'Protestant' gunmen assiduously avoid clearly marked, accessible and unarmed priests and nuns when searching for targets. Individuals engaged in authentic religious wars – during the Inquisition, the Reformation and the Counter-reformation – had no difficulty in despatching heretics to hell.

Religious motivations undoubtedly underlie much of what the Catholic and Protestant clergy do. Many Catholic priests support a united Ireland, and most Protestant clergy support the Union. However, these national preferences are autonomous of religious beliefs. Clerics on both sides, after all, have been socialized in their respective communities. They live, have families and perform pastoral functions within them. It is not surprising, therefore, that they share their flock's political aspirations. As Ian Paisley complained of Cardinal O'Fiaich, 'You can take him out of Crossmaglen but you cannot take Crossmaglen out of him.'[123]

It is important to realize that the external perception that the conflict is religious does not square with local perceptions.[124] The Policy Studies Institute's Survey in 1986 asked respondents: 'What, in your opinion, are the main causes of the current Troubles in Northern Ireland, which began in the late 1960s?' The question was designed to make the respondents think about factors that were still relevant in 1986, and they were able to list more than one cause. The results were classified and are reported in table 5.5. They

196   *Internal Explanations*

are complex, but only 13 per cent of Protestants and 12 per cent of Catholics thought religion was one of the main causes of the troubles, and some of these respondents thought the problem was 'a lack of religion' rather than religious bigotry. Catholics are more likely to hold discrimination, civil rights or socio-economic issues responsible for the conflict, whereas Protestants are more likely to blame violence or terrorism. The classifications listed in table 5.5 overlap, and if categories 1 and 2 and 6 are combined – linking civil rights, discrimination and socio-economic inequalities – then non-religious factors unequivocally emerge as the most important perceived causes of conflict.[125] The overwhelming majority of Northern Irish agree that they are not engaged in a *jihad*. We have heard the response that such evidence should be discounted as collective 'denial', but we find that thesis neither plausible nor testable.

Is Protestantism at the Core of the Conflict?

Protestants believe that the conflict has multiple causes, as table 5.5 demonstrates. We believe, like most of them, that their opposition to a united Ireland, their support for the Union, their unwillingness to accommodate the nationalist minority, and their support for Ian Paisley and the DUP cannot be fundamentally or primarily reduced to their religious values and beliefs.

While cultural differences between Protestant and Catholic may be indiscernible to outsiders, and their historical linguistic differences have long since been eroded, the two blocs have different practices in a range of cultural activities, including music, sport and literature.[126] The Gaelic revival of the late nineteenth century made Irish nationalism more unattractive to Protestants, and this was reinforced by the implementation of a Gaelicizing agenda in independent Ireland – including compulsory knowledge of the Irish language for the educational leaving certificate and certain careers in public service. The anti-British atmosphere in independent Ireland, which led to its departure from the Commonwealth and the declaration

Warring Gods? **197**

Table 5.6 Structured sources of Protestant opposition to a united Ireland in 1978

	% agreeing
'would lose British national identity'	89.6
'standard of living would go down'	77.5
'fear of the power of the Roman Catholic Church'	74.5
'would be in a minority in the Republic'	70.9
'want to keep privileged position in Northern Ireland'	66.1

Source: Moxon-Browne, *Nation, Class and Creed.*

of a Republic, made a united Ireland an additionally uninviting prospect for people who felt themselves British monarchists.[127]

There have always been economic as well as cultural reasons why Ulster Protestants resist incorporation in a united Ireland. The Protestant bourgeoisie and proletariat thought that Irish home rule would mean submergence in a polity whose leaders promised protectionism and import-substitution. Today, Protestants – and some Catholics – continue to believe that their economic position would rapidly deteriorate if they joined a state whose major export seems to be its own citizens. A unified Ireland would turn the present British, unionist, and Protestant majority in Northern Ireland into a political minority and would also denote a victory for their enemy, the Provisional IRA. These fears are sufficient to explain – though they do not justify – why so many Protestants are unwilling to accommodate nationalists.

Professor Bruce's argument that Protestants resist a united Ireland primarily for religious reasons depends on an unprofessional use of data. His apparently powerful claim that 74.5 per cent of unionists give 'fear of the power of the Roman Catholic Church' as their reason for being unionist is misleading.[128] The same data is used elsewhere to argue that fear of the Roman Catholic church's power is the 'main' reason for Protestant opposition to a united Ireland.[129] The impression conveyed is that Protestants have been asked to choose one reason for their opposition to a united Ireland and three-quarters have selected this religious reason as their main reason. However, the survey to which Bruce refers allowed Protestants to select a number of reasons for opposing Irish

198   *Internal Explanations*

unification (see table 5.6). The responses show that Protestants clearly agree on multiple reasons for opposing a united Ireland. Had they been asked whether they opposed a united Ireland because that is what the IRA was fighting for, we can be sure that they would have concurred. The question-wording in table 5.6 does not allow us to infer which fears are of most intense importance to Protestants, but more were concerned that they would 'lose their British identity' and that their 'standard of living would go down' than were worried about the power of the Roman Catholic church. Moreover, 70.9 per cent of Protestants feared 'they would be a minority' in the Republic and an honest 66.1 per cent 'wanted to keep their privileged position in Northern Ireland'. Fear of the Catholic church, therefore, is not the 'main' reason Protestants resist incorporation into an all-Ireland republic – just one of a number which have different weights for each individual Protestant. When Ian Paisley implied, during a radio interview in 1971, that the conflict could be resolved if the political influence of the hierarchy in the Republic was removed, he was forced to make a quick retraction by his confused followers – who had plenty of non-religious reasons for opposing a united Ireland.[130]

Richard Rose's Loyalty Survey is often used to confirm the view that fear of the Roman Catholic church is at the forefront of Protestant minds. Indeed Rose includes the following quotation at the top of his chapter on religion:

Interviewer: What do you have against Roman Catholics?
Belfast Protestant: Are you daft? Why, their religion of course.[131]

When readers recover from the joke they must realize that the question is hardly neutral. Would the same response have been given if the Belfast Protestant had been asked what s/he had against 'republicans' or 'nationalists'? More significantly when asked about the position of the Catholic church in the Republic, 69 per cent of Protestants thought it was 'politically important', 'powerful' or 'too powerful', but when asked what they disliked about the Republic's government only 7.6 per cent of them mentioned interference or dominance by the Roman Catholic church.[132] In any case fear

Warring Gods?   **199**

of the position of the Catholic church in the Republic does not necessarily indicate that the Protestant religion is central to unionism. Rejection of 'Romanism' may be a rationalization of a whole complex of attitudes and interests, ranging from cultural contempt to ardent secular liberalism. Secular unionists, or Protestant atheists as they are colloquially known, vigorously oppose a united Ireland, and have more reason to do so than the bulk of Ulster Protestant believers who share the moral conservatism which historically has been entrenched in the Republic's constitution and public policies.

Protestants' desire to maintain the Union also cannot be reduced to their religion, especially as Great Britain is increasingly less Protestant. Great Britain is now largely secular – only 13 per cent of the English claim any church membership.[133] While Protestants are divided over their national identity, many, indeed most, now regard themselves as British[134] – the same Professor Bruce who argues that 'Ulster Protestants have not developed a clear sense of nationality' provides details of a 1978 survey which indicates that 67 per cent of Protestants consider themselves to be 'British'.[135] Unionists like being part of a large, still relatively powerful, 'Great' British state, and older unionists remain proud of their collective sacrifices during two world wars and of their service to the Empire. Economic self-interest buttresses national identity. Northern Ireland enjoys measurable subsidies and it does not make sense to argue that these have no bearing on Protestant motivations. Determined to stress the salience of religion, Bruce points out that marginalized Protestants remain solid unionists despite the fact that they gain least economically from the Union.[136] However, this argument is economically mistaken: marginalized Protestants may gain least from the Union, but they still gain, so their cost–benefit calculus favours the Union. There is also nothing surprising about marginalized groups acting vehemently to protect what others may regard as meagre economic rewards – consider the behaviour of 'white trash' in the deep South of the USA or poor Afrikaners in South Africa. We are not, however, advancing the counter-error of reducing unionism to economics. In short we agree with those who question whether unionism must have a

200   *Internal Explanations*

fundamental attribute, a dimension more important than any other,[137] but if it has to be given a fundamental attribute then it must be seen as the political expression of an ethno-national community which is religiously demarcated – and not the political expression of *a* religious community.

Unionists' reasons for resisting accommodation with Catholics obviously include religious motivations, but apart from fundamentalists, these reasons are not paramount or widespread. There is a simpler reason: for unionists accommodating Catholics means accommodating nationalists. They were far more perturbed by Terence O'Neill's meeting with Sean Lemass than by his visits to Catholic convents. Their opposition to power-sharing focuses on its linkage to an Irish (nationalist) dimension, not a Vatican dimension. Even loyalist paramilitaries say they are happy to accommodate Catholics if and when they accept the Union.[138] They are far more worried about public policy concessions to nationalists – which may restrain 'their' security forces – than they are about concessions to Catholics *qua* Catholics. When the British government announced in 1992 that Catholic schools would receive 100 per cent capital funding there was no major discontent in the unionist press.[139]

The claim that 'the Northern Ireland conflict is a religious conflict' because 'that is the only conclusion that makes sense of Ian Paisley's career', his electoral success in particular, is also misleading.[140] For a start it proves nothing about what motivates those Protestants who vote for the APNI (approximately 10–12 per cent) and the UUP (between 40 and 60 per cent). To sustain his thesis Professor Bruce seems intent on exaggerating the DUP's support.[141] He acknowledged that only 'half of Ulster's unionist voters' support the DUP, but did not observe that this figure relied on a selective concentration on untypical election results and neglected the Protestant electorate who vote for the APNI.[142] Bruce's favoured electoral illustration is the untypical European parliamentary election,[143] in which Paisley's personal charisma, the nature of the campaign, the electoral system, and the dullness of his UUP opponents, help Paisley receive a proportion of the poll which dwarfs what his party obtains in other regional elections.[144] If instead

Warring Gods? **201**

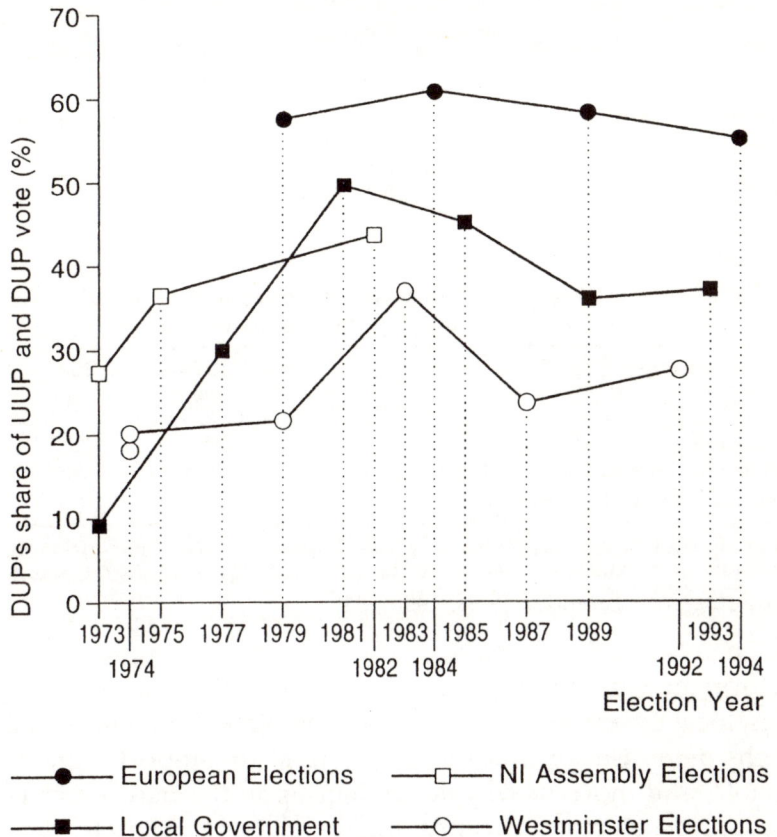

Figure 5.2 The competition for votes between the DUP
and the UUP, 1973–94

we highlighted the DUP's share of the poll at Westminster
elections – which ranged from 8 to 10 per cent during the 1970s
and from 13 to 20 per cent during the 1980s – we could present
a misleading impression of the weakness of the DUP. To do so
would be no worse than the argument adopted by Bruce.

The lesson is simple: sociologists of religion, over-ambitious
to apply their insights, should be more cautious with electoral
data. There are after all political rather than religious reasons
for the variability of the DUP's electoral performance. Figure 5.2 shows the DUP's share of the DUP and UUP vote
in elections held between 1973 and 1994. We have distinguished the DUP's performance in European elections from its

202   *Internal Explanations*

Table 5.7 Members of the Free Presbyterian Church in Northern
Ireland, 1961–91

	1961	1971	1981	1991
Absolute Numbers		7,337	9,621	12,363
Percentage of respondents	0.07	0.4	0.7	0.8

Source: Census of Northern Ireland (1961, 1971, 1981, 1991).

Table 5.8 Electoral support for major unionist parties in the 1975
Convention and the 1982 Assembly

	1975 (%)	1982 (%)
Ulster Unionist Party (UUP)	25.8	29.7
Democratic Unionist Party (DUP)	14.8	23
Vanguard Unionist Party (VUP)	12.7	(–)

Source: B. O'Leary, 'Appendix 4. Party Support in Northern Ireland, 1969–89', in J. McGarry and B. O'Leary (eds), *The Future of Northern Ireland* (Oxford: Clarendon Press, 1990), 343.

performance in other region-wide elections (Westminster elections, local government elections and assembly elections). The graphs demonstrate that the DUP's level of support is more variable, and more heavily dependent upon the nature of the election, the electoral formula and the electoral districts, than Bruce's arguments would suggest. These variations cannot be explained by changes in people's religious commitments. The UUP usually has a higher vote-share than the DUP – except in European elections – though the DUP's weaker performance in Westminster elections results from its decision not to compete in certain constituencies for fear of letting nationalists win them.[145]

The DUP nevertheless enjoys significant electoral support, so *prima facie* evidence for the salience of religion in politics remains. The key question can therefore be put: do Protestants support Ian Paisley and the DUP for religious reasons?[146] Table 5.7 shows the numbers of persons identifying as followers of the Free Presbyterian Church, the church founded by Paisley, in the four censuses held since 1960. The tenfold growth in membership of the Free Presbyterians may be significant, but the Free Presbyterians still make up a tiny fraction of Northern Ireland's population (less than 1 per cent), and there has been a far higher rise in the absolute numbers of those declaring that they have no religion.

It is important to realize that the DUP is not only a party with large numbers of Free Presbyterians in its membership, it is also a hard-line unionist party. It consistently opposes compromise with nationalists, and calls for the 'smashing' of Sinn Féin and the IRA. In the DUP 1982 Assembly manifesto, for example, the party supported majority rule, offered 'the firmest stand against all attempts to force Ulster down the Dublin road', and called for all-out war against the IRA, and the return of the death penalty. Only in the last paragraph was there a reference to the party's support for evangelicalism.[147] The DUP also spearheaded loyalist assaults on the Anglo-Irish Agreement of 1985, and the Joint Peace Declaration of 1993. The message? Unionists can be confident that the DUP will not sell them out. They cannot feel so confident about the UUP, home to such notorious 'Lundies' as Terence O'Neill, James Chichester-Clark, and Brian Faulkner, and individuals like Harry West, Ken Maginnis, and Chris McGimpsey, who have proposed power-sharing with nationalists.

The DUP was not anywhere near as popular in the mid-1970s as it became in the early 1980s (see figure 5.2 and table 5.8). The reason was that in the 1970s the DUP had to compete with the Vanguard Unionist Party (VUP), which was a hard-line loyalist party, and secular. Its leader, William Craig, had even welcomed ecumenism when it emerged in the early 1960s.[148] Until 1976 Craig was far more militant than Paisley, and feared by nationalists as a fascist exponent of independence for 'Ulster'. The VUP collapsed, however, when Craig appeared to compromise in discussions with the SDLP during the Constitutional Convention, opening the field of uncompromising extremism for exclusive occupation by Paisley's party. The DUP became the home of most former VUP supporters after that party disintegrated in the wake of its leader's national, rather than religious, 'treachery', as table 5.8 suggests.

The DUP wins a significant share of the Protestant working-class vote. The party's evangelicalism cannot be the basis of

204   *Internal Explanations*

this electoral success as the urban Protestant working class is not particularly religious.[149] It fears losing the benefits of the Union, dislikes nationalists or Catholics, and distrusts the 'furcoat brigade' in the establishment UUP. The DUP attracts this working-class vote, not by wearing evangelicalism on its sleeve, but by downplaying it. To increase its appeal to non-evangelical Protestants the party changed its name from Protestant Unionist to Democratic Unionist, compromised its commitment to temperance and sabbatarianism, and pushed interventionist rather than free-market economic policies.[150] That Protestants' vote for DUP candidates because 'they like them and what they stand for'[151] has obvious and non-religious explanations.[152]

What of Akenson's thesis that Ulster Protestants are, like Afrikaners and Israeli Jews, a 'covenant people'?[153] First of all Akenson makes a largely historical rather than contemporary argument, maintaining that religion is now much less important for Ulster Protestants than it was. They are no longer a covenant people: the popularity of ecumenism, the increasing moderation of sects other than the Free Presbyterians, doubts about the correctness of discrimination, and the fragmentation of Protestant political unity are increasingly putting the notion of a covenant people into their cultural past. Secondly, and crucially, Akenson's own evidence from South Africa, Israel, and Ulster suggests how neatly the selective use and interpretation of the Old Testament coincided with the ethnic interests of these three settler peoples. In South Africa and Ulster the Protestant settlers, intentionally or otherwise, forgot that Christ's sacrifice was supposed to have transformed God's covenant with the Jews into a universal faith to be preached to Jew and Gentile alike – a covenant between Christ and humanity. The 'chosen people' theme in the history of Ulster Protestantism is therefore capable of being interpreted in a much more hard-headed manner than that customary amongst historians and sociologists of religion. The theological 'covenant' which Protestants invoked to justify their privileged status and discriminatory behaviour was a conveniently group-interested misinterpretation of Christianity, in which ethnic politics shaped religious world-views more than vice versa, and in which religion was selectively used as an ideological power-resource rather than propagated as an authentic and universal belief system.

Is Catholicism at the Core of the Conflict?

The Catholic church has considerable influence and power in the Republic, even if its role has been exaggerated by unsympathetic commentators.[154] This power and influence, even though it is waning,[155] undoubtedly buttresses unionist opposition to a united Ireland. However, it cannot be validly inferred that successive revolts by northern nationalists have had religious causes, or that the aims of Irish nationalists are synonymous with those of the Catholic church.

Discrimination against their religion *qua* religion played little part in motivating Catholics to boycott the Northern Ireland parliament after 1921. Almost all explicitly religious discrimination in the UK had been legally abolished before partition in 1920. While nationalists and Catholics were on the receiving end of substantial discrimination,[156] Catholics were relatively well treated *qua* Catholics. Catholics were discriminated against because they were perceived as disloyal nationalists/republicans, not because they said the rosary or believed in the doctrine of transubstantiation. Even Michael Farrell, who has documented exhaustively the maltreatment of the northern minority, believes – oddly – that Catholics did rather well in educational provision.[157] Schools were segregated, with the approval, or even the insistence, of the Catholic hierarchy. Catholic schools and hospitals did not receive the same level of funding as state institutions – and this was an issue in northern nationalist politics during the Stormont era and after[158] – but full state support for voluntary or religious schools was infrequent in English-speaking democracies and dominions, and non-existent in the USA.[159]

It is redundant to seek religious explanations for Catholics' political hostility to the Stormont regime. They had more than enough non-religious reasons to consider revolt or protest.

206   *Internal Explanations*

It is sufficient to refer to the disadvantages they suffered, politically, legally, economically, and culturally, to explain their political attitudes.[160] Moreover, the disparities between Catholics and Protestants in recruitment and positions in employment cannot be significantly attributed to differing religious values and methods of education, as some Protestants and unionist commentators believe.[161] These disparities were (and are) mostly because of direct and indirect discrimination, as we shall subsequently discuss.[162]

Conspiracy theories which held the Catholic church responsible for critically supporting republican violence are just incredible. The Catholic church, world-wide, has been noticeably (and notoriously) willing to accept and work with all types of regimes, at least before World War II. The Catholic church did not enthusiastically endorse the partition of Ireland, and could not have done so without alienating most of its constituency. However, in practice the Catholic hierarchy reached various accommodations with the unionist regime, including appointing a chaplain to the Stormont parliament in 1963.[163] The Irish hierarchy has exacerbated communal divisions by its continuing insistence that the Constitution and public policy in the Republic should enforce Catholic doctrine as far as possible, and by its position on mixed marriages. However, Catholic churches have advocated these public policies everywhere in the world. They can scarcely, on their own, account for conflict, violence and stalemate in Northern Ireland.

The argument that the Church is, however indirectly, responsible for republican violence is difficult to substantiate, and scoffed at by republican paramilitaries.[164] The Church's lack of control over the IRA was demonstrated most spectacularly by the failure of Pope John Paul II's plea for peace made in September 1979, made on bended knees as he said mass in Drogheda.[165] The Catholic clergy condemn unjustified state violence, but they have also consistently condemned the IRA.[166] It is difficult to see how this dual condemnation legitimized the violence of the IRA, as several critics have argued, any more than it justifies the excesses of the security forces. Such criticism, directed against the Catholic church by

Paisleyites and others, is substantially the same as that levelled against the SDLP by unionists. The only way for the Catholic church (and the SDLP) to avoid these criticisms, it appears, is for them to become uncritical supporters of British state authority.

Is Religion Responsible for the Social Boundary in Northern Ireland?

It is difficult to imagine, despite one political scientist's argument to the contrary, that the two communities that have co-existed in Ulster since the seventeenth century would have been able to maintain their separateness so successfully in the absence of religious differences.[167] There are, despite Belfast folk wisdom, no phenotypical differences distinguishing the two communities; and linguistic differences were eroded relatively quickly after the plantation, even though some claim to detect differences in accents and dialects between Protestants and Catholics from the same areas, and it is a local shibboleth that Protestants and Catholics pronounce the letter 'H' differently. However, though we accept the salience of religion as an ethnic marker it cannot be over-emphasized that ethnic divisions cannot be reduced to religion, or church policy on education, or mixed marriages.

The high rates of endogamy in Northern Ireland, at least in urban areas, owe as much to residential segregation and the resulting lack of social interaction, as to church policy;[168] and residential segregation in rural areas extends back in time to the colonial plantations. If Catholics do not meet Protestants, and vice versa, they are unlikely to want to marry them. In a zone of ethnic conflict where people emphasize solidarity and maintaining numbers, and display distrust if not hatred of the 'other side', endogamous practices prevail even among those who do not practise their religion.[169] Endogamy makes it more likely that the offspring will not only be of the same religion, but of the same political views. Marriage across religious lines carries more than dangers of religious censure – it can mean

208   *Internal Explanations*

social ostracism, accusations of treachery and, in the most
extreme cases, assassination.[170]

The conflict, in our judgement, cannot be attributed to
the segregated education system. To begin with, research on
whether the segregated education system has exacerbated
community divisions is inconclusive.[171] Children attending
different school systems have opposing political attitudes but
it has not been proved that this difference follows from their
school experiences.[172] Integrated education elsewhere in the
world does not necessarily lead to the diminution of ethnic
conflict. The curricular differences between the two dominant
schooling systems, including the controversial area of history,
have been exaggerated. The most important factor affecting
curricular procedures are external examinations, and these are
common to both school systems.[173] While Gaelic games are
exclusive to Catholic schools, many sports, such as field athletics, basketball, and soccer, are played in common. The Catholic
church's argument that a Catholic education promotes pacifism[174] may be hard to swallow given the activity of some of
its alumni, but it does not follow that a Catholic or a separate
education causes or increases violence. For one thing, the conflict between the ethnic communities, which were defined over
three centuries ago, predates the modern education system
by two centuries. Both communities maintained segregation
and animosities without formally segregated education – and
could do so in the future. Contrary cross-national evidence
on the alleged link between denominational education and
communal conflict also exists. The cases of the Netherlands
and Canada demonstrate that denominational educational
systems may be characterized by peaceful co-existence. The
worst that can be said about the segregated education system,
though a serious enough charge, is that it makes no significant
contribution to breaking down ethnic stereotypes produced by
other forms of socialization, and may reinforce them.[175]

Sophisticated critics of segregated education recognize
these arguments but maintain that the need to promote
inter-communal understanding makes a denominational system less justified than it may be in more placid societies.
However, even they recognize that a deliberate move towards

integrated education, through coercion or through severely biasing the public funding of educational finance, might not produce any positive consequences, and would probably be counterproductive. The minority community apparently enjoyed better relations with the Northern Ireland Department of Education than with other government departments during the Stormont period. For all their understandable complaints about facing the 'double burden' they paid – supporting their own schools and paying taxes for schools their children did not attend – education was the one policy sector in which minority self-government was permitted. It remains this way today. This cultural autonomy is often considered essential by minorities – as it is by Protestants in the Republic. Similar arrangements have formed essential parts of political settlements in Canada and the Netherlands.[176] The segregated education system has also provided stable, relatively prestigious jobs for Catholics when many other sectors have been relatively closed – and a disproportionate number of the Catholic middle class is employed here.[177] When the civil-rights campaign emerged in the 1960s, it was led by the products of the Catholic education system. Their complaint was not that they had received a bad education, or had been denied access to state schools and universities, but that they were not receiving the jobs for which their qualifications entitled them.

Though surveys show that both communities would accept integrated education,[178] this support is exceptionally soft. Previous attempts to form an integrated education system, in Ireland in 1831 and Northern Ireland in 1923, foundered on the rock of serious opposition within both communities.[179] When one member of the power-sharing executive floated a trial balloon on integrated education in 1974, there was no significant interest,[180] and there was no noticeable response to legislation in 1978 which provided funding for integrated schools where sufficient demand existed.[181] Few parents have sought changes to the present system,[182] and it has not been a burning issue for political elites. Moreover, mixing the children of Catholics and nationalists, and Protestants and unionists, would not necessarily have positive consequences. Research points in several directions. The 1968 Loyalty Survey revealed

210   *Internal Explanations*

that those who experienced integrated education were not significantly more tolerant than those who did not – a conclusion
consistent with studies in other countries.[183] This judgement
has been supported by subsequent research.[184]

The interaction of blacks and whites in the United States
is said by a psychologist to have increased prejudice there –
although he does not believe the same would happen in societies where differences are not ascriptive.[185] One recent study
claims that children develop more moderate attitudes as they
progress through integrated schools.[186] However, integrated
schools can also provide additional 'interfaces' for conflict
to those which already exist. Contact can confirm or even
increase prejudice rather than reduce it. 'A Catholic in a
mixed school may learn that when Protestants say "Not an
Inch" they mean it, just as a Protestant may learn that his
Catholic schoolmates refuse to regard the Union Jack as the
flag to which they give allegiance.'[187] It is worth remembering
that those who suffered most in 1969 were the Catholics and
Protestants housed outside their respective ghettos. Sometimes
'good fences make good neighbours'.

Policy-makers have three feasible options in the education
field. They can:

- impose integrated education, by abolishing the segregated
  system, or by depriving it of the funds to operate;
- bias funding towards the integrated sector, to which parents could send their children on a voluntary basis; or
- support all three sectors, the integrated, and the two
  denominational systems, equally, while preserving a common educational curriculum.

The first option risks explosive consequences. It could only
work if integration was sought by overwhelming and determined majorities on both sides, i.e. if there were already a consensus. There is not. Coercive integration would be regarded
by sizeable groups as prejudicial to their culture and/or religion. It would be opposed by Catholics in a political system with
a Protestant majority; but also by Protestants, because in many
areas of Northern Ireland their children are now a minority in

all age-cohorts.[188] Increased funding for voluntary integration poses fewer problems, but it is no panacea. It appeared to be the policy on which the Conservative government embarked in 1988. The problem is that those who use integrated education may be those who least need it. The more intransigent parents hold back. Even if they do not, a significant integrated system has to overcome the consequences of widespread residential segregation. Parents balk when faced with the prospect of bussing or chauffering their children into 'enemy territory'; and without this, secondary education would remain segregated.

Equality of funding for all educational systems – integrated and denominational – is the best foundation of cultural security for all, and we therefore welcome the agreement reached in late 1992 between the Catholic church and the British government which will, for the first time, enable equality of funding for all schools in the region.[189] A recent study by the Standing Advisory Commission on Human Rights has shown that the failure of Catholic schools to prepare students for certain scientific courses and occupations owed more to capital underfunding than to any intrinsic Catholic propensity to avoid teaching science.[190] Equality of funding for the Catholic sector – with funding to make up for past inequalities in resources – will go further to resolving conflict than more heroic changes to the schools. There are other modest steps which can be developed in the education system. There is room for more inter-cultural activity in arts, games, athletics, and debates, and for joint fieldwork in relevant subjects. History and religion can be taught with less sectarian and more cross-cultural content. The Education Reform (Northern Ireland) Order, passed in February 1990, sensibly insists on a cross-curricular approach which encourages mutual understanding of both cultures.

Conclusion: Putting the Gods in their Place

Interpretations of Northern Ireland which emphasize the primacy of religion err by ignoring the multiple nature of the

212   *Internal Explanations*

divisions between the two communities, and by understating the evidence which shows the national conflict to have greater salience. Protestants and Catholics are divided by religion, by definition, but they are also divided by differences in economic and political power, by historical experience, and, most intensely, by national political identity.

The thesis that religious motivations are not primary for either nationalists or unionists, or for republican or loyalist paramilitaries, is in our judgement convincing. Religion is the key ethnic marker, facilitating the residential, marital and educational segregation which helps reproduce the two ethnic/national communities. Because religion is the key marker its importance is exaggerated. It is an analytical mistake to endow the boundary-marker with more significance than the fact that there is a boundary. People belong to 'religious communities' irrespective of their actual religious or non-religious convictions, because the religious label is an ethnic label, whence the well-known, and only half-joking references to Protestant and Catholic atheists.

No social scientist has satisfactorily demonstrated that theological beliefs are particularly important either individually or in aggregate in explaining political violence in the region. Although we share the liberal prejudice that religious fanaticism and dogma are likely to be productive of violence, we are not persuaded that they are the keys to understanding violence in Northern Ireland. If one wants to argue that there is an important religious dimension to the conflict it is more prudent to argue that there exists a conflict between 'civil religions' or 'secular religions', i.e. to maintain that each community worships its own nation and does so in an exclusivist manner. Whether the disposition to sacralize the nation is greater in more religious communities is not something which has been properly investigated.[191] Nevertheless it is an argument which states that religion reinforces nationalism, not the other way around. We would be happy to accept this formula if it is demonstrated – because we deny the primacy of religion this does not mean that we think religion is irrelevant, unimportant, epiphenomenal or a red herring.

If it is incorrect to believe that the two communities are only or essentially fighting over religion, that Protestantism is at the core of unionism, that Catholicism is at the heart of national-ism, and that the churches are responsible for social divisions in Northern Ireland, what follows? Increasing secularization or ecumenism will not bring a sustained peace, as neither deal with the material concerns of both communities or the political question of national identity and the national character of the state. Secularization and/or ecumenism should be welcomed for their own sake, not for their presumed by-products.[192] The consolidation of a pluralist Republic should be developed for its own sake, not because it will attract Protestants into a united Ireland. Depicting nationalists as zealous Catholics will solve nothing, and will not address their subordinate political and economic position or their aspiration for a united Ireland. Finally, even if the churches can be persuaded to change their policies on intermarriage and education, these changes alone will not significantly improve relations between the antagonistic communities.

Explanations which accord primacy to religion create blind-alleys for policy-makers and inhibit understanding. They absolve important political agents of responsibility. If the antagonisms are religious, then they cannot have been caused by the historic legacies of colonial conquest, plantation and oppression, by the Stormont regime's practice of political and economic discrimination against nationalists, by successive British governments' mismanagement in Ireland before and after 1972, or by British political institutions. If the conflict is religious then the historic nature of the Republic's nationalism, as opposed to its Catholicism, receives less attention than it should. Explanations which emphasize the primacy of religion therefore need to be exposed to strong light. When that happens, they evaporate, leaving little residue.

Notes to pp. 171–6   **463**

1   Conor Cruise O'Brien, *States of Ireland* (London: Panther Books, 1974), 149.
2   Richard Rose, *Governing without Consensus: An Irish Perspective* (London: Faber and Faber, 1971), 248.
3   Simon Lee, 'Unholy Wars need Holy Solutions', *Fortnight*, 292 (1991), 13.
4   Donald H. Akenson, *God's Peoples: Covenant and Land in South Africa, Israel and Ulster* (Ithaca, N.Y.: Cornell University Press, 1992), 9.
5   It could be argued, and it has been, that one or more religious factions are aided or provoked by external co-religionists, and that the relevant religions were originally cultural imports.
6   Unless otherwise stated we use Catholic to refer to an adherent of the Roman Catholic and Apostolic Church, and Protestant to refer to all other (non-Orthodox or Coptic) Christian believers.
7   Rose, *Governing without Consensus*, 248, 264, 427.
8   David Smith and Gerald Chambers, *Inequality in Northern Ireland* (Oxford: Clarendon Press, 1991), 35.
9   John Fulton, *The Tragedy of Belief* (Oxford: Clarendon Press, 1991), 9–12; Rose, *Governing without Consensus*, 264–5; Smith and Chambers, *Inequality in Northern Ireland*, 36; Peter Stringer and Gillian Robinson (eds), *Social Attitudes in Northern Ireland, 1990–91 Edition* (Belfast: Blackstaff, 1991); and *Social Attitudes in Northern Ireland, the Second Report, 1991–92* (Belfast: Blackstaff, 1991).
10 Ed Cairns, 'Is Northern Ireland a Conservative Society', in Stringer and Robinson (eds), *Social Attitudes in Northern Ireland, 1990–91 Edition*, 145. The survey was explicitly designed to elicit religiosity: 'Apart from special occasions such as weddings, funerals and baptisms, how often nowadays do you attend services or meetings connected with your religion?' Consequently the responses are not exactly comparable to the questions asked by Rose in *Governing without Consensus*, or by Edward Moxon-Browne in *Nation, Class and Creed in Northern Ireland* (Aldershot: Gower, 1983).
11 See, for instance, Padraig O'Malley, *Ireland: The Uncivil Wars* (Belfast: Blackstaff Press, 1983), 118; and Sabine Wichert, *Northern Ireland since 1945* (Harlow: Longman, 1991).
12 If every Protestant had voted Unionist and no Catholic had done so, the index of religious voting would be 100. If Catholics had voted for the Unionists in the same proportions as Protestants, the index would have been zero.
13 Arend Lijphart, 'Review Article: The Northern Ireland Problem: Cases, Theories and Solution', *British Journal of Political Science*, 5, 3 (1975), 87.
14 Anthony Heath, Bridget Taylor and Gabor Toka, 'Religion, Morality and Politics', in R. Jowell, L. Brook, and L. Dowds (eds), *International Social Attitudes: the 10th BSA Report* (Aldershot: Dartmouth, 1993), 49–80.
15 See, for example, S. W. Beach, 'Religion and Political Change in Northern Ireland', *Sociological Analysis*, 38 (1977), 37–48. The same shortcut would define the Lebanese and Serbo-Croat-Bosnian conflicts as religious.
16 Not the Catholic Archbishop of Canterbury, as stated by O'Malley in *Ireland*, 185.
17 Edward Pearce, 'One Long Piece of Perplexity', *Fortnight*, 296 (1991), 15. He explains that the English, by contrast, have had their 'religious passion' drained out of them 'like watered beer out of a staved-in barrel'. Pearce, like another British columnist, Alan Watkins, consistently interprets the conflict as religious – and consistently displays Cathophobic passions.
18 *Fortnight* (April 1991), 21.

464   *Notes to pp. 176–80*

19   Andrew Boyd, *Holy War in Belfast* (Tralee: Anvil Books, 1969).
20   B. Mawhinney and R. Wells, *Conflict and Christianity in Northern Ireland* (Grand
      Rapids, Michigan: Eerdman, 1975); Duncan Morrow, 'Pastors and Politics',
      Fortnight, 296 (1991), 'Special Supplement: Religion in Ireland', 3–4.
21   'In a world in which Protestant and Catholic leaders endorse ecumenical efforts
      to draw together Christians of all denominations, Northern Ireland remains a
      monument to an earlier age of faith and wars of faith', Rose, *Governing without
      Consensus*, 247. 'The peculiarity . . . is that the conflict which took place in the
      remainder of Europe and in the United States some centuries ago is taking
      place in the province *now*.' John Hickey, *Religion and the Northern Ireland Problem*
      (Dublin: Gill and Macmillan, 1984), 81.
22   Lee, 'Unholy Wars need Holy Solutions', 13.
23   Morrow, 'Pastors and Politics'.
24   David Rapoport, 'Some General Observations on Religion and Violence',
      Terrorism and Political Violence, 3, 3 (1991), 118–40.
25   Ibid., 119.
26   Ibid., 121.
27   Rapoport is sympathetic, if reserved, about René Girard's argument that
      religion originates in the attempt to manage violence in kin-based societies: the
      function of religious ritual is to keep violence outside the religious community
      and to control the otherwise destructive norm of vengeance, *Violence and the
      Sacred* (London: Athlone, 1981).
28   Cited in John Darby, *Conflict in Northern Ireland: the Development of a Polarised
      Community* (Dublin: Gill and Macmillan, 1976), 114.
29   Rose, *Governing without Consensus*, 401.
30   Fulton, *The Tragedy of Belief*, 125–31.
31   Lee, 'Unholy Wars need Holy Solutions', 13; Mawhinney and Wells, *Conflict
      and Christianity in Northern Ireland*.
32   Mawhinney and Wells, *Conflict and Christianity in Northern Ireland*, 7.
33   Ken Heskin, *Northern Ireland: A Psychological Analysis* (Dublin: Gill and
      Macmillan, 1980), 24.
34   Wilson, *Ulster: Conflict and Consensus* (Oxford: Basil Blackwell, 1989), 211.
35   Patrick Buckland, *A Short History of Northern Ireland* (New York: Holmes and
      Meier, 1981), 100.
36   Heskin, *Northern Ireland*, 47.
37   O'Malley, *Ireland*, 178.
38   O'Brien, *States of Ireland*, 168.
39   Rose, *Governing without Consensus*, 216–17.
40   Heskin, *Northern Ireland*, 42–4.
41   The shift in the religious balance between 1961 and 1991 was disguised by the
      imperfections of the 1971 and 1981 censuses, but must also be partly attributed
      to a change in the comparative communal rates of migration. Between 1921
      and 1971 Catholics migrated absolutely and relatively more than Protestants.
      Over the last two decades this pattern *may* have been reduced – for example
      some claim that a Protestant 'brain-drain' is now under way; Protestants, who
      are more likely to go to British universities, are more likely to decide to stay
      in Great Britain. See also pp. 502–3, n. 24
42   O'Brien, *States of Ireland*, 168.
43   Ibid., 168; Wright, 'Protestant Ideology and Politics in Ulster', *European Journal
      of Sociology*, 14 (1972), 213–80.
44   Rose, *Governing without Consensus*, 216–17.
45   Steve Bruce, *God Save Ulster! The Religion and Politics of Paisleyism* (Oxford:

Oxford University Press, 1986); Roy Wallis, Steve Bruce, and David Taylor, 'Ethnicity and Evangelicalism: Ian Paisley and Protestant Politics in Ulster', *Comparative Studies in Society and History*, 29 (1987), 293–313.

46   Bruce, *God Save Ulster!*, 249.

47   Ibid., 263.

48   Ibid.

49   In a subsequent book Bruce emphasizes that the core of Paisley's church is anti-ecumenical, and sees the clash with Catholicism as a test of the elect status of Ulster Protestants, see *The Edge of the Union: the Ulster Loyalist Political Vision* (Oxford: Oxford University Press, 1994).

50   *God Save Ulster!*, 123; and Steve Bruce, 'Ulster Loyalism and Religiosity', *Political Studies*, 35, 4 (1987), 643; see also Heskin, *Northern Ireland*, 37.

51   Bruce's view is derived from Rose, who argues that the vast majority of Catholics regard themselves as Irish by national identity whereas Protestants, unsure of their nationality, fall back on their religion for symbols of identity, *Governing without Consensus*, 216–17.

52   Bruce, *God Save Ulster!*, 251.

53   Ibid., 253.

54   Ibid., 264.

55   Akenson, *God's Peoples*.

56   Ibid., 16, 23, 118, 137, 193.

57   Ibid., 258.

58   Nationalists differ about how to produce this happy state of affairs. For civic nationalists 'The Irish problem is quite simply the fruit of Northern Protestant reluctance to become part of what they regard as an authoritarian Southern Catholic State', Garret FitzGerald, *Towards a New Ireland* (London: Charles Knight, 1972), 88. Republicans argue that partition allowed clerical empire-builders to run amok in both parts of Ireland, exacerbating religious divisions. They support Wolfe Tone's prophesy that an independent and united Ireland would 'unite the whole people of Ireland . . . abolish the memory of all past dissensions and . . . substitute the common name of Irishman in place of the denominations of Protestant, Catholic and Dissenter' – see, for example, Hilda McThomas, 'Neutral Wins Few Converts', *Fortnight*, 292 (1991), 17.

59   See table 5.3 and O'Leary and McGarry, *The Politics of Antagonism*, 136–8.

60   This view is shared by FitzGerald, *Towards a New Ireland*, 35.

61   Fulton, *The Tragedy of Belief*, ch. 5.

62   Wilson, *Ulster*, 213–14.

63   Conor Cruise O'Brien, *God Land: Reflections on Religion and Nationalism* (Cambridge, Mass.: Harvard University Press, 1988). O'Brien does not specify to what type of holy nationalism, if any, unionist ideology belongs, and has apparently reversed his previous opinion, expressed in *States of Ireland*, that unionism is more impregnated by Protestantism than Irish nationalism is with Catholicism.

64   Hickey, *Religion and the Northern Ireland Problem*, 84–5.

65   The fact that many nationalist militants, including those in the INLA, IPLO and Official IRA, are more Marxist than Christian causes no problem *if* communism is also regarded as a Catholic conspiracy – just as it was regarded as a Jewish conspiracy in Nazi Germany (Heskin, *Northern Ireland*, 27). Fundamentalist Protestants regard both communism and Roman Catholicism as godless forms of paganism.

66   Ian Paisley, 'Submission by Dr. Paisley, M.P., M.E.P. at Plenary Session of Strand One Talks, Stormont, June 1991' (mimeo), 3.

67 One DUP spokesperson regarded the visit by Pope John Paul's special envoy to persuade the hunger-strikers to abandon their fast as a direct attempt to strengthen their resolve! – O'Malley, *Ireland*, 90.

68 Ibid., 189.

69 J. Allister, *Irish Unification Anathema: the Reasons why Northern Ireland Rejects Unification with the Republic of Ireland* (Belfast: Crown Publications, n.d), 20–1.

70 See Arthur Aughey, *Under Siege: Ulster Unionism and the Anglo-Irish Agreement* (London: Hurst, 1989); and Hugh Roberts, *Northern Ireland and the Algerian Analogy: A Suitable Case for Gaullism?* (Belfast: Athol Books, 1986).

71 Hugh Roberts turns the tables in the debate over which community is more religious by arguing that Protestant persecution of Catholics in Ireland, *in so far as it existed*, was directed at destroying their political power not their religion. He claims that, by contrast, Catholics have been preoccupied with extirpating Protestant religious heresy. 'To come under the Republic is to come under the hegemony of the Roman Catholic church ... There can be no doubt that the ideological core of anti-British nationalism in Ireland was furnished by Roman Catholicism', *Northern Ireland and the Algerian Analogy*, 41, 35 and 38.

72 Bruce maintains that the British do not understand Northern Ireland because they are unaware of the central importance of the Protestant religion for unionists ('Ulster Loyalism and Religiosity', 643). His project is to educate them. He is preaching to the converted – as Arthur Aughey has pointed out.

73 Aughey approvingly cites Robert McCartney's view that the Unionist tradition has as much in common with the ideas of Paine, Mill and the framers of the US Constitution as it has with Calvin, Luther, or Paisley, see *Under Siege*, 10.

74 Ibid., 8.

75 Ibid., 28, and see chapter 3, pp. 126–8, above.

76 Aughey, *Under Siege*, 7, 12. Similarly Henry Patterson writes that 'for many republicans, nationality and Catholicism were integrally linked ... "secular" republicanism was very much a minority creed', *The Politics of Illusion: Socialism and Republicanism in Modern Ireland* (London: Hutchinson, 1989), 64. The British and Irish Communist Organizations also attempted to discredit the claim that republicanism had solid secular foundations – see chapter 4, *passim*.

77 Aughey, *Under Siege*, 11.

78 An exemplary early anthropological study, set in rural 'Ballybeg', is Rosemary Harris's *Prejudice and Tolerance in Ulster* (Manchester: Manchester University Press, 1972).

79 Some activities organized by the Catholic church, such as bingo, attract mass followings from both sides of the ethnic boundary.

80 Fulton, *The Tragedy of Belief*, 131; also see Richard Jenkins, 'Northern Ireland: In what sense "Religions" in Conflict?', in R. Jenkins, H. Donnan, and G. McFarlane, *The Sectarian Divide in Northern Ireland Today* (London: Royal Anthropological Institute of Great Britain and Ireland, Occasional Paper No. 41, 1986), 6–7.

81 Rose, *Governing without Consensus*, 329; also see John Whyte, *Interpreting Northern Ireland* (Oxford: Clarendon Press, 1990), 40.

82 Fulton, *The Tragedy of Belief*, 199.

83 Whyte, *Interpreting Northern Ireland*, 42.

84 Fulton, *The Tragedy of Belief*, 223.

85 Rupert Taylor, 'The Queen's University of Belfast and "the Troubles": the Limits of Liberalism', PhD thesis, University of Kent at Canterbury; and see 'The Limits of Liberalism: the Case of Queen's Academics and the "Troubles"', *Politics*, 7, 2 (1987), 28–34.

86 Darby, *Conflict in Northern Ireland*, 130.
87 Cardinal William Conway, *Catholic Schools* (Dublin: Catholic Communications Institute, 1970).
88 Fulton, *The Tragedy of Belief*, 185.
89 Rose provides an example of this misperception: 'Protestants often complain that the existence of separate schools causes or helps maintain political conflict in Northern Ireland. Many Catholics reject this argument', *Governing without Consensus*, 335.
90 Darby, *Conflict in Northern Ireland*, 126–7; Arthur, *The Government and Politics of Northern Ireland* (London: Longman, 1984), 38; E. Gallagher and S. Worrall, *Christians in Ulster, 1968–1980* (Oxford: Oxford University Press, 1982), 154; Dominic Murray, *Worlds Apart: Segregated Schools in Northern Ireland* (Belfast: Appletree Press, 1983), 141–2; and Michael McGrath, 'The Price of Faith: the Catholic Church and Catholic Schools in Northern Ireland since 1920', London: PhD thesis, London School of Economics and Political Science (1995).
91 John Sugden and Alan Bairner, *Sport, Sectarianism and Society in a Divided Ireland* (Leicester: Leicester University Press, 1993).
92 R. J. Cormack and R. D. Osborne (eds), *Religion, Education and Employment in Northern Ireland* (Belfast: Appletree Press, 1983).
93 Murray, *Worlds Apart*, 149.
94 Darby, *Conflict in Northern Ireland*, 130–1.
95 International media frequently assume that segregated education is the cause of conflict, and argue that if only integration could be adopted, then Northern Ireland's troubles would be over. In October 1993, after the IRA killed ten people in the Shankill Road, a BBC film was widely shown around the world in which the explanatory theme was that Catholic and Protestant children went to separate schools. The faith which hard-boiled journalists display in educational solutions is often touching.
96 Heskin, *Northern Ireland*, 155.
97 Terence O'Neill, *The Autobiography of Terence O'Neill* (London: Hart Davies, 1972), 79.
98 Robert G. Crawford, *Loyal to King Billy: A Portrait of the Ulster Protestants* (London: Hurst, 1987), 32, 121; Morris Fraser, *Children in Conflict* (Harmondsworth: Penguin, 1973); Fulton, *The Tragedy of Belief*; Jenkins, 'Northern Ireland: In what sense "religions in conflict"?'; C. Irwin, *Education and the Development of Social Integration in Divided Societies* (Belfast: Queen's University Press, 1991).
99 'Ulster – The Need for a New Outlook', *The Tablet*, 13 September 1975.
100 Gallagher and Worrall, *Christians in Ulster*, 166; Crawford, *Loyal to King Billy*, 66.
101 Gerald McElroy, *The Catholic Church and the Northern Ireland Crisis* (Dublin: Gill and Macmillan, 1991), 86.
102 Rose, *Governing without Consensus*, 336.
103 Moxon-Browne, *Nation, Class and Creed in Northern Ireland*, 134.
104 A. M. Gallagher and S. Dunn, 'Community Relations in Northern Ireland: Attitudes to Contact and Integration', in Peter Stringer and Gillian Robinson (eds), *Social Attitudes in Northern Ireland*, 1990–91 edition (Belfast: Blackstaff Press, 1991), 16.
105 Gallagher and Worrall, *Christians in Ulster*, 193; Heath, Taylor and Toka, 'Religion, Morality and Politics'.
106 Smith and Chambers, *Inequality in Northern Ireland*, 36–7.
107 Gallagher and Worrall, *Christians in Ulster*, 193.
108 See Whyte, *Interpreting Northern Ireland*, 27.

109 Wilson, *Ulster*, 204.
110 Sarah Nelson, *Ulster's Uncertain Defenders: Loyalists and the Northern ireland Conflict* (Belfast: Appletree Press, 1984).
111 Bruce, *God Save Ulster!*, 263.
112 O'Leary and McGarry, *The Politics of Antagonism*, figure 1.
113 Gallagher and Worrall, *Christians in Ulster*.
114 Roy Foster, 'Varieties of Irishness', in Maurna Crozier (ed.), *Cultural Traditions in Northern Ireland* (Belfast: Institute of Irish Studies, 1989), 13–14.
115 'Analytically, one of the most surprising findings is the very limited relationship between *individual* regime outlooks and *individual* religious influences. Within each community, exposure to religious influences does not greatly differentiate one Protestant from another, or one Catholic from another. People who are more regular in church attendance, or stronger in their faith, or more fundamentalist in their faith are not much more likely to be ultras, disaffected, or fully allegiant citizens', Rose, *Governing without Consensus*, 274. The result is only surprising if one supposes the primacy of religious explanations. Rose is a very good political scientist so he reports data at odds with his preconceptions. See also the work of his colleague, Ian McAllister, 'The Devil, Miracles and the Afterlife: The Political Sociology of Religion in Northern Ireland', *British Journal of Sociology*, 33, 3 (1982), 340–7.
116 There is a story, probably apocryphal, about an English journalist who enquired of a Catholic farmer why he had voted for Bernadette Devlin, given that she was known to be an atheist. 'Sure', the farmer replied, 'she is a Catholic atheist.'
117 Rose, *Governing without Consensus*, 252.
118 Fulton, *The Tragedy of Belief*, 130.
119 Gallagher and Worrall, *Christians in Ulster*, 59; Wilson, *Ulster*, 215.
120 Anglican Archbishop and Nobel peace-prize winner, Desmond Tutu, has argued that violence against an oppressive state is justified under certain conditions, and would be surprised to hear he was enunciating 'Roman Catholic' doctrine.
121 Frantz Fanon, *The Wretched of the Earth*, with an introduction by Jean-Paul Sartre (Harmondsworth: Penguin, 1963).
122 Rose correctly observed that 'Physical assaults, when they occur, are usually directed at lay Catholics and their property', *Governing without Consensus*, 250. One priest, Father Hugh Murphy, was kidnapped by loyalists and held as a hostage for the safe return of an RUC officer, William Turbitt, held by the IRA. The priest was released unharmed, the officer was found dead – *Fortnight*, 170 (1978), 9.
123 O'Malley, *Ireland*, 198. In an incisive analysis, usually ignored by sociologists of religion and partisans of religious interpretations of the Northern Ireland conflict, Ian McAllister uses data gathered in a 1973 survey to test whether having more or less religious commitment is related to people's political attitudes. He finds little relationship between the political attitudes of Catholics and Protestants and their religious commitment, see Ian McAllister, 'The Devil, Miracles and the Afterlife: The Political Sociology of Religion in Northern Ireland', 330–47.
124 Opinion poll data are imperfect, especially in deeply divided territories. Apart from the problem of loaded questions, for which the assiduous interpreter can control, respondents may be unwilling to reveal what they really think, either because they judge their views deviant or because these views might put them at risk. Opinion polls in Northern Ireland therefore tend to

over-emphasize moderation and downplay extremism, which accounts for the facts that (i) opinion poll support for the moderate Alliance Party is roughly twice what it receives in elections, (ii) power-sharing receives high support in polls while politicians advocating it flounder at elections, and (iii) huge numbers of Protestants vote for Ian Paisley while hesitating to admit it.

125 This evidence supports that of the Commission which reported on the immediate causes of the present conflict, Cameron, *Disturbances in Northern Ireland: Report of the Cameron Commission* (Belfast: HMSO, 1969).

126 See chapter 6.

127 Denis Kennedy, *The Widening Gulf: Northern Attitudes to the Independent Irish State, 1919–49* (Belfast: Blackstaff Press, 1988).

128 Bruce, *God Save Ulster!*, 123.

129 Bruce, 'Ulster Loyalism and Religiosity', 643.

130 'If the 1937 constitution of the Republic was scrapped and if it came to be even that the Catholic hierarchy no longer exercised the power, influence, and control over the government of Dublin, then Protestants in Northern Ireland would look upon the Republic in a different light and there would be good neighbourliness in the highest possible sense', cited in O'Malley, *Ireland*, 192; see also FitzGerald, *Towards a New Ireland*, 89–90.

131 Rose, *Governing without Consensus*, 247.

132 Ibid., 257; Moxon-Browne, *Nation, Class and Creed in Northern Ireland*, 38–9.

133 Smith and Chambers, *Inequality in Northern Ireland*, 35.

134 Rose, *Governing without Consensus*, 485; and see chapter 3, table 3.3, p. 110.

135 Wallis, Bruce, and Taylor, 'Ethnicity and Evangelicalism: Ian Paisley and Protestant Politics in Ulster', 301.

136 Bruce, *God Save Ulster!*, 260–1.

137 Aughey, *Under Siege*, 7.

138 See, for example, the text of the UDA's think-tank, New Ulster Political Research Group, *Common Sense* (Belfast, 1987).

139 Historically the underfunding of Catholic schools by the state has been denied by unionists, and historically loyalists demanded an end to any public funding of Catholic schools which were accused of encouraging disloyalty to the state, see J. F. Galliher and J. L. DeGregory, *Violence in Northern Ireland: Understanding Protestant Perspectives* (Dublin: Gill and Macmillan, 1985), 75.

140 Bruce, *God Save Ulster!*, 249.

141 Ibid., 1–2, 118.

142 Ibid., 267–8.

143 Bruce, 'Ulster Loyalism and Religiosity', 643.

144 See Brendan O'Leary 'Appendix 4. Party Support in Northern Ireland, 1969–1989', in John McGarry and Brendan O'Leary (eds), *The Future of Northern Ireland* (Oxford: Oxford University Press, 1990), 342–57.

145 Ibid. Bruce's judgement may have arisen from the fact that his research was conducted in the early 1980s when the DUP was doing well.

146 Bruce acknowledges that the 'vast majority' of the DUP's supporters are not evangelical Protestants, 'Ulster Loyalism and Religiosity', 645.

147 Bruce presents data inconsistent with his own thesis – *God Save Ulster!*, 136.

148 Probert, *Beyond Orange and Green*, 123.

149 Nelson, *Ulster's Uncertain Defenders*.

150 Some of those active in the DUP are 'so committed to the Union' that they are 'prepared to go some way towards moving some of their evangelical principles into the area of private life and personal choice, rather than alienate

non-evangelical unionists', *God Save Ulster!*, 148. Bruce is right about this, but errs in not spelling out its significance.

151   Bruce, 'Ulster Loyalism and Religiosity', 647.

152   The primary source for Bruce's work was interviews with leading Free Presbyterians, not with secular DUP voters, see *God Save Ulster!*, viii. Others who have researched the loyalist working class in Belfast arrive at significantly different conclusions, see Sarah Nelson, 'Protestant Ideology Reconsidered', *British Sociology Yearbook*, 11 (1975). Hickey's book has similar methodological imperfections. His arguments are constructed from long and tedious quotations from *The Protestant Telegraph* and *The Junior Orangeman's Catechism*. After citing these 'representative' works, he claims that 'enough evidence should have been quoted . . . to show that Paisley's attitude towards the Roman Catholic Church is not untypical of Protestant views in Northern Ireland', Hickey, *Religion and the Northern Ireland Problem*, 78.

153   Akenson, *God's Peoples*.

154   One liberal unionist suggests that the Republic's government 'felt impelled to consult the Papacy before any important decision was taken'!, Wilson, *Ulster*, 208. For an objective assessment of the Roman Catholic church's influence in the Irish Republic, see John Whyte, *Church and State in Modern Ireland, 1923–1979* (Dublin: Gill and Macmillan, 1980), especially 362ff.

155   Tom Inglis, *Moral Monopoly: the Catholic Church in Modern Irish Society* (Dublin: Gill and Macmillan, 1987).

156   O'Leary and McGarry, *The Politics of Antagonism*, ch. 3.

157   Farrell, *The Orange State*, 101.

158   McGrath demonstrates that debates over funding for schools and hospitals figured prominently in the nationalist press during elections and by-elections, especially when rival nationalists were competing, *The Price of Faith*.

159   Few English observers realize that in Scotland Catholic schools were granted full funding as early as 1918.

160   O'Leary and McGarry, *The Politics of Antagonism*, chs 3–4.

161   See Wilson, *Ulster*, 108, and chapter 7 below, pp. 283–5.

162   See chapter 7, pp. 283–5.

163   Darby, *Northern Ireland*, 117–18.

164   See *Fortnight*, 320 (1993), 7.

165   Patrick Bishop and Eamonn Mallie, *The Provisional IRA* (London: Hutchinson, 1987), 344; Gallagher and Worrall, *Christians in Ulster*, 121ff.

166   By 15 February 1971 the Catholic Cardinal claimed to have made statements denouncing violence 23 times, Gallagher and Worrall, *Christians in Ulster*, 60; and see McElroy, *The Catholic Church and the Northern Ireland Crisis*. The DUP's claim that Father John Magee visited the hunger-strikers in 1981 to strengthen their resolve ignores the fact that the envoy's task was to talk the prisoners out of the hunger strike, and that he was unsuccessful.

167   Michael MacDonald, *Children of Wrath*, 12.

168   Whyte, 1986; *Interpreting Northern Ireland*, 33–9.

169   While attaching primary blame to Catholic policy for endogamy, one sociologist acknowledges that Catholics might have other reasons for not marrying Protestants: they may consider them to be 'bigots, or oppressors or ethnic aliens', Fulton, *The Tragedy of Belief*, 226.

170   One mixed marriage required a police escort to protect the 'happy couple' from their families! Whyte, *Interpreting Northern Ireland*, 41.

171   Darby, *Northern Ireland*, 138–9.

172   Murray, *Worlds Apart*, 139.

173 Ibid., 143.
174 Gallagher and Worrall, *Christians in Ulster*, 164–5; Rose, *Governing without Consensus*, 334–5.
175 D. H. Akenson, *Education and Enmity: the Control of Schooling in Northern Ireland* (Newton Abbott: David and Charles, 1973); Darby, *Northern Ireland*, 133.
176 Arend Lijphart, *Democracy in Plural Societies: A Comparative Exploration* (New Haven: Yale University Press, 1977), 39–44. The Canadian Constitution Act of 1867 gives the Protestant minority in Quebec and the Catholic minority outside Quebec the right to have their own educational systems. In Ontario, Catholic schools enjoy full funding from the provincial government.
177 Edmund Aunger, 'Religion and Occupational Class in Northern Ireland', *Economic and Social Review*, 7, 1 (1975), 1–17.
178 Rose, *Governing without Consensus*, 336.
179 Darby, *Northern Ireland*, 139; Gallagher and Worrall, *Christians in Ulster*, 154.
180 Gallagher and Worrall, *Christians in Ulster*, 160–1.
181 Fulton, *The Tragedy of Belief*, 181; Gallagher and Worrall, *Christians in Ulster*, 162–3. The 1978 Act provided machinery to convert segregated into integrated schools managed by a joint committee, on which Catholics and Protestants would be represented in equal numbers.
182 Those who support the state (Protestant) sector in Northern Ireland have not raised the issue of the duplication of resources and high costs involved in a segregated system. On the contrary, Rose's Loyalty Survey indicated that 64 per cent of Protestants would have approved funding Catholic schools on an equal basis to Protestant schools – a fact which Rose curiously interpreted as meaning that Protestants were against segregated education, *Governing without Consensus*, 336.
183 Rose, *Governing without Consensus*, 336–7.
184 J, Darby, D. Murray, D. Batts, S. Dunn, S. Farren, and J. Harris, *Education and Community in Northern Ireland: Schools Apart?* (Coleraine: New University of Ulster, 1977); see also Gallagher and Worrall, *Christians in Ulster*, ch. 10.
185 Heskin, *Northern Ireland: A Psychological Analysis*, 145.
186 Irwin, *Education and the Development of Social Integration in Divided Societies*.
187 Rose, *Governing without Consensus*, 337.
188 Census of Northern Ireland (London: HMSO, 1992).
189 *Irish Times*, 6 November 1992.
190 SACHR (Standing Advisory Commission on Human Rights) (1991).
191 For an unconvincing argument in this vein, see Conor Cruise O'Brien's *God Land*. For him, nationalism as a collective emotional force 'makes its first appearance, with explosive impact, in the Hebrew Bible', in which a land and power are promised to a chosen people, *God Land*, 2. He also believes that once deities and kings are de-sacralized it is nations which inherit their religious charisma. He differentiates three scales of 'holy nationalism' in ascending order of arrogance and exclusivity: the 'chosen people', the 'holy nation' (the chosen people with tenure), and the 'deified nation'. Logical and factual errors in O'Brien's discussion of religion and nationalism are pointed out by Ernest Gellner, 'The Sacred and the National', *LSE Quarterly*, 3, 4 (1989), 357–69; and Brendan O'Leary, 'Review', *Ethnic and Racial Studies*, 12, 4 (1990), 586–8.
192 The Norwegian philosopher Jon Elster has argued that 'willing what cannot be willed', i.e. willing what can only come about as an unintended by-product of other processes, is a paradigm form of irrationality, *Sour Grapes: Studies in the Subversion of Rationality* (Cambridge: Cambridge University Press, 1983), 44–52.

[5]

BUDDHAPUTRA AND BHUMIPUTRA?
DILEMMAS OF MODERN SINHALA BUDDHIST MONKS IN RELATION TO ETHNIC AND POLITICAL CONFLICT

Sarath Amunugama

The ethnic and political conflict in Sri Lanka have created ethical dilemmas for Sinhala monks. They have had to react to a Tamil separatist war, an Indian threat to the country's sovereignty and the extensive use of violence by Sinhala rebel groups and the state. Contrary to common belief Sinhala monks do not act as a monolithic body, particularly on political issues. This essay describes the different organizations within the Sangha, and the Buddhist laity, and their coalition building in order to present an effective response to the above mentioned issues. It also analyses concepts brought into play, particularly by radical young monks, to resolve these dilemmas in terms of Sinhala Buddhist ideology.

On 29 July 1987, India and Sri Lanka entered into an agreement, commonly referred to as the Indo-Sri Lanka Accord, aimed at ending Tamil separatism in Sri Lanka. By this agreement the Sri Lankan authorities agreed to effect changes in the country's constitution and devolve substantial power from the centre to the provinces. Eight Provincial Councils were to be established, one of which—the council of the amalgamated North and Eastern provinces—would be Tamil dominated. This would, in effect, grant a degree of autonomy to the Tamils in what they claimed were their 'traditional homelands'.

The signing of the Accord, with little advance notice or discussion, sparked off mass opposition in Sinhala-dominated parts of the country. These demonstrations were organized by the *Mavbima Surakeeme Viyaparaya* (MSV) or 'The Movement for Safeguarding the Motherland'. Founded in July 1986 the MSV had grown rapidly as a powerful 'umbrella organization' of monks, non-Marxist political parties of the opposition (SLFP, MEP and JVP through its front organizations) and important lay Buddhist associations.

The mass opposition to the Accord, which caught the Government by surprise, led to the rapid deployment of the Indian Peacekeeping Force (IPKF) in the North and East, releasing Sinhala troops for active duty in the South. A few days later the JVP, which had up to now kept a low profile in the MSV, took over the anti-Accord struggle. From then on, till the killing of its top leadership in late 1989, the JVP became the main adversary of the government and the severest critic of the Accord, though they did receive varying

116   *S. Amunugama*

degrees of support from their erstwhile partners in the MSV. Many of the Sangha and lay Buddhist associations which constituted the MSV were sympathetic to the JVP's implacable opposition to President Jayawardene and his policies. A journal of one such group of radical monks, which claimed to be 'the only journal published by Sri Lankan Bhikkus' reports:

> When the correct history of this country is written, the 29 July 1989 will undoubtedly be recorded as a day of special significance. Two aspects of this day will be recognized. On one hand it will denote the betrayal of a land and a people after gagging and chaining them; thereby making them a slave nation.
>
> On the other hand 29 July 1987 will be seen as the day on which the patriotic people, rejecting slavery under a foreign imperialist power and refusing to fall on their feet even with the threat of death, decided to fight the invading foreign power as well as the treacherous, cowardly and power-hungry ruling regime of this country.
>
> That spontaneous uprising of patriotic citizens—who came onto the streets of their towns and villages—has now, two years later, become an organized, broad-based national liberation struggle, drawing towards it all patriotic elements.[1]

In this paper I shall explore the reaction of radical Sinhala Buddhist monks, particularly those groups within the MSV, to ethnic and political issues related to the Accord. How did it affect their perceptions of the role of the Sangha in relation to national problems? What were the consequences of their deep involvement in political activity including, in the case of some monks, armed revolt? What were the elements of Buddhist ideology and symbolism which were highlighted in this encounter? In sum, how did they 'manage' the contradiction between *Buddhaputra* (sons of the Buddha) and *Bhumiputra* (sons of the soil)?

MAVBIMA SURAKEEME VIYAPARAYA

The Tamil struggle for a separate state—Eelam, was predicated on the claim that the Northern and Eastern provinces were their 'traditional homelands'. While the numerical preponderance of Tamils in these two provinces was a demographic reality, the concept of a historical Tamil 'homeland' was bitterly contested by the Sinhalese. The Jayawardene regime itself, up to the time of the Accord, treated it as a non-negotiable issue. Previous negotiations on the ethnic problem (the Jayawardene–Parathasarathy talks as well as Thimpu and Bangalore negotiations) had floundered principally on this issue.

The MSV also treated this question as the centrepiece of its policy. It insisted that it was a non-negotiable issue, in its very first policy statement:

> Sri Lanka is the mother country of us all—Sinhalese, Tamils, Muslims, etc. We have lived together for over a thousand years on that basis. It should be so in the future as well. Today we face a secret national and international conspiracy

to divide the motherland. By implementing the proposal to divide power on the basis of race, and cutting the country into two out of 'nationalist sectarianism' the whole country will be destroyed. Let us defeat murderous Eelamism and national and international conspiracies to divide the country. Our great hope is that all races will live in friendship, peace, and amity. After all, wealth is distributed on this basis in our country.

Though President Jayawardene was finally compelled to treat the 'strong centre vs. traditional homelands' issue as basically a political and demographic problem for purposes of obtaining a settlement, it was one which went to the heart of Sinhala-Buddhist consciousness. The ferocity of Sinhala-Buddhist opposition to the Accord can be understood only by examining the depth of this concern. According to Sinhala-Buddhist tradition, fashioned largely by *Vamsa* literature, Sri Lanka is the *Dharmadvipa* (the island of faith), consecrated by the Buddha himself as the land in which his teachings would flourish. The *Mahavamsa* states that on the very day of the Buddha's death, Vijaya—the founder of the Sinhala race—landed in Sri Lanka, as if to bear witness to the Buddha's prediction.[2] Furthermore, it was believed that the Buddha had visited the island thrice. One of those visits was to Nagadipa in the northernmost part of the Jaffna peninsula. (Ironically, to establish concord between two quarrelling kinsmen.)[3] The north was thereby firmly established within the sacred geography of Buddhists. Till the beginning of the ethnic war Nagadipa was an important pilgrimage centre for Sinhala Buddhists on a par with Mahiyangana and Kelaniya.

Centres of Buddhist pilgrimage provided dramatic evidence of Buddhist claims to the North and East. Some of these sites continued to be centres of Buddhist worship. Others, such as the legendary Gokanna Temple in Trincomalee, had been transformed into centres of Hindu religiosity. Most were in ruins. But they were identified and perpetuated in Buddhist consciousness through the repertory of *Vandana gatha* (worship stanzas) known to most Buddhists.

These feelings of religious inclusion were strengthened by a twentieth century phenomenon. Buddhist and Hindu lay organizations (sabhas) began to reclaim historic sites and rebuild religious edifices. For the Buddhists, the classic example was Anagarika Dharmapala's attempt to reclaim and restore sacred Buddhist sites in India, particularly the Temple at Buddha Gaya. Following him, Valisinghe Harischandra campaigned to 'save' the eight sacred sites or *Atamasthana* in Anuradhapura.[4] Modern Buddhists, concentrated in the South and Southwest of Sri Lanka, discovered that most of their sacred sites were located in the North Central, Northern and Eastern parts of the country. In the pre-independence period Buddhists restored ancient sites at their own expense (for example the restoration of Ruvanveli

Seya). With independence, and particularly after 1956, these reconstructions were undertaken either directly by government or by senior government officials, particularly Government Agents, who could mobilize the resources of the state on an informal basis as well as draw contributions from local entrepreneurs. (Among such officials were Nissanka Wijeratne who established the 'sacred city' in Anuradhapura, Ridgeway Tillekeratne who repaired the Somawathie Chaitya in Polonnaruwa and Somapala Gunadheera who restored temples in Trincomalee District). Thus to most Buddhists the North and East constituted a part of their patrimony, a land from which they had been driven off by the Tamils, as graphically described in the *Vamsa* literature.

President Jayawardene had a reputation as a hardliner on the ethnic issue. A student of archaeology, passionately involved in Buddhist historical research, and a former office bearer of the Anagarika Dharmapala Trust, he was very sympathetic to the Buddhist view. But he was fast running out of options. As a clever politician, he had come to the realization that the ethnic impasse could not be overcome without a concession on the 'homelands' issue.

The MSV was formed at this junction with a variety of manifest and latent objectives. Buddhist leaders feared that there would be a 'sell out' by way of a negotiated settlement, which gave recognition to the Tamil 'homeland' concept. They had by now, come to dislike and distrust Jayawardene. In particular they felt that he was not hard enough in prosecuting the war against Tamil separatists. In their estimation he was not a person who would ultimately give way to the Buddhist leaders. The MSV was also aware that Marxist parties and their allies—the LSSP, CP, NLSSP, and SLMP, would support the President in reducing the power of the centre and devolving powers to Provincial councils. At the all-party conference convened by the President in 1986, devolution of power had been discussed and endorsed by the Left. Buddhist leaders felt that the need of the hour was a coalition which would be powerful enough to influence political events. Up to now they had acted independently, with little effect on government policy. The MSV was therefore primarily designed to be 'the voice' of the unified Buddhists. It was to be a pressure group which no power in the country could ignore. To the non-Marxist opposition (SLFP and MEP) pursuing its own agenda, the SMV provided an opportunity of building a broad coalition against the UNP. The new electoral system, for both the Presidency and Parliament, did not favour a single party approach. The SLFP which had emerged as the only credible alternative to the UNP, realized that it had to reach out to voters beyond its party vote bank. Traditionally 'nationalistic', it saw great electoral possibilities in this new configuration.

In many ways the strongest backers of the MSV were a group of Sinhala-Buddhist politicians and professionals who could not be accommodated in the old hierarchy bound parties of both the Right and Left. They could see in this new coalition a leadership role for themselves based on possession of modern skills (e.g. Dinesh Gunawardene, Gamini Iriyagolla, Nath Amarakone, Gamini Wijesekera and Rupa Saparamadu). For instance, though Dinesh Gunawardene is a charismatic politician, the new electoral system appeared to portend the demise of his small party. The SMV appeared to him to be a good platform to gather a wider constituency, leading later perhaps to an electoral arrangement with the SLFP.

What were the constituent elements of the MSV and how was it organized? We could classify those constituting the SMV under three heads: Political organizations, Sangha associations and Buddhist lay associations.[5]

Political organizations	*Represented by*
1 Sri Lanka Freedom Party (SLFP)	Sirimavo Bandaranaike Lakshman Jayakody
2. Mahajana Eksath Peramuna (MEP)	Dinesh Gunawardene
3. Sinhala Bala Mandalaya (SBM)	Nath Amerakone
4. Sinhala Janata Peramuna	
5. Sri Lanka Deshapremi Peramuna	(JVP oriented)
Sangha associations	
1. Deshapremi Taruna Bhikshu Sanvidanaya	(JVP oriented)
2. Manava Hitavadi Bhikshu Sanvidanaya	(JVP oriented)
3. Samastha Lanka Pragatisili Bhikshu Peramuna	(MEP oriented)
Lay-Buddhist associations	
1. Loka Sáma Maha Sammelanaya	(SLFP oriented)
2. Sri Lanka Eksat Bauddha Maha Sammelanaya	
3. Sinhala Sanvardana Sanvidanaya	Businessmen's organization (Senanayake UNP oriented)
4. Eksat Tri Sinhala Vimukti Sanvidanaya	
5. Dudley Senanayake Gunanusmarana Sangamaya	(Senanayake UNP oriented)

120   *S. Amunugama*

6.	Sinhala Taruna Peramuna	(SLFP oriented)
7.	Sinhala Janata Vatu Kamkaru Sangamaya	
8.	Bauddha Saba Sammelanaya	
9.	Kelanipura Bauddha Bala Mandalaya	
10.	Anagarika Dharmapala Taruna Samitiya	
11.	Sri Lanka Bauddha Samiti Niyojita Sammelenaya	
12.	Buddhist Theosophical Society	(Gamini Iriyagolla)
13.	Sinhala Kantha Peramuna	(Mrs Indrani Iriyagolla)

Though the MSV proposed an elaborate organization on paper, reflecting perhaps the preponderance of Sinhala Buddhist professionals who acted as 'back room boys'—lawyers, civil servants, engineers and businessmen, in practice each of the constituent parts continued to maintain their identity though, they did coordinate information and publicity. With well attended meetings, press statements, articles, pamphlets and links with mainstream Sinhala newspapers, they were able to present themselves as the voice of Buddhist opinion. They were also successful in getting the endorsement of Sangha chiefs (*Mahanayakes*). Palipane Chandananda Mahanayake of Asgiriya chapter emerged as the strongest clerical supporter of the MSV. His pre-eminent role in the movement was recognized by the International media which dubbed him, 'Sri Lanka's Buddhist Khomeini'.

The stated objectives of the MSV were an encapsulation of the demands, of organized Sinhala groups on the ethnic issue.[6] The *Vinivida* magazine lists 29 points as a draft of a common programme amplifying the following core objectives:

> Prevention of Sri Lanka becoming a colony of the Indian Empire; the establishment of national unity in the basis of independence, territorial integrity, sovereignty of the people, democracy, freedom and basic human rights.

Let us analyse how these 'code words' create dilemmas for the Sinhala monks and examine the ways in which they seek to resolve them within the realm of Buddhist ideology and symbolism.

THE ROLE OF INDIA

The traditional view is that Sinhala-Buddhist ideology is deeply permeated with anti-Indian feeling. We need however to examine countervailing beliefs within the same ideology. India is the land of the Buddha. President Jayawardene's oft stated pronouncement, 'I am a lover of India and a follower of her greatest son' represents an important strand of Sinhala-Buddhist thinking. India is *Aryavarta*, the land of the Aryans with whom the Sinhalese claimed kinship, thereby excluding 'the other'—Dravidian Tamils. Even more significantly, it was from India that the gift of *Buddha Dharma*—the most precious of gifts, was brought by the Thera Mahinda. In modern times Anagarika Dharmapala devoted the best years of his life to rekindling the flame in India, restoring sacred sites and making a pilgrimage to Buddha Gaya—'the Buddhist Jerusalem'—the touchstone of a Sinhala Buddhist commitment.

Dharmapala also set in motion a significant political trend by inducting young Sinhala Bhikkus for missionary activity in India. Several such monks, who were trained in Bengal, were fascinated by revolutionary politics in the province and the struggle for Indian independence. Vidyalankara Pirivena, a major centre of Buddhist learning, established strong links with India.

The Centenary Commemoration Volume of Vidyalankara Pirivena refers to these links, which were strengthened during the time of its third principal Lunupokune Dharmananda.

> It is impossible to describe his contribution to Buddhist missionary activity in India. The world will recognize its value only in the future. A large number of Indian intellectuals came to him to study Buddhism. Many of them were so convinced by the doctrine that they entered the monkhood. Today they are engaged in Buddhist missionary activity in India. Though Buddhist missionary activity in India has a long history there was no interest in translating Dharma texts into local languages, till his students entered this field . . . Today the better part of the Tripitaka has been translated into Hindu. All this was done by his students.

With the establishment of a department of Pali studies in the university of Calcutta, again thanks to Anagarika Dharmapala, several Sinhala scholar monks came to India to teach (Rambukwelle Siddharta, Walpola Rahula). Some others came to study Sanskrit. They were associated with the Vidyalankara Pirivena and were the driving force behind the pathbreaking Vidyalankara declaration of 1946, which justified the active social intervention of the Bhikku. (Among these monks were Walpola Rahula, Naravila Dhammaratane, Kotahene Pannakitti, and Bambarandc Siri Sivali.) This declaration is taken as a charter by radical monks today.[7]

Thus to 'progressive' monks, India was essentially a friendly country counterbalancing the alleged 'pro-western' bias of UNP regimes. For these monks the India of Subhas Chandra Bose and Nehru, with its socialist objectives and traditional cultural symbols, was an attractive model. They first supported the dominant socialist party of the Forties, the LSSP. Later they threw their support to S.W.R.D. Bandaranaike, whose SLFP claimed a close affinity with the policies of the Indian Congress.

With the escalation of ethnic conflict however Sinhala opinion—encouraged by both government and private media—took a distinctly anti-Indian turn. Each of the Indian moves in this area were perceived as anti-Sinhalese. Let us examine the chronology of events. The growing estrangement between the two communities was intensified by the anti-Tamil riots of July/August 1983.[8] The immediate provocation for this communal violence was the death of 18 Sinhalese soldiers, blown up by a land mine in Jaffna. These claymore mines and other sophisticated weapons were supplied by India as a way of escalating the civil war. The 1983 riots led to a new phase of Indian intervention in Sri Lankan affairs. An estimated 130 000 Tamils fled to India, particularly to Tamil Nadu.[9] This strengthened India's hand as a 'broker' in the ethnic confrontation. From 1983 India engaged in a series of acts which showed up the inability of the Sinhalese to control events. Tamil guerilla groups were trained and equipped by India, Tamil leaders were received in India and accorded 'state guest' status in New Delhi, human rights issues were raised in International fora, the Sri Lankan military offensives were halted, food parcels were dropped from Indian planes to counter an economic blockade of the north, Sri Lankan air space was violated and a threat of military invasion was made public. This intervention culminated in the Indo-Sri Lanka accord of 1987 and the arrival of Indian troops.

The majority of Sinhalese looked on these Indian activities as an infringement of the sovereignty of Sri Lanka. Within the UNP itself, a group led by the Prime Minister R. Premadasa accused India of meddling in local affairs and denounced the Accord.

Let us now examine how the monks associated with the MSV looked at this dilemma from a religious perspective, as distinct from the political perspective, which they generally shared with the Sinhalese.

For Sinhala monks the Thera Mahinda, believed by them to be the son of Emperor Asoka and historically the founder of the *sasana* in Sri Lanka, is second in significance only to the Buddha himself. He is called *anubudhu* (like the Buddha) and monks claim ecclesiastical descent from him. How is Mahinda Thera represented in this time of trouble? The Founding Father from India is contrasted strongly with Rajiv Gandhi, son of the 'Empress of India'—Indira Gandhi.

The *Vinivida*, celebrating *Poson*, the festival marking Mahinda's arrival, makes a direct comparison. It highlights Mahinda's words to Devanampiyatissa, the Sinhala King:

> O great King, equal are the followers of Dharmaraja. It is with loving sentiment that I come from Jambudvipa.

The *Vinivida* states,

These friendly words of that great son of India the Arahat Mahinda still ring in our ears. It is a statement of peaceful coexistence. In the past sons of India treated this beautiful island with respect and affection. This was because we had within our country the strength to safeguard that noble religion which saw birth in India. Political and religious emissaries of that time had no desire to subjugate us. They made us the heirs to their [religious] inheritance for the benefit of mankind. This sacred trust has been honoured [by us] for over two thousand five hundred years. During this long period India has remained India. Sri Lanka remained Sri Lanka.

Mahinda's compassion is contrasted with the actions of Rajiv Gandhi.

Though we inhabit a small island, due the possession of the Dharma we are treated with respect by the world. Another highborn son of India has sullied this [age old] relationship by acting foolishly; by breaking all ethics of international behaviour by dropping dirt on this country by force.[10]

This same contrast is manifest in a feature in the magazine entitled *Letters to Thera Mahinda* wherein the problems caused by Indian intervention and even the faults of Senior monks who do not openly protest against such injustice, are 'reported' to the founding father.[11] Maduluwawe Sobhita a leading ideologue of the MSV, on the other hand emphasizes the 'Sinhalaness' of the Sangha by turning the spotlight on the Bhikku *Maha Aritta*— the first Sinhala monk. We see how skilfully he makes Maha Aritta important for the present time.

The Sri Lankan Bhikshu Sasana began when Arahat Mahinda arrived in the island and ordained, as a Bhikku, the Sinhala youth Maha Aritta. In the thousands of years since this [event] the Bhikshu Sasana has been the independent, driving force of our nation.[12]

What is noteworthy in this debate is the effort of the Sangha to separate the issue of the Indian origins of Buddhism from the ongoing political crisis with India. What is at issue here is the legitimacy of the Sinhala Sangha itself. Any doubt cast on the value of ecclesiastical succession originating with Mahinda would strike at the very roots of the Sangha organization. The history of each of the three main sects (*Nikayas*) of the Sangha begins with the validation of this succession. When the Mahavihara succession died out in the country, Sinhalese Kings facilitated its resumption by getting down monks from Siam with legitimate succession to give higher ordination to locals. The later sects sought this legitimacy in Burma. The *Amarapura* went to Ava while the Ramanna were first given higher ordination at Pegu in 1861.

The *Tapasa Nikaya* which created a furore in the late 1950s did not believe 'n such ecclesiastical succession.[13] Its leader *Tapasa Himi* claimed the right to ordain monks even though he himself had not received 'Legitimate' ordination. Nor had he received higher ordination. This was one of the main arguments used by other sects against the *Tapasa* monks. The ethnic war was a crucial period for the Sangha. They were not only leading Sinhala opinion, they were also reacting to strong lay sentiment. Any dissonance could call into question their closely guarded claims to traditional charisma. Due to the Sinhala monks identifying themselves strongly with Sinhala anti-Indian and anti-Tamil political sentiment they pre-empted any move to question the grounds of their legitimacy. The need to 'indigenize' the Sangha did not arise.

THE MONK AS A POLITICAL ACTIVIST

The changing role of the monk is an ever present phenomenon in Buddhist society. Though Max Weber, emphasizing the canonical view, defined the Sangha as a 'community of renouncers' they have played an important social role from the very inception. While the salvation seeker (in contemporary terms the meditative forest monk) is held in high esteem as a role model, Buddhist societies have always accommodated village monks (grama-vasi) who have provided religious and social services to the laity. The laity in turn provided sustenance (alms) to these monks in exchange for 'merit' (*punya*). The village monks had to be larger in number as the 'merit' needs of the laity could not be accommodated by 'meditation' monks, whose objectives in any case did not mesh with the needs of the laity.

Thus in Buddhist societies we see two distinct, though interacting, cultures. One is the canonical culture with the *Abhidhamma* as its apex. The other is the culture of *Bahujana Hitaya*—the Sangha's intervention in society which is clear from the *Vamsa Katha* and related Buddhist literature.

A key stage in the Sinhala Sangha's social interventionist culture was reached with the Vidyalankara Declaration of 1946 referred to earlier. This declaration clearly and directly recognized the changed status of the monk:

> Today economic, social, and political conditions are different from the time of the Buddha. So, we must accept that the life of Bhikkus today is different from that of Bhikkus of the Buddha's time.
>
> Then the monks' objective, by and large, was to achieve Nirvana in that birth. Later monks, postponing Nirvana for a later time, involved themselves in both self and social realization.[14]

The monk who postpones his own salvation, it is argued, has found time for social amelioration. Since the 1940s this has meant either pre-occupation with social work (e.g. rural development sponsored by Heenatiyana Dhamma-loka: Sarvodaya monks) or politics.

The Vidyalankara declaration rationalized the Bhikkus involvement in the left politics of that time, despite the strong opposition of the Buddhist establishment. However, it was only with the founding of the SLFP by S. W. R. D Bandaranaike that the radical monks found a party which was close to their concept of politics. They threw themselves into the 1956 election campaign and were largely responsible for creating the SLFP's identity as a 'Sinhala-Buddhist' party. (This was not Bandaranaike's original conception as the first SLFP manifesto and list of office bearers will show.) The election of 1956 was introduced in Buddhist terms by monks who were the chief speakers on SLFP platforms, as a '*Mara Yuddha*', a fight against evil.

With their success at the election, the immediate post-1956 period marks the zenith of Bhikkhu influence in the country. The new Prime Minister Bandaranaike made changes in his cabinet to satisfy the monks. Newly designated ministers started out from Kelaniya temple for their oath taking. A new department of cultural affairs was set up to look after the interests of the monks. Bandaranaike made Sinhala the sole national language with their approval. An agreement reached between Bandaranaike and Chelvanayagam, the Tamil leader, for the resolution of the ethnic problem was 'torn up' unilaterally in deference to the wishes of the monks. The recommendation of a leading monk that all vehicles should carry a Sinhala symbol, a direct affront to the Tamils, was implemented. Vidyalankara and Vidyodaya Pirvena were given university status.

The undoubted success of the monks in 1956 led to the institutionalizing of their political role. Every Sri Lankan party with a Sinhala base used monks in their election campaigns. They also set up 'front' organizations of monks sympathetic to their party position. The UNP, emulating the SLFP, proclaimed that they would create a 'Dharmista' (Righteous) society, a phrase resonant with Buddhist hopes. Bhikku organizations were established by the UNP in every Sinhala electorate, thereby neutralizing the SLFP's advantage.

Though the UNP, after winning the 1977 elections, continued to court the monks, particularly the seniors in the sangha hierarchy, they could not make the same 'connection' that the SLFP established with their monks. Buddhist monks were never comfortable with J. R. Jayawardene who had his own vision of Buddhism drawn from a textual interpretation of the canon. He emphasized canonical concepts and downgraded the ritual and social role of monks. His was an intellectual Buddhism derived from the writings of western scholars like Rhys Davids and Edwin Arnold, as will be discerned in his Buddhist essays (later published as *Golden Threads* (Colombo, 1986)).

What was more significant for the monks however were the consequences of the UNP's 'free market' economy. Though the state sector continued to be the dominant component of the economy, the UNP managed to liberalize the manufacturing and trade sectors leading to an influx of foreign goods

126   *S. Amunugama*

and the creation of wealth and employment. This also meant, however, an increase in inequality in the distribution of income. Traditional positions were downgraded while the 'mudalali' (trader) ethos was on the ascendent. It also meant that monks, intellectuals, artists, etc. who as custodians of traditional culture depended on state patronage, would be challenged by creators of new, more market oriented cultural products. Consumerism was a challenge to the 'modest life style' (alpecca) that Buddhism prescribed.

> New commercial banks, hotels for tourists, newspaper advertisements and TV commercials depict a new economic orientation. The Consumerism that has been established goes beyond meeting day to day needs and tries to enslave the mind . . . Due to this strategy the cities will prosper while villages suffer. This new mentality being entrenched in our society is foreign to us. Short cuts, profit motive, entrepreneurship, selfishness, cunning and instant gratification are its characteristics.[15]

Many of the monks who were later to form the MSV attempted to protest against this growing consumerism. The government broke up many of these meetings.

With the spread of ethnic violence, monks were drawn more forcefully into the arena of political agitation. From the beginning they were reckoned by government as actors in the drama. Parathasarathy, foreign policy advisor to Indira Gandhi, was requested to discuss his proposals for ethnic peace with senior monks. 'They are my Parathasarathy's' said Jayawardene, thereby legitimizing the monks' role as advisors on the ethnic issue. Monks were in the forefront of demonstrations against Indian intervention, often in collusion with government authorities.

However, once they perceived the Jayawardene government as 'unreliable', they began to follow a more independent course, particularly by establishing the MSV. While both the UNP and SLFP were prepared to use the monks, it was the JVP—the Sinhala based revolutionary party that raised their social role to a new intensity. In the case of JVP there was no ambiguity regarding the monks' role. Unlike senior monks who still recognized the need for both self-realization and the discharging of social responsibilities, JVP monks place a premium on their political role. The JVP sangha organization was the first grouping of monks to participate in a May day parade. About a thousand young monks clad in their distinctive saffron red robes walked under the banner of the Socialist Bhikku Front. Recognizing their special role monks were positioned in the parade immediately behind the JVP top leadership. Later monks participated *en masse* in all JVP sponsored demonstrations.

After the signing of the Accord and the launching of the JVP insurrection the slogan 'Motherland above all' became the battle cry. University students adopted 'Motherland first, degree second' as their battle cry and began to boycott classes. Secondary school children amended the slogan to 'Motherland first, school second'. While young monks presented their version: 'Motherland first, Pirivena' second'.

The 1980s then see the rapid politicization of the Sinhala sangha. What started as a trickle in the 1940s had now become a flood. All Sinhala-based political parties have established support organizations among the sangha. They compete for monks' favours by offering material benefits—official residences, Mercedes Benz cars, trips abroad, state appointments and construction of temples. Pirivenas and universities became recruitment centres of monks for different political parties. The ethnic conflict provided an opportunity for the monks to openly engage in social and political activity since it was presented as a problem of national concern. Any doubts regarding their proper role had to be suppressed in a time of crisis. This approach was taken to its logical extreme, as we shall see later in this essay, by the JVP which began to view the monk as another foot soldier in the revolutionary struggle.

MONKS AGAINST 'CATHOLIC ACTION'

Another source of insecurity for the modern monk is the growth of rival religions. The SLFP is usually identified as a defender of Buddhism against the intrusions of other religions. It checked 'Catholic action' in the 1950s, took over denominational schools, evicted catholic nursing nuns, provided Buddhist preachers more time over national radio and secured employment in the higher echelons of the administration and armed services for more Buddhists. It also singled out Buddhism for special status in its 1972 constitution.

The UNP, on the other hand, drawing more support from minorities, including a Roman Catholic block vote, is more suspect. The dragging out of the ethnic war led to the suspicion that the government was unwilling to go all out militarily against the Tamil guerrillas. These fears were compounded when publicity was given in Sinhala media to the involvement of the Catholic Church which provided shelter to the guerrillas, operating in Catholic-dominated areas like Mannar. The trial of a Tamil priest Father Singaraiya and other priests accused of aiding the guerrillas, the statements of Rev. Deogupillai, Bishop of Jaffna and the number of Catholics among the guerrillas were closely monitored by Buddhist monks.[16]

> International conspirators have urged the Catholic Church to enter remote villages of the very poor. A dangerous leopard has donned the white cassock to convert impoverished Buddhist villagers to Catholicism. This is only the first step on the road to Eelam. Those lay Buddhists who used to visit the temple to attend to needs of monks have now fallen before the church and make the sign of the cross.[17]

Unlike the 1950s when Buddhist leaders complained of the influence of 'Catholic action' in the higher strata of government, the present threat is perceived from young Catholic priests who are adherents of 'Liberation Theology'. They live with the poor and in the pursuit of their congregational tasks become a direct rival of the socially oriented monk. What amounts to a case study of such an encounter is found in an article by Tiranagama Ratanasara, a well known Buddhist monk. Ratanasara describes his experiences with a 'liberated' Catholic priest in the *Angunukolawewa* village in the deep south. The priest lives in a poor man's house and rides a bicycle. He teaches in the village school 'where when he arrives the children welcome him with joy'. He brings clothes, milk foods, medicine, and chicken coops to the village. Once a week a meeting of Christian youth are held.[18] When a Buddhist temple is built the 'father' is the first to offer flowers. The article ends on a pessimistic note.

> Today, with Angunukolawewa as its headquarters about twenty villages in the area are being 'developed' by Catholics. This is a 'religious hunt' for poor rural people. Can all this lead to peace in the country?

ON THE USE OF VIOLENCE

Though Buddhist doctrine prescribes *ahimsa* and Buddhist social practice bears its influence we see numerous instances of dilemmas created by this teaching. The tension between the needs of the Buddhist state and the prescriptions of the Dhamma is ever present in Buddhist societies.[19] The classic instance is the dilemma of Dutugemunu.[20]

The decision of Tamil youth to take to violence in their struggle for a separate state, the induction of Indian troops to the island, and the decision of the JVP to use 'revolutionary violence' created dilemmas—of varying degree—for Sinhala monks. Let us examine their responses in each of these instances. In the case of the Sri Lankan, in effect Sinhala, army killing Tamil guerrillas the majority of monks supported it without serious reservation. (There were exceptions—(a) those who lived on the borderlands between Sinhala and Tamil areas organized as the *Saama Bkikshu Padanama*, (b) those who supported the Marxist oriented parties and (c) those associated with the Sarvodaya movement. But they were small both in number and in influence.) Unlike the monk from Pulingurata who, according to the *Mahavamsa* attempted to salve the conscience of Dutugemunu by refusing to grant 'human' status to the slain Damilas, Sinhala monks attempted to resolve the dilemma by making a distinction between non-violent Tamil people and violent Tamil rebels. The Tamil argument that the Sinhalese are 'racist' is turned against them by highlighting the racial basis of Eelam. As Peter Schalk, analysing the MSV manifests puts it, 'Militancy is evident not only in the language (murdering Eelamism) and in its aggressive suspicion (conspiracies), but above all in that the text consciously turns the argument of being racist against the "conspirators" who are credited with wanting to divide the country on a racial basis'.

This approach is given a Buddhist perspective in the *Vinivida* which contrasts racism engendered by colonialism with the experience of Asoka.

> History has cursed us with colonialism which changed our historic path. Today our people are paying for this diversion in blood and bullets. Those who fight for barren earth are nothing but savages. Arhat Mahinda's father, the King Asoka chose Dharma Vijaya because he realized the futility of fighting for land. It being so, we are compelled to characterize those who do not live together but quibble about historic homelands and thereby break up their motherland, as well as those who encourage them, as savages.[21]

The epithet 'savage' (*mlecca*) resonates with anti-Buddhist connotations in the Pali chronicles. For the monks there were immediate reasons for such a usage. They had special reason to fear Tamil attacks. Tamil guerrillas appear to have singled monks out for punishment. The temple at Nagadipa was attacked and Buddhist monks were evicted. Others fled from temples in the North and East. Even those in the border areas were in danger. Tamil guerrillas injured and killed over a hundred worshippers at the Sacred Bo tree in Anuradhapura. An attack on the Temple of the Tooth was anticipated. A busload of monks, returning from a pilgrimage, were brutally murdered at *Arantalawa*, leading to a joint appeal to government by the Mahanayakes seeking military protection for the sangha. Maduluwave Sobhita writes of the insecurities of the sangha,

> Today, the Buddhist monk is assailed from every side. In the North and East Tamil terrorists have flattened Buddhist temples. A few days ago terrorists attacked the Trikonamadu forest hermitage, killed the monk there and offered his flesh as alms to the Buddha. The massacre of Bhikkus at *Arantalawa* is unprecedented in history . . . The heart of Sinhala Buddhism is the Sacred Bo tree. The massacre at this site, hallowed for thousands of years, is an attack on all Buddhists. The sacred site which is usually bathed in incense and water was bathed in blood.[22]

The characterization of Tamil rebels as '*mleccas*' helped the monks to extend their patronage to the armed services. Military commanders, after assuming office, worshipped at the Temple of the Tooth and met the Mahanayakes of Asgiriya and Malvatta to obtain their blessings. Bodhi Pujas were held in leading temples to seek the blessings of gods in ensuring the safety and success of military personnel. Monks officiated at military functions and the central army cantonment at Panagoda saw the erection of an impressive '*chaitya*' (pagoda).

Though the induction of Indian troops (IPKF) helped Sinhalese troops

130   *S. Amunugama*

first by enforcing a ceasefire, and later taking over the fight with the Tamil
guerillas, Buddhist monks were reluctant to recognize this development as
they strongly opposed the Indo-Lanka Accord. Also the terror tactics of the
JVP prevented any favourable, or even objective, assessment of the Indian
contribution. Thus the focus was placed on the misdemeanours of the Indians
and their alleged continuing links with the guerillas. Maduluwewa Sobhita
takes such an approach:

> Ten months ago Indian troops were inducted here saying peace would come in
> seventy-two hours. We know that the Sinhalese of Tricomalee stayed on in
> their lands even amidst great difficulties and threats from terrorists. The IPKF
> came to disarm the Tamil terrorists. But in addition to gifting fifty lakhs of
> rupees [to the Tamil administration] they joined hands with the Tigers and
> have now began to exterminate the remaining Sinhalese and their monks in
> places like Tricomalee.[23]

The violence which was unleashed in the South by the JVP security
forces and vigilante groups on the other hand, created major problems for
the Sangha. While the monks could find a broad consensus in their views
regarding Tamil separatists and the IPKF, the extension of violence to the
South was traumatic.

We can examine this dilemma in terms of (a) the monks and the JVP,
(b) the monks and the UNP regime, (c) differences in perception of violence
in the Sangha hierarchy and (d) the monks and the vigilantes or 'death
squads'.

THE MONKS AND THE JVP

The JVP is a revolutionary party which draws its membership from rural
Sinhala youth. It has launched armed attacks on the state twice (1971 and
1987–89) without success. Obeysekere's observations regarding the social
composition of the JVP in 1971 still holds good.

> In the first place the movement is unequivocally a revolt of the youth of the
> country, and those who actively participated in it were predominantly males . . .
> the statistical information also reveals that the overwhelming majority of sus-
> pected insurgents were Sinhala Buddhists.

He concludes that

> one simply has to view the insurgency as a Sinhala Buddhist movement spear-
> headed by the youth of the country.

Of all the Sri Lankan political parties, it was the JVP that set out deliberately to mobilize the monks as a vital support group. This decision
reflected the party's emphasis on youth, as opposed to the working class, as
the motor of the Sri Lankan revolution. They looked upon universities as

centres of recruitment. For a variety of reasons, young Buddhist monks had come to constitute a significant proportion of the university population. The egalitarian, 'Sinhala Buddhist' ideology of the JVP appealed to the young monks. Referring to the 1971 insurgency, A. C. Alles states that Buddhist temples were used for concealment of arms and ammunition, as hiding places for members of the movement, and as outposts of the JVP. Members were posted to abandoned Buddhist temples to do propaganda work among villagers. The decision to launch an attack on the government forces in 1971 was taken in a Bhikku hostel of a university.

Though the monks did play an important role in 1971, it was in the late 1980s that they became crucial to the JVP. The JVP was proscribed by the government following the anti-Tamil riots of 1983. While the top leadership went 'underground' they maintained their strength through 'front' organizations. Three key 'fronts' of the JVP were (a) university and senior college students, (b) Buddhist monks and (c) women. Each of these 'fronts' had its distinctive constitution, office bearers, budget and publications.

Organization-wise the JVP had three departments. (a) *Zonal organizations*—the country was divided into five zones, i.e. (1) Western and Sabaragamuwa; (2) Central; (3) Rajarata; (4) Uva and Eastern; (5) South. Each of these 'zones' were subdivided into districts and subdistricts. Central committee members were in charge of each district, while each zone had two high level party leaders as political and military secretaries respectively. (b) *National Committees* on education, finance, military organization and propaganda. (c) *Front organizations*, i.e. the three mentioned earlier as well as 'fronts' for workers and youth.

If we take the monks organization for detailed scrutiny we find that each of the territorial divisions—zone, district and subdistrict, had a branch of the JVP Bhikku organization. Thus it could be called the most comprehensive 'non-formal' Sangha grouping outside the traditional Sangha hierarchy, based on *Nikaya*. The JVP organization was radical in that it cross cut *Nikaya* differences by establishing itself as a *Tri-Nikayika* (3-sect) organization throughout the country. Monks from all sects were free to join.

The importance attached by the JVP to its monks organization can be gauged by the fact that it was placed in charge of a top leader D. M. Ananda (alias Dissanayake Mudiyanselage Nandasena), generally reckoned to be the No. 3 in the JVP hierarchy, after the leader Rohana Wijeweera and General Secretary Upatissa Gamanayake. The following description of Ananda's career highlights the various strands of support which gave the JVP its strength.

> A native of Wariyapola, 35 years of age. He graduated in Arts from the University of Kelaniya in 1980. He was a Buddhist monk when he entered the University, but gave up robes in his final year. The leader of the Socialist students union at

Kelaniya University and the Secretary of the inter University students Federation, [He] was the organizer of the countrywide protest against the proposed
white paper on education in 1981. Till the proscription of the party he was the
president of the Socialist students Union of the JVP. His importance increased
tremendously in the years following the proscription and while functionally the
most important man in the organization, he was in the eyes of his party comrades,
No. 3 in the organization.[24]

While the monks were deployed for JVP propaganda, they were particularly useful in agitation on special issues which tended to give the party a good
image among the youth. Monks were in the forefront of agitation against
the White Paper on Education, the privatization of the Medical College,
Pirivena reform and the Indo-Lanka accord. They also participated in student
agitation for higher payments to University scholarship holders, higher
salaries for university teachers and other employees and for the holding of
early general elections. Monks were also used as couriers and many temples
and university Bhikku hostels were used as safe-houses.[25]

However, JVP monks were confronted with a major dilemma when their
party decided on the path of 'revolutionary violence'. There is some
ambiguity created deliberately by the JVP regarding the use of violence,
particularly the assassination of political opponents and government officials.
Wijeweera, the JVP leader, took up the position that the JVP did not engage in
violence. That was the work of the *Deshapremi Janatha Viyaparaya* (DJV)
which he said was

> not the armed division of the JVP. You ask what the connection between the
> DJV and JVP is? As far as we are aware the DJV is a mass peoples organization.
> There are members of the JVP, as well as non-members in it. We believe that
> some members of the UNP, the SLFP and other groups, who are against the
> Indian invading armies, who are against the fifth columnists of the Indians,
> who are against the Tamil Eelam terrorists, who are against India swallowing
> Sri Lanka, who oppose the merger of the North and East, who are against the
> second Kandyan convention of Rajiv Gandhi and Jayawardene, who are against
> the provincial councils and who do not want Sri Lanka to be another Sikkim,
> are also in the DJV.[26]

In reality the DJV carried out decisions of the political sections of the
party taken at the appropriate national, zonal, divisional or sub-divisional
level. This was known to the leaders of JVP Sangha organization, though it
is quite likely that the general membership accepted the official party view.
The JVP's commitment to the DJV, however, was never in doubt.

How did the monks react? Here we must also add another dimension to this
question. While the DJV/JVP did carry out assassinations of its opponents,
it claimed that it was only reacting to state violence.

When the public protested peacefully against the Jayawardene–Gandhi pact of betrayal, 142 people were shot. It is in this situation that the DJV was born on a solid foundation. It cancelled the monopoly that Mr Jayawardene and the Indian fifth columnists held on the use of violence.[27]

It is correct that UNP 'workers' attacked the MSV during the signing of the Indo-Lanka Accord leading the JVP/DJV towards counter violence. Yet many of the organizations in the MSV began to rethink their positions once the JVP began to dominate the anti-Accord opposition and, more significantly, began using widespread terror and violence. The major political organizations—SLFP, MEP and the Sinhala Bala Mandalaya—distanced themselves from the MSV. So did its chief monks, particularly the Mahanayake of Asgiriya, Palipane Chandananda. About this time the elections for President were anounced. The SLFP candidate Mrs Bandaranaike, issued her manifesto. With the support of ethnic minorities in mind, the SLFP pledged to establish two provincial councils in the East—one for the Tamils and another for the Muslims. This raised a storm of protest. The SLFP which opposed the creation of even a single provincial council in the East, when they were in the MSV, were now going even beyond the Accord by agreeing to create two provincial councils. Gamini Iriyagolle, President of the Theosophical Society and a live wire of the MSV, openly repudiated the SLFP and threw his weight behind the UNP. Cyril Matthew, another MSV hero, went further. 'A special hell', he said, 'should be invented for Mrs Bandaranaike and the SLFP for the betrayal of Sinhala Buddhists'.

The withdrawal of the senior monks from the SMV left the JVP monks in a quandary. They could not repudiate the violence of the JVP/DJV. On the other hand, their senior monks did not come to their rescue. In this situation the JVP monks reacted to the impasse in several ways:

(a) allowed the JVP to the assassinate senior monks who were supporters of the UNP or Left parties.

(b) pressured senior monks in their temples, regional organizations and *Karaka Sabhawa's* to desist from supporting the UNP or SLFP.

(c) criticized senior monks who did not support the JVP.

(d) organized a national and international campaign against attacks on JVP monks.

The assassination of senior monks including Pohaddaramulle Pemaloka (patron, SLMP), Thambugala Sumanasiri, Vellatota Pannadassi and Kotikawatte Saddhatissa and many leading priests of regional areas, have been attributed to the DJV/JVP. These monks had broken the rule imposed by the JVP/DJV that they should not lend support to parties which were in favour of the Accord. The *Vinivida* attempts to resolve this dilemma by suggesting to its readers that the JVP was not involved in these killings and drawing attention to state killings of young monks. This response became necessary as senior monks including those in the 'non-violent' sections of

134   *S. Amunugama*

the MSV, openly condemned Pemaloka's murder.

> The assassination of Pemaloka Thero appears to be another step in a political
> conspiracy. We have received information that this was not a killing carried out
> by the Deshapremies; [DJV]. On reading the statement of a certain group of
> monks, published in the *Divayina* of 23rd of December, we came to the con-
> clusion that there is a coterie of monks in this country who are unaware of the
> arrest, torture, disrobing and killing of [young] monks.[28]

Though not visible to laymen, JVP monks were also exerting pressure on
senior monks from both within and outside their traditional organization.
JVP monks organized several *satyagrahas* and fasts at centres of Buddhist
worship. A mass *satyagraha* was arranged near the Temple of the Tooth, a
show of strength which was designed to impress the sangha establishment of
Asgiriya and Malwatta. Soon after this demonstration the highest decision
making bodies (*Karaka Sabha*) of these two establishments passed resolutions
condemning the Accord and seeking protection for the monks who had been
taken into custody by armed services. When the JVP escalated their terror
tactics, leading Buddhist monks were characterized as 'traitors' and sent
'death threats'. As a result some left the island and others drastically curtailed their religious and social activities.

While pressure was being put on chief monks through Sangha Sabhas, a
public campaign criticizing them for 'inaction' was also launched. Buddhist
reformers from the time of Anagarika Dharmapala have been critical of 'the
sloth and lack of commitment' of the Sangha leadership. Later on, reformist
monks, who were sympathizers of socialist parties, criticized their chiefs for
supporting the UNP in exchange for worldly benefits. This critical vocabulary
('lazy, spittoon-filling monks') was resurrected by pro-JVP monks to criticize
their elders.

CRITIQUE OF THE SANGHA LEADERSHIP

In an essay in *Vinivida*, a young monk Kumbalgamuwe Dhammananda
presents a critique of Sangha elders.[29] He begins by broadly classifying
these elders:

> In modern Sri Lanka out of about 30 000 Bhikkus, over a thousand are *Nayakas*.
> Such nayakas have been appointed at provincial, district and sub-district level. In
> each district there are chief, deputy, chief *adhikarana* (adjudicator of ecclesiastical
> law), deputy *adhikarana*, etc. for each of the sects.

He then describes the functions of these Nayakas, which he claims are
incorporated in their *sannas* or letters of appointment. These functions are:

> The protection and enhancement of the *Buddha Sasana*, ensuring the safety of
> the sangha, resolution of conflict among monks in order to safeguard sangha

unity, ensuring the welfare of the Buddhist laity and giving leadership to the Sri Lankan nation.

However, says the writer,

> these leaders have deliberately shirked their duty and have tragically allowed international conspiratorial forces to drag down the country, race and the Buddha sasana.

Contrasting present sloth with the glorious heritage of a Bhikku, he says that in the past monks like Kudapola and Weliwita Sangaraja placed 'the motherland first' because 'without a sovereign territory', language, religion and culture cannot flourish. How then did the Nayakas lose sight of their mission? According to the writer, British colonialists were responsible because they converted sangha or commonly owned property to private ownership of the chief monks, thereby making them selfish and 'this worldly'. Thus the monk lost sight of his 'patriotic tasks' and became a seeker after money and property. The monk who was previously engaged in the *yuga mehwara* (historic task) of protecting the race and sasana now 'began to waste his time in the law courts, litigating with teacher, fellow monk, and lay supporter in order to gain wealth, property and position'. This decline had many consequences. Politicians have used monks for their own ends. The Catholic Church has conducted a subtle campaign to encourage Eelamism, discredit monks and convert Buddhists to their religion. This is due to the weakness of Sangha leadership fragmented on party, sect, caste, and *parshava* (groups within a Nikaya) lines. Learned monks, who obtain doctorates, prefer to go abroad to spread the message to foreigners while their own countrymen suffer.

The writer then comes to his immediate concern,

> When the young monk (*Podi Hamuduruwo*) who entered the university together with the village *Dayaka's* (lay supporter) son begins to fight the anti-Buddhist aggression of international conspirators and agitates against cut backs in free education, killing of unarmed people and the massacre of students, they are assaulted, tortured and imprisoned. Many others are killed and burned. But some Mahanayakes know nothing of this.

Next comes a broadside at the Nayakas:

> Chief priests have no time for these problems. But they have time to invite a Minister to declare open the new temple *Thorana*, pull down the 18-cubit Buddha statue and build [in its place] a 88-cubit Buddha statue, lay a marble floor in the bathroom and trade in the car for a new model Datsun.

The writer contrasts these selfish concerns with the commitment of young monks and concluded by inviting the seniors to relinquish their positions if they cannot fulfil their responsibilities.

MONKS AND ARMED OPPONENTS

When the armed services and vigilante groups launched an offensive against the JVP, young monks faced extreme danger. Unlike their party leaders who had gone underground, monks who had spearheaded public agitation were easy targets. At this stage many of the senior monks, who had borne the brunt of radical attacks, like the one quoted earlier, were not willing to come to their rescue. By this time Mahanayakas' 'bete noir' J. R. Jayawardene was out of power and his successor President R. Premadasa, was quite acceptable to them.

The *Vinivida* is indignant about chief monks who were quoted as saying: 'young monks were more dangerous than the Northern Tamil Terrorists'.[30] According to this journal hundreds of monks were being tortured and killed by their armed opponents. JVP monks responded to this crisis in several ways. Some surrendered, or criticized the JVP for misleading them and became supporters of the government. Their statements were given wide publicity in the media. Some others gave up robes or fled to other countries. It is likely that core supporters gave up robes and joined the JVP guerrillas who had retreated to jungle camps. There were many reports of the disappearance of monks, sightings of laymen with shaven heads and the discovery of discarded robes in public places.

The poetry and short stories published in journals like *Vinivida, Ravaya, Vivarana* and the largest circulation Sinhala newspaper *Divayina* depict the dilemmas of young monks who find their 'holy cause' defeated by violence. In all cases they remain silent on JVP violence and seek to focus attention on the victimization of innocents.

In a short story entitled *A Brief Tale* we meet a young monk, Mahinda. He is his chief monk's favourite. Mahinda gets on very well with the village youths who, despite their difficulties, help the monks to repair the temple and string up coloured lights for *Poson*. When the villagers fail to contribute to temple charity, the chief monk loses his temper. Mahinda pacifies him by explaining that their congregation is poor; yet they never fail to send food for the monks.

One day, the peace of the village temple is shattered. Mahinda's father, a village carpenter, his eyes full of tears, conveys a fateful message

> 'You tell me father that Malli (younger brother) was absolutely innocent.'
> 'You know that he is innocent. He and his friends had fired the brick kiln and were chatting on the Lake Bund when the armed men came. They put hot coals into his mouth and threatened to kill him if he did not give information. I have looked everywhere for him. He's not to be found.'

The father falls at Mahinda's feet in worship and goes looking for his other son. Mahinda, standing very still 'like a rock statue' sees in his mind's eye his younger brother who had unselfishly taken over the burdens of helping his parents. Without the brother's generosity he could not have become a monk. Mahinda's reverie is broken by his friend Gunapala who comes with bad news.

> 'I rowed your father across the river. Near the rubber estate there were a lot of people looking at a body which had washed up. Your father took one look at it and started wailing. It was Piyadasa Malli.'
>
> 'Enough Gunapala. I cannot cry like my father. I had a hunch it would come to this. Do me a favour, please look after my father.'

The following morning Mahinda was gone. His robes were left behind. The chief priest said 'Mahinda is a good person. He may have given up his robes. But he had gone to do good'.[31]

This ending leaves the clear impression that Mahinda has joined the guerrillas. In a poem which has the same theme, the ending is more explicit. The monk sheds his robes, takes a T-56 submachine gun (the T-56 came to symbolize JVP military strength) and disappears into the night.

CONCLUSIONS

Most writings about the Sri Lankan crisis tend to describe the Sinhala Sangha as a monolithic organization having 'clear cut' views on ethnic and political issues. In reality it is not so. At the formal level there are the sangha's institutional structures for the making of pronouncements. It is rare that they make pronouncements on public issues. Informally, monks participate in a variety of organizations with their own agendas for action. Charismatic leaders of the Sangha work to build coalitions of these organizations so that a common position can be articulated. They do not often succeed. Nor does the success of such coalition building depend entirely on the sangha. The strength and commitment of lay groups become crucial.

Second, we see that the notion of Sinhalese 'custodianship' of Buddhism is so strong that monks are willing to rationalize the use of violence against the 'other', even though it contravenes the basic tenets of Buddhism. The arguments and strategies adopted to resolve this dilemma favoured the domain of *realpolitik*. In this they were directly in line with the sangha we encounter in the Pali chronicles who link the fortunes of the Buddhist Church with the Sinhala state. Despite more than a century of 'Protestant Buddhism' its intellectual overlay was stripped as soon as the modern Sinhala 'nation' faced a real crisis.

Third, changes in Bhikku education, particularly in the Pirivenas and universities and changing patterns of recruitment to the Sangha (not analysed in this essay) are creating a new strata of radical socially committed monks. They, however, still operate within the traditional 'Sinhala-Buddhist' axis.

138   *S. Amunugama*

It was this strata which formed an important support group for the JVP. Their membership and influence is likely to increase.

Fourth, though the use of violence against the Tamils, the UNP and the Left was rationalized by the radical monks in terms of the needs of modern 'realpolitik', they attempted to draw on classic Buddhist textual concepts of the inviolability of the monks (anantacharipapakarma) and an interpretation of social intervention (Bahujanahitaya) when they in turn were the subjects of state violence.

Fifth, the commitment to social revolution is so strong among radical monks that they are willing not only to condone the use of violence by the JVP, but also in many cases shed their robes and take up the gun. This phenomenon which has been noticeable in several contemporary Buddhist societies juxtaposes the radical monks persona, Buddhist 'selflessness' and new Buddhist interpretations of social intervention.

Sixth, we see the attempts of Sinhala monks to understand social reality in terms of Buddhist symbolism. When dealing with secular notions like ethnicity, democracy, revolution and violence, monks attempted to relate them to their culturally prescribed world of symbols. They go back to the examples of the monks—Wariyapola, Kudahapola, etc. who confronted state power. Communism is understood in terms of the Buddha's prescription of communal living (absence of private property, sharing of alms, etc.) for the sangha. This leads to the continuous 'oversimplification' of complex contemporary issues.

Finally, in contrast to the conventional view of Sinhala monks as a confident, assertive power group within the national polity we find that they perceive themselves as a deprived, alienated group inadequately recognized by both political authorities and the Buddhist public. They believe that they are 'used' by politicians and unless better organized, would be outmanoeuvered by 'foreign conspiratorial forces' including Eelamists and Roman Catholics.

The intrusion of monks into the arena of revolutionary politics has resulted in a loss of their charisma. Monks are arrested, stripped of their robes, publicly humiliated and even killed by armed Sinhala Buddhists. This change in perception has been noted by the monks themselves.

> When demonstrating monks are teargassed and assaulted they are forced to run for cover with their robes tucked up. When they run about the streets like laymen, will the public exhibit religious devotion? Will not their *bhakti* be destroyed?[32]

This dwindling of social esteem of and for Buddhist monks may have long term implications for recruitment, education, influence, and the religious vocation of the Sinhala Sangha.

NOTES

1 *Vinivida* 24, July 1989, p. 6.
2 *The Mahavamsa*: trans. Wilhelm Geiger, Colombo, Govt. Information Department, 1950.
3 *Mhv.* 1.46.
4 A. C. Alles, *The Trial of Walisinghe Harischandra and Others*, Colombo, Lake House Investments, Ltd, 1989.
5 Peter Schalk, ' "Unity" and "Sovereignity". Key concepts of a militant Buddhist organization in the present conflict in Sri Lanka', *Temenos*, 1989, pp. 55–82.
6 Schalk, 1989, pp. 64–71.
7 *Vinivida* 14, June 1988, pp. 2–6.
8 S. J. Tambiah, *Sri Lanka: Ethnic Fratricide and the Dismantling of Democracy*, Chicago, University of Chicago Press, 1986, pp. 28–33.
9 *New York Times*, 11 March 1990.
10 *Vinivida* 14, June 1988, p. 1.
11 *Vinivida* 24, July 1989, pp. 9, 10.
12 *Vinivida* 13, May 1988, p. 14.
13 Michael Carrithers, *The Forest Monks of Sri Lanka*, Delhi, Oxford University, 1983.
14 *Vidyalankara Pirivena Centenary Volume*, Colombo, Government Press, 1975, p. 61.
15 *Vinivida* 18, November 1988, p. 25.
16 *Vinivida* 18, November 1988, p. 11.
17 *Vinivida* 18, November 1988, p. 12.
18 *Vinivida* 18, November 1988, p. 26.
19 S. J. Tambiah, *World Conqueror and World Renouncer*, London, Cambridge University Press, 1976, p. 47.
20 Gananath Obeysekere, *Meditations on Conscience*, Colombo, Social Scientists Association, 1988.
21 *Vinivida* 14, June 1988, p. 1.
22 *Vinivida* 13, May 1988, p. 15.
23 *Vinivida* 13, May 1988, p. 15.
24 C. A. Chandraprema, 'Profiles of leaders', in *Island*, 5 February 1990.
25 A. C. Alles, *Insurgency 1971*, Colombo, Colombo Apothecaries Ltd., 1976, p. 97.
26 *Sri Lanka Sunday Times*, 13 November 1988.
27 Wijeweera, *Sri Lanka Sunday Times*, 13 November 1988.
28 *Vinivida* 20, January–February 1989, p. 7.
29 *Vinivida* 18, November 1988, p. 3.
30 *Vinivida* 18, November 1988, p. 4.
31 *Vinivida* 24, July 1988, p. 22.
32 *Vinivida* 24, July 1988, p. 17.

SARATH AMUNUGAMA is a fellow of the International Centre for Ethnic Studies, Colombo, Sri Lanka. He holds a Doctorate from the École des Hautes Etudes en Sciences Sociales, Paris. Formerly Director of the International Programme for Communication of UNESCO, Paris, he was a Visiting Scholar at Harvard University in 1990.

50/1, Siripa Road, Colombo 5, Sri Lanka.

[6]

The War in Former Yugoslavia and Religion

SRDJAN VRCAN

I

It is a legitimate, intriguing and urgent challenge to contemporary sociological research to enquire into the role of religion in the Yugoslav crisis. The question involves more than simply the relationship between religion and war: it involves the earlier and wider question of the role of religion in deepening social divisions and cleavages until they reach the point of fracture and in exacerbating social conflicts until they reach maximum incandescence. It also involves the question of the relationship of religious confessions to each other, and to the otherness of the others, in an area with mixed population, multiconfessional, multinational and multicultural.

Two fundamental *a priori* objections may of course be made to asking the question at all.

Firstly, some will point out that the war has been characterised as a religious one by the propaganda apparatus of one or other of the conflicting parties with the purely propagandistic aim of concealing the real nature of the war and creating (at least) confusion in international public opinion. It is more or less obvious, however, that this war has not been a religious war. It is evidently a political war, caused by political strategies which since the beginning of the Yugoslav crisis have been on a collision course. It is a war which fully confirms the well-known formula of Klausewitz that war is but a continuation of politics by other means. However, this does not mean that religion has nothing to do with the war. It is also more or less obvious that the three major confessions of the region, Catholicism, Orthodoxy and Islam, have all been implicated and involved in the conflict in some way and to some degree. Here we see an analogy with the civil war in Lebanon and the chronic conflict in Northern Ireland. In both these cases the wars have not been 'religious' in terms of the classical definition of a 'holy war';[1] but at the same time it has been obvious that religion has not been a purely passive onlooker but has been actively engaged in the conflict. Consequently at an impressionistic level the assertions of F. Vreg sound a convincing note:

> Amongst the demons of destruction of the processes of cultural rapprochement in the European area have been not only growing ethnicism, which frequently turns into the malignant tumour of nationalism, but also religious mysticism. We have seen a brutal eruption not only of national feelings with their political symbols, but of religious feelings and symbols too, and this has been wrongly understood as a religious rebirth. Croatian soldiers wear not only HDZ badges, but Catholic crosses too; Serbian soldiers do not carry photographs of Milošević but Orthodox crosses. Muslim fundamentalists and mujaheddins kill under the slogan of Allah.

368   *Srdjan Vrcan*

In the former Yugoslav area, then, 'new' frontiers are being established between Catholics, Orthodox and Muslims.[2]

There is no doubt that religious symbolism has for some obviously relevant reasons been widely and deliberately used in the armed conflicts in the former Yugoslav area.

Secondly, it is possible to dismiss the whole question with the argument that the war in former Yugoslavia is purely accidental in origin, or that it is an essentially anomalous phenomenon with no symptomatic value and therefore not deserving of any kind of sociological investigation at all. This argument hardly stands up to scrutiny, however. It is more plausible to maintain that the war is the inevitable result of a dominant political logic which has been in operation for some time. We ought also to remember that current developments in former Yugoslavia can hardly be interpreted as constituting a radical novelty in the modern history of the area, but rather as a contemporary repetition of events which have happened before. It is not surprising that Ernest Gellner's descriptions of the situation in some parts of Eastern Europe formulated in the early 1980s are valid for the developments in former Yugoslavia in the early 1990s. It has turned out to be true that obedience to the nationalist imperative must 'involve population exchanges or expulsions, more or less forcible assimilation, and sometimes liquidation, in order to attain that close relation between the state and culture which is the essence of nationalism.'[3] We also need to bear in mind that the war in former Yugoslavia is not the only war of its kind. In 1992 most of the 30 or more wars being waged around the world were of a tribal, racial, ethnic and/or religious character.[4] Some religious thinkers have been taking up the general challenge of the problem of religion and war. Thus Torrelli asks: 'As it emerges from patriotic wars and wars generated by the clash of two ideological messianisms, is the world going to be engulfed by new religious wars?'[5] It is very difficult, then, to argue that the war in former Yugoslavia is a totally anomalous phenomenon. Just the contrary: it may reasonably be claimed that this is a war with highly symptomatic value if, for instance, C. Offe is right in his diagnosis of the situation in Central and Eastern Europe to the effect that 'there the scene is dominated by territorial disputes, migrations, minority or nationality conflicts, and corresponding secessionist longings'.[6] At the same time, it is permissible to connect the events in former Yugoslavia, which have led to a war in which religion plays a visible role, with some developments and changes of a wider extent. 'As the world becomes increasingly interdependent,' writes Kokosalakis,

> and as the utopianism of modernity becomes explicit, ethnic struggles and the assertion of identities become a prominent feature of the contemporary world. Religion at large is inextricably involved in this process almost everywhere and exemplifies the very tensions which are inherent in the matrix of universalism and localism.[7]

The developments in former Yugoslavia may be interpreted as constituting an extreme case of tensions which exist elsewhere. In a stimulating analysis Patrick Michel insists that 'all these contemporary societies are postcommunist societies in the sense that all have to manage the end of a polarity of ultimate references, which have been structuring not only people's behaviour but also their mentality', and that the problems of relationship between particular and universal are today of a crucial urgency.[8]

Some would argue that this war ought to be projected onto the background of the problem of the affirmation of identities and differences and also of their relation to others and to otherness. In this respect, the war in former Yugoslavia may be taken as an extreme case in which the affirmation of identities has turned into a practical denial of the possibility of living together peacefully and on a basis of equality with others and their otherness, as well as an extreme case in which, as Kalscheuer has recently underlined, religious memories and identities have become motives for their bloody self-affirmation.[9]

II

There are at least three major lines of argument which emphasise the specific features of the war in former Yugoslavia and legitimise our enquiry into the role of religion in the crisis.

The first line of argument proceeds from a series of undeniable facts. It is a fact that it is largely religious believers and members of various confessions who have been killing each other, who have been destroying each other's homes and churches, who have been driving each other from their towns and villages. Without their engagement on a mass scale, there would be no war, or at least the war would have been shorter and more confined. It is also true that when religion is important to people it is religion which defines the actual battle-lines.[10] To some degree this has been confirmed by events in former Yugoslavia. Another undeniable fact is that the combatants on all sides have made extensive use of religious symbols as the most appropriate to indicate their identities and to demonstrate the aims they have been fighting for; and religious symbols have also been the best means of identifying legitimate targets for destruction. There can hardly be any doubt that the war has so far been waged in a context of religious symbolism, and that the use of religious symbolism has had the effect of increasing rather than decreasing the conflict potential of the basic confrontation. Conflicts between religious and national groups frequently attain extraordinary vehemence and are the most difficult to abate.[11]

It is, furthermore, an evident fact that the war has so far had some very important consequences for the religious confessions in former Yugoslavia. First of all, there is no doubt that the war has made important changes to the map of the whole area and will continue to do so. It would be naive to believe that these changes will affect only the political map of the area, and will be confined to a redrawing of the borders of the new states. In fact, as the conflicts have become totalised and radicalised, they have been changing all kinds of maps: social, political, demographic, economic, cultural and confessional; even the maps of people's everyday lives. One may therefore predict with certainty that the confessional map of the area which will ultimately emerge will certainly be very different from the previous one.

Secondly, there have been very important changes in the social position of the various confessions within the various institutional frameworks in the area. The churches and religions have moved from an essentially extrasystemic or even countersystemic position to occupy a systemic or suprasystemic position; religion is now the overarching systemic cultural and symbolic aggregate.

Thirdly, there have been important changes in the very content of the operative religious confessions. It is obvious that ecumenical dialogue initiatives have been declining everywhere and in some places have completely ceased; that the balance between universalism and particularism within the different confessional cultures has been radically changing; and that some features of the various religions which were previously of marginal or secondary relevance have become more prominent: the

370   *Srdjan Vrcan*

theme of sacrifice, for instance, becoming so important in the current confessional interpretations of history, as martyrology in Serbian Orthodoxy, as a kind of Calvary in Croatian Catholicism and as a historical holocaust among the Bosnian Muslims.

Fourthly, there have been profound changes in the relations between the various confessions: almost everywhere they have deteriorated.

Fifthly, there have been important changes in the external political, cultural and ideological conditions under which the various confessions operate in the everyday life of society in the various regions of former Yugoslavia. The collapse of all previously existing systemic restrictions led to the affirmation of religious freedom on an abstract level; but this has now been followed by new restrictions and oppressive practices against particular confessions in different parts of the country. As so often in history, the proclamation of religious freedom has not been universal but very selective, increasing the freedom of some but restricting the freedom of others.[12]

Finally, it is a fact that since the mid-1980s the predominant political strategies in Central and Eastern Europe have been orientated towards the aim articulated by Mazzini in the nineteenth century of 'one nation one state'. In former Yugoslavia these strategies have obtained religious legitimacy, withheld for a time only by Bosnian Islam and more recently by part of Croatian Catholicism in Bosnia. The Mazzinian political formula is very close to the Old Testament formula of 'one God, one nation and one land'.[13]

The second line of argument is historico-situationally specific.

Firstly, it is obvious, but needs stressing, that the war in former Yugoslavia is a very peculiar contemporary war. It is being waged not in some distant part of Asia, Africa or Latin America but on European soil, close to the very heart of Europe, an hour by air from major European cities.

Secondly, it is obvious, but needs stressing, that the confessions implicated and engaged in the war are not strange pagan religions or extremist fanatical sects, but well-established and respectable world religions: Christianity in its Catholic and Orthodox versions has shaped European history and Islam has existed on European soil for centuries. Those involved are believers in God in general and in God and Christ in particular.

Thirdly, we should note that this war has another peculiarity. It is a war not between opposing states with more or less delineated frontiers and more or less regular armies, but a war being waged and presented as one between nations as collective entities, involving in a total manner all individuals belonging to those nations and disregarding any other identities they may possess. It is a war which has been depicted and publicly legitimised as a confrontation between presumably irreconcilable types of human culture and civilisation; and in the final analysis, as a legitimate confrontation of totally incompatible worlds. It is a war, therefore, into which the principle of collective responsibility as opposed to that of personal responsibility has been introduced; and this principle has legitimised the elimination of all distinctions between military and civilians, between armed and unarmed, between men and women, between adults and children. It has moreover become legitimate to resort to retaliation on a mass scale as a normal way of waging the war, and to treat all persons and objects identified by a specific national sign as hostile and as legitimate targets. With this aspect of the war being daily underlined by the mass media and the politicians it is not surprising that thousands of people have been murdered, that thousands of houses have been demolished or plundered in regions where no shot has ever been fired, that numerous churches and devotional objects have been destroyed in places otherwise untouched by war operations, that hundreds of thousands of people have been driven from their homes, that thousands of unarmed civilians have been arrested as potential enemies and sent to concentration camps.

Fourthly, another particular feature of the war is that it is not being waged between total strangers against unknown intruders from far away, but between people who yesterday were acquaintances, neighbours, colleagues, friends. Furthermore, the weapons being used are not examples of contemporary high technology that kill and destroy at a distance: these combatants come face to face with their victims and are personal witnesses of the effects of their actions; consequently, the war is waged in an atmosphere of overheated personal emotional commitment. At the same time, this war is not being fought as a strictly professional task requiring only technical knowledge and efficiency: it is more similar to traditional wars which require an emotional commitment on the part of the combatants and their supporters. It is a war, therefore, which feeds on overheated hatred, and it needs the permanent production and reproduction of hatred on a mass scale as its main spiritual fuel. In this sense it is a war in the manner of a *jihad*. A recent commentator has described some current wars as not simply instruments of politics but as signs of identity, expressions of community, ends in themselves.[14] As Torrelli notes, describing modern wars:

> The enemy is the central notion; the war is being waged against him; but in modern wars, in ideological wars, in civil wars the enemy becomes a human type to destroy: he is to be 'converted', or he must disappear; this is a new war between 'believers' and 'heretics'. True religious wars have always been manichaean wars in which the enemy has been satanised.[15]

There is thus no way of avoiding the difficult subject of the role of religion in the production and reproduction of hatred on a mass scale.

Finally, we must take account of the fact that the war is being waged in Europe, in an area that may reasonably be considered, for historical and cultural reasons, as almost the ideal field for practising interconfessional dialogue and ecumenism and working towards multiculturality, multiconfessionality and multinationality as a viable way of life for present and future. The fact is, however, that publicly proclaimed willingness for interconfessional dialogue and ecumenism has not been able to resist increasing social division and conflict. The religious problem is not a failure to agree on the theological interpretation of the *filioque,* or on celibacy, or on the question of women priests or on papal primacy; the problem is a failure to live together in conditions of normality and equality. Interconfessional dialogue and ecumenism seem to belong to history. Never before, except during the Second World War in some regions, has the idea that 'it is impossible to live together with these others' obtained more support or higher legitimacy. Never before has a multinational, multicultural and multiconfessional community been not only declared unviable but stigmatised also as something unnatural, against nature.

The third line of argument to demonstrate the legitimacy of an exploration of the role of religion in the war in former Yugoslavia is predominantly theoretical.

Firstly, the war provides an opportunity for a reexamination of some of Max Weber's ideas and more particularly of their contemporary relevance. I am referring mainly to Weber's idea that an unavoidable polytheism, an irreducible pluralism of gods, or ultimate values, leads inevitably to irreconcilable antagonism as the distinctive feature of the human condition as such. According to A. Giddens, commenting on Weber's ideas, the war in former Yugoslavia seems to suggest that behind ultimate values stands nothing but force, that irreconcilable cultures are defended by conflicting states operating from the home of their power.[16] Have Weber's ideas been superseded by modern history? Are they outdated, or have they preserved their theoretical relevance for the contemporary sociology of religion? We should remember particularly Weber's warning that in the modern age the old gods might well rise again from their tombs and engage once again in their old eternal struggles, leaving to men only the possibility of aligning themselves with one or the other.

Secondly, as Weber did, we should examine the relationship between the religious ethics of human universal brotherliness and politics. Weber concluded that there is an acute tension between the two, which is always connected with power and violence, either manifest or latent.[17] It seems now, in light of recent experience, that this relationship is more complex and more ambivalent. One ought to remember Hobsbawm's thesis that Christianity has been the most fertile greenhouse for universal but competing ideas.[18] Frequently, the acute tension noted by Weber either does not exist, or is easily circumvented, particularly when integral nationalism enters on the scene.[19] At least it seems that the otherness of the 'others' may be easily absolutised in such a way as to put those 'others', with their specific traits, for all practical purposes outside the field otherwise covered by universal human brotherliness. That this is so could, of course, best be demonstrated by an analysis of public reaction to war crimes and misdeeds committed against others by their own side.

Thirdly, we should take note of an interesting set of problems regarding the process of transition to which Patrick Michel draws our attention. Discourse on transition presupposes that the point of departure of the transition as well as the point of arrival have been clearly identified, which is not the case. Michel discusses the role of communism in the development of modern society. On the one hand, there is the view common in the Catholic Church that the Soviet system was the last incarnation of modernity, the last caricature by those who would construct a world without God and the ultimate bastard offspring of the Enlightenment, and that consequently the fall of communism represents the victory of the church over modernity. On the other hand, there is an interpretation of the fall of communism which sees communism as a failed attempt to retard a continuous and global process of disenchantment by substituting a political modality of believing for a religious modality: the fall of communism is thus a further stage in the process of global disenchantment – this time, disenchantment with sacralised politics. According to the latter interpretation, the primary function of religion in the transition from communism has been to compel politics to limit and desacralise itself. Consequently, there are two distinct processes in operation. The first has been inducing the political reinstrumentalisation of religion, which thus becomes one of the reference points for politics and regularly questions the categories of pluralism and therefore of democracy. The second process is longterm, it involves a threefold phenomenon of individualisation, differentiation and rationalisation, and it induces the loss of social relevance of religion. In the final analysis, those who appeal to ultimate and absolute references are facing the champions of democratic politics which, because it operates in conditions of pluralism, has by definition to be located in the relative. After the failure of communism with its ultimate references, sacralised and absolutised, the choice seems to be between politics with ultimate religious references, excluding pluralism (at least at the highest level), and politics with no ultimate references at all, no sacred absolutes, and hence coherently pluralist. Put in the simplest terms, the choice is between politics in a reenchanted and reenchanting world, and politics in a disenchanted and disenchanting world. The consequences of this disjunction are certainly very interesting to examine.[20] The role of religion in the Yugoslav crisis should shed light on the relationship between war and these two alternative types of postcommunist politics.

III

There is no need to develop a lengthy argument in order to show that the major confessions have played an important role in sharpening social divisions and in intensifying social conflict or to demonstrate their involvement in various ways in the war that has broken out. It is, however, important to explore the reasons for this role and involvement. To quote N. Kokosalakis:

> In what was Yugoslavia, of course, the claims for autonomy of the new Republics of Slovenia, Croatia, Servia, Bosnia, etc., and the resultant violent conflicts, are all underpinned by different ethno-religious boundaries between Catholics, Orthodox and Moslems. Now it hardly needs emphasizing that these ethnoreligious identities are immediately connected with the social and political struggles of these people to acquire statehood and a place in a world of scarcity and hard economic realities. Religious conservativism in these circumstances tends to promote political radicalism and violent conflict.[21]

The involvement of the major religious confessions in the war has developed on the basis of the confessional legitimacy previously given to the dominant political strategies. The religious confessions have been variously involved with political strategies in three contexts: firstly, in bringing about the demolition of the atheistic state with the elimination of all previously existing restrictions and institutional pressures on religion and ecclesial organisations and securing complete religious freedom; secondly, in securing independent national states in a complex region where the application of the right to self-determination must disclose the 'chameleonic' nature of this right;[22] and thirdly, in accomplishing radical and rapid transition involving a set of political, economic, ideological and cultural shock therapies.

Conferring confessional legitimacy on such political strategies in general is, however, different from conferring it on a war. To qualify as 'just', a war must traditionally fulfil a number of crucial requirements, including the following: (a) war should be a last resort when all other means have been exhausted; (b) war should clearly be an act of redress of rights actually violated or defence against unjust demands backed by the threat of force; (c) war must be openly and legally declared by properly constituted governments; (d) there must be a reasonable prospect of victory; (e) the means must be proportionate to the ends; (f) the war must be waged in such a way as to distinguish between combatants and noncombatants; (g) the victorious nation must not require the utter humiliation of the vanquished. All the major confessions involved in the war in former Yugoslavia have effectively invoked this same doctrine to legitimate their support for the different and opposed political strategies that have led to the war and consequently for their support for the opposed sides in the war. It should also be noted that the doctrine of 'just war' is being invoked at a time when at least some Christian thinkers have been seriously questioning and revising that doctrine.[23] It is also clear that there are no indications that serious consideration has ever been given to observations such as Reinhold Niebuhr's warning that the Christian faith 'ought to persuade us that political controversies are always conflicts between sinners and not between righteous men and sinners. It ought to mitigate the self-righteousness which is inevitably concomitant to all human conflict.'[24] Finally, it is also important to take into account the generally disregarded possibility that the irony of history may be at work today in the process of transition in this area, as it has been before, involving the possibility of perverse effects of otherwise commendable social

374 *Srdjan Vrcan*

actions.[25] It is thus a legitimate exercise to look more closely at the reasons which have motivated and facilitated confessional options for opposed political strategies, providing religious legitimacy for such strategies and contributing to a more or less total mobilisation of confessional resources for political purposes.

Lying behind this phenomenon is a complex process involving the parallel politicisation of religion and the religionisation of politics, described by R. Robertson as a trend of world dimensions.[26]

Despite occasional criticism and partial dissent, the politicisation of religion has been proceeding steadily in official political circles. It may be detected primarily in a visible political instrumentalisation of religion and in a religious instrumentalisation of politics. The former involves a visible process of mobilisation of all the resources at disposal, including confessional resources, for political purposes in a situation of increasing social conflict. In fact, none of the dominant political strategies that have led to the war had a realistic chance of success without an extended mobilisation of the various existing confessional resources or without obtaining at least some kind of legitimacy in superior religious terms. The latter involves a direct confessional intervention in politics, without which there is no realistic likelihood of a religious *reconquista* of secularised society. This has required the affirmation of each particular confession as the primary legitimating institution, which is able to create and recreate stable loyalty on a mass scale to emerging social and political systems.

The political mobilisation of confessional resources has been brought about in two different ways, described by R. Robertson.[27] A particular religious confession will be favoured as a result of ideological motives and for political purposes which are in themselves of a nonreligious and extrareligious nature; meanwhile a particular political programme will be chosen on the basis of strictly religious commitments and for purely religious motives.

The parallel process of the religionisation of politics has been going on in different ways. The process consists essentially in a tendency to present crucial political concepts as meriting total adherence and unconditional and overheated veneration, in substance religious or parareligious.

The most important aspects of this process have been the following.

1 A systematic and permanent inclination to lend essentially religious attributes and connotations to some key political concepts in everyday usage, even if these are of secular origin, with the evident intention of increasing their non-negotiable attraction and intensifying their emotional charge as well as protecting them by explicit sacralisation from possible political critique and immunising them from public dissent. In this way they are given an ultimate political legitimacy of essentially numinous nature as in political discourse about 'sacred Croatia', 'sacred Serbia', 'celestial Serbia', 'sacred untouchable frontiers', 'sacred will of the nation', 'sacred history of the fatherland' and so on.

2 The ontologising of existing social, political and cultural differences, projecting them on to a metaphysical backdrop. By this means political conflicts are transformed into conflicts, as it were, *sub specie aeternitatis;* they are presented as conflicts between different and opposed human types, between irreconcilable cultures, between antagonistic types of civilisation. The possibility of normal and peaceful coexistence is thus reduced and the acceptable price to be paid for conflict and war is raised.

3 A pervading and systematic manichaeanism is applied to current conflicts, and this leads to one of the opposed parties being portrayed as an angelic personifi-

cation of Good and the other as a diabolic incarnation of Evil. The tendency to depict the two sides as God's and Satan's goes against Weber's expectation that the introduction of God's name into violent political conflicts will be experienced by believers as blasphemy.[28]

4 An interpretation of national history in terms of a sacred martyrology of Calvary made glorious by the quality and quantity of the suffering of the victims that has to be recompensed or revenged in terms of a privileged quasi-salvational historical mission within the eternal plans of Providence, or in terms of a historical dedication of the nation chosen in advance by Heaven in a non-negotiable manner and committed to the celestial cause and spiritual values.

5 The nations involved are eternalised in terms of some kind of *Urvolk* and in terms of their fundamental allegedly suprahistorical immutable qualities.

6 A constant resort in official interpretations of recent political events to a theory of diabolic conspiracy (involving Masons, Jews, the Comintern, the Vatican) against this or that nation.

The end result of this kind of religionisation of politics can be described as the absolutisation and sacralisation of some otherwise controversial political goals or, in Michel's terminology, the reintroduction into politics of ultimate references; the reenchantment of politics. The process is of a structural nature and has social functions which can easily be detected. And it is hard to pretend, in the context of a critical sociological analysis, that such a process has nothing to do with religion.

Behind this whole process lies a very specific concept of the nation which is prevalent in contemporary confessional cultures, Orthodox and Catholic and recently Islamic too. As Schnapper has noted, there are at least two different histories of the nation, two different ideas of the nation which have been permanently opposed to each other, and the histories of the construction of the nation and national ideologies have been different in the eastern and western parts of Europe. 'In various terms theorists of the nation have opposed the nation of Western Europe – civic, voluntary, contractual – to the nation of Eastern Europe – populist, organic, natural, ethnic. The Western European nation of citizens is opposed to the Eastern European nation of ancestors.'[29]

The Western European definition dates back to the French Revolution, and 'defines the nation in non-ethnic terms. This concept of *"nation citoyenne"* is opposed to an ethnically-based definition of the nation.' The crucial element in this definition is 'the idea of the nation as an association of citizens, each of whom possesses certain rights which should be guaranteed and safeguarded by the state.' And this means that the nation is defined on the basis of 'the idea of citizenship and a commitment to pluralism': the nation is not to be understood in terms of a community which is ethnically and culturally homegeneous;[30] it is at least in principle open to all who participate in the common political life. The Eastern European concept of the nation is more ethnic than political, and is based on the idea of exclusive adherence to a collective entity, characterised by cultural homogeneity, which tends to be closed. Political structures are deemed to derive from the *Urvolk*, the preexisting historico-biological community, and the state is seen as the supreme, almost sacred, political incarnation of such a community and its *Wesenswille*, and not necessarily a state based on law and the democratically articulated political will of equal citizens, which is by definition negotiable and open to criticism and contestation as well as to rational and competent public discourse. This latter concept necessarily introduces a discriminatory distinction between citizens of the first order and citizens of the

376   *Srdjan Vrcan*

second order, according to their nationality, or between citizens and subjects, the former enjoying all the rights of citizenship and the latter being denied some of these
basic rights.[31]

Each of the main religions in former Yugoslavia is host to various traditions and
cultural aggregates which can be used, and have been used, to stimulate and legitimate confessional options in support of political strategies in pursuit of the political
ideal of 'one nation, one state, and only one state for each nation' – an ideal which
can hardly be realised in this area without resort to violence. Some of these confessional traditions and cultural aggregates are as follows.

1 There is a tradition which refers to an allegedly insoluble synthesis between the
   respective nationality and confession, insisting that a particular confession has
   been not just one of the important historical and cultural components of the
   nationality in question, but the constituent and constitutive nucleus of the very
   being of that nation as such. An element of transendence and sacredness has
   thus been implanted into the national being itself.
2 There is a traditional belief in the presumed convergence of the national state
   and its particular confession and church, a convergence which leads to the veneration of the national state as such, regardless of how it was established and
   the historical context in which it has developed, and above all regardless of the
   way it is organised and functions. In these circumstances, for a church to stay
   resolutely with its people means that it must also stay resolutely with its
   national state and state politics. The notion of the sacredness of the state has
   been built into the very idea of the national state.
3 There is a tradition which interprets national history as a sacred or quasisacred
   martyrology (in Serbian Orthodoxy) or Calvary (in Croatian Catholicism) of
   the respective nation; this is primarily the consequence of a deliberate historical
   dedication of the nation to religious beliefs and celestial values. In this way
   national history becomes desecularised.
4 There is a tradition which ascribes a specific historical role to a particular nation
   in the history of a particular confession. The nation is described as finding itself
   on a religious frontier, as acting historically as the guardian of this (western or
   eastern) religious frontier and constantly exposed to external threats.
5 There is consequently a well-established tradition of a fundamental historical
   convergence between, on the one hand, the 'national cause' (Serbian or
   Croatian) and, on the other hand, the 'religious cause' (Orthodox or Catholic)
   in the wider arena. And this tradition appears to be reinforced by conditions in
   the modern industrial world. If, as Ernest Gellner argues, the function of the
   nation state in the modern industrial world is essentially that of a necessary
   political roof over a common culture, then there is an important twofold consequence for the former Yugoslav area: firstly, a particular religion as a crucial
   element in a common shared culture requires by necessity a specific political
   national roof over it in an otherwise pluricultural and pluriconfessional region;
   and, secondly, a state which claims to function as a political roof over a shared
   national culture in an otherwise pluricultural and pluriconfessional region must
   obtain an essentially religious legitimacy and generate the required cultural
   homogeneity in religious terms too. There is consequently a mutual reinforcement of two parallel absolutisms: national and confessional.
6 Finally, there is a tradition which regards those of a different confession as
   schismatics, heretics or infidels. This easily leads to the negative absolutisation

of confessional and national 'otherness' and lends a kind of superior legitimacy to political ideas which proclaim the impossibility of living together in a peaceful, democratic and durable way with those of different confessions and nationalities.

In my view we must come to the conclusion that the war in the former Yugoslavia is not a classical religious war of the type well known from history, but is nevertheless a war in which religion is deeply involved and consciously engaged. At the same time, the war has some of the characteristics of a war of faiths, if a war of faiths means a conflict of creed against creed (*'croire contre croire'*, as Michel has put it[32]); but the faiths involved represent a mixture of confessional and worldly components, including absolutisations, sacralisations and reenchantments. It has to be said that the course of events in the Yugoslav crisis has shown that the confessions operating in the area have been more able to divide than to unite, to oppose than to conciliate, to inflame than to placate.[33]

Notes and References

[1] 'The term "holy war" has been, and is, applied to wars which are in some way the contest of God himself. Holy wars appear as wars which have been commanded. Their legitimacy does not allow of any debate: a holy war must lead to the total elimination of the opponent, who is the enemy of God himself ... A holy war is not only a just war; it is more than a necessary evil which ought to be limited; it is a positive good; it contributes to the accomplishment of God's kingdom; it executes God's will.' J. Touscoz, 'La guerre juste: quelques remarques sur les doctrines du judaisme, du catholicism et de l'islam', in M. Torrelli (ed.), *Religion et Guerres* (Mami, Nice, 1992), p. 93.

[2] F. Vreg, 'Iluzije o evropskem multikulturalizmu', *Teorija in praksa*, vol. 30, nos 7–8, 1993, p. 664.

[3] E. Gellner, *Nations and Nationalism* (Basil Blackwell, Oxford, 1986), p. 101.

[4] B. Barber, 'Džihad protiv McWorld', *Teorijia in praksa*, vol. 29, nos. 9–10, 1992, p. 843.

[5] M. Torrelli, 'Introduction', *Religion et Guerres*, p. 9.

[6] C. Offe, 'Capitalism by democratic design? Democratic theory facing the triple transition in East Central Europe', *Social Research*, vol. 58, no. 4, 1991, p. 869.

[7] N. Kokasalakis, 'The historical continuity and cultural specificity of Eastern Orthodox Christianity', in *Conferenza Internazionale su 'Religions sans frontières?' Tendeze presenti e future di migrazione, cultura e comunicazione* (Università degli Studi di Roma 'La Sapienza', Rome, 1993), p. 94.

[8] P. Michel, 'Pour une sociologie des itinéraires de sens: une lecture politique du rapport entre croire et institution', *Archives de sciences sociales des religions*, vol. 82, 1993, pp. 223–38.

[9] O. Kallscheur, *So All European Roads Lead to (West) Rome*, (Institut für Wissenschaften vom Menschen, Vienna, 1993), p. 8.

[10] J. Coleman, 'Social cleavages and religious conflicts', *The Journal of Social Issues*, no. 12, 1956, p. 46.

[11] *loc. cit.*

[12] E. Poulat, *Liberté, laïcité* (du Cerf, Cujas, Paris, 1987). As a credible witness may be taken Ševko Omerpašić, the head of the Islamic community for Croatia and Slovenia. See his interview in *Feral Tribune* (Split), 23 September 1993, p. 3.

[13] J. L. Piveteau, 'L'Ancien Testament a-t-il contribué à la territorialisation de la Suisse?' *Social Compass*, vol. 40, no. 2, 1993, p. 169.

[14] Barber, *op. cit.*, p. 843.

[15] Torrelli, op. cit., p. 23.

[16] A. Giddens, *The Nation State and Violence* (Polity Press, Cambridge, 1992), p. 185.

378   *Srdjan Vrcan*

[17]   H. H. Gerth and C. W. Mills, *From Max Weber: Essays in Sociology* (Oxford University Press, New York, 1958), pp. 333–5.

[18]   Eric Hobsbawm, *Nacije i nacionalizam* (Liber, Zagreb, 1992), p. 71.

[19]   The term 'integral nationalism' is taken from J. Schwarzmantel, who writes that 'traditional or "integral nationalism" has invoked an idea of "one nation, one state", where the nation has been claimed to be totally culturally united, as having supposedly homogeneous character.' J. Schwarzmantel, 'Nation versus class: nationalism and socialism in theory and practice', in J. Oakley (ed.). *The Social Origin of Nationalist Movements* (Sage, London, 1992), p. 57.

[20]   Michel, *op. cit.*

[21]   N. Kokosalakis, 'Religion and the dynamics of social change in contemporary Europe', *Archives de sciences sociales des religions*, no. 81, 1993, p. 145.

[22]   The term is taken from B. Neuberger, 'Samoodločba narodov-konceptualne dileme', *Novarevija*, vol. 13, nos 141–2, 1994, p. 157.

[23]   See, for instance, G. Labouerie, 'A propos de guerre juste', in *Religion et Guerres*, p. 110. He insists that 'there are no just wars, there are inevitable wars, wars connected with our freedom and its practice'. He refers to the Vatican II assertion that 'war must never be regarded as a means of establishing justice among peoples' (*ibid.*, p. 243).

[24]   Quoted in J. B. Elshtan, *Women and War* (Basic Books, Boston, 1987), p. 187.

[25]   R. Boudon, *Il posto del disordine* (Il Mulino, Bologna, 1985), p. 258.

[26]   R. Robertson, 'Globalization, politics and religion', in J. Beckford and T. Luckman (eds), *The Changing Face of Religion* (Sage, London, 1989), p. 12.

[27]   *ibid.* p. 19.

[28]   Gerth and Mills, *op cit.,* p. 334.

[29]   D. Schnapper, 'Les sens de l'ethnico-religieux', *Archives des sciences sociales des religions*, no. 81, 1993, p. 155.

[30]   Schwarzmantel, *loc. cit.*

[31]   J. Habermas has pointed to tensions existing between the generalisation of human rights and nationalism, asserting that 'the abstract generalised idea of democracy and human rights constitutes a solid point of reference upon which traditional national concepts – the language, literature and history of one nation – break down.' J. Habermas, 'Per una idea razionale di patria', *Micromega*, no. 3, 1987, p. 131.

[32]   Michel, *op. cit*, p. 228.

[33]   In this respect we should take into account critical views such as those expressed by Barber (*op. cit.*, p. 844) to the effect that whereas in the past such monotheistic faiths as Judaism, Christianity and Islam were characterised by an enlightened universalism, in their modern incarnations they tend to be parochial rather than cosmopolitan, fuelled by hatred rather than love, proselytic rather than ecumenical, fanatical rather than rational, sectarian rather than deistic, ethnocentric rather than universalist, with the result that as new forms of hypernationalism they are schismatic and secessionist, and never integrative.

[7]

This article questions a widely shared assumption that posits the incompatibility of religious politics and democracy. Using evidence from an analytically significant case, Belgium, it explores the political and institutional conditions under which religiously motivated aliberal political actors integrate successfully into democratic institutions. The interaction of three factors is shown to be crucial: a political shift affecting the religious actor negatively, the existence of competitive institutions, and a centralized religious structure. The main theoretical implication is that democratic consolidation can be the contingent outcome of self-interested political strategy rather than the result of the pursuit of normative principles. The article underlines the institutional and political context in which religious movements are embedded (as opposed to their political theologies) and the centrality of agency and strategic calculation. It advocates placing the study of religion and politics in a more broad theoretical perspective and the study of democratization in a wider historical context.

DEMOCRACY AND RELIGIOUS POLITICS
Evidence From Belgium

STATHIS N. KALYVAS
New York University

I t is a common belief that religious fundamentalism—the appeal for a return to the literal reading of a holy text and its application to politics and society—is a major threat to democracy. Concern about the expansion

AUTHOR'S NOTE: *Research for this article was funded in part by New York University's Institute for Advanced European Studies. I thank Emmanuel Gérard, Staff Hellemans, Emiel Lamberts, and Boris Libois for their help in Belgium and Jan De Maeyer for providing me with access to KADOC's facilities in Leuven. For their comments on previous versions, I am grateful to Stefano Bartolini, Ivan Ermakoff, Staff Hellemans, Marcus Kreuzer, David Laitin, Gabriella Montinola, Adam Przeworski, Alex Schuessler, Daniel Verdier, and Libby Wood as well as participants in the "Catholic Politics and the Politics of Catholicism" panel of the Tenth International Conference of Europeanists, the New York University Politics Research Collo-quium, and the European University Institute's Comparative Politics seminar. The usual caveat applies.*

COMPARATIVE POLITICAL STUDIES, Vol. 31 No. 3, June 1998 292-320
© 1998 Sage Publications, Inc.

and impact of religiously inspired politics is widespread, and the demise of communism has turned Islamism into the most dangerous enemy of liberal democracy (Sartori, 1991). Religious politics is thought to be structurally inimical to democratic development for two reasons. First, it is highly ideological, hence, intolerant and not amenable to compromise—a crucial aspect of democratic politics: The "injection of religion into political controversies tends to hamper working out the pragmatic accommodations needed by a functioning democracy" (Reichley, 1986, p. 801). Second, fundamentalist movements promote an aliberal and antisecular project that openly defies the very foundations of liberal democracy, not to say modernity altogether.

This article presents empirical evidence to qualify the thesis of the structural incompatibility between religious politics and liberal democracy.[1] It demonstrates that under certain political and institutional conditions, successful religious mobilization in politics is compatible with democratic development. Religious movements entering politics with a theocratic and aliberal project can possibly consolidate democracies. In particular, I provide evidence to support the following two claims: Democratic development is possible in the initial absence of an ideological commitment to democracy by major political actors, and the mechanism of the gradual evolution of aliberal political forces toward democracy can be strategic self-interest rather than normative commitment. The main theoretical implication is that democracy can be the contingent outcome of self-interested political strategy rather than the result of the pursuit of normative principles. This article stresses the need for a sustained focus on the institutional and political context in which religious movements are embedded, as opposed to their political theologies and assorted religious scriptures and traditions; it underlines, as well, the centrality of agency and strategic calculation in the process of democratic consolidation.

I provide empirical evidence from the widely overlooked European experience. Nineteenth-century Europe, a region in which extremely intense political conflict coincided with the building of liberal democratic institutions, experienced the rise of aliberal religious movements and parties that challenged the very foundations of the emerging liberal order (Kalyvas, 1996). Explaining the ways in which these movements were incorporated into liberal regimes carries empirical and theoretical relevance that transcends the European 19th century.

1. In this article, democracy is minimally defined as a regime in which governmental offices are filled as a consequence of contested elections (Przeworski, Alvarez, Cheibub, & Limongi, 1995).

I focus on Belgium, an analytically significant case. Linz (1978) has underlined the need to study "old democracies" because they "were once new, beset by the risks facing all new democracies" (p. 8). Belgium is one of the few democratic regimes that have enjoyed a stable existence for more than a generation. Yet, to reach this point it had to overcome formidable challenges, including acutely polarized politics around religion. Although aliberal Catholic movements were created almost everywhere in Europe, only in Belgium did a Catholic party win an electoral majority and govern without allies.[2] Yet, not only did Belgian democracy survive but it gradually expanded. How was that possible, given that it was for a long time supported only by the Liberals and opposed by almost everyone else? I show that three factors combined to create a dynamic that made possible the democratic evolution of the Catholic movement and the consolidation of the fledging democratic regime in Belgium: a political shift negatively affecting the religious actor, the existence of competitive institutions, and a centralized religious structure.

I begin with introductory remarks about religion and democracy. Then, I provide some background on the Catholic movement and the Belgian case. I unpack the Belgian Catholic movement into its three components—moderate political insiders, radical grassroots outsiders, and a centralized church—and analyze the structure of interaction among these actors. I critically examine a number of arguments that address the democratic evolution of the Catholic movement and I introduce an alternative argument based on the interaction between political and institutional contexts. I show that the consolidation of Belgian democracy was the contingent by-product of the self-interested strategic actions of the Church and the moderate Catholics. I close with a discussion of the interaction between ideology and strategy.

RELIGION AND DEMOCRACY, NORMATIVE COMMITMENT, AND SELF- INTEREST

The relationship between religiously motivated politics and democratic development can take four different forms, depending on the ideological underpinning of religious mobilization and the institutional context in which it unfolds: The agent of religious mobilization can be motivated by democratic (or nondemocratic) principles and values, and this mobilization can develop under an authoritarian or democratic regime. Table 1 maps this variation.

2. During the same period, the Netherlands had a government based on a coalition of Protestant and Catholic parties. However, these parties' denominational differences led to their mutual neutralization with respect to their overarching political project.

Table 1
Religious Mobilization

	Democratic	Nondemocratic
Institutional context democratic	DD	DN
Nondemocratic	ND	NN

Note: D = democratic; N= nondemocratic.

Table 1 illustrates a central problem in the study of religion and politics. Research is usually based on a truncated sample in which religion is politically activated by nondemocratic actors in an authoritarian context and results in authoritarian outcomes (Cell NN). In other words, context and values covary in an authoritarian direction. Yet, the outcome is accounted for by an exclusive reference to the values held by the religious movement, leading to a potentially biased inference. Moreover, the results of such research are generalized (often implicitly) to the hypothetical cases of Cell DN (Cell DD is considered to be empty). There is a reason for this bias: Religious mobilization has seldom been successful, particularly under democracy. Electoral majorities are rare instances in general and religious mobilization, like class mobilization, has rarely resulted in electoral victories (Przeworski, 1991, p. 36). Thus, overwhelming attention is paid to very few cases: In this context, Iran looms gigantic.

Instead, I focus on a case in which ideology and institutional context can be disaggregated. I ask the following question: Can religious movements, even when ideologically hostile to liberal democracy, sustain a liberal regime? If yes, how? My intention is to specify when the logic of political competition within a liberal regime and the constraints imposed by competitive politics on political actors shape political action in an opposite direction from that predicted by ideology. If the politicization of religion and the rise of aliberal religious movements is not inherently destructive of democracy, it is necessary to identify the conditions under which ideologically motivated actors make choices that go against their own principles.

The debate about religion and politics is part of the larger issue of democratization. According to the relevant literature, democratic consolidation[3] requires a commitment to democracy by the main political and social actors: "The absence of serious conflict among politically significant groups

3. Democratic regimes become consolidated when "all politically significant groups regard its key political institutions as the only legitimate framework for political contestation, and adhere to the democratic rules of the game" (Gunther, Dianandouros, Nikiforos, & Puhle, 1995, p. 7).

over the acceptability of the basic framework of political contestation [is] central for regime sustainability and democratic persistence" (Gunther et al., 1995, p. 15). Accordingly, a broad indicator of consolidation is "the absence of a politically significant antisystem party or social movement" (Gunther et al., 1995, p. 13; Linz & Stepan, 1996, p. 16). As Przeworski (1991) remarks, "The literature on democracy is full of the language of values and moral commitments" (p. 24). According to this view, democrats make democracies.

It follows that democracies in which significant political forces are antidemocratic remain unconsolidated and their prospects are grim. Demonstrating that democratic development is possible in the initial absence of an ideological commitment to democracy by major political actors lends support to an alternative view of democratization (and democracy), which posits that the compliance of political actors to democratic rules is independent of their ideological preferences and may result from the strategic pursuit of their interests under certain institutional conditions: Democracy is a spontaneous and self-enforced equilibrium (Przeworski, 1991). In other words, democracies make democrats.

Because of their ideological bias, religious movements are an ideal testing ground for determining whether the strategic pursuit of interests is a better predictor of political action than ideology. Furthermore, showing that actors who place an extreme emphasis on doctrine and ideology act strategically on the basis of cost-benefit calculations, even when this means sacrificing their core principles, allows for the specification of the mechanisms through which principles are subverted by pragmatism.

Belgium satisfies the following requirements: It has a religious cleavage coupled with religious mobilization, an ideological preference for an aliberal/nondemocratic regime by the agent of this mobilization, competitive (although not necessarily all-inclusive) political institutions, and democratic consolidation (instead of breakdown) following an electoral victory by a party associated with religious mobilization. By narrowing the empirical focus to a case in which a religiously inspired party had the practical possibility of restricting or destroying a parliamentary regime through its unshared control of the government for a period spanning 30 years, but did not, I isolate the elements that account for the nonauthoritarian evolution of religious politics.

CATHOLICISM, LIBERALISM, AND DEMOCRACY

The ongoing debate on religion and politics has surprisingly overlooked Catholicism. Despite being considered an integral part of the Western tradition, Catholicism has routinely been singled out as hostile to democracy. For instance, Huntington (1991) has pointed out that "Catholicism was associated with the absence of democracy or with limited or late democratic development" (p. 75). During the second half of the 19th century, the Catholic Church produced an ideological project (best expressed in the 1864 papal encyclical *Quanta Cura* and its annex, the *Syllabus Errorum*) whose opposition to political liberalism, democracy, and human rights was "implacable" (Hehir, 1993, p. 15). The Catholic Church (hereafter referred to as the Church) denounced liberalism; the freedoms of speech, conscience, religion, and press; the doctrine of progress; the separation of state and church; the legal equality of cults; the sovereignty of the people; and the modern conception of civilization. It condemned as a grave error the belief that a regime that did not repress the violators of Catholic religion could be good.

The Church became the agent of sustained religious mobilization by building a Catholic mass movement. A political expression of integral or ultramontane Catholicism, this movement acquired a structure equivalent of the Church's: Hierarchical and stratified, it was based on "the absolute power of bishops over priests and priests over laymen" (Gabbert, 1978, p. 643). Built outside of liberal political institutions, this movement sought their destruction. Like early socialists, the Church thought that liberal democracy was not a viable regime. By creating a distinct Catholic society (or subculture) within secular society, a real country that is hostile and opposed to the legal country, it sought to build a *societas christiana* (Christian society) that was based on restrictions of individual freedom, organicist conceptions of representation, and fusion of state and church. Supreme authority would be wielded by spiritual leaders, and all ideological or religious projects contrary to Catholic dogma would be forbidden (Birnbaum, 1991, p. 580; de la Cueva, 1996, p. 248; Zwart, 1997, pp. 243-245). Although such a project appeared utopian to many, the prospect of an authoritarian regime closely associated with the Church was certainly not unrealistic: witness, among others, Franco's Spain, Salazar's Portugal, Concordat, and, later, Dollfuss's Austria and Vichy France.

However, not only did the Catholic movement not destroy democracy but it ended up consolidating it. As Linz (1978) points out, "Some of the political movements identified with the Catholic Church and inspired by the fulminations against the liberal democratic state of the *Syllabus* were to become the strongest supporters of various democratic political systems in the second half of the twentieth century" (p. 29). This paradox has been identified as well by Berger (1987): "Paradoxically, despite the church's hostility to the state and its attempts to encapsulate Catholics in a world as impermeable as possible to the influences of secular and liberal society, the impact of this subcultural development was in many ways to consolidate and stabilize the political and social order" (p. 128). Despite its obvious significance, however, this paradox has never being explained.[4]

An immediate explanation of why Catholic movements did not undermine democracy is simply that they were rarely able to run their countries and, thus, apply their program. Under these conditions, they indeed had to recognize "that their theocratic ideals were no longer realistic" (Zwart, 1997, p. 244). However, this explanation does not hold for the case of Belgium, in which a party supported by and identified with a Catholic movement won a landslide victory in the 1884 elections and governed the country alone and without interruption for the following 30 years. The Belgian Catholic government did not reverse the liberal political institutions that it had inherited and even proved quite moderate in the implementation of clerical reforms, often displeasing the Church. This development stands in sharp contrast to the "slow and arduous journey towards political democracy of the institutional Church" (Papini, 1993, p. 49), which officially accepted democracy only in 1944.

BELGIUM: HISTORICAL BACKGROUND

Belgium was created in 1830, following a revolt against the king of the Netherlands. The new kingdom acquired a liberal constitution, which guaranteed individual freedoms and allowed the Church to develop freely. The compromise between Liberals and pro-Catholic Conservatives, known as unionism, was reflected in the nonpartisan cabinets that governed the country until 1847. Still, this compromise was fragile. It was, moreover, an elite arrangement that excluded the immense nonvoting majority of the Belgian population.

The growing division of the political class led to the emergence of partisan politics. This division was primarily fueled by the Liberals, who first formed a party in 1846, as well as the first partisan Belgian cabinet in 1847. After 1857, they began to challenge the constitutional compromise by introducing policy measures that reduced the power of the Church. Although mild, these measures had a big effect on Catholics who felt that the constitutional pact was violated by the Liberals (Laury, 1979, pp. 51-53). Conservatives, although generally defending the rights of the Church, were not a religious party. When they decided to form a political organization to compete with the Liberals in

4. For instance, it has been argued that the transformation of the Catholic movement was due to "diverse causes and numerous factors," such as the mutations of the Church and the pontificate, general psychological and generational factors, "social mutations," ideological and political pressures from adversaries, and the "will to defeat the liberal supremacy and leave the Catholic ghetto" (Vecchio, 1987, p. 7). Obviously, these arguments beg the question.

1858, they named it *Association Constitutionelle Conservatrice*, a name denoting both their support for the constitution and their conservative (as opposed to openly Catholic) outlook. Although the Liberals grew increasingly anticlerical, the Conservatives kept a moderate stance, thus provoking the ire of the episcopate and the hostility of many Catholics who felt unrepresented (Lamberts, 1984b, p. 52; Simon, 1961b, p. 13). Altogether, the combination of Liberal anticlericalism and Conservative moderation led a growing segment of Catholics to agitate for the formation of a truly Catholic party, which would promote an aliberal constitutional revision as a first step toward a clerical evolution of the regime. Polarization around the issue of religion culminated following the 1878 Liberal victory. Liberals passed an education law that drastically reduced the Church's privileges. The Church responded by mobilizing its flock. The conflict, known as "school war," quickly escalated into a "true ideological civil war" (Witte & Craeybeckx, 1987, p. 54). The Conservative victory in the 1884 elections marked both the mutation of the parliamentary Right into a confessional party based on the mass Catholic movement and the consolidation of the Belgian liberal regime.

Political movements are rarely monolithic, and the Belgian Catholic movement was no exception. To explain its evolution and transformation, it is necessary to focus on its internal dynamics in a way that is sensitive to the political context in which it is nested. Three actors can be distinguished: the Church, expressed by both its national and transnational leadership (the episcopate and the Vatican);[5] the moderates of the parliamentary Conservative Party; and the radicals, controlling the Catholic press and the grassroots associations.

During the late 1870s and early 1880s, a "harsh struggle" (Simon, 1961b, p. 11) took place between moderate conservative parliamentarians and radical Catholics, with the Church acting as the arbiter. The focal issue of this conflict was the aliberal revision of the Belgian constitution. This conflict between "the ultramontanes and the liberal Catholics, anticonstitutionals and constitutionals, [or] intransigent and moderates" (Simon, 1961b, p. 11) was eventually resolved by an intervention of the Church in favor of the moderates prior to the crucial 1884 elections. Radicals were eliminated from the Catholic movement before the Catholic victory at the polls. This intervention accounts for the moderate evolution of the Catholic movement. Understanding, therefore, the trajectory of the Belgian Catholic movement requires a precise answer to the following question: Why did the Church, given its

5. Lay Catholics and low clergy were excluded from the government of the Church. The episcopate maintained the lower clergy in "the strictest obedience" and exercised an authority that was "quasi-dittatoria" (Simon, 1961a, pp. 30-31).

antidemocratic and antiliberal leanings, choose to support the moderates? Fortunately, recent historical research and published archival material allow for a precise answer to this crucial question.

THE ACTORS

The Church

The Church played an active role in the formation of the Belgian state and accepted the 1830 constitution, which preserved its power and influence. Still, it viewed its acceptance of the constitution as a compromise, a modus vivendi, that did not respond to the Catholic ideal (Simon, 1961b, p. 28). As Simon (1961a) points out, "We cannot say that the [bishops] had a constitutional spirit" (p. 29). In the 1860s, as the Vatican became increasingly vocal about its rejection of liberalism, some theologians attempted to cope with the growing contradiction between practical politics and ideological principles. They came up with a distinction between the thesis (i.e., the truly Christian society in which the division between civil and religious spheres did not exist) and the (liberal) hypothesis (i.e., the situation imposed by the circumstances). As long as the Belgian constitution provided a framework within which the Church could freely develop, the hypothesis was accepted. This fragile balance was upset in the 1860s when the Liberals became increasingly anticlerical, challenging the constitutional pact and undermining the Church's support for the constitution. During the 1870s, most bishops adopted at least a moderate version of the ultramontane theses (Lamberts, 1984b, p. 52; Witte & Craeybeckx, 1987, p. 87). By 1878, the episcopate was evenly divided about openly condemning the constitution. However, it permitted the agitation of the radicals against the constitution and the parliamentary Right (Soete, 1986, p. 46).

The Ultramontanes

The Ultramontanes were a small but growing and very influential group composed of deeply faithful lay Catholics, mostly of landed noble or upper bourgeois extraction. They set up close-knit associations whose project, epitomized by the motto *Instaurare omnia in Christo* (Restore everything in Christ), was the "restoration of the social reign of Jesus Christ" (Simon, 1956, p. 108; Vander Vorst-Zeegers, 1965, p. 265).[6] Although relatively few, prob-

6. The most important groups were the Croisés de Saint Pierre (founded in 1871) and the Confrérie de Saint-Michel (founded in 1875). Their chief ideologue was a law professor at the Catholic University of Louvain, Henri Périn (1815-1905). Leaders included the engineer and

ably even a minority among Catholic elites, the Ultramontanes were far from marginal. They enjoyed wide legitimacy within the Catholic world and were taken seriously by their opponents; they were very close to prominent bishops, expressed the aspirations of the lower clergy, controlled almost the totality of the Catholic press, and were building a growing network of popular associations. As a result, their influence was disproportionate to their size. Indeed, the Conservative leader Charles Woeste (1878, p. 166) observed in 1878 that although the radicals were political outsiders, their influence in the country was quickly growing. Likewise, the Liberal leader W. Frère-Orban placed the two groups on equal footing when he remarked in 1879 that "there are two Catholic parties, one favorable and the other hostile to the constitution" (cited in van Zuylen, 1955, p. 1906).

The Ultramontanes' political weight flowed from three sources. The first was their ability to influence public opinion through their newspapers, which dominated the Catholic press.[7] Only one important pro-Catholic newspaper, the *Journal de Bruxelles* (*JdB*), whose influence was limited to the Catholic nobility and upper bourgeoisie of Brussels, supported the parliamentary Right and the constitution; an open war was waged against it by all other Catholic newspapers and many bishops, including the Belgian archbishop Mgr. Dechamps (Vander Vorst-Zeegers, 1965, pp. 295-300, 304). Second, the Ultramontanes had a close, almost intimate, relationship with the Roman Curia during the tenure of Pope Pius IX and were openly supported by half of the Belgian episcopate.[8] In fact, although the bishops were divided about tactics, they were, in terms of ideology, closer to the Ultramontanes than to the moderates. Auguste d'Anethan, a prominent member of the parliamentary Right, complained in a 1878 letter to archbishop Dechamps that "what makes

---

architect Arthur Verhaegen (1847-1917) and the wealthy Ghent textile industrialist Joseph de Hemptinne (1822-1909). This is an example of their ideas: "Question: Can you cite deviations to the law of God which we are never allowed to tolerate? Response: Yes, such are the freedom of consciousness, of cults, of the press, and others of the same kind, proclaimed by the revolutionaries at the end of the last century" (Hemptinne, 1877, pp. 7-8).

7. The ultramontane press included the *Bien Public*, *Le Catholique*, *Le Courrier de Bruxelles* (representing the ideas of the Confrérie Saint-Michel) and the weekly *La Croix*, all funded by de Hemptinne. According to Lamberts (1984a), these militant newspapers diffused the ultramontane ideas among "all strata of the population" (p. 60). P. de Haullevile, the director of the moderate *JdB* (cited in Vander Vorst- Zeegers, 1965), called the *Bien Public* "a work of absolute religious devotion administered, so to speak, by a confraternity of Catholic writers" (p. 168).

8. Pius IX's support for the radicals was open and unequivocal (Lamberts, 1984b). The same was true for most nuncios. According to Simon (1956), the nuncio, Mgr. Cattani, "was one of those responsible for the fervent, even mystical, thrust of the ultramontanes" (p. 37). As van Zuylen (1955) put it, the Ultramontanes "knew that they were encouraged and supported in the Curia by personalities of the first plan and had all reason to consider themselves representatives of the real opinions of the Holy See" (p. 1723).

the situation grave, is that all [ultramontane] newspapers . . . have at least received public encouragement from the bishops . . . whereas the episcopal hostility against the *Journal de Bruxelles* has been evident and, in any case, there has been an instigation to cancel subscriptions to this only instrument of the Parliamentary Right"[9] (cited in Vander Vorst-Zeegers, 1965, p. 257). Moreover, the lower clergy enthusiastically supported the most radical ultramontane theses (Vander Vorst-Zeegers, 1965, p. 175; Woeste, 1927, p. 204).[10] As Vander Vorst-Zeegers (1965) concludes, the "very high level of harshness" reached by the conflict between the two Catholic camps was due to the fact "that the ultramontanes felt supported by ecclesiastical authority" (p. 273). Finally, the publication of the *Syllabus* fueled the growth of ultramontanism. The official outright rejection of liberalism legitimized the ultramontane movement and made possible the open critique of the Belgian regime. After the *Syllabus*, there could be no doubt: Insofar as ideology was concerned, the Ultramontanes represented official Catholicism.

The Conservatives

The Conservatives kept a moderate stance on issues related to state and church relations. Although opposed to liberalism in principle, they recognized that the circumstances forced them to accept the constitutional regime as the least bad (Vander Vorst-Zeegers, 1965, p. 294). As one of them put it, "For us, the ideal would be a Christian monarchy. . . . We can loyally accept a situation which is quite away from this ideal, but under one condition only, that . . . a God-State is not established against us" (Hauleville, 1876, p. 138). Conservatives were concerned about the defense of the Church's rights but not at the cost of their more immediate political goals. They refused to be exclusively associated with religion and the Church, were opposed to the adoption of a religiously oriented political program, and argued that religious agitation would be harmful to both party and church (Kalyvas, 1996, pp. 58-60; Vander Vorst-Zeegers, 1965, p. 294). Above all, Conservatives rejected the formation of a confessional party (Preneel, 1982). As a prominent Conservative, Adolphe Dechamps, said, "The constitution of a Catholic party is a peril, a misfortune for everyone, and particularly for religion" (cited in Soete, 1986, p. 201). As political insiders, the Conservatives were politically stronger than the Ultramontanes. They had total control over candidate

9. In fact, Dechamps rejected d'Anethan's repeated pleas for a public episcopal approval of the *JdB* (Vander Vorst-Zeegers, 1965, p. 257).

10. According to Woeste (1927), *"maints ecclésiastiques négligeaient l'hypothèse pour la thèse"* (p. 149).

nominations for elections, and they used it to lock the Ultramontanes out of parliamentary politics. This situation was resented by the Ultramontanes, who began to challenge the Conservative political dominance.

THE CONFLICT

During the second half of the 1870s, the Ultramontane attacks against the Conservatives and the constitution reached new heights (van Zuylen, 1955, p. 1713). Following a public petition to the king alluding to a constitutional revision in a Christian direction (1875), the Ultramontanes issued a political program and attacked the Conservative Right, thus launching a public debate about the constitution in Catholic newspapers and reviews. The moderates accused the radicals of seeking "to substitute constitutional politics with theological ones," aspiring "to overthrow all our political organization," and "unfurling a revolutionary flag," 1878). This conflict peaked in 1878, creating a climate of "mistrust, even hatred" among Catholics (Vander Vorst-Zeegers, 1965, pp. 253, 297).

The 1878 elections were won by the Liberals who, exceeding all expectations, initiated their most resolutely anticlerical program. On July 10, 1879, they passed the van Humbeck law, which stipulated that the state would take over primary education. The Church was pushed out, particularly through the abolition of its right to inspect schools, the replacement of clerical by lay personnel, and the reduction of religious instruction in primary schools. This law, dubbed by Catholics as *loi de malheur* (law of misfortune), was followed by a government-initiated break of diplomatic relations with the Vatican (1880), a law on secondary education (1881), and a law making attendance in primary schools compulsory (1883). The impact of the Liberal victory and its aftermath was, thus, momentous. Ultramontanes and moderates braced for what appeared to be the most crucial confrontation within the Catholic camp. The former published a political platform, whereas the latter drafted a memorandum to the Vatican. These documents shared one point: the demand for the direct and unequivocal elimination of the other side. For the Church, this amounted to choosing an exclusive political agent.

The Ultramontanes made their most ambitious public bid for the leadership of political Catholicism just before the 1878 elections. In a pamphlet titled *Catholique et Politique*, they laid out their ideas and drafted a realistic ("possible" as they called it) political program (Verhaegen, 1878b, p. 3). Its main thrust was the denial of the possibility of a separation between religion and politics. A central place was reserved for attacking the parliamentary Right, which was accused of being exceedingly moderate when it came to matters of religion and of lacking not only a real program but also the program "of the Church itself" (Verhaegen, 1878b, pp. 4, 6, 8): If Conservatives accepted as individuals the authority of the Church in their private life, they ought to do the same as politicians in their political life. The pamphlet proposed the wholesale and immediate substitution of the parliamentary Right by a truly Catholic party "frankly hoisting the catholic flag in both public and private life" (Verhaegen, 1878b, p. 14). Although they promised to initially respect the constitution, this respect was to be both conditional and temporary. Indeed, they flatly rejected the constitution: "We believe, together with the Church and like the Church, that the principles which flow from the Belgian Constitution are false and subversive, that the separation of Church and State is bad, and that the Constitution, in itself, is bad" (Verhaegen, 1878b, p. 15). They pointed out that the constitution was nothing more than a pact, which was unfair to the Church and carried no moral implications. Therefore, they agreed to "tolerate" it so long as the Catholic Church "would permit us to do so," without forgetting that this toleration was not justified by the constitution itself but by the attitude of the Church (Verhaegen, 1878b, pp. 3, 16). Given the right opportunity, they would seek a constitutional revision.

At the same time, the Ultramontanes sent a confidential memorandum to the episcopate making a clear bid for their entry into party politics or, as they put it, for the "Catholic restoration" of the Conservative Party. They stressed the opposition between the parliamentary Right and the Catholic country, which, they argued, grew every day because both sides "march rapidly in opposite directions." "While Catholics follow the papacy," the memorandum claimed, "the Right becomes *liberal catholic or state catholic*" (cited in Simon, 1955, p. 148). They argued that the Catholic cause was condemned irrespective of the electoral outcome: If it won, the Right would quickly become indistinguishable from the Liberals, whereas if it lost, it would be incapable of inspiring the Catholics. The Church ought to "choose truly catholic candidates [to] modify in a substantial, though gradual way, the deplorable parliamentary situation of the Catholic party" (cited in Simon, 1955, p. 153).

The 1878 Liberal victory intensified the ultramontane offensive because "liberalism in power accomplished the demonstration begun by the previous [Conservative] cabinet, of the incompatibility between constitutional freedoms and freedoms for the Church—even its existence," 1878). The defeat of the Right proved the failure of its moderate strategy and provided the opportunity for its overhaul into a "plainly Catholic party" (Simon, 1956, p. 108; Verhaegen, 1878a, p. 7). The *Bien Public* demanded the introduction of the "integral formula of Christian public law" (Vander Vorst-Zeegers, 1965,

p. 253); regional committees of "Catholic interests" were planned, and in June 1878, the ultramontane leader, Périn, announced that the time had finally come to publicly announce the constitution of a Catholic party (Simon, 1956, p. 326).

Conservatives reacted aggressively. They linked their fate to that of the Church: "If the present situation goes on, the parliamentary right will not be able to continue its mandate; it will be increasingly weakened; the liberals will grow in power and audacity and, under their persistent action, the faith of the populations will be singularly compromised" (Woeste, 1927, p. 160). Reacting to the neutrality of the episcopate, they drafted an official party memorandum (August 20, 1878) asking the pope to condemn the ultramontane attacks against the constitution and their party. They argued that the division among Catholics was detrimental to the interests of the Church and that unity had to be reestablished on a pro-constitutional basis. They switched the debate from values to strategy: "What divides us is not a question of doctrine but one of action (*conduite*)." They finally asked the Holy See to halt the ultramontane attacks and bestow advice of "political wisdom, prudence, and moderation" (cited in van Zuylen, 1955, pp. 1719-1720). The reception of this memorandum in the Vatican was hostile, and the instructions of the papal Secretary of State Cardinal Nina to the nuncio (October 1, 1878) were negative. Nina reiterated the condemnation of the principles of the constitution and recommended no church intervention in the inter-Catholic conflict (Simon, 1956, p. 110).

The papal reaction shows that in 1878 it was by no means obvious what side was going to prevail. While Conservative parliamentarians controlled the political game, the Ultramontanes were making substantial inroads in Catholic public opinion by promising to be implacable on issues related to the Church's interests, by proclaiming their ideological orthodoxy and their commitment to Catholic principles, by advertising their close links to the Vatican, and by connecting to the Catholic masses through their network of charitable organizations and newspapers in a way that Conservatives could only dream.[11] The attitude of the bishops throughout the conflict was "hesitant" and dominated by "incertitude" (Simon, 1961b, p. 25), and they appeared to be swinging over to the radical side. As Simon (1956, p. 111) concludes, the liberal hypothesis was very precarious in 1878.

---

11. In their 1878 memorandum, the Ultramontanes argued that the existing Catholic associations, the Catholic circles, were ready to follow them (Simon, 1955, p. 152). The impressive mobilization of these organizations in the 1884 elections demonstrates the mass potential of radical Catholicism.

THE OUTCOME

The Catholic conflict was resolved by papal intervention on February 22, 1879. In an audience he gave to Belgian journalists, Leo XIII pointed out that although the Belgian constitution consecrated principles that he could not approve of, it had proved good in practice for the Belgian church. Therefore, he asserted, Belgian Catholics should not only abstain from attacking the constitution but should also defend it (van Zuylen, 1955, pp. 1733-1734). This message put an end to the conflict and settled the dispute about the nature of the regime with a clear stand in favor of the liberal institutions; it also spelled the death of the ultramontane movement. Following the papal announcement, the Belgian church openly endorsed the moderates and moved swiftly against the radicals, forcing the ultramontane press to stop its attacks against the constitution and the Conservative party and purging some prominent radical leaders.[12] The Church's decision in favor of the parliamentary Right contributed to the consolidation of the young Belgian democracy. With the help of an unprecedented mass mobilization orchestrated by the Church, the rejuvenated Conservatives (now referred to as the Catholic Party) won the 1884 elections. Although they reversed most of the anticlerical Liberal legislation, they followed a moderate course, refusing to grant the most extremist version of the Church's program. Most important, the Catholic party did not challenge the country's liberal institutions.

Why did the Church abandon the Ultramontanes? Did this decision reflect a shift in its ideological preferences? In the following, I survey a number of arguments that seek to account for the decision of the Church, respectively stressing personalistic or ideological factors, sociostructural variables, the preferences of the electorate, and the effects of the political context. I then introduce and support an alternative explanation that stresses the interaction between political and institutional contexts.

Most historians explain the decision of the Church through a personalistic perspective: The death of the intransigent Pope Pius IX in 1878 and the election of the more pragmatic Leo XIII pushed the Church toward the moderates (Lamberts, 1984b, p. 78; Soete, 1986, pp. 47-48). The papal shift was certainly important: Leo's ascension to the papal throne appears to coincide with the resolution of the intra-Catholic conflict. However, it took

---

12. Some attacks still took place but were marginal instances. Périn was forced to resign his position at the University of Louvain and retire from public life following a papal condemnation (August 3, 1881). This "sounded the end of ultramontanism" and was "a real and definitive victory for the parliamentary Right" (Vander Vorst-Zeegers, 1965, p. 283). In 1881, the *Revue Générale* published a telling article titled "The End of the Catholic-Liberal Dispute."

an entire year for Leo to condemn the attacks against the Belgian constitution.
(He ascended in the papal throne in February 1878 but only pronounced his
decision in February 1879.) In the meantime, the Vatican openly supported
the Ultramontanes as suggested, among others, by Cardinal Nina's negative
reply to the Conservatives' memorandum and the October 1878 congratula-
tory papal telegram to the ultramontane newspaper, *Bien Public* (Simon,
1955, p. 11; 1956, p. 110).[13] This lag strongly suggests that Leo's decision
was more than the product of his personal views. Moreover, and most
important, it is not enough to explain the Vatican's stance. For all its
centralization, Rome still allowed (or was forced to allow) some degree of
autonomy to the national churches. As Simon (1961b) said, "the devotion of
the bishops to the pope was real, but as direct inheritors of the apostles they
were still persuaded that their episcopal rights allowed, even required a
relative originality and a certain independence in the spiritual management
of their dioceses" (p. 27). In the past, the Belgian church had supported the
Belgian constitution despite the Vatican's dislike of it. Now that the constitutional compromise had been challenged by the Liberals, the Church could
have found ways to support the Ultramontanes if it so wanted, in spite of the
papal decision.[14] Therefore, it is necessary to explain what led both the
Vatican and the Belgian church to support the parliamentary Right in 1879.

Another argument stresses sociostructural variables and implies that there
was really no choice for the Church because both capitalism and liberal
democracy were securely established during the second half of the 19th
century and could not be possibly threatened (Witte & Craeybeckx, 1987,

13. See also Nina's (October 1878) comment on the acceptability of "the free doctrinal
discussion of the laws and the eventual modifications that could be brought to these laws" (van
Zuylen, 1955, p. 1727). We also know, from his private discussions with the Belgian *chargé
d'affaires* during the same period (March to September 1878), that Leo displayed a conciliatory
bent (van Zuylen, 1955, pp. 1725-1726). Van Zuylen (1955) correctly refers to "oscillations of
the Curia's pendulum" (p. 2080).

14. The Belgian church ignored Vatican directives in a number of instances: In 1879, it
pursued a hardline strategy against the Liberal education bill despite a papal directive to the
contrary. The Belgian bishop, Mgr. Doutreloux, declared to the nuncio (cited in van Zuylen,
1955), "The Holy-Father cannot order us to do things contrary to our consciousness in order to
serve motivations of temporal order" (p. 2079). As the nuncio remarked to Woeste in this respect,
"I have obtained nothing from the episcopate, despite my efforts" (Woeste, 1927, p. 168).
Likewise, the Liberal leader, Frère-Orban, pointed out to the nuncio (cited in Vander Vorst-
Zeegers, 1965), "What value can I attribute . . . to Rome's promises of mediation? Either they
are dead words, or the bishops laugh at the Holy See's moderation advice" (p. 221). As van
Zuylen (1955) concludes, "The Pope was tired of the resistance of the Bishops. He left them
free to act in their way and under their own responsibility" (p. 2080).

p. 88). This argument exaggerates the stability of the regime[15] and wrongly assumes that capitalism and liberalism go hand in hand. However, given social pressure, liberal institutions have often been sacrificed by the liberal bourgeoisie to save capitalism. A credible socialist threat could have led segments of the liberal bourgeoisie to trade political liberalism for the protection of their economic interests.

The existence of real choice for the Church could also be denied by an argument underlining the moderate and centrist character of the Belgian electorate, which alternated its support between Conservatives and Liberals. In addition, the (majoritarian) electoral system would have heavily penalized a split of the Catholic vote into competing moderate and radical factions. Hence, it was rational for the Church to endorse the moderates, and the radicals stood no chance. This argument was often put forth by the Conservatives in their effort to win the endorsement of the Church: The Conservative leader, Charles Woeste (1878), referred to a "thirty year experience [which] has established that in Belgium, majorities are formed and unformed by the shift of an intermediary group, which has no clear [political] coloration and moves sometimes to the right and sometimes to the left" (p. 170). Yet, Woeste's argument was quickly refuted. In 1884, the Conservatives ran the most clerical campaign in their history (this is when they became the official Catholic party) and won. What is more, they remained in power for the following 30 years. Apparently, the floating intermediary group ceased shifting sides and clung to the Conservatives precisely when the latter moved to the right.

In addition, politics in Belgium during this period can hardly be described as moderate. Passions were heated and politics were acutely polarized. Demonstrations, counterdemonstrations, and street battles between Catholics and Liberals were common. Warnings that a civil war was imminent were frequent (M. V. Lynen, cited in Haulleville, 1876, pp. 128, 139). As the Liberal *Revue de Belgique* put it (June 14, 1876; cited in Haulleville, 1876), "The antagonism of our parties is not a political struggle anymore; it is from now on an essentially religious struggle. . . . It is the 16th century which begins anew. . . . We FATALLY march to CIVIL WAR, with no other possible outcome than the proscription of liberalism or the destruction of the church" (p. 133). This was flamboyant rhetoric but nevertheless reflected the prevailing mood.

On a more general level, the argument about the electorate's moderation assumes that voters' preferences are not affected by the political process.

15. In the beginning of the 1880s, Belgium had a per capita gross national product (GNP) of approximately $600 (in 1960 funds); this is well below Germany's GNP in 1919 ($710) or even 1933 ($1,474 in 1985 funds) (Pound, 1990, p. 353; Przeworski, 1996, p. 5).

However, this is not necessarily the case. Because of its powerful influence over its flock and its huge organizational network, the Church had the unique capacity, even in the context of a system of limited franchise and majority vote, to muster if it so chose considerable support for the radicals—by both increasing turnout and shaping the political preferences of its followers.[16] The image of Belgian peasants marching to the polling station on election day behind their priest is a typical illustration of this influence. In fact, available electoral data indicate that the victory of the church-backed Conservatives in 1884 was the result of the mobilization of the Church and its lay associations (Falter, 1986). Simon (1956) underlines the significance of a Catholic endorsement: "The only way to get efficient action from the Right, was to have it recognized by the Holy See as the most authentically Catholic" (p. 74). Clearly, the Church's backing combined with the climate generated by Liberal anticlericalism could have "clericalized" the Conservative electorate even more, turning radical Catholics into a credible power contender. What was needed was time because setting up a new political organization is a slow and arduous process.

Finally, it is possible to point to the impact of the political context: The Liberal victory in 1878 and the shock of the anticlerical reforms led Catholics to close ranks and join forces. Still, this argument begs the question, Why should Catholic unity have taken place under the Conservatives' banner? Moreover, the Liberal victory did not unite the Catholics. Quite the contrary: As the Conservatives pointed out in their memorandum to the Vatican (August 20, 1878), "It was possible to hope that the results of the 11th June [elections] would dissipate the [ultramontane] blindness. Unfortunately the opposite has happened and the trouble grows from day to day to the great profit of our adversaries" (cited in Woeste, 1927, p. 159).

I introduce an alternative argument that stresses the interaction between political and institutional context: The Church picked the moderates because the Liberal victory, by negatively affecting the Church, increased the utility of a future Conservative cabinet. In addition, the institutional context favored political insiders over outsiders, allowing for the possibility of a future Liberal defeat. In turn, because the Conservatives derived their political credibility and their power vis-à-vis the Church and the Ultramontanes from the liberal institutional context, they made their alliance with the Church conditional on the latter's unequivocal acceptance of the constitution. Hence, the consolidation of the democratic regime in Belgium was the contingent by-product of the self-interested strategic considerations of both the Church

16. In Italy, the Church was able to persuade a very substantial proportion of the electorate to abstain from voting until 1913.

and Conservatives.[17] To elaborate, the Church could support either the Ultramontanes or the parliamentary Right. This choice had crucial political consequences. Supporting the Ultramontanes meant challenging the liberal regime. Although the Church did not possess extra-parliamentary means of subverting the regime, backing the radicals undermined the liberal institutions regardless of the electoral outcome. Even if the Ultramontanes did not win, their mere political presence with the endorsement of the Church would undermine the regime's legitimacy and "drastically reduce the confidence of other actors in democratic institutions" (Przeworski, 1991, p. 28). If, on the other hand, they won, the breakdown of the liberal regime would be likely. If the radicals were allowed to govern, they would go ahead, apply their program, and curtail the liberal institutions; whereas if the Liberals decided not to comply with the electoral result and prevented the radicals from assuming power, they would have undermined the very institutions they sought to promote.

Choosing the Ultramontanes and winning was the Church's preferred outcome because its position would be greatly enhanced. Losing, however, would be costly because of the Liberal's retaliation for its disloyal stance. Backing the parliamentary Right and winning was a second best: The regime would remain liberal and its own position would not vary greatly. Losing would be costly but less than in the ultramontane scenario. Prior to the 1878 Liberal victory, the Church avoided having to choose between moderates and radicals. The bishops could afford to be divided over whom to support and allow the intra-Catholic conflict to linger. The refusal of the Conservative government to deliver policies satisfying the Church made the radicals an attractive option, but the Church hesitated to outrightly side with the radicals, given the risks entailed.

The 1878 Liberal victory altered the political landscape. The initial reaction of the Church included timid but eventually futile efforts to reconcile radicals and moderates. The van Humbeck education bill took the Church by surprise. As the nuncio, Mgr. Vannutelli, pointed out (cited in van Zuylen, 1955), the school bill is "far worse than everyone expected it to be" (p. 1909). Faced with big losses, the Church could no longer afford to waver; it decided to pick and fully back an exclusive political agent and made Catholic unity its top priority. The critical importance of the Liberal victory is confirmed by the most authoritative Belgian historian on this issue, A. Simon. Simon (1956) points out that "it was [the Liberal leader] Frère-Orban who indirectly

17. Although it was a contingent by-product of their self-interested strategic considerations, this outcome was foreseeable, whereas the emergence of a confessional party, also a contingent by-product of similar calculations, was not (Kalyvas, 1996).

provided the opportunity for the political and confessional unity of Catholics. The 1879 education bill and the break-up of diplomatic relations [with the Vatican] were *the decisive instance*" (p. 74, italics added). However, although the Liberal victory explains the Church's decision to choose, it tells us nothing about the content of the choice: Why (and how) did the Church pick the moderates?

The Liberal victory altered the payoffs attached to the Church's two options. The reduction of church privileges meant that the Church's postelectoral status quo was worse than the preelectoral one. Once the Church experienced true anticlericalism, it could no longer accuse Conservatives of being closet Liberals. Moreover, the Conservatives, stung by their electoral defeat and the ultramontane threat, offered concessions to the Church in the form of a more proclerical program. Hence, the utility (to the Church) of a future Conservative government increased. Furthermore, the Church needed to reverse the anticlerical reforms quickly. The Liberals' continuing presence in power represented a big (and rising) cost for the Church and made swift action a necessity. Although the Church set up a vast network of Catholic schools, it could not sustain it for a long time without state financial support: The longer Liberals remained in power, the harder it would be for the Church to provide Catholic education. This factor placed a premium on political actors who could credibly promise to quickly deliver a Catholic victory (i.e., political insiders rather than outsiders). Finally, once the Church committed itself to a single, clearly defined political strategy and fully supported its chosen political agent, it raised its probability of success by enforcing Catholic unity and mobilizing the previously undermobilized faithful, hence making the median voter more clerical. This, rather than structural, personalistic, or ideological factors, best accounts for the decision of the Church. According to Simon (1956), "Leo XIII did not see clearer than Pius IX: the facts were clearer" (p. 31).

The Liberal victory that set the Church in motion was nested in a larger institutional context. Institutions were significant in two ways. First, they made a future Conservative victory plausible because a regime in which "parties lose elections" (Przeworski, 1991, p. 10) was in place: A pro-Catholic victory in the next round could realistically be assigned a nonzero probability. As Przeworski (1991) has observed, "If outcomes were either predetermined or completely indeterminate, there would be no reason for groups to organize as participants" (p. 13). Because institutions define the realm of what is possible, they help shape political strategy. Second, the institutional context made a Conservative victory more plausible than an ultramontane one because existing political institutions favor, at least in the short term, political actors integrated in the political system. The Conservatives already had a political organization in place. The Church's need for a quick reversal of the anticlerical reforms favored political insiders with a long experience and knowledge of the existing political system. Moreover, because of their position within the political system, Conservatives controlled the definition of what was politically possible. As one Conservative wrote to Archbishop Dechamps, "Have therefore, Monseigneur, a little confidence to the politicians who are heading the country's business; they see things from up close . . . and they are, allow me to say, better positioned than the episcopate to know what is politically possible" (cited in Vander Vorst-Zeegers, 1965, p. 164). The Ultramontanes could not supply credible promises to the Church and were at a disadvantage once the Church decided it needed an agent that could produce quick results—a point of which Conservatives did not fail to remind the Church. The radicals would find "not a single man in the Parliament to support them" (d'Anethan to Mgr. Dechamps, cited in Vander Vorst-Zeegers, 1965, p. 178).

The institutional context also had a more indirect, although very significant, effect: It structured the daily behavior of politicians in a way that insidiously subverted their individual ideological preferences. The nuncio, Mgr. Vannutelli, made this point beautifully in a memorandum he sent to the Vatican in 1876 (cited in van Zuylen, 1955).

> [Conservatives], despite their intimate convictions dictated by their faith and their submission to the Holy Father, are often forced in public life to act following opposite principles. This is not the effect of a latent perversion of their consciousness, even less of a will rebellious to the teachings of the Church; it is, rather, a tough necessity of their situation. In fact, by being Ministers, deputies, senators, magistrates, they are forced to act, each in his own sphere, following the principles of the Belgian Constitution and laws. Yet, the Belgian Constitution and the organic laws are based upon the principles of the most narrow liberalism. Thus, it is impossible for the public acts of these functionaries to be presented outside without the mark of liberalism, which is imposed upon them not by their free will as rulers, but really by the necessity to govern following the Constitution. (pp. 1714-1715)

It is now possible to clearly discern the contingency in the process of democratic consolidation. The striking fact is that neither the Church nor the Conservatives had in mind the future of liberal institutions when they engaged in the process described previously. The Church had one overriding concern, its influence in society (i.e., keeping education Catholic and maintaining diplomatic relations between the Vatican and the Belgian state, hence reversing the liberal laws. As Simon (1956) points out, "the Church appeared willing to sacrifice much" (pp. 37-38) to get back the privileges it had lost. Clearly, the Church was not interested in enhancing the regime. "Demanding fidelity to the constitution" was for Leo XIII "the best *practical*) way to preserve the religious interests" (Simon, 1961b, p. 13; italics added). Likewise, the Conservatives did not defend the liberal constitution because they believed in it—in fact, many did not. Even their own justification for supporting the constitution was made in terms of political strategy rather than ideology. They were concerned about loyalty to the liberal institutions for two practical reasons. First, a loyal stance served their goal of reelection by making their action more credible and efficient. As their leader, Charles Woeste (1927), argued, "If we want to stay a political party, exercising its influence upon the destinies of the country, the attacks against the constitution must cease" (p. 155). Second, such a stance strengthened their position within the Catholic camp (i.e., vis-à-vis the Church and the Ultramontanes) because their power was derived from their position in the Liberals' regime. In short, the Belgian case constitutes a clear instance in which the legitimacy of a democratic regime emerges in a contingent way from strategic choices rather than normative values and principles.

No choice would have been possible in the absence of a centralized religious structure. The Church's ability to enforce unity under the leadership of the moderates was crucial.[18] The radicals were silenced and their press altered its political line; Henri Périn, the chief radical ideologue, was forced out of public life. Only a centralized institution like the Church could have achieved such a feat, which simultaneously subdued the radical Catholics and appeased the Liberals. At the same time, the Church managed to keep the radicals within its ranks and under its control. By adopting a tough stance on the question of education, by pushing the Conservatives toward a more clerical direction, and by providing incentives for the radicals to focus on social organizations, the Church displayed a superior ability of management and made sure that most radicals did not desert the Catholic camp after their defeat.

STRATEGY AND IDEOLOGY

The fact that strategic rather than ideological considerations were at the center of this process is discernible in the way that Conservatives convinced the Church to back them up. Both participants and historians note that in reaching its decision, the Church acted in a pragmatic or practical way. For instance, Simon (1956) reports that Mgr. Vannutelli, initially a radical, "abandoned the field of principles to join that of political opportunity"

18. The Church's enforcement ability was later confirmed when a Flemish popular Catholic movement led by Abbé Daens was repressed in a similar fashion during the 1890s.

(p. 37). This is not to say that ideology and values did not matter. Ideological issues pervaded Belgian politics, and political actors were accordingly highly motivated by values. Indeed, the Liberals and the Church aggressively promoted societal projects that were "clearly opposed" from an ideological point of view (Simon, 1961b, p. 29). Even when the Vatican took a stand on the issue of the Belgian constitution, it did so in a way that remained ambivalent. As Simon (1956, pp. 11-12) points out, Leo's support to the constitution was not an admission of the hypothesis, which was implicitly condemned, but rather a tactical move. The importance of ideological concerns and the permeability of the boundaries between religion and politics is further underlined by the presence of many theological considerations in the political debate. For instance, the *JdB* was accused by the Ultramontanes of sinning because it was published on Sundays. The result of this heavily ideological climate was that parliamentarians often had to consult with bishops about a great number of issues (Simon, 1955, p. 25). In turn, the Belgian episcopate was composed of theologians for whom ideas and principles mattered a lot. These were generally not people with an innate (or cultural) attraction to moderation and pragmatism. According to the nuncio, Mgr. Vannutelli (report to Cardinal Nina, cited in van Zuylen, 1955),

> This resistance [of the Belgian bishops to papal directives for moderation] is not the result, in my opinion, of a clear perception of the truth (clearly the opposite). . . . To begin with, the majority of these Bishops always thinks obligated to follow the opinion of the most fanatic and extreme [people]. If professor A, and journalist B argue that all [public] schools must be condemned, how it is possible that we, the Bishops, appear to be less pure and less zealous? This tendency to follow the opinion which is considered the purest, is even more manifest in the episcopal reunions, because everyone fears to be accused by a colleague of servility vis-à-vis the Government, of court flattery, or of lack of zeal and courage. (p. 2076)

The presence of these ideological and cultural attributes is hardly surprising. What is surprising is that these actors entered cost-benefit calculations and ended up acting in a way that can be called pragmatic, despite such attributes. This is an important point that contradicts arguments that discount the likelihood of democratization in the presence of religiously motivated political actors. A quick survey of the debate that followed the 1878 elections illustrates how the Church made the leap from principles to political opportunity and provides insights into the microprocess through which religiously motivated actors make cost-benefit calculations and end up acting in a pragmatic way.

Interestingly, even the radicals felt obliged to make a strategic argument. Right after the elections, they published a pamphlet titled "To Catholics: Defeated, What We Will Do." This pamphlet, which obtained the imprimatur, the Church's official permission to be printed, was widely reproduced in the Catholic press. The parliamentary Right was accused of having failed to "place the political question into the religious field" (Verhaegen, 1878a, p. 4). The way to go was "to definitively abandon the strategy that just collapsed, forego the policy of material interests, concessions, oratory precautions" and form "a political party, Catholic before everything else" (Verhaegen, 1878a, pp. 7-11). However, the radicals, being political outsiders, could not credibly guarantee the Church a quick reversal of the anticlerical reforms; as a result, they reverted to maximalism. As the ultramontane bishop of Tournai, Mgr. Dumont, put it, "In the interest of religion I prefer [electoral] abstention than the triumph of liberal Catholicism [the parliamentary Right], which I have decided to fight all my life as a graver error than open hostility [to the church]" (letter to Robiano, October 13, 1878; cited in Simon, 1955, p. 161). Obviously, most bishops and the Vatican could not share such a view.

Contrast the radicals' arguments to the those put forth by the Conservatives: What divides Catholics, the latter argued, "is not a question of doctrine but of action" (van Zuylen, 1955, p. 1719). Woeste (1927) pointed out that "no doctrinal issue divides [Catholics]; it is a question of action [*conduite*]" (p. 155), whereas the Conservatives' memorandum to the pope reiterated that "it is not a question of doctrine; in that field there can be no disagreement between Catholics. It is a matter of action, a practical question of application" (cited in Woeste, 1927, p. 159). The transition from the world of ideology to that of action was made possible by the distinction between absolute and relative goals. The Conservatives argued that "by wanting that which we regard as the absolute good, we often jeopardize and lose the relative good," (1877). The implication was clear:

> The only efficient mission at this point is to group and reorganize our forces while illuminating liberalism's flaws; not to spend time raising difficult and purely theoretical questions bound to divide us and abate our electoral action. We must never sacrifice principles to love of popularity; but we need with the same care to avoid useless unpopularity. (Woeste, 1878, p. 171)

The point was made that the "confusion between politics and religion" was only benefiting the Liberals (d'Anethan to Mgr. Dechamps, July 4, 1876; cited in Vander Vorst-Zeegers, 1965, p. 237). Of course, switching the terms of the debate from doctrine to strategy could be accomplished because the Liberal victory had altered the political parameters and the institutional context created political insiders who could credibly argue that they were able to deliver the goods. The role of these insiders was crucial: They translated, so to speak, the requirements of political expediency, opportunity structures, and cost-benefit calculations to a language that was understandable by the Church.

CONCLUSION

Once it made its mind, the Church backed the parliamentary Right as its exclusive political agent. Hundreds of associations mobilized, and in 1884, the Conservatives won a resounding victory. Making good on their word, they overturned the liberal educational reforms. Yet, this was a bittersweet victory for the Church. Besides sacrificing its bigger goals, it quickly found that the Conservatives resisted many of its demands (such as the Church's monopoly on education) and governed moderately, a fact that provoked church complaints. Conservatives were able to resist the Church's pressure because they had proved that they were the ones who knew how to beat the Liberals.

The victory of the Conservatives reinforced decisively the democratic institutions of Belgium at the modest cost of a slight clerical bias in governmental policies. An important danger for the regime was eliminated, and new political and social groups were integrated into the liberal institutions. The credibility of the Conservatives was cemented, and the perception that moderation and attachment to the constitution was the Church's best strategy acquired hegemonic status. In Simon's (1956) terms, Conservatives "gave reason to the hopes" of those who supported "the freedoms" as a way to increase the influence of the Church (p. 75). A virtuous cycle was initiated, leading to the construction of a tradition in which the liberal constitution became "one of the central symbols of Belgian nationhood" (Conway, 1996, p. 276). When the 1889 papal instructions to the nuncio mentioned the party's division into hardline and moderate factions, they instructed the nuncio "to maintain the balance between these tendencies without forgetting that it is the moderates who made the electoral victory of the Catholics" (cited in Simon, 1961a, p. 171).

In short, moderation (and through it democracy) became self-enforcing. This is the main reason why interwar "Belgian Catholicism manifested little of the long-standing hostility to liberal parliamentarism evident in many other predominantly Catholic countries" (Conway, 1996, p. 271). This became clear in the 1930s when the Belgian church, contrary to the Italian or Austrian churches, opted for democracy and condemned the fascist movement, REX, despite its Catholic roots. By the same token, this process operated as an evolutionary mechanism that weeded out ideologically motivated actors and reinforced pragmatist ones. The remarkable fact is that this outcome was achieved not as a result of some process of ideological or civic learning but from purely self-interested actions. The consolidation of Belgian democracy was, thus, contingent on the process of political competition. Self-interest ran parallel to the preservation of democratic institutions, and democratic legitimacy was generated endogenously through the political process: Democracy made democrats.

The Belgian case suggests that the presence of a group of politicians integrated into existing institutions and associated with a religious movement reinforces democratic institutions. Their fate is usually linked to the institutions within which they operate. Thus, contrary to conventional wisdom, links between churches/religious movements and parliamentary groups can be conducive to democratic consolidation. The existence of a competitive institutional framework matters a lot, but it has to be reinforced by a particular political context: Paradoxically, the radicalization of the Liberals, by leading to church moderation, proved beneficial to the democratic institutions. Had the Liberals not radicalized when they did, the Church might have remained ambivalent or might have allied with the Ultramontanes, a potentially disastrous prospect for Belgian democracy.

Ideology can be a poor predictor of political action. An exclusive focus on the ideology of the Belgian church would have predicted a totally different course of action from the one actually followed; a similar exclusive focus on the ideology of the Indian or Turkish religious parties can seriously underestimate their capacity to play by the rules of the democratic game. This is why the bias toward ideology in the study of religion and politics can produce extremely misleading results. Values do matter, but they have to be placed in a more broad political and institutional context. This point carries particular relevance for the study of contemporary religious fundamentalism, which is dominated by an overwhelming emphasis on ideas and religious traditions.

In short, democratic consolidation was made possible through the combination of a political shift, which affected the Church negatively; the Church's centralized structure; and the presence of competitive institutions. The implication is that religious mobilization in politics is not necessarily destructive of democracy even when it is permeated by an aliberal and antidemocratic ideology. Interestingly, the situation facing the Catholic Church parallels the predicament of socialist parties. The Church operated within a regime it disliked and under a state controlled by its enemies. This striking analogy is less surprising than the fact that it is negated when it comes to the study of religious politics: Unlike the Left, the main assumption about religious movements has been that they cannot possibly integrate into a liberal democratic framework. The Belgian case suggests that this assumption should be strongly qualified. Clearly, when placed in a more broad theoretical perspective, the study of religion and politics gains as much as the study of democratization gains when it is placed in a wider historical context.

REFERENCES

Berger, Suzanne. (1987). Religious transformation and the future of politics. In Charles S. Maier (Ed.), *Changing boundaries of the political: Essays on the evolving balance between the state and society, public and private in Europe* (pp. 107-149). Cambridge, UK: Cambridge University Press.

Birnbaum, Pierre. (1991). Catholic identity and universal suffrage: The French experience. *Social Science Journal, 129,* 571-582.

Conway, Martin. (1996). The right in inter-war Belgium. *European History Quarterly, 26*(2), 267-292.

de la Cueva, Julio. (1996). The stick and the candle: Clericals and anticlericals in Northern Spain, 1898-1913. *European History Quarterly, 26*(2), 241-265.

Falter, Rolf. (1986). De Kamerverkiezingen van 10 juni 1884 [The parliamentary elections of 10 June 1884]. In Emiel Lamberts & Jacques Lory (Eds.), *1884: Un tournant politique en Belgique: De Machtswisseling van 1884 in Belgie* [1884: A political shift in Belgium] (pp. 9-43). Bruxelles, Belgium: Publications des Facultés Universitaires Saint-Louis.

Gabbert, Mark A. (1978). The limits of French Catholic liberalism: Mgr Sibour and the question of ecclesiology. *French Historical Studies, 10,* 641-663.

Gunther, Richard, Diamandouros, P. Nikiforos, & Puhle, Hans-Jürgen (Eds.). (1995). *The politics of democratic consolidation: Southern Europe in comparative perspective.* Baltimore: Johns Hopkins University Press.

Haulleville, Prosper de. (1876). Vainqueurs que ferons-nous? [Winners, what will we do?]. *Revue Générale, 23,* 125-141.

Hehir, J. Bryan. (1993). Catholicism and democracy: Conflict, change, and collaboration. In John Witte Jr. (Ed.), *Christianity and democracy in global context* (pp. 15-30). Boulder, CO: Westview.

Huntington, Samuel P. (1991). *The third wave: Democratization in the late twentieth century.* Norman: University of Oklahoma Press.

Kalyvas, Stathis N. (1996). *The rise of Christian democracy in Europe.* Ithaca, NY: Cornell University Press.

Lamberts, Emiel. (1984a). Het Ultramontanisme in België, 1830-1914 [Ultramontanism in Belgium, 1830-1914]. In Emiel Lamberts (Ed.), *De Kruistocht tegen het Liberalisme: Facetten van het ultramontanisme in België in de 19e eeuw* [The crusade against liberalism: Facets of ultramontanism in Belgium during the 19th century]. (pp. A[AU: PAGES?]). Leuven, Belgium: Universitaire Pers.

Lamberts, Emiel. (1984b). Une offensive de Pie IX er des Ultramontains radicaux contre la législation matrimoniale en Belgique, 1875 [An attack of Pius IX and the radical ultramontanes against the marriage legislation in Belgium, 1875]. *Revue d'Histoire Ecclesiastique, 79*(1), 50-78.

Laury, Jacques. (1979). *Libéralisme et instruction primaire, 1842-1879: Introduction à l'étude de la lutte scolaire en Belgique* [Liberalism and elementary education: Introduction to the study of the school struggle in Belgium]. Louvain, Belgium: Éditions Nauwelaerts.

Linz, Juan J. (1978). *Crisis, breakdown, and reequilibriation.* Baltimore: Johns Hopkins University Press.

Linz, Juan J., & Stepan, Alfred. (1996). Toward consolidated democracies. *Journal of Democracy, 7*(2), 14-33.

Papini, Roberto. (1993). Christianity and democracy in Europe: The Christian democratic movement. In John Witte Jr. (Ed.), *Christianity and democracy in global context* (pp. 47-63). Boulder, CO: Westview.

Pound, N.J.G. (1990). *An historical geography of Europe.* Cambridge, UK: Cambridge University Press.

Preneel, L. (1982). Mouvements catholiques et expériences des catholiques en Belgique [Catholic movements and experiences of the Catholics in Belgium]. In E. de Jonghe & L. Preneel (Eds.), *Theorie et Language du Mouvement Catholique: Problèmes d'Historiographie* [Theory and discourse of the Catholic movement: Problems of historiography] (pp. 117-137). Leuven, Belgium: Universitaire Pers.

Przeworski, Adam. (1991). *Democracy and the market: Political and economic reforms in Eastern Europe and Latin America.* Cambridge, UK: Cambridge University Press.

Przeworski, Adam. (1996, August/September). *Why democracies survive in affluent countries?* Paper presented at the Annual Meeting of the American Political Science Association, San Francisco.

Przeworski, Adam, Alvarez, Michael, Cheibub, José Antonio, & Limongi, Fernando. (1995). *Economic and institutional conditions of durability of democracy, 1950-1990.* Revised version of a paper prepared for the Conference on Consolidating the Third World Democracies: Trends and Challenges, Taipei, Taiwan.

Reichley, James A. (1986). Democracy and religion. *Political Science and Politics, 19*(4), 801-806.

Sartori, Giovanni. (1991). Rethinking democracy: Bad policy and bad politics. *International Social Science Journal, 129,* 437-450.

Simon, Alois. (1955). *Catholicisme et Politique: Documents Inédits (1832-1909)* [Catholicism and politics: Unpublished documents (1832-1909)]. Wetteren, Belgium: Scaldis.

Simon, Alois. (1956). *L'hypothèse libérale en Belgique: Documents inédits (1839-1907)* [The liberal hypothesis in Belgium: Unpublished documents (1839-1907)]. Wetteren, Belgium: Scaldis.

Simon, Alois. (1961a). *Instructions aux nonces de Bruxelles (1835-1889)* [Instructions to the nuncios in Belgium (1835-1889)]. Bruxelles, Belgium: Institut Historique Belge de Rome.

Simon, Alois. (1961b). *Réunions des évêques de Belgique, 1868-1883: Procès-Vebaux* [Meetings of the Belgian bishops, 1868-1883: Minutes]. Leuven-Louvain, Belgium: Nauwelaerts.

Soete, Jean-Luc. (1986). Les catholiques et la question du programme, 1878-1884 [The Catholics and the question of the program, 1878-1884]. In Emiel Lamberts & Jacques Lory (Eds.), *1884: Un tournant politique en Belgique: De Machtswisseling van 1884 in Belgie* [1884: A political shift in Belgium] (pp. 45-68). Bruxelles, Belgium: Publications des Facultés Universitaires Saint-Louis.

Vander Vorst-Zeegers, J. (1965). *Le "Journal de Bruxelles" de 1871 à 1884* [The "Journal de Bruxelles" from 1871 to 1884]. Leuven-Louvain, Belgium: Nauwelaerts.

van Zuylen, Pierre. (1955). La Belgique et le Vatican en 1879 [Belgium and the Vatican in 1879]. *Revue Générale Belge, 21,* 1707-1734, 1901-1915, 2065-2081.

Vecchio, Giorgio. (1987). *Alla ricerca del partito: Cultura politica ed esperienze dei cattolici italiani nel primo Novecento* [Searching for the party: Political culture and experiences of the Italian Catholics in the first part of the nineteenth century]. Brescia, Italy: Morcelliana.

Verhaegen, Arthur. (1878a). *Aux Catholiques: Vaincusé que ferons-nous?* [To Catholics: Defeated, what will we do?]. Bruges, Belgium: Imprimerie Classique de Saint-Augustin, Desclée de Brouwer et Cie.

Verhaegen, Arthur. (1878b). *Catholique et Politique* [The Catholic and politics]. Bruges, Belgium: Imprimerie Classique de Saint-Augustin, Desclée de Brouwer et Cie.

Witte, Els, & Craeybeckx, Jan. (1987). *La Belgique politique de 1830 à nos jours: Les tensions d'une démocratie bourgeoise* [Politics in Belgium from 1830 to the present: The strains of a bourgeois democracy]. Brussels, Belgium: Editions Labor.

Woeste, Charles. (1878). La Chute du Ministère Malou [The fall of the Malou ministry]. *Revue Générale, 28*, 157-171.

Woeste, Charles. (1927). *Mémoires pour servir à l'Histoire contemporaine de la Belgique, Vol. 1* [Memoirs intended to serve for the contemporary history of Belgium]. Bruxelles, Belgium: Librairie Albert Dewit.

Zwart, R. S. (1997). Christian democracy and political order in the Netherlands. In Emiel Lamberts (Ed.), *Christian democracy in the European Union (1945-1995)* (pp. 242-253). Leuven, Belgium: Leuven University Press.

Stathis N. Kalyvas is assistant professor of politics at New York University. He is the author of The Rise of Christian Democracy in Europe *(1996, Cornell University Press). His research focuses on democracy, religious politics, political conflict, and the formation of collective identities.*

Part II
The Politics of Church–State Relations

[8]

N. J. Demerath III

Religious Capital and Capital Religions: Cross-Cultural and Non-Legal Factors in the Separation of Church and State

THE SEPARATION OF CHURCH AND STATE is a major component of the American political system and its civil religious mythology. As an article of faith, it is widely regarded as a unique American heritage, constitutionally created and legally sustained. This paper challenges both its singularity and its legal dependence by placing the United States in comparative and cross-cultural perspective. Even within such nominally religious states as Indonesia, Pakistan, Sweden, and Thailand, there is far more separation than is widely supposed, as religion provides more political piety than governing influence. Since the similarities with the United States are at least as important as the differences, and since "separation" in these contexts is not a legal phenomenon, a more general sociopolitical explanation seems in order. Hence, this paper offers a series of reasons for the gap between religion and government, drawing both on the politics of the state and on the societal position of religion itself. Not to put too fine a point on the matter, religion's capital is frequently maximized when it is not a capital religion.

COMBATTING PROVINCIALISM

Every society is an enterprise of faith, and often the faith endures despite reality. It is precisely in this civil religious nexus of interpretations and idealizations that societies shape their futures while reshaping their pasts. One fundamental tenet of the American faith

---

N. J. Demerath III is Professor of Sociology at the University of Massachusetts in Amherst.

22   *N. J. Demerath III*

concerns a "separation of church and state"[1] that is generally portrayed as a mythically inviolable and quintessentially American product of our constitutional heritage.

Against such a background, this paper may be seen as impious and heretical. But in questioning some of the basic shibboleths of separation, it falls within the time-honored Weberian tradition of exposing "ideal types" to empirical assessment.[2] The separation of church and state is a construct of political theory rather than a description of governing reality. To what extent does the two-hundred-year-old theory coincide with a still developing reality, not only in the United States but in other nations around the globe?

Max Weber himself offered a beginning point for this assessment. In discussing the "relations between ecclesiastic and secular power," he delineates three major types: *hierocratic, theocratic,* and *caesaropapist.*[3] In the first, secular power is dominant but cloaked in religious legitimacy; in the second, ecclesiastic authority is preeminent; and in the third, secular power holds sway over religion itself. Note that the possibility of actual separation looms as a possible fourth category but is not mentioned by Weber, presumably because it lacks even the minimal empirical credibility necessary to qualify in ideal-typical terms.

Of course, Weber was writing in a quite different political and religious context. But recent American legal scholars have also expressed skepticism on the point. As Samuel Krislov has recently put it: " 'Separation' of church and state is an artificial concept not really capable of easy implementation or logical achievement."[4] Certainly any myth of *absolute* separation is scotched quickly in examining the American experience,[5] and it would be unfair to compare our shibboleths to other societies' realities. American politics have often come wrapped in religious piety. The list of exceptions to both the "free exercise" and the "establishment" clauses of the Constitution's First Amendment defies brief summary. Some reflect a lack of compliance with court decisions (for example, persistent prayer in the public schools), and others have been recently endorsed by the Supreme Court itself (for example, legislative chaplains or Christmas creches on public property). Perhaps it is not surprising that the courts have winked at some of the exceptions while specifically authorizing others. After all, the law entails a different sort of

Religious Capital and Capital Religions   23

ideal-typifying, and consistency is not a virtue of even the Supreme Court's judgments in this area.

Yet asking for a pure distinction is surely asking for too much in an impure world. Even if Jefferson's "wall of separation" is not impenetrable, it remains one principle of American statecraft that is actually honored more in the observance than in the breach. Indeed, "separation" is not just a source of our civic pride but a reasonably reliable guide to our political behavior. While the gap between church and state is not sacrosanct, it is not trivial either. When religion and government are mixed, it is rarely lightly, and the results are often contested whether they involve encroachments on religious liberty or establishment entanglements.

But what of the putative uniqueness and legal grounding of America's separationism? Here we need to invoke cross-national comparisons to place the United States in proper perspective. Of course, one does not have to travel to take a cross-cultural trip. The reports of others are amply available, and some have even been submitted to comparative codification. Consider Krislov's summary of a recent survey of 142 national constitutions around the world conducted by Van Moorseven and Van der Tan:[6]

> A 1978 study of written constitutions (computer analyzed no less) indicates that forty-three (or 30 percent) of those analyzable provided for a national religion and ninety-nine (or 70 percent) did not. Thirty-three countries specified religion, most notably for the office of religious minister. All but twenty had some reference to church or religion. Sixty-one (or 43 percent) guaranteed freedom of religion, while sixty-four (or 47 percent) guaranteed both religious freedom and the right to be affiliated religiously. Only ten (7 percent) have no constitutional provision of this type. Provisions for freedom of religion are much more common than provisions for freedom of thought; indeed, the frequency is almost double that of ... "political freedoms."[7]

This suggests that the American case is not as distinctive as our self-image insists. Some 70 percent have no formal national religion, and all but 7 percent make some constitutional provision for religious freedom. In fact, our First Amendment's prohibition of an "establishment" religion is more unusual than its guarantee of "free exercise"—though, as we shall see shortly, it is perhaps an ironic

24   N. J. Demerath III

comment on constitutions generally that many nations have a better record in avoiding establishments that are not constitutionally banned than in nurturing the free exercise that is constitutionally secured. Indeed, what may be most distinctive about our own constitution is not so much its content as the seriousness with which we regard it. Even Americans who know little of its specifics accord it revered status as both a source and a reflection of our political system. In many other countries, constitutions are a changing gloss, and there are some in which a nation's constitutional commitment reflects the sardonic line from a recent American automobile commercial, "[Constitutions] must be good; we've had six of them in the last twelve years."

IN QUEST OF THE RELIGIOUS STATE

Clearly one must probe behind the formalistic facade to find the true relations between a society's religion and government. With this in mind, I recently supplemented my readings in the secondary literature with research visits to several countries whose relations between religion and the state stand in apparent contrast to the United States. Specifically, I was in search of religious states with officially recognized state religions. This ruled out such countries as India, an officially secular nation whose constitutional provisions concerning religion are very similar to the United States; Italy, whose long-standing concordat with the Vatican was dissolved in 1986; and even Israel, whose Jewish identity is more a function of ethnicity and demography than of religion or legality, though there are whole areas of family law set aside for religious jurisdiction—whether Jewish, Muslim, or Christian.

I visited four countries which appeared to meet the test. In travelling through first Pakistan and then Indonesia, I found myself retracing much of V. S. Naipul's "Islamic journey" for his provocative but strangely haughty volume, *Among the Believers*.[8] Buddhist Thailand offered a window onto a quite different non-Western religious culture. Finally, while Sweden marked a return to the West and to Christianity, its state Lutheranism provides still another contrast with the United States.

Of course, cross-cultural analysis is notoriously vulnerable to distortion. However, a master of the genre, Clifford Geertz, offers

Religious Capital and Capital Religions 25

some encouragement in his shimmering essay on law as "local knowledge." First, he suggests that "apologizing . . . never does any good anyhow."[9] Second, he stands another cautionary maxim on its head:

> Santayana's famous dictum that one compares only when one is unable to get to the heart of the matter seems to me, here at least, the precise reverse of the truth: it is through comparison, and of comparables, that whatever heart we can actually get to is to be reached.[10]

Elsewhere, Geertz stresses the advantages of "thick description" in any ethnographic study.[11] Alas, even a middling account is a casualty of the present format. Without pretending that this research is sufficiently thick in either its earlier uncut incarnation or possible expansion to book length, almost all of the country-by-country details have been deleted here. I am hopeful that a brief summary will serve as a bridge to the more analytic sections which follow.

Comparative scholars invariably enter the field with predispositions, including whether one is prepared to maximize differences or similarities with one's home society. Raised on a diet of liberal cultural relativism, Western social scientists are inclined to look more for contrasts than for similarities, as was I in beginning my quest for religious states. Gradually, however, I began to realize that some similarities were pressing, and that, despite manifold cultural differences among societies, there were a number of shared structural circumstances. Thus, nations are increasingly united not only by their participation in a common international political economy but also by a shared vulnerability to many of the same internal religious and political dynamics. But before pressing the point, let me provide brief introductions to the four societies at issue.

Pakistan offers a case of not only a religious state but a society undergoing religious ferment. This was especially true under the 1977–1988 regime of the late Zia ul-Haq and his campaign for national "Islamization." Yet there were widespread doubts about both the campaign's success and its sincerity. Many who credited the prime minister's private piety were cynical about his public motives.[12] Opposition came particularly from the ranks of those who stood to suffer most from a literal and inflexible reliance on the eighth-century Koran—for example, educated women and the country's economic elite. But there was also restiveness among some members of Paki-

26   N. J. Demerath III

stan's two dominant Muslim communities, the majority Sunnis and the minority Shiites. The two had coexisted relatively amicably since the country's bloody partition from India in 1947. But now that there was a possibility of conferring real power on the Islamic courts and mullahs, conflict quickened as questions arose concerning which Islamic group would define and wield such power. Finally, some government insiders suggested that the campaign itself was a "fraud," and that Zia himself had begun to see its disadvantages. While the "Shariat Bill" remained pending, his policy seemed to be one of keeping the pot simmering without allowing it to come to a boil. While the tension was somewhat reduced during the brief successor reign of Benazir Bhutto, the current prime minister, Nawaz Sharif, has recently raised the political fire once again by announcing renewed support for the bill and the campaign.

Meanwhile, Indonesia presents an instructively different scenario under its longtime President Suharto. Arguably the world's largest Muslim nation, it is also among the world's most religiously pluralistic societies. The paradox is rooted in the common Indonesian's self-description as "Muslim—but not like the Iranians; in fact, I'm also part Buddhist, part Hindu, part Christian and part animist." This mirrors the country's multilayered and syncretic cultural history.[13] The government reflects a similar ambivalence. While acknowledging its Islamic base, it has also sought to snuff the fires of Islamic fundamentalism, against which it has protected itself both culturally and structurally. Culturally, the government requires national fealty to the broadly integrative and panreligious principles of *pancasila,* a politically manipulated civil religion functioning as a vague tabula rasa on which only the government itself can write. Structurally, the government has developed a national political apparatus called *golkar,* which is part party machine, part civil service, and part Big Brother.[14] Here too, then, there is a considerable gap between the state and its official religious system.

Certainly there is no question of Buddhism's cultural dominance within Thailand; however, its relation to the state is problematic. As recent presidential successions have made clear, Thailand's government shares with both Pakistan and Indonesia a closer relation to the military than to religion. It also shares an asymmetry by which the state exerts far more control over religion than does religion over the state.[15] This is partly because of qualities inherent within Buddhism

Religious Capital and Capital Religions   27

itself. Whereas Koranic Islam knows no distinction between religion and power (and hence is especially disadvantaged in the presence of contemporary state structures which set it aside), Buddhism has long observed such a distinction as an ideal (and hence is differently disadvantaged by current political processes). Although Thai Buddhism does have a national administrative structure in the *songha*, it lacks a powerful ecclesiastical agency or ideology. In addition, its tradition of monkish mysticism and anticharismatic humility makes Buddhism an unlikely base for a political movement.[16] Indeed, the Thai government has struck a bargain with the Buddhists which is very much on the government's terms. In return for providing a number of stipends and subventions, the state has secured powers of appointment to important religious posts as well as representation in religious councils, effective veto power over many religious policy decisions, and the right to legal intervention in instances of internal religious disputes. Both despite and because of Buddhism's position at the core of Thai culture, its political and administrative aspects are more appendages to the state than sources of power over it.

Finally, Sweden provides a kind of limiting case for this analysis. A formal religious state under the Lutheran church of Sweden, the country is simultaneously one of the world's most secular societies as measured by almost any criterion of religious behavior or belief. In many respects, Sweden's state religion is more a nostalgic vestige of the past than a vital influence in the present.[17] While the church continues to play "life and death roles," this is actually the straight line for a series of popular witticisms based on several characteristics of the church. First, the clergy earn state support partly by serving the government as census takers enumerating births and passings in their parishes; second, funerals are the one church ritual which continues to be compelling for the majority of the population, as many nonchurch members pay an annual membership tax of several hundred dollars to remain eligible for the rite; third, most active church parishioners are over the age of sixty, and as with American liberal Protestant denominations, this reinforces a moribund quality in the institution. In fact, there is now slow movement in Sweden toward religious disestablishment. This has majority support not only within the country as a whole but even among church leaders who hope separation will prove to be a stimulant. The action remains

28   N. J. Demerath III

low on the political agenda, more because of disinterest than opposition.

Earlier we noted that, even in the American case, the separation between church and state is far from absolute. Now we have seen that the kind and degree of separation that exists in the United States may not be unique. Pakistan, Indonesia, Thailand, and Sweden all share more functional separation of religion and government than either their politics or their legal structures would suggest. This indicates that an explanation does not lie primarily within laws or constitutions themselves. The remainder of this paper discusses a series of nonlegal considerations which may be more important determinants. They are grouped into two categories: first, those concerning the circumstances of politics and government; second, those involving characteristics of the religious sphere itself.

SHOOTING THE GAP POLITICALLY

As much as the "separation of church and state" is ingrained in American culture, it is scarcely imaginable for any leading American politician to follow the example of the leader of Sweden's Liberal party who recently noted that he does not believe in God, though he respects those who do. Indeed, religion has seldom loomed so large in American politics as over the last decade. Beginning with "born-again Christian" Jimmy Carter, and extending through Ronald Reagan under the influence of the "Moral Majority," piety and politics became almost passionate bedfellows. But there is a major difference between religion's role in American politics and its standing within the three branches of American government. As much as the politicians protest their religious devotion, the Court, the Congress, and the Executive Branch have all been criticized for being too secular in response to religious groups and issues. The separation of church and state may seem moribund from the perspective of political rhetoric, but it is alive and kicking within the structure of government itself.

Much the same situation applies in Pakistan, Indonesia, and Thailand, though Sweden remains an ironic exception as a formally religious state in which religion has only a minor political presence. Elsewhere, it is common for political figures to cloak themselves in religious garb, much like Reagan himself. Note, however, that many

Religious Capital and Capital Religions   29

of these same politicians have a quite different religious agenda once off the stump and into state administration. Here religion may be not merely irrelevant but a major liability. Absolute religious principles do not fit well in the "compromise" world of actual governance. Theological constraints on state actions do not sit well with elected officials who seek to preserve a capacity for flexible policy responses to changing circumstances. And if religion must be incorporated into law or state policy, most officials prefer very brief and very general codifications which can be variously interpreted as conditions warrant. It is true that this may leave religion as a loose cannon on the decks of the ship of state, but the politicians have at least temporary control of the fuse.

Even the smallest nation today is heavily implicated in an international political economy that requires reliability and predictability in international terms. Local religious customs such as the Islamic prohibition of financial interest introduce extraneous factors which may alienate potential partners and allies. Partly in response to this international context, Third World governments are increasingly specialized, professionalized, and bureaucratized—though not always in that order. Indeed, perhaps the single most dramatic case of a "religious state" has begun to relax its strictures largely for these reasons. Recent reports out of Iran[18] suggest that its political leadership is quietly deemphasizing the Islamic traditionalism of the late Khomeini as a necessary price for readmission into the world economy.

But even where a nation's political leadership is overtly religious, most governments depend upon a sophisticated civil service that may become a community unto itself, one that is frequently secular and sometimes cynical with respect to its nation's traditional religious patterns. Religious commitments made by political officials can be broken by bureaucratic functionaries. However, politicians are more than capable of breaking their own commitments. There is a well-known political dynamic that offers a counter to Robert Michels' "iron law of oligarchy"[19] in explaining the persistence of elites; elected politicians ultimately lose when "pie-in-the-sky" rhetoric runs afoul of "pie-in-the-face" reality. Politicians often promise more than they can deliver in the search for votes and/or legitimacy, and this portends an almost inevitable fall when they are later held to their own standards. At the risk of metaphoric overkill, any politician who campaigns on the basis of religion is using a double-edged sword.

30   N. J. Demerath III

Any government that seeks legitimacy through religion in the absence of other noncoercive sources may risk long-term losses despite short-term gains. And once religion is introduced into politics, it can be very difficult to pull it back. Not only do its absolute criteria clash with the politics of compromise, but religion tends to be emotionally "hot" and accompanied by its own experts who are frequently difficult to control. Finally, very few state officials relish publicly opposing religious considerations once they have been activated.

All this explains why many politicians want it both ways: that is, public rhetoric on behalf of religion in politics coupled with private efforts to stem the tide within government. This describes recent heads of Pakistan, Indonesia, Thailand, and the United States. But as pointed out by Johnston and Figa, the problem may be paradoxically compounded, because the "less legitimate the regime, the more it needs the church. . . . [and] the more the church may be disposed to oppose it for moral and evangelical reasons."[20]

From the standpoint of the government, religion may be both a *source* and an *object* of administration. It is a source because it offers an institutional network whose tentacles reach both deep and wide across the society. This allows a variety of administrative efficiencies, ranging from the Swedish census to Indonesia's *golkar* apparatus. Perhaps the classic instance involves the British raj in India, during which the colonial government greatly increased the systematic rigidity of the Hindu caste system to enhance record keeping and administrative control over the sprawling country.

As this suggests, religion may also be an administrative object when it represents a potential base of countermobilization which must be dampened. As a cultural wild card in the frequently fixed game of state politics, religion poses a threat to established policies and policy makers. As we have seen, this is a major reason why "state religions" are more common than "religious states." Governments frequently "volunteer" their offices and resources to "assist" with important religious functions, including religious publication and education, pilgrimages such as the Islamic hajj to Mecca, and the maintenance of churches, mosques, and temples. Alliances between government and religion frequently smack of cooptation, and religious groups sometimes prefer to remain outside of the political establishment and state apparatus to preserve their power potential. Meanwhile, laws concerning the free exercise of religion often have

Religious Capital and Capital Religions   31

explicit or implicit contingencies concerning the national interest. Such decisions rarely involve the self-conscious constitutionalism of the US Supreme Court's religious rulings and, for example, its four-step "Lemon" criteria for acceptable state religious coincidence and cooperation; they may sometimes entail the actual suppression of speech and assembly. Still, the basic logic applies in the United States as well as elsewhere.

Despite the emphasis thus far on the state's control over religion rather than vice versa, there is no question that religion may exert power in state matters. Even where religion lacks access to the political instruments of "structural power" (whether coercion, votes, budgets, or networks of influentials), it may wield considerable "cultural power," which Rhys Williams and I have defined as follows:

> "Cultural power" is the capacity to use cultural resources to affect political outcomes. These resources include symbols, ideologies, moral authority and cultural meanings. They can be used to legitimate or delegitimate political outcomes or actors, to keep some issues public and political and others out of the public eye altogether, and to frame the terms with which issues are discussed when they are public.[21]

While this kind of power is often overlooked by political analysts, it can be very potent indeed, especially for issues overlaid with moral salience. Without arguing that politicians are bereft of such power, it tends to be especially emphasized by outsiders, social movements, and religious forces lacking more direct structural levers. If it is true that religion and the state often occupy quite different realms in culture and structure respectively, religion is by no means imprisoned within its cultural sphere.

However, movements and institutions which rely on cultural power tend to be limited in the kind of influence wielded. Thus, religion is more likely to achieve some types of political outcomes than others. Here three further distinctions are important: First, religion is less apt to manifest "positive power" than "negative power," where the former involves the ability to initiate action and create change, and the latter entails blocking or vetoing an impending course. Second, religion is less likely to engage in "primary power" than "secondary power," where the former involves the capacity to seize and carry through a policy-making transaction as the prime

32   N. J. Demerath III

mover, whereas the latter engages in fine-tuning from the sidelines. Third, religion is less likely to wield "public power" than "private power," where the former refers to actions on the part of the government itself and the latter refers to the actions of the citizenry as individuals. Although this boundary differs from society to society, it is rarely absent and rarely without a constraining influence on religion's legitimacy as a social force.

IRONIES OF RELIGIOUS SECULARIZATION, PLURALISM, AND AUTHORITY

So far we have examined a range of reasons why religion may be clutched to the politician's bosom for purposes of legitimacy but held at arms length in the process of actual governance. Formal religious establishments notwithstanding, the "separation of church and state" is by no means a uniquely American political reflex. But if this is so from the political perspective, what about the vantage point of religion itself? Much of this turns on the much-discussed and widely misunderstood issue of *secularization*.

Few conceits have been more enduring in the West than the notion that other societies will inevitably "evolve," "develop," or "modernize." One critical element of this perspective for Western intellectuals involves the secularization motif. Whether defined as the demystification of the sacred, the diminishment of sacred salience, or the sacred's retreat from the societal core, the process denotes a cultural change that many regard as the inevitable result of such basic developmental processes as Weberian rationalization and Durkheimian differentiation. Imagine, then, the rush to reconsider following the religious recrudescence of the last decade. As religion has seemed to reemerge as a major political force throughout the world, and as a "fundamentalist" revival (however mislabeled) has loomed within virtually every world faith, theories of secularization have been assaulted.[22]

Of course, much of this corrective was deserved; any implication that religion follows a linear course through decline to disappearance is off the mark. At the same time, religion's mere persistence—even its perfervid resurgence—is by no means a clinching rebuttal to a more reasoned secularization thesis. Paradoxically, secularization may be an actual *precondition* for religious vitality in at least three senses:

Religious Capital and Capital Religions   33

First, any religious group must continually adapt to changing secular circumstances if it is to remain relevant to its adherents. Secularization is basically an adaptive process. Many "modernist" religious groups faulted for being overly accommodating to their social contexts would only have fewer members served less meaningfully without such compromises. Indeed, this describes the single most common dynamic and largest faction of each of the world's religions—sensationalist news reporting notwithstanding. It characterizes the Islamic majority in both Pakistan and Indonesia as well as Buddhists in Thailand and Christians in Sweden and the United States.

Second, however, religious revivals are frequently direct responses to secularization itself. Every retreat into the past is inevitably a dialectic with the present. Certainly this is true of those who seek a return to some prior and purer religious alternative to the present, as in the fundamentalist case. Note that these movements generally involve persons marginal to—and not to be confused with—the cultural mainstream. Precisely because of their marginality, these groups and their leaders typically lack the broad political credibility necessary to convert sparks into fire. This is true of the leadership of both the American religious Right and the traditionalist mullahs of many Islamic societies.[23] There is a sense in which charges of fundamentalism from the secular camp resemble the charges of communist conspiracy from the political Right. Fundamentalists and secularists occupy identical positions in each others' demonology, and, as Roland Robertson has noted, fundamentalism itself is largely an inverse function of modernism.[24] However, none of this is to deny the force of such religious movements, especially if their elemental flame burns long enough to survive the secularizing tendencies which accompany their mobility into higher status ranks and the ways of conventional politics. In fact, some religious movements have had the ironic effect of increasing modernization in the surrounding society, a point that Arvind Sharma makes with regard to Hinduism in India.[25]

Finally, a third way in which secularity may produce religious vitality concerns the extent to which religious movements serve as surrogates for secular concerns. It is sometimes difficult to disentangle such overlapping causes as religion, power, ethnicity, social class, regionalism, nationalism, and even anti-Westernism. There are in-

34   N. J. Demerath III

stances in which religion is politicized as the only permitted form of social protest, hence a serious masquerade for less "legitimate" grievances. Sometimes this is cynical on the part of protest leaders; at other points it is because religion offers the only available vocabulary and resources for such movements. For whatever reason, cases of public religious conflict may be culturally encoded with secular subtexts and agendas. Thus, some of the force behind Islamic fundamentalism in countries such as Pakistan, Egypt, and Iran represents the favored option of traditionalism generally and is akin to the political platform of the American "Moral Majority" in favoring a return to bygone familial, sexual, and economic relations. On the other hand, Islamic fundamentalism in countries such as Indonesia and Malaysia serves some student activists as a permissible proxy for prohibited left-wing antigovernment and anti-Western protest. Here, as with social movements generally, recruitment may say more about local social and political networks than about religious sentiment itself.[26] Of course, a leftist political ideology also describes the "base communities" of Latin American Catholicism, where it is sometimes difficult to know which comes first, the ideology or the theology.

Yet the relationship between the secularization and politicization of religion is complex and in part curvilinear. At one extreme, a strictly traditional religion may be so otherworldly and so out of touch with secular issues as to turn its back on politics altogether. At the other extreme, a highly secularized religion may lack the galvanizing force needed for political influence despite the private political concerns of its nominal adherents. Religious groups in the middle of the continuum are most often politically implicated; here secularization has gone far enough to admit political concerns but not so far as to be politically enervating.

Secularization is related to the kind of politicization as well as the degree. In general, secularization tends to be more pronounced among those with greater education, higher status, and more contact with the West—those who are more rewarded by the status quo and hence more likely to favor it politically. Ironically, then, those forms of religion which are most likely to be allied with the state tend to be more secularized rather than less, or less traditionally religious rather than more. Conversely, politically mobilized religion is more apt to be in opposition to the state than in partnership with it.

Religious Capital and Capital Religions   35

Meanwhile, secularization is by no means the only major variable at work here; another involves *religious pluralism*. While few societies are as religiously heterogeneous as Indonesia, India, or the United States, virtually none is religiously monolithic. Even where a nation is dominated by a single faith tradition—for example, Christian, Hindu, Islamic, Jewish—major differences within the faith frequently loom large—for example, Catholic versus Protestant; Hindu versus Sikh; Sunni versus Shiite; Orthodox versus Reform. How does the degree of heterogeneity bear upon religion's relation to the state?

This issue too is rimmed with irony. In the pure case of total religious homogeneity, a religious alliance with the state would seem a structural redundancy of a cultural fait accompli. Of course, such cases rarely occur outside the imagination of Emile Durkheim. And yet a number of countries offer approximations in which the dominance of a single religious faith is so encompassing as to reduce the urgency of its governmental ties. Even when the government itself begins to undergo secularization, there is little sense of alarm over the absence of perceived religious competition, as both Sweden and Thailand attest.

But, of course, competition is key. Where there is very little, an alliance with the state does not matter; where there is a great deal, such an alliance may matter too much. Moreover, the very prospect of one religion or religious group gaining establishment status may be sufficient to activate a religious conflict that has been previously quiescent. Earlier we saw the increase in Sunni-Shiite conflict in Pakistan as talk of Islamization escalated. But perhaps the classic case involves the Hindu-Muslim rivalry on the eve of Indian independence and the partitioning of Pakistan in 1947. For centuries prior to and during British colonial rule, Hinduism and Islam had coexisted relatively calmly—indeed, there is a sense in which these two quite different religions were mutually complementary in serving India's long-term cultural development. However, once autonomous power was at stake, the conflict between the two led to bloody rupture.

Here, then, is another major consideration that favors effective separation. To put the matter slightly differently, in those cases where the political stakes of a state religion are low, at least a symbolic form may develop and persist. But in more pluralistic instances where the

36   N. J. Demerath III

political stakes are high and zero-sum as the gain in one religion's influence is accompanied by the loss of another's, competition itself may ward off the eventuality. Post–World War II Indonesia and the United States are both cases in point. In the former, Islam is pitted against Hinduism, Buddhism, Christianity, and animism with all of their extrareligious connotations; in the United States, it was not until the 1940s and the development of Catholicism as a looming threat to established Protestantism that church-state litigation began in earnest, following a period of some 150 years of litigious lassitude.

However ironic, it is not accidental that the concept of *civil religion* has its most conspicuous applications in Indonesia and the United States, two of the world's most religiously pluralistic societies. Both the American concept of a Judeo-Christian heritage and the Indonesian umbrella of *pancasila* are to some extent cultural fabrications. Each is used to impose a sense of unity over the reality of diversity; both are "civil" in Cuddahy's sense of putting a polite face on a conflicted situation. The two also share a tendency to substitute the symbols of religious influence for its reality.

Finally, another nest of factors related to religion and the state involves the matter of *religious authority*. It is, of course, Christocentric to discuss the "separation of *church* and state" worldwide, though the phrase has become a global shorthand for the generic issue. The ecclesiastical and organizational implications of a "church" are by no means the least of Christianity's distinguishing characteristics. Yet the extent of a hierarchical structure is best regarded as a variable rather than an absolute. Within Christianity itself, there are wide and obvious differences between "episcopal" top-down structures, on the one hand, and "congregational" bottom-up models of local autonomy on the other. But similar variations occur within other religious traditions. Within Islam, this is a fundamental distinction between the more authoritatively structured Shiites and the more locally autonomous Sunnis. Hinduism is more centrally organized in Indonesia's Bali than in India. Buddhism's *songha* in Thailand differs from Buddhism's organizational form in Tibet, let alone within the "greater vehicle" of China or Japan.

Meanwhile, there is a second distinction that is equally pertinent to the issue of authority, and it is encapsulated in Weber's dichotomy

Religious Capital and Capital Religions 37

between "emissary" and "exemplary" prophecy.[27] Whereas the former involves ascetic activism in the search for redress and reform in this world, the latter exemplifies the passive pursuit of virtue through mysticism and contemplation. Here the Christian, Judaic, and Islamic faiths tend toward the ethical ideal, while Hinduism and Buddhism are more inclined to the exemplary. Once again, however, there is variation within each tradition.

In fact, these two distinctions can be harnessed for the purposes at hand. From the standpoint of sheer political potency, the combination with the greatest potential is ethical prophecy embedded within and protected by a hierarchical ecclesiastical structure (for example, eighth-century Islam or pre-Reformation Catholicism). Conversely, the least likely source of political power is emissary prophecy without organizational trappings (for example, the Hindu guru). Note, however, that the remaining two combinations are important. Ethical prophecy without the reinforcement of an organizational structure may amount to spitting in the political wind. And an elaborate ecclesiastical structure *without* an ethically prophetic spark is particularly vulnerable to state cooptation. After all, those who make it to the top of such ecclesiastical ladders are selectively recruited, gradually socialized, and generally rewarded for their loyalty to the political status quo.

This last scenario suggests one final irony of separation: those religious groups with the greatest organizational resources to place at the disposal of a political perspective rarely fulfill their political potential. If they retain their independence outside of the government, they are more likely to whisper than shout, for fear of being overheard. If they are taken into the hall of state itself, they may never be heard from again in anything approximating a prophetic voice; after gaining so much, they now have too much to lose. Illustrations here are widespread, for this is perhaps the most common saga in religion's continuing but ambivalent groping for secular power. From the standpoint of church and state, then, seeming power may sometimes become powerlessness, and on the other hand, religions outside the state's cold embrace can occasionally become very powerful indeed. This is a major reason why cults and sectarian movements on the fringes of society sometimes exert disproportionate influence by refusing the path of compromise and cooptation. It

38   N. J. Demerath III

is in this sense that religion's capital is often maximized when it is not a capital religion.

CONCLUSION

It is with indebtedness to Thomas Jefferson and his concern for a "wall of separation" between church and state that this paper has offered a "wall-eyed" view of religion and power. In focusing on a very limited question, it has received a somewhat surprising response. Despite religion's prominence as a source of political legitimacy and campaign rhetoric, it is rarely a dominant factor in the affairs of state. The United States is less distinctive in this regard than many Americans suppose, and insofar as its own tradition of "church-state separation" continues, this may owe less to legal and constitutional requirements than to a range of social and political constraints which we share with other nations.

In reviewing a series of political and religious factors which bear on the relation between sacred agencies and secular power, this paper seeks more to begin discussion than to end it. Indeed, its most fundamental conviction is that both the subject and the style of the research are worthwhile. Religion and its relation to society have too often been explored through the dark lens of single societies treated singularly. It is only by widening our perspective that we may deepen it.

ENDNOTES

[1] The phrase itself comes not from the First Amendment of the Constitution, as is widely supposed, but from a letter written by Thomas Jefferson to a friend in 1802 in which he refers to a "desirable wall of separation" between the realms.

[2] Max Weber, *The Methodology of the Social Sciences* (New York: The Free Press, 1949), 90–113.

[3] Max Weber, *Economy and Society*, 2 vols. (Berkeley: University of California Press, 1978), 1159–60.

[4] Samuel Krislov, "Alternatives to Separation of Church and State in Countries Outside the United States," in James E. Wood, Jr., *Religion and the State* (Waco, Tex.: Baylor University Press, 1985).

[5] For an elaboration of this point, see N. J. Demerath III and Rhys H. Williams, *A Bridging of Faiths: Religion and Power in a New England City* (Princeton: Princeton University Press, 1992).

Religious Capital and Capital Religions   39

6Hen C. Van Moorseven and Ger Van der Tan, *Written Constitutions: A Comparative Study* (Dobbs Ferry, N.Y.: Oceana Publishers, 1978).

7Krislov.

8V. S. Naipul, *Among the Believers* (New York: Random House, 1981).

9Clifford Geertz, *Local Knowledge* (New York: Basic Books, 1983), 186.

10Ibid., 233.

11Clifford Geertz, *The Interpretation of Cultures* (New York: Basic Books, 1973).

12Cf. Henry J. Korson, "Islamization and Social Policy in Pakistan," in *Journal of South Asian and Middle Eastern Studies*, 6 (2) (1982): 71–90; Anita M. Weiss, ed., *Islamic Reassertion in Pakistan* (Syracuse: Syracuse University Press, 1986); and Lawrence Zimring, "Public Policy Dilemmas and Pakistan's Nationality Problem: The Legacy of Zia ul-Haq," in *Asian Survey*, 28 (8) (1986): 795–812; Hamza Alavi, "Ethnicity, Muslim Society, and the Pakistan Ideology," in Weiss, 21–48.

13For a tour de force through Indonesia's cultural history in a single sentence, see Geertz, *Local Knowledge*, 226.

14Cf. Donald E. Weatherbee, "Indonesia in 1985: Chills and Thaws," in *Asian Survey*, 26 (2) (1986): 141–49.

15For an excellent analysis of the *songha* in relation to the Thai state, see Samboon Suksamran, *Buddhism and Politics in Thailand* (Singapore: Institute of Southeast Asian Studies, 1982).

16See, for example, Prasert Yamklingfung, "Family, Religion, and Socio-Economic Change in Thailand," in *East Asian Cultural Studies*, 13 (1974): 20–31.

17For examples, see John T. S. Madeley, "Scandinavian Christian Democracy: Throwback or Portent?" in *European Journal of Political Research*, 5 (1977): 267–86; Lennart Ejerfelt, "Civil Religion: Made in Sweden," in Bela Harmati, ed., *The Church and Civil Religion in the Nordic Countries of Europe* (Geneva: Lutheran World Foundation, 1984); and Goran Goransson, "Church and Nation: A Changing Relationship in Sweden," in Harmati, 72–78.

18Cf. *New York Times*, 8 April 1991, 1.

19Robert Michels, *Political Parties* (New York: Free Press, 1911).

20Hank Johnston and Jozef Figa, "The Church and Political Opposition: Comparative Perspectives on Mobilization against Authoritarian Regimes," in *Journal for the Scientific Study of Religion* 27 (1) (1988): 32–47.

21Demerath and Williams.

22Phillip E. Hammond, ed., *The Sacred in a Secular Age* (Berkeley: University of California Press: 1985).

23Cf. Said Amir Arjomand, "Social Change and Movements of Revitalization in Contemporary Islam," in James A. Beckford, ed., *New Religious Movements and Rapid Social Change* (London: Sage/UNESCO Publishers, 1986), 87–112; and Nader Saiedi, "What is Islamic Fundamentalism," in Jeffrey K. Hadden and

40   *N. J. Demerath III*

Anson Shupe, eds., *Prophetic Religion and Politics* (New York: Paragon House, 1986).

[24]Roland Robertson, "Considerations from within the American Context on the Significance of Church-State Tension," in *Sociological Analysis,* 42 (3) (1981): 193–208.

[25]Arvind Sharma, "New Hindu Religious Movements in India," in Beckford, ed., 20–39.

[26]K. D. Jackson, *Traditional Authority, Islam and Rebellion* (Berkeley: University of California Press, 1980); Judith Nagata, "Indices of the Islamic Resurgence in Malaysia," in Richard T. Anton and Mary Elaine Hegland, *Religious Resurgence: Contemporary Cases in Islam, Christianity, and Judaism* (Syracuse: Syracuse University Press, 1987).

[27]Cf. Max Weber, *The Sociology of Religion* (Boston: Beacon, 1963), 46–59.

[9]

Nikki R. Keddie

Secularism and the State: Towards Clarity and Global Comparison

Debates about the process of secularization have, in recent years, centred on the work of a group of sociologists and historians, mostly British, who have put forth and debated what is known as 'the secularization thesis'.[1] This correlates modernization with secularization, and generally measures secularization primarily through declining church membership and declared religious beliefs. In most of this discussion, secularization is attributed almost exclusively to socio-economic change, without significant reference to the state, to ideas, or to political movements. While there have been modifications of the thesis over time, one recent definition shows that it still retains its essential characteristics: the secularization thesis is a 'research programme with, at its core, an explanatory model' which 'asserts that the social significance of religion diminishes in response to the operation of three salient features of modernization, namely 1) social differentiation, 2) societalization, and 3) rationalization'.[2] These factors are defined later, but clearly all three involve societal change rather than changes in ideas, political movements or the state. Advocates of the secularization thesis have also tended to see it as a progressive one-way process; societies and their constituent members become more secular as they become more modernized. This article, in contrast, contends that such an overwhelmingly 'societal' and non-political view cannot adequately explain secularization. Furthermore, it cannot explain the rise in recent decades and in many parts of the world of anti-secular movements and ideas.

The secularization thesis concentrates heavily on Great Britain, with some attention to western Europe. Its advocates attribute American exceptionalism to such factors as a multiplicity of churches and ethnicity, or to the supposedly secular nature of American church teachings.[3] The non-Christian and non-Western worlds are generally omitted from this debate. There secularization has, as I will show, been more influenced by government action than by autonomous societal changes, and trends toward secularization have sometimes been dramatically reversed. The original secularization thesis, and even its modifications, tended to see secularization as a one-way street. Religious revivals in the US or elsewhere were generally ignored or explained away. A leader of this school even wrote a book on the rise and fall of the US religious Right, published in 1988.[4] Reversing the old saying, one might comment, 'I'll see it when I believe it'.

The Complex Nature of Secularism

It is not just the conclusions of the secularization thesis that can be challenged, but also its limited concept of secularization and the secular which centres on declining religious belief and church membership. Secularization theory shares the linear-progressive viewpoint of modernization theory, and is really a sub-category of that theoretical approach. Although it is broadly true that societal secularization has usually accompanied modernization, the theory is undialectical and plays down contradictory forces. Hardly noted are the counter-examples to the view, including the fact that government secularization policies often bring about anti-secular reactions, especially among certain classes and groups. In recent decades, rapid modernization has contributed not only to secularism but to major anti-secularizing trends, especially in countries with growing fundamentalist movements.

---

[1] This article had its origins in a paper written for a conference on past and future *fins de siècle* held at the Library of Congress in late 1994 and organized by Bruce Mazlish and Alvin Kibel. Thanks for helpful suggestions are due to them and the other participants, and also to others who have read and commented on the paper, including Charles Tilly, Perry Anderson, Robin Blackburn and Theda Skocpol.
[2] Roy Wallis and Steve Bruce, 'Secularization: The Orthodox Model', in Steve Bruce, ed., *Religion and Modernization: Sociologists and Historians Debate the Secularization Thesis*, Oxford 1994, pp. 8–9.
[3] For the secularization thesis and some articles critical of it, see especially Bruce, *Religion and Modernization*; the US is the focus of Roger Finke's contribution, 'An Unsecular America', pp. 145–69. The whole idea of a uniform process of secularization is attacked in David Martin, *The Religious and the Secular: Studies in Secularization*, London 1969.
[4] Steve Bruce, *The Rise and Fall of the New Christian Right: Conservative Protestant Politics in America 1978–1988*, Oxford 1988. The book does make valid points about the narrow base and legislative failures of the Christian Right.

Even Bryan R. Wilson, a founding father of the secularization thesis, notes that many who write of it limit their evidence to church membership, their subject of study to Christianity, and their idea of secularization to just one of its many meanings.[5] One may add that even such major Christian countries as France and Italy are rarely mentioned in such works. Nor is history much mentioned by the sociologists involved.

One may agree with these sociologists that modernization and its subcategories of urbanization, migration, and industrialization were by and large associated in the West with a weakening of religious institutions and belief. But we might find other modernizing forces that correlate with secularization, including such cultural factors as the rise of literacy and public education, and the emergence of new types of reading material and entertainment. There seems no reason to pick some aspects of modernization and not others as causing secularization.

Further, there is little reason to think that levels of church membership or declared belief are sufficient measures of secularization. Secular attitudes and behaviour are characteristic of many church members and believers. In many societies, modernization has produced two major cultures in each religion, roughly, that of the secular and that of the true believer, and in many areas there has been a reaction against secular nationalist culture and rule. Particularly in the US, in some ex-communist countries, and some non-Western ones there has been a religious reaction which also has political implications. Studies including more countries might yield more complex and dialectical generalizations than those posed by the secularization thesis.[6]

A different trend in the scholarly study of secularization and secularism is to stress the role and writings of intellectuals like Locke, Milton, Voltaire, Jefferson and others. While, like the purely sociological view, this outlook contains some truth, both views greatly understate the role of politics and the state in both social secularization and the spread of secularist views.

Secularism and the State

While the word 'secularization' is commonly used mainly for a social trend and the word 'secular' is applied largely to governmental policy, the two are profoundly, if dialectically, related in a way not covered by the secularization thesis. A secularized population encourages a secular state, but secular states also encourage mass secularization, especially of the schools and of those receiving schooling. Some consideration of the secularization of the state and of politics is needed to understand the secularization of society.

---

[5] Bryan R. Wilson, 'Reflections on a Many-Sided Controversy', in Bruce, *Religion and Modernization*.

[6] Some of the pros and cons of the secularization thesis are discussed in various articles by Karel Dobbelaere, who also provides bibliographies: 'Secularization: A Multi-Dimensional Concept', *Current Sociology*, vol. 29, no. 2, Summer 1981, pp. 1–213; 'Secularization Theories and Sociological Paradigms: A Reformulation of the Private-Public Dichotomy and the Problem of Societal Integration', *Sociological Analysis*, vol. 46, no. 4, Winter 1985, pp. 377–386; 'Some Trends in European Sociology of Religion: The Secularization Debate', *Sociological Analysis*, same issue, pp. 107–37.

No state today is entirely secular or entirely non-secular. The very strengthening of a state demanded by modern economies requires considerable state control of public education, civil law, welfare and other spheres that is more secular than anything that existed in the past. A large degree of secularism is a necessary concomitant of the modern industrial .world. Even fundamentalist Iran soon adopted a series of essentially secular laws and procedures, and Khomeini in a sense secularized religion, especially in his startling 1988 decree which stated that Qur'anic obligations, like daily prayer, could give way to reasons of state.[7] A similar secularization will probably occur in any fundamentalist government that hopes to keep power. At the opposite extreme, no state yet seen has been purely secular, whether the word is used to mean state separation from religion or state control of religion. (State separation and state control are not absolutes, and do not exhaust all the political meanings of secularism, which is a contested and changing concept.)[8]

The two currently salient political meanings of state control and state separation are often not distinguished. For many Westerners the word 'secular' means essentially the 'separation of church and state'—to use the American formulation. Secularists in this sense are those who believe in that separation, whatever their private religious beliefs. This wording of a common idea is especially American, and America may come closer to such a separation than any other major Western country. Americans can note that this separation has not hurt religion in the US, but has allowed for the flowering of a variety of sects and churches, both Christian and non-Christian. Even this formulation, no matter how it is worded, may not be an adequate description of reality which is much more varied than any such phrase would imply. First, to judge by the situation in some of the most secular Western countries, church and state are nowhere wholly separate, and usually have important ties, whether or not the church-state relationships favour a single established or dominant religion. (For purposes of brevity, the word 'church' here will be taken to mean the institutions of all organized religions, and the word 'state' will refer to all levels of government—central, provincial and local.) In Germany and Spain, for example, the state collects reli-

---

[7] See especially Ervand Abrahamian, *Khomeinism: Essays on the Islamic Republic*, Berkeley 1993, p. 57: 'The government in Islam', Khomeini elaborated, 'is a primary rule having precedence over secondary rulings such as praying, fasting, and performing the *hajj*...' In short, the state, so long as it was a truly Islamic state, could overrule the highest-ranking clerics and their interpretation of the sacred law'.

[8] In John Ruedy's excellent summary, 'Secular is a term used to distinguish the temporal or worldly from the spiritual, while secularism has come to denote a philosophy that privileges the domain of the temporal and diminishes that of the spiritual. The former grows to cover civil affairs and education, while the latter is increasingly restricted to the areas of private belief, worship, and conduct. While secularism as a philosophy is central to the Western experience, it should be borne in mind that the concept has evolved historically and that it is still doing so. What was considered the proper province of human rational decision was different in the fifteenth century than in the nineteenth century and is even more different in the late twentieth. Secondly, it should be stressed that the struggle over the frontier between the secular and the religious is one characterized by continuous tension and that, up to now, the exact line of the frontier between the two has never been agreed upon. One must also recognize that in the West there has seldom been agreement among secularists as a group, nor among the religious as a group, as to where exactly that frontier should be'. Introduction to John Ruedy, ed., *Islamism and Secularism in North Africa*, New York 1994, p. xiv.

24

gious taxes that are used to support the church; in France the state helps support churches and some mosques; and in Great Britain there is an established religion, a law of blasphemy—however rarely employed— that covers only the majority religion, and state support for various forms of religious education.[9]

Even in the US, which at least since the 1962 Supreme Court decision against prayer in the schools has been arguably the most secular of major Western countries, the state indirectly supports the vast network of church schools and institutions by exempting them from taxes as non-profit organizations and by certain other indirect subsidies. Nor is what may seem like a strict church-state separation always rigorously enforced; prayer in schools, for example, is still quite widespread in several areas of the US despite its being illegal.[10] And in 1997 the Supreme Court may have heralded a less-strict church-state separation when it reversed a recent decision of a past Supreme Court and said that public school teachers could teach certain special classes in parochial school classrooms. (An apparently 'anti-religious' Supreme Court decision also in 1997 seems more limited in its church-state implications.) Another church-state issue coming to the fore both federally and at state level is the proposal, already enacted in a few states, for state-subsidized vouchers for poor children to attend private—mostly religious—schools. Such a provision has recently been successfully challenged as unconstitutional in a Wisconsin appeals court, but voucher proposals remain very much alive. In the US, and to a degree elsewhere, state-school issues have been central to conflicts over secularism, and the lines of acceptance and conflict on these and other questions are continually changing.

Besides the ambiguity of such concepts as separation of church and state, particularly when the ideal is compared to actual conditions, there is the fact that some applications of 'secularism' in practice mean something quite antithetical to the ideal of church-state separation. They produce instead increasing control of the church by the state. This is clearest in a number of non-Western countries, including modern Turkey, Pahlavi Iran, Bourguiba's Tunisia, and Nasser's Egypt. In such countries, with strong religious institutions that formerly controlled of much of law, education and social welfare, the state had to take power from those institutions to introduce modernizing and centralizing changes. Such

---

[9] Peter G. Forster, 'Secularization in the English Context: Some Conceptual and Empirical Problems', *The Sociological Review*, vol. 20, no. 2, May 1972, pp. 153–68. Forster notes that sociologists tend to dismiss the importance of English state defense of the Church, but that it includes 'the position of the monarch as head of church as well as state, the bishops in the House of Lords, the Mayor's Sunday, the oath in court, religious broadcasting on the BBC, church parades in the armed forces, subsidies to church schools, and above all the collective worship and religious instruction in state schools. Though these observances are not generally obligatory, one must generally contract out to avoid them... Nearly every English child is exposed to the religious component of dominant values... when the truth of Christianity is affirmed at morning assembly'. (pp. 164–5) Recent writers have noted the frequent use in urban schools of legally allotted religious time to teach things other than Christianity, however.

[10] One article estimates that 25 per cent of US schools still begin with Bible or prayer reading, and many end with released time for religious instruction. N.J. Demerath III and Rhys H. Williams, 'A Mythical Past and an Uncertain Future', *Church-State Relations— Tensions and Transitions*, New Brunswick 1987.

state control of religious institutions has been more important in the West than is usually realized, with the modern state taking over much of education, including parts formerly controlled by churches, and regulating church behaviour in a variety of ways. Especially in 'backward' European countries whose rulers wanted to catch up with the West—such as Russia both before and under communism—state control and manipulation of religion and the church were notable. Communist countries are often not referred to as secular, perhaps because the state control of the church was so obvious, and yet on this point there was little to choose between communist countries and Ataturk's 'secular' Turkey which, if anything, more forcibly changed religion and permissible religious practices. On this point, as on some others mentioned, there appears to be a continuum—from countries with little control by the state over the church to countries with a great deal of control—and it is not always clear which countries should be called secular.

The phenomenon of continuities and continuums between the secular and the non-secular exists in belief as well as in practice. It is nonetheless true that in the realm of belief there are clusters on each end of the continuum—on the one side, those who do not believe religion should mix in politics at all, and, on the other, those who strongly believe that it should. The latter are often referred to as 'fundamentalists'. Many secularists are ideological and politically committed, as are anti-secularists. Indeed, secularism has been called an ideology, and some secularists behave in ideological fashion.

The Non-Western Experience of Secularism

The usual procedure in making comparisons covering both Western and non-Western countries in modern times is to begin with the West, where a whole series of modern developments came earliest, and then proceed eastward. This is a logical approach but, in the case of secularism, an important new perspective may be gained if we first turn to what happened in the past two centuries in many non-Western countries where secularization was an important issue, and then see if this sheds light on Western developments.

In the non-Western world, secularism, whether or not the word was widely used, seems to have been especially important in Muslim countries and in South Asia. The basic reasons for its importance in Muslim countries are not hard to find. First, as in Judaism and Christianity, the prevailing religion was monotheistic and scriptual, implying a basic minimum of common belief and practice among believers. In all three religions, education, law, and social practice all had strong religious elements, involving both considerable control by religious institutions and a set of beliefs guiding ideology and activity. In addition, Christianity and Islam had religious institutions with considerable economic and political power. Such cultural, political, and economic power in the hands of religious institutions was tied to traditional ways of doing things which affected both economic and political structures. Thus, as modernization developed, the old religious institutions came under attack by intellectuals and rulers. These institutions were inadequate to, and could not quickly adapt to, modern technology,

26

science, centralized and bureaucratic political structures. This is a simplified and schematic picture of the rise of political secularization in both the Christian and Muslim worlds, and, to a degree, of that in Judaism. Islamic history is different from Western Christian history, partly because modernizing trends began earlier and have been more gradual in the West, and also because Islam has not had a strong secular legal tradition. These are two of the factors that have made secularization more difficult and contentious in recent decades in the Islamic world than in the West, while all the main scriptural monotheistic religions have been more resistant to secularization than have other religious traditions.

In India there was a variation on the above pattern. Hinduism was far from scriptural or monotheistic, and it has even been argued that it was not, in premodern times, really a religion at all, if religion is taken to mean a common body of beliefs.[11] Its institutions were more local and varied than were those of Christianity or Islam, but they were, often allied with government, law and education. In India, the rise of secularism, before and after independence, was largely tied to the creation of a nation-state, originally as part of the anti-British struggle. If identities remained primarily religious, there was no chance of creating a unified nation. And if Hinduism was to be openly favoured over other religions, there was similarly no chance of developing a multi-religious national liberation struggle, or of keeping the nation united after independence. The fact that other religions, notably Islam, Christianity, and Sikhism, were more scriptural and unified gave the Hindus who took the secular approach of the Indian National Congress and later the Congress Party all the more reason to work to keep religion out of politics.

Western works about secularism usually stress intellectual or social belief, but in non-Western countries these were less important than governmental—and sometimes oppositional—political motivations, often tied to economic interests. There were relatively few intellectual figures with relatively little influence espousing secularism before it became a major political or governmental cause. As for popular belief, there is no doubt but that non-Western modernizing governments greatly preceded their populations in secularist beliefs and practices. This primacy of governments in secularization has been somewhat obscured by the fact that not only Western but also indigenous scholars often prefer to discuss the achievements of intellectuals rather than those of governments. While more intellectuals preceded governments in secularism in the West, even in this field scholarship often overstates the role of intellectuals.

A brief summary of secularization in the Middle East since the nineteenth century may illustrate my point. Here the stress will be on the Ottoman Empire and Turkey, which had the longest and ultimately the most radical secularization process; but the trends discussed were found elsewhere, and other countries will be mentioned.

---

[11] See especially the chapters by Guenther D. Sontheimer and Robert Eric Frykenberg in Sontheimer and Hermann Kulke, eds, *Hinduism Reconsidered*, Delhi 1959.

Secularization in the Middle East

Secularization in the Middle East is inseparable both from Westernization and from efforts to strengthen the central state. While it is often
said that state and church were inseparably intertwined in pre-modern
Islam, this is not really true. In the first Islamic centuries, after the first
four pious caliphs, dynasties often paid little attention to what was said
by Islam or the religious classes—at most no more attention than pre-
modern Western rulers did to Christianity.[12] Administration and foreign
relations were carried out with minimal attention to Islam. While there
was much less non-religious law than in the West, Islamic rulers did
have large legal spheres in which the state, not the religious judges,
made decisions, and some basis in tradition or in writing by which such
law worked. In the period called 'early modern' in the West, the Safavid
dynasty in Iran and the Ottomans in the Ottoman Empire ruled states in
which the religious classes, or *ulama*, were more a corporate body than
ever before. Especially in the Ottoman Empire, there were governing
institutions with considerable independence of religious bodies. These
societies were not, however, secular in any modern sense, as dominant
ideas took a religious form; the *ulama* controlled most education, law,
and social services, and also had possession of religious taxes and of
inalienable donations of so-called vaqf land and goods. Not only were
religious institutions and intellectual hegemony far stronger than in
most modern societies, but the central state was weaker and, at least in
most periods, more decentralized.

In its early centuries, the Ottoman state had a series of major and minor
military victories over European Christians, and felt no need to emulate
the West. Beginning in the late-seventeenth century, however, it began
to suffer the reversals that continued over the next two centuries. The
treaties of Karlowitz in 1699 and Kuchuk Kaynarca in 1774 marked
major losses to Austria and Russia. In the nineteenth century, liberation
movements among the Ottoman Balkan Christians cut away long-held
territory, and further territory was lost in the late nineteenth and early
twentieth century.

Along with a growing realization of the strength of the West, this series
of defeats created two opposite reactions from the eighteenth century
onwards. One was to try to emulate the West, especially in military matters. The other was to react against unsuccessful Westernizing reforms
by reasserting the old ways.[13] Governmental reforms began as early as
the early eighteenth century; one of them was to introduce a printing
press with (Arabic) Ottoman characters. Like many other reforms that
may not appear to us as attacks on religion and the religious classes, this

---

[12] On Islam and the state, see especially Nikki R. Keddie, *Iran and the Muslim World:
Resistance and Revolution*, London 1995, ch. 15, and the sources cited therein. Among the
best-informed are Sami Zubaida, *Islam, The People and the State*, London 1989; Nazih N.
Ayubi, *Political Islam: Religion and Politics in the Arab World*, London 1991 and 'Rethinking the Public/Private Dichotomy: Radical Islam and Civil Society in the Middle East,
Contention, vol. 4, no. 2, Winter 1995, pp. 79–105; and Ira Lapidus, 'The Separation of
State and Religion in the Development of Early Islamic Society, *IJMES*, vol. 6, no. 4, 1975,
pp. 363–85.
[13] Niyazi Berkes, *The Development of Secularism in Turkey*, Montreal 1964, ch. 2.

was taken as such. It was said that holy texts might be disseminated widely and be sullied, but there was also concern that the spread of learning beyond the religious classes would weaken their position. When wars with the West recommenced, the reforms of the so-called 'Tulip Period' were largely abandoned under conservative pressure.

Both the Ottoman and the Egyptian experience show that Westernizing governmental reforms depended for success on a change in the structure of the ruling classes. The old regimes in both areas were dependent until the nineteenth century on military groups who opposed the adoption of Western-style military forces—in Egypt the Mamelukes and in the Ottoman Empire the janissaries. Napoleon's invasion of Egypt defeated and weakened the Mamelukes, making it possible for Mohammad Ali (1805–48) to deal them the final blow and then to strengthen and Westernize his armed forces. In the Ottoman Empire there was no similar early weakening of the janissaries, and they overthrew the first reforming sultan, Selim III. Sultan Mahmud II (1808–39) spent years preparing to oppose the janissaries, and then massacred them in 1826, after which he undertook a series of primarily military reforms.

Secularism and Military Education

The military reforms of Mohammad Ali and Mahmud are not usually presented under the heading of secularization, but this was their result. Western uniforms and drill offended many of the *ulama*, and the first new, Westernized schools that were set up outside religious institutions were aimed at servicing the armed forces. These were military medical schools, technical schools, and attached translation bureaux. It was impossible to modernize without reducing the prerogatives of *ulama* and their—often elite—allies, and undermining traditions increasingly identified as 'Islamic'.

The pragmatic and governmental impetus to early secularization was far more important than the ideological impact of the French Revolution or Enlightenment thinking.[14] Other governmental reforms in nineteenth-century Egypt and the Ottoman Empire also had secular connotations: the bringing of *vaqf* and of religious taxes under greater government control, the extension of modern, state-controlled education, the adoption of secular codes especially for trade, reforms in Islamic law and the beginnings of its codification. Such reforms were needed to strengthen the state in the face of Western incursion and internal revolt. Even a ruler seen as a religious reactionary, Abdul Hamid II who reigned in the late nineteenth century, implemented many such self-strengthening measures. They were, however, particularly associated with Mahmud II and

---

[14] Keddie, *Iran and the Muslim World*, ch. 15. In a famous article, important for information other than its main thesis, Bernard Lewis argues that the French Revolution was quickly influential in Ottoman Turkey and could be so because its ideas were secular, not Christian. I have contested this idea in *Iran and the Muslim World*, as have other scholars. See 'The Impact of the French Revolution on Turkey', *Journal of World History*, vol. 1, July 1953, pp. 105–25; also Serif Mardin, *The Genesis of Young Ottoman Thought*, Princeton 1962, 169ff; Niyazi Berkes, *Secularism*, pp. 83–5; and Ibrahim Abu Lughod, *The Arab Rediscovery of Europe*, Princeton 1963, p. 134, n. 28.

with the leading statesmen of the subsequent period, called the *tanzimat* or 'ordering', in 1839–76. In nineteenth-century Egypt such centralizing measures were undertaken especially by rulers—Mohammad Ali and later Isma'il.[15]

In none of these undertakings did the limited utterances of intellectuals or changes in popular opinion regarding religion or church-state relations play a significant role. Modernization of the military, education and trade was carried out—at first entirely and, even in the twentieth century, predominantly—from the top, so that past secularization in the Middle East should be seen as primarily a phenomenon of the state and politics, rather than of intellectual life or social belief and practice.

Such secularization from above was a necessary accompaniment of the economic transformations taking place in these countries, which the old religio-legal structures with their lack of modern or secular law and their ties to agrarian society could not cope with. These transformations, like secularization, had to be heavily promoted by governments, given the weakness of indigenous capitalist classes and the strength of European economic competition. The economic changes achieved did not reach the stage of full-blown, much less free-market, capitalism.

In the Middle East, the dominant form of secularization—that initiated by states—was not at all liberal and was rarely democratic. Not all liberal intellectual opinion in these countries was secularist. True, in states where such secularization was relatively slow in coming—such as Iran, or even Egypt after the post-Mohammad Ali retreat on modernization—a few nineteenth-century intellectuals were both liberal and anti-clerical. In the Ottoman centre, however, the first independent political intellectuals—the Young Ottomans—attacked the over-centralization brought in by the *tanzimat*, including its religious policies. Their leading intellectual, Namik Kemal, constructed an Ottoman past with the equivalent of a Western-style of separation of powers, in which the *ulama* played a key role. The Young Ottomans were constitutionalists, and most of them believed in a constitution that would be less centralizing and secularist than were the *tanzimat* statesmen.[16] In their search for more democratic and decentralized structures, the Young Ottomans did not adopt an anti-clerical position. The story of the Young Ottomans is one of several reminders that although secularism in the West is usually associated with the Left and with liberalism, this association is not inevitable, particularly when secularization is government-controlled. When such secularization is in conflict with constitutionalism and democratization, it may give rise to defences of religion not only from the Right but also from the Left.

---

[15] On Egyptian nineteenth-century reform and secularism see Juan R.I. Cole, *Colonialism and Revolution in the Middle East: Social and Cultural Origins of Egypt's 'Urabi Movement*, Princeton 1993; Albert Hourani, *A History of the Arab Peoples*, Cambridge, Mass. 1990; Afaf Lutfi al Sayyid Marsot, *Egypt in the Reign of Muhammad 'Ali*, Cambridge 1984, and the works they cite.

[16] On Ottoman developments since the eighteenth century, including the Young Ottomans, see especially Berkes, *Secularism in Turkey*, and Bernard Lewis, *The Emergence of Modern Turkey*, London 1961. On the Young Ottomans see especially Mardin, *The Genesis of Young Ottoman Thought*.

Secularization Under Ataturk

Twentieth-century Ottoman history saw further governmental secularization, first under the rule of the so-called Young Turks. They retained, however, an uneasy compromise with religious institutions. Since the late nineteenth century, the Sultan had pushed his claim to be the caliph of all Muslims, and the government was loath to take radical measures against religious institutions. This changed with the transformations brought in by Mustafa Kemal Ataturk, who inaugurated the most secular state in the Islamic world. Ataturk, unlike the rulers of other Middle Eastern countries, was in a position to do this for a number of reasons: 1) the sultan-caliph was compromised by his dependence on Western powers, especially England; 2) the sultan-caliph had acquiesced in the Allied dismemberment, not only of the Arab parts of the Ottoman Empire, but, more seriously, of Anatolia itself where regions had been given to Armenians, Kurds, and Greeks; these developments had fatally compromised the old regime and its religious allies; 3) Mustafa Kemal was a victorious general in World War I, and his fame and ability helped him to rally the Turks to retake much of the territory occupied by the Greeks and others—he was thus seen as a strong national hero, unmatched in any other Muslim country; 4) defeat in war had weakened the entire old regime, making it possible to build a quasi-revolutionary state structure—something that would have been far more difficult in any other Muslim country; 5) the Ottoman Turks had a longer and stronger history of governmental modernization than any other Middle Eastern people, leaving them more prepared for further changes.

After a short period in which Ataturk used traditional religious language and did not attack the caliphate, from 1923 onwards, he moved to abolishing first the sultanate and then the caliphate and then, up until his death in 1938, getting parliament to pass a series of measures that thoroughly undermined the power of religious institutions. The Arabic call to prayer and the Arabic alphabet were outlawed, Turkish was romanized and there was a purge of Arabic and Persian words and elements—these changes all had religious implications. For a time, there was no higher religious education permitted, and lower-level religious education was severely curtailed. Alone among Muslim countries, Turkey abolished use of the *sharia*, religious law which by then in Turkey, as in several Muslim countries, essentially covered only family and personal status matters. It was replaced by a slightly altered Swiss civil code. Women got equal rights in divorce and child custody; polygamy was outlawed; veiling was heavily discouraged; and women got to vote in national elections in 1934, well before they did in France, Italy and Switzerland. Such developments are signs of government-sponsored secularism, as traditional religious groups back patriarchal interpretations of their doctrines, and see in women's rights a weakening of their power.

Probably the best work on secularism in any Muslim country, Niyazi Berkes's *The Development of Secularism in Turkey*, reads: 'Two myths have sprung up and become established concerning the nature of the secularism emerging from the Kemalist Revolution. One is the belief that this secularism means the separation of religion and state after the fashion of French laicism; the other is the belief that it was a policy of irreligion

31

aiming at the liquidation of Islam.'[17] I would agree that neither the separation of religion and state nor irreligion is a correct characterization of Ataturk's programme, but I disagree with Berkes's subsequent point that the programme is best characterized as one aiming at ending the former bifurcation of religious and secular spheres, and at producing a more modern and rational Islam.[18] Such a description does not capture the essence of what Ataturk was doing: the establishment of state control over religion and the religious classes. This included controlling and limiting religious education, outlawing religious brotherhoods, profoundly altering family and personal status matters and putting them under new state laws instead of religious laws, severely limiting forms of male and female dress associated with Islam, and decreeing new forms of 'secular' Western dress. These were all to a large degree questions of control and of power, words that all too rarely enter the discussions of secularism.

Berkes also suggests that Ataturk was trying to follow the popular will, but his acts clearly went far beyond what people would have asked for. Changes in the economy and society, such as rapidly increasing urbanization and the growth in capitalist relations, had created new middle and bureaucratic classes that backed secularizing changes. There were also intellectuals before and during the Ataturk period whose secularism was independent of the government. But the government under Ataturk moved considerably beyond what the majority of the population would have wanted or voted for. This is suggested, among other things, by the reintroduction of certain aspects of religion in the period following World War II when a multi-party system and free elections were established, and new parties challenged elements of Ataturkist secularism, culminating in an electoral plurality for the religious Welfare Party in December 1995.

Secularism is a principle of the Turkish constitution, and secularists including the military forced the resignation of Welfare Party Prime Minister Erbakan in 1997. Some threatened to outlaw the party on the basis of acts they considered unconstitutional. Such acts, including expanding religious education and allowing more women to veil, would not cause any stir in most Muslim countries, or indeed most Western ones, but a real struggle for power is involved. In August 1977, a secular government proposal to expand the number of years all children must spend in secular public schools, to the detriment of religious schools and their views, aroused extensive conflict. There is no doubt, however, that most Turks became more secular and less religiously observant in the decades since 1925, and that the state's secular policies, including education, were largely responsible for this.

Secularization in Other Muslim Countries

Government-initiated secularism is found in a number of other twentieth-century Muslim countries, even though none went as far as Ataturk. The most dramatic changes came when old regimes were overthrown—the Qajar dynasty in Iran by Reza Shah in 1925; the Egyptian monarchy by Naguib and Nasser in 1952; the Iraqi monarchy in

---

[17] Berkes, *Secularism*, p. 479.
[18] Ibid., ch. 17.

32

1958 with the eventual victory of the Baath Party under Saddam Hussein; and the Dutch by nationalists in Indonesia. The old regimes had often tried to placate the *ulama* and other religious leaders and believers. The new regimes, in contrast, were more centralizing and nationalist, and they, like Ataturk, wanted to use the government to change the economy, whether calling their policies statism, socialism or something else. To establish governmental power over society, it was necessary to limit the power of the religious classes, including their ideological power. Primarily Islamic ideologies were often abandoned in favour of nationalist ones, as had also happened in Turkey over time, or were reformulated as adjuncts to nationalism, as in the widespread modern formula 'Arab-Islamic', which privileges an Arab nationalist view of Islam.

Reza Shah (1925–41), like Ataturk, ruled a country that was formally independent, whereas in the Arab countries mentioned above there were various forms of foreign control, so that independent policies of secular nationalism could not be pursued until after World War II. Iran was a far less developed and more decentralized country than Turkey, and Reza ·Shah's first task was to build up an army and disarm potential separatists, especially nomadic tribes. Later he took a series of steps partly modelled on Ataturk's, including imposed dress reform for both men and women—though stricter for women than in Turkey—the extension of state education, control of *vaqfs*, and an official ideology of nationalism, stressing the pre-Islamic periods and denigrating Arabs and, by implication, Islam. Autocratic secular nationalism was continued by his son, Mohammad Reza (1941–79). In Iran, however, partly because it had much less modern history of reform, modernization, and socio-economic change than did Turkey and because the *ulama* was far stronger and more independent, there developed a larger backlash to secularization.

Here is not the place to give the story of the 1978–79 revolution except to say that in many ways it has retained a number of secular features and has not meant a return to a traditional past. On the other hand, it expressed a phenomenon typical of the modern Middle East, which to some degree exists also in the US and many other countries—the importance of 'two cultures', secular and religious; Western-oriented and traditionalist. In Iran and the Middle East this split is largely tied to certain social classes — the popular classes and traditional bourgeoisie, on one side, and the new bourgeoisie and intellectuals, on the other. Iranian rule is now becoming more pragmatic and secular despite continued religious pretensions, and it seems possible that the Islamic revolution will ultimately secularize larger segments of society than it desecularizes—both those recoiling from government policies and those newly educated and participating in public life. This is suggested by the large majority achieved in the presidential elections of 1997 by the liberal cleric Khatami, followed by parliament's acceptance in August of a cabinet including moderates, with men who had spoken out for greater freedoms in the key posts of Minister of Interior and Minister of Culture and Islamic Guidance.[19]

---

[19] On the 1997 elections and cabinet, in addition to accounts in major newspapers, see the August 1997 analyses on the Internet by Gary G. Sick, (9952@columbia.edu). There is a vast literature on Iran since Reza Shah, and only a few relevant works not cited elsewhere in this article can be mentioned here: J.-P. Digard, B. Hourcade, and Y. Richard, *L'Iran au*

Gamal Abdel Nasser, like Ataturk and Reza Shah a man of military
background with goals of national independence and rapid modernization, also pushed Egypt further toward secularism via the path of
growing state control over religion. This was shown especially in the
expansion of the ancient Islamic university, al-Azhar, to include secular
subjects and its increased control by the state. The Azhar sheikhs were
ever-willing to issue decrees supporting government actions when
needed, rather in the manner of the leaders of various religions in the
Soviet Union.

Syrian and Iraqi revolutionary leaders in recent decades have similarly
followed a path of nationalism, economic statism, and secularism. The
secularism of Middle Eastern governments tended to better the position
of religious minorities, who had toleration but second-class status under
traditional Muslim law, and so minorities, including Shi'i Muslims in
countries with Sunni majorities, have tended to favour secular governments, even though the most secular of these governments were usually
also partly or wholly autocratic.[20]

Secular Government in India

In India, the position of minorities is crucial in explaining the secularism
of the national movement and later the national government. While
there were several movements that stressed Hinduism or Islam in pre-
partition India, the strongest national movement of the late nineteenth
and early twentieth century was that of the secular Indian National
Congress. India had never been united with its contemporary borders,
and Indian nationalism was essentially a creation of the anti-British
struggle. To create unity among India's numerous castes and religions, a
nationality without religious or caste preference had to be created. The
Congress has always found it difficult to maintain this secularist balance,
however; Mahatma Gandhi incorporated a number of Hindu beliefs and
practices into his programme, and the Congress provincial governments
of the late 1930s often discriminated against Muslims, thus contributing to the support of the movement for the creation of Pakistan. More
recently secularist rulers of India have been accused of granting too much
to Muslims and to outcasts—to the latter by 'affirmative action' style
education and employment programmes, and to the former by allowing
aspects of Muslim family law to be enforced in the Muslim community.[21]

XXe Siècle,Paris 1996; E. Abrahamian, *Iran between Two Revolutions*, Princeton 1982; Said
Amir Arjomand, *The Turban for the Crown*, New York 1988; Shaul Bakhash, *The Reign of
the Ayatollahs*, revised ed., New York 1990; H.E. Chehabi, *Iranian Politics and Religious
Modernism: The Liberation Movement in Iran under the Shah and Khomeini*, Ithaca 1990; Nikki
R. Keddie, *Roots of Revolution*, New Haven 1981. Recent events are thus far best covered in
major newspapers and in magazines and journals.
[20] On the secularism of (particularly Shi'i) minorities, see Nikki R. Keddie, *Iran and
the Muslim World*, ch. 10 and Keddie, 'The Shi'a of Pakistan', Von Grunebaum Center
Working Paper, Los Angeles 1993.
[21] On Indian communalism, see especially Tapan Raychaudhuri, 'Shadows of the
Swastika', *Contention* vol. 4, no. 2, Winter 1995; Daniel Gold, 'Organized Hinduisms:
From Vedic Truth to Hindu Nation', in Martin E. Marty and Scott Appleby, eds,
Fundamentalisms Observed, Chicago 1991; Sucheta Mazumdar, unpublished paper on
gender and fundamentalism; Achin Vanaik, *The Furies of Indian Communalism*, Verso,
London 1997.

However fragile Indian secularism has been, there seems no peaceful alternative in a country with about 100 million Muslims—more than in Pakistan—and millions of Sikhs, not to mention other groups. The rise of militant Hindu nationalism or fundamentalism is a threat to non-Hindus, and is paralleled by anti-secular fundamentalist movements in nearly all Muslim countries. All these movements suggest that top-down, government-controlled secularism has not satisfied large parts of their populations. In many of the countries discussed, after periods when secular nationalist, sometimes socialist, oppositional ideologies were popular, there is growing appeal of ideologies recommending a return to religion.

What all these non-Western examples suggest is that the needs, first, of governmental self-strengthening and then of nationalist movements and states were the primary factors in secularist policies, changes and achievements. Although some secularist intellectuals and secularizing social trends existed in most of these countries before secularism was adopted by a twentieth-century movement or state, these were not the main forces in the decisions to adopt secularizing policies. In all the above countries, secularism was tied to nationalism, to modernization, and to the centralization of control over politics, economic life, ideology, and society.

The above non-Western examples also indicate that actual policies followed by governments are often significantly either more or less secular than are their ideologies. In contemporary Iran, for example, many policies are more secular than ideology indicates. What may be the most resistant to change in such circumstances are the highly visible badges of Islam, like veiling, which immediately leads everyone to think this is an 'Islamic' state. On the other hand, recent eyewitness accounts indicate that even within this highly visible and symbolic sphere, with its theoretical injunction to hide hair and body, women are increasingly bending the rules by uncovering some hair, wearing semi-transparent and stylish chadors, or wearing various forms of tribal or regional dress. In France, at the other extreme, official devotion to a 'laic' ideology leads to official action against veiling in schools, while at the same time some Islamic and other religious institutions get state subsidies. Iran exemplifies states that are more secular than they claim, and France those that are less so.

Even though this discussion has stressed examples from Asia, there is no clear or absolute line of demarcation regarding secularization from above between Asia and Europe. Autocratic state-sponsored secularization as a necessary accompaniment of other aspects of modernization was as characteristic of Russia from Peter the Great through Stalin as it was of modern Turkey or Iran.

Secularism in the West

The focus on secularism and nationalist centralizing government in non-Western countries raises the question of whether anything similar may be discerned in the West. In virtually all countries that have experienced secularism we find, in different degrees, the three areas of secularism and secularization that have been discussed in this article: intellectual, societal and governmental-political. In non-Western areas, where modernization was often defensive and primarily state-sponsored, we find government-sponsored or nationalist movement-sponsored secularization stronger and earlier than significant intellectual or societal secularization. In the West, although intellectual and societal secularization have generally been more significant than they are elsewhere, government-sponsored secularization has been far more important than is usually recognized in works on secularism or secularization. Hence, while secularism is frequently traced to intellectual roots, in Locke and Mill on toleration, or Voltaire and other Enlightenment figures who attacked the Church and organized religion, it could equally be traced to Henry VIII, who confiscated monasteries and increased state control of the church, to enlightened despots who sponsored power over the Church, and certainly to the activities of the French Revolution, Napoleon, the new American republic, and increasingly secular European governments. These governmental actions included measures of toleration such as the emancipation of the Jews—and of Catholics in Protestant countries and vice versa—and reduced privileges for the majority religion. All had a strong, often central, political and governmental element.

States that are growing in strength and that want to extend their control to all who live within their borders have reasons to secularize, including the granting of relatively equal treatment to all religions and building up a non-religious national ideology and symbols. In older, less centralized, structures members of non-established religions could be ignored, persecuted or allowed considerable autonomy. In more modern states, however, with the growth of national markets, economies, and cultures, governments wanted contented and essentially interchangeable citizens of an increasingly unified state and society, which required that the rules of treatment be essentially uniform for different groups.

In addition, modern states and their leaders want the primary loyalty of citizens to be to their state or nation, and help build up ideologies—if on a lesser scale than in the non-Western or communist worlds—that stress such loyalty to the state and nation rather than the church. (Those embraced by the 'nation' usually came to mean those within its existing boundaries, sometimes with an irredentist addition of some beyond the boundaries, but never subtracting ethnic or religious groups that might want independence or unity with some other entity.) Nationalism, it has been noted, is in part a modern substitute for religion, and as such it must play down the role of religion in life, thought and government. By the seventeenth or eighteenth century, religious conflicts, whether in the religious wars in Europe or in persecutions in US colonies, had come to be seen as bloody, indecisive and inimical to national unity, so that it was increasingly felt best by governments to find a place for all religious groups. Modern states have tended to encourage nationalism irrespective of how strong this trend was among the general population or among intellectuals—the two groups that scholars have tended to stress in nationalism as in secularism. Nationalism or even national identity has been shown to be weaker and to emerge later among the general popula-

36

tion than most scholars previously thought.[22] Most national identities are secular—except when a church has been tied to a nationalist movement, as in Poland and Ireland—and nationalist ideologies are usually secularist in their effect. Furthermore, religious toleration, favoured by most modern governments, is tied to a weakening of belief, as it is difficult, if one is a true believer, also to believe that followers of false doctrines should have the same freedoms and privileges as do the righteous.

Naturally, things are not quite this simple, or we would find many governments promoting atheism and taking radical steps against religion in order to carry the discouragement of religious loyalties to its logical conclusion. Instead, governments in power find it useful to be on good terms with various religious institutions, once their wings are clipped, and there remained among rulers, as among many 'enlightened' intellectuals, the idea that the masses of the population should be religious to keep them orderly. (This idea was, until the revival of fundamentalism, popular in the non-Western world. Several non-religious Iranians used to tell me that it was good that the masses were religious as otherwise they would become revolutionary!) Hence Western governments rarely go all the way towards suppressing religion, promoting atheism, or the like. There is a general liking by governments for moderate religions that can inculcate civic virtues, and a dislike only for radical 'sects', or 'foreign' religions, like Islam in Western countries, that might threaten militancy or intrude on the old order.

Secularism and Fundamentalism

A comparison that concerns society more than the state has to do with organized and politicized religious attacks on secularism which, like the fundamentalisms that encourage such attacks, have in this century thus far occurred chiefly in four parts of the world—the Muslim world, South Asia, Israel, and the US. They have not as yet been strong in Europe. There are not necessarily similar causes for these attacks in each region, but it is worth seeing if any comparisons can be made.

The US is often seen as needing secularism because it houses so many religious denominations, including several of fairly equal strength. After some experience of repression in the colonial period by stronger denominations, most states and then the federal government opted for freedom of religion. The first amendment to the US constitution, saying that 'Congress shall make no law' for the establishment of religion or interfering with the free exercise of religion followed many similar state laws, but these were not generally interpreted by state and federal governments to mean the strict secularism that recent supreme court rulings have tended to favour. The Bill of Rights was not intended to interfere with acts by state governments, and Congress only began to rule on free speech questions in the states in the late 1920s, and on religious establishment questions in the 1940s. The decision against prayer in the schools is as recent as 1962. In 1925, when the American Civil Liberties Union (ACLU) brought on the Scopes case to challenge a Tennessee law

---

[22] For a striking study of one case, see Eugen Weber, *Peasants into Frenchmen: The Modernization of Rural France 1870–1914*, Stanford 1976.

forbidding the teaching of evolution, the Court had never ruled on religious freedoms or free speech in the states. Although the first appeals
court's reversal of Scopes's conviction meant that the case, and hence the
constitutional issue, could not be appealed further, and the Tennessee
law remained on the books for decades, the ACLU soon achieved some key
Supreme Court rulings on Bill of Rights questions.[23] Nearly all laws
touching free speech and religion were state and local laws, so the
Supreme Court's agreement to rule on them was crucial.

This is the situation as summarized by Leonard Levy:

> Those who framed and ratified the First Amendment meant that
> the establishment clause, like the rest of the Bill of Rights, should
> apply to the National Government only... According to the
> Fourteenth Amendment [1868], no state may deprive any person of
> liberty without due process of law. The preponderance of evidence
> suggests that the framers of the Fourteenth Amendment neither
> intended its provisions to incorporate any part of the Bill of Rights
> nor to impose on the states the same limitations previously imposed
> on the United States only. However, the language of the Fourteenth
> Amendment allowed for the possibility that the Constitution pre-
> vented the states, as well as the United States, from violating the
> First Amendment.[24]

By a rule known as the incorporation doctrine, the Fourteenth Amendment was said to incorporate First Amendment rights. In the 1947
Everson case, the court laid down principles it has generally stuck to—
that aid to all religions was an illegal establishment of religion; and that
no tax can be used to support religious activities or institutions. Further
decisions have followed, and it is clear that the US now outlaws—as
many individual US states previously did—a number of practices common in western Europe. On the other hand, the court's rulings since
1947 have been far more mixed and contradictory and less uniformly
favourable to strict church-state separation than most people imagine.[25]
This mixed trend has thus far continued under the current court.

In the US there has been in the twentieth century 'two cultures', even
among Christians. While certain ideas were held in common by the
main Protestant churches through most of the nineteenth century,
beginning at the end of the century there was a rapid development in one
stream of various Protestant denominations away from biblical literalism
and toward religious modernism, liberalism, and the social gospel. This
group tended to secularism in their attitude toward both church-state
relations and everyday life. On the other hand, those who wanted to preserve old beliefs became more militant than they had ever been before.
Their ideas included a group of Christian doctrines that in the early
twentieth century were named the Fundamentals. There now developed
a schism between the traditionalists, who tended to have less modern

---

[23] Walker, *In Defense of American Liberties*, ch. 4.
[24] Leonard Levy, *The Establishment Clause: Religion and the First Amendment*, New York
1986, pp. 122–3.
[25] Ibid., pp. 162–3.

education, to be centred in the south and midwest, and to be more
rural in origin, and the modernists and secularists, centred among the
better-educated urban groups. There was some correlation between
religious denominations and degree of fundamentalism, but it was not
complete.[26]

A Dialectical Conflict

Secularism and fundamentalism appear to have a dialectical relationship
with one another in the US and elsewhere. The early development of
modernism and secularism in the late nineteenth century was followed
by a rise in fundamentalism, which was in large part a reaction to various
facets of modernism and to rapid urbanization and socio-economic
changes and dislocations. A new wave of change, especially in civil rights
and sexual and family questions beginning in the 1960s, was followed
by a new wave of fundamentalism beginning in the 1970s.

Such developments were far less sharp in Europe, for a variety of reasons.
These included the much lower levels of religious belief and church affiliation in Europe; to have a large body of fundamentalists it is necessary to
have a large body of believers, or, as in India and Israel, of believers in
religious nationalism (communalism). Also important are the weakness
in Europe, as compared to the US, of both the liberal to radical Protestant
groups that veered toward liberalism and modernism and especially of
evangelical Christians, who tended toward fundamentalism. In polls and
in church membership figures, the US has always been shown to be far
higher in both religious belief and church membership—including regular church attendance—than any western European country. This
means that what is probably the most secular of major Western countries
in its legal practice is also the most religious, whether this is measured
by church membership and attendance or by religious opinions.[27] Either
general widespread religious adherence, as in the US and much of the
Muslim world, or exclusivist religious nationalism (communalism), as in
South Asia or Israel/Palestine provide the necessary basis for large-scale
fundamentalism, whether in the East or the West.[28]

---

[26] See Walker, *In Defense of American Liberties*, ch. 4.
[27] A variety of poll data show religious belief, including belief in a number of 'irrational'
ideas like Creationism, and also church membership and attendance are far higher in the
US than in any other Western country. A Gallup poll in 1981 asking 'Are you affiliated
with a church or religious organization?' got a 57 per cent positive response from
Americans, as compared to 4 per cent of French, 5 per cent of Italians, 13 per cent of West
Germans, 15 per cent of Spaniards, and 22 per cent of the British. For the most complete
survey data on religion in America, see Barry A. Kosmin and Seymour P. Lachman, *One
Nation Under God: Religion in Contemporary American Society*, New York 1993; the Gallup
poll is reported on p. 9.
[28] The similarities and differences between the areas characterized by religiosity and those
characterized by religious nationalism (communalism) are discussed in Nikki R. Keddie,
'The New Religious Politics: Where, When, and Why do "Fundamentalisms" Appear?'
forthcoming in *Comparative Studies in Society and History*. In that article I also propose
replacing the term 'fundamentalism', to which there are some valid objections, with 'New
Religious Politics' and the adjective 'religio-political', both defined for such discussions
as excluding predominantly liberal or socialist religious politics. I have not adopted this
change here, as it requires a lengthy explanation and justification. My own objections to
the term 'fundamentalism' are not strong enough to preclude my using it when it is still
the only widely accepted common global term.

The dialectical relationship between the growth, first, of secularism and then of fundamentalism appears dramatically in the non-Western world. Although this can be discussed only briefly, it appears that secular nationalist governments, such as those of the Pahlavis, Bourguiba, and the Congress in India helped create a traditionalist-fundamentalist opposition that could point to the governments' favouring of minorities and of Western ways and their undermining of religious traditions as ideological points on which to build religious and political opposition movements. Governments that culturally modernized in a more modest fashion saw less religious opposition—true thus far of most governments in the Arabian peninsula, for example. Governments in India also called forth religious and political opposition especially focused on these governments' 'anti-Hindu' favouring of minority religions and outcasts. Other factors also favour fundamentalist movements, including such socio-economic ones as the rapid urbanization of more traditional and often marginal rural people, under-employment among the growing educated classes, and increased income inequality, and such political factors as resentments against the Western powers, Israel, and a variety of government policies.

In the US, too, some of the upsurge of political fundamentalism is a response to state action, such as Supreme Court rulings on abortion or aspects of sexuality. Yet state-encouraged secularization of thought has surely been greater over time than has the religious backlash. State power and action are not notable mainly for giving rise to religious reactions. Rather, this paper makes three main points. First, the history of secularism and the spread or retreat of secular culture cannot be understood without a serious discussion of the role of the state and politics. Second, the role of state secularism is dialectically interrelated with other factors, such as economic change, which both allows states to centralize and secularize and encourages secularized states to launch further economic change. Social and intellectual changes and perceptions of international and minority problems also often encourage—and recently may discourage—state secularization which in turn further affects those spheres. Third state secularization has on the whole tended to increase the secularization of the population, even though there has been a serious backlash under certain historical conditions.

This article has not seen states as the only important driving force behind secularization, but says that the state and other political forces are more important to secularization than is often stated. We should not be satisfied either with sociological discussions that are limited to large impersonal trends or with overwhelmingly intellectual interpretations.[29]

---

[29] This brief treatment of complex comparative issues is necessarily simplified. There is only space to mention two further complexities: first, the state, like any institution, is not independent of intellectual and social forces that this article sees it as chiefly as acting upon, and the complexities of these interrelationships can barely be suggested here. Second, the role of the state in encouraging both secularism and anti-secularism may have a counterpart in a paradoxical role of religious politics in encouraging secularization. Some have suggested that Protestantism, which first encouraged religiosity and even religious politics, was an inadvertent cause of a later rise in secularism. And in contemporary Iran, religious politics has probably increased secularism both from widespread disgust with the government and from bringing new groups and classes into a now essentially secular politics. Just as state secularism may bring a reaction, so too may state religiosity. These examples support the general thesis of this article that secularism can only be understood with a comparative, dialectical, and comprehensive approach that includes the roles of politics and the state.

[10]

The New Religious State

Mark Juergensmeyer

One of the most interesting—some would say disturbing—features of the post-Cold War era is the resurgence of religious politics. It appears as a dark cloud over what many regard as the near-global victory of liberal democracy following the collapse of the Soviet Empire.[1] It fuels regional disputes in North Africa, the Middle East, and South Asia and may be leading toward what Samuel Huntington has apocalyptically called "the clash of civilizations."[2] It has led to some impressive gains: radical religious parties are now firmly established not only in Iran but in Algeria, Sudan, Egypt, India, Afghanistan, Pakistan, the incipient Palestine, and elsewhere in what was once called the Third World. Although it is tempting to dismiss the religious activists involved in these uprisings as "fundamentalists," their goals and their motivations are as political as they are religious. For this reason I prefer to call them "religious nationalists," implying that they are political actors striving for new forms of national order based on religious values.[3]

The question I will pursue in this essay is how religious nationalists conceive this relationship between religion and politics. In the past several years, I have examined various movements of religious nationalism, including Hindu and Sikh partisans in India, militant Buddhists in Sri Lanka and Mongolia, Christian activists in eastern Europe and Latin America, right-wing Jewish politicians in Israel, and Islamic activists in the Middle East and Central Asia. I have described some of these movements in other essays and in a recent book.[4] Therefore, I will not discuss these cases in depth here, but rather will explore an issue that I believe is central to virtually all of these movements: their assumption that religion can replace liberal democracy in providing the ideological glue that holds a nation together and that it can provide the justification for a modern religious state.

In this essay I will first describe how traditional religion can play the same ideological role that secular nationalist theories play in providing a theoretical basis for a nation-state. Because of this ideological role, I will then show, religion and liberal democratic ideas are seen as competitive in both the West and the Third World. Finally, I will explore a kind of resolution of this competition: the rise of a potent new synthesis between the nation-state and religion.

The Confrontation of Two Ideologies of Order

One of the most striking features of religious nationalists' rhetoric is the way that it juxtaposes religion with western notions of national ideology. Secular nationalism is "a kind of religion," one of the leaders of the Iranian revolution proclaimed.[5] He and other religious nationalists regard secularism not only as a religion, but as one peculiar to the West.[6] They assume that secular nationalism responds to the same sorts of needs for collective identity,

379

ultimate loyalty, and moral authority to which religion has traditionally responded. Some go further and state that the western form of secular nationalism is simply a cover for Christianity. For evidence, they offer the fact that the word "Christian" is used in the title of some political parties in Europe. But whether or not secular nationalism in the West is overtly labeled Christian, most religious activists see it as occupying the same place in human experience as Islam in Muslin societies, Buddhism in Theravada Buddhist societies, and Hinduism and Sikhism in Indian society. To these Muslims, Buddhists, Hindus, and Sikhs it is perfectly obvious: the West's secular nationalism competes in every way with religion as they know it.

Behind this charge is a certain vision of social reality, one that involves a series of concentric circles. The smallest are families and clans; then come ethnic groups and nations; the largest, and implicitly most important, are global civilizations. Among these civilizations are to be found Islam, Buddhism, and what some who hold this view call "Christendom" and others call "western civilization." Particular nations such as Germany, France, and the United States, in this conceptualization, stand as subsets of Christendom/western civilization; similarly, Egypt, Iran, Pakistan, and other nations are subsets of Islamic civilization.

Are they correct in this assessment, that the social functions of traditional religion and secular nationalism are so similar they both can be regarded as two aspects of a similar phenomenon? Huntington's recent essay seems to agree.[7] Earlier, Benedict Anderson suggested that religion and secular nationalism are both "imagined communities;" Ninian Smart regarded them both as "world-views."[8] In an interesting way, these scholars concur with religious nationalists' understanding of the social character of religion: like secular nationalism, religion has the ability to command communal loyalty and to legitimize authority. To this extent I agree with Anderson and Smart—and with many religious nationalists—that religion and secular nationalism are species of the same genus. I prefer to call this genus "ideologies of order."

My use of the word "ideology" should not be misconstrued as an effort to revive the meanings attached to it by Karl Marx or Karl Mannheim or by those identified with the "end of ideology" debate some years ago.[9] Rather, I use it in the original, late eighteenth century sense. At that time a group of French *idéologues*, as they called themselves, were attempting to build a science of ideas based on the theories of Francis Bacon, Thomas Hobbes, John Locke, and René Descartes that would be sufficiently comprehensive to replace religion. According to one of the *idéologues*, Destutt de Tracy, whose book *Elements of Ideology* introduced the term to the world, "logic" was to be the sole basis of "the moral and political sciences."[10] In proposing their own "science of ideas" as a replacement for religion, the *idéologues* were in fact putting what they called ideology and what we call religion on an equal plane. Perhaps Clifford Geertz, among modern users of the term, has come closest to its original meaning by speaking of ideology as a "cultural system."[11]

To make clear that I am referring to the original meaning of the term and not to "political ideology" in a narrow sense or to a Marxian or Mannheimian notion of ideology, I will refer to what I have in mind as "ideologies of order." Both religious and secular nationalistic frameworks of thought are ideologies of order in the following ways: they both conceive of the world around them as a coherent, manageable system; they both suggest that there are levels of meaning beneath the day-to-day world that explain things unseen; they both provide

Mark Juergensmeyer

identity for and evoke loyalty from secular communities; and they both provide the authority that gives social and political order a reason for being. In doing so they define how an individual should properly act in the world, and they relate persons to the social whole.

I have defined both nationalism and religion in terms of order as well as ideology. For this definition there is ample precedent. Regarding nationalism, Karl Deutsch has pointed out the importance of orderly systems of communication in fostering a sense of nationalism.[12] Ernest Gellner argues that the political and economic network of a nation-state requires a spirit of nationalism that draws upon a homogeneous culture, a unified pattern of communication, and a common system of education.[13] Other social scientists have stressed the psychological aspect of national identity: the sense of historical location that is engendered when individuals feel they are a part of a larger, national history.[14] But behind these notions of community are also images of order, for nationalism always involves the loyalty to an authority who, as Max Weber observed, holds a monopoly over the "legitimate use of physical force" in a given society.[15] Anthony Giddens describes nationalism as the "cultural sensibility of sovereignty," implying that the awareness of being subject to such an authority—an authority invested with the power of life and death—is what gives nationalism its potency.[16] It is not only an attachment to a spirit of social order but also an act of submission to an ordering agent.

Religion has also been defined in terms of order, albeit in a conceptual more than a political or social sense. Clifford Geertz, for example, sees religion as the effort to integrate messy everyday reality into a pattern of coherence that takes shape at a deeper level.[17] Robert Bellah also thinks of religion as an attempt to reach beyond ordinary phenomena in a "risk of faith" that allows people to act "in the face of uncertainty and unpredictability" on the basis of a higher order of reality.[18] Peter Berger specifies that such faith is an affirmation of the sacred, which acts as a doorway to a more certain kind of truth.[19] Louis Dupré prefers to avoid the term "sacred" but integrates elements of both Berger's and Bellah's definitions in his description of religion as "a commitment to the transcendent as to *another* reality."[20] In all of these cases there is a tension between this imperfect, disorderly world and a perfected, orderly one to be found at a higher, transcendent state or in a cumulative moment in time. As Durkheim, whose thought is fundamental to each of these thinkers, was adamant in observing, religion has a more encompassing force than can be suggested by any dichotomization of the sacred and the profane. To Durkheim, the religious point of view includes both the notion that there is such a dichotomy and the belief that the sacred side will always, ultimately, reign supreme.[21]

From this perspective, both religion and secular nationalism are about order. They are therefore potential rivals. Either could claim to be the guarantor of orderliness within a society; either could claim to be the ultimate authority for social order. Such claims carry with them an extraordinary degree of power, for contained within them is the right to give moral sanction for life and death decisions, including the right to kill. When either nationalism or religion assumes this role by itself, it reduces the other to a peripheral social role.

The rivalry has historical roots. Earlier in history it was often religion that denied moral authority to secular politicians, but in recent centuries, especially in the West, it has been the other way around. Political authorities now attempt to monopolize the authority to sanction violence. They asserted this authority long before the advent of the nation-state, but usually in collusion with religious authority, not in defiance of it. What is unusual about the modern period is how victorious the secular state has been in denying the right of religious authorities to be ultimate moral arbiters. In the modern state, the state alone is given the moral power to kill (albeit for limited purposes, military defense, police protection, and capital punishment). Yet all of the rest of the state's power to persuade and to shape the social order is derived from these fundamental powers. In Max Weber's view, the monopoly over legitimate violence in a society is the very definition of a state.[22] But the secular state did not always enjoy a monopoly over this right, and in challenging its authority, today's religious activists, wherever they assert themselves around the world, reclaim the traditional right of religious authorities to say when violence is moral and when it is not.

Religious conflict is one indication of the power of religion to sanction killing. The parties in such an encounter may command a greater degree of loyalty than contestants in a purely political war. Their interests can subsume national interests. In some cases a religious battle may preface the attempt to establish a new religious state. It is interesting to note, in this regard, that the best known incidents of religious violence throughout the contemporary world have occurred in places where it is difficult to define or accept the idea of a nation-state. Palestine, the Punjab, and Sri Lanka are the most obvious examples, but the revolutions in Iran, Nicaragua, Afghanistan, Tajikistan, and the countries of eastern Europe also concern themselves with what the state should be like and what elements of society should lead it. In these instances, religion provides the basis for a new national consensus and a new kind of leadership.

Modern religious activists are thereby reasserting the role of religion in most traditional societies where religion, as Donald E. Smith puts it, "answers the question of political legitimacy."[23] In the modern West, this legitimacy is provided by nationalism, a secular nationalism. But even here, religion continues to wait in the wings, a potential challenge to the nationalism based on secular assumptions. Perhaps nothing indicates the continuing challenge of religion more than the persistence of religious politics in American society, including most recently the rise of politically active religious fundamentalists in the 1980s and the potency of the Christian right in the 1992 and 1994 national elections.[24] Religion is ready to demonstrate that, like secular nationalism, it can provide a faith in the unitary nature of a society that will authenticate both political rebellion and political rule.

Competition between Religion and Secular Nationalism in the West

Putting aside the recent electoral victories of America's religious right, secular nationalism has largely been the victor in the competition between religion and secular nationalism that has been going on in the West for several centuries now. At one time, the medieval church possessed "many aspects of a state," as one historian put it, and it had commanded more political power "than most of its secular rivals."[25] Perhaps more important, religion provided the legitimacy on which the power of monarchy and civil order was based. By the mid nineteenth century, however, the Christian church had ceased to have much influence on European or American politics. The church—the great medieval monument of Christendom with all its social and political panoply—had been replaced by churches, various denominations of Protestantism and a largely depoliticized version of Roman

Mark Juergensmeyer

Catholicism. These churches functioned like religious clubs, voluntary associations for the spiritual edification of individuals in their leisure time, rarely cognizant of the social and political world around them.

Secular nationalism began to replace religion several centuries ago as the ideological agent of political legitimacy.[26] But the form in which we know it today—as the ideological ally of the nation-state—did not appear in England and America until the eighteenth century. Only by then had the nation-state taken root deeply enough to nurture an ideological loyalty of its own, unassisted by religious or ethnic identifications, and only by then had the political and military apparatus of the nation-state expanded sufficiently to encompass a large geographic region. Prior to that time, as Giddens explains, "the administrative reach" of the political center was so limited that rulers did not govern in "the modern sense."[27] Until the advent of the nation-state, the authority of a political center did not systematically and equally cover an entire population, so that what appeared to be a single homogeneous polity was in fact a congeries of fiefdoms. The further one got from the center of power, the weaker was the grip of centralized political influence, until at the periphery whole sections of a country might exist as a political no man's land. Therefore, one should speak of countries prior to the modern nation-state as having frontiers rather than boundaries.[28]

The changes of the late eighteenth and nineteenth centuries included the development of the technical ability to knit a country together through roads, rivers, and other means of transportation and communication, the economic ability to do so through an increasingly integrated market structure, an emerging world economic system which was based on the building blocks of nation-states,[29] the development of mass education which socialized each generation of youth into a homogeneous society, and the emergence of parliamentary democracy as a system of representation and an expression of the will of people. The glue that held all these changes together was secular nationalism: the notion that individuals naturally associate with the people and place of their ancestral birth in an economic and political system identified with a nation-state. Secular nationalism was thought to be not only natural, but also universally applicable and morally right. Although it was regarded almost as a natural law, secular nationalism was ultimately viewed as an expression of neither god nor nature but of the will of a nation's citizens. The ideas of John Locke about the origins of a civil community and the "social contract" theories of Jean-Jacques Rousseau required very little commitment to religious belief.[30] Although they allowed for a divine order that made the rights of humans possible, their ideas did not directly buttress the power of the church and its priestly administrators, and they had the effect of taking religion—at least church religion—out of public life.

At the same time religion was becoming less political, secular nationalism was becoming more religious. It became clothed in romantic and xenophobic images that would have startled its Enlightenment forbears. The French Revolution, the model for much of the nationalist fervor that developed in the nineteenth century, infused a religious zeal into revolutionary democracy, which took on the trappings of church religion in the priestly power meted out to its demagogic leaders and in the slavish devotion to what it called "the temple of reason." According to Alexis de Tocqueville, the French Revolution "assumed many of the aspects of a religious revolution."[31] The American Revolution also had a religious side: many of its leaders had been influenced by eighteenth century Deism, a

Comparative Politics   July 1995

religion of science and natural law which was "devoted to exposing [church] religion to the light of knowledge."[32] As in France, American nationalism developed its own religious characteristics, blending the ideals of secular nationalism and the symbols of Christianity into a "civil religion."

The nineteenth century fulfilled de Tocqueville's prophecy that the "strange religion" of secular nationalism would, "like Islam, overrun the whole world with its apostles, militants, and martyrs."[33] It was spread throughout the world with an almost missionary zeal and was shipped to the newly colonized areas of Asia, Africa, and Latin America as part of the ideological freight of colonialism. It became the ideological partner of what came to be known as "nation-building." As the colonial governments provided their colonies with the political and economic infrastructures to turn territories into nation-states, the ideology of secular nationalism emerged as a by-product of the colonial nation-building experience. As it had in the West in previous centuries, secular nationalism in the colonized countries in the nineteenth and twentieth centuries came to represent one side of a great encounter between two vastly different ways of perceiving the sociopolitical order and the relationship of the individual to the state: one informed by religion, the other by a notion of a secular compact.

In the mid twentieth century, when the colonial powers retreated, they left behind the geographical boundaries they had drawn and the political institutions they had fashioned. Created as administrative units of the Ottoman, Hapsburg, French, and British empires, the borders of most Third World nations continued after independence, even if they failed to follow the natural divisions among ethnic and linguistic communities. By the second half of the twentieth century, it seemed as if the cultural goals of the colonial era had been reached: although the political ties were severed, the new nations retained all the accoutrements of westernized countries. The only substantial empire to remain virtually intact until 1990 was the Soviet Union. It was based on a different vision of political order, of course, in which international socialism was supposed to replace a network of capitalist nations. Yet the perception of many members of the Soviet states was that their nations were not so much integral units in a new internationalism as they were colonies in a secular Russian version of imperialism. This perception became dramatically clear after the breakup of the Soviet Union and its sphere of influence in the early 1990s, when old ethnic and national loyalties sprang to the fore.

Competition between Religion and Secular Nationalism in the Third World

The new nations that emerged as the "Third World" in the middle of the twentieth century had to confront the same competition between religion and nationalism as the West has had to confront, but in a very short period of time, and they simultaneously had to contend with the political by-products of colonial rule. If accommodating religion was difficult for the West, efforts to bridle religion in the new nations were a thousand times more problematic. There, the political competition of religion was much more obvious. Given religious histories that were part of national heritages, religious institutions that were sometimes the nations' most effective systems of communication, and religious leaders who were often more devoted, efficient, and intelligent than government officials, religion could not be ignored. The attempts to accommodate it, however, have not always been successful, as the following examples indicate.

384

Mark Juergensmeyer

In Egypt, following the revolution of 1952, Nasser was caught in a double bind. Since his support came from both the Muslim Brotherhood and the modern elite, he was expected to create a Muslim state and a modern secular state at the same time. His approach was to paint an image of an Egypt that was culturally Muslim and politically secular, and he cheerfully went about "Egyptizing along with modernizing," as a professor in Cairo put it.[34] The compromise did not work, and especially after Nasser attempted to institute "scientific socialism," which the Muslim Brotherhood regarded as anti-Islamic, the Brotherhood became Nasser's foe. Nasser's successor, Anwar al-Sadat, repeated the pattern, which turned out to be a tragic and fatal mistake. Like Nasser, Sadat raised Muslim expectations by currying favors with the Muslim Brotherhood. In 1971 he released many of them from jail. But by 1974 he and the Brotherhood were at loggerheads, and again the organization was outlawed. Sadat attempted to wear the mantle of Islam by calling himself "Upholder of the Faith," announcing that his first name was really Muhammad rather than Anwar, and promoting religious schools. None of his attempts really worked. Sadat was thought to be a Muslim turncoat. With this image in mind, members of the al-Jihad, a radical fringe group of the Muslim Brotherhood, assassinated him in 1981. His successor, Hosni Mubarak, tried to steer more of a middle course, making no promises to the Muslim activists, but no new secular or socialist departures either.[35]

In India, three generations of prime ministers in the Nehru dynasty—Jawaharlal, his daughter Indira Gandhi, and her son Rajiv—have all tried to accommodate religion as little as possible. Yet there have been times when they have been forced to make concessions to religious forces almost against their wills. Jawaharlal Nehru seemed virtually allergic to religion, putting secularism alongside socialism as his great political goal. Nonetheless, the Indian constitution and subsequent parliamentary actions have given a great deal of public support to religious entities.[36] Religious political parties have elected legislators to national and state assemblies; religious schools have been affiliated with the state; and temples and mosques have received direct public support. In general, the Indian government's attitude has been defined, not by indifference, but instead by an effort to treat each religion with equanimity; as Ainslie Embree puts it, "advocates of secularism in India always insisted . . . that far from being hostile to religion, they valued it."[37] Even so, these concessions have not been sufficient to stem the tide of religious politics in India. The 1980s was a decade of tragedy in this regard. Hindu nationalists wanted more and more access to power, prompting defensiveness on the part of Muslim and Christian minorities and a bloody rebellion on the part of the Sikhs. The assassinations of Prime Minister Indira Gandhi and her son Rajiv did not put an end to their sense of dissatisfaction, and the election of 1991, which brought to power a Hindu nationalist party in several of India's states, demonstrated the potency of the Hindu right.

In Sri Lanka following independence, the urbane and western-educated leaders of the new nation realized that they would have to give a Sinhalese Buddhist aura to their secular political stance in order for it to be widely accepted. Perhaps no Sri Lankan leader attempted to give in to Buddhist demands as much as did S. W. R. D. Bandaranaike, but even he lost his life at the hands of an irate Buddhist monk. The present rulers in Sri Lanka face the same dilemma as their predecessors: they need Sinhalese support, but they feel they can not go so far as to alienate the Tamils and other minority groups. They have been attacked viciously by Sinhalese Buddhist nationalists for attempting to achieve what might be impossible: a national entity that is both Buddhist and secular. The use of Buddhist symbols is meant to appeal to the Sinhalese, and the adoption of a secular political ideology is supposed to mollify everyone else.

The problem with all these attempts of secular leaders to accommodate religion is that they lead to a double frustration: the leaders are considered traitors from both a religious and a secular point of view. Moreover, these compromises suggest that spiritual and political matters are separate, which most religious activists see as a capitulation to the secularist point of view. They sense that behind the compromises is a basic allegiance to secular nationalism rather than to religion.

A New Synthesis: The Religious Nation-State

Religious activists are well aware that, if a nation starts with the premise of secular nationalism, religion is often made marginal to the political order. This marginality is especially onerous from many revolutionary religious perspectives, including the Iranian, the Sikh, and the Sinhalese, because they regard the two ideologies as unequal: the religious one is far superior. Rather than to start with secular nationalism, they prefer to begin with religion.

The implication of this way of speaking is not that religion is antithetical to nationalism, but that religious rather than secular nationalism is the appropriate premise on which to build a nation, even a modern nation-state. In fact, virtually every reference to nationhood used by religious nationalists assumes that the modern nation-state is the only way in which a nation can be construed.

Although the link between religion and nationalism has historical precedents, the present attempt to forge an alliance between religion and the modern democratic nation-state is a new development in the history of nationalism, and it immediately raises the question whether it is possible: whether what we in the West think of as a modern nation—a unified, democratically controlled system of economic and political administration—can in fact be accommodated within religion. Many western observers would automatically answer no. Even as acute an interpreter of modern society as Giddens regarded most religious cultures as at best a syncreticism between "tribal cultures, on the one hand, and modern societies, on the other."[38]

Yet by Giddens' own definition of a modern nation-state, postrevolutionary Iran would qualify: the Islamic revolution in Iran has solidified not just a central power but a systematic control over the population that is more conducive to nationhood than the monarchical political order of the shah. A new national entity came into being that was quite different from both the polity under the old Muslim rulers and the nation the shah ineptly attempted to build. The shah dreamed of creating Ataturk's Turkey in Iran and bringing to his country what he perceived as the instant modernity brought to Turkey by Ataturk. Ironically, Khomeini—along with his integrative religious ideology and his grass-roots network of mullahs—ultimately accomplished the unity and national organization that the shah had sought.

A similar claim is made in India, where Hindu nationalists are emphatic on the point that "Hindutva," as they call Hindu national culture, is the defining characteristic of Indian

Mark Juergensmeyer

nationalism. In Sri Lanka, according to one Sinhalese writer, "it is clear that the unifying, healing, progressive principle" that held together the entity known as Ceylon throughout the years has always been "the Buddhist faith."[39] The writer goes on to say that religion in Sri Lanka continues to provide the basis for a "liberating nationalism" and that Sinhalese Buddhism is "the only patriotism worthy of the name, worth fighting for or dying for."[40] Similar sentiments are echoed in movements of religious nationalism in Egypt, Israel, and elsewhere in the world.

In these efforts to accommodate modern politics, has religion compromised its purity? Some religious leaders think that it has. In favoring the nation-state over a particular religious congregation as its major community of reference, religion loses the exclusivity held by smaller, subnational religious communities, and the leaders of those communities lose some of their autonomy. Many religious leaders are therefore suspicious of religious nationalism. Among them are religious utopians who would rather build their own isolated political societies than to deal with the problems of a whole nation, religious liberals who are satisfied with the secular nation-state the way it is, and religious conservatives who would rather ignore politics altogether. Some Muslims have accused Khomeini of making Islam into a political ideology and reducing it to the terms of modern politics. Moreover, as Bernard Lewis claims, most Islamic rebellions are aimed in the opposite direction: to shed Islam of the alien idea of the nation-state.[41] Yet, even if that is their aim, one of the curious consequences of their way of thinking is the appropriation of many of the most salient elements of modern nationhood into an Islamic frame of reference. Rather than ridding Islam of the nation-state, they too have created a new synthesis.

Modern movements of religious nationalism, therefore, are subjects of controversy within both religious and secular circles. The marriage between religious faith and the nation-state is an interesting turn in modern history, frought with dangers, for even if it is possible, the radical accommodation of religion to nationalism may not necessarily be a good thing. A merger of the absolutism of nationalism with the absolutism of religion might create a rule so vaunted and potent that it might destroy itself and its neighbors as well. The actions of religious terrorists in the 1980s and early 1990s in South Asia and the Middle East warrant some of those fears. When a society's secular state and its religious community are both strong and respected, the power of life and death that is commanded by any single absolute authority—be it secular or religious—may be held tenuously in check. Without that balance, an absolute power of the worst sort could claim its most evil deeds to be legitimate moral duties. The revolutionary religious movements that have emerged in many parts of the world in the 1980s and 1990s exhibit some of those dangers—as well as many of the more hopeful aspects—of the religious nationalists' synthesis between the two great ideologies of order.

Modernity and the Religious State

One of the reasons why it is difficult to gauge whether the new religious states will become congenial members of the family of nations is that the few that have come into existence in recent years—such as Iran, Afghanistan, and Sudan—are still in the process of formation. Movements that favor religious nationalism in other countries are even more unspecific about what kind of detailed governmental rules and limitations their religion prescribes:

there is no single model of religious politics. Some have claimed that religion—Buddhism in the case of Sri Lanka, for example—has a strong affinity with socialism.[42] Others have asserted that it is compatible with capitalism: the constitution of the Islamic Republic of Iran, for instance, guarantees the right of private property.[43] In India, Hindu nationalists have made a distinction between nation and state, claiming that, as long as the country has a clear sense of national identity and moral purpose, the specific political framework and policies of the state matter little.[44] The policy stands of the Hindu BJP party during the 1991 election campaign were remarkably similar to those of secular political parties: it stated that, despite its affirmation of Hinduism as the ideological glue that holds the nation together, it has no intention of "running a Hindu government."[45] The political role of religion is primarily in formulating national identity and purpose, and some religious nationalists claim that, as long as government leaders are "in touch with the God behind the justice and the truth that the government espouses," as one Jewish nationalist put it, they will be satisfied.[46]

There are, however, differing points of view within religious nationalist movements, and one of the differences is over the role that religion should play in day-to-day governmental affairs. In Iran, the influence of the clergy has waned since the mid 1980s. In India, there is a tension between the often ragtag band of religious mendicants who help get out the vote for Hindu parties and the middle class urbanites who lead them. Among the latter are what the Indian press during the 1991 elections referred to as "Scuppies," saffron-clad yuppies; they are successful businessmen and administrators who see in Hindu political parties a stabilizing influence on the country and not a narrow dogmatism.[47] In other movements of religious nationalism one can also find this "Scuppie" pattern of an educated, urban religious elite linked with a large, disenfranchised rural constituency. In Sri Lanka, for instance, uneducated rural youth were tied to groups of urban student allies. In Palestine, many of the Muslim leaders were educated and trained abroad. The same was true of the Islamic Front in Algeria, where many participants in the 1991–92 uprising were highly educated doctors, scientists, and university professors. According to one of them, Fouad Delissi, a forty-year-old party leader in the popular quarter of bab al-Oued who worked as a maintenance director for Algeria's petroleum products retailing company, "if there are people who consider themselves democrats . . . it's us." The Muslim leader's circle of comrades included a majority who had studied in the United States or in France, and their interest in being involved in the Islamic political movement was to help "guide the country in a scientific, normal, modern way."[48]

Since they appear to have a broad outlook on their own society and its role within the larger international context, can we take these Algerian religious nationalists at their word and accept them as "modern"? The answer to that question depends in large measure on what is meant by "modern." A number of scholars has insisted on distinguishing between "modernity," largely defined as the acceptance of bureaucratic forms of organization and the acquisition of new technology, and "modernism," described as embracing the ideology of individualism and a relativist view of moral values. This distinction allows us to observe that religious nationalists are modern without being modernist.[49] Although they reject what they regard as the perverse and alienating features of modernity, they are in every other way creatures of the modern age.

In Giddens' frame of reference, it is perhaps inevitable that this be so. Nationalism, from his point of view, is a condition for entry into a modern world political and economic system

Mark Juergensmeyer

based on the building blocks of nation-states. It is unthinkable that a political or economic entity can function without some relationship to large patterns of international commerce and political alignment, and this relationship requires strong centralized control on a national level in order for it to be maintained. Since movements for religious nationalism aim at strengthening national identities, they can be seen as highly compatible with the modern system.

Religious nationalism, then, may be viewed as one way of bringing heretofore unreconcilable elements—traditional religion and modern politics—into collusion with one another. Those religious movements that are not nationalist and not political have been hostile to the nation-state, and they can legitimize the views of those who oppose the notion of a global nation-state system. In a similar vein, Wilfred Cantwell Smith contended in the mid 1950s that there was a fundamental opposition between Islam and modernity, by which he meant not only the attributes of modernism that Lawrence has mentioned, but also the fact that the transnationalism of Islamic culture has mitigated against the nation-state.[50] Recent movements of Islamic nationalism, however, have been surprisingly particular to individual nation-states and provide a remarkable synthesis of Islamic culture and modern nationalism. As one observer of the Iranian revolution remarked, it has "no precedent" in modern history.[51] Since the revolution, however, there has been a number of attempts in other parts of the world to achieve the kind of synthesis of traditional culture and modern politics to which the Iranian revolution aspires.

Currently throughout the world, the nation-state continues to be critical to global politics. Rather than challenging this fact, the new religious politics accommodates itself to it. It does so in the Third World as well as in the West, not only for ideological reasons but also for economic ones, since nation-states are the essential units of a global market system. In the past, religion had very little role to play in this scheme, and when it did become involved, it often threatened it. Contemporary religious politics, then, is the result of an almost Hegelian dialect between two competing frameworks of social order: secular nationalism (allied with the nation-state) and religion (allied with large ethnic communities). The clashes between them have often been destructive, but they have also offered possibilities for accommodation. These encounters have given birth, in some parts of the world, to a synthesis, in which religion has become the new ally of the nation-state.

NOTES

1. For the optimistic point of view that liberal democracy has triumphed, see Francis Fukuyama, "The End of History," *The National Interest*, 16 (Summer 1989), 3–18; and *The End of History and the Last Man* (New York: The Free Press, 1992), pp. xi–xxiii.

2. Samuel P. Huntington, "The Clash of Civilizations?," *Foreign Affairs*, 72 (Summer 1993), 2–11; and "If Not Civilizations, What? Paradigms of the Post-Cold War World," *Foreign Affairs*, 72 (November–December 1993), 186–94.

3. See Mark Juergensmeyer, "Why Religious Nationalists Are Not Fundamentalists," *Religion*, 23 (Spring 1993).

4. See Mark Juergensmeyer, "The Logic of Religious Violence," in David C. Rapoport, ed., *Inside Terrorist Organizations* (London: Frank Cass, 1988), pp. 172–93; "What the Bhikkhu Said: Reflections on the Rise of Militant Religious Nationalism," *Religion*, 20 (1990), 53–75; and *The New Cold War? Religious Nationalism Confronts the Secular State* (Berkeley: University of California Press, 1993). Some of the book's arguments and revised segments from it have been incorporated into this essay.

Comparative Politics   July 1995

5. Abolhassan Banisadr, *The Fundamental Principles and Precepts of Islamic Government* (Lexington: Mazda Publishers, 1981), p. 40.

6. Interview with Dr. Essem el Arian, Member of the National Assembly, Cairo, January 11, 1989; Sheik Ahmed Yassin, Gaza, January 14, 1989; and Bhikkhu Udawawala Chandrananda, Kandy, Sri Lanka, January 5, 1991.

7. Huntington, "Clash of Civilizations?."

8. Benedict Anderson, *Imagined Communities: Reflections on the Origin and Spread of Nationalism* (London: Verso, 1983); and Ninian Smart, *Worldviews: Crosscultural Explorations of Human Beliefs* (New York: Scribner's, 1983).

9. Karl Marx and Friedrich Engels, *The German Ideology* (New York: International Publishers, 1939); Karl Mannheim, *Ideology and Utopia* (New York: Harcourt, Brace and World, 1936); David Aptner, ed., *Ideology and Discontent* (New York: The Free Press, 1964); and Chaim I. Waxman, ed., *The End of Ideology Debate* (New York: Simon and Schuster, 1964).

10. Destutt de Tracy, *Elements of Ideology*, in Richard H. Cox, *Ideology, Politics, and Political Theory* (Belmont: Wadsworth Publishing Company, 1969), p. 17.

11. Clifford Geertz, "Ideology as a Cultural System," in Apter, ed.

12. Karl Deutsch, *Nationalism and Social Communication* (Cambridge, Mass.: MIT Press, 1966).

13. Ernest Gellner, *Nations and Nationalism* (Oxford: Basil Blackwell, 1983), p. 140.

14. Anthony D. Smith, *Nationalism in the Twentieth Century* (Oxford: Martin Robertson, 1979), p. 3. See also L. Doob, *Patriotism and Nationalism* (New Haven: Yale University Press, 1964).

15. Max Weber, "Politics as a Vocation," in Hans H. Gerth and C. Wright Mills, eds., *From Max Weber: Essays in Sociology* (New York: Oxford University Press, 1946), p. 78. Regarding the state's monopoly on violence, see John Breuilly, *Nationalism and the State* (Manchester: Manchester University Press, 1982); and Anthony D. Smith, *Theories of Nationalism* (London: Duckworth, 1971).

16. Anthony Giddens, *A Contemporary Critique of Historical Materialism, Volume Two: The Nation-State and Violence* (Berkeley: University of California Press, 1985), p. 219.

17. Clifford Geertz, "Religion as a Cultural System," reprinted in William A. Lessa and Evon Z. Vogt, eds., *Reader in Comparative Religion: An Anthropological Approach*, 3rd ed. (New York: Harper and Row, 1972), p. 168.

18. Robert Bellah, "Transcendence in Contemporary Piety," in Donald R. Cutler, *The Religious Situation: 1969* (Boston: Beacon Press, 1969), p. 907.

19. Peter Berger, *The Heretical Imperative* (New York: Doubleday, 1980), p. 38. See also Peter Berger, *Sacred Canopy: Elements of a Sociological Theory of Religion* (Garden City: Doubleday, 1967).

20. Louis Dupré, *Transcendent Selfhood: The Loss and Rediscovery of the Inner Life* (New York: Seabury Press, 1976), p. 26. For a discussion of Berger's and Dupré's definitions, see Mary Douglas, "The Effects of Modernization on Religious Change," *Daedalus*, 111 (Winter 1982), 1–19.

21. Émile Durkheim, *The Elementary Forms of the Religious Life* (London: George Allen and Unwin, 1976), pp. 38–39.

22. Weber, "Politics as a Vocation," p. 78.

·23. Donald E. Smith, ed., *Religion, Politics, and Social Change in the Third World: A Sourcebook* (New York: The Free Press, 1971), p. 11.

24. See Randall Balmer, *Mine Eyes Have Seen the Glory: A Journey into the Evangelical Subculture in America* (New York: Oxford University Press, 1989); Bruce Lawrence, *Defenders of God: The Fundamentalist Revolt against the Modern Age* (San Francisco: Harper and Row, 1989).

25. Joseph Strayer, *Medieval Statecraft and the Perspectives of History* (Princeton: Princeton University Press, 1971), p. 323.

26. Strayer, *Medieval Statecraft*, pp. 262–65.

27. Giddens, *Nation-State*, p. 4.

28. Ibid., p. 4. See also "Frontiers into Boundaries: The Evolution of the Modern State," ch. 5 of Ainslie T. Embree, *Imagining India* (New York: Oxford University Press, 1989), pp. 67–84.

29. Giddens, *Nation-State*, pp. 255ff. See also Immanuel Wallerstein, *The Modern World-System: Capitalist Agriculture and the Origins of the European World-Economy in the Sixteenth Century* (New York: Academic Press, 1974); Immanuel Wallerstein, *The Modern World-System II: Mercantilism and the Consolidation of the European World-Economy, 1600–1750* (New York: Academic Press, 1980); and Sidney Pollard, *Peaceful Conquest: The Industrialization of Europe, 1760–1970* (New York: Oxford University Press, 1981).

30. John Locke, *The Second Treatise on Government*, ch. 8, "Of the Beginnings of Political Societies" (New York:

Mark Juergensmeyer

Cambridge University Press, 1960), p. 375; Jean-Jacques Rousseau, *Social Contract*, ch. 8, "On the Civil State" (New York: Pocket Books, 1967), p. 23.

31. Alexis de Tocqueville, *The Old Regime and the French Revolution* (New York: Doubleday Anchor Books, 1955), p. 11. See also John McManners, *The French Revolution and the Church* (Westport: Greenwood Press, 1969).

32. Ernst Cassirer, *The Philosophy of the Enlightenment* (Boston: Beacon Press, 1955), p. 171. Among the devotees of Deism were Thomas Jefferson, Benjamin Franklin, and other founding fathers of America.

33. De Tocqueville, *The Old Regime*, p. 13.

34. Interview with Professor Leila el-Hamamsy, American University, Cairo, January 10, 1989.

35. Interview with Professor Saad Ibrahim, Cairo, January 10, 1989.

36. See Donald E. Smith, *India as a Secular State* (Princeton: Princeton University Press, 1963), which details the many concessions the government has made.

37. Ainslie Embree, *Utopias in Conflict: Religion and Nationalism in Modern India* (Berkeley: University of California Press, 1990), p. 88.

38. Giddens, *The Nation-State*, p. 71.

39. D. C. Vejayavardhana, *The Revolt in the Temple: Composed to Commemorate 2,500 Years of the Land, the Race, and the Faith* (Colombo: Sinha Publications, 1953), reprinted in Smith, ed., *Religion, Politics and Social Change*, p. 105.

40. Vejayavardhana, *The Revolt in the Temple*, p. 105.

41. Bernard Lewis, *The Political Language of Islam* (Chicago: University of Chicago Press, 1988).

42. Stanley Tambiah, *Buddhism Betrayed?*, pp. 117–18.

43. *Constitution of the Islamic Republic of Iran* (Berkeley: Mizan Press, 1980), Article 47, p. 46.

44. See Ainslie T. Embree, "The Function of the Rashtriya Swayamsevak Sangh: To Define the Hindu Nation," in Martin E. Marty and R. Scott Appleby, eds., *Accounting for Fundamentalisms* (Chicago: University of Chicago Press, 1993), p. 5.

45. Zafar Agha, "BJP Government: What Will It Be Like?," *India Today*, May 15, 1991, pp. 20–21.

46. Interview with Rabbi Levinger, a leader of the Gush Emunim, Jerusalem, January 16, 1989.

47. Madhu Jain, "BJP Supporters: Invasion of the Scuppies," *India Today*, May 15, 1991, pp. 18–19.

48. Kim Murphy, "Algerian Election to Test Strength of Radical Islam," *Los Angeles Times*, Dec. 26, 1991, p. 19.

49. Lawrence, *Defenders of God*, p. 27.

50. Wilfed Cantwell Smith, *Islam in Modern History* (Princeton: Princeton University Press, 1957), p. 47.

51. Sick, *All Fall Down*, p. 185.

[11]

The Politics of Ideology: The Papal Struggle with Liberalism[1]

Gene Burns
Princeton University

Social actors are drawn to ideological formulations that justify a defense or expansion of their own autonomy and power. Changes in distributions of power can close some avenues of ideological autonomy and open others; thus actors will have varying degrees of control over different issues within a given ideology. In response to the rise of liberal states in 19th-century Europe, the papacy was forced to avoid sociopolitical issues if it was to avoid persistent church-state conflict. Gradually reformulating Catholic ideology within the limited structural autonomy they had, popes subordinated sociopolitical issues to more purely religious and moral issues while constructing a new ideological opposition to liberalism.

The social context of belief systems, or ideology,[2] has only recently and occasionally been an important topic in political sociology (e.g., Sewell 1985; Skocpol 1982, 1985), and then sometimes only indirectly (Block 1985; Block and Burns 1986; Jones 1983; Laclau and Mouffe 1985; Luker 1984). However, political change is also ideological change (Wuthnow 1987, p. 62): Can we, for example, imagine the U.S. civil rights movement without the growth of an ideological commitment to racial equality? Can we imagine modern feminism without the process of consciousness raising (Evans 1979)? But, while political sociologists have developed

[1] I would like to thank Fred Block, Elizabeth McLean Petras, Ewa Morawska, Braulio Muñoz, John Noakes, Libby Schweber, Stephen Chiu, anonymous *AJS* reviewers, and the members of the Princeton University Culture Workshop during the 1988–89 academic year for helpful comments at various stages of my research and writing. Requests for reprints should be sent to Gene Burns, Department of Sociology, Princeton University, Princeton, New Jersey 08544.

[2] I am using the term "ideology" rather than "belief systems" because I want to stress the sociological tradition emphasizing structural influences, which tends to use the former term. My use, however, does not imply that ideology is a system of "false" beliefs (Mannheim [1929] 1936), only that one can understand it in the context of a given social structure. I do, however, mean to speak broadly of the various components of belief systems, e.g., values, within the context of the analysis of social change.

American Journal of Sociology

powerful structural[3] models of social and political change, they have not adequately applied structural insights to the study of ideology. The need for a more sophisticated conceptualization of ideology has become increasingly clear (Sewell 1985; Skocpol 1985). This paper argues that ideology is best understood within a political, structural framework, but one in which limited degrees of ideological autonomy exist within any given structural constraints.

Structural approaches have tended to argue (or, often, simply assume) a number of views of ideology, most of which negate the necessity of studying specific, empirical change within ideologies. One can argue that ideology is irrelevant to the main dynamics of social change (Skocpol 1979), fully determined by material factors (as Marx's earlier writings often argued), or so all-encompassing in its ability to dominate subordinate social groups that it serves a very similar function to "latent pattern maintenance" in the Parsonian framework (Abercrombie, Hill, and Turner 1980). In this last option, prevalent in notions of the "embeddedness" of ideology in social practice and material forces (Gramsci 1971, pp. 175, 326–27; Althusser 1969, 1971; Laclau and Mouffe 1985, pp. 108–13; Jones 1983, pp. 21–22; Sewell 1985), ideological dominance is so pervasive that ideology itself is not easily distinguished from other social processes. In none of these scenarios, then, is ideology both causally important *and* easily distinguishable from other social processes (Burns 1988).

Yet no major theoretical scheme within sociology would deny the basic sociological observation that people depend on ideology to make sense of social experience, including politics. Even Marxist views imply that people use ideology to justify and understand their experiences, even if that ideology does not always correspond to reality and does not act as an independent variable.

How, then, should we talk about ideology? To understand ideology, we must remember both that social actors develop ideologies as they attempt to understand the world *and* that structural constraints partly

---

[3] By "structure" I mean impersonal, persistent patterns of constraints. (I am indebted to Fred Block and John Noakes for providing similar conceptualizations.) Constraints are to be understood as patterns of costs for actions; a person might choose to act against structural constraints but at a cost. Thus, if a certain action in a particular society will result in imprisonment, we can reliably predict that most people under most circumstances will avoid such action. But taking such action might be important enough to some persons that they are willing to suffer the costs. My conception of structure ultimately shares more characteristics with a Marxist view of structure than with an anthropological or linguistic view because I refer exclusively to structures that operate through the organization of social relations. But I differ from the Marxist view in that structures need not be only material forces; patterns of costs can, e.g., emerge from the fact that most persons in a society are socialized to disapprove of a certain type of action.

Politics of Ideology

limit ideological freedom of movement. This article argues that the most important constraints originate in distributions of power; change in those distributions of power forces social actors to make sense of, and to survive within, a new set of constraints. But we must remember that such change is as likely to *weaken* the constraints on some actors as it is to strengthen them. While many social actors may be forced into ideological reformulation, we can expect that they will attempt to take advantage of what structural (and thus political) autonomy they have, refashioning their own ideological understandings of the world in opposition to threatening or hostile ideologies.

The argument here draws upon Swidler's (1986) discussion of agency in the manipulation of cultural resources as well as upon Lukes's (1977) and Sewell's (1985) arguments for a conception of agency within social structures. But we would have to qualify—though not necessarily completely reject—any notion of voluntarist choice among ideological alternatives, for two reasons. First, as I have already implied, agency must be considered in the context of the organizational and political constraints on the paths of ideological change (Fulbrook 1983; Zaret 1985). The expression and propagation of some ideologies will face repression, or their propagation may encounter insurmountable organizational obstacles. Second, the political context of ideological change implies that, because ideology allows social actors to make political sense of a changing world, they will be drawn to ideological reformulations that justify a defense or expansion of their own autonomy and power.

The Catholic church serves as an excellent case study of structural constraints on ideological change and the ideological options available to social actors as they are forced to adapt to changing constraints. I attempt to explain the political dynamics whereby the papal struggle with liberalism[4] in the late 19th and early 20th centuries led to two important developments in Catholic ideology—one primarily forced by the changing political constraints on church ideology, the second resulting from the papal defense of its political autonomy.

First, there was an increased differentiation of fundamental doctrine on the "faith and morals" of individuals and families from less central matters of macropolitics and economics, a differentiation the papacy op-

---

[4] Throughout this article, I use the term "liberalism," not in its contemporary sense of a moderately left-of-center perspective, but in its classical sense. Liberalism was not, of course, simply one movement, but a number of more or less similar trends, associated with the rise of bourgeois classes and modern states, which affected the Catholic church throughout Europe. Liberal economics (in the form of capitalism), liberal politics (especially republican forms separating church and state), and liberal ideology (e.g., freedom of conscience, freedom of religious practice) all threatened the ancien régime privileges of the church.

American Journal of Sociology

posed but could not prevent if it was to avoid dangerous conflict with European states. And yet, ultimately, the papal concentration of control over matters of faith and morals, now free from state control, actually enabled Rome to increase its centralization of authority within the church itself.

Second, the papacy developed a perspective on social issues that opposed liberalism with a neofeudal worldview. Within that perspective, "social doctrine" became a distinct doctrinal category to address such issues.[5] Popes avoided conflict with liberal states by devaluing doctrine on social and political issues and making it vague enough to avoid specific policy commitments. Yet, by retaining precapitalist, organic views of society, the papacy preserved for the church an independence from liberal ideologies.

To summarize the argument on the first point, through most of the 19th century the Catholic differentiation between spiritual and temporal concerns was not as sharp as it is today. Today, for example, Pope John Paul II is forbidding priests and nuns to hold political office (Kolbenschlag 1985); in his view, holding such office detracts from their spiritual concerns. He bases this prohibition on a particular reading of a declaration of the Second Vatican Council (1962–65) that the church's role in the world does not include temporal government (see the Vatican II documents *Gaudium et Spes*[6] and *Ad Gentes* in Abbott [1966], pp. 287–89, 599).

The absolute primacy of the spiritual mission of the church is today, then, a fundamental tenet of Rome and of Catholic conservatives, in opposition to church reformers and radicals who want to emphasize the church's obligation to transform political and social structures. But a century ago, the political division in the church was almost completely reversed; popes and conservatives condemned those who argued that the church had no role in temporal government, most famously in Pope Pius IX's *Syllabus of Errors,* issued in 1864.

[5] Not all doctrine dealing with matters of macropolitics and economics falls under the category of social doctrine. For example, just-war theory would probably be considered moral doctrine. However, despite the fact that official doctrinal categories and the ideological categories dealt with in this paper do not completely coincide, all modern doctrine dealing with such macro issues shares the properties of avoiding specific policy comitments. Thus, such doctrine does not really bind individual Catholics in the way that doctrine about the faith and morals of individuals does. For example, this is true of just-war theory. It is easiest to make the argument understandable to those unfamiliar with Catholic history by focusing on social doctrine, but ultimately this article is making an argument about ideology, not doctrine per se.

[6] It is customary to refer to church documents by a brief title taken from the first few words of the document in the language of the official text, usually Latin. *Gaudium et Spes* is the "Pastoral Constitution on the Church in the Modern World," *Ad Gentes,* the "Decree on the Church's Missionary Activity."

Politics of Ideology

The reversal occurred because the rights that the church still possesses, and thus is able to conserve, have changed in response to modern political forces that came to exclude the church from its former privileged role in the European political economy. The old feudal order declined, and an increasing secularization of politics also grew to threaten the church's role. Although the church did not welcome such a process, the actions even of conservative popes could not stop—in fact, at times, even aided—a changing political context whereby it was easiest for Rome to increase control over central doctrinal issues within the church while deemphasizing Catholic participation in modern European politics. In a process similar to the "boundary work" that Gieryn and his colleagues have observed in the professionalization of science (Gieryn 1983; Gieryn, Bevins, and Zehr 1985), the Catholic church was forced to specify further its hierarchy of doctrinal priorities. The church faced a world hostile to Catholicism's role in the ancien régime, and one that had already removed many of the church's feudal economic privileges. But secular opponents were willing to exchange church religious autonomy for a withdrawal from temporal politics. Interestingly, however, the papacy used the opportunity of greater autonomy to centralize power in the church further, as well as to develop a clear *ideological* autonomy from temporal forces.

The Catholic church never participated in the liberal social order, which brings us to the second important effect of the struggle with liberalism. Having never been an active partner in bourgeois politics and economics, as it had been in the medieval social order, the church never absorbed liberal ideology, the ideology of its perceived enemies. The papacy thus filled the newly emerging social doctrine with a content derived from its traditional neofeudal perspective. Ideologically, 19th-century social doctrine opposed liberalism from the Right.

Throughout this process of ideological reformulation, the papacy consistently failed whenever it attempted to reintegrate the church into European politics, while it was quite successful in developing a new ideological opposition to liberalism. The widened separation of church and state had been forced upon Rome by changing European political structures; Rome's own attempts to circumvent those changes thus, ironically, failed so badly that they served only to reinforce the church's isolation from secular politics. But, as long as Rome remained within its politically determined social boundaries, it had the autonomy to develop new ideological forms and even expand its authority over what had been politically defined as religious issues.

An understanding of the constraints and opportunities of the papacy's ideological reformulations lies in the history of the church's conflict with modern states, to which I now turn.

American Journal of Sociology

THE PAPACY'S TEMPORAL POWER

At least from the conversion to Christianity of the emperor Constantine in
A.D. 312 until approximately 1870, the Catholic church was a distinct
part of the European sociopolitical order. Although doctrinally the
church always emphasized the importance of the spiritual over the temporal, in fact its religious authority was heavily intertwined with the
temporal order. Major European Catholic powers heavily influenced not
only papal policies but even papal elections. Up until 1903, when Pope
Pius X declared it invalid, France, Spain, and Austria even possessed the
officially accepted right to veto any candidate in a papal conclave. (Use of
the veto was common in the 18th and 19th centuries.) Popes were heavily
dependent on such nations to conduct their policies, and Catholic sovereigns occasionally had to fear the loss of their thrones should the pope
come to oppose them (Chadwick 1981, pp. 253–341; Graham 1959, pp.
17–18, 107). As another example of the intertwining of spiritual and
temporal authority, the central role of the church in European feudalism
of course hardly needs mention.

As a result of the church's status in the European order, Catholic
doctrine and practice very much valued and sanctioned the temporal
prerogatives of the church. For example, into the 19th century it was not
uncommon for the papal secretary of state, second in rank in Rome after
the pope himself, to be a layman with experience and ability in managing
the pope's kingdom in central Italy. This was despite the fact that the
holder of the office was automatically a cardinal; the very powerful secretary of state during most of Pius IX's reign (1846–78), Giacomo Cardinal
Antonelli, for instance, was never a priest. It is, of course, impossible to
imagine a lay person holding such a high Vatican post today, as papal
authority is centered much more on purely religious concerns than on
those of state management. (Into the 19th century, it had even been
acceptable for unordained Roman bureaucrats to wear clerical clothing as
professional uniform [Graham 1959, p. 141].)

Perhaps a more important indication of the intertwined relationship of
temporal and religious authority is the fact that the papacy and its supporters argued fervently through the 19th century that the religious sovereignty and independence of the pope very much depended on his having
his own temporal kingdom, so that he would be the subject of no other
ruler (Graham 1959, pp. 158, 175–77). This perspective dominated
church ideology from the French Revolution to the early 20th century.
The perspective had existed long before 1789, but it became the central
axis of Catholic ideology once political change threatened Rome's place in
the European sociopolitical order.

With the French Revolution, one of the most powerful European states

Politics of Ideology

attempted to destroy the influence of Christianity, not only ideologically but, probably more important, institutionally. The church was to suffer a number of defeats and humiliations. In a country whose monarch had long claimed the title "Eldest Son of the Church," church lands were confiscated, and the early years of the Revolution seemed to promise the extinction of all clerical presence, let alone privileges. Eventually Napoleon made peace with the church, the church was granted control over most primary education, and priests became employees of the state. But in the meantime Napoleon's forces had taken over the Papal States, Pope Pius VI (1775–99) died in French exile, and Napoleon imprisoned Pope Pius VII (1800–1823) from 1809 to 1814. Closer relations wih the state during the Restoration were to be reversed again in 1830 (Moody 1953b; O'Dwyer 1985).

Reacting against the revolutionary threat, Pope Pius VI officially condemned the events and principles of the Revolution as early as 1791 (Moody 1953b, p. 111); that the church would take such a position is hardly surprising. The legacy of the Revolution was that liberal politics, from the church's point of view, not only threatened the church's role in any specific society—a role that seemed entirely natural to priests, bishops, and popes of the time—but also threatened the very existence of the church. In papal eyes, liberal political principles of rationalism, freedom of thought, freedom of religion, and so forth were nothing but declarations of war on the Catholic faith, both as belief system and as institution. And the imprisonment of two popes seemed good evidence to church conservatives that the papacy needed temporal independence.

Events in the 19th century did little to reconcile the church to liberalism. Interested nations, as well as political forces in the Papal States of central Italy, pressured Rome to institute the kind of constitutional system gaining favor in other countries (Jemolo 1960, pp. 4–6; Graham 1959, p. 134). Such popes as Gregory XVI (1831–46) were hardly receptive. A few weeks after his election, Gregory called in Austrian troops to suppress a liberal revolt in his dominion. In 1832, in an explicit rejection of great-power recommendations that he reform the Papal States (Wallace 1966, p. 18), Gregory published the encyclical *Mirari vos* (in Carlen 1981a, pp. 235–41), which condemned the principles of separation of church and state, freedom of the press, and freedom of religion (Camp 1969, p. 7; Jemolo 1960, p. 2). Despite some minor concessions, Gregory made no moves toward separating the papacy's religious rights from its temporal control of central Italy.

Gregory's successor, Pius IX (1846–78), showed conduct as a bishop that was less authoritarian than Gregory's (Wallace 1966, p. 19), but, despite European hopes that a liberal pope had finally come to power, it is unlikely that Pius was ever a liberal (Camp 1969, p. 8). For example, his

1129

American Journal of Sociology

very first encyclical, *Qui Pluribus* (in Carlen 1981*a*, pp. 277–84), criticized the Enlightenment championing of reason over faith.

Nevertheless, in response to pressure from within the Papal States, Pius IX instituted in his kingdom a short-lived division of jurisdiction between secular and religious ministries. The political goals of the papacy and of the Italian republicans of the secular cabinet, however, were hopelessly contradictory: the Papal States were of course a major impediment to Italian unification. The results of the power sharing thus were disastrous, as the secular cabinet wanted to wage an Italian war of unification on Austria, an important papal ally. Pius, having initiated the secular ministries in May 1848, abolished them in August (Hales 1954, pp. 58–67; Halperin 1939; Graham 1959, pp. 136–39).

As if this experiment in dividing religious from temporal sovereignty were not enough to sour Pius IX on liberalism, toward the end of 1848 Rome, like much of Europe, experienced a republican uprising. The pope fled the city, fearing for his life. Although he was restored to power by an enemy of Italian republicanism (Napoleon III), in 1859 the emerging Italian republic took from Pius all the papal territories except for Rome itself. Upon the withdrawal of French troops to fight in the Franco-Prussian War in 1870, the republic annexed Rome, leaving the pope only the Vatican and a few small properties in and around Rome (Moody 1953*a;* Halperin 1939).

It is possible, but unlikely, that another pope might have chosen a more conciliatory posture, but Pius IX opted for intransigence in the face of modern political forces that boded ill for the church, declaring himself a prisoner of the Vatican. He ignored those who argued that by identifying itself with an archaic political order, the church would lose the people, as he hoped for what Italian republicans feared (Wallace 1966, p. 260), that is, foreign intervention to restore his kingdom.

In reaction to his losses, Pius IX issued in December 1864 the famed *Syllabus of Errors* condemning most of the tenets popularly associated with liberalism, including freedom of worship. The *Syllabus* was an appendix to the encyclical *Quanta cura* (in Carlen 1981*a*, pp. 381–86), which insisted on the evils of separating church and state and of tolerating any but "the true religion." In 1870 came the *non-expedit*, that is, the papal prohibition of Catholics' voting in the republican elections, which remained in force until Pope Benedict XV lifted it in 1919 (though by that time it had been increasingly disregarded for at least a couple of decades).

Beginning a pattern that lasted through Pope Pius XI (1922–39), Pius IX's own attempts to oppose liberalism ironically reinforced the separation of church and state. Although the *non-expedit* was consistent with the view that the Italian republic had grievously sinned against the pa-

Politics of Ideology

pacy, it prevented those most faithful to the cause of the pope from having any influence on the government that was to legislate the future relationship between the republic and the church. Italian nationalists who still considered themselves devout Catholics, despite disagreements with the pope, still of course voted and held office. But political participation by the staunchest supporters of the papacy, those who obeyed the *non-expedit,* might have exerted pressure toward a compromise more favorable to Pius IX's position. The widening separation of church and state, then, was beyond papal control; attempts to oppose it only reinforced it.

Despite Pius IX's opposition, the 1871 Law of Guarantees was not unreasonable; it offered the papacy greater autonomy in religious affairs in exchange for noninterference in temporal politics. The law, whose validity the Vatican never formally accepted, granted the pope sovereign status, so that he could not be prosecuted under Italian law, and allowed him to conduct international diplomacy. He was to receive a stipend from the Italian government (which Pius IX refused) and to have complete freedom of international communication; control of communication of domestic decrees was liberalized but not completely eliminated. Participants in papal conclaves, even if from nations hostile to Italy, were guaranteed freedom of assembly. The state was no longer to nominate candidates for the Italian episcopacy, and bishops no longer had to take an oath of allegiance to the king. Nevertheless, Pius IX and his secretary of state, Cardinal Antonelli, treated the Law of Guarantees as essentially blasphemous. Pius IX's successors were less openly hostile; however, disputes continued, in some cases for decades, especially over the place of the church in Italian education, the property and privileges of religious orders, and marriage laws (Halperin 1939, chaps. 2–4; Jemolo 1960, chap. 2).

Many anticlericals, as well as devout liberal Catholics, had hoped that widening the separation of church and state would also liberalize the church, giving the papacy less to be autocratic about. The irony was that liberal attack upon the church (that, in Italy, took the pope's kingdom) internationally had the opposite effect. It increased Pius IX's autonomy within the institutional church, allowing him further to centralize and increase internal papal power: episcopacies no longer institutionally intertwined with the state became more dependent on the Vatican's protection against hostile governments than they did on the state's protection against the papacy (O'Connell 1984). The papacy became less dependent on, or hampered by, the privileges that states had controlled (e.g., the nomination of episcopal candidates) for perhaps centuries, allowing it to exert further control. Ironically, then, just as the papacy's resistance to

American Journal of Sociology

liberalism contributed to the separation of church and state, liberal states'
attacks on Catholicism made the church, internally, even more Roman
and less liberal.

Of course, Pius IX could use the argument that it was essential to close
ranks when the church was under attack. Thus he began the church's
period of greatest centralization, which was to last at least until the
Second Vatican Council and which, in some respects, continues. Pius
concentrated decision making in the Curia, the Vatican's bureaucracy
(O'Connell 1984, p. 201), but the most important centralizing accomplishment was the formal declaration of the doctrine of papal infallibility. This
doctrine involved a shifting of power away from the episcopacy in favor
of the papacy; a serious challenge would not come until Vatican II. To
make this fundamental doctrinal declaration, Pius IX called Vatican I,
the first ecumenical council—a meeting of the world's bishops—since the
16th-century Council of Trent met to inaugurate the Counter-Reformation.

On the one hand, the doctrine of infallibility reflects the ideological
priority of the faith and morals of individuals and families over concerns
of temporal politics and economics, a prioritization that legitimately can
be said to have a long history (see, e.g., Kerwin 1960, pp. 15–52; Ehler
and Morrall 1954). Thus infallibility—while it lends an aura to all papal
statements—officially applies only when formally invoked for fundamental doctrinal declarations of faith and morals, which in practice means
specific religious and moral doctrines distinct (in papal eyes) from mac-
ropolitical or economic issues. However, while there has always been
some distinction between "faith and morals" and more "temporal" issues,
at the time of Vatican I (1869–70) the two were much less distinct in
Catholic ideology than they are today. Thus, what is interesting about the
declaration of infallibility is that Pius IX felt the need to declare it precisely when his temporal authority was crumbling. Primary (and controversial) on the Vatican I agenda were two issues: the formal declaration of
infallibility and church-state relations in the wake of Italian unification
(Hales 1958, pp. 141–56).

Rome was trying to keep both issues under control, but it was easier to
emphasize religious questions, as the church was being forced out of
temporal government, thus gaining an increased (but unwanted) autonomy from states. Contemplating the end of Pius IX's reign, Catholic
powers considered using their veto to prevent the election of another pope
as intransigent as he (Engel-Janosi 1953), that is, to make sure the papacy
would accept the autonomy it had so far rejected.

The church would continue to encounter states trying to limit its involvement in temporal politics in turn-of-the-century France, revolution-

Politics of Ideology

ary Mexico, Fascist Italy, and Nazi Germany, among others. Pius IX's successors, dealing with the aftermath, would gradually widen the differentiation between religious and temporal issues, decentralizing macropolitics and economics—two areas where the church's formerly large influence had receded—away from the ideological core. In the next section, I examine the process whereby, given the changed political and social structure of Europe, the actions even of popes who had no sympathy for the separation of church and state ultimately reinforced that separation. Without necessarily intending to widen the distinction between religious and temporal matters, such popes increasingly differentiated their authority on matters of faith and morals, on the one hand, from their authority on matters of macropolitics and economics, on the other.

DIFFERENTIATION AND THE LOSS OF TEMPORAL POWER

The world had changed, the alliance of throne and altar gone forever, but the papacy did not fully accept this fact until Vatican II (1962–65). With the possible exception of Benedict XV (1915–22), the church between Vatican I and Vatican II was ruled by a series of popes with little sympathy for the modern separation of church and state. Leo XIII (1878–1903), Pius IX's immediate successor, had a personal preference for monarchical government (Arnal 1980, p. 201), and an ancien régime perspective was clear in his views of the obligation of the state to protect no religion but Catholicism and to repress error and immorality in the press (Leo XIII 1940, pp. 129–130, 239). As pope, though he recognized that the U.S. church had prospered by the separation of church and state there, he told Americans that it was much preferable, and beneficial for the church, for Catholicism to enjoy the protection and patronage of the state (Ellis 1983, p. 55; Leo XIII 1940, pp. 68, 74–77, 81–82, 127–28).

Unsurprisingly, then, Leo was authoritarian on religious matters. In a move that some have interpreted as an effort to stimulate Catholic philosophical studies (Camp 1969, p. 11; Falconi 1967, p. 5), he mandated that only Thomism was to be studied, an action that was fairly repressive (Daly 1980, pp. 9–10, 18–19). As a bishop, the future pope had been a very important inspiration for the *Syllabus* and the dogma of papal infallibility (O'Connell 1984, p. 208; Wallace 1966, p. 81). Furthermore, in 1899 Leo condemned doctrines of "Americanism," which argued for greater religious toleration and a more liberal view of the church's role in society. Such doctrines, which were generally popular in the United States but which were just as much a product of European (especially French) liberal Catholics who exaggerated American Catholic outlooks,

American Journal of Sociology

were threatening because they affirmed church-state separation and attempted to legitimate freedom of religion (Curran 1980; McAvoy 1945; Smith 1969, pp. 495–96).

And yet Leo was more conciliatory than Pius IX on the matter of temporal sovereignty. In Belgium, France, and Spain, he was willing to exchange the local churches' cessation of overt political agitation in return for peaceful church-state relations, even when this entailed prohibiting clergy from actively advocating a return to monarchy, despite his own personal preference for monarchy (Wallace 1966, pp. 277–308). In Italy, while he continued to argue that temporal power was essential to his independence, he spoke only of recovering the city of Rome, implicitly accepting the 1859 losses as a fait accompli (Leo XIII 1940, pp. 3, 7–8, 79; Jemolo 1960, p. 54). Thus Leo had no interest in democratizing the papacy's religious authority, but he began a slow, halting withdrawal of the church's temporal claims.

The most interesting aspect of Leo's pontificate, however, is the birth of what was, in effect, a new branch of doctrine, known as social doctrine, with his 1891 encyclical *Rerum novarum* (Leo XIII 1940, pp. 167–204). Although the term "social doctrine" apparently did not become common until the pontificate of Pius XI (1922–39), and some recent popes and other Catholics have preferred the term "social teaching," it was, in any case, not until Leo XIII that "the Church's social concerns were given a systematic philosophical and theological justification" separate from that of other doctrine (McCormick 1982, p. 99). And Catholics interested in such issues universally cite Leo as the parent of such concerns (e.g., Moody 1961, p. 73; Griffin 1987, p. 227). Social doctrine deals generally with questions of politics and economics on the societal level, as opposed to the religious and moral obligations of individuals and families. And although social doctrine implied a new Catholic view of the moral standards for conduct in modern society, the hierarchy has always regarded it as the least binding level of doctrine, one allowing disagreement at the specific level of policy, considered outside the church's competence.[7] (The more recent, common preference for the term "social teaching" demonstrates the progressive trend to make social doctrine even more flexible and nondogmatic [Curran 1985; Dorr 1983, p. 9]. This is in great contrast to doctrine that concerns the faith and morals of individuals and families,

---

[7] To point out that social doctrine deals with politics and economics at the societal level is all that needs to be said for the discussion here. The content of social doctrine is dealt with below in a separate section; the particulars are more relevant to an analysis of the medieval heritage that remained with Catholic thought as it reacted against liberalism.

Politics of Ideology

such as sexual morality, which deals very much in particulars within binding, supposedly unchanging doctrinal requirements [see, e.g., Mc-Cormick 1982, p. 100; Burns 1988].) *Rerum novarum*—and papal ideology on social and political issues ever since—avoids specific policy questions, arguing instead that the church's role is to teach a moral outlook that transcends historical and political particulars (Leo XIII 1940, p. 182).

Thus Leo stated that social doctrine does not address economic issues per se but their moral dimensions and that Catholic parties derive their Catholic identification from their *moral* principles, which do not imply any preference for a system of government (Leo XIII 1940, pp. 232–34; Schmandt 1961, pp. 30–31). While Pius IX had attempted very much to retain the connections between obligatory political opinions and religious devotion, Leo began to separate them.

It was not until the reign of Pius XII (1939–58) that ideological differentiation progressed to the point that the church's religious authority came to be defined as virtually separate from the temporal realm. In the period between Leo XIII and Pius XII, such differentiation developed haltingly; nevertheless, papal policy gradually contributed to the church's withdrawal from temporal prerogatives, even when the opposite result was intended. Simultaneously, popes increased Vatican control over faith and morals. Let us examine this process in the pontificates of Pius X (1903–15), Benedict XV (1915–22), and Pius XI (1922–39).

Leo's successor, Pius X, very much saw his role as one of silencing dissent. Pius X condemned some of the same views designated by Leo as aspects of Americanism, but his dragnet was wider and its effects more vicious. Eager to exterminate a somewhat imaginary conspiracy of theological dissenters grouped under the heading of "modernism," he had no qualms about ruining scores of ecclesiastical careers in the process (Carlen 1981*b*, pp. 71–98; Falconi 1967, pp. 32–71; Daly 1980; Kurtz 1983, 1986).

However, Pius X's attempt to control all aspects of Catholic life could be successful only on these more purely religious and theological matters. The inquisition against modernism can be understood as a part of the Vatican reaction against the loss of its standing within European social structure, a reaction that served to further consolidate the centralization of institutional power in Rome (Lyng and Kurtz 1985, p. 906). But European party politics were beyond papal grasp; thus Pius X's attempts to control Catholic political groups served only to reinforce the separation of church and state.

Pius X wanted hierarchical control over any political group that claimed Catholic inspiration, especially liberal groups; he was more lenient with the semifascistic *Action française,* in that its royalism was

American Journal of Sociology

compatible with his idealization of the ancien régime (Arnal 1980, pp. 193–96; Agócs 1973, p. 77–78; Camp 1969, p. 35).[8] But Pius X's refusal to allow Catholic participation in politics, in a world in which even the Catholic laity desired freedom from the hierarchy on matters of temporal politics, was in practice nearly equivalent to the prohibition of all explicitly Catholic political participation. Pius X prohibited the reformist *Sillon* in France and the Christian Democrats in Italy, and he prohibited Christian Democratic priests from serving in legislatures (Arnal 1980, pp. 189, 197; Falconi 1967, p. 57) or, in general, from being active politically (Jemolo 1960, p. 119). Thus, in a world where Catholic lay groups were interested in political organization only if allowed some autonomy from hierarchical control, Pius X's refusal to sanction such groups simply meant that there would be no organized, political participation explicitly oriented toward furthering Catholic goals.

Christian Democratic groups throughout Europe were explicitly attempting to differentiate secular political activities, even when inspired by Catholic principles, from moral or religious issues, which came under the jurisdiction of the hierarchy (Breunig 1957, p. 240). Pius X's response was to force political withdrawal. Ironically, Pius X in practice contributed to the separation of church and state by prohibiting precisely those groups' attempting to differentiate religious from political concerns. Similarly, in France, his hostility to liberalism contributed to the withdrawal of the church from politics. Although much less conciliatory than Leo XIII toward France in church-state disputes, his refusal to deal with the French government de facto reinforced the church's exclusion from political influence.

But outside the realm of macropolitics and economics, Pius X—like all popes since Pius IX—was able to strengthen church autonomy in those matters that did not challenge the widening separation of church and state. In fact, he could increase church autonomy by contributing to that separation. Thus, in reaction to Austria's exercising a veto in the 1903 conclave, he quickly acted to eliminate the privilege, thereby extracting the church from one aspect of state domination (Camp 1969, pp. 13–14; Engel-Janosi 1954, p. 271).

Yet Pius X was not hostile toward the Italian republic; he was basically

---

[8] Part of the mythology about Pius X is that he was little concerned with politics because he believed that the church should concentrate on spiritual concerns (Falconi 1967, pp. 11–23, 74, 79; Hebblethwaite 1986, pp. 26–27). Although a partial truth, this view is fairly misleading; it is a misunderstanding of the nature of the church's involvement in secular politics at the time. In fact, we shall see that Pius X wanted to control any political groups that called themselves Catholic, especially those that challenged the ancien régime perspective with which he, like previous popes, sympathized.

Politics of Ideology

inactive on the "Roman Question," though he did feel it needed to be settled; perhaps even a conservative like Pius X began to recognize that only "in the realm of fantasy or dreams" did anyone expect the church's temporal power to be restored (Jemolo 1960, p. 85; see also pp. 100, 109, 112; Agócs 1973, pp. 76–77). Perhaps this explains why he did not seem troubled by the lack of political effectiveness that resulted from his refusal to allow Catholics ideological freedom on political questions. In any case, Pius X himself tended to focus his energy on purely religious issues, such as liturgy, church music, and canon law (Falconi 1967, pp. 21–25; Camp 1969, p. 15; Jemolo 1960, p. 112), issues over which, of course, he had almost complete control.

Pius X, then, without necessarily intending so, contributed to a church withdrawal from politics while emphasizing the religious authority of the papacy. His withdrawal, however, did not increase individual Catholics' freedom on social and political questions, as Leo XIII had begun to do. But, by the early 20th century, the stage was set for further differentiation between religious and temporal concerns, the latter expressed doctrinally in an increasingly distinct, and less binding, way. Secular politicians came to care less about the internal workings of a church rapidly losing its temporal power base, and even church conservatives began to see some clear advantages, for example, a newly found autonomy from interfering states, that came with the loss of temporal power (Jemolo 1960, pp. 114–15, 170).

Later popes, then, continued to ease the official hostility toward Italy, and they went further than Pius X in seeking to resolve the situation. Benedict XV (1915–22), despite the brevity of his reign and the fact that it was dominated by World War I, did make a conciliatory gesture. He set aside the papal policy of refusing to meet with Catholic heads of state who implicitly recognized Italy's sovereignty over Rome by meeting with the king in that city. Benedict also encouraged official discussions to settle the Roman Question (Jemolo 1960, p. 168; Falconi 1967, p. 127).

Benedict was followed by a conservative pope who ruled with an iron hand. But because of the changed status of the Roman Question, we find that with Pius XI (1922–39) the nature of conservatism in the church had changed. Pius XI retained an antidemocratic view of the world, and his clear preference—as we shall see in his dealings with Mussolini—was for a church-state alliance rather than liberal arrangements. Yet he saw the unrealistic aspirations toward temporal sovereignty as obstacles to be eliminated; he had little patience with fellow prelates who echoed Pius IX's intransigence. And, we shall see, when Pius XI did try to reestablish a church-state alliance, his attempts backfired, demonstrating that it was no longer possible for the church to enforce its religious authority through temporal, political means. Pius XI's failed policy made clear that the

American Journal of Sociology

church would be wiser to protect its autonomy than to romanticize its past.

Pius XI settled the Roman Question by signing the Lateran Treaty with Mussolini in 1929, and yet he did so because his sole interest was the protection of the institutional church, preferably by protection from a confessional state. He had no commitment to church-state separation in principle—quite the opposite (Falconi 1967, pp. 161–62, 187; Pius XI 1942, p. 171).

Pius XI clearly admired Mussolini from early on not only as a man who could guarantee the church's independence, so Pius XI thought, while unpredictable democratic governments could not, but also as "a man who lacked the prejudices of the liberal school," that is, hostility toward the church (Jemolo 1960, p. 232; Rhodes 1973, p. 46). On paper, the Lateran Treaty and the accompanying concordat seemed highly favorable to the church; in return for little more than papal recognition of Italian sovereignty over the former papal territories, the state granted the primacy of religious over civil marriage, freedom for religious orders, a large money settlement, and the presence of religion in education. Mussolini even agreed that persons in official disfavor with the church (e.g., defrocked priests) would lose civil rights and that the state would recognize and enforce canon law. At the time, it seemed that Pius XI was indeed correct that fascism could offer what a liberal government could not, that is, a return to the confessional state (Falconi 1967, pp. 289–92; Rhodes 1973, pp. 37–52; Vaillancourt 1980, p. 248).

In his eagerness to reach an agreement with the church's apparent temporal savior, Pius XI bargained away the existence of the Catholic political party, the Popular party, guaranteeing that the church would not interfere with the Fascist state. He preferred groups directly under hierarchical control, such as Catholic Action, over the Popular party in any case (Falconi 1967, p. 189). Under Pius XI, the Vatican secretariat of state was in a flurry of activity in negotiating concordats with authoritarian governments. But, in Italy at least, he did not realize that, without any real temporal power base, the church was in reality bargaining away its ability to counter political suppression, its ability to defend itself should the Fascists not uphold the confessional state.[9]

Pius XI had surrendered the right of any Catholic organizations to challenge fascism and, more important, agreed to dismantle those organizations in exchange for an agreement that Mussolini, like Hitler, had no

---

[9] His administration seemed more realistic in negotiating with Germany. There, the church signed a concordat with a government whose good faith was of course questionable from the beginning, but it was fairly clear that refusal to sign would have meant unrelenting persecution (Harrigan 1961; Kent 1964).

Politics of Ideology

intention of keeping when it became inconvenient. The dictators signed to gain international prestige and, at least temporarily, to remove the Catholic church from the ranks of the domestic opposition. This complete bad faith in signing explains why Mussolini, like Hitler, would assent to an accord that on paper seemed so favorable to the church. Although after the war the church would receive state protection of its privileges concerning education and marriage laws, and de facto civil recognition, a full return to the confessional state, especially a truly authoritarian alliance, was unrealistic in Western Europe. The government that Pius XI thought would rebuild the church-state alliance could persecute the church much more viciously than liberals ever had, for the church had already lost the means to retaliate effectively. Pius XI was not a medieval pope who could force Mussolini to abdicate, and the failure of his attempt at a church-state authoritarian alliance demonstrated only how outdated such policy was.

The pontificate of Pius XI, then, somewhat repeated the pattern of Pius X's, but—given the Fascist context—with much graver results. He held authoritarian control over matters of faith and morals, and he preferred hierarchical control over Catholic lay political parties. But there was a contrast with Pius *IX* that points to an increasing differentiation between religious and temporal matters. While it is true that Pius IX and Pius XI were both interested primarily in defending the church's religious and institutional prerogatives and thought that an alliance of throne and altar was the best method of doing so, Pius XI (as well as, to a lesser degree, Pius X) took a much more strategic than doctrinaire approach to relations with modern states. He was willing to assure that the church would withdraw from overt political activity if, in particular nations (such as France), that was the only option by which the church could escape state hostility (Falconi 1967, pp. 197–98). A church-state alliance remained only an ideal, one that he mistakenly believed he could achieve in Fascist Italy.

Thus the reign of Pius XI, who quite clearly had no sympathy for liberalism either as it pertained to church-state separation or to republican forms of government, demonstrates the two important effects of the legacy of the papacy's struggle with liberalism. His important contribution to social doctrine, the 1931 encyclical *Quadragesimo Anno* (Pius XI 1942, pp. 178–234), states that the church is interested in presenting the moral principles of social order, not in dealing with temporal particulars. Unlike Pius IX's, Pius XI's preferences for church-state alliance remained *preferences* rather than doctrinal obligations in that his social doctrine argues that it is not within the church's competence to advocate a particular state arrangement. In addition, the encyclical continues Leo's criticism of capitalism from a neofeudal perspective, emphasizing the glories

American Journal of Sociology

of the old guild system. But before I address the particulars of the neofeudal content of that social doctrine, let us examine the pontificate of Pius XI's successor, in which the distinction between the church's religious authority and temporal involvement grew more pronounced than ever.

Pius XI's secretary of state, Eugenio Pacelli, succeeded him as Pius XII (1939–58). Pius XII's embattled reign during World War II remains a controversial one, especially over his attitudes and actions concerning the Holocaust (e.g., Falconi 1970; Friedlander 1966; Lichten 1963; Lewy 1964; Rhodes 1973, pp. 337–52; Vaillancourt 1980, pp. 293–95; Zahn 1962). But of main interest here is that under Pius XII, Catholic ideology reached perhaps its most distinct differentiation.

Initially, Pius XII's approach to temporal issues may appear to resemble Pius IX's, that is, in involving the church in temporal state politics. Pius XII clearly allied the church politically with the West and was obsessed by anticommunism (see, e.g., Dorr 1983, pp. 76–86). He was similar, as well, to his immediate predecessor, Pius XI, insofar as he almost surely preferred a church protected by and allied with the state; in fact, in postwar Italy he worked hard, and successfully, to guarantee church privileges under the Christian Democrats (Jemolo 1960, pp. 278–319).

But, unlike Pius IX, Pius XII did not intertwine temporal and "religious" issues. Most important, he did not give formal doctrinal sanction to his political ideals and activities. His concern with communism and his political alliance with the West are best understood as means to protect the Catholic church and contain what he saw as the evils of atheism, rather than as an intertwining of church and state functions.[10] Thus, while he made infrequent references to (especially Leo XIII's) social doctrine, his concern with temporal issues—for example, social reform, democratic participation, or particular state policies—did not go beyond the advocacy of a general political alliance with Western democracy. That is to say, the church was to ally itself with the West so that good Christians could carry on their religious mission, not so that the church itself could focus on temporal issues. Thus Pius XII, while concerned with geopolitics, did not pay much attention to social doctrine. Pius XII conceived the

---

[10] There is the possible exception of his involvement in postwar Italy; reflecting his preference for church-state alliance, other things being equal, he worked for the acceptance of Catholicism as, in effect, the official religion. But to do so he had to act within, and accept, a basically liberal political structure, quite different from the ancien régime or fascism. And, in other countries, other things were not equal, and so overall his activity on behalf of church-state alliance was considerably weaker than Pius XI's.

Politics of Ideology

church as a more purely religious, hierarchical institution than did perhaps any other modern pope.

The papacy of Pius XII is, therefore, of most interest for culminating the centralization of religious authority that had begun with Vatican I. Pius XII was the first, and so far only, pope to formally invoke the infallibility defined at Vatican I, in his 1950 declaration of the dogma of the bodily Assumption of Mary into heaven. It is interesting to note how often, in at least five separate encyclicals, Pius cites Vatican I, the council of infallibility and centralization (Carlen 1981*b*, pp. 39, 53, 65, 109, 179, 370). Pius XII in fact emphasized the divine nature of the papacy and of the church more than any pope since at least Pius IX. His conception of the church as the "Mystical Body of Christ" (in his encyclical *Mystici Corporis Christi*, in Carlen [1981*b*], pp. 37–63) emphasizes a church that is very distinct from the world around it by virtue of that divine presence.

For Pius XII's conception of the church's purpose primarily concerned spiritual matters, as well as moral matters, especially those affecting the family (e.g., Carlen 1981*b*, p. 27). But this otherworldly spirituality was to be under the firm authority of a hierarchical church. So his emphasis on the church as physical institution was not an emphasis on temporal involvement, strange as that may seem to non-Catholics. The hierarchy, then, was to be in firm control of spiritual matters, whereas such issues as the specifics of the social order, though Pius XII certainly referred to them, were simply not high priorities. Even Pius XII's acceptance of democracy in the fight against communism seemed to be less an absolute moral commitment than a strategic, realistic acceptance of the best option available at the time. Thus, for example, he did not display any great concern for the specifics of democratic processes (Dorr 1983, pp. 84–86).

Even when he argued explicitly that social and economic matters are within the domain of the church, Pius XII implicitly recognized the hierarchy of ideological levels that harks back to Leo XIII, in that such matters are of concern only insofar as they have moral implications (Carlen 1981*b*, p. 368). That is, the Catholic view of the world is through the lens of morality, not focusing much on issues that have no clear moral implications in Catholic moral theology. In any case, Pius XII did not generally emphasize these social concerns.

Falconi (1967, pp. 282–83) likens Pius XII's encyclical *Humani generis* (Carlen 1981*b*, pp. 175–84) to Pius X's campaign against modernism in that it aimed to restrict new developments in theological and biblical research. In this encyclical, Pius XII argued that, because human intellect is often hampered by desire and must be properly trained, the hierarchy's pronouncements on faith and morals had to be the starting point of all theology and Catholic philosophy, implying of course infallibility (Carlen 1981*b*, pp. 175, 180). In fact, he stated, citing Pius IX, that the job of

American Journal of Sociology

theologians was to demonstrate the sources in revelation of doctrine already defined by the church (meaning the hierarchy). So as not to leave any ambiguity, *Humani generis* also stated explicitly that encyclicals—many of which Catholic theologians treat more as points of discussion than as unalterable truth—have dogmatic status (Carlen 1981*b*, pp. 178–79). *Mystici Corporis Christi* had earlier clearly implied that the church never makes a doctrinal error, whether or not formally invoking infallibility (Carlen 1981*b*, p. 43). Yet, implicitly acknowledging an ideological hierarchy of priorities, *Humani generis* notes that there is much in philosophical investigation "that neither directly nor indirectly touches faith or morals, and which consequently the Church leaves to the free discussion of experts" (Carlen 1981*b*, p. 180). Thus he very clearly distinguished Roman authority over matters of faith and morals, which cannot be questioned, from other issues that are much more open to debate. Among those were issues of social reform, which, at least under Pius XII, were not often papal concerns.

In his desire to centralize authority in the papacy, Pius XII, born two years before Pius IX died, was very much a 20th-century version of his papal namesake. But the world had changed, creating a different context and a different meaning for the same institutional authoritarianism. Pius IX increased theological and institutional centralization in reaction to temporal threats. By the mid-20th century, defending papal temporal power was no longer a concern, and so centralization meant making the papacy, and the church, even more divine and less worldly.

STRUCTURAL AUTONOMY AND THE STRUGGLE WITH LIBERALISM: A NEOFEUDAL SOCIAL DOCTRINE

The ideological history of the Catholic church confirms Fulbrook's (1983) finding that a church's perspective on the temporal world very much depends on whether it is allied with or alienated from state structures. Having been very much a part of the feudal social order, the medieval church granted doctrinal sanction to the economic and social hierarchies of the age. Being politically and economically intertwined with the medieval social order, ideologically the church reflected a very close affinity with temporal sovereigns and ruling classes.

But with the emergence of the modern state system and industrial capitalism, the church gradually was excluded from political and economic power. It never was an important partner in liberal politics or liberal economics. This process of exclusion, we have seen, led to an ideological differentiation that more clearly distinguished macropolitics and economics from central religious beliefs. But social doctrine, as it became more distinct, needed content. The church, in analyzing the mod-

Politics of Ideology

ern political and economic order, unsurprisingly, did not turn to the dominant liberalism of the day to supply that content, for liberalism was its sworn enemy. As noted above, Leo XIII, who founded social doctrine as a distinct ideological category, was certainly no liberal, and he did not abandon claims of the necessity of temporal sovereignty for his religious independence (Leo XIII 1940, pp. 3, 7–8, 79).

It is contemporary moderate and Left-leaning Catholics who most often emphasize social doctrine, but the two most important (pre–Vatican II) contributors to social doctrine were Leo XIII, the monarchist (in his 1891 encyclical *Rerum novarum*), and Pius XI, the pope eager to form an alliance with fascism.[11] The development of social doctrine allowed the papacy to give a general analysis of social issues that remained ideologically independent of liberalism without addressing specific, controversial policy issues.

Leo's paternalistic discussion of the plight of workers in industrial society was, despite its basic conservatism (discussed below), a great contrast to previous church approaches to social issues. It opened the door to Catholic advocacy of proletarian causes. Leo was the first modern pope not to rule central Italy, and thus the first for whom the attempt to gain the allegiance of the working class would not encounter the fundamental contradiction that the church was closely intertwined with the ruling classes and ruling sovereigns of Europe. Thus, Leo made small moves toward a new political alliance, given that the church had been forced out of its old alliance with preliberal states and social classes.

Those whom Leo turned to for advice on the ideas that influenced *Rerum novarum* might initially appear to have been progressive social reformers (Vidler 1964, pp. 125–29), and, within a paternalistic world view, they did advocate social reform. But they appear more accurately to be characterized as conservative aristocrats, critical of capitalism from the Right, not the Left (Wallace 1966, pp. 262–67; Moody 1961, pp. 78–79). Leo himself came from an aristocratic background likely to

---

[11] Modern reform-minded Catholics often assume that the development of social doctrine as a distinct ideological category meant that the papacy was heightening the value of reforming the world. But nearly the opposite was the case, since social doctrine became distinct by becoming ideologically subordinate to faith and morals. Thus some popes (e.g., Pius X, Pius XII) could put little effort into refining social doctrine, while none, of course, has neglected faith and morals. After Vatican II, the situation changed somewhat because that council reemphasized participation in the world (esp. *Gaudium et Spes,* in Abbott [1966], pp. 199–316). Vatican II, however, did not question the basic ideological differentiation subordinating social concerns to faith and morals, the latter remaining the ideological property of Rome, thus leading to a certain amount of political tension in the church whereby some groups are attempting to reorder the ideological priorities. But that is another story, too large to include in this paper.

American Journal of Sociology

emphasize preindustrial values and lived in a relatively undeveloped country; his personal style was likewise aristocratic, sometimes even snobbish (Falconi 1967, pp. 15–16; Schmandt 1961, p. 33).

Although there was a true, paternalistic concern for the plight of the working class, *Rerum novarum* was an attempt to apply to the contemporary world a somewhat romanticized view of medieval social organization (Leo XIII 1940, pp. 195–98), in which the church was a crucial link. The "lessons" of that social organization still have an important legacy in Catholic social doctrine, a fact that contemporary observers of the church often miss. Liberalism, a force perceived as very hostile to the church, could not, in a pope's eyes, provide answers to modern social problems. Would not the days when the church was at its zenith—at the center of European civilization—the days of guilds, before church-state separation, provide a better model?

Thus we find that essential to Leo's approach was the role of the institutional church and religious morality in the social order. *Rerum novarum* argues that modern social problems are the result of the decline of religion, an argument he had been making for decades (Wallace 1966, pp. 80, 91, 278–79; Leo XIII 1940, pp. 49–62, 86–87), and one that, not too surprisingly, remains a strong influence on Catholic social doctrine: "Public institutions and laws set aside the ancient religion. Hence by degrees it has come to pass that working men have been given over, isolated and defenceless, to the callousness of employers and the greed of unrestrained competition" (*Rerum novarum,* in Leo XIII 1940, p. 168). To someone outside the Catholic worldview, the second sentence probably does not follow from the first as clearly and convincingly as it does for Leo; this logic, however, remains important in Catholic social doctrine. The solution to industrial and social conflict, the argument goes, begins with a return to religion (Leo XIII 1940, pp. 175, 203–4; see also *Graves de Communi,* pp. 234–35). Religious devotion, reflecting the modern differentiation of Catholic ideology, is always primary to technical questions of policy; the church, so the argument goes, leaves the details of policy—where disagreement is allowed because such details are not very important—to temporal authorities. Thus *Rerum novarum,* and social doctrine in general, avoids questions of policy and often exhorts society to return to religion.

While avoiding such specific issues, social doctrine is, however, clearly opposed to libertarian views of the market; it is not up to owners to do whatever they wish with property (Leo XIII 1940, p. 178); the interests of society must be kept in mind. Employers are to pay a fair wage, enough to support a worker and family; Leo rejected a purely market wage (pp. 192–94).

Continuing the essentially neofeudal perspective, Leo argued that the

Politics of Ideology

wealthy are obliged to practice Christian charity to aid workers; the continued amassing of profits, as well as usury, was immoral (Leo XIII 1940, pp. 168, 180). Social reform, then, is to occur paternalistically, through charity (p. 180) and noblesse oblige, although preferably in a more regular, dependable manner than simple almsgiving (p. 237). Denying that class conflict was inevitable (pp. 177, 182), and assuming that the class structure of society was natural (pp. 176–77; Camp 1969, pp. 30–32; Wallace 1966, pp. 113, 272), Leo argued that the state is to work to the benefit of all classes (see also *Graves de Communi,* in Leo XIII 1940, p. 233). The state is to intervene if necessary to protect the workers' welfare, including the workers' ability (e.g., being physically healthy) to practice religion. It is the moral duty of all classes to work together in harmony. Pre–Vatican II social doctrine, reflecting the church's lack of direct experience in managing modern liberal economies or states, argued a simplistic and romantic social theory that saw state partisanship toward particular classes, as well as class conflict in general, as moral, not structural, failings.

Thus Leo legitimated few concrete means, other than increasing their religious devotion (Leo XIII 1940, pp. 189–90), by which the working class, whose cause he was supposedly championing, could improve their position. He argued that the conditions that lead workers to strike should be removed, but in practice he did not seem to approve of strikes (Camp 1969, p. 116). He pronounced on the moral obligations of owners but was not specific on exactly how the state should regulate the market.

After Leo, political developments, as we have already seen, continued to contribute to the church-state separation that opened the ideological door for social doctrine. But given the low ideological priority of that category of doctrine, there were few significant contributions to it until Pius XI's *Quadragesimo Anno,* in 1931 (in Pius XI 1942, pp. 178–234). *Quadragesimo Anno* was more reform-minded than *Rerum novarum,* for example, in its insistence that charity is essential but not enough to achieve justice (pp. 179, 229), that opposition to unions is criminal (p. 187), and with even a hint that the developing world (not, of course, his term) is poor because of exploitation by colonial industry (p. 200).

How was it that a pope with such apparent right-wing sympathies could produce such a document? Pius XI inherited Leo's neofeudal perspective, a perspective that was critical of capitalism and the laissez-faire state, but he updated it. And by Pius XI's time, the church in Europe was even more distant from liberalism, socially and politically, than it had been under Leo. Leo had still hoped to win some concessions from the Italian republic, but Pius XI more optimistically hoped for the end of liberalism and had definite admiration for the corporatist critiques of capitalism that had become quite common, and that merged rather well

American Journal of Sociology

with romanticized notions of medieval guilds. (Pius XI, however, was no revolutionary and so urged the reform, not the abolition, of capitalism [1942, pp. 214–15].)

Like Leo, Pius XI was insistent that no solution could be found without the church (1942, p. 181), specifically through a religious and moral reform that preceded social reform, even within unions (pp. 182, 188, 224). He even stated that a source of the social problem was that people are *too* preoccupied with temporal matters (p. 230). He was quite conscious that Catholic social doctrine is born of an opposition to liberalism, in both its political and economic forms (pp. 182, 185, 211), and stated that unions are only one form of desired association, which should not be restricted to just one class (p. 190).

Like Leo, Pius XI argued for the inviolability of property while stressing the social obligations of ownership, again rejecting the idea that property is simply a commodity to produce profits, and thus distinguishing between rights of ownership and rights of use. The state has a right to ensure the social uses of property (1942, pp. 193–96) and to control property whose domination by individuals would lead to social harm (p. 220). An important reform is that all be able to acquire property (p. 201). Seeming to imply that class differences are inevitable and just, he repeated Leo's argument that no one is morally entitled to income "which he does not need in order to live as becomes his station" (p. 196). He argued a theme later repeated by John Paul II (in the encyclical *Laborem exercens,* in Carlen 1981c, p. 312), that both capital and labor are essential, each deserving a just, but not total, share, the worker's being enough to support a family (pp. 196–99, 203). But Pius XI seemed more attuned than Leo to the requirements of the market (pp. 201, 203–4).

On ideological differentiation, again Pius XI was more explicit than Leo in noting that the church's authority concerns not technical matters, but the moral aspects of social and economic questions—clearly rejecting, however, the notion that it is possible to talk of technical matters completely independently of moral questions (1942, pp. 192–93).

What Pius XI presented in *Quadragesimo Anno* was a vision of a corporatist social order (1942, pp. 207, 212) in which workers share in ownership (p. 202) yet are forbidden to strike because the state would prevent class conflict (p. 213), an order that he explicitly asserts once existed (p. 206), that is, in medieval times. Members of society were to be joined in ways that cut across class divisions; thus once again papal social doctrine was denying that market or class divisions necessarily became social and moral divisions (pp. 209, 211). This pope, then, attempted to reinstitute the ancient régime in an alliance with fascism—but, as we have

Politics of Ideology

seen, failed—and continued the critique of capitalism from the ancien régime perspective.

CONCLUSION

The development of a new papal perspective on social and political issues was a complex process that involved structural constraints that limited, but did not completely determine, Catholic ideological options. The strategy of reestablishing the central role of the church hierarchy in secular politics consistently failed and, in fact, ironically served to reinforce a widening separation of church and state. But the development of an independent ideology that respected the separation of church and state was quite successful. The papacy managed to further centralize control over issues concerning the faith and morals of Catholic individuals and Catholic families but could do so only by subordinating issues of macropolitics and economics. Even on these issues, however, as long as the church avoided specific policy issues that might initiate conflict with powerful secular forces, the papacy could successfully develop an independent Catholic ideology that opposed liberal perspectives while drawing upon centuries-old Catholic conceptions of a corporatist society.[12]

Ideological change in the modern Catholic church involved a political process in which a defensive posture against modern states allowed popes to increase the centralization of authority within the church itself, as well as to develop an antiliberal social doctrine. Studies by Kurtz (1983, 1986)

[12] As mentioned in n. 11, the Second Vatican Council (1962–65) made more ambiguous the ideological differentiation that was partially forced upon the papacy and that was partially the result of papal initiative. This council accepted as official doctrine a fact that had been established decades before, i.e., that the church does not belong in temporal government. But it also called for increased church commitment to social justice. As a result, the papacy, while criticizing unbridled capitalism (e.g., in John Paul II's 1988 encyclical *Sollicitudo Rei Socialis*), the arms race, etc., in *general* terms, has attempted to restrain some bishops and other members of the church from addressing policy issues in ways that seem to morally sanction specific policy options while excluding others. For example, the Vatican intervened to ensure that the U.S. bishops' pastoral letter on peace (National Conference of Catholic Bishops 1983) made clear the distinction between binding moral *principles* and particular policy *preferences* (see *National Catholic Reporter,* April 22, 1983; *Origins,* April 7, 1983). It is no accident that Vatican II would question this ideological differentiation while also (again, with ambiguous results) questioning the extreme centralization of institutional power in the papacy. That is, the papacy had used this ideological differentiation partially to ensure that the central ideological issues would be under Roman control; ideological readjustment would thus require a redistribution of power. But the ideological politics of the Catholic church since Vatican II (see Burns 1988) are much too complex to be addressed in this paper.

Religion and Politics

American Journal of Sociology

and Lyng and Kurtz (1985) of the modernist heresy have noted the relationship between defensiveness and centralization, but they have not
specified that the papacy's actions were not *only* defensive or, furthermore, that popes could not define orthodoxy and centralize ideological
control any way they chose. The papacy could not control the changing
political structure of Europe, but it successfully augmented its own power
within the constraints of that structure. But to expand its own power, the
papacy unwittingly participated in an ideological differentiation that it
had, in fact, initially resisted. Some of its own resistance contributed to
the widened separation of church and state, a separation ultimately
reflected in a widened ideological differentiation. In that differentiation,
the papacy subordinated issues of macropolitics and economics. But, as
long as Rome avoided specific denunciations of European (especially
Italian) state policy, it could fill its newly created social doctrine with
preliberal and antiliberal themes. Those themes of course held great appeal for popes who perceived a harsh political climate filled with liberal
persecutors.

   This example of the interaction of structural constraints, political
power, and ideological change suggests a number of important themes for
the political sociology of ideology. For example, it suggests that understanding political structure is essential to the understanding of ideological
boundaries. In fact, attention to political structure builds upon the study
of cultural boundaries while helping to correct the overly Durkheimian
approach of some such work (Douglas 1966; Erikson 1966). While it
remains true that social conflict is likely to emerge around problematic
ideological or cultural boundaries (see Darnton 1984), those boundaries
may in fact often be determined by larger political transformations. A
boundary becomes problematic not necessarily because it is inherently or
logically ambiguous, but because changing political balances place new
structural constraints on ideologies. Thus, a widened church-state separation enforced by temporal powers pushed the church to sharpen the
ideological boundary between faith and moral issues, on the one hand,
and social and political issues, on the other. (In this context, see the
interesting studies of the ideological construction of scientific boundaries
by Gieryn [1983] and Gieryn et al. [1985].)

   The issue of ideological boundaries raises another point. As mentioned
at the beginning of this article, some approaches emphasize the relationship between power and ideology but too easily assume that ideology
serves as a unitary, legitimating force, as Wuthnow (1985, pp. 815–16)
points out. As Abercrombie et al. (1980) note, an assumption that dominant ideologies pervade and organize all social life has appeared in both
Parsonian and Marxist approaches (see also Skocpol's critique of such
approaches [1985]). Some analysts of the Catholic church even argue that

Politics of Ideology

Catholic ideology has existed primarily to legitimate capitalism, even at times when rising bourgeoisies attacked church privileges (Gismondi 1986; Kearney 1986). Just as it is important to understand that Catholic ideology has internal boundaries prioritizing different types of issues, as do many ideologies, so we must keep in mind that fragmentation of power will always allow the possibility of competing ideologies in society as a whole. Attempts to control competing powers can, in fact, as in the case of liberal attacks on Catholic privileges, help produce new forms of oppositional ideology. Attention to structural constraints on ideological options suggests the need to emphasize how changing social conditions can restrain ideological freedom of movement and yet, simultaneously, allow the possibility of important ideological change.

REFERENCES

Abbott, Walter M., S.J., ed. 1966. *The Documents of Vatican II.* Piscataway, N.J.: New Century.
Abercrombie, Nicholas, Stephen Hill, and Bryan S. Turner. 1980. *The Dominant Ideology Thesis.* London: George Allen & Unwin.
Agócs, Sandor. 1973. "Christian Democracy and Social Modernism in Italy during the Papacy of Pius X." *Church History* 42:73–88.
Althusser, Louis. 1969. *For Marx.* London: Allen Lane.
———. 1971. "Ideology and Ideological State Apparatuses (Notes toward an Investigation)." Pp. 127–86 in *Lenin and Philosophy and Other Essays,* translated by Ben Brewster. New York and London: Monthly Review.
Arnal, Oscar L. 1980. "Why the French Christian Democrats Were Condemned." *Church History* 49:188–202.
Block, Fred. 1985. "Postindustrial Development and the Obsolescence of Economic Categories." *Politics and Society* 14:71–104.
Block, Fred, and Gene A. Burns. 1986. "Productivity as a Social Problem: The Uses and Misuses of Social Science Indicators." *American Sociological Review* 51:767–80.
Breunig, Charles. 1957. "The Condemnation of the *Sillon:* An Episode in the History of Christian-Democracy in France." *Church History* 26:227–44.
Burns, Gene. 1988. "The Political Structure of Ideological Change: Roman and American Catholicism." Ph.D. dissertation. University of Pennsylvania, Department of Sociology.
Camp, Richard L. 1969. *The Papal Ideology of Social Reform: A Study in Historical Development, 1878–1967.* Leiden: E.J. Brill.
Carlen, Claudia, IHM, ed. 1981a. *The Papal Encyclicals.*Vol. 1, *1740–1878.* Salem, N.H.: McGrath.
———. 1981b. *The Papal Encyclicals.* Vol. 4, *1939–1958.* Salem, N.H.: McGrath.
———. 1981c. *The Papal Encyclicals.* Vol. 5, *1958–1981.* Salem, N.H.: McGrath.
Chadwick, Owen. 1981. *The Popes and European Revolution.* Oxford: Clarendon.
Curran, Charles E. 1985. "The Changing Anthropological Bases of Catholic Social Ethics." Pp. 5–42 in Curran, *Directions in Social Ethics.* Notre Dame, Ind.: Notre Dame University Press.
Curran, Robert Emmett, S.J. 1980. "The McGlynn Affair and the Shaping of the New Conservatism in American Catholicism." *Catholic Historical Review* 66:184–204.

American Journal of Sociology

Daly, Gabriel, O.S.A. 1980. *Transcendence and Immanence: A Study in Catholic Modernism and Integralism*. Oxford: Clarendon.

Darnton, Robert. 1984. "Philosophers Trim the Tree of Knowledge: The Epistemological Strategy of the *Encyclopédie*." Pp. 191–213 in *The Great Cat Massacre and Other Episodes in French Cultural History*. New York: Basic.

Dorr, Donal. 1983. *Option for the Poor: A Hundred Years of Vatican Social Teaching*. Dublin: Gill & Macmillan; Maryknoll, N.Y.: Orbis.

Douglas, Mary. 1966. *Purity and Danger: An Analysis of the Concepts of Pollution and Taboo*. New York: Pantheon.

Ehler, Sidney Z., and John B. Morrall, trans. and eds. 1954. *Church and State through the Centuries*. Westminster, Md.: Newman.

Ellis, John Tracy. 1983. "Review Article: From the Enlightenment to the Present: Papal Policy Seen through the Encyclicals." *Catholic Historical Review* 69:51–58.

Engel-Janosi, Friedrich. 1953. "Austria and the Conclave of 1878." *Catholic Historical Review* 39:142–66.

———. 1954. "The Roman Question in the First Years of Benedict XV." *Catholic Historical Review* 40:269–85.

Erikson, Kai. 1966. *Wayward Puritans*. New York: Wiley.

Evans, Sara. 1979. *Personal Politics: The Roots of Women's Liberation in the Civil Rights Movement and the New Left*. New York: Vintage.

Falconi, Carlo. 1967. *The Popes in the Twentieth Century: From Pius X to John XXIII*, translated by Muriel Grindrod. Boston: Little, Brown.

———. 1970. *The Silence of Pius XII*. Boston: Little, Brown.

Friedlander, Saul. 1966. *Pius XII and the Third Reich*. New York: Knopf.

Fulbrook, Mary. 1983. *Piety and Politics: Religion and the Rise of Absolutism in England, Württemberg and Prussia*. Cambridge: Cambridge University Press.

Gieryn, Thomas F. 1983. "Boundary-Work and the Demarcation of Science from Non-Science: Strains and Interests in Professional Ideologies of Scientists." *American Sociological Review* 48:781–95.

Gieryn, Thomas F., George M. Bevins, and Stephen C. Zehr. 1985. "Professionalization of American Scientists: Public Science in the Creation/Evolution Trials." *American Sociological Review* 50:392–409.

Gismondi, Michael A. 1986. "Transformations in the Holy: Religious Resistance and Hegemonic Struggles in the Nicaraguan Revolution." *Latin American Perspectives* 13 (3): 13–36.

Graham, Robert A., S.J. 1959. *Vatican Diplomacy: A Study of Church and State on the International Plane*. Princeton, N.J.: Princeton University Press.

Gramsci, Antonio. 1971. *Selections from the Prison Notebooks*, edited and translated by Quintin Hoare and Geoffrey Nowell Smith. New York: International.

Griffin, Leslie. 1987. "The Integration of Spiritual and Temporal: Contemporary Roman Catholic Church-State Theory." *Theological Studies* 48:225–57.

Hales, E. E. Y. 1954. *Pio Nono*. London: Eyre.

———. 1958. *The Catholic Church in the Modern World*. London: Eyre & Spottiswoode.

Halperin, S. William. 1939. *Italy and the Vatican at War: A Study of Their Relations from the Outbreak of the Franco-Prussian War to the Death of Pius IX*. Chicago: University of Chicago Press.

Harrigan, William M. 1961. "Nazi Germany and the Holy See, 1933–1936: The Historical Background of *Mit brennender Sorge*." *Catholic Historical Review* 47:166–98.

Hebblethwaite, Peter. 1986. *In the Vatican*. Bethesda, Md.: Adler & Adler.

Jemolo, A. C. 1960. *Church and State in Italy, 1850–1950*, translated by David Moore. Philadelphia: Dufour.

Politics of Ideology

Jones, Gareth Stedman. 1983. *Languages of Class: Studies in English Working Class History, 1832–1932*. Cambridge: Cambridge University Press.

Kearney, Michael. 1986. "Religion, Ideology, and Revolution in Latin America." *Latin American Perspectives* 13 (3): 3–12.

Kent, George O. 1964. "Pope Pius XII and Germany: Some Aspects of German-Vatican Relations." *American Historical Review* 70:59–78.

Kerwin, Jerome G. 1960. *Catholic Viewpoint on Church and State*. Garden City, N.Y.: Hanover House/Doubleday.

Kolbenschlag, Madonna, ed. 1985. *Between God and Caesar: Priests, Sisters and Political Office in the United States*. New York: Paulist Press.

Kurtz, Lester R. 1983. "The Politics of Heresy." *American Journal of Sociology* 88:1085–115.

———. 1986. *The Politics of Heresy: The Modernist Crisis in Roman Catholicism*. Berkeley and Los Angeles: University of California Press.

Laclau, Ernesto, and Chantal Mouffe. 1985. *Hegemony and Socialist Strategy*. London: Verso.

Leo XIII, Pope. 1940. *Social Wellsprings: Fourteen Epochal Documents by Pope Leo XIII*, edited by Joseph Husslein, S.J. Milwaukee: Bruce.

Lewy, Guenther. 1964. "Pius XII, the Jews and the German Catholic Church." Pp. 195–217 in *The Storm over* The Deputy, edited by Eric Bentley. New York: Grove.

Lichten, Joseph L. 1963. *A Question of Judgement: Pius XII and the Jews*. Washington, D.C.: National Catholic Welfare Conference.

Luker, Kristin. 1984. *Abortion and the Politics of Motherhood*. Berkeley and Los Angeles: University of California Press.

Lukes, Steven. 1977. "Power and Structure." Pp. 3–29 in *Essays in Social Theory*. London: Macmillan.

Lyng, Stephen G., and Lester R. Kurtz. 1985. "Bureaucratic Insurgency: The Vatican and the Crisis of Modernism." *Social Forces* 63:901–22.

Mannheim, Karl. (1929) 1936. *Ideology and Utopia*, translated by Louis Wirth and E. A. Shils. New York: Harcourt, Brace & World.

McAvoy, Thomas T. 1945. "Americanism, Fact and Fiction." *Catholic Historical Review* 31:133–53.

McCormick, Richard A., S.J. 1982. "*Laborem Exercens* and Social Morality." *Theological Studies* 43:92–103.

Moody, Rt. Rev. Joseph N. 1953a. "The Church and the New Forces in Western Europe and Italy." Pp. 21–92 in *Church and Society*, edited by J. N. Moody. New York: Arts.

———. 1953b. "From Old Regime to Democratic Society." Pp. 95–186 in *Church and Society*, edited by J. N. Moody. New York: Arts.

———. 1961. "Leo XIII and the Social Crisis." Pp. 65–86 in *Leo XIII and the Modern World*, edited by Edward T. Gargan. New York: Sheed & Ward.

National Conference of Catholic Bishops. 1983. *The Challenge of Peace: God's Promise and Our Response*. Washington, D.C.: United States Catholic Conference.

O'Connell, Marvin R. 1984. "Ultramontanism and Dupanloup: The Compromise of 1865." *Church History* 53:200–217.

O'Dwyer, Margaret M. 1985. *The Papacy in the Age of Napoleon and the Restoration*. Lanham, Md.: University Press of America.

Pius XI, Pope. 1942. *Social Wellsprings*. Vol. 2: *Eighteen Encyclicals of Social Reconstruction by Pope Pius XI*, edited by Joseph Husslein, S.J. Milwaukee: Bruce.

Rhodes, Anthony. 1973. *The Vatican in the Age of the Dictators, 1922–1945*. London: Hodder & Stoughton.

Schmandt, Raymond H. 1961. "The Life and Work of Leo XIII." Pp. 15–48 in *Leo*

American Journal of Sociology

XIII and the Modern World, edited by Edward T. Gargan. New York: Sheed & Ward.

Sewell, William H., Jr. 1985. "Ideologies and Social Revolutions: Reflections on the French Case." *Journal of Modern History* 57:57–85.

Skocpol, Theda. 1979. *States and Social Revolutions.* Cambridge: Cambridge University Press.

———. 1982. "Rentier State and Shi'a Islam in the Iranian Revolution." *Theory and Society* 11:265–83.

———. 1985. "Cultural Idioms and Political Ideologies in the Revolutionary Reconstruction of State Power: A Rejoinder to Sewell." *Journal of Modern History* 57:86–96.

Smith, Elwyn A. 1969. "The Fundamental Church-State Tradition of the Catholic Church in the United States." *Church History* 38:486–505.

Swidler, Ann. 1986. "Culture in Action: Symbols and Strategies." *American Sociological Review* 51:273–86.

Vaillancourt, Jean-Guy. 1980. *Papal Power: A Study of Vatican Control over Lay Catholic Elites.* Berkeley and Los Angeles: University of California Press.

Vidler, A. R. 1964. *A Century of Social Catholicism, 1820–1920.* London: S.P.C.K.

Wallace, Lillian Parker. 1966. *Leo XIII and the Rise of Socialism.* College Station, N.C.: Duke University Press.

Wuthnow, Robert. 1985. "State Structures and Ideological Outcomes." *American Sociological Review* 50:799–821.

———. 1987. *Meaning and Moral Order: Explorations in Cultural Analysis.* Berkeley and Los Angeles: University of California Press.

Zahn, Gordon. 1962. *German Catholics and Hitler's War.* New York: Sheed & Ward.

Zaret, David. 1985. *The Heavenly Contract: Ideology and Organization in Pre-Revolutionary Puritanism.* Chicago: University of Chicago Press.

[12]

Jewish Messianism, Religious Zionism and Israeli Politics: The Impact and Origins of Gush Emunim

Eliezer Don-Yehiya

Almost from its very beginning in 1974, the Gush Emunim movement has attracted wide public attention, reflected in the extensive coverage of the movement's views and actions by the Israeli media. The interest in Gush Emunim extends beyond Israel's borders, and has also been manifested in the field of academic research. While most of the literature on the subject is in Hebrew, recently there have been several books published in English which deal with Gush Emunim, or with the political conditions and developments which gave rise to this movement.

THE IMPACT OF GUSH EMUNIM

How are we to account for the extraordinary attention accorded to a new group led by young and politically inexperienced religious people? The answer may lie in the unique impact of Gush Emunim on Israeli society and politics. But this, in turn, begs the question of the nature and sources of Gush Emunim's impact on the Israeli polity. This issue, indeed, is the subject of a collection of articles edited by David Newman of Tel-Aviv University.[1] In his preface, the editor states that the volume is 'an attempt to understand the Gush Emunim dynamic and its relation with Israeli society and Judaism at large'. The 14 contributions to the book are divided into two sections: the first is concerned with ideological and political aspects of Gush Emunim, the second with the implementation of its settlement policies in the Israeli occupied territories.

In Newman's opinion, Gush Emunim has played a very influential role in Israeli public life. 'The Gush has been responsible for major changes in both society and space in Israel', and it 'has become a powerful actor on the political stage'. This is reflected in the very remarkable achievements of Gush Emunim on the ideological and the practical levels.[2]

The problem is that Newman makes no attempt to base his unequivocal statements on a discussion and analysis of relevant empirical facts presented by himself or other contributors to the book. This is all the more regrettable since Newman's views on the actual impact of Gush Emunim and the sources of its ideology are not shared by all students of that movement. In fact, even among the contributors to the book there are those whose conclusions seem to contradict its editor's opinions on the subject.

One of the contributors, Gershon Shafir, claims that 'as a settlement organization Gush Emunim remained a sect of middle-class Ashkenazim, with higher religious and secular education, unable to broaden its base'.[3] He further argues that since the beginning of the Likud's second term in office in 1981, governmental and other settlement organizations have replaced Gush Emunim as the leading force in the settlement activities in the West Bank.[4]

216   MIDDLE EASTERN STUDIES

These arguments are hardly compatible with Newman's assertion that 'there can be no doubt' that Gush Emunim 'constituted and remains the major force' behind the settlement enterprise in the West Bank.[5]

Admittedly, there are other and different assessments of Gush Emunim's impact, which tend to confirm Newman's views. Another contributor, Ehud Shprinzak, claims that 'the leaders of Gush Emunim acquired tremendous political power, which made it possible for them to accomplish all their controversial goals'.[6]

Differences of opinion between various contributors to the same book are legitimate, and an editor may, of course, disagree with the analysis and conclusions of other contributors, provided that he acknowledges the existence of these different views, and explains the reasons for his own preferences. Unfortunately this has not been done by Newman, though another contributor, Myron Aronoff, does note the various points of view regarding the actual impact of Gush Emunim.[7]

It is important here to make a distinction, implicit in Aronoff's careful and thorough analysis, between the historical role of Gush Emunim and its present impact. There is hardly anyone who would deny the historical significance of Gush Emunim as manifested in its pioneering role in the settlement of the West Bank and the enlistment of public and political support on its behalf. The problem is: to what extent has Gush Emunim managed to maintain its influential role in Israeli politics? In my opinion, there is a strong case for the claim that as an institutional and distinctive political movement, Gush Emunim no longer plays a significant role in Israel.

The organizational decline of Gush Emunim in recent years has been manifested in several ways. First, there is the growing tendency of the move-ment's founders and leaders to conduct their political and settlement activities outside the organizational framework of Gush Emunim. As Aronoff points out, many of the central activists joined the newly formed Tehiya Party in 1981, 'leaving control of Gush Emunim in the hands of secondary echelon leaders'. Other leaders preferred to maintain their links with the National Religious Party, while later, in 1983, some chose to join Morasha, the newly created religious-nationalistic party.

In the area of settlement, too, the focus of activity has shifted from Gush Emunim itself to specialized bodies such as Amana or Yesha – the council of settlements in Judea and Samaria. These changes in the nature of Gush Emunim's activities are presented by Aronoff as processes of 'routinization, bureaucraticization and diversification' of an ideological movement.[8]

The change, however, has not been merely the result of a voluntary transference of power and functions to related specialized agencies. To a large extent, the organizational decline of Gush Emunim can be attributed to internal controversies and differences of opinion regarding strategy and tactics.

Contrary to its public image, Gush Emunim is far from being a monolithic group in terms of political attitudes. The controversy over the political activity of Gush Emunim leaders in the Tehiya party has been one such divisive issue, based on differing attitudes towards active membership in a political party as an effective means for the realization of Gush Emunim's goals. This controversy also reflects differences of opinion on the issue of cooperation

THE IMPACT AND ORIGINS OF GUSH EMUNIM   217

between religious and secularist Jews in the same political party. Gush Emunim leaders were also divided in their reaction to crucial events such as the withdrawal from Sinai, and in particular the emergence of the so-called 'Jewish underground' in the West Bank.

Admittedly, these very issues are presented by Aronoff as an indication that Gush Emunim still has an important role to play in Israeli political life, manifested and activated mainly in crisis situations.[9] However, the fact is that the withdrawal from Sinai and the evacuation of the Jewish settlements from the Yamit area and particularly the Jewish underground affair have revealed the organizational weakness and internal divisions of Gush Emunim rather than its strength and unity.

The detention in 1984 of Gush Emunim activists engaged in terrorist activities against Arabs on the West Bank plunged the entire movement into a serious crisis. The reactions of various leaders reflected differing views on central issues, such as relations with Arabs, attitudes towards governmental institutions, and the use of violent and illegal means for the attainment of ideological goals.[10]

Internal divisions are of course a common feature of any political movement. But while an established and well-organized movement may overcome its internal conflicts and retain its organizational integrity and identity and its political capacity, this is a far more difficult task for a movement of which the initial organizational basis is not well developed. Gush Emunim had been primarily a spontaneous protest movement rather than an established institutionalized organization. This very fact contributed to the initial success of Gush Emunim when the need for protest activities and intensive political struggle was evident and deeply felt by supporters of the movement, united by a basic consensus on goals and means of action. This was not the case later, following the change in government which brought to power a political leadership which was much more sympathetic to the settlement enterprise in the West Bank.

Under Labour rule (1974–77), Gush Emunim's settlement activities were in themselves a kind of illegal protest activity which drew widespread public support, particularly among young people. Following the Likud's rise to power, settlement activities in the West Bank became a legal and almost routine activity. On highly controversial issues, Gush Emunim was unable to take a firm stand because of internal differences, while on an issue such as settlement, where there was broad internal consensus, the leading role was taken over not only by voluntary specialized agencies, but by the government itself.

Paradoxically, then, it seems as though the very success of Gush Emunim in achieving its operative goals was the major cause of its decline as a distinct political organization. But can we indeed conclude that Gush Emunim achieved its major operative goals, even if its role was later taken over by others? A negative answer is given by Gershon Shafir. In his view, Gush Emunim has failed to fulfill its central aims and implement its major policies. The main reason is the unwillingness of most Jews in Israel to follow the lead of Gush Emunim in joining the settlement enterprise in the West Bank. 'Gush Emunim never succeeded in creating a mass movement of settlers' and it has failed to win 'the serious and sustained type (of support) required in uprooting and moving to the West Bank'.[11]

But can the success or failure of an ideological movement be judged merely by assessing its immediate achievements in the practical field, or its ability to command the total commitment of its supporters? The fact that Gush Emunim has not succeeded in launching a mass settlement movement in the West Bank should come as no surprise. Idealism in the sense of personal sacrifice for the sake of a collective vision is not a common virtue, and it is not willingly shared by the masses. Hence the very ability of a social movement to gain widespread public support for its aims and activities can be considered a measure of its success, even if only a minority of its supporters actually demonstrate a total dedication and commitment to the ideals and way of life of the movement.

In spite of its passive character, the mass moral support for the aims and actions of a few idealists could in certain circumstances, be translated into a powerful political force. The political importance of the settlement enterprise in the West Bank cannot be measured by the actual number of settlers. We must also consider the significant public support for this enterprise, which may well render very difficult any attempt at a political solution that would entail the evacuation of Jewish settlements in the West Bank.

Acknowledging the political significance of Jewish settlement in the West Bank cannot, however, serve as an adequate measure for assessing Gush Emunim's ideological and political impact. Jewish settlement in the West Bank has become, to a considerable extent, an autonomous factor, with a political importance of its own. Despite the pioneering role of Gush Emunim in this area, many of the settlers today are not associated – organizationally or even ideologically – to this movement. The Council of Jewish Settlements in Judea, Samaria and Gaza (Yesha) reflects a variety of opinions and ways of life. Nevertheless it has managed to become the main representative and spokesman of the settlers on economic and political questions of common interest.

These questions, which include the maintenance and development of West Bank settlements and the improvement of security conditions in the area, are shared by many settlers who do not adhere to the Gush Emunim ideology. In his interesting article, 'American Settlers in the Territories', Chaim Waxman reports that of these settlers, 'the majority was not primarily motivated by ideological factors. Rather, they were primarily motivated by associational and/or other economic factors'. Waxman cites these findings to confirm Shafir's thesis that the Jewish settlement of the territories was primarily 'the consequence of the policies of the Israeli government rather than the ideology and activities of Gush Emunim'.[12]

The fact that, for many settlers, ideology is no longer the primary motivation in their decision to settle on the West Bank is not to deny, however, the central role that ideology played in the pioneering efforts of the Gush Emunim activists who laid the foundations for Jewish settlement in the West Bank. It can be said that the dedication and self-sacrifice of the first Gush Emunim settlers, based on their deep ideological convictions, played a vital role in creating conditions which, at a later stage, could provide non-ideological motivations for a different type of settler. Despite the declining role of the Gush Emunim ideology as a motivating force for settlement, it still exerts a profound impact in this sphere, particularly evident in the highly controversial issue of Jewish settlement in areas of dense Arab population.

THE IMPACT AND ORIGINS OF GUSH EMUNIM 219

In this sense, the ideological factor may still prove of important practical consequence in the spheres of settlement and politics. As Shafir points out, the political potential of the Gush Emunim ideology may in the future be brought to bear in crisis situations, which result from controversial decisions concerning Jewish settlement in the occupied territories.[13] I refer here to the impact of Gush Emunim's ideology rather than the impact of Gush Emunim, because it is the nature of its ideology which gives this movement its continued influence despite its organizational weakness.

THE IDEOLOGICAL ORIGINS

The significance of Gush Emunim ideology should not be judged solely by the practical consequences of its ideology in the spheres of settlement and politics. The impact of Gush Emunim must also be judged by its ability to influence or even transform Israeli political culture through its ideology. A careful study of this ideology is therefore necessary in order to properly assess and understand the role of Gush Emunim in Israeli society. It is particularly important to trace the intellectual and social origins of Gush Emunim's ideology, in order to evaluate the degree of its uniqueness and originality and to account for its influence. Such a study might suggest an answer to the important question: to what extent can Gush Emunim be perceived as representing and effecting a genuine change in the area of ideology and political culture in Israel?

Unfortunately the above questions are not dealt with adequately in the book edited by Newman. In his introduction, Newman states that the major impact of Gush Emunim has been felt in its practical achievements in the settlement of the West Bank. Yet he also speaks of Gush Emunim's role in 'bringing to life an ideology which existed, but had been dormant within the national religious society'.[14]

Such a conclusion should be based on historical findings and analysis, tracing the ideology of Gush Emunim to its origins in Zionist or religious thought. But the editor and other contributors fail to discuss at any length the historical origins of the movement which is the subject of their study. The importance of such a discussion is all the more evident, since other contributors claim that Gush Emunim's impact on the ideological level is far more significant than Newman suggests.

Such a view is implied in David Shnall's claim that 'Gush Emunim has had an important impact on contemporary Judaism'.[15] Another contributor, Lilly Weissbrod, goes so far as to present Gush Emunim's ideas as a 'revolutionary ideology, which have become the "New Zionism" of the Jewish people in Israel'.[16]

The problem with the above arguments is that they, too, are not based on a careful analysis of Gush Emunim's ideological origins. But where should we look for these origins? Ehud Shprinzak argues that while the influence of Gush Emunim has been felt in most segments of Israeli society, the movement has deep roots in the Jewish-religious subculture, which explains its remarkable political success. 'It is the support of this subculture which made Gush Emunim so effective and irresistible.'[17]

While Shprinzak's assertion of Gush Emunim's 'irresistibility' is debatable, he is quite right in emphasizing the importance of the movement's links with religious circles in Israel. It is significant that most Gush Emunim leaders were members of the National Religious Party, and in its earliest days the movement was in fact a group within the NRP. Even after Gush Emunim's leadership renounced its official ties with the NRP, quite strong unofficial links remained between the two movements, which have a common origin in the religious-Zionist subculture. This subculture, known in Israel as the 'religious camp', has for many years been characterized by wide-ranging interrelated institutions and activities in the social, educational, religious and political spheres.[18]

Gush Emunim's links to the religious camp can be traced to the religious basis of its ideology, which perceived Jewish settlement in the West Bank as playing a central role in a God-ordained process of messianic redemption in which every Jew is oblige to take an active part. The question is: how can we reconcile the prominent role played by the religious Zionist subculture in the formation and consolidation of Gush Emunim, with the commonly held assumption of the traditionally low level of involvement and moderate stance of the religious Zionist party (the NRP) in matters of foreign and defense policy? The answer, of course, might be that there has been a profound change in the ideology and policies of religious Zionist circles culminating in the rise of Gush Emunim. Among the supporters of this view are those who go so far as to argue that the ideology and politics of Gush Emunim run counter to the original Zionist principles, and are a gross distortion of the basic ideas of authentic religious Zionism.

These arguments are the main thesis of a book which has recently been published (in its English version) by the Israeli Minister of Communications, Amnon Rubinstein.[19] According to Rubinstein, the historic leaders of religious Zionism shared with their secular counterparts a national and universal outlook, irreconcilable with the political messianism and the highly particularistic and chauvinistic attitudes of Gush Emunim. In Rubinstein's view, 'religious Zionists share with their secular colleagues a philosophy which saw Jewish nationalism in a universal and humanistic context'.[20] Rubinstein further argues that the religious Zionist leaders 'accepted the political aims of secular Zionism, including the return to the family of nations within the framework of a secular nation state'. This was manifested in the attitudes of religious leaders and thinkers whose words 'bore the message of humanism and universalism bequeathed by enlightened Zionism'.[21] In Rubinstein's view, never — until the emergence of Gush Emunim — were Jewish national activities in the Land of Israel 'clothed with a messianic meaning'.

This nationalistic-pragmatic approach, according to Rubinstein, was also reflected in the political behavior of the religious parties, which 'never resorted to mystical terms' but complied with the 'underlying Herzlian premises of Zionist thought', and, before the 1967 war, were even 'the spokesmen for moderation and restraint in the country's foreign and defense policy'.

Rubinstein concludes that the political messianism of Gush Emunim reflects a 'new religious tenor', radically different from the original outlook and attitudes of religious Zionism, which is in 'open defiance of Herzlian Zionism'. Rubinstein argues that Gush Emunim succeeded 'not only within the religious

THE IMPACT AND ORIGINS OF GUSH EMUNIM 221

segment, transforming it from a moderate force to the vanguard of extremism, but also within large parts of the secular sector'.[22] Despite its polemical style, Rubinstein's book is an interesting and thought-provoking essay. The problem is that he fails to provide historical evidence to confirm his arguments, apart from several occasional citations from the writings of certain religious thinkers.

The question as to what extent Gush Emunim represents a profound change in the ideology and politics of religious Zionism, can only be answered by a careful historical study of the political attitudes and behavior of the religious Zionist movement, particularly in the area of foreign and defense policy. Such a study can be useful in assessing the degree of Gush Emunim's uniqueness and novelty, and it might serve to account for the widespread influence of Gush Emunim both within and beyond the ranks of religious Zionism.

MESSIANISM AND PRAGMATISM IN RELIGIOUS ZIONISM

The historical study of religious Zionist attitudes on foreign policy affairs is the subject of a recent book by Stuart Reiser.[23] In his study, Reiser traces the development of foreign policy within the religious Zionist movement since its foundation in 1902, concluding that the changes which have occurred in this area cannot be presented as a clear-cut and one-directional change from a moderate political stance to a militant and extremist one. In Reiser's view, the political history of religious Zionism has been characterized by an oscillation between moderate and extremist styles of politics. Thus, several different periods can be distinguished in the history of the religious movement.

In its early years, under the leadership of its founder Rabbi Yitzhak Yaakov Reines, the movement pursued a moderate and pragmatic approach to political issues. According to Reiser, 'The initial pragmatic approach of the 'Mizrahi' movement [the predecessor of the NRP as the religious Zionist party], was one based on its leaders' assessments of the practical needs of world Jewry rather than an attempt to link Zionism to the messianic component of prophetic Judaism'.[24] This was clearly demonstrated by Mizrahi's support of the British proposal for Jewish settlement in Uganda.

In a later period, however, Mizrahi experienced a shift from pragmatic to messianic Zionism. This was manifested in the movement's endorsement of Rav Kook's philosophy which accorded a religious messianic significance to the Zionist enterprise. It was under the influence of Rav Kook's messianic ideology that Mizrahi endorsed 'a powerful religious nationalism', manifested in its activist political attitudes, such as the rejection of earlier proposals for the partition of Palestine between Jews and Arabs.

Shortly before the establishment of the state of Israel, however, there occurred yet another shift in Mizrahi's political stance, expressed in the movement's acceptance of the partition of Palestine in accordance with the UN resolution of 29 November 1947. In Reiser's view this signalled a retreat to the earlier pragmatic approach, which had characterized the religious Zionist movement in its first years. This renewed pragmatic style endured for the following two decades, until the 1967 Six-Day War. It is Reiser's contention that the territorial results of the 1967 war 'contributed to the reawakening of the messianic forces that were once a vital part of the earlier Mizrahi movement'.[25]

Reiser, then, perceives political developments within religious Zionism as a series of modulations between periods of moderate and pragmatic political behavior and periods of militant, active and extremist politics motivated by a messianic ideology. This cycle is far from complex. Indeed, Reiser notices signs of a second retreat to a pragmatic approach among the ranks of the religious Zionists, following the experience of the Lebanon War.

Reiser's thesis is rather interesting, and his book is highly relevant for a discussion of Gush Emunim and its ideological origins. Hence, it is all the more regrettable that Reiser's analysis is not based on an accurate and properly documented presentation of his subject. As a matter of fact, it is rather surprising that an author of a book on the politics of an Israeli party has no access to relevant material written in Hebrew, as suggested by the failure of the author to cite any Hebrew source in his book. The author's exclusive reliance on secondary sources in the English language has resulted in errors of information and interpretation unworthy of a scholarly work.

Our main concern here, however, is with Reiser's aforementioned argument that the 'Gush Emunim phenomenon' is not to be interpreted as a revolutionary change, but rather as another link in a series of shifts and fluctuations in the political attitudes of religious Zionism, from pragmatism to messianism and vice versa.

There is indeed abundant historical evidence to substantiate the claim that, contrary to Rubinstein's argument, political maximalism and messianism are not a new phenomenon in religious Zionism. This conclusion in itself cannot however be used to confirm the claim that the recent religious-nationalistic awakening, represented by Gush Emunim, in fact represents a reversion to positions held by religious Zionists in the pre-state period. Similarly, although, until the Six-Day War, religious Zionists in the State of Israel adopted a moderate political style, this does not confirm Reiser's argument that, in so doing, they were retreating from their pre-state messianism to the political pragmatism which had dominated the Mizrahi movement in its early years.

As a matter of fact, there is no inherent contradiction between 'messiansim' as such, and a pragmatic and realistic approach to the concrete issues of practical politics. Various kinds of messianic theology can be distinguished on the basis of their potential for radical politics. There is the passive form, in which the messianic vision is not translated into political action; indeed, such action may even be prohibited, viewed as a violation of God's will. While this passive approach cannot of course be reconciled with radical politics, not all the forms of 'active messianism' should lead necessarily to the endorsement of an extremist or radical political style. 'Active messianism' in its various forms is a theory or model of historical interpretation which has clear and deliberate political implications. Such a theory may include a comprehensive and radical program of political action for the immediate and full-scale realization of the messianic vision. But it might also be compatible with a moderate and pragmatic approach, which takes into consideration the conditions of social and political reality.

Messianism as the belief in the heavenly ordained redemption of the Jewish people and the whole of mankind is a central tenet of Judaism.[26] The traditional concept of Jewish messianism reflected a passive and a-political attitude, which obliged Jews to await patiently the miraculous coming of the Messiah. The novelty of religious Zionism was that it reintroduced the political dimension into Jewish messianic tradition, by insisting on the religious right and obligation of Jews in the post-emancipation period to take an active part in the process of God-ordained national redemption. This was to be accomplished by political, economic and other activities aimed at resettling the Jews in the Land of Israel, and regaining their national independence.

The early religious Zionists interpreted such historical events as the emancipation of European Jews as an indication of an imminent redemption, in which all Jews should involve themselves by joining the movement for the return to Zion. In later periods, the Zionist reawakening and its profound achievements — manifested in such events as the Balfour declaration, the mass settlement of Palestine by Jews, the establishment of the State of Israel and its military victories over the Arabs — were interpreted by religious Zionists as signs of the beginnings of messianic redemption. In broad terms, this political-messianic approach, which accorded a sacred meaning and purpose to the Zionist enterprise and the State of Israel, has been the dominant trend in the religious Zionist movement for most of its history.

Admittedly, in its early years, the Mizrahi movement led by its founder Rabbi Reines, had adopted a clearly non-messianic and highly pragmatic perception of Zionism, conceiving it as a purely political movement, whose sole purpose was to rescue Jews from oppression and persecution in the diaspora by establishing a secure haven for them in the Land of Israel.[27] This was, however, the only period in the history of religious Zionism in which this movement was dominated by a pragmatic conception of the very essence and purpose of Zionism. Here it should be noted that the history of religious Zionism began long before the establishment of the Mizrahi movement. The first religious Zionists, the so called 'forerunners of Zionism', Rabbis Kalisher and Alkalai, were already preaching the idea of the 'return to Zion' in the years 1860–80,[28] while Mizrahi was founded by Rabbi Reines only in 1902, as part of the Zionist movement established by Herzl in 1897.

Contrary to the pragmatic conception of Zionism held by Rabbi Reines and other early Mizrachi leaders, Kalisher and Alkalai formulated their Zionist message in explicit messianic terms. But their kind of messianism was not at all of a militant or radical nature, and was compatible with a realistic and pragmatic style of politics. Here we should distinguish between 'pragmatism' as a principle or theory which interprets and legitimises aims and goals, and 'pragmatism' as a political strategy or tactic which is concerned with the realistic, practical and effective ways and means to attain predefined goals in a given situation.

In Reines' conception of Zionism, the essence and goals of this movement were perceived in pragmatic terms. Hence, this form of religious Zionism is incompatible with a messianic approach which sanctifies Zionism and the State of Israel as part of the process of heavenly redemption. Such an approach can however be reconciled, with a pragmatic style or strategy of politics.

Contrary to Reiser's argument, the moderate stand of religious parties in Israel on foreign policy issues is not to be conceived as a reversion to the non-messianic approach of the Mizrahi movement under the leadership of Rabbi

Reines. Most religious Zionists have perceived the State of Israel, ever since its establishment, as a manifestation and embodiment of the beginning of redemption. In this they follow the traditional messianic conception of Zionism, held by most religious Zionists in the pre-state period, except for the early years of the Mizrahi movement.

The question is: to what extent did the 'political maximalism' of the pre-state Mizrahi movement reflect a radical conception of messianism different from the kind of messianic ideology which had been held by Kalisher and Alkalal and was later adopted by Israeli religious parties? Just as messianic theology should not necessarily lead to extremist political attitudes, so might political maximalism or activism be held independently of theological views, and be compatible with a 'non-radical messianism' or even a non-messianic outlook.

Here we should draw a distinction between 'messianism' as a theory, a principle of historical interpretation, and 'messianism' which is also an operative program for political action. While the first may also have practical political implications, in this case it is the nature of the desired goals and purposes which is defined by the messianic vision, and not the political means for their realization, which are to be decided upon and implemented in accordance with practical and rationalistic considerations. By contrast, messianism as a political program means that not only the goals, but also the means for their attainment, are governed by messianic ideas and attitudes. Hence, in this approach radical politics are an integral part of the messianic theology which legitimizes and prescribes this style of politics.

As a matter of fact, the shift in Mizrahi's policy in 1947 did not reflect profound change in the level of political theology. Indeed, those leaders of Mizrahi who claimed the historical and religious right of Jews to the entire Land of Israel, did not present their views as part of a comprehensive program for the immediate realization of the messianic vision 'here and now', regardless of political, military or moral conditions. Their initial position was that Jews should not renounce their legitimate rights in the Land of Israel by accepting the partition proposals. In this, they shared the attitude held by many non-religious Zionists prior to 1947. Indeed, 'maximalism' in the sense of a Jewish claim to political sovereignty over the entire Land of Israel had become, in effect, official Zionist policy following the Biltmore resolution of 1942, though this does not mean that the Zionist leaders adopted the radical politics of the Revisionist movement. The same can be said of the majority of the Mizrahi leaders, who, in spite of their 'maximalist' approach, were strongly opposed to the extremist politics of the Revisionists with regard to the British, and they sharply condemned the terrorist activities of the Jewish underground organizations.

Admittedly, the maximalist position of the religious Zionists was based to a large extent on religious arguments, such as the divine right of Jews to the Holy Land in its entirety. But as it became evident that the partition proposal represented the only real chance for gaining Jewish independence, the Mizrahi leaders, albeit rather reluctantly, joined the other Zionist leaders in support of the partition proposals, as endorsed by the UN General Assembly in its resolution of 29 November 1947.

It follows then that Gush Emunim cannot be viewed as a reversion to pre-state religious Zionist messianism. It is indeed a unique and novel phenomenon, and its uniqueness and novelty lies not in its 'political radicalism', nor in its messianism as such, but rather in its transformation of the Jewish messianic vision into a radical and all-embracing political programme to be fully implemented 'here and now'.

We have noted that the ideas of Gush Emunim never became an influential political current within the ranks of religious Zionism before 1967. This does not, however, mean that these ideas do not originate in the teachings of certain religious Zionist thinkers.

MESSIANIC THEOLOGY AND RADICAL POLITICS – RAV KOOK, FATHER AND SON AND THEIR DISCIPLES

In his above-mentioned article, Shprinzak traces the origins of Gush Emunim ideology to the teachings of Rabbi Avraham Yitzhak Hakohen Kook ('Rav Kook'), who began his literary and public activity in the early years of the twentieth century, and who has come to be known as one of the greatest Jewish thinkers and spiritual leaders in the modern era. Shprinzak does not base his argument on a study of Rav Kook's writings. Instead he relies on the testimony of Gush Emunim leaders, who 'reveal the deep impact of Rav Kook's ideas on their beliefs'. In addition, the fact that most of Gush Emunim's founders were educated in Merkaz Harav (a Talmudic academy established by Rav Kook) is taken by Shprinzak as a further indication of the great influence of Rav Kook's ideas on Gush Emunim's ideology.[29]

Concerning the first point, it is true that Rav Kook has been greatly admired by Gush Emunim leaders and followers, who frequently refer to his writings as their source of inspiration and legitimization. But this in itself cannot be taken as conclusive evidence that Gush Emunim ideology has indeed been grounded in Rav Kook's teachings.

As for the second point, those founders of Gush Emunim who were students or graduates of Merkaz Harav have indeed been greatly influenced by the sort of education they received. But their major, direct source of inspiration was not the writings of Rabbi Avraham Yitzhak Kook, but rather the teachings and personality of his son and successor as head of Merkaz Harav – Rabbi Zvi Yehuda Kook.

The impact of the younger Rabbi Kook on Gush Emunim has indeed been enormous. Shprinzak relates that 'given Gush Emunim's commitment to a unique worldview, it is surprising how little it has published about its ideology'. Hence 'even careful research would reveal only a scant ideological harvest'. The fact is, however, that Gush Emunim ideology is to be found almost in its entirety in the teachings of Rabbi Zvi Yehuda Kook. Admittedly, many Gush Emunim adherents are not familiar with Rav Zvi Yehuda's discourses and articles, which are phrased in very difficult language, particularly for those without a thorough knowledge of Jewish traditional sources. But those disciples of Rav Zvi Yehuda who have become leaders and propagandists of Gush Emunim, popularized the ideas of their spiritual mentor, and endeavored to put them into effect.

226

It can still be argued that the ideas of Rav Kook the father played a significant role in the formation of Gush Emunim ideology, through their impact on the teachings of his son. Indeed, Rav Zvi Yehuda himself maintained that his teachings were mainly a commentary and an elaboration on the ideas of his revered father. On the more theoretical level, some of Rav Zvi Yehuda's ideas and concepts do indeed have their origins in the philosophy of his father. Those theoretical concepts of the father have, however, been translated and applied by his son to the level of operative attitudes in such a radical manner as largely to transcend or transform their original meaning or intent. It is significant here that the operative-political dimension receives much greater emphasis in Rav Zvi Yehuda's teachings than in those of his father, who concentrated mainly on theological issues of a theoretical nature, although they might have practical implications.[30] Both father and son share a messianic theology which is distinct in its strong emphasis on the unique and holy nature of the Jewish people, characterized in their view by inherently sacred qualities to be found in every Jew, regardless of his attitudes and behavior. Confronted with the seemingly secular nature of the Zionist enterprise, which he conceived as the beginning of divine redemption, Rav A.Y. Kook argued that even those Zionists who were divorced from Jewish religious tradition, had nevertheless been motivated by the 'inner divine spark' in their soul, although they were not yet ready to admit or acknowledge this fact.

Holiness is also the defining characteristic of the Land of Israel, and even of the Jewish state. Long before the establishment of the State of Israel Rav A.Y. Kook described it as 'the greatest happiness of man and the embodiment of his noblest ideas'. In this statement, however, he was referring to an ideal state 'whose only wish is that God shall be one and his name one'. After the State of Israel came into being, Rav Zvi Yehuda Kook and his disciples applied the notion of holiness and redemption to the existing state and its institutions.

This example reflects the difference between the concept of 'holiness' in the teachings of the two rabbis. In Rav A.Y. Kook's conception, holiness is perceived as a potential latent in the Jewish nation, to be realized by governing its actions by the Torah. In Rav Zvi Yehuda's approach, holiness is perceived not as an inner potential, but as a given fact. This is why the state of Israel can be considered a holy state and the concrete expression of divine redemption, in spite of its seemingly secular character.

Rav Zvi Yehuda's conception of holiness is reflected in the strong emphasis which he places on the territorial-political dimension of Jewish redemption. In Rav Zvi Yehuda's view the sacred nature of the Land of Israel obliges Jews to fulfill the 'commandment of conquest' by settling the whole land and defending Jewish sovereignty over it. Since the fulfillment of that commandment is considered a significant part of the redemption process, any territorial compromise is conceived as a serious interruption in this God-ordained messianic process, and hence should be resisted by every available means with no regard for the attitudes and reactions of other nations. This is consistent with Rav Zvi Yehuda's conception of the inherently profound differences and antagonism distinguishing Jews as a 'nation set apart' from the other nations of the world.

In this too, Rav Zvi Yehuda's approach differs from that of his father. The emphasis of Rav A.Y. Kook on the unique and sacred nature of the Jewish people did not lead him to endorse a strongly particularistic attitude towards other nations. In fact, Rav Kook's messianic theology integrates universalistic elements, such as the insistence on Jewish obligations towards all mankind, his warnings against the moral dangers of unchecked narrow nationalism, and his perception of Jewish national redemption as a prelude to the redemption of all mankind.

Rav Zvi Yehuda's unique brand of radical messianic nationalism was greatly influenced by the experience of two crucial events in modern Jewish history – the Holocaust of European Jewry, and the establishment of the State of Israel only a few years later. Rav Zvi Yehuda's attitude to Jewish-Gentile relations reflects his perception of the Holocaust as the expression of the evil of the gentiles and their deep hatred of Jews. The Holocaust also signifies for him the total, radical severance of the Jews from the diaspora, confirmed in a positive way by the establishment of the State of Israel.

The establishment of Jewish independence in the Jewish homeland in the wake of the most tragic event in Jewish history signalled for Rav Zvi Yehuda the actual beginning of the messianic era, and with it, the divine obligation incumbent on all Jews to take part in the continuing process of redemption by defending and extending Jewish presence and sovereignty in the land of Israel. This obligation pertains to every Jew, whatever his religious beliefs, but it confers a special responsibility on observant Jews. The latter are obliged to undertake a very active role, in co-operation with secular Jews, in those areas of settlement and political activity which are a vital part of the process of redemption.

The different views of father and son are also manifested in the role of religious people in national political activities. While Rav Kook the father encouraged observant Jews to take part in all spheres of life, he emphasized the special obligation of religious Jews to concentrate on the spiritual dimension of the Jewish national awakening. This is in line with Rav Kook's conception of holiness as an inner spiritual potential which will be realized with the evolution of the redemption process. Rav A.Y. Kook called upon religious Jews to do their best to contribute to this spiritual awakening, which would lead to a mass movement of return to Jewish religion.

While Rav Zvi Yehuda also hoped for a religious awakening, he placed much more emphasis than his father on the active and even leading role which observant Jews should play in the political dimension of the national-messianic enterprise. The impact of this approach was manifested on the operative level in the leading role of Rav Zvi Yehuda's disciples and other religious adherents of Gush Emunim in settlement and political activities aimed at defending and consolidating Jewish sovereignty over the entire land of Israel.

.How can we account for the very strong impact of Rav Zvi Yehuda's teachings on his Merkaz Harav students and through them, on wide circles both inside and outside the religious public in Israel? In discussing the background for the establishment of Gush Emunim, Shprinzak notes the special importance of a 'unique, almost miraculous event', which deeply impressed and influenced Rav Zvi Yehuda's students in Merkaz Harav.

On the eve of Independence Day 1967, Rav Zvi Yehuda delivered a festive sermon to his Yeshiva students and graduates. He lamented Arab rule over a large part of Eretz Yisrael and expressed his strong belief in the imminent liberation of all these territories, including the Jewish holy places in Jerusalem and the West Bank.

'When three weeks later, in June 1967, they discovered themselves to be citizens of an enlarged state of Israel, the graduates of Merkaz Harav were convinced that a genuine spirit of prophecy had come over their Rabbi on Independence Day.' In this way, Shprinzak argues further, those 'faithful students became holy emissaries equipped with unshakable confidence ... in the divine backing for their activities'.[31]

This interesting story cannot, however, explain the remarkable success of these 'holy emissaries' from Merkaz Harav in winning the active support of many and diverse circles in Israeli society. It should also be noted that Merkaz Harav students and graduates were aware of Rav Zvi Yehuda's radical messianic views long before that Independence Day of 1967. Indeed, Rav Zvi Yehuda had expressed such views in a very coherent and consistent manner ever since the establishment of the State of Israel. This coherence and consistency, which was characteristic of the whole of Rav Zvi Yehuda's teaching and personality, was one of the main reasons for the enormous influence he exerted on his disciples.

DEVELOPMENT AND CHANGE IN RELIGIOUS AND POLITICAL CULTURE

The question still remains: how do we account for the great spread of Rav Zvi Yehuda's views beyond the circle of his students, following the Six-Day War? It can be argued that Rav Zvi Yehuda's disciples propagated his ideas through their activities in the state-religious educational system and the religious-Zionist youth movement of Bnei-Akiva. Indeed, Shprinzak and Aronoff stress the crucial role of the autonomous system of religious education, particularly the high school yeshivot, in socializing religious youth to the political values of Gush Emunim.[32] A significant development to be noted at this point is the increasing political involvement of religious educators holding radical-messianic views.

The radical views of those engaged in teaching can be explained by the fact that in contrast to professional politicians, they are not called to confront directly the conditions and pressures of social and political reality, and hence are free to take firm positions on fundamental issues, without having to compromise their principles. To a certain extent, this might also help to explain the differences between the two rabbis. In his role as head of a yeshiva, Rav Zvi Yehuda was more inclined to hold firm and consistent positions on matters of principle and to draw radical political conclusions from theological conceptions than his father, the Chief Rabbi of Eretz-Yisrael.

We must still, however, account for the growing political involvement and political radicalization of religious educators and other religious groups, and for their increasing impact on Israeli society and political culture since the Six-Day War.

Lilly Weissbrod relates the success of 'Gush Emunim's new Zionism' to the 'crisis of identity' which, in her view, occurred in Israel in the wake of the Six-Day War. Weissbrod argues that 'a separate secular Israeli identity constituted no serious problem until the occupation of the West Bank in the Six Day War of 1967.' This secular national identity was based on early labor Zionism, 'the dominant ideology in Israel until recently', which 'restated the entire messianic message in secular terms'. However the ability of labor Zionist ideology to provide legitimacy and support for the national identity of Israeli Jews was seriously impaired in the wake of the Six-Day War.

That secularist ideology, which rejected Israelis' links to Jewish tradition and to Jews in the diaspora, 'could not justify Israel's occupation of foreign land. Only Jewishnes could do so'. Hence the emergence of a new and powerful ideology, which stresses the central role of Jewish religious tradition in the national identity of Israelis, and legitimizes the Israeli claim to West Bank territories in terms of Jewish traditional values and Jewish history. This ideology is 'Gush Emunim's new Zionism', which, in Weissbrod's view, is becoming 'the dominant ideology in Israel'.[33]

Weissbrod's analysis is interesting, but misleading. First, if the problem indeed was that 'Israelis who identified themselves as Israelis had no moral claim on the Holy land', then how did those Israelis have a moral claim to the territories under their rule prior to the Six-Day War? Second, why could they not justify the occupation of the West Bank in military-strategic terms, as was done by many Israeli politicians and army officers? It seems inconceivable that political interests related to Israeli rule over the occupied territories should have played a major role in a widespread endorsement of a messianic theology by non-religious Jews.

The main point is that the marked decline in the impact of labor Zionism on Israeli political culture had begun long before 1967, and the occupation of West Bank territories did not play a major role in that 'crisis of identity', which in fact preceded the Six-Day War. This crisis in the secular definition of Israeli national identity did indeed have an effect on the national-religious awakening which gave rise to Gush Emunim. But the crisis itself was mainly a product of social processes which had begun in the early years of Israeli statehood, and were reflected in the failure of secular systems of values and symbols to replace traditional Judaism as an adequate source of integration and legitimization for Israeli state and society. This led to a growing tendency on the part of Israeli Jews to turn again to Jewish traditional values and symbols in order to invest their Jewish identity with content and meaning and provide a firm basis for their sense of national solidarity.[34]

This process was greatly enhanced by the Six-Day War, which aroused strong feelings of Jewish identification and solidarity in all segments of Israeli-Jewish society. However, the growing penetration of Israeli political culture by traditional symbols of Jewishnes is not to be conceived of as a religious-political awakening like that of Gush Emunim. As a matter of fact, the emerging new system of values and symbols constituted a rather 'low-key' mixture of religious and nationalistic elements which could not draw that kind of deep and total commitment which had been invoked by traditional Judaism on the one hand, or labor Zionism on the other.

Contrary to Weissbrod's claim, it is not the 'new Zionism' of Gush

Emunim, but rather a kind of tradition-oriented symbol system which can be defined as Israel's 'new civil religion', that has come to dominate Israeli political culture. Although the emerging civil religion could not satisfy those who sought an inspiring vision and demanding belief system, it nevertheless paved the way for the approval of Gush Emunim ideology. While this ideology also integrates religious and national elements, it is a hotted up synthesis, which imposes on its adherents deep and total commitments in both the religious and national spheres. The demanding nature of Gush Emunim ideology, its call for self-sacrifice and total devotion to the collective ideal, the pioneering spirit of its activists and their exemplary leadership – all these made a great impact on wide circles in Israeli society. Among those who were deeply impressed by Gush Emunim are many non-observant Jews, who have nevertheless acknowledged the leading role of religious people and a religiously based messianic ideology in what they considered to be a movement of national awakening.

Shprinzak and Aronoff have noted the success of Gush Emunim in gaining recognition and support as an authentic revitalization movement among many non-religious Jews.[35] This does not mean that the secular supporters of Gush Emunim actually adopted its ideology or even fully comprehended its basic principles, which were grounded in the messianic theology of Rav Zvi Yehuda Kook. Admittedly, as Shprinzak and Aronoff indicate, Gush Emunim ideology integrated values and symbols which originated in labor Zionism. But the enthusiastic disciples of Rav Zvi Yehuda transformed the content and meaning of those concepts and symbols which they had borrowed from Labor Zionism, adapting them to their messianic theology. The decline of ideological secularism and the concomitant 'Judaization' of Israeli political culture have nevertheless enabled and encouraged many non-religious Israelis to cooperate with Gush Emunim's religious members, and to admire their idealism and self sacrifice, inspired as they were by a religious-messianic theology.

The willingness of non-religious Jews to support Gush Emunim and acknowledge its leading role in the 'struggle for Eretz-Yisrael' was, however, largely dependent on the willingness of Gush Emunim's religious members to co-operate with non-observant Jews in the struggle for the common cause of Eretz-Yisrael, and to assume the dominant role in that struggle. This willingness, which has become one of the defining characteristics of Gush Emunim, has its origins in earlier developments in the Israeli religious camp.

The predominance of secular ideologies and moods in the pre-state period and the early years of statehood resulted in the adoption of the mentality and attitudes of a 'belligerent minority' by the religious public and parties. This was manifested in the defensive approach which characterized the political attitudes of the religious circles during that period, their preoccupation with religious issues and concerns, and their low level of involvement in political matters of a general nature.

There is another related factor which helps to account for the low profile of the religious parties in matters of foreign and defense policy, before 1967. In the early formative years of Israeli statehood, the religious parties acknowledged the need to concentrate their efforts on the struggle for the preservation and enhancement of the role of religion in public life by means of state and local legislation and inter-party arrangements. This resulted in the virtual neglect of other political issues, facilitated by the fact that, before 1967, the major Israeli political parties were not deeply divided on fundamental operative issues of foreign and defense policy.

In his book Reiser mentions the role played by the 'Young Faction' of the NRP in initiating the changes which occurred in this party's political style. Reiser, however, does not provide an adequate analysis of the background, attitudes and motivation of this group, and their impact on religious Zionism.

The important point is that changes in the political stance of religious Zionist circles had been introduced by the 'Young Guard' of the NRP before the 1967 war. Those young party members who in 1963 established themselves as a separate faction in the NRP denounced the pragmatic and conservative style of the veteran leaders, as well as their willingness to 'compromise on principles', and their defensive and segregationist strategies. The Young Guard urged party members and the religious public as a whole to become much more involved in Israeli society and culture; to take an active part in political debates and decisions; and to form independent and clear-cut attitudes on public issues of general concern. This view reflected the growing self-confidence of the religious youth, leading them to claim a much more influential role in Israeli society and politics. This self-confidence itself was a product of the above-mentioned changes in Israeli society and political culture: the decline of secular ideologies and the growing 'traditionalization' of Israeli culture. To this we may add the significant expansion of the system of intensive religious socialization known as the 'high-school Yeshivot', and the personal background of the young religious generation of native-born Israelis, who were much more a part of the 'general' Israeli society than was the older generation.

The Six-Day War, and the religious-national awakening which followed, greatly enhanced the impact of the Young Guards' claim for much greater involvement of the religious public in political issues of general national concern, grounded in a religious worldview. This claim, which before the 1967 war had been phrased in general and somewhat abstract terms, was given concrete and operative content and form after the war by the insistence on the sacred principle of the territorial integrity of Eretz-Yisrael.

These developments dislodged the religious Zionists from their former marginal position in Israeli society and politics, and for the first time they became the leading vanguard in a political struggle for a general national cause. This was the basis for the close co-operation between the leaders of the NRP 'young faction' and those Aerkaz Harav students and graduates who, even before 1967, had been deeply influenced by the messianic teachings of Rav Zvi Yehuda Kook.

The great victory of the Six-Day War — the liberation of Jerusalem, the Jewish holy places and the conquest of the West Bank — aroused great enthusiasm in wide religious circles, where the events were interpreted as a miraculous manifestation of the process of divine redemption. But the impact of the Six-Day War lay not only in its military and territorial achievements. The war had been preceded by a 'waiting period', when Jews in Israel and the diaspora were anxious as to the fate of the Jewish state. The war strengthened the sense of national solidarity among Jews in Israel and abroad, while reinforcing the unique, separate nature and position of the Jewish people and the irreconcilable gap and the antagonism between Jews and other nations. These views, articulated long before in the teachings of Rav Zvi Yehuda Kook, were even further enhanced as a result of the 1973 war. After the 1973 war, Rav Zvi Yehuda's disciples were instilled with a sense of great urgency, which stemmed from the imminent threat posed by the war to the entire messianic enterprise and the process of Jewish national revival. The lesson which the founders of Gush Emunim have drawn from the Yom Kippur War was: the urgent need for decisive and immediate action to consolidate and enlarge the Jewish presence and Jewish rule throughout the entire land of Israel.

It is this sense of urgency which led Rav Zvi Yehuda's disciples to found 'Gush Emunim' several months after the Yom Kippur War. It also influenced their decision to establish themselves as a separate group outside the ranks of the NRP. The founders of Gush Emunim felt that the NRP leaders were not aware of the urgent need to wage an uncompromising battle for the sake of the land of Israel. They also believed that all Jews, whatever their belief, were obliged to co-operate in a common effort for the revival and redemption of the Jewish people and the Holy Land. Hence limiting their activity to the framework of one religious party seemed to Gush Emunim leaders to be detrimental to the cause of national solidarity and the struggle for Eretz-Yisrael.

Gush Emunim members perceived cooperation with non-religious Jews in the name of Jewish national unity as a sacred value in itself. In this they were also influenced by the teachings of Rav Zvi Yehuda. It is instructive at this point, once again, to compare Rav Zvi Yehuda Kook with his father, the Chief Rabbi of Eretz-Yisrael. Rav A. Y. Kook had indeed legitimized co-operation with non-observant Jews by his perception of 'secularism' as a superficial phenomenon to be overcome by the inner forces of holiness, which is the special quality of the Jewish people and the genuine source of the Zionist enterprise. But, despite the bold and innovative nature of Rav Kook's theoretical views, his operative attitudes reflected a rather cautious and pragmatic approach. This was manifested in his willingness to co-operate with non-observant Jews only in a rather limited and reserved way.

This approach was also manifested in the actual attitudes and policies of religious Zionism towards non-religious individuals and groups. While in theory religious Zionists rejected the segregationist approach of the non-Zionist 'Agudat Yisrael' party, in practice they were unwilling to admit non-observant Jews to parties, settlements and other institutions or organizations founded by religious elements. This approach was to a large extent the product of the defensive strategy adopted by the religious public in a society which was dominated by a militant secular ideology.

On this and other points, Rav Zvi Yehuda Kook and his disciples in Gush Emunim were willing to implement theoretical principles and conceptions implied in the teachings of Rav A.Y. Kook in a much more determined, consistent and radical way than he himself had been prepared to. This was manifested in the willingness of Gush Emunim leaders to accept non-observant members and even to establish 'mixed settlements' of religious and non-religious settlers. Here too, the above-mentioned changes in the role of

THE IMPACT AND ORIGINS OF GUSH EMUNIM 233

religion in Israeli society have encouraged Rav Zvi Yehuda's disciples to put into effect his ideas concerning the sacred value of Jewish solidarity and co-operation in the God ordained process of national redemption.

However this very example of close co-operation between religious and secular Jews in the name of messianic ideas indicates that, even in relatively favourable conditions, an attempt to implement theoretical concepts and principles in a systematic and consistent manner may come up against difficulties and antagonisms. As Julien Bauer implies in his article in the volume edited by Newman, the 'mixed settlements' have not been a 'success story'. Conflicts have erupted in several settlements and, in some cases, have resulted in a split between religious and non-religious settlers.[36] Co-operation with non-observant Jews in a 'mixed political party' has also been a controversial issue within the ranks of the religious leaders and members of Gush Emunim.

This and other disputes over the practical implications and applications of Gush Emunim's messianic ideology have been the main reasons for this movement's organizational decline – a point to which we have referred above. This in itself did not entail a decline in the commitment of Gush Emunim adherents to the basic principles of its ideology. The radical messianism which originated in Rav Zvi Yehuda's teachings has played a central role as the main driving force which motivated and inspired the pioneering settlement activities of the founders of Gush Emunim; and it was this 'spirit of Gush Emunim' which gained it widespread public support and social-political impact, despite its organizational weakness.

There are, none the less, indications that the public appeal of Gush Emunim ideology has also been negatively affected by such events as the Lebanon War and the Jewish underground affair. It seems too early, however, to predict whether Gush Emunim will overcome its present difficulties and regain, or even enhance, its prominent role in the Israeli political culture.

NOTES

1. David Newman (ed.), *The Impact of Gush Emunim* (London: Croom Helm, 1985).
2. Newman, 'Preface', pp. 1–2 and 'Introduction', p. 1.
3. Gershon Shafir, 'Institutional and Spontaneous Settlement Driver: Did Gush Emunim Make a Difference?' in Newman, pp. 159–60.
4. Ibid., p. 166.
5. Newman, 'Introduction', p. 2.
6. Ehud Sprinzak, 'The Iceberg Model of Political Extremism', in Newman, p. 27.
7. Myron J. Aronoff, 'The Institutionalisation and Cooperation of a Charismatic, Messianic, Religious-Political Revitalization Movement', ibid., p. 60.
8. Ibid., p. 59.
9. Ibid., p. 60.
10. These conclusions are based on a study of Gush Emunim's literature, particularly the monthly periodical *Nekuda* (in Hebrew). See for example: *Nekuda*, 80 (November 1984) and 89 (July 1985).
11. Shafir, p. 161.
12. Chaim Waxman, 'Political and Social Attitudes of Americans Among the Settlers in the Territories', in Newman, pp. 210–11.
13. Shafir, p. 169.
14. Newman, 'Introduction', p. 2.

15. David Schnall, 'An Impact Assessment' in Newman, p. 20.
16. Lilly Weissbrod, 'Core Values and Revolutionary Change', in ibid., p. 72.
17. Shprinzak, p. 27.
18. An analysis of the 'religious camp' in Israel can be found in my article 'Stability and change in a "camp party": The N.R.P. and the Young-Guard Revolution', *Medina, Mimshal Veyehasim Bein Leumvvim* 14 (1977), (in Hebrew).
19. Amnon Rubinstein, *The Zionist Dream Revisited: From Herzl to Gush Emunim and Back* (New York: Schocken Books, 1984).
20. Ibid., p. 104.
21. Ibid., p. 47.
22. Ibid., pp. 105–6.
23. Stewart Reiser, *The Politics of Leverage: The National Religious Party of Israel and its influence on Foreign Policy* (Cambridge, MA: Center for Middle Eastern Studies, Harvard University, 1984).
24. Ibid., p. 11.
25. Ibid., p. 16.
26. See for example: Gershon Sholem, *The Messianic Idea in Judaism* (New York: Schocken, 1971).
27. See my article 'Ideology and Policy in Religious Zionism – Rabbi Y. Y. Reines' Conception of Zionism and the Policy of the Mizrahi Under his Leadership', in *Hatzionut* (Tel Aviv: Hakibbutz Hameuchad, 1983), Vol. 8, pp. 103–46 (in Hebrew).
28. See Jacob Katz, *Jewish Nationalism: Essays and Studies.* (Jerusalem, Sifria Tsionit, 1979), pp. 263–356 (in Hebrew).
29. Shprinzak, p. 28.
30. See my article, 'Jewish Orthodoxy, Zionism and the State of Israel', *The Jerusalem Quarterly*, 31 (Spring 1984), esp. 22–8.
31. Shprinzak, pp. 37–8.
32. Shprinzak, op. cit., p. 37; Aronoff, op. cit., p. 48.
33. Weissbrod, op. cit., pp. 72–3.
34. See Charles S. Liebman and Eliezer Don-Yehiya, *Civil Religion in Israel: Traditional Judaism and Political Culture in the Jewish State* (Berkeley: University of California Press, 1983).
35. Shprinzak, op. cit., pp. 30–31; Aronoff, op. cit., p. 50.
36. Julien Bauer, 'A New Approach to Religious-Secular Relationships?' in Newman, pp. 98–9.

[13]

The Evolving Regulatory Structure of European Church-State Relationships

JOHN G. FRANCIS

In Western Europe, many contemporary churches have achieved remarkable levels of administrative autonomy and tangible resource support. Yet paradoxically, public participation in the traditional churches appears marginal. In Eastern Europe under Communism, churches experienced varying levels of hostility and bare toleration. Yet also paradoxically, some Eastern European churches nevertheless sustained membership growth. Since the fall of the Soviet communist regimes, moreover, a number of churches have re-emerged as vibrant forces in their respective nations. Is the inference to be drawn that state hostility produces strength while state support produces neglect? Of course, an impressive number of factors other than the state help shape the organizational presence of a church. The concern of this essay, however, is the state regulation of churches and the consequences of the regulatory environment, often unintended, for both state and church.

This essay explores the consequences of the regulatory patterns that have emerged in eastern and western European church-state relations since the end of the Second World War. The aim is to see if an understanding of these regulatory regimes can help in understanding the apparent paradoxes in European church-state regulatory relationships. It is argued that the regulatory regimes that have developed in Europe have created incentives for European churches to play roles in society other than that of mobilizing participation in institutionalized religion. Traditional European churches have responded to the regulatory environment by becoming more involved in educa-

• JOHN G. FRANCIS (B.A., Stanford University; M.A., Ph.D., University of Michigan) is professor of political science at University of Utah. He has co-authored *Western Public Lands* and *The Politics of Realignment* and is the author of *The Politics of Comparative Regulation*. His articles have appeared in *Political Studies, Perspectives, Political Studies Journal*, and *Natural Resources*. Special interests include comparative public policy and European and North American regulatory issues.

tion, charity, and political commentary, rather than in the direct encouragement of religious life.

REGULATION AND RELIGION

Regulation, as defined in this essay, is the setting of limits on group or individual conduct for public purposes. Through regulation, the state sets limits rather than proscribing behavior. Theodore J. Lowi has argued that regulation may be seen as morally ambiguous if the behavior to be regulated is deeply controversial. Groups engaged in the activity will resent the activity being constrained, while critics of the activity will question why it has not been proscribed.[1] Thus, if religion is judged as the opiate of the people, opponents of churches will question why churches are not banned rather than regulated. If freedom of religion is of paramount value, supporters of a church may object to regulation.

Regulation may embrace a remarkable range of activities. We most frequently think about regulation in the economic sphere. Here the state's intervention is most likely to occur when there is market failure. A firm or combination of firms has established a monopoly that allows them to set higher prices for a product or a service at lower levels of production than would be found in a competitive market environment. Through regulation, the state establishes a structure to review the behavior of the firm. On the basis of the information gathered, the state may establish production guidelines and ceilings on prices. The state may also establish standards to maintain the quality of the product and process by which the product is produced.

Regulation has its critics.[2] Indeed, a theory of regulatory failure has developed; a central point in this theory is that regulation becomes ineffective over time and often works to the advantage of the regulated rather than the regulators. It is in the tradition of this critique of regulation that this essay seeks to apply regulatory analysis to church-state relationships.

Three recurring themes found in studies of regulatory failure are really variations on the theme of the ineffectiveness of regulation. First is that of capture. Over time — perhaps indeed from the inception of regulation — the firm or the industry can

1.   Theodore J. Lowi, "Liberal and Conservative Theories of Regulation," in G.C. Bryner and D.L. Thompson, eds., *The Constitution and the Regulation of Society* (Provo, Utah: Brigham Young University Press, 1988), 7-42.
2.   Alfred E. Kahn, *The Economics of Regulation: Principles and Institutions* (Cambridge, Mass.: M.I.T. Press, 1988).

STRUCTURE OF CHURCH-STATE RELATIONSHIPS   777

secure state resources and insulate itself from competition because of a number of advantages that it has over the designated
regulatory agency. Most notably, these advantages are information and political power.[3]

The second theme is that of adaptation. The regulated enterprise adapts to the variety of incentives and disincentives
created by the regulatory regime. For example, if regulation of
telecommunications governs local calls but not long distance
calls, then the telecommunications firm's energies are likely to
be directed at realizing income from its long distance service. If
state subsidies are available for certain services but not for
others, the regulated telecommunications firm is likely to adapt
its commitments to services with the enhanced return provided
by subsidies. Adaptation to the regulatory environment may undermine the objectives identified in establishing the original
regulatory regime.

The third theme is that ineffectiveness may be brought
about by over-regulation. So complex a set of responsibilities
may be placed on the regulators that the end result is under-
regulation. The state elaborates a set of objectives to regulate a
specific industry but finds that it has created far too demanding
a regulatory framework. This leads in turn to the paradox of
under-regulation as the state's regulators retreat from the
daunting task of regulation. For example, the competing objectives of universal service, cost control, and environmental quality often pose formidable challenges to the task of regulators.
Regulation of utilities is a contemporary example of how the
complexity of regulation, with the competing goals of universal
service, rate setting, and air quality, can produce regulatory
quandaries.[4]

There are of course limits to the parallel between the regulation of firms and the regulation of churches. A basic difference
is that a church draws its support on the basis of religious commitment — presumably a quite different source of commitment
than consumer preference for many people. In the fundamental
relationship between the church and its members, there is no
clear unit of exchange that lends itself to quantification. Perhaps much more so than firms, however, churches have the capacity to mobilize their memberships on behalf of their

3.   George J. Stigler, "The Theory of Economic Regulation," *Bell Journal of Economics and Management Science* 2 (Spring 1971): 3-21.
4.   Terry M. Moe, "Control and Feedback in Economic Regulation: The Case of
the NLRB," *American Political Science Review* 79 (December 1985): 1094-116.

objectives in negotiating with the state. Another difference is that states' seeking to regulate churches often lack doctrinal competence. They may be ill-equipped to understand the church's mission and lack information as to church resources and the best uses of those resources. Finally, another principal difference is that the relationship between a nation and the religious commitments of its citizens is the consequence of many forces acting over long periods of time. These forces may have created in a population religious commitments of singular intensity or, on the other hand, apparent disinterest that has little to do with the direction of contemporary state regulation of religion. Despite these differences, however, the case can still be made that regulatory theory is relevant to the understanding of church-state relationships. This essay argues that the direction of contemporary state regulation may help shape the direction of a church's priorities and activities independently of the condition of the population's religious commitment. Churches as organizations will respond to regulatory incentives and costs, just as they respond to the political environment.

Why do states seek to regulate churches? Historically, as will be shown below, rulers may have sought to impose on their subjects their own respective judgments about the correct institutional expression of their faith. States have seen regulation as a means to weed out corruption or to redress the distribution of resources in their society. Quite often, states have appeared to fear churches as challenges to the political order that need to be contained.

Historically, regulation of churches by European states has embraced some or all of a number of areas. States have played significant roles in regulating or ultimately selecting senior church leaderships within the country. States have assumed the power to determine the numbers and types of clergy allowed to practice their religious responsibilities within the nation. The state's approval has been sought in determining the boundaries of church administrative territories. The state's acquiescence has played a role in church reform of doctrine or liturgy. States have from time to time set limits on the nature of church participation in education, public communication, social welfare, and health care. Finally, states have limited — or enhanced — churches' ability to own property or businesses.

At this time, virtually every church, at least in Western Europe, has achieved a remarkable measure of autonomy in the determination of its leadership, its size, and the direction of its

STRUCTURE OF CHURCH-STATE RELATIONSHIPS 779

clergy. By contrast, historically in Roman Catholic countries, the state or the aristocracy controlled higher-level clerical appointments or shared in appointment decisions with the Vatican. In many Protestant states, the state exercised the power of appointment with relatively little formal consultation with church hierarchies. At the same time, the capacity of the church to establish a central role in a society's institutions has diminished and a review of church attendance in Western Europe suggests remarkable declines in membership.

Churches may find that regulation benefits their own positions in society. In many cases these churches confront receding memberships. Catholic churches in nearly all Western European states enjoy sustained and significant declines in the conflicts with state authorities that were recurring crises during the nineteenth and a good deal of the twentieth century. This decline in conflict undoubtedly is related to the effective dechurching of many of the European populations. Regulation in these cases appears to be actively sought by churches as a means of sustaining resource flows. This relationship of negotiating support in exchange for some measure of regulation appears to be the emerging norm of convergence in state-church policy throughout Europe. But it raises the perplexing question of how new churches will respond to a structure of church-state relations that does not reflect the neutral tradition of liberalism but rather expresses clear although measured support for some churches over others in practice and often in theory as well.

A church may seek several objectives in regulation. These objectives may undergo change as the regulatory context shifts. A church may conclude that regulation provides a competitive advantage in dealing with competition with other churches. Established, long-existing churches that now enjoy some measure of recognition from the state may wish to stabilize the situation by delimiting the boundaries of state recognition from newer or missionary churches that threaten the membership base of the established churches. The established churches may simply be concerned with maintaining their existing obligations to staffs, buildings, and educational programs. The longer established the church, presumably the greater the obligations it has to sustain existing organizations. The theory of regulatory capture would predict these observations. There is always the risk, however, that the capture model of regulation is not predictive of future state-church relationships, given the possibilities for new directions coming from within the state or from groups found neither in established church(es) nor in the state. New churches are the most likely sources of pressure for changes in the direction of regulation.

HYPOTHESES

On the basis of this understanding of regulation, four working hypotheses are derived to focus the analysis of church-state relationships in contemporary Europe:

A.   If a state sternly regulates a church or churches and is able to suppress effectively all other significant independent social and economic organizations, then there is a reasonable probability that the church or churches will become focal points for both secular and religious opposition to the state.

B.   If a state regulates churches in part by providing state income for the churches' provision of education, health care, or other forms of social care, but for no other church activity, then it is increasingly likely that the churches will direct their energies toward these areas of endeavor and will be identified with these fields of activity.

C.   If a state provides funds to pay for stipends of the clergy, then there is a greater likelihood that the hierarchy will enjoy greater independence from the laity in making decisions and place much less emphasis on maintaining church memberships.

D.   If a church leadership has over time reduced the role of state intervention in the affairs of the church, but has been able to sustain material benefits or other measures of preferment, then it is a reasonable inference that the church benefits from regulation rather than or in addition to the state or the broader community.

THE CONTEXT OF EUROPEAN CHURCH-STATE RELATIONS

This section sets the context for testing the hypotheses. Historically, church-state relationships have been a recurring and significant source of political controversy in European states. The outcomes of these controversies may be viewed in terms of the following taxonomy: the *Erastian model*, in which the state has assumed responsibility for the direction of the church; the *liberal model*, in which the state is secular and neutral in its relationships with the church(es) found in its society; the *theocratic model*, in which the church has achieved supremacy in religious and secular affairs; the *spheres model*, in which the

STRUCTURE OF CHURCH-STATE RELATIONSHIPS   781

church prevails in some spheres and the state in other spheres of society; and the *anti-church model*, in which the state stands in opposition to the church and seeks to curtail or eliminate religion.

The Erastian model. On this model, the state seeks to organize the church as a department of the state. This model is commonly associated with the Protestant German states of the Reformation. The Erastian model confronts the problem of internal religious change, perhaps expressed in controversies over liturgy or doctrinal controversies. From the regulatory perspective, two broad responses to internal change may be taken by the Erastian state. First, the state may simply tolerate a good deal of doctrinal variation within the church viewed as a common religious house. Second, the state may seek to play the role of arbiter or imprimatur in determining the correctness of certain positions in theological disputes. Both positions run the risk of reduced credibility for both the church and the state.

The liberal model. The liberal model argues for neutrality of the state in the affairs of churches. It conceives the state as one in which there is no privileged relationship between the state and any particular church. Although the liberal model has its origins in European thought, it may be argued that it has rarely been found in European countries. Few European regimes have adopted neutrality as the basis for church-state regulation. The United States is often judged to be a better example than European nations of the application of the liberal tradition to church-state relations.[5]

The United States also is a nation with one of the highest rates of church attendance on either side of the North Atlantic. Does the fact that the American state constructs church-state relations as a wall of separation contribute to the apparently greater American public willingness to attend church and to attach importance to religion? Roger Finke has argued that the deregulation of churches in the United States has promoted religious individualism; that is, for an American church to survive it must attract communicants in the open market by responding to the individual's understanding of religion as one of personal conversion.[6]

The theocratic model. Here the church assumes or is given a

5. Robert Audi, "The Separation of Church and State and the Obligations of Citizenship," *Philosophy and Public Affairs* 18 (Summer 1989): 259-96.
6. Roger Finke, "Religious Deregulation: Origins and Consequences," *Journal of Church and State* 32 (Summer 1990): 609-26.

sphere of influence that embraces both religious and secular spheres. As with the state in the Erastian model, the church is supreme and so the question of the state's defining boundaries does not arise. The church's autonomy in determining public policy is not confined to its membership but embraces the broader community in which the church is located. This model may exist in regions within a state but certainly is not characteristic of nations in Europe today. The best example of a European theocracy in the last century was the Papal states in what is now modern Italy.

The spheres model. This model can best be described by saying what it is not. It is not the liberal tradition or the Erastian or the theocratic. Rather, it may be described as the situation in which the society is understood as made up of competing or perhaps complementary spheres. Conflicts between the Holy Roman Emperors and religious hierarchies often reflected this battle over spheres of autonomy. Variations of this model are found in a remarkably wide range of European nations today. These range from nations that profess to be of a certain church, to others that are critical of a specific church. Samuel Krislov argues that the determination of boundaries between church and state is enormously difficult in any system that seeks to recognize separate spheres of responsibility between a church and a state.[7] It is probably useful to conceptualize the spheres model as a continuum. At one end are the Roman Catholic Churches in Ireland and in today's Poland, where the sphere of church influence is quite large and embraces many areas of public policy making. At the other end of the continuum are Scandinavian churches which have narrowly-defined spheres of influence in public policy making.

The anti-church model. This final model is one in which the state is deeply critical if not in outright opposition to the church. The former regimes of Eastern Europe reflected an oppositional tradition as historically did the nineteenth and early twentieth century regimes in Mexico and in France which often sought to disestablish or to curtail church life severely. Examples of opposition include expulsion of religious orders, seizure of church resources, and prohibition of many church-sponsored activities.

There are two critical points concerning these models and

---

7. Samuel Krislov, "Alternatives to Separation of Church and State in Countries Outside the United States," in *Religion and the State: Essays in Honor of Leo Pfeffer*, ed. James E. Wood, Jr. (Waco, Texas: Baylor University Press, 1985), 421-40.

STRUCTURE OF CHURCH-STATE RELATIONSHIPS 783

their relevance to the examination of the hypotheses put forth in this essay. First, in practice the liberal model has not characterized the political relationships between the state and major churches, although liberalism has been advocated by significant numbers of people within European nations. Second, most European nations at different eras have experienced more than one of the other models of church-state relationships. The implication that these two point for testing the hypotheses is that there are very real and long-standing traditions in European politics, characterized by sharp conflicts or at other times by close identification between church and state. The heritage for church-state relations can mean deep suspicion of churches by portions of the population. For others, the heritage may be a very deep suspicion of the state's policies toward a specific church. This tradition of distrust directed at the state has been compounded by conflicts among different churches. The intensity of church-state politics increased in the nineteenth century with the emergence of political movements of the Left that were often committed to anti-church programs. This heritage of conflict and collaboration, but never remoteness, between church and state has structured the regulatory regimes that formed in Europe after the Second World War. In the aftermath of the War, there was an interest on the part of many church leaders and political leaders, particularly on the continent, to search for some measure of accommodation and stability in church-state relationships.

The aim in the analysis that follows is not a testing, but an exploration of the four hypotheses. The exploration relies on accounts of policies and events pertinent to church-state relationships in major European states. In addition, public opinion survey data is used to assess priorities in popular attitudes towards participation in church life.

The regulatory relationships that have developed in many parts of Europe are the result of regimes formed by the respective states and the main Protestant and Catholic churches found within their borders. These relationships reflect the longstanding, interwoven relationships between the churches and their respective states. It is suggested in the analysis that follows that the regulatory regimes which have developed have given preferment to the traditional churches. This preferment has taken the form of tangible resources and state-sanctioned social roles. At the same time, there has been a diminished presence of state involvement within the doctrinal and administrative concerns

of the respective churches. But Europe, as will be described below, is changing as new churches outside the regulatory regime
gain in numbers while older churches that have enjoyed regulatory preferment have come to experience declining active
memberships. The hypotheses are designed to use the regulatory literature to help explain where churches have gained preferment while increasing their administrative independence
from the states. It is further contended that the current regulatory regime has contributed to deemphasis on mobilizing members in the traditional churches.

The countries selected for this examination of church-state
relations are Italy, France, Germany, and England (not the
United Kingdom). Illustrations will also be drawn from a
number of other European countries in order to offer a general
assessment of the hypotheses concerning the consequences of
state regulation for church activity. The four nations selected
for this analysis are among the major European societies. All
four have experienced at different times quite different church-
state regulatory regimes. Italy is composed of former states,
some of which have long traditions of church-state relations
characterized by the theocratic model. Italy is a society with
strong liberal and anti-church movements as well. France since
the Revolution has witnessed a series of regimes, sometimes
characterized by the anti-church model and other times by the
spheres model, as well as by significant numbers of liberal supporters in the population. Both Germany, at least in the Prussian lands, and Britain in the English lands have had state-
established churches. In the case of England, a state church
continues to exist. A re-unified Germany brings to this analysis a
national region that experienced a regime characterized by the
anti-church model for forty years. These rich and varied traditions of church-state politics provide for an assessment of the
regulatory regimes that have evolved over the past three decades in Western Europe's four principal powers.

Italy. In the first half of the nineteenth century the papacy
was, as it had been for centuries, the temporal ruler of central
Italy. Since Italian unification, the papacy has ceased to be a
temporal power of any significance. Of course, the pope continues to be the spiritual leader of Catholics within Italy and
throughout the world. This unique relationship between modern Italy and the Vatican has deeply influenced church-state
politics. Since unification was completed in 1870, Italian governments have held from time to time quite different judg-

STRUCTURE OF CHURCH-STATE RELATIONSHIPS   785

ments as to the role of the Vatican. In the late nineteenth century, the Vatican was judged as a threat to unification. In the 1920s, the Fascists regarded the church as an institution obstructing Mussolini's aim of achieving a monopoly on political power. In the postwar Italian Republic, the Vatican was closely identified with the ruling Christian Democratic regime, which recognized Catholicism as the religion of the Italian people. Opposition parties were often critical of this close identification between the Catholic Church and the ruling party.

In 1984, a new era began with negotiations culminating between the Vatican and the ruling coalition in signing a new concordat. Negotiations were prompted by Italian political leaders, who were much less interested in intervening in church affairs than had been their predecessors. At the same time, Vatican officials were concerned with the Catholic Church's close identification with the ruling party coalition, specifically the Christian Democratic party. The Christian Democrats had been the mainstay of every government since the formation of the Italian Republic. Nonetheless, in the 1984 concordat negotiations, the Church sought to maintain a large measure of its recognition by the state.

The Italian relationship between church and state is complicated by the role of the Vatican as seat of the pope. A significant factor in the estrangement between the Catholic Church and the Italian state was the loss of the papal states during the wars of Italian unification and the perceived threat of a liberal Italian state to the position and values of the Church. The papacy was estranged from the Italian state from the 1860s until the 1920s, when a concordat between the Vatican and the Fascist state was signed. The treaty outlined the formal relationship between the Church and the Italian state. Church-state relations continued to be strained during the Fascist era with Mussolini's push for a monopoly on power. Relations improved a great deal after the fall of Mussolini and with the creation of the Italian Republic, especially with the close alliance between the Christian Democratic party and the Catholic Church. Deep divisions remained between the Church and the significant sectors of Italian society which were critical of religion in general and of the Catholic Church hierarchy in particular.

The concordat approved by the Italian state and the Vatican in 1927 recognized Catholicism as the religion of the Italian people. The Vatican was recognized as a sovereign state with extra-territorial rights to a number of other buildings in Italy.

The state was given consultative power and some powers to reject episcopal nominees. Religious education was required in
Italian state schools with some possibility for opting out. Diocesan boundary changes were subject to civil approval. Canon law
was granted the force of civil law in a number of areas. Clergy
were to receive stipends from the state. Italian youth and lay
organizations were permitted to promote religious activities.
This was an especially important concession on the part of the
Fascist state in negotiating the concordat, because the Fascists
were opposed to the presence of non-Fascist groups in the Italian nation. Finally, in the concordat non-Catholic churches
were allowed to operate in Italy with the approval of the state.

The 1927 concordat had the effect of strengthening the ultimate political role of the Catholic Church during the Fascist
period, for few other organizations were allowed to operate
outside the state. During the 1930s and 1940s, Catholic action
became the recruiting ground for many future Italian politicians
who formed under church support the Christian Democratic
party in the postwar period. In a sense, the Catholic Church and
the Communist party were the two principal beneficiaries of the
aftermath of Fascism, for both were able to function during
the Fascist era — the one above ground and the other below
ground.

The Christian Democratic party has been the major actor in
the over fifty postwar governments that have been formed in
the Italian Republic since its establishment in the late 1940s.
This has led some to conclude that there is significant identification between the Christian Democratic party and the Catholic
Church. During periods of scandal or dissatisfaction with the
ruling party, particularly during the 1970s, popular discontent
seemed to spill over from the party to the Church. The Church
itself was surprised at its declining influence when it suffered
two successive defeats in referenda permitting divorce and
abortion in the 1970s. The capacity of the Church to be influential in Parliament was not reflected in balloting in the Italian
electorate at large. In Vatican circles, the defeats were viewed
as strengthening the case for rebuilding the Church in Italy and
distancing the Church from the Christian Democratic party.

At least since the 1960s, there were demands from a number
of groups to revise the 1927 concordat. The election of a Polish
pope and the rise of the first Socialist prime minister brought

STRUCTURE OF CHURCH-STATE RELATIONSHIPS   787

the process of revision to closure in 1984.[8] The revised concordat continued the basic terms of the 1927 pact, along with some important changes that appeared to allow greater distance between church and state. For example, religious instruction was still to be a component of Italian state education but it became much easier for students, their parents, or their guardians to opt out of the instruction. The state also surrendered its oversight of ecclesiastical appointments with the exception of the requirement that appointments to Italian positions have Italian citizenship.

The major development in current Italian church-state relations is a shift in how the state supports the stipends of the clergy. The arrangement that is about to take effect shifts financial support over time from direct payments to the clergy to a system that is not unlike the German one of voluntary taxation in support of churches, described later in this essay. Under the new system, Italian citizens may opt to have support for the Church collected as part of their tax obligations. Thus the Church may no longer assume that its revenue is a given. Instead, financial support for the Church must reflect in part the commitment of communicants.

The revised concordat appeared to give new standing to non-Catholic churches in that it made their recognition by the state nearly automatic. Cemeteries that had been Protestant or Jewish, but under the old concordat had to be managed by the Catholic Church, were now turned over to their respective faiths. But it is also clear that small Protestant churches have come to regard the revised concordat as giving far greater support to the Catholic Church than to other churches. For example, under the revised concordat if a Protestant family elected to have their child not receive Catholic instruction, the child was required to take additional classes in another subject matter. Protestants demonstrated in favor of having the child released from school rather than being given additional school work.[9] Recently the Italian Constitutional Court ruled that classes in the instruction of the Catholic faith should not become a reason for discrimination; students, therefore, should be allowed to leave the school grounds instead of attending the

8.   Maria Elisabetta de Franciscus, *Italy and the Vatican: The 1984 Concordat Between Church and State* (New York: Peter Lang, 1989).
9.   Rosalie Beck and David Hendon, "Notes on Church and State Affairs," *Journal of Church and State* 31 (Autumn 1989): 581-23.

classes.[10] The head of the Italian Bishops' Conference regretted the decision as weakening the transmission of values and violating the 1984 Concordat. Protestants have also objected to Catholic calls for state support for private Roman Catholic schools.

France. At the turn of this century, France experienced a move to a stance somewhere between a liberal and an anti-church model. The likely political consequences of this move provoked considerable debate. It is reasonable to conclude that few in 1900 would have predicted the course that church-state relations have taken in France. In the years since disestablishment, the French state has moved gradually towards a spheres model of church-state relationships. The Roman Catholic Church has regained a position of preferment, it is argued below, for some of the services it provides French society. The most noteworthy of these services is education. The discussion that follows focuses on the predictions of hypotheses B and D, concerning the effects of the regulation of services and the provision of subsidies in understanding how churches adapt to a regulatory environment.

Historically, the relationship between the church and the French state has undergone a series of dramatic changes. The French Revolution of two centuries ago brought about an era of sharp controversy over not only the Catholic Church but religion itself. Portions of France were dechristianized, while other sections, notably Brittany, became intensely Catholic and anti-Revolutionary. The Church regained a good deal of its former institutional position when Napoleon signed a concordat with the Vatican in order to establish the legitimacy of his regime. In successive regimes, the Napoleonic concordat was alternately criticized and threatened with denunciation, or relied upon and strengthened.

These shifts in church-state relationships reflected the sharply different value systems that characterized changing French regimes. In the period up to the First World War and, some would say, up to the Second World War, the Church was identified with the monarchist right in politics. The Napoleonic concordat was sustained by the restored monarchies, the Second Empire, and part of the Third Republic. But in leftist circles, the Church was seen as pursuing an active strategy of challenging the secular institutions of the French state. The controversy

---

10. AU Bulletin, "Italian Students Can Opt out of Religion Classes, Says Court," *Church and State* 44 (May 1991): 21.

STRUCTURE OF CHURCH-STATE RELATIONSHIPS 789

reached a critical point in 1905, when the French Church was disestablished. An important point is to ask why the Church was not disestablished earlier. Part of the explanation lies in the view of some on the Left that as long as the state paid the clergy the state could exercise some control over the political activities of the clergy.

The 1905 separation did give the Catholic Church the power of appointment of bishops but very little else. Religious orders were expelled and the state quit paying the stipends of the clergy. Cathedrals and churches were declared state property. The Church's income was greatly reduced as a result of the separation. Ironically, the French Catholic Church lacked any national institutions because of the mutual fear of the state and the Vatican that a French national bishops conference would challenge either the state or Papal power. In the aftermath of separation, a national bishops conference was established to direct Catholic policy in France. The period after the First World War brought a new stability to church-state relations. The Council of State sustained rulings that churches could only be used for religious purposes. Some funds were also made available for church organizations. Other churches were able to operate in France but the levels of support available to the Catholic Church even after the separation were much greater than those available to non-Catholic churches.

In the aftermath of the 1905 separation, the Catholic Church itself began to create missions in parts of France.[11] Efforts were made in the 1920s and onwards to establish a renewed Catholic intellectual presence in France. Ultimately, with the coming of the Fifth Republic the Church was much harder to characterize ideologically . Experiments with worker-priest movements in the 1940s, participation in center parties, and the record of many Catholics in the Resistance, eroded the distrust that had long characterized the attitude of the parties of the Left toward the Catholic Church.[12] The Church's efforts in private education during the 1950s were encouraged by many Catholic families but criticized by advocates of a uniform national educational system. The creation of the Fifth Republic in 1958, with the devoutly-Catholic Charles De Gaulle as president, resulted in

11. John McManners, *Church and State in France, 1870-1914* (New York: Harper Torchbooks, 1972).
12. William Bosworth, *Catholicism and Crisis in Modern France: French Catholic Groups on the Threshold of the Fifth Republic* (Princeton, N.J.: Princeton University Press, 1962).

the state's assuming the cost of instruction in Catholic schools. In the decades that followed, Catholic schools became important to many not as institutions of religion but as providers of traditional education in an age of widening controversy over the direction of the state school sector.[13]

In 1981, the Socialists came to power for the first time in the history of the Fifth Republic. Their secular tradition brought about the introduction of a bill that apparently would have brought church schools much more under state control. Reaction was swift and massive. In perhaps the largest demonstrations in the history of France, approximately 2 million people took to the streets in Paris in favor of autonomous church-run schools with state support. A pro-government counter demonstration drew only seventy-five thousand people. The government was forced to abandon its relatively mild bill. Education has clearly been the success story of the Catholic Church in France.[14]

The emerging issue on the agenda of French church-state relations will be the Moslem community, which is the largest in Western Europe. Controversies over dress codes and religious instruction steadily grow.[15] The levels of support available to Roman Catholics simply are not available to Moslems in the state that declares support for the separation of church and state.

Germany. Germany, more so than any other other country in Western Europe, contains within its frequently changing boundaries all of the major issue found in church-state relations throughout Europe — in addition to the historic conflicts between Protestants and Catholics; between Protestant Empire and Catholic hierarchy, and between the Third Reich and churches.

The new challenge for Germany is the integration of the former East Germany which for the most part possess an antichurch model. Present-day major German Churches in large measure, as a result of state support, are among the wealthiest churches in Europe. The discussion of church-state relations that follows embraces all of the four hypotheses. The East Ger-

---

13.   J.E. Flower, "The Church," in *France Today: Introductory Studies*, 6th ed., ed. J.E. Flower (London: Methuen, 1987), 172-95.
14.   Julius W. Friend, *Seven Years in France: Francois Mitterand and the Unintended Revolution* (Boulder, Colo.: Westview Press, 1989).
15.   AU Bulletin, "France Approves Religious Garb for Islamic Students," *Church and State* 43 (January 1990): 22.

STRUCTURE OF CHURCH-STATE RELATIONSHIPS 791

man experience allows for the an examination of a church as focal point for opposition of experience. The German churches are deeply involved in both charitable works and social issues and yet church attendance is not impressive. German state involvement in matters of doctrine and church administration has steadily diminished in the postwar years.

Both Italy and France are countries in which the terms of the church-state debate have been the conflict between Catholic and secular forces over what should be the role of the state (if any) in supporting the institutions of the Church. In Germany, a nation unified at the same time as Italy in the 1860s, two contending religious traditions had coexisted since the Reformation. In the Empire created by Prince Otto Von Bismarck, about two-thirds of the population was Protestant and one-third Roman Catholic.

The church-state tradition in the German states, particularly the Protestant tradition, placed responsibility for the church in the hands of the prince. Prussian monarchs assumed leading roles in combining different confessions, notably Lutheran and Calvinist, into one church. The conflicts of the Reformation had established the role of the German princes in determining church membership and church structure within their respective states. The practice in both Catholic and Protestant states was quite similar in assigning a pivotal role to the ruling prince. The fundamental difference between Catholic and Protestant states was the role of the Vatican as a supranational church body.

In the enlarging lands of the Prussian state, the King — who would later be given the title of Emperor of Germany — became the head of the Evangelical Church in 1871. The state assumed responsibility for the material and doctrinal condition of the church within its lands. The challenge of German unification was the challenge for the Protestant king/emperor to respond to his Catholic subjects who were not members of the church he headed. Indeed, the course of public policy decisions throughout the relatively short history of the Second Empire often produced considerable concern among Catholics that they were second-class citizens.

The so-called cultural conflict between Chancellor Bismarck's government and the Roman Catholic Church over educational policy after the formation of the Empire in 1871 revealed a sharp clash between the Erastic model and the spheres model — that is, between state control of church activi-

ties and separate arenas of respective church and state autonomy. Bismarck ultimately gave way. The Catholic hierarchy
participated in electoral politics by helping to establish the
Center party. The collapse of the Empire in 1918 left the Protestant Church without the king/emperor as its organizational
head, ending an arrangement that had lasted for four hundred
years. The Protestant Church was rebuilt after 1918 but was
clearly a troubled organization that was seriously challenged by
the coming of the Nazi period. The Nazis sought to create their
own version of the Protestant German church, which divided
even further a church still dealing with the consequences of the
Empire's collapse in 1918.[16]

The end of the Second World War left a German Protestant
church led by people committed to making a break with the
past. Initially, Protestant church leaders sought to maintain the
unity of the church in a Germany divided into zones by the Allies. Ultimately, the Protestant leadership in the West had to accept that the organizational division of their church would
conform to the new boundaries of West and East Germanies.

In contrast to the Protestant experience, the Roman Catholic
Church gained a reputation of organizational strength during
both the Weimar Republic and the Third Reich. The Roman
Catholic hierarchy seemed to be confident in dealing with the
Nazis. The Vatican negotiated a concordat with the Nazi regime
that caused criticism that the Church was legitimizing the Nazi
state. The concordat was defended as providing protection to
Catholics during the Nazi period.

In postwar West Germany, the Catholics emerged with a
better reputation and a stronger church. The newly-created
West Germany was about equally divided between Catholics
and Protestants and there was considerable sympathy for
strengthening the role of religion in the new German state. The
Roman Catholic hierarchy received support for a number of its
concerns from American occupational authorities. Both the
Catholic and the Protestant Churches sought to establish strong
relationships with the new state. The drafters of the post-Second
World War West German constitution adopted the financial arrangements that had been established in the Weimar constitution. The state was authorized to collect tithes from baptized

---

16. Gordon Craig, *Germany: 1866-1945* (New York: Oxford University Press,
1978).

STRUCTURE OF CHURCH-STATE RELATIONSHIPS   793

Christians.[17]

Both the Protestant and the Catholic Church received fairly generous terms of support and recognition from the newly-formed West German state. Church-run hospitals and other charities were supported by government funding. The Vatican was able to retain concordats signed both at the land level (the German states) and to retain the accord signed between the Third Reich and the Vatican. Thus state-church regulation now can occur at both the state and the federal levels of German government. Funds were also made available for the maintenance of church buildings and salaries for bishops of both churches as well as for the maintenance of episcopal residences. There is little doubt today that West German churches are among the wealthiest in Europe.

During the 1960s, debate developed over the role of state support for confessional schools. Much attention was paid to what was said to be lower levels of academic success of German Catholics in comparison to German Protestants. Some Catholics argued that this disparity in academic performance was attributable to the inferior quality of Catholic confessional schools. This critique occurred at a time when the Social Democratic party was itself concerned over the maintenance of confessional schools. In the course of the debate, it became increasingly evident that the only group in strong support of maintaining the confessional schools was the Roman Catholic hierarchy. Catholic laity and Protestants both favored the abolition of confessional schools and the substitution of religious instruction in state schools. The debate did result in the phasing out of confessional schools in state after state in the Federal Republic. This result demonstrated the decline of the state as a negative external unifier in sustaining the power of the hierarchy in speaking for German Catholics. The new sympathetic regulatory environment of post-War Germany had gone a long way toward reducing the perception of Catholics that they were second class citizens. A new common identity for both Catholics and Protestants emerged: citizens of a new Germany. One consequence of this new common identity was a decline in the capacity of Roman Catholic bishops to speak politically for their communicants, as Catholic Germans saw that they had other effective

---

17.   Frederick Spotts, *The Churches and Politics in Germany* (Middletown, Conn.: Wesleyan University Press, 1973).

identities in the West German state.[18]

Few Catholics lived in East Germany and the separated Protestant churches did not suffer the regulatory severity imposed on churches in some other Eastern European countries. Nonetheless, the East German state did not support the churches financially and they came to be known as voluntary churches. The normalization of relations between the Germanys in the early 1970s was helpful to the East German churches as funds flowed east from the wealthy West German Protestant churches to their much poorer brethren in the East.[19] The East German Protestant churches became a focal point in the peace movement in the early 1980s and many of their leaders played an important role in the transition to democracy in 1989.

But the voluntary East German Protestant churches seemed unable to survive the unification of the two Germanys. Funds were no longer transferred East and the extension of tithe collection through taxation resulted in an estimated 5 million people leaving the former East German churches. There is confusion as to why East Germans left their Protestant churches. Some argue it was because the East Germans understood that the church tax would give 9 percent of their individual income to the state rather than 9 percent of what they pay in taxes.[20] Public opinion surveys suggest that very few German young people see much value in any sort of religious commitment.[21] Compounding the challenges facing the East German Protestant churches is the influx of many mission churches from the West who see in this former communist land the prospects of conversion of eastern Germans to their respective faiths. Estimates put the number of churches now active in the East at 250 to 350.[22]

But the generous material recognition of the two main churches, Protestant and Catholic, is a larger question for all of Germany. This state support has strengthened the churches as institutions. Both main churches are deeply committed to a vast

---

18. Ibid.
19. A.G. Roeber, "Churches in the New Germany," *The Christian Century* 107 (July-August 1990): 692-93.
20. Rosalie Beck and David Hendon, "Notes on Church-State Affairs," *Journal of Church and State* 33 (Winter 1991): 183-91.
21. Maria Frise, "Growing Up Without God in a Post-Marx Society," *The German Tribune*, 4 November 1990, 14-15.
22. Nora Miethka, "The Sects Step in to Exploit the Social Uncertainties in the Eastern Laender,"*The German Tribune*, 2 June 1991, 15.

STRUCTURE OF CHURCH-STATE RELATIONSHIPS 795

number of social and health care organizations. These church-sponsored organizations are funded by federal and state funds but are run by the two churches that are both closely identified with social welfare policy issues. But what of other churches which simply lack the scale and range of state support?

A case in point is the growing Islamic community. It is estimated that close to 1.5 million Moslems are in Germany, with close to fifteen hundred mosques. Many of the mosques appear to be run by Islamic Fundamentalists.

Petitions are being circulated in Germany to have Islam recognized as a religion, which would entitle mosque authorities to receive the church tax. The challenge for German authorities is that they would be collecting revenues from a religious organization that is committed to enlarging the size of its community.[23] The two old established churches appear to have lost interest in conversion and increasingly put their efforts into social welfare, environmental, and other public policy issues in a state that has established a regulatory framework that is clearly favorable to the two main churches but not to all churches.

Britain. Britain has a heritage of inter- and intra-faith conflicts that rivals that of Germany. In the course of the last century, Britain has seen a decline in inter-church conflict consonant with the growth of state toleration of other churches. The legacy of earlier intolerance is, of course, Northern Ireland. Among the four main countries examined, Britain is the only one that possesses established churches, and then they are only in two of the lands that compose the United Kingdom, England, and Scotland. Scotland recognizes the Presbyterian Church. The Church of England's role is unique, for not only is it the state Church of England but it is formally a part of the United Kingdom's political institutions through episcopal representation in Parliament and regular involvement in the political rituals of the nation.

The Church of England, although it is the state church, has nonetheless witnessed steadily diminishing involvement on the part of the British state in regulating doctrine and administrative appointments. Nonetheless, there has not been any correlative reduction in tangible resources provided by the state to the church. The Anglican church is very much at the center of major public policy debates in the nation, but it is not a church that

---

23. Baha Gungor, "Islamic Fundamentalism Flexes Its Muscles Among Turks in Germany," *The German Tribune*, 9 December 1990, 14.

provides significant social, health-related, or educational services. As predicted in hypotheses C and D, the Church of England receives a considerable portion of income from state-
managed funds and enjoys a good deal of autonomy from state
intervention.

Nonetheless, the British controversies were different from
controversies in the other countries of this study in that the
Anglican Church was often challenged in some policy areas such
as education by two other groups, the Roman Catholic minority
and the nonconformists (that is, the other major Protestant denominations). A good deal of nineteenth century church regulation consisted of opening up political participation and
appointments to non-Anglicans. Debates within the Anglican
Church over liturgy and theological interpretation were also
heated. Such debates could and did have consequences for
prime ministers who then as now have the power of appointment of bishops.

In contemporary England, the Anglican Church is formally
headed by the monarch. As is the case in so many other areas,
formal attribution of power to the monarch really means attribution of power to Parliament. The power of episcopal appointment has been weakened by requiring widespread consultation
and the development of a short list of candidates for an episcopal vacancy prepared by a list of senior churchmen. Strongly
supported candidates would present a difficult challenge for a
prime minister to reject. Funding for the Anglican Church
comes in part from revenues earned from church lands and
other investments. It is estimated that the annual income pays
for approximately one-half the salaries of the clergy.[24] The
House of Lords contains twenty-six Anglican bishops who are
the lords spiritual, while the life, hereditary, and law peers are
the lords temporal. The synod of the Anglican Church has responsibility for doctrinal and liturgical matters but ultimately
Parliament disposes. A major issue for the synod in 1992 is the
ordination of women. If the synod were to approve the ordination of women — which is unlikely — the change would then
likely require Parliamentary approval. It is unlikely that a mod-
ern-day Parliament would overturn the judgment reached by
the synod on this or other controversial issues.

The Anglican Church plays a relatively modest role in British

---

24. Rupert E. Davies, *The Church of England Observed* (London: SCM Press,
1984).

STRUCTURE OF CHURCH-STATE RELATIONSHIPS 797

education at this stage. Religious instruction, though a component of the state school system, is quite broadly conceived and efforts in the recent educational reform to bill to tighten religious instruction failed. The one region of Britain where negative reaction resulted in the filing of a law suit against the Education Reform Act of the late 1980s was Northern Ireland, where Catholic bishops objected to the provision of the Act that if a confessional school parent association opted to have its school join the state system, the state would assume the costs of running the school. The Anglican Church leadership has escaped from having its ranks filled with government patronage appointments and from recruiting only from the upper reaches of English society. Since the 1940s, the church has also taken an increasing critical and independent role as a critic of public policy while retaining its role in the political institutional life of the nation.[25] In 1990, the Anglican Church published the latest in a series of reports on issues of major public policy concern. The report, entitled "Living Faith in the City," is a critical assessment of the conservative government's urban policy.[26] It is clearly critical of the Conservative government. Supporters of the government pointed out that a church in which no more more than 1.5 million of its members regularly attend services would gain little attention for issuing such a report unless it was the established church.[27]

In short, the Anglican Church that separated from the Roman Catholic Church in the sixteenth century has achieved a good deal of autonomy in the power of appointment and in managing its own funds. There is apparently little interest among its leadership in disestablishing the church with the likely consequence of being reduced to the sectarian role of a minor church. Its critics nevertheless argue that if the Church is to regain any sort of religious momentum it needs to be disestablished.[28]

25. Kenneth Medhurst and George Moyser, *Church and Politics in a Secular Age* (Oxford: Clarendon Press, 1988).
26. Archbishop of Canterbury's Advisory Group on Urban Priority Areas, "Living Faith in the City," (London: General Synod of the Church of England, 1990).
27. David J. Smith, "Faith in the City and Mrs. Thatcher," *Policy Studies* 11 (Summer 1990): 18-23.
28. Clifford Longley, "Manacled to a Spiritual Corpse: Why the Church of England's Decline Is so Clearly Established," *Church and State* 43 (March 1990): 19-20.

798   JOURNAL OF CHURCH AND STATE

A Comparative Exploration of the Hypotheses

Students of European church-state relations would be hard pressed not to conclude that the regulatory climate in contemporary Europe is unfavorable to the mainline churches. Silvio Ferrari points out that state budgets provide for some religious denominations in Spain, Italy (the religious tax is to come into effect later), Greece, Belgium, and Luxembourg. A religious tax provides income, as has been noted, in Germany; and also in Austria, Switzerland, Denmark, Norway, and Finland. Indirect support is provided in France, Great Britain, the Netherlands, and Sweden. Church access to television and radio is available without charge in much of Europe.[29] For the most part, the principal churches of Europe have secured considerable autonomy and regulatory terms that grant them considerable resources. It is true in the case of Sweden that the courts ruled that the Lutheran Church could not refuse to re-admit a self-proclaimed atheist.[30] Yet, while the principal churches may, as institutions, have achieved reasonable economic security, they have not thrived as focal points for their respective national populations.

As discussed earlier, the United States remains a remarkably singular nation in church attendance. Although weekly church attendance has fallen in the United States in the past thirty years, nonetheless, American church attendance remains higher at 43 percent in 1986 than attendance in most Western European nations. In the four countries of this study, weekly church attendance in 1986 was, respectively, Italy 36 percent, France 12 percent, (West) Germany 21 percent, and England 14 percent.[31] When young people (defined as late teens and early twenties) were asked in the late 1980s how important religion should be in life, 9 percent in West Germany said very important while in France and in Britain it was only 8 percent respectively. In sharp contrast, 47 percent of young people in the United States claimed religion should be very important.[32]

A common pattern in all four states is the attenuation of the

---

29. Silvio Ferrari, "Separation of Church and State in Contemporary European Society," *Journal of Church and State* 30 (Autumn 1988): 533-48.
30. Rosalie Beck and David Hendon, "Notes on Church and State Affairs," *Journal of Church and State* 31 (Autumn 1989): 581-23.
31. Princeton Religion Research Center, *Emerging Trends* (Princeton, N.J.: Princeton Religion Research Center, 1988).
32. Princeton Religion Research Center, *Emerging Trends* (Princeton, N.J.: Princeton Religion Research Center, 1989).

STRUCTURE OF CHURCH-STATE RELATIONSHIPS   799

state role in selection of church hierarchies as well as in doctrinal and policy concerns of the church. Churches in Europe enjoy organizational autonomy that is remarkable given the past.

Moreover, it is apparent that churches in three of the states — Germany, France, and England — are now identified with quite different activities respectively. These activities, this essay argues, need to be explained in reference to church interests and the pattern of regulatory relationships that has evolved in the postwar period. In France, where the separation of church and state has existed for most of this century, the Catholic Church by the most recent decade has been able to define itself in part as a producer of quality education rather than as principally a political advocate of a former regime. The public appears to accept the judgment that church schools produce a level of education that may be superior to that found in the troubled state system. This support for church-run schools does not result from their being viewed as bastions of faith and morals, but from the quality of the secular education offered in these schools. The French Church receives financial support from the state in running the Church school system. It is in the area of education that the French Catholic Church has been most successful in securing its position in what it took to be a challenge from the French government in the early 1980s.

The German churches also no longer define themselves in support or in opposition in a particular regime. Instead, churches in Germany emphasize issues in which they have a substantive incentive, especially social welfare policy. Their arena is not education but health care and social need. These are areas in which both major churches have assumed a public policy role and in which they receive state funding. The dramatic change in the fortunes of the East German Protestant churches may reflect the experience of other Eastern European churches where the churches assumed a political role in society in part because of the absence of alternatives. The East German churches were partially subsidized by the West German churches, which strengthened their position in a society short on resources. The unification of the two nations left the church abandoned by its membership and overtaken by secular organizations who have assumed much of its political role. But over time it may be observed that the Protestant churches in East Germany will begin to carve a role in social welfare concerns as it stabilizes support from both the state and the local population.

800   JOURNAL OF CHURCH AND STATE

This avenue will not be easy to follow for the competing sects that have entered the old East Germany in last few years.

In England, the Anglican Church has little incentive to be actively engaged in education without antagonizing other confessions. The state has a preemptive role in health care, and private charities or the state assume significant roles in social welfare. The Anglican Church's principal arena that sets it apart from other churches, indeed from the churches in the other states discussed herein, is its established role in the nation's governing institutions and ceremonials. The Anglican Church has enjoyed, as has been noted, increasing insulation in being used by the state as a source of patronage. The Anglican Church is thus allowed to increasingly define its role as a sort of official clerical opposition or assessor of social conditions and public policies.

In Italy, the Vatican would appear to have concluded that the earlier concordat had resulted in too close an identification with the fortunes of the perpetually-in-office Christian Democrats. The interest of the Vatican in supranational concerns may have promoted distancing of the Italian Catholic Church from the party structure it had helped to create after the Second World War. This venture in partial deregulation has seen the Italian Catholic Church move to act a good deal more like its counterparts in other European countries — de-emphasizing the partisan role for the role of a quasi-interest group seeking resources from the state.   Similarly, the Spanish Catholic Church receives substantial economic support from a Socialist government that two generations ago sought to disestablish the Catholic Church there.[33] If these brief accounts reflect the condition of the principal churches in these nations, then a reasonable inference is that over time the state has receded in regulation of churches partly as a result of increasing secularization, and partly because of the complexity of the state's becoming immersed in questions of doctrine and personal selection. This is the risk of over-regulation leading to less regulation. Finally, in part because of the challenge of regulating a church when the state lacks information and resources to sustain regulatory rigor, the church is enabled to begin to reinterpret regulations on favorable grounds. Even in France, where separation has existed since 1905, the state has been facilitative of the

---

33.   Robert Graham, *Spain: A Nation Comes of Age* (New York: St. Martin's Press, 1984), 220-21.

STRUCTURE OF CHURCH-STATE RELATIONSHIPS   801

Catholic Church through its maintenance of church buildings and support of church-run schools.

In reviewing the four hypotheses outlined earlier, some very tentative assessments can be made. There is some support for the first hypotheses that where a church is sternly regulated but secular organizations proscribed, the church will play a broader political role. That would appear to have been the case in East Germany where the Protestant churches were a voluntary institution capable of a range of social and political expressions. There is evidence in support of the second hypothesis that regulatory windows of opportunity become attractive for churches as institutions. In Germany, France, and Britain, churches have assumed new roles in moving away from partisan politics to the provision of services or specific areas of public policy competence. It would appear that the Italian Catholic Church may be moving in the same direction by reducing its partisan role and assuming other responsibilities such as education. It is a process of regulatory adaptation that has enabled churches as institutions to realize opportunities found in the regulatory environment that has emerged in the decades after the Second World War.

The third hypothesis, that church hierarchy is more likely to be independent when it receives state support, may be true. Certainly the Anglican Church's income for those in official positions may afford the church leadership a freedom from raising funds from church members that churches without state support lack. Both German and English church leaders are significant commentators on social and political issues. But for this third hypothesis to be sustained, there is need to consider the final hypothesis — the decline in state intervention in matters of doctrine and personal. The record seems quite clear in state after European state governments have surrendered their role for in the determination of church leaderships, church administrative boundaries, the number of clergy, and many other clerical activities. Even in Britain the state has greatly greatly reduced its role in episcopal selection. In the wealthy and influential diocess of Cologne, Germany, there were serious objections among Roman Catholic leaders to the Vatican's appointment of a particular Roman Catholic Bishop. However, the protest was to no avail. One can easily imagine a time when the state leadership could intervene to block the appointment. Indeed, it seems that the fourth hypothesis is the most persuasively supported, for the evidence seems solid that the principal churches have achieved autonomy at the expense of state control without losing financial support and often privileged positions in their respective nations.

Future prospects for discontent in these countries lie in the increasingly active role of smaller churches and other religions in European societies. The European tradition has never really adopted the liberal principle of neutrality towards churches. Relations between the state and churches vary greatly from one church to another. Non-Catholic churches in Italy have pressed for greater separation between the state and the Roman Catholic Church. This position has been echoed in Spain and in Britain.[34] The Swedes have sought to deal with the issue of their state church and other religions by offering cash subventions to other churches that demonstrate that their respective memberships are over three thousand.[35] But the Swedish solution may not always be well received with the structure of concordats and patterns of support that exist in other nations now confronted with increasing members of Christian churches that are non-European in origin or with the return of Islam to Europe.[36] The issue in the future will be the return to the debate over neutrality as a stance for the state.

An unintended consequence of the anti-church model as found in some of the former Communist regimes of Eastern Europe is that the church may gain from the severe regulatory climate if, even though it is seriously and heavily regulated, it nonetheless can function to an extent not possible for other secular organizations. Under such conditions, the church may have the advantage of becoming an institutional magnet for those critical of the state. Paradoxically, therefore, the state may strengthen the church as a force in opposition to the state. But this advantage may only emerge when the church has an antecedent identification as a communal force as opposed to, say, a center of individuals seeking retreat from the world.[37] If the church were associated with a prior distrusted regime, its

34. AU Bulletin, "British Parliament Rejects Parochiaid Expansion," *Church and State* 44 (July-August 1991): 165; AU Bulletin, "Spanish Protestants, Jews Refuse Tax Aid," *Church and State* 43 (April 1990): 93.

35. Swedish Institute, "Religion in Sweden," *Fact Sheets on Sweden* (Stockholm: Swedish Institute, 1991).

36. Kevin Piecuch, "Islam Finds a New Home in Western Europe," *Christianity Today* 34 (March 1990): 40-41.

37. Pedro Ramet, *Cross and Commissar: The Politics of Religion in Eastern Europe and the U.S.S.R.* (Champaign-Urbana, Il.: University of Illinois Press, 1987).

STRUCTURE OF CHURCH-STATE RELATIONSHIPS 803

credibility may be severely reduced in becoming a focal point for a broad coalition of opposition forces.

Both the Irish and the Polish Catholic Churches enjoy considerable support in their respective nations. The position of these two churches surely has been strengthened over time by their identification with the national aspirations of their respective populations. Both Ireland and Poland have histories of occupation by foreign powers. Thus the severity of regulation would confront a church firmly rooted in the population and would blunt the effectiveness of the state's regulatory strategy. In other nations, where the church's support in the population was marginal prior to the rise of an anti-church regime, the severity of regulation may actually weaken an already fragile church. This may be the case, for example, in Cuba.

In Eastern Europe today, the discussion has returned to what it was in Western Europe two generations ago, where churches that were tolerated and severely regulated now see the opportunity to negotiate newly favorable terms of regulation between church and state. There are divisions as is already seen in the objections of smaller Protestant churches to ties between between the Roman Catholic Church and the Polish, Czech, and Slovak states respectively. But the larger issue is the extent to which, in the case of Poland, the state will undertake to realize Catholic values in public policy areas such as education, marriage, or abortion.[38] The test will be the capacity of the Catholic Church that played such a critical role in sustaining opposition to the Communist state to retain its power in an environment where secular organizations now have the opportunity to rebuild civil society.

CONCLUSION

Today there is remarkable convergence in the regulatory practices of a number of European states in the West. The model is likely to be adopted by some states in the post-communist East. In the nineteenth century, churches were often the organizational expressions of religious movements that in some cases defended the state as a protector of a religious society or condemned the existing state as threatening the religious foundations of society. Today few western European politicians are likely to see *churches* as representing such inclusive ideological movements. Rather, they are more likely to see them as inter-

---

38. Waldemar Chrostowski, "The Desert and After," *Voice*, 9 July 1991, 10.

est groups who also possess moral issue agendas but also who compete for resources and regulatory sympathy. This is not to say that religious leaders fail to speak out on the issues of the day. If anything, religious leaders probably believe that they have greater freedom to speak out today than their predecessors had in the past. But such leaders speak from insulated positions as moral authorities rather than as heads of broad-based movements challenging or sustaining the very core assumptions of the state. States possessing the institutional responsibility to govern the internal affairs of churches either by concordat or by the terms of establishment of the national church have uniformly beat a sharp regulatory retreat, seeing greater costs than benefits in the regulatory enterprise. Thus, churches possess a good deal of internal autonomy and have been able to retain, and in some cases increase their claims on their respective states for material resources and regulatory preferment. It is this author's judgment that the postwar regulatory regime in Europe has had the consequence of many of the old European churches undergoing a period of adjustment and emerging, in part, as successfully incorporated interest groups in their respective societies.

[14]

Juan J. Linz

Church and State in Spain from the Civil War to the Return of Democracy

[In the last sixty years] the mutation of the Spanish Catholic Church has been extraordinary. It is as though we had been watching a play of several acts, complete with changes of scenery, of the plot, and of the personality of the characters and even the emotional tone: furious in the thirties, exalted in the forties and fifties, troubled and inquiring in the sixties, moderately euphoric throughout the seventies and discrete, with a sense both of satisfaction and disillusion in the eighties.
—Víctor Pérez Díaz

"Iglesia y Religión en la España Contemporánea" [1]

THE RELIGIOUS-POLITICAL CRISIS OF THE THIRTIES

SPANISH CATHOLICISM FACED THE CRISIS of the 1930s with a strange mixture of weakness and strength. Compared to Catholic Germany, Belgium, the Netherlands, Switzerland, and even Italy, Catholics in Spain had not been organized for political and social action. Spanish Catholicism had been living under the protection of a government that had given the church hierarchy a share in power in the Senate, had assured public recognition of the Catholic

---

Juan J. Linz is Sterling Professor of Political and Social Science at Yale University.

160   *Juan J. Linz*

church, had limited competition from other churches, and, except for an occasional crisis, had guaranteed the free development of its activities. Part of that bargain had been, however, the continued existence of the traditional royal *patronato,* which had assured government influence on episcopal appointments.[2]

Efforts to create Catholic workers' organizations and trade unions had not been successful since they were bitterly contested by the anarchist movement and the Socialist unions. The weakness of lay organizations facilitated the victory of the Republican-Socialist coalition in the 1931 elections. While longtime dependence on the state under the monarchy made it difficult for the church hierarchy to accept the change of regime, the Vatican, the elite of Catholic lay organizations, and the nuncio quickly applied the doctrine of Leo XIII of indifference toward forms of government and asked for the recognition of the new regime. The electoral defeat of pro-Catholic candidates made way for the approval of an anticlerical constitution, but that victory was deceptive since lay activists and the clergy were still able to mobilize mass electoral support for the defense of the church in 1931.[3]

The Catholic reaction to the 1931 elections cannot be understood without examining the renewed intensity of anticlericalism, whose roots are complex and difficult to understand. While the connection of the church with the monarchy and the Primo de Rivera dictatorship certainly contributed to the general public's suspicion of the church, the intense anticlericalism of the bourgeois Left Republicans had other roots.

To a large extent, both the "officialization" of Catholicism and popular anticlericalism were embedded in rural community life. To people living in those areas, the fusion of the local power structure and the church seemed natural. In the context of the ongoing social conflict—the protests of the lower classes against the power structure, the legal system, and the police—that fusion appeared as illegitimate, immoral, and profane. Irrespective of their personal religiosity, many people rejected the church as an ally of the powerful and the rich, who were religious conformists or devout, which led to violent anticlericalism and a readiness to follow an antireligious intelligentsia. Those sentiments were not limited to rural society but also extended to the working class of the growing industrial centers.

Church and State in Spain   161

On another level we find an intellectual rejection of Catholic dominance in Spanish intellectual and cultural life. Many attributed the scientific and cultural backwardness of Spain, in comparison to other Western nations, to the influence of the Counter-Reformation and the insensitivity of the church to accept many trends in modern science and culture. Socialists who had not been particularly concerned with the clerical issue, which they considered a diversion by the bourgeoisie of the working class from the real class conflict, began to back the anticlericalism of the petty bourgeois, while the anarchists, their main competitors for the support of the workers, expressed enthusiastic anticlerical and antireligious feelings.

The self-definition of the Republic as a regime one of whose priorities was the laicization-secularization of Spain and whose leaders insisted on the support of that republic in order to participate in the polity obliged Catholics to mobilize all their resources in the electoral struggle of 1933. A series of circumstances, including the extension of suffrage to women, gave an electoral victory to the Right, making the Catholic party, the CEDA, the largest in parliament; however, the ambiguity of the CEDA in relation to the monarchy-republic issue, its refusal to identify with the Republic as defined by the republicans, and the distrust of the president of the Republic prevented the entry of CEDA ministers into government until October of 1934. After initial efforts by the nuncio and some churchmen to reach an understanding with the Republic, Catholics failed to achieve their goals despite massive votes, leading to an even more everyday conflictual attitude. Violence against the church, its clergy, and its buildings increased after the Popular Front electoral victory in 1936. Hostility against the church had erupted somewhat sporadically under the Republic and, at times, was almost tolerated by the authorities, but in the October 1934 revolution against the entry of the CEDA into the government, thirty-seven priests and seminarians lost their lives.

The military uprising in July 1936, conceived as a *pronunciamiento* which soon would become a civil war, unleashed a bloody and destructive persecution in a matter of hours.[4] Some clerics reacted by going as far as to revive the classic doctrine of just rebellion, but the news of the burning of churches and convents and the massacre of priests and nuns made it clear to everyone in the church, to the clergy and most practicing Catholics, which side they

162   *Juan J. Linz*

were on. The tragic events that followed were interpreted by church-men as mainly being the result of anticlerical propaganda and the actions of agitators, if not a conspiracy. They believed that most people in Spain were still Christian, even the working class. For others who were more perceptive it was the belief that the church was allied with their enemies, the privileged, and that it was class interest that kept people away from the church. To their opponents, how-ever, most of Spain was alienated from religion and only clericalism maintained the Catholic presence. Both perspectives led to radical and intolerant responses: the first, the destruction of the enemy—the Left—and later a social interpretation of the religious mission, particularly in the last years of the Franco regime; the second, the militant anticlericalism of the thirties and in the civil war.

The Nationalists reestablished the presence of religion in educa-tion, abolished divorce, authorized jurisdiction in marital cases to ecclesiastical courts, gave public funds to pay clerical salaries, and subsidized the reconstruction of churches and convents. Religious symbols dominated the landscape. Bishops and priests occupied a prominent place in any official ceremony, and the authorities at-tended ex officio religious ceremonies. All those who had opposed or persecuted the church, in turn, were persecuted themselves. The intellectual life, media, and school textbooks were subject to govern-ment censorship to exclude any criticism of the church. The state had become in many areas the secular arm of the church, while the church in *a do et des* contributed to the legitimation of the regime.[5]

A complex issue in the development of religion and politics in Europe in the interwar years is the relationship of the churches and the faithful with fascist movements. Spanish fascism, despite its earlier insignificance electorally and as a mass movement, had an important role during this period due to the civil war and the hegemony of the Axis in Europe. The fascist party, the Falange, was a heterogeneous movement created from the union of different groups. Falangist nationalists saw the influence of the Vatican in internal affairs as a threat and felt a deep distrust and dislike for the CEDA, who reciprocated that dislike. Their mutual animosity would contribute later to the conflicts and squabbles of the "political families" in the Franco coalition. Some members of the hierarchy,

Church and State in Spain 163

reflecting the Vatican's hostility to Nazism, expressed their misgivings about the "statism" of the fascists and the potentially dangerous influence of foreign-pagan ideas. On the other hand, the Falange found in the church a limit to its totalitarian ambitions and attempted to save or strengthen the party's political space by claiming to be as Catholic as the "professional Catholics," thereby making its contribution to the hegemony of public religion in those years. Even so, on many issues, mainly in the field of education and cultural life, some fascists provided a brake to the ambitions of proclerical reactionary Catholics and the hierarchy supporting them.[6]

It is this background that explains a period of tensions between the Vatican and the Franco regime that would last until 1945.[7] A typical issue during this period, for example, was the refusal by the church to take an oath of allegiance to the head of state, an oath that the new primate never made but on which the church finally gave in.

Any analysis of religion and politics has to deal with the relationship between religion and nationalism. One extreme, the position of many European liberals and fascists, sees the church, especially the transnational church, as a threat to national integration. On the other end of the spectrum are those churchmen and laypeople who see an identity between the church and the nation, between being a religious person and a nationalist, excluding from the community those who question that identity. That line of thought might be reached by different paths. One sees the identification of the church with a nation as a way to defend a culture, a language, and the national self against alien cultural and ideological influences—a pattern that is characteristic of defensive nationalism in the peripheries of nations, like Catalonia and the Basque Country in Spain. The other begins with a more complex religiously based claim: that the greatness of a nation, its historical success, is linked with its loyalty to the faith and the church; secularization becomes a threat not only to the church but to the nation. Spanish national-Catholicism is probably closer to the second pole.

The "triumphant" church born in the civil war was made possible by the Franco regime, but one could also say that the regime in large part was made possible, stable, and long lasting thanks to that religious legitimation. What could have been a *pronunciamiento* became for many a crusade. What could have been a military

164   *Juan J. Linz*

dictatorship became a complex regime with a form of organic statism that was able to survive for decades.

NATIONAL-CATHOLICISM IN POWER

The period from 1945 to 1957 was the high point of Catholic triumphalism, of the public identification of the church with the Franco regime. After delays and hesitations, the Vatican finally signed a concordat that, together with the bases agreement with the United States, ended the international isolation of the regime. It is also a time when the seeds of future tensions were planted.[8]

How did this marriage of religion and politics, church and state, emerge? Foremost was the whole process by which the Spanish church identified itself with the Nationalists in the course of the civil war. In addition, the weakening of the fascist component of the regime as a result of the defeat of the Axis led to an attempt by the Catholics to recuperate the areas in which the Falangists exercised some influence. There are, however, more specific reasons as to why Franco wanted to make efforts to co-opt political Catholicism and through it to strengthen the support of the church hierarchy and, if possible, that of the Vatican. In May 1945 and subsequent months the hostility of the Allies and many Western politicians had threatened the regime on account of the regime's ideological affinity, connection, and collaboration with defeated fascist powers. The regime needed to incorporate people who could contact foreign governments (let us not forget that Christian Democracy was on the rise in Europe) and who would be able to neutralize the monarchial pressure. Catholics who were to be co-opted, however, wanted to be assured of some of their own goals, including the evolution of the regime toward a monarchy, thereby ensuring continuity after Franco. They also had more immediate objectives, in particular, the placement of their people in key positions.

Events in 1945 and their impact on Spanish society represented a total victory for clerical-political Catholicism. Looked at more closely, using the private papers of the actors, one realizes that it was also a victory for Franco, as he was able to consolidate his power despite an emerging opposition of monarchists, a pretender, and some of his advisers, who were even contemplating, albeit with great hesitation, a future democracy. Politically, it was a complex co-

Church and State in Spain 165

optation of an elite, some of whose members would end disillusioned and in the democratic opposition to Franco. National-Catholicism would be one of the many factors that would make the emergence of a Christian Democratic party impossible in 1975–1977.

The closeness of religion and politics led to conflicts which might seem incidental from the outside: the clergy was insatiable in demanding obedience of religious laypeople in politics on the basis of their commitment to the church, and the lay religious politicians, upset by any sign of independent judgment in matters affecting them, were equally relentless in demanding support from the hierarchy, even the Vatican.

The hegemony of Catholicism, paradoxically, also was apparent in the ways that cultural matters were affected by the narrow-minded views of many members of the religious orders and the church hierarchy, which contributed to the crisis of national-Catholicism in the universities and the assertion of a more independent Catholic intelligentsia.[9] The fact that re-Catholicization from above ultimately did not assure the conversion of those defeated in the civil war made some who had been involved in the missionary effort realize that perhaps that strategy was unviable, was not in the interest of the evangelic mission of the church, and was possibly even un-Christian.

Efforts of Catholic organizations to reach the working class and the criticism of the monopolistic conception of official trade unions would generate a new dynamic in the church of great importance years later.

The triumphalism of the church was particularly oppressive when exercised by a hierarchy and clergy largely of peasant background who were trained in seminaries with little contact with the secular culture and who often lacked esthetic sensitivity. They had been formed mainly in canon law and had made their careers mostly in ecclesiastical administration. Due to their rural lower-class background, they were reverential to those who had power and money, people who had made their own social ascent possible through fellowships and influence. That background explains this anti-intellectualism that was even extended to Catholic intellectuals and a new generation of priests with prior academic training, and led to condemnations and attacks against leading thinkers and the ridiculous censorship of movies and books. At times their asceticism,

166   *Juan J. Linz*

rigidity, sense of power, and dignity led the clergy into conflicts with Franco and the authorities.

The cooperation with the Vatican led to new ecclesiastical appointments, among them bishops who would undertake the disengagement of the church from the state and would provide a new pastoral outlook. At the end of this period the church, together with the army, was able to defeat the constitutionalization of a single party as the center of power. The success of such an attempt would probably have made the dismantling of the regime after Franco's death more difficult.

The identification of the state with Catholicism, or as the state interpreted it, the use of Catholicism and the support of the church to legitimize the regime, became a weakness for the regime. It was clear that the Spanish hierarchy and much of the clergy were not to question the mutually convenient alliance; however, the interpretation of Catholic political-social thought was heteronomous and was not in their hands. Since alternate Catholic interpretations were religiously legitimate as long as the Vatican did not condemn them, they could be rejected but not exorcised. As alternate interpretations were inevitably present, Spanish Catholics, both churchmen and laypeople, eventually began to discover them. They would read Maritain and other Catholic thinkers and use their ideas to question the regime. After Vatican II, as increasingly wider circles introduced ideas that clearly undermined the claims of the regime, Franco's government began to find itself on the defensive in its own arena. Even those churchpeople who were sympathetic to Franco could not fully support the violent reaction of the authorities and, instead, would defend organizations and individuals who were "good Catholics" but did not share regime-supporting interpretations of their Catholicism. The more the regime attempted to suppress such threatening tendencies, the more it risked a collision with the church, which would result in the church's declaration of independence from the state. Nothing within the regime disturbed its claim of legitimacy more than the questioning of its monopoly of Catholicism and led to demands that a changing church should reaffirm earlier positions. At the same time, its claim to be a Catholic regime limited the capacity of authorities to repress Catholic dissidence, although it would ultimately do so. In the last years of the regime the government was fining priests for their sermons, jailing members of the clergy, and

Church and State in Spain 167

considering the expulsion of a bishop, thereby risking the excommunication of the government.

The situation of the Spanish Catholic church and the Franco regime in the postwar period has important implications for the analysis of religion and politics everywhere. Any regime that relies on a religious basis of legitimation—particularly of transnational religion—risks a crisis of legitimacy should the political ethic of the religion change, in other words, should emerging clerics, religious intellectuals, and ecclesiastic leaders question the interpretation that served the regime. The heteronomous character of religion with respect to the polity is always a latent challenge.

The national-Catholic project in Spain, in spite of its apparent success, encountered limits and resistance within the regime itself. It was impossible to delete the legacy of a liberal secular culture in the same way as an anticlerical and anti-Catholic culture. The writers and thinkers of half a century could not be ignored nor the important impact of European intellectual life erased. The memory of another culture, one that was different but was not intentionally opposed to a clerically dominated culture, was kept alive by Ortega y Gasset, Unamuno, Baroja, and other writers. Specific works could be censored or suppressed but they remained an essential part of the national culture. As Spain attempted to incorporate itself into the Western world, its borders became more permeable and those seeds of dissent flourished. New generations of Catholic intellectuals defended their national secular legacy against the more obscurantist tendencies in the church. The intellectual poverty and the lack of aesthetic sensibility and artistic creativity of Spanish Catholicism over decades, with honorable exceptions, generated the dissent of the intellectuals, which would later spread to the student movement.

Although the Falange and its organizations did not challenge the triumphant church of the fifties, they provided a cover for some of the critics of hegemonic clericalism. The convergence of some men coming from that sector within the regime with more liberal Catholics provoked a crisis in the late fifties. It was no accident that a new cohort of Catholic conservative intellectual members of the Opus Dei would direct their hostility against those tendencies by trying to present their own efforts abroad as a "liberal" attack against the legacy of fascism. However, since fascism as an ideological alternative was now dead, many among those people slowly moved toward

168   *Juan J. Linz*

a liberal or social-democratic democracy, opposing the regime. In the meantime, their students, attracted by Marxism, were moving toward more radical positions. The Opus Dei intellectuals, with the support of the state, attempted to recover their initiative, but their conservative message did not find a large audience. The Opus could not revive the by now exhausted national-Catholic project without the support of the hierarchy that was experiencing the impact of Vatican II and other changes in the universal church and had personal links with Catholics expelled from power.

THE CRISIS OF NATIONAL-CATHOLICISM

The crisis of the "reactionary" church was initiated by a new cohort of clerics and Catholic intellectuals, who were in contact with the more liberal Falangist intelligentsia and, through them, with the non-Catholic intellectual heritage. This group would directly, and more often indirectly, play a political role that was, paradoxically, a result of the post–civil war Catholic triumphalism.

The reaffirmation of the Catholic identity under persecution and the hope for a religious revival led some of that generation, after they had finished their secular studies, had lived through the war, and had established social relations outside the clerical world, to choose late vocations in the church. They reacted to the atmosphere of the seminary—its life-style and intellectual poverty, the authoritarianism of superiors, and their efforts to isolate seminarians from the world, even the Catholic world outside—with a new curiosity and openness to other religious interpretations and established new networks among themselves. Not everyone in this generation would completely reject national-Catholicism. Some stopped at their loyalty to the regime, and a few, threatened by later more radical innovators, turned back to earlier reactionary positions, but the seeds for pluralism and openness had been planted.

Spanish bishops at the time of Vatican II were basically conservatives but they were affected by it as much as other episcopacies. They were possibly even more eager than those from other countries to find out what other bishops were thinking. Perhaps their previous isolation and their desire to be with "the church," that is, with the majority consensus, contributed to their openness.[10]

Church and State in Spain   169

The changed position first of the clergy and later of part of the hierarchy cannot be understood without reference to a profound social change that began in the late fifties and accelerated in the sixties. Because of the ways these changes were affecting the views of its members, the church was forced to recognize rather than ignore them. This was particularly true for those involved with the working class. The Catholic Action organizations of workers in Spain would experience the same evolution as those in France, generating conflict between the church and the regime when the hierarchy defended them, and within the church when it felt that it had lost its control. The lay Catholic working-class activists would later become the leaders of illegal trade unions and a new working-class movement.

In 1968 the church's response to the proposed trade union law aroused some tension. In the following years the problems would cumulate: those derived from the appointment of bishops, the Basque problem, sit-ins in the churches, the joint assembly of bishops and priests, the presence of bishops in the Franco Cortes, and so on. A declaration by the church in 1973 represented a decisive step in its thinking. As summarized by Cardinal Tarancón, it was a clear defense of the plurality of political options that could be derived from faith and commitment to justice, church participation in the transformation of the world as an integral part of the preaching of the gospel, mutual independence of the church and the political community, and the healthy cooperation of both in the common service to mankind. This was a new language.[11]

In Europe conflicts between church and state generally have been a result of policies of the state, liberal or Left anticlericalism, efforts of secularization, and "state paganism." In the late Franco regime there was no change in the position of the state initiating the conflict but a profound change in the church.

The motivation of that change was a religious *examen de conciencia*—an examination which, in view of the position of the church in the society and the ideology of national-Catholicism, had to lead to a critical analysis of the relation of the church with the society and the polity. The unrest among the clergy led the hierarchy to convene a joint consultative meeting of bishops and priests after preparatory assemblies in the dioceses.[12] The representatives were neither the radicals nor the ultraconservatives who had voluntarily isolated

170   *Juan J. Linz*

themselves. On September 13, 1971, this joint meeting of bishops
and 169 priests representing the dioceses voted for a proposition:

> We humbly recognize and ask for pardon because we did not know
> [how] to be, at its [due] time; true ministers of reconciliation in the
> midst of our people, divided by a war among brothers.

The necessary two-thirds vote was not obtained and the resolution
went back to the committee. The assembly generated a complex
intrigue in the Vatican by Spanish churchmen, but the Pope publicly
disauthorized maneuvers by conservative members of the *curia* and
the regime. A few days later Cardinal Tarancón was elected Chairman of the Episcopal Commission. It is difficult to convey the
hostility that the independent position of the church, led by Tarancón, generated among right wing radicals with the support of some
clergymen, the sympathy of some bishops, and a tolerant government. After the funeral of Prime Minister Carrero Blanco, who had
been assasinated by ETA terrorists, the hostility culminated in threats
and demonstrations under the slogan "Tarancón al paredón":
Tarancón to the execution wall.

Under the leadership of Tarancón, with the support of the majority
in the Episcopal Conference, the hierarchy was able to maintain its
solidarity with fellow bishops who were now stepping beyond more
pastoral concerns. It was a solidarity based ultimately on a commitment to the integrity and independence of the institution. But it was
also this affirmation of independence which was so challenging to the
regime and was the source of its disappointment and feelings of
betrayal. Tarancón recalls that in a conversation with a cabinet
member who argued about what was in the best interest of the
church, he had to tell him: "Remember, Mr. Minister, that here the
bishop is me. You should defend the interests of the state and let me
state which should be the position of the church."

One of the paradoxes of the late years of the Franco regime is that
the regime's opponents, many of whom had never had ties with the
church or had stopped being practicing Catholics, needed and found
support in the church. They wrote for publications sponsored or born
in the religious realm, held their meetings in convents, and sponsored
assemblies of strikers and sit-ins in churches. Funerals of victims of
the struggle and repression became political events, and the church
intervened on behalf of those being tried and sentenced by the

government for insurrection. It was the longtime autonomy of the ecclesiastical realm and a commitment to the church that allowed the opposition to claim its political space, sometimes even the most radical.

It is important to emphasize that while the actions of individual priests were based on sincere moral convictions, the actions of their defenders, although they did not share their sentiments and were even less approving of their actions, were not moved by opportunism either, as the Francoites often said, but by a mixture of respect for the sincerity of those men and women, the insistence on the sacred status of the priests and even more of a bishop, the sanctity of ecclesiastic premises, and so on. It is ironic that a very "clerical" conception of the church was used to protect those who put traditional clericalism into question.

THE CHURCH IN THE NEW DEMOCRACY

The death of Franco (1975), the transition to a democracy (1975–1977), the new Constitution (1978), and the coming to power of the Socialists (1982) was not as traumatic to the church as the proclamation of the Republic in 1931, nor even a significant threat. Important changes in the church had taken place in the late years of the Franco regime, and for years its leadership had been preparing for the transition. The same was true for the opposition, particularly the Communist party, which wanted to avoid a confrontation with the church. The contrast with 1931 could not be greater.

A decisive factor was this time people in the church and Catholic organizations were involved in the opposition of the regime. In addition, the embittered reaction of the authorities had ended the church's identification with the government. The carefully planned private mass for Franco and the public homily of Cardinal Tarancón on the occasion of the proclamation of King Juan Carlos set the tone of the church toward the transition.

In refusing to encourage or support a Christian Democratic party, the Spanish Catholic church took a position that differentiates it from the Catholic church in other Western European countries and in Chile.[13] In 1976–1977, without the support of the church, the already fragmented Christian Democratic forces could not wage a successful organizational and electoral drive. With only 1.4 percent

172   *Juan J. Linz*

of the vote, their fate was sealed. These facts made it obvious that any further discussion about a "church party" would be irrelevant.

In the context of moderate democratic politics, the acceptable compromise on church-state relations in the Constitution, the absence of a communist menace, and the post-Vaticanum church, the lack of success of the Christian Democratic party gave the church the advantage of greater independence and the ability to take positions without appearing partisan, although perhaps at the cost of a more limited influence.

The drafting of a new constitution was a potential threat since it involved the separation of church and state and "mixed matters" like education, in which the stakes for the church were high. After some tensions, in which the actors were the parties and their representatives rather than the hierarchy or the public, the basic texts that were eventually chosen were acceptable to the church and were perhaps more favorable than could have been expected.[14]

Separation of church and state is one of the ideas that many associate with democracy. A number of democracies however have established churches or relations of cooperation between state and church, and others like Spain in 1931 have, invoking that principle, legislated profusely on religious matters and deprived religious organizations and their members of rights recognized to all citizens, like holding certain offices, engaging in teaching and commercial pursuits, and the right to property and compensation in case of expropriation. To say therefore that separation of church and state goes with democracy is an oversimplification, and to describe the pattern of relations in those terms without specifying it further is misleading.

The 1978 Spanish Constitution, like that of 1931, formally separates religion and the state, but the specific norms and above all the spirit with which this principle was introduced are fundamentally different. Nothing can convey that difference better than the texts themselves; for example, Article 6 of the 1978 Constitution reads:

> (1) Freedom of ideology, religion, and worship of individuals and communities is guaranteed with no more restrictions on their expression as may be necessary in order to maintain public order protected by law.

> (2) Nobody may be compelled to make declarations regarding his religion, beliefs, or ideologies.

Church and State in Spain   173

(3) There shall be no state religion. The public authorities shall take the religious beliefs of Spanish Society into account and shall maintain the consequent relations of cooperation with the Catholic Church and other confessions.

The 1931 Constitution had simply stated in Article 5: "The Spanish State has no official religion," and it was in these terms that religious freedom was stated and *regulated* in Article 27:

The freedom of conscience and the right to profess and practice freely any religion is guaranteed in the Spanish territory except for the respect due to the demands of public morals. Cemeteries shall be subject exclusively to civil jurisdiction. There cannot be in them separation of enclosures for religious reasons. All the confessions can exercise their cults privately. The public manifestations of cult shall be, in each case, authorized by the government. No one can be compelled to declare officially his religious beliefs. The religious condition will not constitute a modifying circumstance of civil and political personality, except in what is stated in this Constitution for the appointment of President of the Republic and to be President of the Council of Ministers.

The different conception of religion in 1978 is reflected in the recognition granted to the rights not only of individuals but "communities," in the mention of the religious belief of the society, in the injunction in favor of "cooperation" (in contrast to the individualistic and private rather than public character of religions in 1931), and in the inclusion in the article on religious freedom of 1931 of a public regulation and exclusion from the religious sphere of sacred areas like cemeteries.

In Catholicism, as in a number of other religions, in contrast to most Protestant churches and sects, religious orders are an essential part of the institution and their activities are central to its religious mission; therefore, any regulation affecting them touches religious freedom as defined by the church. The 1978 Constitution, in contrast to that of 1931, does not separately regulate the right to create or join religious orders, nor their property, nor their activities, and it is assumed that their rights fall under the general regulation of freedom of association and other freedoms.

Article 26 of the 1931 Constitution of the Republic had regulated the status of religious orders by stipulating that they were to be prohibited from engaging in industry, commerce, or teaching. The

174   *Juan J. Linz*

Prime Minister Azaña was aware of the importance of the last prohibition when he said: "that will displease the liberals" and said that it was the obligation of republicans, of Spaniards, to prevent it at all costs, by closing his statement with: "Don't tell me that this is contrary to freedom because this is a question of public health."[15] In all Catholic countries and in many non-Catholic ones the freedom to teach and to establish, within certain limits, educational institutions has been one of the most controversial issues between churches and governments. On this point also the 1978 Constitution differs radically from that of 1931. The monopoly of *escuela pública única*, still maintained in the Socialist party program in 1976, was abandoned, and public support of educational centers was allowed under certain conditions, although this would continue to be the object of prolonged debate.

Today Spain is the model of a friendly or at least nonantagonistic separation of church and state, in a way that is similar to the Federal Republic of Germany. This has been the result of a break with the long tradition of church establishment and the legally privileged position of the church but also of a clear rejection of a laicist state that would want to push religion into the private realm and control its public manifestation and influence, for example, in education. It is normatively different from the American model of separation in the sense that it allows cooperation between the church and the state and recognizes the special position of Catholicism in Spanish society.

HOW TO CHARACTERIZE THE POSITION OF THE CHURCH IN CONTEMPORARY SPANISH SOCIETY

The Spanish Catholic church has successfully weathered the potential threats—feared for many years—of the change of an authoritarian regime it had been identified with to a democratic state. Moreover, the Catholic church claims, and to some extent its claim is valid, to have facilitated and even to have contributed to the change. The hierarchy and the mass of the faithful have accepted and supported the new regime and have not condoned attempts of involution. (This does not mean that some segments of the extreme Right have not continued to identify themselves with Catholicism.) The church as an institution and a large number of practicing Catholics have not completely rejected the past regime, but it is now merely a more or

Church and State in Spain 175

less favorable memory which becomes more faded with the passing of time. Few desire a return of national-Catholicism. While the church is obviously unhappy with constitutional provisions on church and state and laws like divorce and limited legalization of abortion, it has not made concerted efforts to question them and does not openly advocate their revision.

This development has been possible in part because of changes in the church after Vatican II but is also a result of changes in the secular and even areligious political forces. The church has not wanted to be associated with clericalism, intolerance, and rigidity, and the Left has not wanted to resurrect the specter of anticlericalism and religious persecution, both associated with the memory of the conflict in the thirties and the civil war. All parties have agreed on "never again." There have been some discordant voices in the broad consensus achieved by the Episcopal Conference, as well as shifts within that consensus, but those voices have not been able to disturb the relations of church and state, nor have they been able to polarize the clergy and the faithful.

The church is not apolitical, it never can be, but it is as nonpartisan as possible, and that is what most of the faithful and those who are nonpracticing and religiously indifferent expect from it. This nonpartisanship is both a weakness and a strength. It could be argued that caution in the transition and the internal heterogeneity and conflicts within the clergy were decisive in achieving the political neutrality of the church. But this neutral position has also resulted from a certain unwillingness of large segments of the faithful to follow the advice of the church in political matters. We now find a church that is outside main political controversies, although it is not silent on issues it considers central, when it hopes to influence the faithful rather than push itself into the political sphere. That withdrawal, which might not be permanent, has made the church less relevant to those who do not count among its faithful and has allowed them to be benevolently indifferent to it.[16]

One of the basic components of the present pattern of church and state relations in Spain is the fact that most debates are not formulated in ideological terms. Neither the church nor the state will make references to past conflicts and positions in order to strengthen their case, and, instead, will limit their debates to the constitutionality of specific norms and their compatibility with the spirit of the constitu-

176   *Juan J. Linz*

tion, which reflects a consensus and is upheld by all as an ideal not to be abandoned. In using the constitution to resolve disagreements, the parties involved take their issues to the Tribunal Constitucional, which has managed to gain considerable respect and whose decisions have not been challenged. This tendency to "juridify" conflicts, however, makes them less meaningful to the average citizen and contributes to a certain depoliticization that characterizes Spanish democracy today, especially in contrast to the overheated political atmosphere of the thirties.

The need to show the relevance of religion to the modern world and to avoid the reduction of religion to the sphere of private morality has led the church to a more progressive stance on social and economic issues, the third world, and peace. These are areas which allow room for convergence with the Left but also for strong postures with little political cost.

One conclusion that might be drawn from the experience of the Spanish Catholic church in the twentieth century is that if a society changes profoundly—by evolution, rather than revolution—the church like other institutions is able to adapt and even participate in that change, especially if the change is social and cultural rather than political. That might explain why the Republic (1931–1936) did not generate change like that in the late years of the Franco regime and democracy, when political change and change within the church was a result of slow but massive changes in society. Secularization in the thirties required a militant secularizing authority undermining what it perceived as control by the church of the uneducated masses, the women, the peasantry, the lower middle class, and the elites through the confessional. The goal could only be achieved through anticlerical propaganda, by isolating the church, preventing it from educating the youth, and so on. In contrast, the secularization of Spain today is the result of social, economic, and cultural change rather than massive political upheaval.

ENDNOTES

[1]The long essay "Iglesia y Religión en la España contemporánea" by Victor Pérez Díaz in *El retorno de la sociedad civil* (Madrid: Instituto de Estudios Económicos, 1987), 411–66, is the most insightful analysis of the church in Spanish society. In many respects it could take the place of this essay. I have felt tempted to reproduce

Church and State in Spain   177

his arguments almost verbatim since I am in substantial agreement with his excellent analysis.

2The best book on the Spanish church is Stanley G. Payne, *Spanish Catholicism: An Historical Overview* (Madison: University of Wisconsin Press, 1984).

3On the conflict between the church and the Second Republic, see José M. Sánchez, *Reform and Reaction: The Politico Religious Background of the Spanish Civil War* (Chapel Hill: University of North Carolina Press, 1964). For the constitutional debate in 1931, see the excellent study by Víctor Manuel Arbeloa, *La semana trágica de la iglesia en España (1931)* (Barcelona: Galba, 1976). Incidentally, Arbeloa is a priest, now leader of the PSOE in Navarra and member of parliament. Miguel Larazony de la Rosa, et. al., eds., *Legislación Española: Leyes religiosas según los textos oficiales* (Madrid: J. M. Yagües, 1935).

4On the persecution of the church in the civil war, Antonio Montero Moreno, *Historia de la persecución religiosa en España 1936–1939* (Madrid: Biblioteca de Autores Cristianos, 1961). The persecution in the civil war cost the lives of 4,184 members of the secular clergy, including seminarians, 2,365 male members of religious orders, and 283 female members—a total of 6,832 religious persons. This means 13 percent of the priests and 23 percent of the members of the orders of the Spanish total, even though only part of the country was controlled by the revolutionaries. In some dioceses the proportion of regular clergy killed reached over 80 percent.

5Jesús Iribarren, ed., *Documentos colectivos del episcopado español 1870–1974* (Madrid: Biblioteca de Autores Cristianos, 1974); Ramón Comas, *Isidro Gomá, Francese Vidal i Barraquer: Dos visiones antagónicas de la Iglesia española de 1939* (Salamanca: Sígueme, 1977); Cardenal Isidro Gomá y Tomás, *Pastorales de la guerra de España* (Madrid: Rialp, 1955). For a history of the regime, see Stanley G. Payne, *The Franco Regime, 1936–1976* (Madison, University of Wisconsin Press, 1987); and Javier Tusell, *La dictadura de Franco* (Madrid: Alianza Editorial, 1988).

6On the incorporation of Catholicism into Spanish fascism and its reservations toward "foreign movements of a similar type," see Payne, *The Franco Regime,* 203–6.

7Antonio Marquina Barrio, *La diplomacia vaticana y la España de Franco* (Madrid: Consejo Superior de Investigaciones Científicas, 1983).

8Javier Tusell, *Franco y los católicos: La política interior española entre 1945 y 1957* (Madrid: Alianza, 1984) is the best historical monograph on this crucial period based on published and private archival sources. Guy Hermet, *Les catholiques dans l'Espagne franquiste* 2 vols. (Paris: Presses de la Fondation Nationale des Sciences Politiques, 1980–1981) is the best and most documented monograph on the subject.

9Federico Sopeña, *Defensa de una generación* (Madrid: Taurus, 1978).

10Rock Caporale, *Vatican II: Last of the Councils* (Baltimore: Helicon, 1964).

11The best sources to understand the period 1971 to 1981, when Vicente Enrique Tarancón was president of the Episcopal Conference, is the book-length interview/dialogue: J. L. Martín Descalzo, *Tarancón, el cardenal del cambio* (Barce-

178   *Juan J. Linz*

lona: Planeta, 1982); see also the collective work, *Al servicio de la Iglesia y del pueblo, Homenaje al Cardenal Tarancón en su 75 aniversario* (Madrid: Narcea, 1984), which includes an essay by him, "Perspectivas de la Iglesia en España" and a bibliography of his writings. A first volume of memoirs: Vicente Enrique y Tarancón, *Recuerdos de juventud* (Barcelona: Grijalbo, 1984) is a revealing document on the experience of the years before and up to the end of the civil war. His book *¿Examen de conciencia o "autocritica"?* (Madrid: Euroamérica, 1955) includes pastoral letters of 1955 and 1956 and is useful in understanding the development of his thought.

[12]*Asamblea Conjunta. Obispos-sacerdote: Historia de la Asamblea,* Edición preparada por el Secretario General del Clero (Madrid: Biblioteca de Autores Cristianos, Editorial Católica S. A., 1971).

[13]On the absence of a Christian Democratic party and the presence of Christian Democratic politicians see, Carlos Huneeus *La Unión de Centro Democrático y la transición a la democracia en España* (Madrid: Centro de Investigaciones Sociológicas-Siglo XXI de España, 1985). On the relation between religiosity, political attitudes, and electoral behavior in democratic Spain, see J. Linz, "Religion and Politics in Spain: From Conflict to Consensus above Cleavage," *Social Compas* 27 (2–3) (1980): 255–77; see also Richard Gunther, and J. Linz, "Religión y política," in J. Linz and José R. Montero, eds., *Crisis y cambio: Electores y partidos en la España de los años ochenta* (Madrid: Instituto de Estudios Constitucionales, 1986), 201–56; this is based on a 1982 election survey.

[14]Richard Gunther and Roger Blough, "Religious Conflict and Consensus in Spain: A Tale of Two Constitutions," *World Affairs* 143 (Spring 1981); Jaime Pérez-Llantada y Gutiérrez, "La dialéctica 'Estado-Religión' ante el momento constitucional," in Tomás R. Fernández Rodríguez, ed., *Lecturas sobre la Constitución española* vol. 2 (Madrid: Universidad Nacional de Educación a Distancia, Facultad de Derecho, 1978), 129–62. On the church and state tensions on education, see Luis Gómez Llorente, *Alternativa socialista a la enseñanza,* Club Siglo XXI (Madrid: Unión Editorial, 1979); Documentos Colectivos del Episcopado Español sobre Formación Religiosa y Educación 1969–1980, Comisión Episcopal de Enseñanza y Catequesis; and Oscar Alzaga, *Por la libertad de enseñanza* (Barcelona: Planeta, 1985).

[15]Manuel Azaña, *Obras completas: Una política en el poder y en la oposición* vol. 2 (Mexico: Oasis, 1966), 49–58.

[16]On the role of religion in the society in the eighties, Francisco Andrés Orizo, *España, entre la apatía y el cambio social: Una encuesta sobre el sistema europeo de valores: el caso español* (Madrid: MAPFRE, 1983), 145–96. For an excellent overview by a close collaborator of Tarancón, see José María Martín Patino, "La Iglesia en la sociedad española," in J. Linz, ed., *España, un presente para el futuro: La sociedad* (Madrid: Instituto de Estudios Económicos, 1984), 151–212. See also, Vicente E. y Tarancón and Marcelo González y Narciso Jubany, *Iglesia y política en la España de hoy,* with foreward and introduction by Olegario González de Cardedal (Salamanca, Ediciones Sígueme, 1980).

Part III
Religion and Electoral Politics

[15]

Regional and Religious Support of Political Parties and Effects on their Issue Positions

KENNETH JANDA

ABSTRACT. Political sociology assumes that social cleavages are manifested in political alignments. This research focuses on the cleavage factors of region and religion in group support of national political parties. It discusses problems in analyzing these factors across cultures and illustrates the problems by analyzing social support for approximately 150 parties in 53 nations in all cultural-geographical areas of the world. Regional and religious patterns of support clearly affect parties' positions on issues. Regionally homogeneous parties tend to oppose national integration, and religiously homogeneous parties tend to oppose the secularization of society. Moreover, parties' positions on secularization also depend heavily on their specific religious composition.

In their pioneering work, Lipset and Rokkan (1967) contend that patterns of support for political parties may be determined by four decisive lines of cleavage: center–periphery, state–church, land–industry, and owner–worker. This formulation of cleavages is based on political issues rather than sociological divisions. Lipset and Rokkan also refer to political alignments based solely on indicators of cultural diversity, such as region, class, and religious denomination (p. 3). Nordlinger (1972) distinguishes social divisions based on *class* (wealth, income, occupation, and education) from those based on *communal* factors (race, tribe, religion, language, and ethnicity). Nordlinger's dichotomy needs to be supplemented by *spatial* factors, such as region and urban–rural place. Although there are probably other bases of social divisions, this is already an impressive list of factors to study for their effects on party support and issue positions across the world.

The Study of Social and Political Cleavages

Of all the possible bases of social cleavage, social class (in some variant) has loomed largest in the analysis of party support. Lipset once claimed, "On a world scale, the principal generalization which can be made is that parties are primarily based on either the lower classes or the middle and upper classes" (1960: 220). Research on the cross-national analysis of party support by social class, compared with research on communal factors, is aided by two facts:

0192-5121/89/04 0349–22

1. *The influence of social class is pervasive*—virtually every society is divided into social classes. In contrast, communal factors are inherently limited in scope; not every society can be meaningfully divided into racial, tribal, religious, language, and ethnic groupings. Where such divisions are meaningful, they may not travel well across societies. Religion, for example, is politically important in India, Lebanon, and France—but in quite different ways.

2. *Social class can be measured on an ordered metric*—from lower to upper. Ordinality is obvious when wealth, income, or education are used as indicators of class, but even occupation (normally a nominal variable) can be ordered for cross-national analysis (low to high prestige). In contrast, communal factors are inherently nominal variables and resist ordered classification even in a single society.

Spatial factors (region and urban–rural) fall somewhere between class and communal factors in their tractability for cross-national analysis. Spatial variables apply to virtually every country, for only the smallest (e.g., San Marino) lack regional or urban–rural variation. But the two variables present different problems in measurement. Region is the quintessential nominal variable—deriving its meaning for political analysis from the geography, history, and administrative structure peculiar to each country. Consequently, regions that have similar names—for example, "south" and "north"—usually lack any basis for comparison across nations. So it makes little sense to compare parties with strong support in the south of the United States even with those that are strong in the south of England—much less in the south of India.

On the other hand, the urban–rural variable is inherently orderable, and the ordinal categories travel well in analysis across nations. It is reasonable to compare parties with strong support in urban areas in the United States with those that have strong support in cities in Britain. However, it is more difficult to obtain data on party support by urban and rural areas than party support by region. Because election results are usually reported by administrative districts, they can almost always be aggregated into regions to measure party support. But election results cannot be aggregated into homogeneous urban and rural areas as easily.

This paper addresses the cross-national analysis of party support by region and religion. Both types of variable are difficult to employ across nations because they are stubbornly nominal, but they differ in their tractability in other ways. Whereas suitable data are more readily available for region than for religion, religious classifications have more capacity for cross-national comparisons than regional categories. Before analyzing parties across the world for regional and religious support, we would benefit from reviewing major studies of party support in Western nations, where the data are better but the scope more limited.

Party Support in Western Europe

I will briefly review three studies of the social bases of party support in Western Europe. The approaches and findings of these studies provide background for a broader analysis of region and religion in party support.

Social Cohesion in Western Parties. In their pioneering work, Rose and Urwin (1969) analyzed social cohesion of 76 political parties in 17 Western nations on five differentiators: religious, regional, communal (ethnic and linguistic), urban–rural, and class. Among these possible bases of social division, they found only region relevant for analyzing party support in every nation. Occupation was a basis of distinction in every country except Ireland (but one suspects that the lack of good data on party support by occupation for Ireland also contributed to its omission). Urban–rural divisions were relevant as a basis of party distinction in all but three nations, and religion was politically relevant in all but five. On the other hand, true communal divisions in party support were lacking in 12 of the 17 nations.

After identifying relevant bases of party support in each nation, Rose and Urwin computed the percentage that each subgroup contributed to the party's composition, while adjusting for the subgroup's size in the population. They defined a party as "socially cohesive" if some minimum percentage (usually 67 percent) of its supporters shared a given characteristic *and* if they did so beyond some minimum percentage of that social group's size in the country.[1] For example, although 85 percent of the supporters of the Australian Liberal-Country party were Protestant, Protestants also accounted for 76 percent of the population. Consequently, Rose and Urwin did not score the Liberal-Country party as distinctively cohesive on religion. In contrast, the Democratic Labor party, which was 60 percent Catholic, qualified as religiously cohesive.

Rose and Urwin calculated that religion figured in the social cohesion of 35 parties, class in 33 parties, region in 8, communalism in 7, and urban–rural in only 4. Their findings challenged Lipset's claim that social class was the dominant basis of party support across nations. At least in their study of Western nations, Rose and Urwin found that parties were more cohesive on religion than on any other social factor. However, by demanding that parties meet their arbitrary standard of cohesion, they may have set the criterion too high to detect the more subtle but more pervasive effects of social class.

Regionalism. In subsequent research, Rose and Urwin focused on region as a factor in party support, noting that "all states other than city-states have some kind of territorial differentiation" (1975: 5). This time they analyzed regional patterns in voting for 108 parties in 19 nations over two elections—one in the 1940s and the other around 1970. (Note that Rose and Urwin were able to expand their study over time and space because of the ready availability of electoral data by regions.) Although they frequently found subtle-to-strong patterns of support for different parties by regions, Rose and Urwin—using a somewhat different methodology— again did not find much regional cohesion among the parties. Focusing on only those parties contesting the second election, they wrote:

> In practice, "party dominant" regions are rare in Western nations today. Six countries . . . have no party winning as many as two-thirds of the seats in a single region. Overall, only 17 of 94 Western parties took as many as two-thirds of the seats in at least one region within their nation (1975: 32).
>
> The findings are consistent: Political regionalism, in the sense of areas giving nearly all their support to one party, does not exist in the Western world today and only a small number of countries (e.g., Canada, Switzerland and Belgium) have very distinctive regional parties (1975: 38).

By requiring areas to give "nearly all their support to one party," Rose and Urwin again demanded a great deal to establish regional effects. Although this strict criterion conformed to their major interest in studying separatist threats to national units, a more flexible approach would certainly have detected regional influences in party support in many more cases. Of course, more flexible methods would have produced problems in disentangling regional effects from the effects of other variables that are confounded with regional boundaries.

Region and Religion. Ersson, Janda, and Lane (1985) designed a study to separate regional effects on party support from the effects of social factors. They analyzed votes cast by region for 93 parties in 16 Western nations over three successive elections ranging from the late 1960s to the late 1970s. Their regional data included variables on employment in industry and agriculture, distribution of income, religion, and ethnic structure. They sought to assess the explanatory potential of regions versus the other social factors through two modes of analysis.

One mode used the regions in each country as nominal variables in a one-way analysis of variance, using the votes cast for each party over all three elections as the dependent variable. In this simple test, region emerged as a very potent independent variable, explaining an average of 75 percent of the variance in party support for all 16 countries.[2] The strongest regional effects were observed in Belgium, where 91 percent of the variance in party voting across 30 districts was associated with individual districts. In fact, region explained more than 60 percent of the variance in every country except Spain (48 percent) and Greece (40 percent).

The other mode of analysis used ecological data on three to five social variables (depending on the country) in ordinary multiple regression to predict the results for the same three elections. Taken together, these social factors explained only an average of 40 percent of the variance in party support for all 16 countries. Again, the variables worked best for Belgium, where five regional indicators of industrial employment, farming activity, income, religion, and Dutch language explained an average of 71 percent of the variance in votes cast for six parties. These factors worked poorest in Greece, where three indicators of industrial employment, farming, and wealth explained only an average of 6 percent of the variance over four parties.

Commenting on the superiority of region over the other social variables in predicting to party support, the authors noted that region was not merely a spatial variable but a stand-in for political tradition and a host of other hidden factors, some of which interact with one another. When used to analyze party support, region substitutes for a complex mix of variables. Even if the mix of variables were known, it would probably exceed the capabilities of ordinary multiple regression. Rather than wondering why a set of three to five social variables explains only 40 percent of party support, one might wonder why it explains so much.

The authors analyzed the patterns of the largest coefficients in all 93 regression analyses to determine which social factors had the greatest effects on party support. They found that religion and industrial employment were present as cleavage dimensions in most West European countries (Ersson, Janda, and Lane, 1985: 186). Interpreting percent employed in industry as a surrogate for social class, Ersson, Janda, and Lane—using very different methodology—thus confirmed the conclusions of Rose and Urwin in identifying both religion and class as major bases of party alignments in Western societies.

Holonational Research on Party Support

In political sociology, cross-national analysis is usually limited to Western nations—Western Europe plus the Anglo-American democracies of Australia, Canada, New

Zealand, and the United States. Much can be learned from such comparative analysis across nations with similar cultures. But to extend our powers of analysis, we should also compare political systems across nations with different cultures. This requires using a sample of nations drawn from various cultural-geographical regions of the world. The anthropologist Raoul Naroll (1972) used the term "holonational" to describe cross-national studies that employ worldwide representative samples.

Comparative research can uncover problems in conceptualization and analysis that escape notice by scholars who focus on a given country. For example, survey research on voting behavior in the United States has employed a unidimensional scale of party identification (Democrats at one end, Independents in the middle, Republicans at the other) that ignores problems in measuring party identification in systems with more than two parties. As a result, the most widely used scale of party identification in the United States treats Independents as a middle category, which produces difficulties in analysis. Perhaps if the original measure had been developed in systems with more than two parties, we would now have better measures of party identification in the United States extending over a longer period of time.

Holonational research on support for political parties across different cultures very quickly uncovers problems of conceptualization and analysis. Some problems can be readily resolved; some cannot. But whether or not they can be readily resolved, confronting problems in cross-cultural analysis usually increases the generality of analysis.

The data for this holonational study of party support come from the International Comparative Political Parties (ICPP) Project (Janda, 1979). The ICPP Project surveyed 158 parties operating in 53 countries during 1950–62. Fifty of these nations were drawn at random in lots of five from each of ten cultural-geographical areas of the world. The other three nations—Britain, the United States, and Canada—were added to the sample for substantive reasons. All parties in each nation that won 5 percent of the legislative seats over two consecutive elections were included in the study. The parties were coded separately for two time periods (1950–56 and 1957–62) for 111 variables (Janda, 1980). This study focuses on only the 147 parties that existed in the later period and on only a few of the available variables.

Conceptualizing and Measuring Social Support

Support for political parties by social groups was assessed according to six potential dimensions of cleavage: (1) socioeconomic status (usually occupation), (2) religion, (3) ethnicity (including language and race), (4) region, (5) urban-rural, and (6) education. The particular groups coded within each of these dimensions varied from country to country, depending on both the historical circumstances of the country and the availability of data resources for coding the parties. Thus, in a Western country the religious groups might be "Catholic", "Protestant," or "Other," while in a Third World country the categories might be "Devout Muslim" or "Nominal Muslim". For all parties within a given country, however, the groups for any given cleavage were identical.

The procedure for scoring the parties on social cleavages can be described with reference to Table 1, which outlines the general case for any country. The columns at the top contained the categories for a given dimension in that country, and the rows contained the parties operating in that country. Party support is conceptualized as adult citizens who identify with the party, not just party members. There are two

354   *Regional and Religious Support of Political Parties and Effects on their Issue Positions*

Table 1. *Support for* n *Parties across* k *Social Groups.*

	Group₁	Group₂	....	Groupₖ	Total %
Party₁	xx	xx	.	xx	100
Party₂	xx	xx	.	xx	100
.		.	.	.	.
.		.	.	.	.
Partyₙ	xx	xx	.	xx	100
Total %	100	100	.	100	

$$(1)\ Social\ Attraction = 1 - \cfrac{\dfrac{\overset{k}{\underset{j=1}{\Sigma}} |X_j - \overline{X}|}{k} \Big/ \overline{X}}{\dfrac{2(k-1)}{k}},$$

Where k is the number of subgroups within the cleavage dimension included in the analysis; X_j is the proportion of the jth group's support given to the party; and $\overline{X}$ is the mean proportion of support for the party, calculated over all social groupings, k.

Method 1 is used to create a measure of *social attraction*, as defined by Formula 1. This measures the extent to which the party attracts supports evenly from each significant subgroup within any cleavage dimension. It ranges from 0.0 to 1.0, with higher values meaning higher attraction. A score of 1.0 is achieved only if there is *no* variation in the percentages of support received by the party from the different social groups in the analysis. A score of 0 results only if a party receives *all* the support of one group while winning *no* support from any other.

$$(2)\ Social\ Concentration = \cfrac{\overset{k}{\underset{j=1}{\Sigma}} Y_j^2 - 1/k}{1 - 1/k},$$

Where k is the number of subgroups within the cleavage dimension included in the analysis and Y_j is the proportion of the party's support coming from the jth subgroup of k groups.

Method 2 is used to create a measure of *social concentration*, as defined by Formula 2. This measures the extent to which party supporters are concentrated in specific subgroups within a cleavage dimension. It ranges from 0.0–when the party's support comes equally from the competing groups– to 1.0, when one group contributes all the party's supporters.

ways of assessing party support from this data table: (1) by computing support as a percent of the *group's* preferences for a party, or (2) by computing support from each group as a percent of the party's *total* preferences. Computing percentages by columns conforms to method 1; computing percentages by rows conforms to method 2.

Wherever possible, the ICPP Project used data from official records or sample surveys to score each party on each potential base of support. Although survey data were best for this purpose, such data, even when available, did not guarantee our scoring a party on a base of support. If the survey researchers did not think the social factor was politically important, it was usually omitted from the survey. In the absence of survey data, we used facts and statements in the literature to estimate party support.[3] Again, if authors did not regard a social factor as important, they tended not to mention it as a basis of party support. Although the lack of suitable data (particularly in Third World nations) undoubtedly decreased our overall ability to code parties for support, our success in scoring parties on social factors indicates the relevance of each potential social factor for party alignment.[4]

KENNETH JANDA   355

I will illustrate how the attraction and concentration formulas were applied with an example of two parties coded for religious support. Based on authors' comments in the literature on Indonesian politics in the early 1960s, I scored the Indonesian Nationalist Party (PNI) as attracting 7 percent of the Devout Muslims (Santri), 33 percent of the larger group of Nominal Muslims (Abangan), and 10 percent of the small minority professing "Other" religions.[5] When these figures were entered into the attraction formula, the PNI obtained a score of 0.50. This was higher than the attraction score of 0.34 obtained by the Muslim Scholars Party (Nahdatul Ulama, NU), which drew support less evenly from Devout Muslims (40 percent), Nominal Muslims (12 percent), and those of Other religions (virtually none).

When the data were recalculated to express the percent of the parties' support that came from each religious group, Devout and Nominal Muslims respectively accounted for 9 and 88 percent of the PNI, compared with 63 and 37 percent of the NU. Entered into the concentration score, these figures produce a value of 0.65 for the PNI and 0.30 for the NU. The PNI's higher score indicates that nearly all of its support was concentrated within a particular group, Nominal Muslims (a point I will discuss later).

Except at the extremes of certain limiting conditions, the attraction and concentration measures are free to vary independently of each other, thus offering two different perspectives from which to evaluate the social bases of party support. Social attraction can be conceived as a measure of party "heterogeneity," and parties high on attraction can be regarded as socially "diverse" or "catch-all" in nature. Social concentration, on the other hand, is a measure of party "homogeneity," and parties high on concentration can be regarded as socially "cohesive," in the sense used by Rose and Urwin (1969). As expected, these measures are negatively related empirically.[6]

As Figure 1 illustrates, we scored more parties for support on occupation and region than for any other social factor. In the case of occupation, this probably reflects the pervasiveness of social class in party politics, as Lipset contended. In the case of region, the high incidence of scoring undoubtedly reflects the existence of electoral data from official records. To some extent, our success in scoring parties according to urban–rural divisions also comes from election results published for major cities.

We were much less successful in scoring parties for religion and education, and least successful by far in scoring parties for ethnicity. With education, we usually suffered from the lack of hard data or an absence of writers' comments on its relevance to party cleavages. Religion and ethnicity are a different story, however. Even lacking good data, writers usually stated whether parties were divided by the communal factors of religion and ethnicity. Whenever writers mentioned these factors as bases of party division, we scored the parties from their statements.

Because the lack of writers' comments about religious bases of party support implies the lack of cleavage, religion appears to be less important than occupation in differentiating parties throughout the world. That is, religion appears to be unimportant when judged by the criterion of pervasiveness (frequency of mention). By that criterion, region—not religion—appears to rival occupation in importance.

Scholars regard the social composition of a party as important because they assume that the structure of social support affects party policies and actions. Whether either regional or religious support for political parties affects their positions on regional or religious issues remains to be demonstrated. We will consider first the case of regionalism.

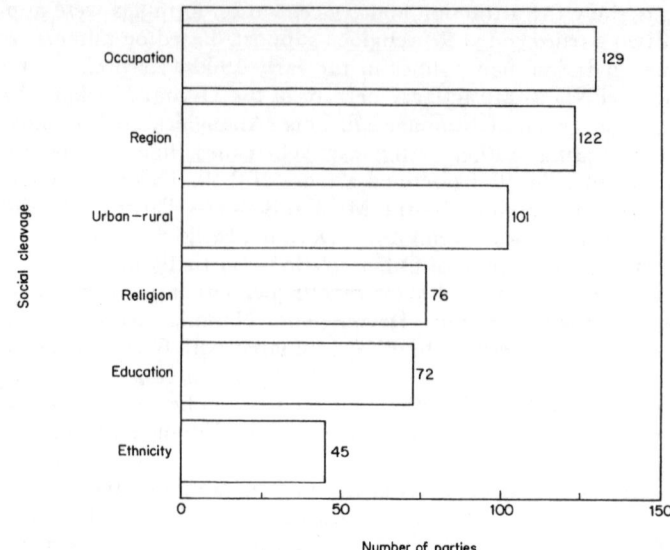

Figure 1. *Success in coding parties on six bases of social support (1957–1962).*

Regionalism in Party Support and Policies

Region is a difficult variable to use in cross-national analysis, because regional categories—e.g., north, Bavaria, highlands, Stockholm—are inherently nominal and are not comparable across countries. Consequently, I avoided analyzing support by specific region and followed the standard approach used by Rose and Urwin, assessing the overall pattern of regional support. My analysis differed, however, by studying a much wider set of countries and by relying on the attraction and concentration scores generated from the ICPP Project. These scores measured whether parties (1) attracted their supporters equally from all regions (however the regions were determined for each country), or (2) had their support concentrated within a single region.

Regionalism in Party Support

To interpret the parties' scores on these measures, we need some benchmarks. The most appropriate ones are the parties' scores for the same measures on the other potential bases of social support. As shown in Figure 2, regionalism is not a powerful differentiator among political parties across nations. Compared with their scores on occupational groupings, for example, political parties attract support more evenly across regional categories and have less support concentrated within any particular regional category. Among the social differentiators, only education shows as little potential for political cleavage among political parties.

This finding for 122 parties across 45 nations reinforces the findings of Rose and Urwin in their study of Western parties. Although regionalism is pervasive in its

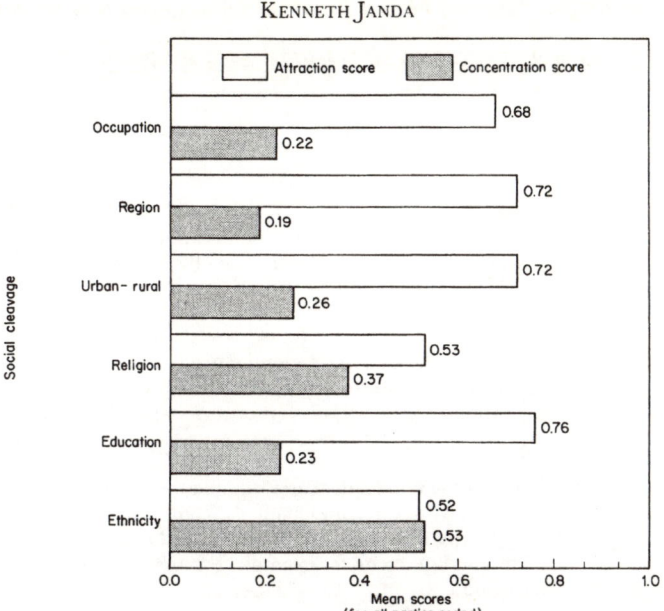

Figure 2. *Indices of party support on six social bases.*

effects on support for political parties, those effects are not very strong when compared with the effects of other potential differentiators. The relative weakness of regionalism in party politics can be explored further by assessing the effect of regionalism on the political issue of national integration.

Regionalism and National Integration

The parties in the ICPP Project were scored on thirteen different issues: (1) government ownership of means of production, (2) government role in economic planning, (3) redistribution of wealth, (4) social welfare, (5) secularization of society, (6) support of the military, (7) alignment with East–West blocs, (8) anticolonialism, (9) supranational integration, (10) national integration, (11) electoral participation, (12) protection of civil rights, and (13) interference with civil liberties. Factor analysis showed that all but two of these issues could be subsumed under two factors: Marxism (representing an economic orientation), and Liberalism (representing a social order dimension).

Quite understandably, the issue of "national integration," which is most relevant to our interest in regionalism, did not relate to either Marxism or Liberalism. Lipset and Rokkan define the issue of national integration as "the conflict between the central nation-building culture and the increasing resistance of the ethnically, linguistically, or religiously distinct subject populations in the provinces and the peripheries" (1967: 14). This concept focuses on the party's predisposition towards the preservation or reduction of distinctive cultural and regional characteristics, exclusive of class.

National integration focuses on the functional and symbolic authority advocated by the party, specifically whether national or subnational influences predominate.

Table 2. *Issue of National Integration: Codes and Results*

Stance toward National Integration	Code		Number of Parties
PRO-strong	+5	*Extreme nationalist:* Advocates obliterating subnational authority, completely assimilating all segments into a national political culture	23
	+4	Intermediate score	4
PRO-moderate	+3	*Nationalist:* Advocates predominance of national authority structures and combined with reluctant toleration of some expression of regional authority	25
	+2	Intermediate score	5
PRO-weak	+1	*Nationalist/localist:* Advocates dominance of national authority structures and symbols, combined with recognizing subnational distinctions *and* an effort to accommodate them, for example, through differential legislation	29
Neutral	0	Or stance is ambiguous or contradictory	10
CON-weak	−1	*Federalist:* Advocates vitual sharing of decision making authority between national and subnational power centers	13
	−2	Intermediate score	3
CON-moderate	−3	*Confederationist:* Advocates sacrifice of some subnational authority to a confederal government, maintaining distinct schools, law enforcement agencies, and the like	4
	−4	Intermediate score	0
CON-strong	−5	*Separationist:* Advocates perpetuating subnational autonomy through secession	3
		Total number of parties scored	119

The extreme nationalist position advocates obliterating subnational loyalties, whether regional, ethnic, linguistic, traditional, or some combination thereof. The Kemalist revolution led by the Turkish People's Party in the 1920s followed such a program, Turkifying ethnic minorities and revitalizing the Turkish nation through political, legal, and educational reform.[7] The extreme disintegrative position on this issue is the assertion of subnational autonomy, that is, separatism.

A total of 119 parties operating during 1957–62 were coded for their stance on national integration according to the categories in Table 2. The mean score of all 119 parties scored on national integration was 1.67, suggesting that most parties favored national unity and that few tended towards separatism.

Data on regional support were available for 99 of these 119 parties, permitting a broad test of the relationship between the parties' regional support and their positions on national integration. Cleavage theory predicts that parties that are regionally heterogeneous would tend to favor national integration more than parties that are regionally homogeneous. The observed correlations between the two measures of regional support and national integration were low, but both coefficients were in the expected directions ($r = +0.33$ for regional attraction and $r = -0.32$ for regional concentration). These correlations conform to cleavage theory, demonstrating a significant, but limited, effect of regional patterns of party support on the positions taken by parties on the issue of national integration.

Squaring the correlation coefficients calculates the proportion of variance in one variable explained by the other. By this measure, only about 10 percent of the variance in parties' positions on national integration can be explained by either the homogeneous or heterogeneous nature of their regional support. Combining the two support measures in multiple regression analysis did not materially improve the explanation. Presumably other factors, such as the *particular* regions that supported parties in particular countries, would explain additional variation if they could be brought into the analysis somehow. That is not easy across nations, due to the idiosyncratic nature of the regional variable. Later, however, I will explore the explanatory effects of particular *religious* groups on issue positions.

Overall, this analysis conforms to the findings of Rose and Urwin and those of Ersson, Janda, and Lane. They detected regional effects in party support in almost every country. "Region," however, is primarily a surrogate for other social factors— class, religion, ethnicity, and so on. In its extreme form, political regionalism can produce separatism, and separatist parties, when they exist, can threaten national integration. Fortunately for government stability, separatist parties are not common. Although regionalism is pervasive, previous studies showed that regionalism is not a critical factor in support of political parties. This study shows that when regionalism is measured by homogeneity or heterogeneity of party supporters, it is also limited in explaining parties' position on national integration.

Religion in Party Support and Policies

Religion is also a difficult variable to use in cross-national analysis. Like regionalism, it is primarily a nominal variable whose categories depend on the history of the country. Unlike regionalism, however, religion offers some basis for comparability of categories across nations. For example, Catholicism, Islam, and major Protestant denominations are prominent in several nations. Unfortunately, there are many variations on religious themes, making religion a challenging variable for cross-national analysis, particularly holonational analysis.

Religion in Party Support

As reported previously in Figure 1, religion is not a pervasive differentiator of party support. Only 76 of the 147 parties in the 1957–62 time period were coded on religious categories. However, when religion *is* politically relevant, it is a powerful differentiator. The attraction and concentration scores graphed in Figure 2 show that parties tend to attract support less evenly across different religions than different occupations, and that parties have more support concentrated within particular religions than occupations. Parties show more cleavage in support on religion than on any other differentiator except ethnicity. However, ethnicity was coded for only 45 parties and was distinctly limited in its effects.

These findings for religious support of political parties across cultures support previous research cited for Western nations: religion is a pervasive basis of party support with pronounced effects on political alignments. The present research extends the study of religion in party support by examining more closely the patterns of support across Western and non-Western nations.

Religion and Secularization of Society

"Secularization of society" was one of the thirteen issues on which parties were scored in the ICPP Project. Although factor analysis identified secularization as one of seven issues in a Marxism factor, it had the lowest average intercorrelations with the other six and correlated only 0.50 with the underlying factor. Thus the parties' positions on secularization of society often varied from their positions on the other issues, such as ownership of the means of production, economic planning, and so on.

Presumably, the religious structure of party support explains the parties' positions on this issue, which reflects what Lipset and Rokkan called "the conflict between the centralizing, standardizing, and mobilizing nation-state and the historically established corporate privileges of the Church" (1967: 14). They note that "parties of religious defense" resisted attempts by secular parties "to create direct links of influence and control between the nation-state and the individual citizen" (1967:15).

The religious variable becomes politically critical in the presence of an institutionalized church. Thus the issue is blunted in India not only by the traditional Hindu view, separating religious and secular authority, but also by the fact, as Weiner has put it, that "since Hinduism has no church, the power of the Brahmin was that of an individual rather than of an institution" (1960: 161). The Islamic tradition, by contrast, makes no distinction between religious and secular life. Hence, although "Indian and Ceylonese politicians continue to exploit Hinduism and Buddhism with little fear that an organized Hindu or Buddhist clergy or church will displace them . . . Pakistani politicians must handle the religious issue with great care . . ." to avoid the creation of an Islamic state (Weiner, 1960: 162).

The secularization variable measures the party's posture towards the privileges of the church. Among the various views of secularization proposed by Broughton and Rudd (1984), it conforms best to their concept of "laicization." Parties were coded for stances ranging from support for government expropriation of church property or official discouragement of religious practices at one extreme to a preference for a state religion at the other. Intermediate categories express the party's attitude towards state support of the church. The coding scheme and the success in coding the parties is detailed in Table 3. A total of 111 of 147 parties operating during 1957–62 were coded on secularization of society. The mean score of all 111 parties scored was −0.67, almost at the middle point of the scale but slightly opposed to secularization.

To assess the effect of religious basis of support on the issue of secularization of society, I analyzed the 64 parties scored on both religion and secularization.[8] Each party's score on secularization of society was correlated with the measures of attraction and concentration over all relevant categories of religious support within each country. According to the theory of cross-cutting cleavages, parties that attract

KENNETH JANDA 361

Table 3. *Issue of Secularization of Society: Codes and Results*

Stance toward Secularization	Code		Number of Parties
PRO-strong	+5	Advocates expropriation of church property or official discouragement of religious practices	6
	+4	Intermediate score	3
PRO-moderate	+3	Advocates abolition of parochial educational systems or punitive taxation of church property	11
	+2	Intermediate score	3
PRO-weak	+1	Advocates removal of state aid to parochial schools, clergy, or church operations or taxation of church property at non-punitive rates	10
Neutral	0	Or stance is ambiguous or contradictory	14
CON-weak	−1	Takes generally benevolent attitude toward religion; advocates exemption of church property from taxation	18
	−2	Intermediate score	6
CON-moderate	−3	Advocates state monetary support of parochial schools, clergy, or church property	32
	−4	Intermediate score	1
CON-strong	−5	Advocates establishing a state religion; imposes a system of laws based on religious prescription	7
		Total number of parties scored	111

support evenly from various religions will tend to have higher secularization scores than those whose support is uneven. Also, parties whose supporters are concentrated among particular religions will tend to have lower secularization scores than those whose composition is spread over religions. The observed coefficients were low but in the expected directions: for attraction, $r = +0.39$, and for concentration, $r = -0.33$.

These results were similar to those obtained when analyzing regional effects on national integration. But the low values for secularization in particular illuminate a problem in using any formula that aggregates party support over groups without identifying the particular groups that heavily influence the aggregate score. Because nominal Muslims accounted for 88 percent of its supporters, the Indonesian PNI received a higher religious concentration score than the NU, mostly a party of devout Muslims. What appears to be a straightforward test of cleavage theory, using measures of social attraction and concentration to predict party positions on related issues, really misclassifies parties that deviate from the assumed pattern of group influence.

A Step Further: The Effects of Specific Religious Groups

So far, I have relied on aggregate measures of attraction and concentration to assess regional and religious effects on the issues of national integration and secularization of society. Because regional categories cannot be compared across countries, the effects of regionalism cannot be examined much further. But religious categories *do* have some cross-national comparability. If, as assumed, the structure of social support affects party policies, the parties' scores on support from comparable religious groups should be able to explain their positions on secularization of society, even across cultures.

I know of no previous attempt to assess the effects of religious support on party positions across cultures, so this step in the analysis was frankly exploratory. Figure 3 illustrates the problem of studying religion across nations by graphing the religious composition of the 24 nations in the ICPP study whose 76 parties were coded for religious support. The nations are arranged in decreasing order of percent Christian and roughly in increasing order of percent Muslim. The presence of Muslim, Hindu, and Buddhist nations in this holonational study complicates cross-national analysis, overwhelming the simple Catholic/Protestant categories applied to mostly Christian Western nations.

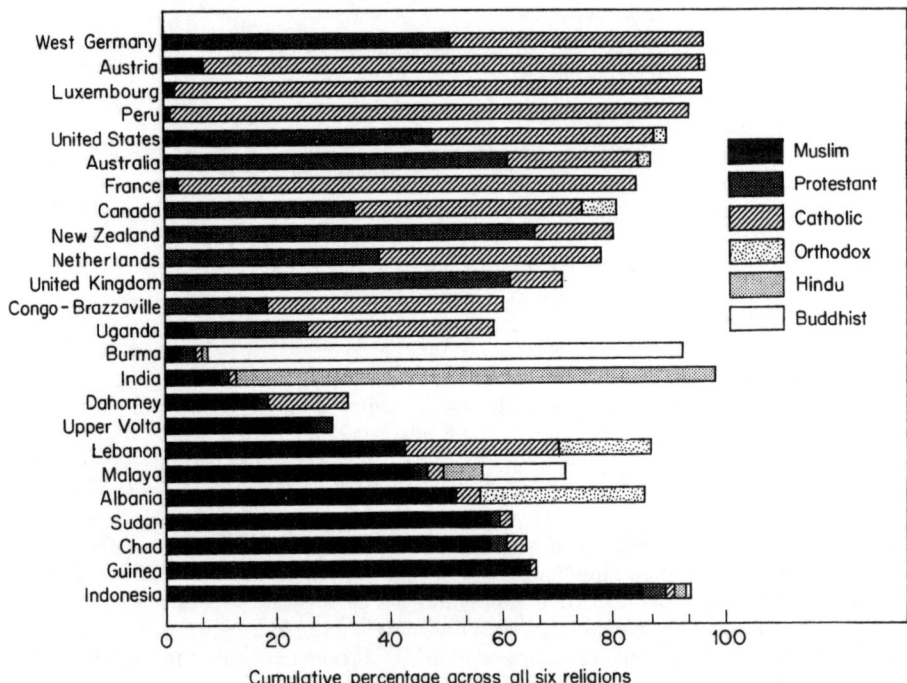

Figure 3. *Variety in religions across the world.*

Sources: Charles Lewis Taylor and Michael C. Hudson, *World Handbook of Political and Social Indicators, II* (Ann Arbor, MI: Interuniversity Consortium for Political and Social Research, 1973); and *The Worldmark Encyclopaedia of the Nations* (New York: Worldmark Press, 1960).

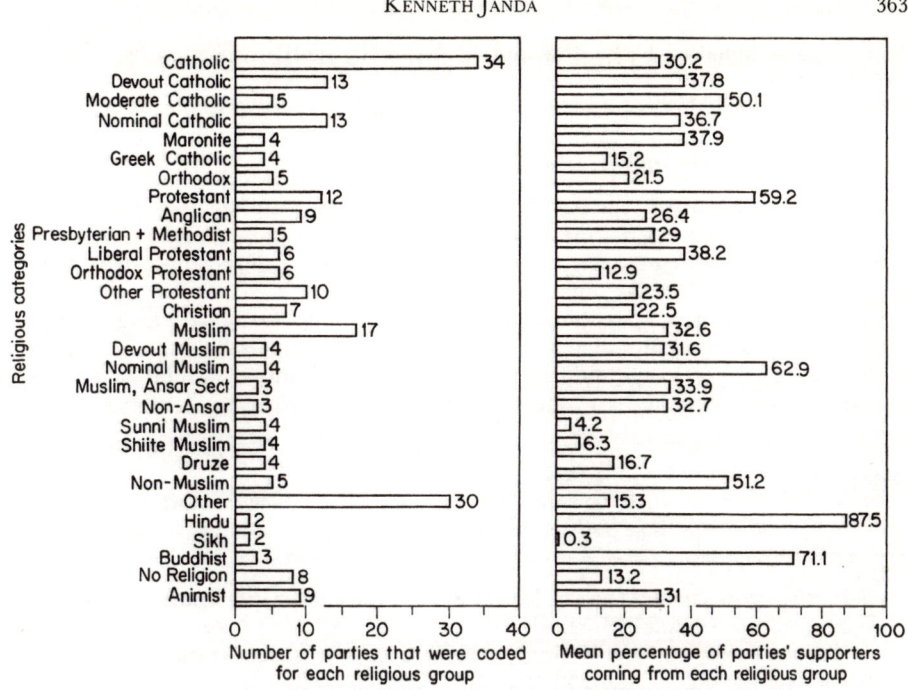

Figure 4. *Coding parties on support from 29 religious groups.*

Figure 4 graphs the 29 distinct religious categories coded for all the parties for which we have data.[9] The most common category, Catholic, applied to 34 parties in eleven countries. The undifferentiated Muslim category also was heavily used, figuring in 17 parties in seven countries. Other categories, such as the Druze and the Maronite Christians in the Lebanon, are largely idiosyncratic to a country. These categories were attached to only the four Lebanese parties. In fact, the Lebanon's four parties also accounted for the appearance of the Sunni and Shi'ite Muslims and the Orthodox and Greek Catholic categories.

A Devotional Theory of Party Positions on Secularization

Little theory exists that predicts which of the 29 nominal categories of religious groups would favor or oppose secularization. Within any type of religion, however, one can theorize that the parties' positions on secularization would depend on the religious devotion of their supporters: *the more devout the religious supporters of a political party, the more they oppose secularization.*

This general theory implies separate sets of hypotheses for each type of religion. Unfortunately, the ICPP data limits the distinctions that can be made among the devotion of supporters within religious types. For example, one is hard-pressed to assess religiosity among the seven diverse groups of Protestants listed in Figure 4. Similarly, one cannot easily claim that Buddhists are more devout than Hindus. The only meaningful distinctions in religiosity in the ICPP data apply to Catholics and

Muslims. Consequently, I formulate only two sets of hypotheses for testing with the available data.

For Catholics, the theory translates as *the more devout the Catholicism of party supporters, the more opposed the party is to secularization of society.* The data allow testing four hypotheses consistent with this theory:

> 1. Parties supported by Devout Catholics oppose secularization more than parties supported by Moderate Catholics.
> 2. Parties supported by Moderate Catholics oppose secularization more than parties supported by Nominal Catholics.
> 3. By implication, parties supported by Devout Catholics also oppose secularization more than parties supported by Nominal Catholics.
> 4. Parties supported by undifferentiated "Catholics" oppose secularization less than Devout Catholics but more than Nominal Catholics.

Devotion to Catholicism was measured differently depending on the country, but it usually reflected frequency of church attendance.

For Muslims, the theory becomes, *the more devout the Islamic orientation of party supporters, the more opposed the party is to secularization of society.* The data allow testing four parallel hypotheses:

> 5. Parties supported by Devout Muslims oppose secularization more than parties supported by Nominal Muslims.
> 6. Parties supported by Nominal Muslims oppose secularization more than parties supported by Non-Muslims.
> 7. By implication, parties supported by Devout Muslims will also oppose secularization more than party supported by Non-Muslims.
> 8. Parties supported by undifferentiated "Muslims" will oppose secularization less than Devout Muslims but more than Nominal Muslims.

Devotion to Islam among party supporters was assessed by authors' comments on each party system.

The Analysis of Religious Effects on Secularization

Ordinary regression analysis was used to estimate religious effects on secularization. The first step involved computing the proportion of a party's support that came from each religious group. This procedure conforms to computing percentages by rows in Table 1. It is the basis of the ICPP measure of concentration, and it follows the procedure that Rose and Urwin used in assessing party cohesion. To emphasize the dominant position of majority groups in a party, however, the proportions of the party's support from each group were squared, which gave extra weight to larger groups.[10]

If the religious group did not apply to a party, the party's score for that variable was set to 0.0 rather than treated as missing. In this way, all parties coded for religion were coded for *each* of the 29 religious groups. However, a group would be activated in the analysis only if the party's support from that group were greater than zero. In a sense, the religious groups were treated like so-called dummy variables in regression analysis, except that the religious support variables ranged in decimal values from 0.0 to 1.0, not just the binary values of 0 or 1. Although there were 29 groups, fewer than six contributed to the support of any particular party.

As anyone who has done regression analysis knows, a researcher has many options in executing the analysis and often conducts many analyses before choosing one to report. Virtually all the analyses conducted tended to support the hypotheses, but with different coefficients and degrees of fit in explaining secularization. Obviously, with 29 variables and only 64 parties coded for secularization, there is considerable potential for high explanation.[11] One analysis that used all the religious variables accounted for 87 percent of the variance in parties' positions on secularization of society.[12]

The analysis reported here eliminates some of the line-fitting consequences of using many variables by combining religious categories in keeping with the hypotheses to be tested. Thus, the Maronites in the Lebanon were eliminated as a distinct variable and were put in the generic "Catholic" category.[13] This change, which affected only the four Lebanese parties, raised the number of generic Catholic parties from 34 identified in Figure 4 to 38. Similarly, the Sunni, Shi'ite, and Druze brands of Islam in the Lebanon and the Answar and Non-Answar sects in the Sudan were put in the generic "Muslim" category. This second change, which affected only seven parties (four Lebanese and three Sudanese), dropped five more variables and raised the number of generic Muslim parties from the 17 parties identified in Figure 4 to 24. Finally, the Sikhs, who were coded for only two Indian parties, were put into the Other religious group.[14] Overall, these changes tended to decrease the explained variance by eliminating party-specific variables from the analysis.

After combining various Catholic and Muslim groups into the generic categories and allowing for data peculiarities, the original 29 religious groups were reduced to 22. Finally, all 22 religious variables were entered into a multiple regression analysis of the positions on secularization of society taken by 64 parties. The resulting equation produced an R^2 of 0.57 with an adjusted R^2 of 0.34. Expressed in words, more than half the variance in party positions on the secularization issue can be explained by the proportions of their supporters who come from these religious groups.

Figure 5 plots the secularization scores assigned to each of the 64 parties against their scores predicted by their religious composition according to the regression equation. Two Marxist parties, the Albanian Workers Party and the Democratic Party of Guinea, were among those that deviated the most from their predicted score and towards secularization. The prevalence of Islam in Albania led to a high concentration of Muslims within the membership of the Workers Party, but communist ideology dictated the party's position on secularization. To a lesser extent, this was true in one-party Guinea, where the PDG was mostly Muslim. Some of the other parties that favor secularization more than expected by their religious makeup can also be explained by historical factors.

On the other hand, most of the parties opposed to secularization are close to the predicted regression line. Some obviously religious parties—the French Catholic MRP, Dutch Anti-Revolutionary Party, Dutch Christian Historical Union—fall neatly into place in the lower left-hand section of the plot. Note in particular the placements of the Indonesian Nationalist and the Indonesian NU (the PNI and Muslim Scholars' Party discussed earlier). The regression line reflects the strong presence of Nominal Muslims in the PNI and Devout Muslims in the NU, predicting the parties' positions on secularization almost exactly.

Given that there is considerable measurement error both in coding parties on issues and in scoring them on religious composition, this is a striking confirmation of the

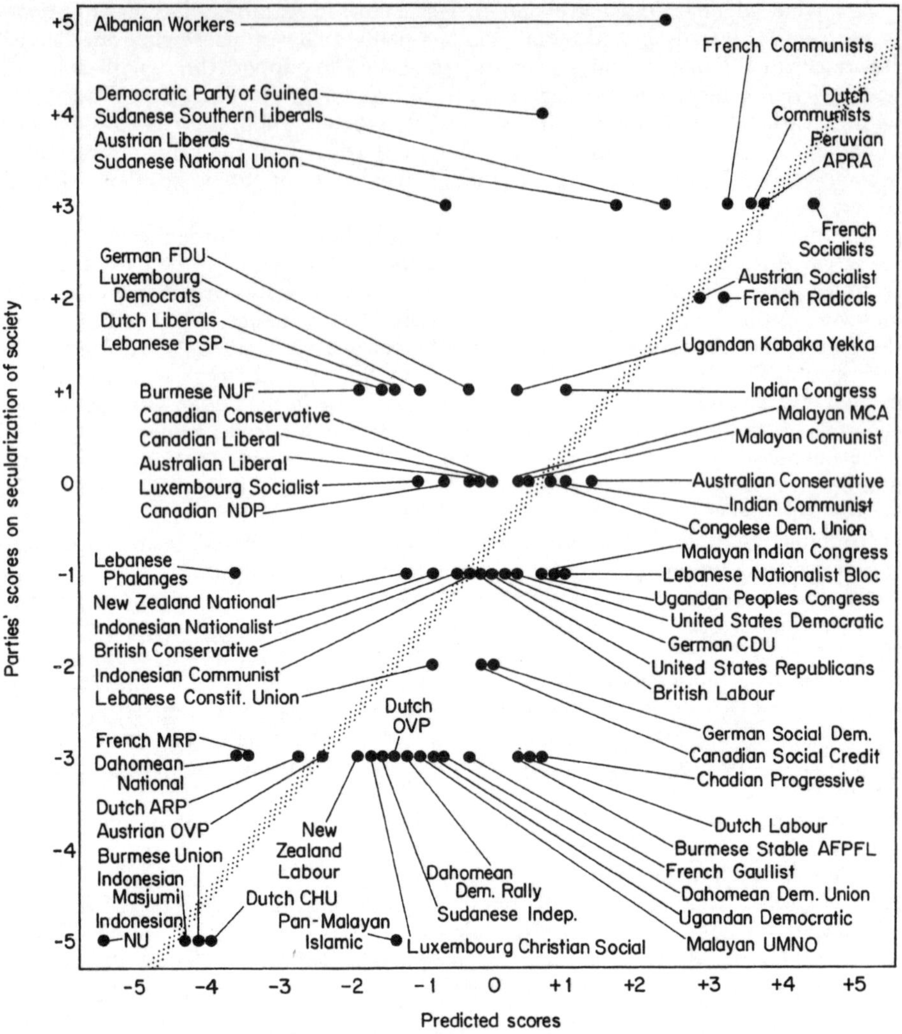

Parties' scores on secularization of society (y-axis)

+5 Albanian Workers —————————————————— ● French Communists

+4 Democratic Party of Guinea —
    Sudanese Southern Liberals —
    Austrian Liberals —
    Sudanese National Union —
    Dutch Communists
    Peruvian APRA

+3 French Socialists

+2 German FDU —
    Luxembourg Democrats —
    Dutch Liberals —
    Lebanese PSP —
    Austrian Socialist
    French Radicals
    Ugandan Kabaka Yekka

+1 Burmese NUF —
    Canadian Conservative —
    Canadian Liberal —
    Australian Liberal —
    Luxembourg Socialist —
    Canadian NDP —
    Indian Congress
    Malayan MCA
    Malayan Comunist

0   Australian Conservative
    Indian Communist
    Congolese Dem. Union
    Malayan Indian Congress

-1 Lebanese Phalanges
    New Zealand National —
    Indonesian Nationalist —
    British Conservative —
    Indonesian Communist —
    Lebanese Constit. Union —
    Lebanese Nationalist Bloc
    Ugandan Peoples Congress
    United States Democratic
    German CDU

-2 United States Republicans
    British Labour
    Dutch OVP
    German Social Dem.

-3 French MRP —
    Dahomean National —
    Dutch ARP —
    Austrian OVP —
    Canadian Social Credit
    Chadian Progressive

-4 Burmese Union
    Indonesian Masjumi
    Indonesian NU
    New Zealand Labour
    Dutch CHU
    Pan-Malayan Islamic
    Dahomean Dem. Rally
    Sudanese Indep.
    Dutch Labour
    Burmese Stable AFPFL
    French Gaullist
    Dahomean Dem. Union
    Ugandan Democratic

-5 ● —NU   Luxembourg Christian Social   Malayan UMNO

-5 -4 -3 -2 -1 0 +1 +2 +3 +4 +5

Predicted scores

Figure 5. *Assigned secularization scores regressed against predicted scores for 64 parties, $R^2=0.57$.*

assumption that the social composition of political parties affects their issue positions. Even more impressive is the pattern of beta coefficients produced by the regression equation. As shown in Figure 6, the coefficients in the shaded areas for Catholics and Muslims support all eight hypotheses generated by the devotional theory of party positions on secularization. The coefficients of −0.30 and −0.37 respectively associated with Devout Catholics and Devout Muslims state the standardized effects of these variables on secularization. For each standardized unit of increase in Catholic or Muslim support, parties tend to *decrease* −0.30 and −0.37 standardized units, respectively, in their support of secularization.[15]

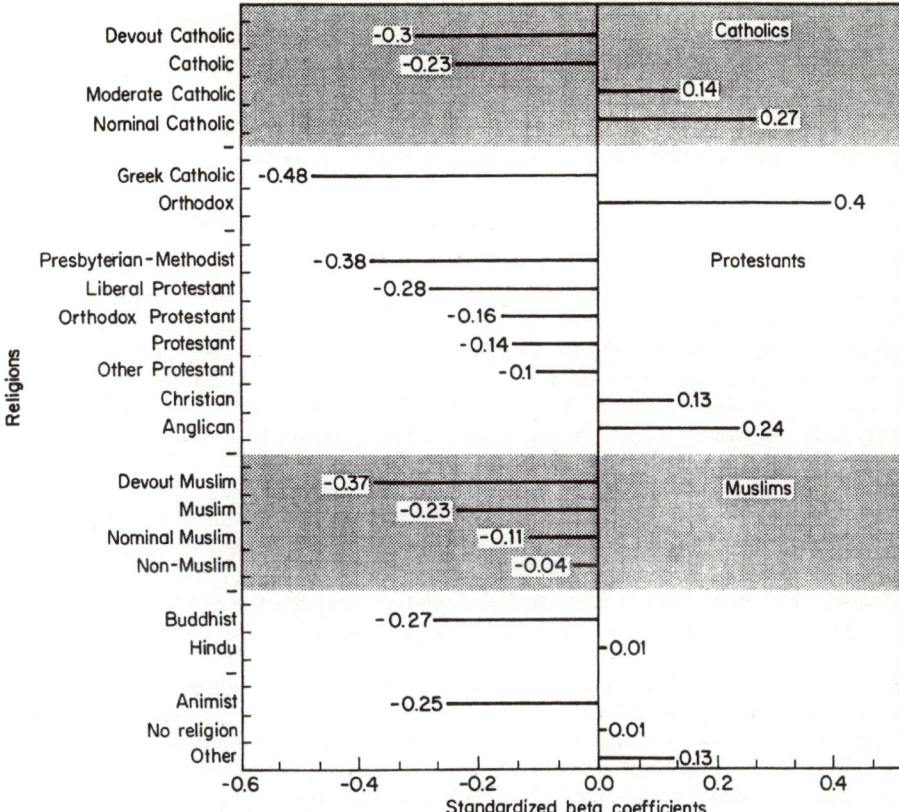

Figure 6. *Effects of 22 religious groups on parties' positions on secularization of society.**

$R^2=0.57$, adjusted $R^2=0.34$. *In some cases, the beta coefficients pertain to data coded for only a few parties. See Figure 4 for the number of parties coded for each religious group.

To help clarify the patterns in the regression equation, the coefficients for all the other groups have been ordered from large negative to large positive values.[16] The large and opposing effects of the Greek Catholic and Orthodox variables reflect the idiosyncracies of Lebanese politics and do not merit more general interpretation. The negative coefficients for most of the Protestant groups, which apply mostly to Western parties, suggest that parties with strong Protestant components tend to oppose secularization. The exceptions are parties that are strongly Anglican and those that are vaguely "Christian," which are exclusively in the Third World. The Buddhist and Hindu variables are tied solely to three parties in Burma and two in India—not enough to offer interpretations. Although the large negative coefficient for the Animist variable (coded for nine parties) is surprising, we expect the positive coefficients produced for No Religion and Other, for these groups are not thought to benefit from secularization.

These results, while theoretically satisfying, should be viewed as exploratory. The analysis needs to be replicated with more parties using better data. Because it may prove harder to score parties for secularization than for religious composition, the initial effort might go into scoring the forty-seven ICPP parties that were coded for secularization but not for religious composition. Ideally, new research would be undertaken to score contemporary parties for both the dependent and independent variables. While this may be done with moderate effort for parties in Western countries, it is a major undertaking for parties in the Third World, which must be included to broaden the study of religious influences in politics.

Conclusion

Previous studies of the social bases of party support in Western nations suggest that region and religion are, along with social class, worthy of analysis. However, the variables of region and religion are more difficult than class to include in a cross-national analysis of the effects of social cleavages on political cleavages. Both variables are inherently nominal and resist comparison across nations. Comparability has been achieved in research by studying whether parties are regionally or religiously "homogeneous" rather than "heterogeneous," without paying close attention to the categories used in the analysis.

Following this basic approach, this holonational analysis of region and religion as bases of party support confirms the basic findings from the more limited analyses across Western nations. The influence of region on party support is pervasive but not particularly salient or critical. The influence of religion on party support is less pervasive but more salient or critical when it occurs. Both regional and religious homogeneity among party supporters predict modestly to parties' positions, respectively, on issues of national integration and secularization of society.

This study extends the analysis of party support beyond aggregate measures of social heterogeneity and homogeneity to explore the effects of particular religious groups in a party on its position on secularization. This approach, which tested eight hypotheses from a devotional theory of secularization, produced findings that were theoretically satisfying. A set of 22 variables, each representing a religious group, explained 57 percent of the variance in the parties' position on secularization. Moreover, all eight hypotheses were supported by the coefficients generated from the regression analysis. These exploratory findings invite additional cross-cultural research on the effects of religious support on parties' issue positions.

Notes

1. Their criteria were somewhat more involved than this. See the five points they list on pages 10–11.
2. The regions were nominal variables in a one-way analysis of variance, predicting to party strength in each of three elections. Eta-squared was used to estimate the percentage of variance attributable to regions.
3. My assistant and I estimated party support through fairly rigorous procedures. We first created a table with empty cells but with fixed totals for the rows and columns. The row totals reported the strength (in percent) of each party in the country, determined mainly from reliable electoral data. The column totals contained the strength (in percent) of each subgroup in the population, determined mainly from census data. We were forced to enter our estimates of party support as percentages of the entire society—such that the entries would sum appropriately to the row and column totals. This constraint ensured that our estimates were internally consistent and thus helped improve their accuracy.
4. The ICPP Project used still a third measure of social support, social reflection. See Gillies

and Janda (1975), Gillies (1979), and Janda (1980) for additional discussion of these measures and their application to the analysis of political parties.

5. I chose the Indonesian case to illustrate how parties were scored for religious composition in the absence of survey data. The Indonesian population was estimated to be 90 percent Muslim. The literature notes that the Santri, Devout Muslims, are greatly outnumbered by the Abangan, or Nominal Muslims. For coding purposes, I assumed a one-third to two-thirds split, but that was obviously a crude estimate. One source said that the Santri backed religious parties, such as NU and Masjumi, while Abangan voted for non-religious parties, such as PNI and PKI (Sjadzali, 1959: 48). Other sources (Kahin, 1952: 157; McVey, 1963: 158) corroborated these observations, which led to estimates of party support that were internally consistent with the scoring matrix of Table 1. (See Janda, 1980: 711.)

6. See Janda (1980: 145–47) for a discussion of the extent of interrelationships across the range of social dimensions.

7. The secularizing aspects of the movement are coded in the secularization variable, discussed in the next section.

8. The number of parties was reduced from 76 to 64 due to missing data on the dependent variable, secularization of society.

9. Two categories, Animist/Other and Non-Animist, were excluded. They only applied to one party, and it was excluded from the later analysis for lack of data on secularization.

10. Squaring proportions to measuring dominance or concentration is a common technique. A parallel analysis done with simple proportions produced similar results, but this analysis is theoretically more appropriate and the results are slightly more satisfying.

11. However, the number of variables is misleading. Although each of 29 different religious groups constitutes a variable in this analysis, most of these variables are coded 0 for any given party. In fact, the number of applicable variables ranges from two to six, for all parties in the analysis are coded for support from at least two groups, and no parties are coded for support from more than six groups.

12. This analysis was reported in Janda (1988). It included nearly all the religious groups plus four variables for the percent Catholic, Protestant, Muslim, and Orthodox in the nation's population. Despite using 31 variables to produce an R^2 of 0.87, the adjusted R^2 was 0.69.

13. In hindsight, the Greek Catholics also probably should have been placed in the generic Catholic group for this analysis, but they were treated separately.

14. The Sikhs, who were coded only for the Congress and Communist parties in India, had to be dropped from separate consideration due to instability of their regression coefficients from analysis to analysis. There simply were not enough observations on Sikhs as a group to warrant including them in this part of the study.

15. A standardized unit refers to a standard deviation. The statement in the text could be rephrased to say that an increase of one standard deviation in group support would result in -0.30 or -0.37 standard deviation changes in secularization. Figure 6 reports standardized (beta) coefficients in the regression equation rather than unstandardized coefficients because of wide differences in the number of parties coded for each religious group, which greatly affects the standard deviation for each variable. Note also that group support is measured in proportions *squared*.

16. Seven of the coefficients were significant at the 0.10 level, and five of these were significant at the 0.05 level. Given only 64 cases and 22 variables, I am less concerned about their significance levels and more concerned with their overall pattern in accordance with the eight hypotheses.

References

Broughton, D. and C. Rudd (1984). "Secularization and Partisan Preferences: Definition and Operationalization," *European Journal of Political Research* 12: 445–450.

370 *Regional and Religious Support of Political Parties and Effects on their Issue Positions*

Ersson, S., K. Janda, and J.-E. Lane (1985). "Ecology of Party Strength in Western Europe: A Regional Analysis," *Comparative Political Studies* 18 (July): 170–205.

Gillies, R. (1979). "Social Diversity of Political Parties: Sources and Consequences." Ph.D. Dissertation, Northwestern University.

Gillies, R. and K. Janda (1975). "Social Aggregation, Articulation, and Representation of Political Parties: A Cross-National Analysis." Paper delivered at the Annual Meeting of the American Political Science Association, San Francisco.

Janda, K. (1979). *Comparative Political Parties Data 1950–1962* Ann Arbor, MI.: Interuniversity Consortium for Political and Social Research, Study 7534.

Janda, K. (1980). *Political Parties: A Cross-National Survey*. New York: The Free Press.

Janda, K. (1988). "Region and Religion as Factors Underlying Support for National Political Parties." Paper prepared for presentation at the XIVth World Congress of the International Political Science Association, Sheraton-Washington Hotel, Washington, D.C., August 28 to September 1.

Kahin, G.M. (1952). *Nationalism and Revolution in Indonesia*. Ithaca, N.Y.: Cornell University Press.

Lipset, S.M. (1960). *Political Man*. Garden City, N.Y.: Doubleday.

Lipset, S.M. and S. Rokkan, eds. (1967). *Party Systems and Voter Alignments*. New York: The Free Press.

McVey, R. (1963). "Indonesian Communism and the Transition to Guided Democracy." In *Communist Strategies in Asia* (A. Doak Barnett, ed.) New York: Frederick A. Praeger.

Naroll, R. (1972). "A Holonational Bibliography." *Comparative Political Studies* 5 (July): 211–230.

Nordlinger, E. (1972). *Conflict Regulation in Divided Societies*. Cambridge, MA: Harvard University, Occasional Papers in International Affairs, no. 29.

Rose, R. and D. Urwin (1969). "Social Cohesion, Political Parties and Strains on Regimes." *Comparative Political Studies* 2 (April): 7–67.

Rose, R. and D. Urwin (1975). *Regional Differentiation and Political Unity in Western Nations*. Beverly Hills, CA.: Sage Publications.

Sjadzali, M. (1959). "Indonesia's Muslim Parties and Their Political Concepts." Washington, D.C.: Georgetown University, unpublished M.A. Thesis.

Weiner, M. (1960). "The Politics of South Asia." In *The Politics of the Developing Areas*, (G. Almond and J.S. Coleman eds.). Princeton, N.J.: Princeton University Press: 153–246.

Biographical Note

KENNETH JANDA is Payson S. Wild Professor of Political Science at Northwestern University. His major substantive interests divide between American government and comparative political parties. His latest book is *The Challenge of Democracy: Government in America* (1989, co-authored with Jeffrey Berry and Jeff Goldman). In comparative politics, his last book was *Parties and Their Environments: Limits to Reform?* (1982, co-authored with Robert Harmel). ADDRESS: Department of Political Science, Northwestern University, Evanston, IL 60208, U.S.A.

Acknowledgment. A preliminary report on this research was contained in a paper presented at the XIV World Congress of the International Political Science Association (Janda, 1988). This paper substantially revises and extends the analysis reported there.

[16]

Religious vs. Linguistic vs. Class Voting: The "Crucial Experiment" of Comparing Belgium, Canada, South Africa, and Switzerland*

AREND LIJPHART
University of California, San Diego

For the purpose of determining the relative influence of the three potentially most important social and demographic factors on party choice—social class, religion, and language—a comparison of Belgium, Canada, South Africa, and Switzerland provides a "crucial experiment," because these three variables are simultaneously present in all four countries. Building on the major earlier research achievements in comparative electoral behavior, this four-country multivariate analysis compares the indices of voting and the party choice "trees" on the basis of national sample surveys conducted in the 1970s. From this crucial contest among the three determinants of party choice, religion emerges as the victor, language as a strong runner-up, and class as a distant third. The surprising strength of the religious factor can be explained in terms of the "freezing" of past conflict dimensions in the party system and the presence of alternative, regional-federal, structures for the expression of linguistic interests.

The major overall conclusion which emerges from comparative studies of the social and demographic bases of voting behavior is that there are two especially important determinants of party choice: social class and religion. Compared to these two strong factors, the influence of other social and demographic

I wish to thank the scholars and the organizations who made the data collected by them or tabulations based on these data available to me for the purpose of this study. The Belgian data were part of the 1970 and 1973 European Communities Studies of which Ronald Inglehart and Jacques-René Rabier were the principal investigators. The data of the 1974 Canadian national election survey were originally collected by Harold Clarke, Jane Jenson, Lawrence LeDuc, and Jon Pammett. The South African data were collected in 1974 by Market Research Africa (Pty) Ltd. under the guidance of Lawrence Schlemmer. The Swiss national election study of 1972 was organized by the Department of Political Science of the University of Geneva and the Sozialforschungsstelle of the University of Zurich under the direction of Henry H. Kerr, Jr., Dusan Sidjanski, and Gerhard Schmidtchen. The Belgian and Canadian data were obtained from the Inter-University Consortium for Political and Social Research. Neither the original collectors of the data nor the Consortium bear any responsibility for the analyses or interpretations presented here. I should also like to express my appreciation to Galen A. Irwin and Jan Verhoef for their advice and assistance, to the Netherlands Institute for Advanced Study in the Humanities and the Social Sciences in Wassenaar, where I was a Fellow in 1974–75 and where I did part of the research for this article, and to the Netherlands Foundation for the Advancement of Pure Research (Z.W.O.) for its financial support.

variables tends to be much weaker. However, a third potentially powerful variable—language—has received scant attention so far. The main reason for this undeserved neglect appears to be that linguistic cleavages are relatively rare in Western democracies.

There are several Western countries with small linguistic minorities, but only three that can really be said to be linguistically divided: Belgium, Canada, and Switzerland. Hence these three countries are obvious candidates for comparison with regard to the impact of linguistic divisions on voting (see Hill, 1974, p. 100). An interesting fourth case that can be added is the Republic of South Africa. This country—or, more precisely, its white electorate—fits all three of the theoretical criteria used by Richard Rose (1974b, pp. 5–6) to demarcate the universe of countries suitable for inclusion in his comparative handbook on *Electoral Behavior:* the persistence of competitive free elections since 1945, a high rank on the conventional socioeconomic indicators of industrialization, and Christian cultural origins.

Another reason why these four countries are especially interesting is that they present an outstanding opportunity for a multivariate analysis of the *relative* weights of the linguistic, religious, and class variables, since all four countries are divided along all of these dimensions. In addition to their linguistic cleavages and the socioeconomic or class differences present in all industrialized societies, there is a Protestant-Catholic division in Canada, South Africa, and Switzerland, and a religious-secular split in homogeneously Catholic Belgium. The latter cleavage is at least as important as the

398   *Religion and Politics*

1979   Religious vs. Linguistic vs. Class Voting   443

denominational difference in the other three countries. In fact, the analysis of Belgian social and political structure in terms of the three cleavages of religiosity, class, and language can be said to have become the standard approach (Lorwin, 1966; Urwin, 1970; Huyse, 1975; Frognier, 1976).[1]

This study will use recent survey data—all collected in the 1970s—for a systematic comparison of the influence of language, religion, and class on party choice in Belgium, Canada, South Africa, and Switzerland. It is explicitly designed to be a cumulative effort and to build onto such prior research achievements in comparative voting behavior as Rose's handbook (1974a) and Robert R. Alford's analysis (1963) of class voting in the Anglo-American democracies. The methods and indices that have proved valuable in these earlier studies will be used here again: in particular, the AID (automatic interaction detector) technique, also known as tree analysis, which is the major multivariate statistical method employed in the Rose volume, and Alford's well-known index of class voting and similar indices for measuring linguistic and religious voting.

Alternative Comparative Strategies: The Value of a "Crucial Experiment"

Religion and social class have been recognized as prime determinants of party choice from the very beginning of comparative voting behavior research, but no consensus has emerged about which of the two variables is the *better* predictor. The two earliest cross-national analyses reached diametrically opposite conclusions. Seymour Martin Lipset (1960, pp. 220, 223–24) found that although religious differences could also contribute to party support, "on a world scale, the principal generalization which can be made is that parties are primarily based on either the lower classes or the middle and upper classes." And he added: "More than anything else the party struggle is a conflict among classes, and the most impressive single fact about political party support is that in virtually every economically developed country

the lower-income groups vote mainly for parties of the left, while the higher-income groups vote mainly for parties of the right." But J. J. de Jong (1956, p. 160)—in what was probably the very first broadly comparative analysis of voting behavior, based on survey results from eleven European countries—concluded that religion was of primary significance and that class, although important, occupied a lower place in the hierarchy of voting determinants: "For the explanation of electoral behavior both in our own country [the Netherlands] and abroad, we always have to pay attention first to the religious factor."

The evidence on which these early generalizations were based was fragmentary and of uneven quality. Later and more systematic cross-national analyses that could benefit from more and better survey findings, have not been able to resolve the disagreement although they have been considerably more cautious in stating their conclusions. Two cross-national analyses, of four and eight countries, respectively, find that class voting tends to be stronger than religious voting (Alford, 1963; Budge and Farlie, 1976), but two other comparative studies, of fourteen and ten nations, respectively, conclude that religion tends to be the stronger factor (Rose and Urwin, 1969; Lijphart, 1971).[2] A fifth attempt to compare the relative influence of class and religion on party choice in twelve countries finds the two variables to be of about equal strength (Lancelot, 1975). These studies differ in several ways, but the critically important explanation of their divergent findings is that they are based on very different samples of countries: the religious factor is especially strong in the continental European countries with the exception of Scandinavia, and the proportion of these core continental European states in the different samples is highly unequal, ranging from zero percent in Alford's study to 60 percent in Lijphart's. The percentages are in perfect agreement with the conclusions of the five studies: zero percent and 25 percent, respectively, in the Alford and Budge-Farlie analyses that emphasize social class as the stronger variable, 33 percent in Lancelot's "neutral" study, and 43 and 60 percent, respectively, in the Rose-Urwin and Lijphart studies that find religion to be the better predictor.

---

[1] Another reason for the comparative analysis of these four countries is that they have been rather neglected by students of voting behavior. Even Rose's (1974a) ambitiously wide-ranging volume treats only two of them: Belgium and Canada. And the chapter on Belgium in the Rose handbook is seriously handicapped by the absence of a question on language in the 1968 national election survey on which most of its findings are based.

[2] Rose and Urwin (1969) actually present findings on 17 countries, but data on the religious basis of party choice are lacking in two cases (Denmark and Finland), and one case is not a "country" on a par with the other sovereign states (Northern Ireland).

What are the reasons for this wide variation in the composition of the samples? Alford (1963, p. 4) chose his four countries, all of them outside continental Europe, because they are comparable cases: "The common political culture of the Anglo-American countries means that a comparative study of political cleavages is not complicated by widely varying political values and traditions." The other authors applied a looser standard of comparability and tried to maximize the size of their samples by including all Western countries with Christian traditions on which appropriate data were available, but Budge and Farlie also included Japan.

In order to arrive at a definitive conclusion about the relative influence of class and religion on party choice, one might take either of two alternative approaches. One approach would be to attempt to maximize the sample to such an extent that it would closely approximate or, ideally, coincide with the universe of countries with free electoral competition. The disadvantage of this strategy is that, while it appears to be impartial, it actually gives social class a better chance to emerge as the more significant predictor: class cleavages are present and politically salient to at least some extent everywhere, whereas denominational differences may be absent and differences in religiosity, though in principle present everywhere, are politically relevant mainly in the continental European countries with their traditions of religious-anticlerical conflict.

The logical alternative is therefore to focus the analysis on those countries where the forces of class and religion actually compete with each other. These cases may be labeled "comparable," not in the usual sense of being similar in a large number of background characteristics and dissimilar with respect to the operative variables (see Lijphart, 1975), but in the sense that all of the variables which the researcher tries to relate to each other are present—and hence truly operative—in all cases. This strategy resembles what Raoul Naroll (1966, p. 336) calls a "crucial experiment," in which cases may be selected "because certain variables happen to be present together." Philip E. Converse is thinking in terms of this alternative approach when he states: "The general rule seems to be that religious differentiation intrudes on partisan political alignments in unexpectedly powerful degree *wherever it conceivably can*" (1974, p. 734, emphasis added). Similarly, Giovanni Sartori argues that class may have a strong influence on party choice only when there are no powerful competing influences, and that therefore "the correct

formulation of the problem is: *Given a multiplicity of cleavages,* can it be shown that there is a hierarchy of cleavages according to which the class cleavage tends to prevail?" (1969, p. 76, emphasis added.)

The contrast between the two approaches is even more striking when language is added as a possible predictor of party choice, because linguistic differences are relatively rare. Rose and Urwin (1969, p. 14) exemplify the first approach when they conclude that "linguistic or ethnic communalism is not today a major source of social cohesion for parties in Western countries." This conclusion is entirely legitimate and empirically correct for the universe of countries with free elections. But although linguistic and ethnic heterogeneity is rather infrequent, "where it occurs, ... it seems to become expressed in partisan cleavages as persistently and vigorously as religious differentiation" (Converse, 1974, p. 735). This study adopts the perspective exemplified by the latter statement: it is a "crucial experiment" of the relative impact of language, religion, and class on party choice in the four countries where all of these variables are simultaneously present.

Four Multidimensional Multiparty Systems

In order to compute Alford's index of class voting, one must divide the voters into manual and non-manual workers and the political parties into left and right parties.[3] Similarly, the calculation of the indices of religious and linguistic voting requires the dichotomous division of the voters into Protestants and Catholics, frequent churchgoers (attending at least twice a month) and those attending church only infrequently or never, and people speaking the majority language vs. those speaking the minority language, as well as the dichotomization of the parties along the Protestant-Catholic, religious-secular, and linguistic dimensions. The classification of the respondents presents few problems. The only difficulty worth noting is that multilingual Switzerland is treated as bilingual, but among the Swiss voting population the Italian-speakers and Romansh-speakers constitute a minority of only about five percent, and it is therefore permissible to focus exclusively on the German-French dichotomy. Further details about the operational definition

---

[3]The following rule is used to compute the index of class voting: "Subtract the percentage of persons in non-manual occupations voting for Left parties from the percentage of persons in manual occupations voting for Left parties" (Alford, 1963, pp. 79–80).

400   *Religion and Politics*

1979   Religious vs. Linguistic vs. Class Voting   445

of the variables and the characteristics of the survey data are given in the appendix.

Table 1 presents the classification of the political parties in the four multiparty systems along the left-right, Catholic-Protestant, religious-secular, and majority-minority language dimensions.[4] Many of the parties can be classified easily on the basis of their programs and traditions. For instance, as far as the left-right cleavage is concerned, the Belgian and Swiss Socialists and the Canadian New Democratic Party (NDP) clearly belong to the left, and the Belgian Liberals, the Swiss Radicals and Liberals, and the Canadian Conservatives to the right. With regard to the two religious dimensions, the Belgian Christian Social party and the Swiss Christian Conservative and Christian Social parties obviously fit the Catholic and religious categories, whereas the Belgian and Swiss Socialists, Radicals, and Liberals are traditionally secular parties. The linguistic cleavage divides the Flemish Volksunie (VU) from the Brussels Francophone party (FDF) and Walloon Rally (RW) in Belgium; similarly, the National party (NP) and its extremist offshoot, the Reconstituted National party (HNP), are Afrikaner parties of linguistic-ethnic defense. The smaller Swiss parties, which are regionally concentrated, can also be assigned easily to a linguistic category: the Liberals, who are particularly strong in francophone Switzerland, the Farmers (PAB) with special strength in Berne, and the mainly Zurich-based Independents.

In more doubtful cases, the criterion of classification is the inductive one of maximizing the indices of class, religious, and linguistic voting. The results contain no great surprises or anomalies. The only possibly controversial classifications in Table 1 are the left-right divisions in Canada and South Africa. The inductively drawn Canadian dichotomy that yields the highest index of class voting, interchanges the Liberals and Social Credit (SC) in Alford's left-right classification of Liberals and NDP vs. Conservatives and Social Credit. However, it is just as reasonable to assign the basically centrist Liberals to the right as to the left, and, although most scholars place Social Credit on the extreme right, the voters feel much less certain about this matter (Elkins, 1974, pp. 502–11; Laponce, 1970, pp. 483–85). For South Africa, the placement of the Nationalists and HNP on the left and the

United (UP) and Progressive (PP) parties on the right reverses the usual classification of these parties on the liberalism-conservatism scale, but the latter classification is based on attitudes toward ethnic and racial issues rather than class issues (Peele and Morse, 1974, pp. 1532–34). In terms of class-based support, the Nationalists have traditionally received more lower-class votes than their opponents (see van der Merwe and Buitendag, 1973, pp. 201–04).[5]

With regard to the party dichotomies on the two religious dimensions, it should be noted that the dividing lines coincide in all three countries in which both a Catholic-Protestant and a religious-secular split occurs, but that the descriptive labels differ: the "Catholic" parties are also the "religious" parties in Canada and Switzerland, but they are the "secular" parties in South Africa. Finally, the linguistic dichotomy is identical with the religious dichotomies in all countries except Switzerland.

Class Voting, Religious Voting, and Linguistic Voting

The indices of class, religious, and linguistic voting for the four countries are presented in Table 2. The top half of the table contains the unadjusted (uncontrolled) indices that are basically the same measures as are used by Alford. The adjusted indices of voting in the lower half represent the "pure" voting index of a particular independent variable when the other independent variables are controlled.[6]

The most striking result that emerges from the array of indices is the weakness of class voting. In all four countries, the unadjusted indices of religious and linguistic voting all reach higher levels. The only relatively high index of class voting is the Swiss index of +21,

---

[4]Only the more important parties are taken into consideration, and the very small parties that received less than roughly three percent of the votes in the elections of the early 1970s are disregarded.

[5]In recent years, the South African United and Progressive parties have regrouped: the left wing of the United party has merged with the Progressives to form the Progressive Federal party; its center has combined with the small Democratic party into the New Republic party; and its right wing continues as the South African party.

[6]Alford's indices of voting, which are differences in proportions, can also be interpreted as the regression coefficients for the regression of party choice on the independent variables if these dichotomized variables are given the numerical values of 0 and 1 (Alker, 1965, pp. 59, 84–85; Särlvik, 1969, p. 132; Korpi, 1972, p. 631). This important characteristic of the index makes it possible to use multiple regression analysis to compute controlled indices of voting.

Table 1. Classification of 21 Parties in Four Countries According to Four Dimensions of Cleavage

	Class Dimension		Religious Dimension I		Religious Dimension II		Linguistic Dimension*	
	Left	Right	Protestant	Catholic	Secular	Religious	Majority	Minority
Belgium	Socialist	Christian Social Liberal Volksunie Walloon Rally Francophone Front	–	–	Socialist Liberal Walloon Rally Francophone Front	Christian Social Volksunie	Christian Social Volksunie	Socialist Liberal Walloon Rally Francophone Front
Canada	New Democratic Social Credit	Liberal Conservative	Conservative New Democratic	Liberal Social Credit	Conservative New Democratic	Liberal Social Credit	Conservative New Democratic	Liberal Social Credit
South Africa	National Reconstituted National	United Progressive	National Reconstituted National	United Progressive	United Progressive	National Reconstituted National	National Reconstituted National	United Progressive
Switzerland	Socialist	Christian Conservative Christian Social Radical Liberal Farmers Independent	Socialist Radical Liberal Farmers Independent	Christian Conservative Christian Social	Socialist Radical Liberal Farmers Independent	Christian Conservative Christian Social	Christian Conservative Christian Social Farmers Independent	Socialist Radical Liberal

Source: Classification by the author on the basis of the parties' programs and traditions and the maximization of the indices of class, religious, and linguistic voting. The majority and minority languages are, respectively: Dutch and French (Belgium), English and French (Canada), Afrikaans and English (South Africa), and German and French (Switzerland).

but even here the other indices surpass it.[7] When the indices of class voting are adjusted for the influence of church affiliation, church attendance, and language, they undergo only a slight further weakening, or none at all, but the other adjusted indices remain stronger with the exception of the two religious voting indices in South Africa and the Canadian index based on church attendance.

Whereas it is easy to identify class as the weakest variable, it is much more difficult to say which is the strongest of the independent variables. Three different patterns appear among the unadjusted indices: religion as the strongest factor (Switzerland), language as the strongest factor (South Africa), and religion and language with approximately equal strength (Belgium and Canada). The Belgian and Canadian patterns fit the third category, but they are not exactly alike: in each of the countries, one of the religious variables and language are almost equally strong, but the strong religious

[7]On the basis of the same data, Henry H. Kerr (1974, p. 7) finds class, religious (church attendance), and linguistic indices with almost identical values: +22, +21, and +23, respectively. The explanation of this discrepancy is partly that Kerr includes a few minor parties in his analysis in addition to the more important ones considered here, but mainly that he uses the dichotomy of Socialists and Communists versus the other parties for all of his indices; this left-right dichotomy maximizes the index of class voting but is far from optimal for attaining high values for the indices of religious and linguistic voting. See also Sidjanski et al., 1975, pp. 45–61.

variable is church attendance in the former case and church affiliation in the latter.

The adjusted indices of religious and linguistic voting differ considerably from the unadjusted indices, but the overall patterns remain the same for three of the four countries. The Belgian indices both decrease in value by about equal amounts, and hence they remain close together. The predominance of language in South Africa is accentuated by the introduction of controls: the index of linguistic voting stays at its very high level whereas the other indices are reduced to insignificance. This finding for South Africa as a whole confirms the earlier conclusion by Stanton Peele and Stanley J. Morse (1974, p. 1537), based on a voting study of three Cape Town constituencies, that "ethnicity [or language] is the major determinant of party vote. . . . Party vote also varies with other demographic categories (SES, religion, place of origin), but this is largely because these factors covary with ethnicity. When ethnicity is held constant, therefore, all these variables lose their predictive power." In Switzerland, church affiliation remains the most potent variable, but the difference with the linguistic voting index has narrowed. Also, church attendance and language are now at the same level. In Canada, finally, the pattern of equal religious and linguistic indices is changed by the introduction of controls. In line with the findings of most other Canadian studies of voting (see Irvine, 1974), church affiliation now emerges as the strongest factor.

Since the religious and linguistic variables appear to be closely interrelated, a further

Table 2. Unadjusted and Adjusted Indices of Class, Religious, and Linguistic Voting in Four Countries

| | Unadjusted Indices | | | |
	Class	Church Affiliation	Church Attendance	Language
Belgium	+10	–	+49	+46
Canada	+ 7	+33	+14	+33
South Africa	+ 9	+27	+23	+66
Switzerland	+21	+49	+46	+25

| | Adjusted Indices | | | |
	Class	Church Affiliation	Church Attendance	Language
Belgium	+ 9	–	+39	+37
Canada	+ 6	+23	+ 5	+15
South Africa	+ 4	–10	+ 3	+67
Switzerland	+21	+37	+27	+27

Source: Data from the European Communities surveys conducted in Belgium in 1970 and 1973, the Canadian national election study of 1974, surveys conducted by Market Research Africa in 1974, and the Swiss national election study of 1972.

examination of the patterns of their influence on party choice is needed. The first step is to take a closer look at the religious factors. Table 3 presents the percentages of support for the "religious" parties among the respondents classified by four frequencies of church attendance and by church affiliation.[8] Switzerland and Catholic Belgium, the two countries with the highest indices of religious voting (church attendance), show very strong monotonic relationships between the frequency of churchgoing and party choice. The differences are smaller and also somewhat uneven in the other two countries. The further classification into Catholics and Protestants in Table 3 shows that frequency of church attendance is an especially important factor only for either the Catholics or the Protestants in each country: for the Catholics in Switzerland and, albeit less strongly, in Canada, and for the Protestants in South Africa. For the other religious groups in these three countries, it is of negligible importance.

Table 3 also shows where the main lines of cleavage appear when church affiliation and church attendance are considered together. In Canada, there are differences in party support *within* both the Protestant and the Catholic communities, but the far greater difference is

[8]The category of very frequent churchgoers includes those attending more than once a week (Belgium) or at least once a week (the other three countries).

that *between* Protestants and Catholics. In South Africa, the party choice of non-churchgoing Protestants is very similar to that of the Catholics, and the most obvious cleavage here is between churchgoing Protestants and all others. A similar pattern emerges in the Swiss case: nonpracticing Catholics behave very much like Protestants and unlike their more faithful coreligionists.

These distinctions can be used to compare the relative impact of religion and language on party choice. This is done in Table 4 which presents the percentages of support for the "religious" parties cross-tabulated according to religion, as classified in the previous paragraph, and language. The "religious" parties are also the parties representing linguistic majorities or minorities except in Switzerland where the two dichotomies do not coincide; for this reason, two matrices are given for the Swiss case.

Religion and language are mutually reinforcing determinants of party choice in Belgium, Canada, and Switzerland. In terms of their relative strength, religion has a slight edge over language in Belgium: the indices of religious voting within the Dutch and French linguistic communities are +38 and +44, respectively, whereas the indices of linguistic voting within the frequent church-attending group and the less frequently and nonpracticing group are a somewhat lower +32 and +38, respectively. The Canadian percentages are more difficult to interpret because there are hardly any French-

Table 3. Percentage Support for the "Religious" Parties Among Respondents with Different Frequencies of Church Attendance in Four Counrties

Church Affiliation	How Often Attending	Percent Supporting the "Religious" Parties in:			
		Belgium	Canada	South Africa	Switzerland
Catholic and Protestant	Very frequently	—	72	73	72
	Frequently	—	61	76	42
	Infrequently	—	56	62	15
	Never	—	57	38	9
Catholic	Very frequently	95	84	}41*	86
	Frequently	75	82		63
	Infrequently	43	74	}36*	36
	Never	16	74		10
Protestant	Very frequently	—	42	77	5
	Frequently	—	52	78	13
	Infrequently	—	45	63	8
	Never	—	49	40	9

Source: Data from the European Communities surveys conducted in Belgium in 1970 and 1973, the Canadian national election study of 1974, surveys conducted by Market Research Africa in 1974, and the Swiss national election study of 1972.

*These categories had to be combined, because there were not enough cases to present reliable percentages for each of the four categories separately.

speaking Protestants in the country. Nevertheless, religion emerges as the more important variable because there is relatively less difference between francophone and anglophone Catholics than between Catholic and Protestant anglophones. In Switzerland, religion is clearly the more powerful predictor in Table 4d, but this is not surprising since the parties are here dichotomized in such a way as to accentuate the religious differences. It is therefore of decisive importance that in Table 4e, where the party system dichotomization has the opposite bias in favor of linguistic differences, religion remains the stronger determinant: the two indices of religious voting within the linguistic groups are +36 and +43 compared with the lower indices of linguistic voting of +23 and +30 within the two religious categories.

In South Africa, language and religion do not reinforce each other. In the Afrikaner community, there is a slightly weaker tendency to support the two Nationalist parties among Catholics and nonpracticing Protestants than among practicing Protestants, whereas in the anglophone group the pattern is reversed. The more important conclusion from Table 4c, however, is that language is the overwhelmingly powerful determinant of party support among white South Africans.

The overall pattern of the relative strength of religion and language in the four countries in Table 4 reinforces the earlier conclusions based on the adjusted voting indices of Table 2. Religion is the better predictor in two countries (Canada and Switzerland); language is stronger in only one country (South Africa); and the two factors have approximately the same strength in one of the countries (Belgium). In the group of four countries, religion therefore emerges as the more important determinant.

Tree Analyses of the Patterns of Party Choice

Further evidence, which slightly modifies but generally supports the above conclusion, is provided by the tree analyses in Figures 1 to 4. The party choice dichotomy used in all four country trees is the division between "religious" and "secular" parties, which, it should be remembered, coincides with the division between the linguistic majority and minority parties in all countries except Switzerland. This dichotomy produces the highest total proportion of the variance that is explained by the independent variables. In order to make the results comparable with the analysis of the indices of voting, we have dichotomized the

Table 4. Percentage Support for the "Religious" Parties Among Religious and Linguistic Groups in Four Countries (and Support for the "German Majority" Parties in Switzerland)

a. Belgium	Dutch	French
(Very) frequent churchgoers	84%	52%
Infrequent and non-churchgoers	46	8
b. Canada	French	English
Catholics	85%	70%
Protestants	*	46
c. South Africa	Afrikaans	English
Practicing Protestants	94%	24%
Catholics and non-practicing Protestants	91	31
d. Switzerland (support for the "religious" parties)	German	French
Practicing Catholics	64%	52%
Protestants and non-practicing Catholics	9	8
e. Switzerland (support for the "German majority" parties)	German	French
Practicing Catholics	76%	53%
Protestants and non-practicing Catholics	40	10

Source: Data from the European Communities surveys conducted in Belgium in 1970 and 1973, the Canadian national election study of 1974, surveys conducted by Market Research Africa in 1974, and the Swiss national election study of 1972.

*Insufficient number of cases.

independent variables in exactly the same way. The process of splitting the samples into subgroups was continued until no predictor could be found that reduced the variance by at least another 0.3 percent.[9]

The results of the tree analyses are summarized in Table 5, which presents the proportion of the variance in party choice explained by each of the independent variables separately and by all of them together. The table also gives the comparable proportions of the variance explained by the stepwise multiple regression method which, unlike tree analysis, assumes additivity and cannot detect interaction effects. It should be pointed out that for the purpose of this table the tree analysis was extended to the 0.1 percent level, since the variance explained by regression is also measured in tenths of a percent. The two sets of percentages turn out to be remarkably similar. The logic of the two methods necessarily leads to identical percentages of the variance explained by the strongest variable. As far as the other variables and the total reduction of variance are concerned, the tree analysis yields consistently but only slightly higher percentages. This means that interac-

[9] This cutting-off point is lower than the 0.6 percent threshold recommended by the designers of the AID method (Sonquist, Baker, and Morgan, 1971, p. 10), but the lower level has been used in several voting studies (see Rose, 1974a, pp. 214, 261, 309, 644; Liepelt, 1971, pp. 188–89).

tion effects play a rather small role.

Before we turn to an inspection of the individual country trees, we can state a number of general conclusions. First, it is worth noting that three of the four tree analyses explain a high proportion of the variance in party choice. In Western countries generally the total variance explained is about 25 percent on the average (Lancelot, 1975, pp. 419–20), and, by comparison, the Belgian, Swiss, and South African percentages are very high indeed. This result is especially remarkable because the present analysis considers only four independent variables (and only three in the Belgian case) in contrast to the dozens of social and demographic variables that are usually applied in tree analyses of voting. The exception is Canada where a below-average total of only about 13 percent of the variance can be explained, reflecting "the lack of social definition in the Canadian party system" (Irvine, 1976, p. 355).

Second, the class factor once again turns out to be extremely weak. Tree analyses were also carried out with the parties dichotomized so as to highlight class differences. These trees are not presented here for reasons of space, but the results can be briefly summarized. In the three countries in which the dichotomies favorable to class differ from the dichotomies used in Table 5—Belgium, Canada, and Switzerland—the total proportion of the variance explained is now reduced to 19.5, 3.9, and 17.3 percent, respectively, and the percentage explained by class is

Table 5. Percentages of the Explained Variance in Party Choice
("Religious" vs. "Secular" Parties) in Four Countries

	Tree Analysis*				
	Class	Church Affiliation	Church Attendance	Language	Total
Belgium	1.6%	–	23.6%	10.8%	35.9%
Canada	0.3	11.3%	0.4	1.1	13.1
South Africa	0.5	0.6	0.3	46.6	48.0
Switzerland	1.0	28.0	9.8	0.3	38.9
	Stepwise Multiple Regression				
	Class	Church Affiliation	Church Attendance	Language	Total
Belgium	0.6%	–	23.6%	10.7%	34.9%
Canada	0.0	11.3%	0.2	1.1	12.7
South Africa	0.1	0.4	0.1	46.6	47.2
Switzerland	0.0	28.0	6.3	0.3	34.6

Source: Data from the European Communities surveys conducted in Belgium in 1970 and 1973, the Canadian national election study of 1974, surveys conducted by Market Research Africa in 1974, and the Swiss national election study of 1972.

*The percentages tend to be slightly higher than in Figures 1–4 because the analysis was continued to the 0.1 percent level of explained variance (instead of the 0.3 percent level used in the figures).

only 1.2, 1.1, and 5.2, respectively. The religious variables remain the strongest determinants of party choice in all three cases.

Third, religion now emerges more clearly as the strongest factor. Church affiliation and/or church attendance explain a much higher proportion of the variance than language not only in Canada and Switzerland, but also in Belgium. This conclusion is not changed by the use of the party choice dichotomy more favorable to language in the Swiss case; the total proportion of variance explained is 20.8 percent, in which church affiliation has the highest share of 11.2 percent and language only a modest 4.5 percent. In South Africa, language remains the overwhelmingly powerful predictor.

Fourth, all of the country trees show relatively simple patterns. With four independent variables (three in the Belgian case) it would have been theoretically possible to find as many as sixteen (or, for Belgium, eight) end groups. In fact, the trees have only from four to six end groups. This means that the high total propor-

tions of explained variance are not the result of many small cumulative additions but of large shares of variance explained especially on the first split.

The Belgian tree in Figure 1 is, unlike the other three trees, almost symmetrical. Neither the order of the successive splits nor the nature of these splits contains any surprises: church attendance accounts for the first split, followed by language and class at the second and third levels of splitting, and the frequent churchgoers, Dutch speakers, and non-manual workers are consistently the people who prefer the "religious" to the "secular" parties.[10] The Canadian, South African, and Swiss trees are all

[10]It is surprising that in the tree presented by Keith Hill (1974, p. 103) language does not emerge as a differentiating factor. The most likely explanation is that Hill dichotomizes party choice as left versus right, and that he includes region, which to a considerable extent coincides with language, among his variables.

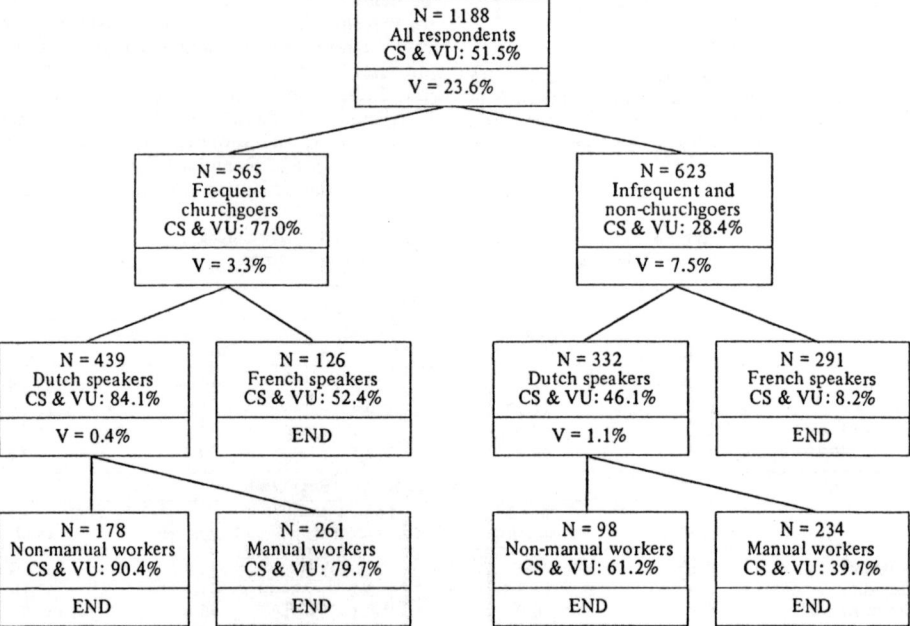

Source: Data from the European Communities surveys conducted in Belgium in 1970 and 1973.

Note: Total variance reduced by 35.8 percent.

Figure 1. A Tree Analysis of Party Choice in Belgium
(Christian Social Party and Volksunie)

asymmetrical. In the last two of these cases, this is caused by the fact that the initial split yields a group that cannot be split further because it is highly homogeneous with regard to party choice and contains very little variance: the Swiss Protestants who overwhelmingly reject the Catholic parties, and the Afrikaners who overwhelmingly support the two Nationalist parties. Compared with the Afrikaners' political unanimity, the English speakers can be characterized as "political refracted" (Charton, 1975, p. 118; see also Lever, 1972, pp. 24–26; van der Merwe and Buitendag, 1973, p. 198). The most striking aspect of the South African tree is the great strength of the linguistic factor: close to half of the variance is explained on the first split. The asymmetry of the Canadian tree is not owing to the virtual absence of variance in party choice among the Protestants. In fact, the Protestant group contains much more variance than the Catholics; however, it is linguistically homogeneous, and neither of the remain-

ing variables emerges as a significant differentiator, whereas the Catholic group can be split further—albeit without contributing impressively to the amount of explained variance. The general pattern of the Canadian tree is similar to that of a series of trees based on surveys between 1957 and 1968 presented by Laponce (1972, p. 277): religion consistently emerges on the first split, and region—which, of course, closely corresponds to language—on the second split.

Conclusion: Comparative Theory and the Paradox of Religious Voting

This four-country comparison was described earlier as a "crucial experiment" in Naroll's sense of the term. It may also be likened to a decisive trial of strength, in which religion turns out to be victorious, language is a strong runner-up, and class finishes as a distant third.

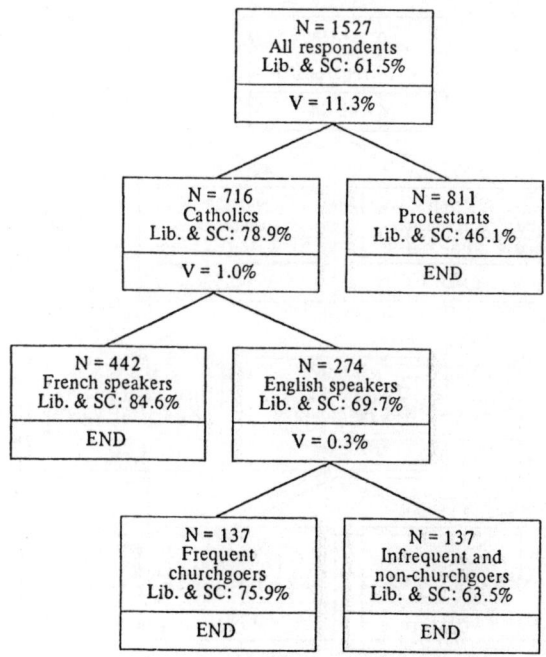

Source: Data from the Canadian election study of 1974.
Note: Total variance reduced by 12.6 percent.

**Figure 2. A Tree Analysis of Party Choice in Canada
(Liberal and Social Credit Parties)**

Can these findings be explained and interpreted in a broader theoretical framework?

The conspicuous weakness of class voting compared with religious and linguistic voting is not really surprising. True, even without a Marxist bias, one would not be unreasonable to assume that elections in Western industrialized societies are, or should be, "the expression of the democratic class struggle" (Lipset, 1960, p. 220), and to regard religious and linguistic attachments as pre-modern forces. However, such "primordial" communal loyalties can be extremely tenacious even in the modern world, and they constitute a formidable obstacle to the development of competing cleavages based on objective socioeconomic interests (see Geertz, 1963, pp. 109–13). As was pointed out above, it is significant that wherever social class and religion are alternative bases of party choice, particularly in the core continental European countries, class voting tends to be weak. And even in the Anglo-American democracies, it can be argued—on the basis of

Alford's own evidence on class voting in these countries—that "class is the major determinant of voting behavior *only if* no other cleavage happens to be present" (Sartori, 1969, p. 76). Social class is clearly no more than a secondary and subsidiary influence on party choice, and it can become a factor of importance only in the absence of potent rivals such as religion and language.

Neither is it surprising that linguistic voting turns out to be relatively strong in the four linguistically divided countries. A shared language is regarded as one of the principal building blocks of nationalism both in the traditional literature on this subject and in Karl W. Deutsch's (1953) more refined concept of a nation as an intensive network of communication. Because language is a crucial differentiator among nations, it is bound to be a major cleavage and a strong source of partisan differences in "nations" that are not linguistically homogeneous. The finding that language is a strong determinant of party choice also accords

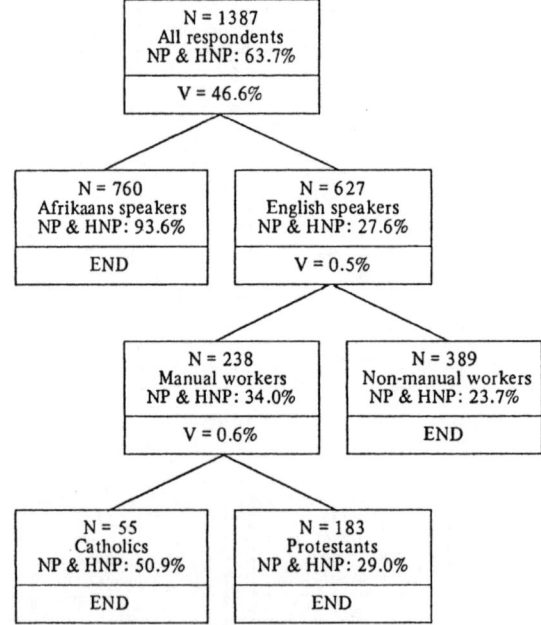

Source: Data from surveys conducted by Market Research Africa in 1974.

Note: Total variance reduced by 47.8 percent.

Figure 3. A Tree Analysis of Party Choice in South Africa
(National and Reconstituted National Parties)

454   The American Political Science Review   Vol. 73

with the developmental theory of cleavage structures and party systems expounded by Seymour M. Lipset and Stein Rokkan (1967): cultural-territorial conflicts are one of the four basic sources of party system cleavages that they distinguish.

The more surprising—and the theoretically more interesting and challenging—empirical finding concerns the relative strength of religious and linguistic voting: religion emerges as the more important dimension of party choice in the 1970s, whereas especially in Belgium and Canada the linguistic-ethnic cleavage has been the more salient dimension of political conflict in recent years. For instance, Meisel (1974, p.

9) considers religion to be "of virtually no political importance in contemporary federal politics" in Canada, whereas, of course, the conflict between francophone and anglophone Canada is of the greatest political significance. Similarly, linguistic issues have in recent years been much more prominent than religious problems in Belgium. Conversely, language has remained the paramount determinant of party choice in South Africa, although, as Hendrik van der Merwe and J. J. Buitendag (1973, p. 190) observe, "there is much evidence that the traditional divisions between the two language groups are tending to become muted." Switzerland is a more doubtful case. In recent years,

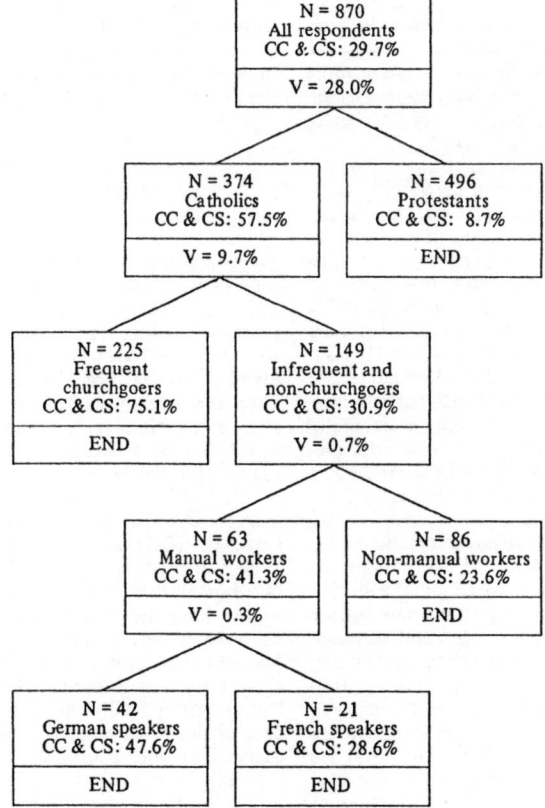

Source: Data from the Swiss national election study of 1972.

Note: Total variance reduced by 38.6 percent.

Figure 4. A Tree Analysis of Party Choice in Switzerland (Christian Conservative and Christian Social Parties)

410   *Religion and Politics*

1979   Religious vs. Linguistic vs. Class Voting   455

the Jura problem has called attention to the fact that even Swiss politics is not immune to linguistic tensions, but the Jura question is primarily a regional rather than a national issue and it is also just as much a religious as a linguistic problem. At the national level, neither religious nor linguistic issues can be said to have high salience.

Two explanations of the paradox may be offered. One follows the well-known argument of Lipset and Rokkan (1967, pp. 50–51) that party systems tend to reflect the political cleavages of the periods in which the parties came into existence, instead of the dimensions of contemporary political conflict. The conflicts of the past have structured the political parties and the differences between them, and are able to survive as entrenched atavisms in the party systems. The party systems in turn structure the electoral contests, even when other political dimensions have become more salient. Following this line of reasoning, Mildred Schwartz (1974, p. 589) argues that in Canada "class-based voting exists; it is consistent class-based parties that are missing." Similarly, one can say that in Belgium, Canada, and Switzerland, the potential strength of linguistic voting is suppressed by the religiously oriented structure of the party systems. The Belgian case also demonstrates, however, that the "freezing" of the party system in the 1920s was not absolute: Flemish linguistic parties already made their appearance in 1919 and have survived in the form of the Volksunie, but the Walloon and Francophone parties originated in the 1960s in a long and solidly established party system. Of course, the presence of these specifically linguistic parties also accounts for the considerable strength of linguistic voting in Belgium, which does not lag very far behind the strength of religious voting.

The second explanation of the paradox of strong religious voting is based on the notion that political parties are important, but not the only, vehicles for the articulation and representation of various kinds of interests. In Belgium, Canada, and Switzerland, a significant difference between the religious and linguistic communities is that the former tend to be geographically dispersed whereas the latter are regionally more concentrated. Consequently, the most suitable organs for the representation of religious interests have been the political parties, whereas the strongest organs for the representation of the linguistic interests could be the subnational governments, especially if they possessed or acquired a high degree of political autonomy: the provincial and cantonal governments in federal Canada and Switzerland

and the recently established cultural councils in semi-federal Belgium (Dunn, 1972; Lijphart, 1977, pp. 90–97, 121–24). The deviant case of South Africa with its extremely strong linguistic voting patterns significantly reinforces this argument: because South Africa has a unitary form of government and because its linguistic communities are geographically interspersed to a high extent, the linguistic interests have had to protect themselves mainly through the party system.

Hence the greater strength of religious compared with linguistic voting in Belgium, Canada, and Switzerland is neither the result of the greater contemporary salience of religious issues in these countries (with the partial exception of Switzerland), nor exclusively the outcome of an atavistic survival of past religious conflicts. At least to some extent, it is also the effect of the presence of alternative, regional-federal, structures for the articulation and representation of the linguistic interests.

Appendix: Survey Data and Operational Definitions

(a) *The data.* The surveys were conducted at approximately the same time: the Belgian surveys in 1970 and 1973, the Swiss survey in 1972, and the Canadian and South African surveys in 1974. The Canadian and the Swiss surveys were election studies, although the Swiss survey was not held until several months after the elections. The South African data were collected in an election year but not in connection with explicit electoral research. The only major Belgian election study done so far, in 1968, could not be used because it did not include any question about the respondents' language (Delruelle, Evalenko, and Fraeys, 1970); instead, two more recent sociopolitical, but non-election, surveys had to be used. It would have been desirable to compare the major social determinants of party choice in the four countries not only in the 1970s but also their trends over extended periods of time. Unfortunately, with the exception of Canada, data of sufficient quality for such a diachronic analysis of voting in these countries are not available.

The multivariate nature of the analysis and the choice of methods required that the sizes of the national samples be relatively large. This is the reason why, in the Belgian case, two similar surveys conducted in 1970 and 1973 were combined. However, no additional data were available to increase the size of the South African sample. In fact, the latter already consists of two separate subsamples of about equal size (a sample of Afrikaners and one of English-speaking white South Africans to whom similar questionnaires were administered) which could ·be combined by applying appropriate weighting procedures. The South African data were collected in cities, towns, and villages, and exclude the rural, mainly farming, population, but this does not affect their comparability with the data from the other three countries because the manual versus non-manual classification that was used required the exclusion of farmers from these samples, too. All four samples can therefore be regarded as representative samples of the national voting populations. The exact numbers of respondents in the samples are as follows: Belgium (1970), N = 1296; Belgium (1973), N = 1266; Canada (1974), N = 2562, weighted N = 2445; South Africa (1974), N = 641 (Afrikaners) + 659 (English speakers) = 1300, weighted N = 2175; Switzerland (1972), N = 1917.

(b) *Operational definitions of the variables.* Social class was operationally defined in terms of the occupation of the head of the household to which the respondent belonged. In order to assign these occupations to the manual and non-manual strata, we used the criteria listed by Alford (1963, pp. 70–71). Farmers are the only significant group that cannot be accommodated in this dichotomous classification.

The two religious variables that were considered are church affiliation and church attendance. The former was dichotomized into Protestant and Catholic categories with all respondents of other faiths and without religious affiliation being left out of consideration. This is the most meaningful and obvious classification for the Canadian and Swiss cases. It may be argued that the more significant dividing line in South Africa lies between the adherents of the Dutch Reformed churches on the one hand and Anglicans, Methodists, Catholics, and Jews on the other hand. Such a dichotomy coincides so closely with the linguistic-ethnic difference between Afrikaners and English speakers, however, that it turns church affiliation into a virtual replica of the linguistic variable (see Peele and Morse, 1974, p. 1526). For the sake of comparative consistency, too, it makes more sense to use the Catholic-Protestant dichotomy in all three countries.

The dichotomization of the church attendance variable presented slightly more serious problems because the categories in the various surveys were not always the same. To keep the dichotomy as simple and straightforward as possible, we drew the dividing line between frequent churchgoers (attending at least twice a month) and those attending church only infrequently or never.

The linguistic variable was operationally defined as the language usually spoken at home or the mother tongue. A question about the home language was asked in the Belgian, Canadian, and South African surveys, but the Swiss survey only inquired into the mother tongue of the respondents. It is a reasonable assumption, however, that the mother tongue and the usual language spoken at home coincide in the vast majority of cases.

The respondents' choice of political party may be elicited by means of several different questions. The principal possibilities are: the respondents' last vote, their intended vote (if an election is to take place in the near future), their probable vote (in answer to the hypothetical question about how they would vote if an election were held at the time of the survey), and their general party preference or party identification. In American voting behavior research a clear conceptual distinction is usually drawn between these variants, especially between party identification and actual voting choice. In other countries, there tends to be such a close relationship between the two that they are virtually indistinguishable. As Budge and Farlie (1976, p. 123) point out, party identification in non-American political contexts predicts actual voting so well that one must "suspect its empirical independence of voting choice, its conceptual antecedence and its explanatory capacity." Because the data of the present study were collected partly in election surveys and partly in non-election surveys, the best method to maximize comparability on this dimension was to avoid the intended or most recent votes as indicators of party choice and to use party preference (Canada and Switzerland), the probable vote (South Africa), or a combination of the two (Belgium).

References

Alford, Robert R. (1963). *Party and Society: The Anglo-American Democracies.* Chicago: Rand McNally.

Alker, Hayward R., Jr. (1965). *Mathematics and Politics.* New York: Macmillan.

Budge, Ian, and Dennis Farlie (1976). "A Comparative Analysis of Factors Correlated with Turnout and Voting Choice." In Ian Budge, Ivor Crewe, and Dennis Farlie (eds.), *Party Identification and Beyond: Representations of Voting and Party Competition.* London: Wiley.

412   *Religion and Politics*

1979   Religious vs. Linguistic vs. Class Voting   457

Charton, Nancy (1975). "English-Speaking White Elites in South African Politics." *Politikon* 2: 115–28.

Converse, Philip E. (1974). "Some Priority Variables in Comparative Electoral Research." In Richard Rose (ed.), *Electoral Behavior: A Comparative Handbook.* New York: Free Press.

de Jong, J. J. (1956). *Overheid en onderdaan.* Wageningen: Zomer en Keunings.

Delruelle, Nicole, René Evalenko, and William Fraeys (1970). *Le comportement politique des électeurs belges.* Brussels: Institut de Sociologie de l'Université Libre de Bruxelles.

Deutsch, Karl W. (1953). *Nationalism and Social Communication: An Inquiry into the Foundations of Nationality.* Cambridge, Mass.: Technology Press.

Dunn, James A., Jr. (1972). "'Consociational Democracy' and Language Conflict: A Comparison of the Belgian and Swiss Experiences." *Comparative Political Studies* 5: 3–39.

Elkins, David J. (1974). "The Perceived Structure of the Canadian Party Systems." *Canadian Journal of Political Science* 7: 502–24.

Frognier, André-Paul (1976). "Party Preference Spaces and Voting Change in Belgium." In Ian Budge, Ivor Crewe, and Dennis Farlie (eds.), *Party Identification and Beyond: Representations of Voting and Party Competition.* London: Wiley.

Geertz, Clifford (1963). "The Integrative Revolution: Primordial Sentiments and Civil Politics in the New States." In Clifford Geertz (ed.), *Old Societies and New States: The Quest for Modernity in Asia and Africa.* New York: Free Press.

Hill, Keith (1974). "Belgium: Political Change in a Segmented Society." In Richard Rose (ed.), *Electoral Behavior: A Comparative Handbook.* New York: Free Press.

Huyse, Luc (1975). "Vijftien Angelsaksische auteurs over politiek, verzuiling en compromisvorming in Belgie." *Res Publica* 17: 413–31.

Irvine, William P. (1974). "Explaining the Religious Basis of the Canadian Partisan Identity: Success on the Third Try." *Canadian Journal of Political Science* 7: 560–63.

———— (1976). "Testing Models of Voting Choice in Canada." In Ian Budge, Ivor Crewe, and Dennis Farlie (eds.), *Party Identification and Beyond: Representations of Voting and Party Competition.* London: Wiley.

Kerr, Henry H., Jr. (1974). *Switzerland: Social Cleavages and Partisan Conflict.* Sage Professional Papers in Contemporary Political Sociology, Vol. 1, No. 06–002. London and Beverly Hills: Sage.

Korpi, Walter (1972). "Some Problems in the Measurement of Class Voting." *American Journal of Sociology* 78: 627–42.

Lancelot, Alain (1975). "Comparative Electoral Behavior." *European Journal of Political Research* 3: 413–24.

Laponce, J. A. (1970). "Note on the Use of the Left-Right Dimension." *Comparative Political Studies* 2: 481–502.

———— (1972). "Post-Dicting Electoral Cleavages in Canadian Federal Elections, 1949–68: Material for

a Footnote." *Canadian Journal of Political Science* 5: 270–86.

Lever, H. (1972). *The South African Voter: Some Aspects of Voting Behavior, With Special Reference to the General Elections of 1966 and 1970.* Cape Town: Juta.

Liepelt, Klaus (1971). "The Infra-Structure of Party Support in Germany and Austria." In Mattei Dogan and Richard Rose (eds.), *European Politics: A Reader.* Boston: Little, Brown.

Lijphart, Arend (1971). *Class Voting and Religious Voting in the European Democracies: A Preliminary Report.* Occasional Paper No. 8, Survey Research Centre. Glasgow: University of Strathclyde.

———— (1975). "The Comparable-Cases Strategy in Comparative Research." *Comparative Political Studies* 8: 158–77.

———— (1977). *Democracy in Plural Societies: A Comparative Exploration.* New Haven: Yale University Press.

Lipset, Seymour Martin (1960). *Political Man: The Social Bases of Politics.* Garden City: Doubleday.

———— and Stein Rokkan (1967). "Cleavage Structures, Party Systems, and Voter Alignments: An Introduction." In Seymour M. Lipset and Stein Rokkan (eds.), *Party Systems and Voter Alignments: Cross-National Perspectives.* New York: Free Press.

Lorwin, Val R. (1966). "Belgium: Religion, Class, and Language in National Politics." In Robert A. Dahl (ed.), *Political Oppositions in Western Democracies.* New Haven: Yale University Press.

Meisel, John (1974). *Cleavages, Parties and Values in Canada.* Sage Professional Papers in Contemporary Political Sociology, Vol. 1, No. 06–003. London and Beverly Hills: Sage.

Naroll, Raoul (1966). "Scientific Comparative Politics and International Relations." In R. Barry Farrell (ed.), *Approaches to Comparative and International Politics.* Evanston, Ill.: Northwestern University Press.

Peele, Stanton, and Stanley J. Morse (1974). "Ethnic Voting and Political Change in South Africa." *American Political Science Review* 68: 1520–41.

Rose, Richard, ed. (1974a). *Electoral Behavior: A Comparative Handbook.* New York: Free Press.

———— (1974b). "Comparability in Electoral Studies." In Richard Rose (ed.), *Electoral Behavior: A Comparative Handbook.* New York: Free Press.

———— and Derek W. Urwin (1969). "Social Cohesion, Political Parties and Strains in Regimes." *Comparative Political Studies* 2: 7–67.

Särlvik, Bo (1969). "Socioeconomic Determinants of Voting Behavior in the Swedish Electorate." *Comparative Political Studies* 2: 99–135.

Sartori, Giovanni (1969). "From the Sociology of Politics to Political Sociology." In Seymour Martin Lipset (ed.), *Politics and the Social Sciences.* New York: Oxford University Press.

Schwartz, Mildred A. (1974). "Canadian Voting Behavior." In Richard Rose (ed.), *Electoral Behavior: A Comparative Handbook.* New York: Free Press.

Sidjanski, Dusan, Charles Roig, Henry Kerr, Ronald Inglehart, and Jacques Nicola (1975). *Les Suisses et la politique: Enquête sur les attitudes d'électeurs suisses.* Berne: Herbert Lang.

Sonquist, John A., Elizabeth Lauh Baker, and James N. Morgan (1971). *Searching for Structure (Alias–AID–III).* Ann Arbor: Survey Research Center, Institute for Social Research, University of Michigan.

Urwin, Derek W. (1970). "Social Cleavages and Politi-
cal Parties in Belgium: Problems of Institutionalization." *Political Studies* 18:320–40.

van der Merwe, Hendrik, and J. J. Buitendag (1973). "Political, Ethnic and Structural Differences among White South Africans." In Association for Sociology in Southern Africa, *Sociology Southern Africa 1973.* Durban: University of Natal.

[17]

Politics and the Pulpit: The Case of Protestant Europe

John Madeley

Confounding the assumptions and doctrines of Enlightenment secularism (in both its original liberal-bourgeois and later Marxist guises), religion has continued to play an important role in the politics of the 'Old World'. Both Northern Ireland and Poland stand as contemporary reminders that, despite rumours to the contrary, God is not dead so far as European politics is concerned. The partial retardation of secularising processes by revivals of different kinds in Catholicism and Protestantism in the nineteenth century, not only confounded the expectations of secularist thinkers, it also had significant political effects in the formative years of the European party systems, which reflected the continuing importance of religious cleavages and the contemporary salience of religious issues in politics. These religious elements in partisan politics have shown a remarkable ability to survive, despite general trends toward secularisation; and even where they have declined or disappeared, the religious factor in a number of significant cases continues to operate as a sort of 'hidden agenda' in the pattern of voting behaviour.[1]

In an important 1969 article on social cohesion, political parties and strains in regimes, Rose and Urwin attempted to assess the relative impact of religion on politics with the aid of quantitative data. They developed a measure for the social cohesiveness of political parties and applied it to the secondary analysis of broadly comparable survey data from seventeen different Western countries.[2] This analysis showed that religion—measured variously in terms of confessional affiliation, church attendance and pro/anti-clerical opinion— provided a positive basis for cohesiveness in a greater number of parties than any other variable, including class. They were thus able to conclude that, contrary to Lipset's well-known claim for the primacy of the class factor in democratic politics, 'religious divisions, not class, are the main social basis of parties in the Western world today'.[3] Two years later a complementary study by Lijphart of the political cohesion of social groups (i.e., the reverse relationship), which was based on a secondary analysis of data from ten European countries, confirmed the contemporary political importance of the religious factor.[4] He concluded that by contrast with divisions based on age, sex and urban/rural residence 'class and religion are clearly the most significant variables'.[5]

In addition to demonstrating the overall importance of the religious factor in post-war European politics, the Rose-Urwin and Lijphart studies also provided a basis for measuring its incidence as between the different regions of Europe. In terms of the broad confessional categories of Catholic and Protestant, Western Europe has, as Rokkan pointed out, been divided into three major areas since the Reformation and the Thirty Years War: 'a Protestant north (Denmark-Norway, Sweden-Finland, Prussia); a religiously mixed zone from Ireland to the Alps (Britain-Ireland, the Low Countries, the Rhineland, large sections of France until 1685, the Swiss cantons); and the counter-Reformation countries in the east and south (the Hapsburg territories, Spain and the Italian territories, France after 1685).[6] This subdivision has remained remarkably stable, at least in so far as the various populations are concerned, even though the state boundaries have shifted as recently as 1945 in such a way as to affect the confessional balance in individual states. Despite the changes entailed in the unification and division of Germany, and the secession from the United Kingdom of the Republic of Ireland, the basic lines of subdivision are still such as to provide the most natural breakdown of Europe into confessional culture areas.

The Rose-Urwin European data (augmented from other sources) are aggregated in Table 1 in terms of these areas. There is clearly a wide variation between the three areas in the distribution of parties cohesive by religion and class. In the Catholic and mixed-confession groups of countries an equal proportion of all parties (72 per cent) are cohesive by religion, while in the Protestant group an almost identical proportion (71 per cent) are not. Cohesiveness by class shows the reverse pattern though not quite as strongly: in the Protestant group, 64 per cent of parties are cohesive by class, as against less than half that proportion (28 per cent) in the other two areas. Lijphart's data, augmented from other sources (see Table 2), reflect a similar pattern: 'Class voting and religious voting are negatively correlated with each other. In general, the higher the index of class voting the lower the indices of religious voting, although this relationship is by no means perfect.'[7] In all cases, class voting is markedly higher than religious voting in Protestant countries, while in the mixed-confession and Catholic countries the reverse is the case.

This contrast in the overall weight of the religious factor between the largely mono-religious Protestant countries and those countries with at least a significant minority of Catholic citizens, is well known and is reflected in the fact that most of the work on the religious factor in European politics has focused on Catholic populations and the largely Catholic post-war phenomenon of Christian Democratic parties.[8] Any attempt to provide a general explanation for the varying incidence of the religious factor must, however, account for its relative weakness in the north of Europe, as well as its relative strength in the middle and south. It must take account of the exceptional, but nonetheless significant, cases where religion has provided the base for Protestant confessional parties in the north. Such an undertaking is made difficult by the fact that what will here be called 'Protestant Europe' has historically contained a much greater variety of confessional types, patterns of Church-State relations, degrees of religious pluralism and levels of religious observance, than has been the case in Catholic or counter-Reformation Europe. This article is a first attempt to redress the balance in studies of the religious factor by: (a) providing a summary overview of the most salient features of the religious structures and cultures of Protestant Europe; and (b) relating these constellations to the emergence or non-emergence of the religious factor in politics.

The term Protestant Europe is used here to identify collectively both the mono-religious Protestant countries of the north and the mixed-confession

TABLE 1

COHESIVENESS OF PARTIES IN FOURTEEN

WEST EUROPEAN COUNTRIES BY RELIGION AND CLASS

	Cohesive by religion only	Cohesive by both religion and class	Cohesive by class only	Other	Total
Protestant countries					
Britain 1966			Lab	Con,Lib	3
Denmark 1956/70	Christians*	Left Socs[+]	Soc,Con,Lib	Rad	6
Finland 1966	Christians*	SKDL +	Soc,Agn,Lib,Con	SPP	7
Norway 1965	Christians	CP	Lab,Agn,Con	Lib	6
Sweden 1964	Christians	CP	Soc,Con,Lib	Agn	6
Total and percentage	4=14%	4=14%	14=50%	6=21%	28=99%
Mixed-confession countries					
Germany 1965	FDP	SDP		CDU	3
Netherlands 1964	KVP,ARP,CHU	PVDA,VVD		Farmers	6
Switzerland 1972**	EVP,Cath,Rad	Soc		Indep, Nat Actn	6
N.Ireland 1968	Unionist, Nationalist		NLIP		3
Total and percentage	9=50%	4=22%	1=6%	4=22%	18=100%
Catholic countries					
Austria 1968	OVP	SPO		FPO	3
Belgium 1965	PSC,Volks-U, Lib	Soc,CP			5
France 1956	SFIO,Rad, MRP,RPF,Ind	PCF			6
Ireland 1965				FG,FF,Lab	3
Italy 1963/67	DCI,PRI,MSI	PCI,PSI	PLI	PSDI,Mon	8
Total and percentage	12=48%	6=24%	1=4%	6=24%	25=100%
All country total	25=35%	14=20%	16=23%	16=23%	71=101%

* These parties did not compete in national elections until the early 1970s

+ These attributions are made on the basis of Rose and Urwin (1969),p.45, Note 1.

**Data for Switzerland are reported in H.Kerr, <u>Switzerland: Social Cleavages and Partisan Conflict</u>, Sage Professional Paper in Comparative Political Sociology, Vol.1, No.06,002.

152   RELIGION IN WEST EUROPEAN POLITICS

TABLE 2

INDICES OF PARTISAN CHOICE IN ELEVEN COUNTRIES OF WESTERN EUROPE

	Class	Church affiliation (Cath/Prot)	Church attendance
Mono-religious, Protestant			
Gt. Britain 1959	+ 37	+ 7	- 1
Sweden 1955	+ 53	—	+ 16
Norway 1957	+ 46	—*	+ 21
Mean scores	+ 34	+ 2	+ 12
Mixed Protestant and Catholic			
W. Germany 1959	+ 27	+ 29	+ 40
Netherlands 1956	+ 26	+ 50	+ 73
Switzerland 1963, 1972[x]	+ 26	+ 15	+ 59
N. Ireland 1968[**]	+ 14	+ 82	n.d.
Mean scores	+ 23	+ 44	+ 57
Mono-religious, Catholic			
Italy 1959	+ 19	—	+ 51
France 1956	+ 15	—	+ 59
Belgium 1956	+ 25	—	+ 72
Austria 1967	+ 31	—	+ 54
Mean scores	+ 22	—	+ 59

* Lijphart gives a score of + 26 here but it is based on
  an expected correlation between membership in fundamentalist
  and dissenters' associations and conservative voting in
  Norway and does not refer to Catholic-Protestant divisions;
  Lijphart (1971) pp.7-8.

[x] The figures for class and church attendance voting are from
  Lijphart, based on a 1963 survey: Lijphart (1971), p.8.
  The figure for church affiliation voting comes from Kerr
  (1974) and is based on a 1972 survey.

[**] The Northern Ireland figures are calculated from the table
  in Rose and Urwin (1969), p.64.

countries of the middle belt. The Westphalian settlement of 1648 finally established the *cuius regio eius religio* rule recognising the right of state authorities to establish as the religion of each state the particular confessional form to which the State's ruler(s) adhered. The application of this rule meant that in the mixed-confession territories of Europe, one or other Protestant church was established as the institutional expression of the official religion. Thus in the Netherlands and Switzerland large regionally-based Catholic minorities were constrained by the existence of a Protestant official religion and Protestant central elites deriving from Protestant majorities. Ireland with its largely Catholic native population also suffered (until 1869) from the imposition of a Protestant state church. Only after 1921 did it take its place among the Catholic countries, while the north of the country remained part of the United Kingdom, dominated by a self-consciously Protestant local elite. In Germany the intricate patchwork of states, principalities and free cities, each with their own established religion, was simplified only in 1870 by the German Reich under the leadership of Protestant Prussia.

THE RELIGIOUS STRUCTURES AND CULTURES OF PROTESTANT EUROPE

The religious settlements of the mid-seventeenth century not only marked the broad spatial subdivision of Europe between Catholic and Protestant populations, they also cemented the divisions within Protestant Europe between different types of confession and different patterns of Church-State relationship. While Lutheran state churches were maintained in Scandinavia and northern Germany, Anglican state churches were re-established in England, Wales and Ireland, and Calvinist church establishments were confirmed in Scotland (1690), the Netherlands and Switzerland. These differences in confessional culture and ecclesiastical structure provided the context for the emergence of quite distinct patterns of religious cleavage among the several Protestant populations in more recent times.

Each of the major types of Protestant confession possessed certain distinct features which *a priori* might be expected to have affected the impact of religion on modern electoral politics.[9] Among the characteristic features of Calvinism are its activist ethos and its insistence on the will of God as expressed in the Bible as the absolute guide for all human conduct. The combination of these two features has been a particularly powerful historical force. Mainstream Lutheranism, by contrast, has tended to be marked by a quietist ethos, an emphasis on personal piety and, through the doctrine of the calling, the belief that the Christian can best serve God by obediently and conscientiously performing the duties attaching to his or her social position which God himself has determined. Anglicanism is distinguished from the other two confessional types by its claim to represent a *via media* between all extremes, including those of activism and quietism. Its historic ability to embrace diverse elements within a single pattern of liturgical order is associated with its origin as the national Church of a single country (England) which, in the century after the Reformation, attempted to achieve comprehensive membership among a religiously diverse population.

Lipset has implied that confessional type does indeed provide part of the

explanation for the differential propensity of particular populations to
generate religious parties. He focuses, however, less on ethos than on the
different confessions' doctrines and their implications for Church-State
relations:

> The more a church conceives of itself as God-ordained and has an
> ecclesiastical constitution that is completely separated from state power,
> the more likely is it to be interested in government action. In the West,
> the Catholic Church best fits these conditions. As a church in the
> sociological sense, it assumes that it is God-ordained, and it claims
> authority over all persons born within it, rather than (as with Protestant
> denominations, which have sectarian origins) over those who
> voluntarily give it allegiance. Unlike other Christian *churches* (the
> Lutheran, the Anglican and the Greek Orthodox), it is genuinely
> supranational, accepting an authority outside the nation: the Pope. The
> other state-supported churches have been closely linked to those who
> hold power in the state and their tie to state power prevents them from
> playing an independent political role.[10]

Among non-Catholic churches, however, 'seemingly Calvinism where it
retains its ancient strong faith, retains more of the attributes of the God-
ordained universalistic Church than any other Protestant group', and in the
Netherlands it provides the basis for two independent confessional parties.[11]
Lutheran churches, on the other hand, seem to diverge most from this pattern
and demonstrate a very low potential for generating political involvement in
the form of support for explicitly religious parties.

This hypothesis is problematic, particularly if the range of variations found
in Protestant Europe is considered. First, almost all churches, or for that
matter sects, denominations or cults, regard themselves to be in some sense
'God-ordained', and there are difficulties in judging to what *degree* a religious
body conceives of itself in this way. Second, with regard to the 'structural'
element of the hypothesis, it is by no means clear that churches with a
'constitution that is completely separated from state power' have tended to be
more 'interested in government action' than, for example, state churches
which depend for their support on government action. Other things being
equal, church independence from state power is likely to be significant in so
far as it affects: (a) the ability of religious communities to act independently;
and (b) the probability that a religious community will see its own interests as
being distinct from those of the State. Third, Lipset's claim that Calvinists
have more consistently provided support for religious parties, raises the
question of the contrast between the relative weakness of the Evangelical
People's Party in Calvinist Switzerland and the relative strength of the
Christian People's Party in Lutheran Norway. This comparison suggests that
variations are perhaps to be accounted for, less by the confessional character
of the dominant churches, than by other factors which only partially, if at all,
coincide with confessional type. Lastly, and most importantly, by restricting
the scope of his hypothesis to churches, Lipset fails to take account of nonchurch religious groups such as independent denominations or groups within

churches which have been a feature of Protestant countries and have occasionally, as will be seen, provided the inspiration and support for religious parties.[12] Despite these problems, the hypothesis does raise interesting questions about the influence of narrowly religious and ecclesiastical factors on the development of patterns of political opposition.

Lipset also proposes a supplementary hypothesis to help explain the likelihood that religious parties will arise within any given population: 'Where a cultural community is threatened by outside values, and there is a close identity between the community and a given religion, religious parties are more likely to emerge.'[13] He adds that this generalisation applies particularly to the situation of various colonial peoples in the Third World, but it would seem to apply equally well to the situation of certain religious communities in Western Europe at junctures which have been crucial for the development of religious parties, for example, the Catholics in the German Reich during the *Kulturkampf*, and both Catholic and Protestant communities in the various parts of Ireland at different times. This point does not only apply to situations where Catholic and Protestant communities coexist, however. As will be seen, the religious cultures of Protestant Europe have generated a wide range of separate religious traditions and communities within certain Protestant populations which were once largely uniform in matters of religion. It will consequently be interesting to examine the degree to which the pluralisation of religious forms is associated with the development of competing communal identities.

Taken together, Lipset's two hypotheses provide a useful starting point for the examination of the preconditions for the emergence (and non-emergence) of the religious factor in the politics of Protestant Europe. The first suggests the importance of the varying confessional and ecclesiastical heritages of the different countries, while the second directs attention to the linkages between the national and other forms of religion and developing elements of cultural and subcultural identity. The rest of this section considers these features. Since the territory of Protestant Europe as defined above contains eleven modern nations, this can of course be undertaken only in the most summary way. The analysis is, however, facilitated if these countries are grouped according to confessional and ecclesiastical type.

Despite the differences of confession (Anglican, Lutheran and Calvinist) and the traditional association of each with contrasting theories or doctrines regarding the proper relations between the Church and the State, these relationships were, in Europe of the late eighteenth century, remarkably uniform. If 1770 is taken as a first datum point for comparing these patterns, the similarities among all confessional areas, including the Catholic, are striking. There was a near-universal tendency for church and state establishments to be closely interlocked even where, as in Calvinist Holland or Catholic France, the dominant confession encapsulated claims for church independence.[14] If the triangular relationship between Church, State and Nation is examined, on the other hand, broad contrasts between Catholic and Protestant Europe begin to emerge. Despite the attempts of eighteenth-century Catholic monarchs to claim power over the Catholic Church within their own countries, they never succeeded in binding the myths of Church and

Nation together in the Protestant manner. The Reformation had brought the
use of vernacular languages into the churches of Protestant Europe at a time
when the spread of printing facilitated the development of national literatures
and cultures. In the cases of the Calvinist Netherlands and Scotland, Anglican
England and Lutheran Sweden, the myths of Nation and Church had been
further bonded by struggles for national autonomy and power during the wars
of religion. In Protestant as opposed to Catholic Europe, therefore, the
established churches tended to be strongly national as well as state dominated.

In the following century (1770 to 1870), a range of patterns of religious and
social cleavage developed under the impact of the forces unleashed by the
French and Industrial Revolutions (in particular secularist radicalism,
nationalism and various strains of religious revivalism). The variations in
these patterns in large part account for the uneven incidence of the religious
factor in the era of mass politics (beginning roughly in 1870). In all parts of
Europe liberalising reforms were introduced but their manner and timing had
important and varying consequences for the resultant cleavage structures.[15] In
line with the broad implications of Lipset's first hypothesis, a factor of
particular importance in accounting for the contrasting patterns appears to be
the degree of independence from the State which different types of church
establishment enjoyed. There were two polar types: countries (usually
Protestant) which inherited Erastian church regimes, where the Church was
directly subject to the authority of the State; and independent church regimes
(Catholic and Protestant), where the established Churches retained a
significant degree of autonomy. In Catholic Europe where, during the
nineteenth century, the Church managed to regain much of the independence
it had tended to lose in the eighteenth, the patterns have been much studied.
The central tendency there was toward what Martin describes as 'spirals of
antagonism' resulting in situations of conflict where 'coherent and massive
secularism confronts coherent and massive religiosity'.[16] The case of
Protestant Europe has received less attention, at least in comparative terms,
and we now turn to examine the more varied contexts to be found there. First
the broad patterns of Church-State relations are described, then the
characteristic types of religious cleavage system which developed within the
frameworks set by the constitutional patterns.

In the Lutheran states of Scandinavia and northern Germany, the classic
pattern of Church-State relations dates back to the Reformation when the
reduction of the Catholic Church had been carried through particularly
thoroughly. Not only were church properties sequestered, religious orders
suppressed, and the authority of the Pope rejected, but the succession
churches were laid completely under the crown, even the vestigial rights of
local parish autonomy in appointments soon disappearing. The classic
Lutheran doctrine of the institutional Church which legitimated this
subjection, stated that the Church constituted only the human framework for
the working of God's free grace; it possessed as an institution no inherent or
derived authority to dispense miraculous benefits or to interpret the will of
God, such as was claimed by the Catholic Church. The prince, as father of his
people in spiritual as in secular matters, was responsible to God alone for his
stewardship as *summus episcopus* of the Church. No longer a state within a

state, the Church ceased to exist as an independent legal corporation and became instead a branch of the royal bureaucracy, charged with the proper administration of the sacraments, the preaching of the word and the general oversight of the moral welfare of the population. Until the late eighteenth century this arrangement provided for almost complete uniformity and a relatively high degree of conformity in religious matters. The church officials' trade-off of church independence for a complete monopoly of religious functions, guaranteed and upheld by the civil power, ensured them a central role in their localities, while their responsibility for the administration of numerous state functions further reinforced a secure and exalted position in the framework of traditional society.[17]

The Anglican succession churches of England, Wales and Ireland were also stripped of any effective independence from the State, although the clergy there did not take on the same character of an ecclesiastical state bureaucracy. While bishops were appointed by the Crown, and the Church lost all influence in the process of their election before appointment, the episcopal office retained a greater degree of dignity and larger independent means. The existence of a wide range of patronage rights vested in the bishops, landowners, colleges and corporations (as well as the Crown) also made for a less rigid subservience to the State, while the development of parliamentary government with jurisdiction over the Church made for a much less uniform style of religious establishment than was the case in the absolutist states of Lutheran Europe. The early development of religious toleration, although it did not dislocate the relationship between the establishments in Church and State, did ensure the freedom of most dissenting Protestant minorities to enjoy their own forms of worship.

The Calvinist countries of Europe—Scotland, the Netherlands and Switzerland—exhibited a wide range of church regimes. Although the theory of Presbyterian church government through a hierarchy of independent synods was anchored in the creed of the Calvinist churches, only in Scotland in the eighteenth century was the theory approximated in practice. There, after the struggles of the previous two centuries against episcopalianism, a structure of local consistories, regional synods and national ecclesiastical courts, headed by the General Assembly in Edinburgh, maintained a degree of independence from the State unknown elsewhere in Protestant Europe. An established Church, supported with a wide range of guarantees by the civil power, it refused to accept the authority of the Crown in its internal affairs, although in the eighteenth century the Crown-in-Parliament did encroach in the matter of church appointments. In the Netherlands, by contrast, the national church synod was not convened for almost 200 years after 1619, and the government of the Church at local and regional level was inextricably intertwined with the civil administration. The denial to religious minorities— including the large Catholic minority in the south—of the rights of citizenship ensured that only members of the Dutch Reformed Church were involved in the management of civil and ecclesiastical functions, but this scarcely compensated the Church for the truncation of its synod structure.

In Switzerland the creeds of the Protestant cantonal churches were Calvinist, but the church constitutions generally took the form of the other,

Zwinglian branch of the Swiss Reformation. The thirty-sixth of Zwingli's sixty-seven theses ran: 'the jurisdiction which churchmen have unduly claimed belongs entirely to the secular authority, provided it is Christian', and it was a Zwinglian theorist of Church-State relations, Erastus, whose name has conventionally been given to the most thorough-going state control over churches. In the Catholic cantons, however, the Church retained more of its wonted independence, protected by the territorial segmentation of political authority from the attentions of the Protestant national majority.[18]

Around 1800 several contrasting changes occurred in the patterns of Church-State relations in the Continental part of Protestant Europe where the impact of the French Revolution was most directly experienced. In northern Germany, for example, the Hohenzollern monarchy imposed throughout its expanded territories a unification of Lutheran and Calvinist churches in a demonstration of pure Erastian statecraft. The effect of this policy was to re-establish a uniform, albeit hybrid, identity of Church and State after the territorial gains had led to the presence in the Hohenzollern territories of a degree of ecclesiastical pluralism. In the Netherlands, on the other hand, after a period of Church-State separation during the French occupation, the national synod of the Dutch Reformed Church was finally reconvened in 1816 and, although its jurisdiction was initially closely circumscribed, in 1852 many, and in 1876 most, of the restrictions were removed. It thus eventually became an independent established church on the pattern of its sister Calvinist church in Scotland.

The significance of the contrasting patterns of Church-State relations for modern politics appears most clearly when the church authorities' responses to the challenges of religious revivalism on the one hand, and secular indifference or hostility on the other, are examined. The introduction of religious toleration at various times was part cause, part consequence of very diverse patterns of religious cleavage. Toleration in all cases entailed a renunciation on the part of state authorities of the effort to maintain conformity and orthodoxy. It was generally conceded or promoted by political elites whose own attachment to confessional orthodoxy was suspect, and many of the groups which took advantage of the new toleration did so in order to revive or re-establish the orthodoxy which latitudinarian church leaderships had ceased to guard. Orthodox Protestant dissent was generally born in opposition to the laxity of the official church authorities and, from the late eighteenth century on, this conflict was fairly common in large areas of Protestant Europe. Its form and its consequences varied widely, however, as between Erastian and independent Protestant churches.

The classic Erastian response is best seen in Scandinavia, northern Germany and Protestant Switzerland.[19] In these countries religious revivalism in various guises had generally already appeared before religious toleration; indeed toleration itself was often the product of wearying experience on the part of the authorities with the difficulties of imposing conformity against the resistance of revivalist groups. One consequence of the relatively late timing of toleration in these countries was that the growth of non-conformity, and the pluralisation of the religious cultures which attended it, occurred largely within the ambit of the state churches and in this way the ideal of comprehensiveness, according to which all members of a society were to be accommodated within a single Church, was maintained. Thus while many small sectarian groups took advantage of eventual toleration to establish their own identity outside the official churches, the groups who were mobilised by the revivalist movements tended to remain within. State church authorities were generally willing to accommodate them, owing to a greater concern for comprehensiveness than for the maintenance of orthodoxy.

In the independent Protestant national churches of the Netherlands and Scotland on the other hand, a different pattern emerged. With their independent Presbyterian modes of self-government, the conflict between revivalist elements and latitudinarian church leadership led initially to bitter struggles within the ecclesiastical governing bodies, constituted as they were to allow representation of varying church views. The schisms which resulted led to the establishment by uncompromising revivalists of a remarkable number of rival churches, each claiming to embody the true national church and maintain traditional orthodoxy. Thus by contrast with the intra-ecclesiastical pluralism of the Erastian churches, there developed a competitive, institutional pluralism. Paradoxically this institutional pluralism did not lead to the proliferation of confessions, except at the margin; in both countries the religious culture remained overwhelmingly Calvinist.

Developments in the United Kingdom, taken as a whole, followed neither of these patterns exclusively. There, religious toleration had been introduced as early as the late seventeenth century after a period of indecisive struggle between national church authorities and dissenting bodies. In Scotland the independent Presbyterian Church was established, while elsewhere the Erastian Anglican Church retained its established status. The early abandonment of the effort to impose religious uniformity meant that when evangelical revivalism appeared with Methodism in the mid-eighteenth century, it was able to develop outside the state Church alongside the old dissenting sects. Unlike the situation in the Netherlands and Scotland, the competitive pluralism generated by a series of important religious revivals did lead to increasing confessional diversity. Furthermore revivalism had an impact within the state Church, and this was accommodated in the same way as in the other Erastian churches. Thus within a single political community one had intra-ecclesiastical pluralism as in the other Erastian churches *and* competitive pluralism as in countries with independent Protestant church regimes. As will be seen, this degree of religious fragmentation was to have important political consequences, in part, because of the association of some alternative traditions with the cultural identity of subgroups, defined variously by class, region, and nationality.

By 1870, therefore, the religious structures and cultures of Protestant Europe showed a much greater degree of variation both within and between different countries than a century before. In the mixed-confession countries, Catholic minorities which had benefited from measures of religious toleration continued to represent distinct religious (and regional) subcultures, made all the more assertive by the revival of ultramontanism and papalism from around mid-century. In the Protestant populations of Switzerland, northern Germany and Scandinavia, both religious revivalism and secularism had developed (albeit at different rates and to different degrees) in the space allowed by the relaxation of the old religious laws, although most of the religious revivalist groups had remained within the ambit of the relatively tolerant Erastian churches. In the Netherlands and Scotland, on the other hand, the challenges of revivalism had led to the emergence of a number of schismatic counter-churches in direct competition with the independent established churches. As in the case of the Erastian countries just mentioned, though not quite to the same extent, religious division had meanwhile failed to generate a wide range of confessional contrasts, Calvinism retaining its historic dominance as the embodiment of the national religious tradition. Finally, in England, Wales and Ireland, while the Anglican Church retained its established status (in the case of Ireland only up to 1869), a greater variety of religious contrasts had emerged by 1870. In addition to the traditions of Irish Catholicism and of Old Dissent which had already been present a century before, a large number of distinct alternative religious traditions developed, spanning a far greater range and embracing a far higher proportion of the population than in any other part of Protestant Europe.

What was the significance of these different patterns for the development of political parties and voting behaviour in the new era of mass politics which was emerging around 1870?

THE TRANSLATION OF RELIGIOUS INTEREST AND VALUE CLEAVAGES INTO POLITICS

Religious groups, like groups identified by ethnicity, class, spatial location and so forth, have certain interests, which are usually legitimised by an explicit doctrine or implicit theory about the world and the group's place within it. In the view of the theory or doctrine, these interests appear not simply as claims but as rights. Where different religious groups develop in situations of religious inequality, such as still existed in Protestant Europe around 1870, the rights of one group often conflict with the pretended rights of another. Most centrally, for example, the rights of established churches as 'the conscience of the state' (as in Anglican and Lutheran countries) or as the guardian of a national covenant with God (as in Calvinist countries), will conflict with the rights claimed by dissident groups, whether within or outside the confessional tradition of the dominant church. The rights of dissident groups within the same confessional tradition will generally be based on claims to represent the *true* conscience of the state or to be the *proper* guardians of a national covenant with God. The rights of dissident groups of a different confessional colour, on the other hand, will generally be argued on the grounds of natural law or other theories of human rights.

Religious groups or institutions differ from other types of collectivity in that they are classic value-generating bodies.[20] The theories or doctrines embodied in their belief systems are of interest not only because they have generally been used to justify individual group or church claims to particular rights, but also because they typically provide the basis for what are claimed to be universal values. In the case of Roman Catholicism these universal values derive from an ancient tradition of social teaching which spans most aspects of human life but which also emphasises the universal status of the Catholic Church as the vehicle of divine grace. In divided Protestantism these universal values have been refracted through the particular ethos of the different confessions: in Calvinism, obedience to the commands of God as revealed in the Bible; in Lutheranism, the patient dependence on divine grace unrelated to works; and in Anglicanism, the cultivation of spiritual life in connection with the ministrations of the Church. By virtue of common ancestry, however, all these Christian traditions also hold a large number of universal values in common—most notably, in recent times at least, values related to what one might broadly call family morality.[21] The development of alternative non-religious value and belief systems, particularly since the French Revolution, has challenged these common claims to represent values of universal application and relevance; and these contests have become a source of ideological political conflict.

In examining the impact of the religious factor on the politics of Protestant Europe, there have been two modes or phases in the 'translation' of religious cleavages which are associated with the dual nature of religious groups as the proponents of interest and value claims; historically, interest claims have always tended to be pressed first.

By 1870 the enforced religious uniformity which had once characterised the Protestant population of northern Europe had largely disappeared, but the privileges and penalties which had once underpinned it had nowhere been completely removed. The religious monopoly provisions of the established churches had been virtually dismantled, more or less gradually in various countries. In the mixed confession countries, large Catholic populations had managed throughout to maintain, and then more and more to assert, their separate religious identity, despite a range of disabilities and disadvantages. Among the Protestant populations the elementary right of religious toleration—to leave the established church and join some other religious body or none—was conceded as early as 1689 in the United Kingdom, and as recently as 1923 in overwhelmingly Lutheran Finland.[22] In most countries this dates to the middle or late eighteenth century. However, the concession of this elementary right hardly touched the main body of laws and provisions which supported the special status of the established churches and their members. The juxtaposition of an emergent religious pluralism with the remaining legal, financial, and other advantages of the dominant churches (and the corresponding disabilities and disadvantages of non-established groups) was in the nineteenth century to prove a most fertile source of contentious religious-political issues. The broadening of the franchise and the opening of access to parliamentary representation for members of disadvantaged groups facilitated the translation of these interest issues into political cleavages. The emergence of a secularist opinion opposed to any connection between the state and religious bodies, reinforced the tendency for these contentions over interest to become political questions.

Three broad types of issue associated with the interests or rights of religious bodies encouraged the oppositional alignment of church establishments, disadvantaged religious groups, and secularists. First, there was the basic issue of the elementary right of religious toleration. Second, there was the removal of the many legal and other disabilities attaching to religious non-conformity and dissent, such as the denial of the right to perform wedding or burial services or the obligation of all to contribute to the upkeep of the established churches through tithes, dues, and taxes. Third, there was the demand for positive equality of treatment for the members of all religious groups, and none. This third type of issue became a particularly potent source of political conflict with the development, in the late nineteenth century, of public education.

The value claims of churches and other religious groups tend to be distinct from their interest or right claims, in so far as they are taken to be of universal rather than particular or sectional scope. Struggles to promote or defend the right of religious communities to follow their own forms of religious service or to influence the religious education of their children, are essentially self-regarding, whatever the tendency to identify the interests of whole societies with the interest of particular groups. Struggles to promote or defend such values as human dignity or social welfare which different religious groups have converted into campaigns against alcohol or pornography or for the defence of the Christian religion generally, are, by contrast, typically oriented to altering arrangements affecting whole societies. While groups or parties organised initially to pursue religious interest claims will usually also make value claims and vice versa, the earlier appearance of interest claim groups and their closer association with particular religious constituencies provide them with a stronger and more stable hold on their electorates.

The structures of religious cleavage reviewed above, define the number, strength, and type of religious groups which by their very existence could be the source of interest claims, the pursuit of which might affect the patterns of political opposition. On *a priori* grounds one would expect religious interest claims to have a political impact proportional to: (a) the numerical and organisational strength of the religious group concerned; (b) the degree of difference in confessional type which distinguishes it, if at all, from that of the established church; and (c) the extent of the disadvantages and disabilities suffered. The impact of religious value claims, on the other hand, should be related to more general factors, such as the overall level of secularisation within a society and the countervailing strength of mainstream religious opinion. Because of their more general character, religious value movements often differ according to whether religious groups, previously divided by competing interest claims, have been able to combine and pool their strengths. Value movements are often characterised by cross-group cooperation among the different religious groups of a particular society; where this cooperation is not achieved for whatever reason, such movements will be correspondingly weak or non-existent.

The emergence of the Catholic parties of Protestant Europe was directly related to the emergence of religious interest issues on the political agenda. The Catholic populations of Ireland, the Netherlands, Germany and Switzerland were characterised by a numerical and organisational strength which was associated with their relative geographic concentration, by the fact that they were confessionally quite distinct from the Protestant established churches, and by the significant extent of the disabilities from which they suffered. In predominantly Protestant Germany, Bismarck's attempt to

TABLE 3: SUMMARY, BACKGROUND CONDITIONS, RELIGIOUS PARTIES, RELIGIOUS VOTING AND ISSUE TYPES

	Background conditions (ca. 1870)			Interests of Religious Groups	Values of the Religious community	Parties
	Dominant confession	Church regime	Religious Pluralism			
England	Anglican	Erastian	High; internal and external	XO		
Wales	Anglican	Erastian	High; external	X		
Scotland	Calvinist	Independent	High; external	XO		
Ireland (after 1921 N. Ireland)	Anglican	Erastian	High; external (+ Catholics)	000 (Nationalists, SDLP); XXX (Unionists, DUP)		Social Democratic Labour Party; Democratic Unionist Party
Denmark	Lutheran	Erastian	Low	X	XX (CCP)	Christian People's Party
Finland	Lutheran	Erastian	Low	X	XX (FCL)	Finland's Christian League
Norway	Lutheran	Erastian	Moderate; internal	XX (Mod. Left P.)——	XXX (CPP)	Christian People's Party
Sweden	Lutheran	Erastian	Low	X	XX (CDL)	Christian Democratic League
Germany	predominantly Lutheran	Erastian	Low; (+ Catholics)	XX (SCWP)——; 000 (Zentrum)——	CDU	Social Christian Workers' Party; Christian Democratic Union
Netherlands	Calvinist	Independent	High; external (+ Catholics)	000 (KVP)——; XXX (ARP)——	CDA; XXX (CHU); XX (SGP); XX (GPV)	Catholic People's Party(KVP); Anti-Revolutionary Party; Christian Historical Union; Christian Democratic Appeal; Political Reformed Party(SGP); Reformed Political League (GPV)
Switzerland	Calvinist	Erastian	Low; (+ Catholics)	000 (SCPP)——	(CDPP)——; XX (EVP)	Swiss Conservative People's Party; Christian Democratic People's Party; Evangelical People's Party (EVP)

Legend: X indicates Protestant; 0 indicates Catholic
X or 0: impact on voting
XX or 00: minor religious party
XXX or 000: major religious party

subject the Catholic Church to the new State raised all three types of interest issue simultaneously. Although he did not attempt to suppress the mass as such, he did expel the Jesuits, tried to control the church's organisation and forbade churchmen to speak from the pulpit on matters of State. On those who resisted these and other attacks on the autonomy of the Catholic Church, which included several bishops and hundreds of priests, the civil courts imposed severe penalties. An important element in the campaign was the attempt to deprive the Church of its former control over primary education. These assaults led directly to the founding and explosive growth of the Catholics' own party of religious defence, the Zentrum, which was to last until the end of the Weimar Republic.[23]

In Switzerland also the Catholic Church came under attack from a liberal Protestant elite. After the Catholic secession war of the 1840s, the Jesuit Order was expelled (1848) and in 1874, in imitation of Bismarck's campaign, restrictions were placed on the freedom of monastic orders. The result was the same as in Germany: a Catholic party was set up which rapidly became the second largest party in the country. Despite its electoral success, the Swiss Conservative People's Party (since 1971 known as the Christian Democratic People's Party) failed to achieve the removal of the anti-Catholic clauses of the constitution. Today it remains a Catholic interest party, though it has also engaged itself in more general religious value issues.

In the Netherlands where in 1815 formal religious toleration had been granted and in 1848 full freedom of religious organisation conceded, the Catholic Church was not subjected to the same sort of attack from the Protestant liberal elite, although the re-establishment of the hierarchy in the 1850s led to a storm of protest. It was, instead, the third type of interest issue, education, that led to the organisation of the Catholic party alongside the orthodox Calvinists of the ARP (see below). Since 1945 this party has been called the Catholic People's Party (KVP).[24]

In Ireland the three types of interest issue arose separately. The first Catholic political organisations were concerned initially with the struggle which led to the Catholic Emancipation Act (1829), and then with the fight to remove the remaining disabilities. This fight focused on relief from the obligation to pay tithes for the upkeep of the established (Anglican) church and culminated in disestablishment in 1869. The education issue, remarkably, was less contentious. The government established a system of state schools, managed by a national board representative of both Catholic and Protestant communities, and clergymen of the different confessions participated in this system for the purposes of religious instruction. Because of the relatively early settlement of the religious group interest issues, the nationalist movement and party did not develop as an explicitly Catholic organisation. But the nationalist movement did derive much of its strength from the historic association of foreign domination and discrimination against Irish Catholics *qua* Catholics, and the resulting identity between Catholicism and Irish Nationalism has ever since reinforced the religio-political polarisation which has dominated the affairs of Northern Ireland since its creation in 1921. Although religious group interest issues continue to feature in the rhetoric of conflict among the militant Protestants there, the bitterness of the protracted conflict between Catholics and Protestants apparently owes more to the dynamics of competing nationalisms, to which religion is essentially incidental, than to the dynamics of religious group interest conflicts.

Among the Protestant populations of Protestant Europe there was by 1870, as has been seen, a wide variation in the number, strength and type of religious groups. Few non-conformist groups, either singly or collectively, approached the numerical or organisational strength of the Catholic minorities, however, and even in the exceptional cases, such as late nineteenth-century Wales where they did, the degree of difference in confessional type between the established church and non-conformity was less than that obtaining between Catholic and Protestant in the mixed-confession territories. Finally, the extent of the disabilities suffered by Protestant non-conformity was rarely as great as that experienced by Catholics. It is therefore not surprising that the translation of religious into political cleavages was much less common among Protestants than among Catholics. Certain translations did nevertheless occur.

In Switzerland and Germany, where the degree of religious pluralism, both internal and external to the established Erastian churches, was relatively low, the comparative absence of important cleavages between religious groups accounts for the weakness of Protestant religious parties. Tension between Church and State was also low because the interests of the established churches were generally well served by precisely those privileges and penalties which elsewhere were a cause of resentment to significant religious minorities (including of course Swiss and German Catholics).[25] Although the usual intra-ecclesiastical differences subsisted between liberals, latitudinarians, high churchmen and more or less orthodox revivalists, these had generally been accommodated in the classic Erastian manner. Religious revivalism furthermore tended to take the form either of world-renouncing pietism or of humanitarian inner-mission movements. Certain religious group interest issues, nevertheless, did emerge to affect patterns of political alignment. Thus Stoecker, despite his Lutheran background and his position (until 1890) as court preacher in Berlin, voiced demands for giving the established church a measure of autonomy, albeit under the authority of the Kaiser as *summus episcopus*.[26] Stoecker's Christian Social Workers' Party, which received its greatest support among the old Reformed (i.e. Calvinist) groups within the Church in Siegerland, was thus, in part at least, a religious interest party. It was also, however, like the short-lived Christian People's Service Party of the Weimar period, as much or more concerned to promote universal religious-social values, particularly social welfare. Like the Swiss Evangelical People's Party (EVP) (which still exists), these parties remained extremely small.[27] In West Germany the religious-political tradition of these parties was taken up in 1945 by the Protestant groups which combined with Catholic Christian Democrats to form the modern CDU. This inter-confessional party has been a classic religious value party, principally committed so far as religion is concerned to promote non-sectarian Christian values, although its development into a catch-all conservative party tends to overshadow its specifically religious character.

The weakness and strength of the religious factor among the Protestant populations of Switzerland and the Netherlands—both overwhelmingly

Calvinist in confession—is instructive. The orthodox Protestants of the Netherlands with a history of independent church government and schism have, throughout the modern period, provided the basis for strikingly successful religious parties.[29] As for the Dutch Catholics, the issue of education provided the initial stimulus when, in 1878, a Liberal government attempted to bar denominational religious education from the school system. A massive petition campaign on this one issue led to the foundation of the country's first mass party, the Anti-Revolutionary Party (ARP). Its founder, Kuyper, was an orthodox clergyman who was as opposed to the lukewarm leadership of the established church as to the programmatic liberalism of the government. Within a decade of founding the party, he had also led the latest in a series of fundamentalist secessions from the Church. The fissiparousness of Dutch Calvinism was also reflected in politics. In 1894 the ARP split when the Christian Historical Union was founded by the politically more conservative, but religiously less fundamentalist, Calvinists who continued to identify with the Dutch Reformed Church. Other smaller parties were formed in 1918 (SGP, the Political Reformed Party) and 1948 (GPV, the Reformed Political League). Their base has been among the smaller Calvinist sects, which have been able to secure separate representation only because of the extremely low-threshold electoral system.[30] Among Protestants as among the more cohesive Catholics, therefore, the Netherlands has seen the direct transposition of religious into political cleavages.[31]

For most of the twentieth century the main confessional parties (ARP, CHU and KVP) have cooperated in government and jointly entrenched the interests of their respective religious constituencies. In 1976, they allied to form the interconfessional Christian Democratic Appeal (CDA). The steady loss of support, which they had suffered collectively, precipitated the foundation of the CDA, but it also reflects the contemporary irrelevance of religious group interest conflicts as traditional Christian values come under attack by movements, for example, to liberalise, the abortion laws.[32] Here, as in Germany, one sees a shift from political patterns set in the period of interest conflicts to patterns more suited to the defence of values which are held in common by all the mainstream denominations.

In the other predominantly Calvinist country, Scotland, a pattern of religious cleavages similar to the Dutch produced quite different consequences. The pattern of a Calvinist church establishment faced by a number of rival secessionist bodies, each claiming to be the true representatives of the national religious tradition, failed to produce a religious political party partly, at least, because religious group interest issues were handled so differently. The 1872 Education Act, which entailed state control of the schools provided by the different Presbyterian churches, safeguarded confessional education on the basis of the 'shorter catechism' which was common to all of the principal groups. The issue of disestablishment, on the other hand, proved more divisive and led for a time to the alignment of free and established church opinion behind the Liberal and Conservative parties respectively. The failure of the disestablishment campaign and the re-unification of the several leading Calvinist bodies with the established church, has since removed this issue from politics, however.

In the rest of the United Kingdom where the Anglican Church had long enjoyed the privileges of established status, religious interest issues were rather more contentious. The survival of Catholicism in Ireland and the early granting of toleration to Protestant dissenters had produced a pattern of dissent external to the Church which was matched in the nineteenth century by the growth of religious divisions within it. The first religious political campaigns, which aligned dissenters with the Whigs and Liberals, and the supporters of Anglican privileges with the Conservatives, concerned the removal of civil disabilities, finally achieved between 1828 and 1871.[33] Thereafter education and disestablishment were the issues which affected the differential support of the various religious groups for the major parties. In Wales, where non-conformity, boosted by religious revivals such as those of 1859 and 1904-5, became a vehicle for the resurgence of a sense of distinctive national identity, both issues became major determinants of party alignment.[34] The 1870 and 1902 Education Acts, the second of which occasioned a 'Welsh revolt', led to major political campaigns by dissenting groups opposed to the public subvention of denominational religious education in areas with no state schools. The issue of disestablishment further reinforced the alignment of massive non-conformity with the Liberal party between 1868 and 1914 when the act disestablishing the Anglican Church in Wales was finally passed.

In England the alignment of non-conformity with the Liberal party before 1914 was also largely related to the emergence of religious group interest issues.[35] Disestablishment was a less central issue in England than in Wales because non-conformity and Anglicanism were closer in strength and there was no complicating nationalist factor. The education issue, however, became almost equally disruptive. Non-conformist reactions to the 1902 Education Act led, as in Wales, to a massive campaign which played a great part in the Liberal landslide of 1906. By the time of the 1944 Education Act, the various religious groups were concerned less with denominational differences than with the maintenance of religious education, as such, within state schools.[36]

In terms of religious value issues, temperance played a large part in reinforcing the association of Welsh and English non-conformity with the Liberal and, later, Labour parties in the period before World War I when it was a political issue of some importance.[37] More recently, however, the emergence of such moral issues as pornography and abortion has only led to the foundation of small campaigning organisations like the Festival of Light and the Society for the Protection of the Unborn Child. Because the interest issues were settled early, these organisations have been unable to capitalise on pre-existing religious-political cleavages. Both of the current major parties have treated the value issues as matters for the conscience of individual MPs and have thereby been able to remove them from party-political debate. The failure of any major party to adopt strong positions on them, not least because of strong intra-party differences of opinion, has meant that the religious factor in modern British politics is a mere vestige of old patterns of alignment, surviving principally among the oldest cohorts of voters.[38]

In Northern Ireland, as has already been noted, the impact of interest issues was, from early on, complicated by the national question. Thus, for example, certain non-conformist leaders opposed disestablishment on the grounds that it would undermine the role of Protestantism in Ireland.[39] The education issue, which ceased to be divisive in the rest of the United Kingdom after World War I, was also treated as merely one aspect of continuing conflict between Catholic nationalism and Protestant loyalism. Owing to pressure from Protestant leaders in the 1920s the state schools effectively became denominational, but this subvention of Protestant religious education did not prevent Unionist politicians attacking subsidies for Catholic schools. Thus Ian Paisley's Democratic Unionist Party (DUP) founded in 1970, continues to oppose these subsidies. Over the last decade statements from both sides condemning the use of violence would seem to reflect an emergent interdenominational consensus on common moral and religious values, but the survival of religious interest conflicts within a context of intense community conflict undermines the prospects for a realignment on this new axis.

In Scandinavia as in the other countries with Erastian church systems, conservative politicians and officials in the late nineteenth century regarded support for the established Lutheran churches as a natural corollary of their defence of the status quo.[40] In this they found themselves ranged against not only secular liberals and social democrats but also lay revivalists within the churches and the small groups of dissenters without. Settlement of the issues of toleration and the removal of non-conformist disabilities was achieved relatively late (earliest in Norway in the 1840s, latest in Finland in the 1920s). Only in Norway, however, was a group of fundamentalist revivalists sufficiently large to provide an independent basis for a religious party. In 1888 they broke from the Left (Liberal) party to form the Moderate Left party when it became clear that their interest in church reform and the maintenance of religious orthodoxy was not shared by their more secular former allies. Led initially by vigorous religious entrepreneurs—like Kuyper in the Netherlands, they were revivalist clergymen—the party soon faded and moved to the Right as the national question came to dominate the political agenda. Throughout Scandinavia conflicts between clerical conservatives, 'churchly' revivalists, radical revivalists and dissenters among the religious activists, each with their own particular interests, undermined any attempt to set up a successful religious party. The maintenance of the privileges of the established churches, including the use of state schools for confessional religious instruction, also meant that in the absence of a large body of dissenters outside the state churches there was no basis in a fundamental grievance. The value issue of temperance which, as in Britain, was adopted by Liberal and Social Democratic parties in the early part of this century, did lead orthodox revivalists and dissenters to give a disproportionate support to these parties, although the parties' support for other more traditional religious values was occasionally suspect.

The recent emergence of a range of moral-religious value issues has been reflected in the rise of expressly Christian parties. In Norway as early as the 1930s a Christian People's Party was founded to combat the secularism of the Left, the latitudinarian policies of the church authorities, and the evils of drink. Originating in Norway's Bible belt in the south and west of the country which had earlier been the base area of the Moderate Left party, it became a national organisation in 1945. Its overriding emphasis on religious and moral questions in which religious activists of most backgrounds have a common interest has made it the representative of interdenominational religious opinion on such matters as temperance, abortion and pornography. Furthermore, its success as the leading centrist party has encouraged groups with similar views and concerns in the three other Scandinavian countries to form Christian parties on the basis of common religious values.

This overview has necessarily been brief despite its relatively narrow focus. Taking Lipset's cue we have concentrated on the religious and ecclesiastical preconditions for the impact of religion upon the politics of Protestant Europe. Table 3 attempts a schematic representation of the major patterns. Clearly a full analysis would also have to include many other aspects of the social and political systems within which the religious factor has operated. But this approach has helped to clarify certain centrally important elements which political analysts might otherwise leave for consideration only by ecclesiastical and social historians. The relative strength and weakness of religion in the modern politics of Catholic and Protestant Europe suggested, on first view, the importance of confessional differences but these cannot alone account for a number of significant variations across time and space. It has been argued that the nature of historically entrenched patterns of Church-State relationships and their associated religious cleavage systems, which are only incidentally related to confessional type, must also be brought into any analysis of the preconditions for the translation of religious into political effects. Such translations vary considerably in form, depending on whether religious interests or values are judged to be at stake. While interest conflicts account for the earliest cases, value conflicts have become most common in recent politics.

Perhaps, as Burke declared, 'politics and the pulpit are terms that have little agreement', but in certain times and certain places it is clearly difficult to understand the operation of one without the other.

NOTES

1. This term is used by Converse to describe the operation of 'religious animosities' on the main trends in American party alignments. P. Converse, 'Some Priority Variables in Comparative Research', in R.Rose (ed.), *Electoral Behaviour: A Comparative Handbook*. London: Macmillan, 1974, p. 733.
2. R. Rose and D. Urwin, 'Social Cohesion, Political Parties and Strains in Regimes', *Comparative Political Studies*, Vol. 2, No. 1, (April, 1969).
3. Ibid., p. 12.
4. A. Lijphart, 'Class Voting and Religious Voting in European Democracies', University of Strathclyde, Glasgow, 1971.
5. Ibid., p. 7.
6. S. Rokkan, 'The Structuring of Mass Politics in the Smaller European Democracies. A Developmental Typology', in O. Stammer (ed.), *Party Systems, Party Organisations and the Politics of the New Masses*. Berlin: Institute of Political Science of the Free University, 1968, p. 52. Much of what follows owes a great deal to insights developed in this and other

seminal articles by Rokkan. Most of these articles are listed in the bibliography appended to S. Rokkan, *Citizens, Elections and Parties*. Oslo: Universitetsforl., 1970.

7. Lijphart, op.cit., p. 9.
8. See, for example, M.P. Fogarty, *Christian Democracy in Western Europe, 1820-1953*. London: RKP, 1957; R.E.M. Irving, *The Christian Democratic Parties of Western Europe*. London: Allen and Unwin, 1979; and J.H. Whyte, 'The Catholic Factor in the Politics of Democratic States', *American Behavioral Scientist*, Vol.17, No. 6, (1974). See also the review article by G. Pridham, 'Christian Democracy in Western Europe: a Bibliographical Survey', *West European Politics*, (October 1980).
9. The classic work on this subject is E. Troetsch, *The Social Teachings of the Christian Churches*. (trans. by O. Wyon), London: Allen and Unwin, 1931. A shorter presentation of the same subject can be found in E. Molland, *Christendom*. London: Mowbray, 1959.
10. S.M. Lipset, *Revolution and Counter-Revolution*. New York: Basic Books, 1968, p. 219.
11. Ibid., p. 220.
12. I have argued elsewhere that Lipset's hypothesis should be reformulated in terms of the differential nature and location of authority in or over religious communities. Martin summarises my argument in D. Martin, *A General Theory of Secularization*. Oxford: Blackwell, 1980, p. 97.
13. Lipset, op.cit., p. 220.
14. 'While the churches continued to exercise their traditional functions, it was increasingly as an arm of the secular state. Everywhere, whether in Catholic, Protestant or Greek Orthodox lands, kings and rulers were asserting their authority over their churches and prelates.' G. Rudé, *Europe in the Eighteenth Century*. London: Cardinal, 1974, pp. 159-60.
15. As will be seen liberalisation was not in all cases a unilinear development without reversals. In the three Continental mixed-confession countries, significant deviations occurred.
16. D. Martin, op.cit., p. 6.
17. A useful review of Church-State relations in Scandinavia can be found in A. Aarflot (ed.), *Kirke og Stat i de Nordiske Land*. Oslo: Univ. forl., 1971.
18. Until the nineteenth century Switzerland maintained at the cantonal level the *cuius regio* rule, which had obtained in the rest of Europe as between states.
19. For the history of revivalism and the Protestant churches throughout Europe, see K.S. Latourette, *Christianity in a Revolutionary Age, Vol. II*. London: Eyre and Spottiswoode, 1960.
20. Lipset, op.cit., p. 215. This idea is a commonplace of religious sociology.
21. It is in this field that the mainstream Christian denominations have been most able to make common cause. Secularists have been concerned to remove the traditional bias of legal systems towards the support of religion-based morality and it is in conflict with these that the different religious groups have tended to define their most distinctive value claims.
22. The 1689 Toleration Act only applied to Protestant dissenting groups which accepted the doctrine of the Trinity. In Finland a degree of religious toleration had been introduced in 1869, but only in 1923 was the right to belong to no religious body formally conceded.
23. The Zentrum in fact included a small number of prominent Protestants such as Ludwig von Gerlach in its early period. For most of its history it was unable to avoid the image of being a Catholic ghetto party. See K. Buchheim, *Geschichte der Christlichen Parteien in Deutschland*. Munich: Kösel, 1953.
24. Daalder indicates the development of the KVP from a mere Catholic interest party: 'It started out with a single aim "religious freedom for the children", and developed into a compendious party with a full set of doctrines.' H. Daalder, 'Parties and Politics in the Netherlands', *Political Studies*, (1955), p. 2.
25. The entrenchment of established church interests made for the identification of privileged church groups with conservative political elites but provided no basis for specifically religious parties—only for the association of religious, economic, and social elements within the dominant blocs.
26. See Buchheim, op.cit., pp. 266-7.
27. Gruber identifies the EVP's principal dilemma thus: 'What political options will a party have that has inscribed on its banner not the interests of the farmers, the workers or industry [or even the interests of a strong religious group—J.M.] but pre-eminently, always and everywhere the interests of God?' C. Gruber, *Die Politischen Parteien der Schweiz im Zweiten Weltkrieg*. Vienna: Europa, 1966, p. 166.

28. Heidenheimer argues that the 'relationship between an underlying set of moral values and an elastic fund of working doctrines' has contributed to the adaptability of German Christian Democracy. A.J. Heidenheimer, *Adenauer and the CDU*. The Hague: Nijhoff, 1960; p. 17.

29. See J.P. Kruijt, 'The Influence of Denominationalism on Social and Organisational Patterns', *Archives de Sociologie des Religions*, Vol. 4, No.8, (1959). Like more recent work, he stresses the penetration of confession-based organisations into a wide range of sectors of Dutch society.

30. A. Lijphart, 'The Netherlands: Continuity and Change in Voting Behaviour', p. 235 in R. Rose (ed.), op.cit. Due to lack of information it is difficult to know whether SGP and GPV should be seen as initially interest or value parties.

31. Lorwin uses the term 'segmented pluralism' to describe the organisation of societies along lines of religious and ideological cleavages and points out that the Dutch first developed a vocabulary for describing it. He also implies that it was the churches' interest in 'preserving the faith' that encouraged its development. V.R. Lorwin, 'Segmented Pluralism: Ideological Cleavages and Political Cohesion in Smaller European Democracies', reprinted in K. McRae, *Consociational Democracy*. Ottawa: Carleton Library, 1974.

32. Irving, op.cit., pp. 207-12 emphasises the pragmatic aspects, while mentioning problems associated with contrasting ethos.

33. In 1871 the Universities Tests Act removed 'one of [the Church of England's] last obviously anachronistic privileges' according to one historian. As in the case of Irish disestablishment it was passed by a Liberal government led by Gladstone—himself not merely a staunch Anglican but a High-Church one to boot. His great popularity among non-conformists derived from his image as a Christian statesman. See D.W. Bebbington, 'Gladstone and the Nonconformists', in D. Baker (ed.), *Church, Society and Politics*. Oxford: Blackwell, 1975.

34. See K.O. Morgan, *Wales in British Politics, 1868-1922*. Cardiff: University of Wales Press, 1963.

35. See S. Koss, *Nonconformity in Modern British Politics*. London: Batsford, 1975.

36. Non-conformist dissatisfaction with the 1944 Act was met with the argument: 'The question is not whether people will be Anglicans or Nonconformists, but whether they will be Christians at all'. Quoted in Koss, op.cit., p. 222.

37. In certain peripheral parts of the country temperance retains a degree of importance. See for example P.J. Madgwick with others, *The Politics of Rural Wales*. London: Hutchinson, 1973.

38. D. Butler and D. Stokes, *Political Change in Britain*. London: Penguin, 1971, p. 170.

39. K.S. Latourette, op.cit., p. 399.

40. For a comparative study of the origins and nature of the religious factor in Scandinavian politics, see J. Madeley 'Scandinavian Christian Democracy: Throwback or Portent?' *European Journal of Political Research* (1977). A recent study of the Finnish case is reported in D. Arter, 'The Finnish Christian League: Party or Anti-Party?', *Scandinavian Political Studies*, No. 2, (1980).

[18]

In From the Cold? Christian Parties in Scandinavia

Lauri Karvonen, Åbo Academy

The combination of extreme religious homogeneity and advanced secularization is a special feature of the Scandinavian societies as compared to the rest of Europe. This difference largely explains why Christian parties have remained small compared to the rest of Europe. This article surveys the creation and popular following of the Christian parties in Denmark, Finland, Norway and Sweden. The four parties acquired an image of "moral vigilantes" from the beginning. Their best electoral results, however, are a result of a more general political protest. Despite the recent success of the Swedish party, the parties are not likely to reach a position beyond that of a minor party with basically a moralist image.

The strongholds of European Christian parties are to be found outside Scandinavia.[1] For a religiously based organization to rise to prominence, religious *conflicts* are necessary. Thus, in countries where the relationship between Church and State was a central bone of contention over long periods of time, Christian parties established themselves to defend the Church's point of view. In Central Europe, for example, separate parties originally emerged as representatives of the Protestant and Catholic populations. In several cases this cleavage has been bridged during recent decades; instead of representing catholicism or protestantism, these parties today promote general Christian values in politics. The historical background for these parties is nevertheless to be found in important contradictions involving Church, State and religious affiliation.

The Scandinavian region, by comparison, largely lacks experience with overarching political conflicts related to religion. The four countries are confessionally extremely homogeneous. Moreover, the level of secularization in terms of religious *activity* in Scandinavia is higher today than in basically any other world region. Finally, the Lutheran Church itself is mainly a state institution rather than a conspicuously religious actor (Gustafsson 1985, 238–65; Flanagan & Dalton 1990, 233; Lijphart 1990, 259; Madeley 1982, 149–153; Madeley 1977). This being the case, it is somewhat surprising that at present Christian parties share in government power in two of the four Nordic countries – Finland and Sweden. In Denmark, furthermore, the Christian People's Party (*Kristeligt Folkeparti*)

25

participated in Poul Schlüter's four-party cabinet from 1982 until 1988. Norway, finally, has electorally the strongest Christian party in all of Scandinavia; the Norwegian Christian People's Party (*Kristelig Folkeparti*) can scarcely be characterized as a minor party in the Scandinavian multi-party context. Are we witnessing a breakthrough for the Christian parties in Scandinavian politics? If that is the case, what is the background for this development? Have the Christian parties managed to activate a politically relevant cleavage based on religiously defined values? From where does their popular following originate? And finally, what are the prospects for continued growth of the Christian element in the Scandinavian party setting? These are the questions addressed in this article.

From Nil to Small to Medium-sized?

Religious parties are "latecomers" in the political arena of Scandinavia. When they emerged the population had to a large extent already been mobilized by the older parties. The Christian parties have therefore faced major difficulties in gaining a foothold among the electorate, as is readily demonstrated in Table 1.

Because of its long history and its relatively strong electoral position, the

Table 1. Results of Scandinavian Christian parties in Parliamentary Elections, 1933–91 (Percent of Valid Votes).

Norway		Finland		Sweden		Denmark	
Year	Percent	Year	Percent	Year	Percent	Year	Percent
1933	0.7	1958	0.2	1964	1.8	1971	2.0
1936	1.3	1962	0.8	1968	1.5	1973	4.0
1945	7.9	1966	0.4	1970	1.8	1975	5.3
1949	8.4	1970	1.1	1973	1.8	1977	3.4
1953	10.5	1972	2.5	1976	1.4	1979	2.6
1957	10.2	1975	3.3	1979	1.4	1981	2.3
1961	9.6	1979	4.8	1982	1.9	1984	2.7
1965	8.1	1983	3.0	1985	2.5*	1987	2.4
1969	9.4	1987	2.6	1988	2.9	1990	2.7
1973	12.3	1991	3.1	1991	7.1		
1977	12.4						
1981	8.9						
1985	8.3						
1989	8.5						

The parties are in Norway: *Kristelig Folkeparti*, in Finland: *Suomen Kristillinen Liitto* (*SKL*), in Sweden: *Kristen Demokratisk Samling*, since 1991 *Kristdemokratiska Samhällspartiet* (*KDS*) and in Denmark: *Kristeligt Folkeparti*.
  * KDS share of ballots cast for the electoral alliance with the Center Party (Source: Wörlund 1988, 80).

Norwegian Christian People's Party constitutes a special case among the Nordic Christian parties. This party was established in 1933 in Western Norway, and during its first ten years was basically a regional party for the Hordaland area. In the first post-war election, however, the party rose to national significance, a position which it has been able to maintain and even to some extent strengthen since then. The Christian League (SKL) in Finland has never gained comparable shares of the popular vote. Nevertheless, in 1970 the party won its first seat in parliament, and it has managed to maintain parliamentary representation ever since. The Christian Democratic Union (KDS) in Sweden also remained a peripheral party over a long period; its chances of exceeding the 4 percent threshold required for representation in parliament seemed decidedly poor. In the 1985 election, however, the KDS joined forces with the Center Party. This electoral alliance gave the Christian party leader Alf Svensson a seat in parliament. But in the following elections, the two parties again ran on separate tickets, and Svensson failed to maintain his seat. Against this background, the 1991 election result was all the more sensational. The Christian Democratic Union had no trouble exceeding the 4 percent barrier clause on its own, and the party suddenly commanded 26 seats in parliament. As for the Christian People's Party in Denmark, its electoral peak seems to have occurred in the 1970s. The party, nevertheless, has managed to stay above the 2 percent limit required for representation in *Folketinget*, the Danish parliament, and it presently holds four seats.

A Frame of Reference – on Critical Thresholds

Every political movement must pass certain critical thresholds in order to be able to gain significance. Conversely, every party must strive not to fall below these limits again. These thresholds are particularly awkward from the point of view of movements and parties which have not been part of the political scene "from the beginning", that is, from the first crucial phase of mass democracy during which basic party constellations were established. Mogens Pedersen is one of the authors who has theorized in terms of such thresholds, and he writes among other things about the *threshold of declaration*, the *threshold of representation* and the *threshold of relevance* (Pedersen 1982, 6–9).

The first threshold, the *threshold of declaration*, simply implies that a group of citizens get together in a conscious and openly declared attempt to organize a political party, to participate in elections and to seek to influence the use of social and political power. Their ability to do this naturally depends on their resources – economic and social as well as other kinds of resources. How successful the establishment of a party is and what character it attains is also largely influenced by the historical and political situation in which the attempt is made. The historical opportunities for different movements naturally vary to a great extent. The context in which a party constituted itself frequently marks its activities and orientation for many years to come.

As for the *threshold of representation*, it goes without saying that numeric strength is of crucial importance. However, many other factors play a role as well. Some parties enjoy the support of clearly defined segments of the population, while others rely on a more varied popular following. The foothold that a party manages to gain in the social structure is often crucial for the stability of its electoral support and for its possibilities to enter into cooperation with intermediate organizations, such as interest groups and popular movements. Geographic strongholds are also important, but sometimes problematic: on the one hand, a party with nation-wide ambitions will not wish to be too strongly associated with a particular geographic region; on the other hand, regionalism is often the best guarantee for the fundamental stability of a party's electoral following. Of particular significance for newly introduced parties is whether they can win relatively stable electoral segments from other parties or whether they are compelled to create an electoral base from a variety of social and geographic elements. In connection with these considerations, Fisher's (1980, 610) proposition about the decline of major parties is also worth examining. According to Fisher, "several of the conditions associated with the decline of the major parties in Western political systems appear conducive to increased minority party activity and success". The counter-hypothesis would be that the electoral gains of the Christian parties originate from the losses of other marginal parties rather than from the decline of the largest parties.

Crucial to the *threshold of relevance* of parties is quite obviously their "raw force" in terms of parliamentary representation. As for Scandinavia, the period during which one-party parliamentary majorities were a distinct possibility definitely seems to have become a matter of history. The question of which parties are to be reckoned with in the parliamentary game is therefore quite complicated. Parties with limited parliamentary representation may, depending on the interplay between arithmetic constellations and political distance, suddenly emerge as highly relevant partners or opponents.

To what extent and in which situations have the Christian parties been able to posit themselves as "relevant coalition partners" in the parliamentary game? What are the prospects for them to establish themselves as recurrent "*cabinet makers*" in Scandinavia? Is their best hope one of attaining the status of *supplementary parties* in relation to the larger parties? What risk do they run to be defined as permanent *outsiders* in parliamentary coalition politics? It is to these questions which we may now turn.

28

"Declaration" – the Emergence of the Christian Parties

The Christian People's Party in Norway is not only the oldest and electorally strongest Christian party in Scandinavia. Its emergence and activities also came to influence the rise and orientation of the three other parties. The process of its establishment displays several features which are characteristic of the "declaratory phase" of Scandinavian Christian democracy at large.

Especially in West Norway, Low Church opinion strongly associated with revivalism and missionary activities had rallied behind the agrarian liberal party *Venstre* after the introduction of universal suffrage. From the point of view of the religious activists, however, the Liberal Party's profile concerning moral and religious questions was somewhat problematic. The party was known to be "culturally radical" in the Oslo region, and it did not make things better that the party leader Johan Mowinckel was a well-known free-thinker. Attempts at placing *"Christians"* sufficiently high on the Liberal Party's tickets had not been successful. It seems to have been particularly significant that perhaps the most respected Christian activist, the Bible School principal Nils Lavik, had been placed so low on the Liberal ticket in Hordaland that he failed to gain a seat in parliament. The calls for a separate Christian party, which had been voiced for some time already, now gained momentum (Lomeland 1971, 19–30).

The decisive impetus behind the establishment of a Christian party, however, seems to have originated from a conflict about a theater play. It would later turn out that these kinds of conflicts frequently provoked active Christian elements to voice protests in Scandinavian politics. In the fall of 1932 it became known that the National Theater of Oslo would present "The Green Pastures, A Fable" by Marc Connelly. This caused an outcry among active Christians, who regarded the play as strongly blasphemous. The protest grew to be somewhat of a popular mass movement. The leading Liberal daily *Dagbladet*, which had, among other things, carried articles in support of the play criticizing narrow-minded Christians, was in this connection subjected to severe criticism (Sæter 1985, 8–10; Lomeland 1971, 35–43).

Popular protest gave rise to a parliamentary debate resulting in a resolution asking the cabinet to assure effective enforcement of legislation against blasphemy. The cabinet failed, however, to respond by adopting any clear standpoints or measures. Instead, eight out of the nine Liberal ministers accepted an invitation to attend a special performance of the play. In religious quarters this was perceived as still another example of a nonchalant attitude towards Christian opinion. Those who worked for the establishment of a separate Christian party had one more argument at their disposal (Johansson 1985, 72).

This opinion was reinforced by what was known as the Överland Contro-

29

versy. Arnulf Överland, a well-known author, had appeared before student associations with a speech carrying the strongly provocative title "Christianity – the Tenth Plague". In the debate about this question a conflict arose between Christian opinion and, among others, the Liberal daily *Bergens Tidende* (Sæter 1985, 9–10).

In addition to these "scandals", there were controversies concerning the democratization of congregational work and differences between the Liberal Party leadership and Christian party activists on temperance policy. Taken together these events constituted the immediate historical background of the establishment of the Christian People's Party in the province of Hordaland in 1933. This marked the beginning of a political movement which was to gain national significance in the immediate aftermath of the Second World War.

As is frequently the case in comparative Nordic studies, it is necessary to take into account the phenomenon of *diffusion* (Karvonen 1981) when studying the character and background of the Christian parties in Scandinavia. The second oldest of the four parties, the Finnish Christian League (SKL), was founded in 1958 under strong inspiration from the Norwegian Christian movement. In fact, the first program of the SKL turned out to be more or less a verbatim translation of the corresponding Norwegian document (Arter 1980, 146). The political and historical context in which the Finnish party came into existence, however, displayed some special features.

Indeed, it would seem as if the *general political background* was of somewhat greater importance in Finland than in the case of the other three parties. The entire post-war era had been a strongly offensive period for the Finnish Communists. In the second half of the 1950s they experienced a strong upward trend among the electorate, which was to result in their best electoral performance ever in 1958. At this election the Communists won 50 seats in the *Eduskunta*, the Finnish parliament, a result which made them the largest party in parliament. The Communists and their allies, the "People's Democrats", conducted a strongly "system critical" line of policy, meaning, among other things, that the system with an Established Church as well as the strongly conservative profile of the Church were subjected to severe criticism. Withdrawals from Church membership increased markedly towards the end of the 1950s, and this tendency was clearly connected to communist electoral strongholds (Sundback 1991, 277–278).

The fact that Christian activists in Finland chose to establish a separate party instead of trying to work through existing bourgeois parties appears to be related to the social foundation on which the party was supposed to be based (Johansson 1985, 24). The strong position of atheist communism in the labor movement had evidently alienated Christian workers and smallholders. It was primarily these people that the SKL wished to appeal

30

to, and these population segments could not be expected to rally behind the established bourgeois parties.

Generally speaking, in short, perhaps the most important impetus behind the creation of a Christian party in Finland was the proliferation of politically motivated secularism and atheism. In the course of the 1960s, the party gradually attained a clearer image of a "moral vigilante" as various "scandals" became topical on the political agenda and important issues concerning such matters as religious instruction in schools were to be decided (Arter 1980, 148; Arter 1987, 32).

The emergence of the Christian Democratic Union (KDS) in Sweden is closely associated with several heated debates on religion and morality. At the beginning of 1964 there was a debate around what was known as the Petition of the 140 Doctors, a document signed by professors of medicine as well as by practicing physicians. The petitioners expressed their concern about increasing promiscuity, the proliferation of venereal diseases and the increased number of abortions. According to the petitioners, sexual instruction given in the schools, and the cultural and sexual policies of the government bore a major responsibility for this state of affairs. The ensuing debate became highly polarized, especially with respect to the question of abortion. The 140 doctors received strong support from Christian organizations and debaters.

Parallel to this development, a memorandum from the National Board of Social Affairs about a religious sect known as Maranata gave cause to additional friction between religious activists and the government. The Board had deemed it necessary to advise all municipalities to take proper measures to prevent children under 16 years of age from attending "ecstatic meetings" (Johansson 1985, 80). In non-conformist circles this was seen as an attempt to limit the freedom of religion.

The question of religious instruction at schools was still another incentive behind the decision to create a political organization based on explicit Christian values. A plan aiming at reforming the curriculum of the secondary schools proposed a reduction of the share of religious instruction. Moreover, the subject itself was to have a character of an objective social science only loosely connected with confessional protestantism. Those who protested against this plan decided to launch a mass petition in order to stop it from being implemented. This turned out to be a highly succesful enterprise, inasmuch as 2.1 million people (out of some five million adult citizens in toto) signed the petition in the course of a few months. This fast mobilization represented a hopeful sign from the point of view of those who argued for the establishment of a separate Christian party.

Still another debate on morality caused by the film "491" helped mobilize the Christian opinion. This picture, which among other things contained advanced sex scenes, was first prohibited altogether by the Government

31

Motion Picture Agency. Later, however, the cabinet decided to lift the ban after certain scenes were cut. Christian activists were at the forefront of this debate, and several of them have later underlined the importance of this question for the decision to create the Christian Democratic Union in 1964 (Johansson 1985, 90–95).

The early history of the Christian People's Party in Denmark in many ways repeats what has been said about the Christian Democratic Union in Sweden. The 1960s had witnessed a considerable radicalization, especially with respect to issues relating to sexuality and morality. This process entailed the liberalization of, among other things, legislation on pornography and abortion. "Danish sin" became a widely known concept throughout the world. Parallel to this, school reform plans proposed a steadily decreasing share for religious instruction in school curricula (Riis 1985, 29). The Christian People's Party was established in 1970 as a direct and explicit reaction against these tendencies in Danish society. The struggle against liberal abortion policies seems to have been particularly important. The program presented by the party, moreover, stressed the importance of continued confessional religious instruction at all levels of the school system, sexual instruction was to be "marriage oriented", "border control of hippies" was to be made tougher, both private and public consumption was to be cut back, and tax and inheritance legislation was to encourage people to save (*Nordisk kontakt* 1971:10, 615).

In sum, the emergence of Christian parties in Scandinavia can be characterized in the following manner:

1. The Norwegian party became the archetype which largely set the standards for the programmatic orientation of the parties, and it inspired the establishment of the other parties.
2. The parties acquired the character of "protest parties" from the beginning; they capitalized on negative reactions to current social phenomena and gathered strength from debates on these questions.
3. The parties at no time represented the "official standpoint of the church" or some sort of an average opinion among church members. The center of gravity at all times lay among nonconformist and revivalist groups and among the lay activists of the Lutheran State churches. There were some clearly negative reactions on the part of the Church against the formation of the parties. This was at least in part explicable in terms of the support the Church had traditionally received from the conservative and agrarian parties, which were now presented with competition. Seen from the point of view of the average voter or church member, the Christian parties can be said to have stood out as a fairly *exclusive society*. In contradistinction to the Christian democratic parties on the

continent, the Nordic Christian parties represented a demonstratively and offensively Christian posture in their national settings.

"Representation" – Sources of Strength and Weakness

Electoral Law and The Christian Parties

Since 1945, when the Norwegian party launched its first nation-wide electoral campaign, it has never had less than ten seats in the *Stortinget*, the national parliament.[2] The peak was reached in 1973 with 21 seats. Since the 1989 election the party has been represented by 14 MPs. The absence of a barrier clause which would stipulate a minimum share of the vote necessary for parliamentary representation from the very beginning made the Christian People's Party a realistic alternative for the electorate.

The Finnish Christian League has also benefited from liberal electoral laws. To be sure, the d'Hont Method, which continues to be applied in Finland (the other three countries have switched to the Saint Laguë variety) to a certain extent favors the largest parties. On the other hand, there is no barrier clause in Finland, either. Moreover, the parties are entirely free to form electoral alliances with each other, and this is decided at the constituency level depending on the regional constellations among the parties. Despite the low Christian share of the total vote, the Finnish Christian League received its first seat in parliament in 1970 through an electoral alliance with the Center Party. Since then, the party has been one of the most active and successful participants in electoral alliances (Noponen 1988, 111). Since the 1991 election, the Christian League has had eight seats in the 200 seat *Eduskunta*, a result of highly favorable electoral alliances.

It is in Sweden that electoral law has created a major obstacle for the Christian party. The first electoral result of the Christian Democratic Union, 1.8 percent in 1964, was as such far from impressive. Still, it brought the party reasonably close to its first seat in parliament. Four years later, after a thorough constitutional reform, the prospects seemed hopeless despite the fact that the party had maintained its share of the vote. The 4 percent barrier clause introduced in connection with the reform seemed at once to put parliamentary representation far beyond the reach of the Christian Democrats (Johansson 1985, 221–41). An electoral alliance between the Christian Democratic Union and the Center Party in 1985, which gave the Christians their first seat in *Riksdagen*, the Swedish parliament, was criticized by the Social Democrats as unlawful. The 1991 election, however, finally lifted KDS easily over the threshold and made the party a factor to be taken into account even from the point of view of electoral arithmetic.

The Danish party just barely reached the 2 percent limit required for representation in 1971, but it fell a few hundred votes short of a seat in parliament. In elections since then, it has managed to gain and maintain parliamentary representation, although in a few instances its share of the vote has fallen dangerously close to the 2 percent threshold. The 1990 election entailed the same number of seats (four) as the previous election.

Electoral Peaks: Christian Parties as a "System Protest"

The 1970s entailed the greatest electoral success yet for the Danish, Norwegian and Finnish parties. In the first two countries, the rise started in 1973 and reached its peak in the following elections (1975 and 1977 respectively). The Finnish party followed suit a couple of years later. In Sweden, by contrast, the corresponding rise of the Christian Democratic Union came considerably later. There was, to be sure, a weak but noticeable upward trend through the 1980s. However, this trend was dwarfed by the electoral success of the KDS in 1991.

The fact that the Swedish party suddenly managed to surpass the electoral threshold quite without the help of electoral alliances, can only be comprehended in terms of a more general electoral protest against the "system". It can be argued, however, that the best electoral results of Scandinavian Christian democracy can in *all cases* be seen as an expression of such a protest. The ascendancy started in 1973 in Norway and Denmark in the wake of a heated debate about EC membership. Parallel to this, the dominant Social Democrats met with their greatest electoral disasters in the entire post-war era. The Danish Social Democrats, for example, plunged from some 37 percent of the vote to some 25 percent two years later, whereas in Norway, the Labor Party lost 11 percentage points as compared to 1969 and wound up with 35 percent of the vote in 1973.

When Sweden repeated the pattern in 1991, the Social Democrats did not suffer quite as dramatic a loss: they retreated from 43.3 percent in 1988 to 37.6 percent. Nevertheless, this was the poorest electoral performance of the Social Democrats since 1928. The election was preceded by a number of "scandals" and debates about betrayed promises in which the Social Democratic Party was portrayed in a very awkward light. The dominant atmosphere surrounding the election, it would seem, was one of fatigue with prolonged social democratic rule in the country.

The Finnish party system lacks a clearly dominant party comparable to the social democratic parties in the other three countries. Nevertheless, the Christian electoral peak in 1979 can be interpreted in terms of a similar protest against the political "establishment". The year before, the position

34

of President Urho Kekkonen as the real power center in Finnish politics had been manifested in a demonstrative way, as all major parties rallied behind him in the presidential elections. The Christian League, however, had nominated its own candidate for the presidency, the party leader Raino Westerholm. His campaign was generally deemed to be competent and serious, and his share of the vote was more than double the Christian vote in the 1975 parliamentary elections. A major part of the protest against the lack of real alternatives in the 1978 presidential elections had apparently been expressed through votes for Westerholm (whom nobody really expected to be able to challenge Kekkonen). In the 1979 election, the Christian League evidently managed to hold some of the "extra votes" its presidential candidate had brought home the year before.

The electoral successes of the Scandinavian Christian parties seem to confirm Fisher's proposition about the connection between the proliferation of minor parties and the decline of major parties. In Denmark, Norway and Sweden, the Christian electoral peak coincides with a protest against the dominant party. Generally speaking, these electoral successes can be explained with reference to the fact that the parties managed to capitalize on – in addition to the original moral protest – a more general *political protest*.

Electoral geography

The electoral geography of Scandinavian Christian democracy is fairly stable over time, but one can hardly speak of an unambiguous Scandinavian pattern. The strongholds of the Norwegian party have always been the Western and Southern parts of the country, particularly Hordaland county in the West (see Fig. 1). Large portions of the narrow coastal strip in central and Northern Norway have also displayed Christian voting above the national average. The weak spots of the party are equally easy to pinpoint: East Norway, i.e. Oslo and the counties surrounding it in the North and the East, has consistently displayed Christian shares of the vote below the national average. The exception has been Östfold county in the extreme Southeast. In Stein Rokkan's classic conceptual map of Norwegian politics (1967, 367–444), the Christian People's Party is undoubtedly a part of the "cultural periphery" in the West and South.

A look at the electoral geography of the Finnish Christian League may at first glance point in the opposite direction: it is in the Southern half of the country that the party's electoral support has reached the highest level. In the real periphery of the North and the East it has been considerably more difficult for the SKL to gain an electoral foothold. In particular, Oulu and Lapland counties in the North have been difficult to conquer electorally. This is notable, since these are the strongholds of Leastadianism, one of

35

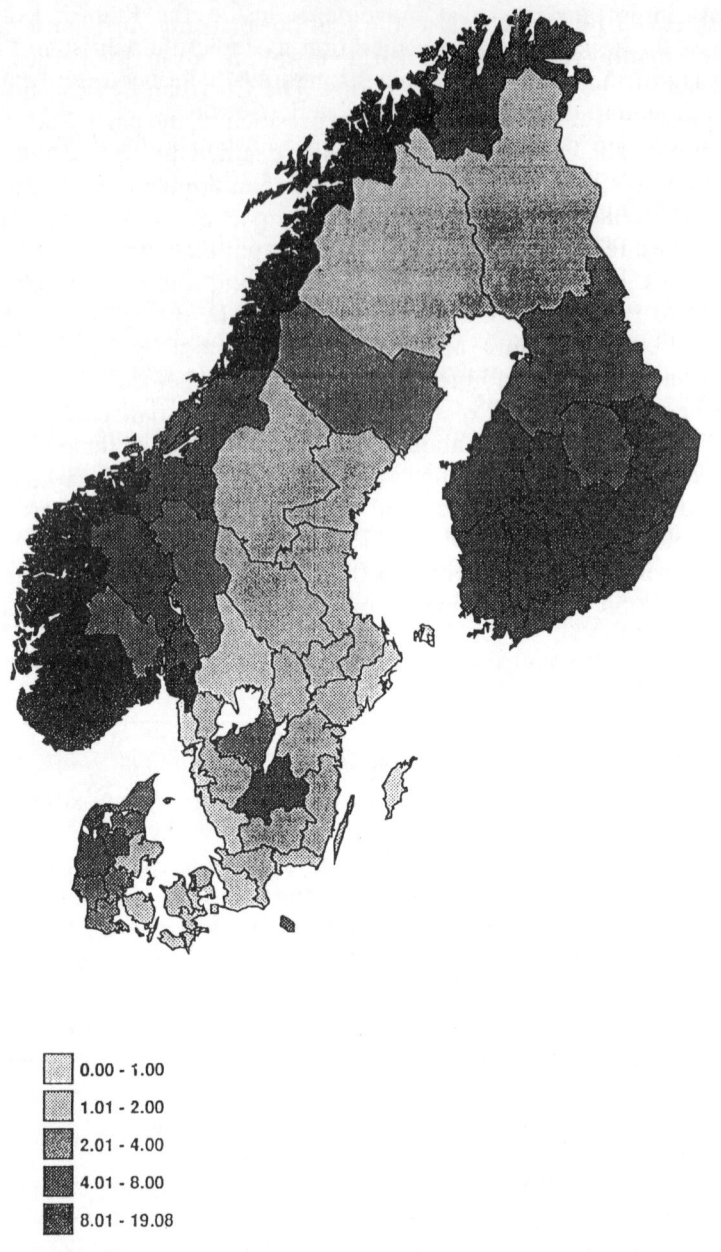

	0.00 - 1.00
	1.01 - 2.00
	2.01 - 4.00
	4.01 - 8.00
	8.01 - 19.08

Fig. 1. Regional Distribution of the Christian Vote in Scandinavia About 1980 (Percent of Valid Votes).

36

the most important revivalist movements inside the Finnish Lutheran Church. Still, it would be an exaggeration to depict the Christian League as "a party of the center". Its main strongholds have been the Kymi and St. Michael counties. Although situated in the Southern half of the country, they certainly do not belong to the core of urban Finland. Rather, the electoral geography of the Finnish Christian party might be characterized as "semi-peripheral".

Over a long period, the electoral geography of the Christian Democratic Union bore a striking resemblance to the map of Swedish non-conformism: the counties of Västerbotten and Jönköping in the North and in central South Sweden, respectively, were the main strongholds of both. This means that the party electorally relied more on the periphery than on the center, although at least Jönköping cannot be considered as a part of the extreme periphery. The 1991 election brought about a major change, however,as the party advanced strongly and uniformly across the entire country, including such previously weak spots as Stockholm and the areas surrounding it. Nevertheless, the greatest percentage growth occurred in the traditional stronghold in Jönköping county. In this electoral district, the KDS is now the third largest party, quite comparable to the Conservatives. Only the Social Democrats are clearly stronger in this region.

The Danish Christian Party has consistently had its strongholds on the West coast of Jutland. The island of Bornholm in the Baltic Sea has also displayed figures above the national average. In other parts of the country, particularly in the Copenhagen area, the Christian People's Party has met with little success. The Danish party clearly repeats the Norwegian and earlier Swedish pattern with strongholds in the non-conformist and revivalist areas of the periphery.

In sum, it appears as if the Norwegian and Danish parties face the greatest difficulties of electoral mobilization in the populous areas in and around the national capitals. Until the last election, this was true of the Christian Democratic Union in Sweden as well. The Finnish party, by contrast, has had higher shares of the vote in the southern half of the country than in the northern periphery.

Voters and Sympathizers

When it comes to individual-level data, Norway once again occupies a special position thanks to the simple fact that the Christian People's Party is large enough to be represented by a sufficient number of respondents in a normal survey sample. Generally, access to individual-level data has been best for Norway and Denmark and most limited for Finland. Since identical data sets do not exist for the four countries, no strict numerical comparison will be presented here. Instead, characteristic features of Christian party

37

voters and sympathizers will be presented in a less stringent form for each country separately.

Data for Norway are drawn from electoral surveys conducted in connection with the 1973 and 1989 parliamentary elections (Norwegian Election Studies 1973, 1989; N: 1973=177, 1989=107). The continuity to be observed over the decade and a half is striking. The prototype of a Christian party supporter in Norway 20 years ago as well as today is an elderly woman in Western Norway who is married or a widow. She frequently speaks the more peripheral "new Norwegian" (*nynorsk*) and is against Norwegian membership in the European Community. By the same token, one would not expect to find a Christian party sympathizer who is a younger industrial worker, divorced and living in Eastern Norway.

In moral questions – here represented by the attitude towards alcohol – the followers of the Christian People's Party are in a category of their own. By contrast, they hardly differ from national averages concerning socio-economic characteristics or general political and social views. They are least numerous in industrial occupations, and especially in 1973 they were overrepresented in the lower income brackets. Generally speaking, however, their distribution over occupational groups and social classes came close to the national statistical average. Moreover, as to class identification, political interest and attitudes towards immigration, Christian party sympathizers represent a middle course. Unfortunately, longitudinal data are not available on all these questions. The "deviations" on moral questions, as well as age, sex and regional location, do not spill over to general political attitudes, however. In the light of this empirical evidence its seems reasonable to characterize the Christian People's Party as a party of the political center.

Danish surveys available for the present study contain a limited number of Christian party voters. In the 1981 Danish Election Study only 25 respondents said they had voted for the Christian People's Party and survey data for the 1988 election contain only 63 Christian party voters. Even given these limitations, it seems rather clear that the Danish party is also a "women's party", and that particularly the youngest age cohorts (under 30 years) are clearly underrepresented. In the 1981 sample, Western Jutland and the island of Lolland seem somewhat overrepresented. The 1988 survey similarly points to an underrepresentation for Zealand including the Copenhagen area and for the island of Funen, whereas Northern and Western Jutland again are overrepresented. Also in Denmark, married and widowed people are overrepresented among Christian party voters. As to occupation and income level, there is some overrepresentation in 1988 for functionaries and pensioners. In 1973 as well as 15 years later, Christian voters represented the lower rather than the higher income brackets. Again, as to political interest and attitudes towards social and economic policies, Christian voters came close to the national average.

38

As for Sweden, Göran Johansson's dissertation (1985, 221–279) contains data for all elections from 1964 until 1982. However, only two variables are included: occupational group and previous party choice. Sample size is limited, providing between 35 and 60 Christian Democratic Union voters depending on the election. In one respect the results are nevertheless unambiguous: the largest single group of KDS voters during this period consisted of mid-level functionaries. This group was consistently over-represented among the party's voters. A survey carried out by Swedish Television in connection with the 1991 election, however, shows that the Christian Democratic Union has managed to make inroads into all occupational categories. The percentage change was greatest among farmers, but in absolute figures the greatest gains came from functionaries (Valu91/STV). It has already been noted that in 1991 the KDS achieved a general breakthrough in the geography of Swedish elections. The survey results suggest that the party managed to break some barriers in a socio-economic respect as well.

Finnish survey data are scarce and the smallness of the samples is troublesome if one wishes to study Finnish Christian League voters. The number of respondents who say that they vote for the party is usually 20–30 in a normal survey. This being the case, questions pertaining to socio-economic or attitudinal correlates of SKL voting are difficult to analyze in a statistically reliable way. Yet, even with these limitations in mind, one may note that SKL voters in both 1973 and in 1991 came closer to the national average than the supporters of any other party in terms of occupational distribution. In 1973 the majority (64 percent) of Christian League voters were workers, whereas in 1991 functionaries were the largest category (54 percent) (Sänkiaho 1991, 38). This corresponds to the general social change in Finland. As to class identification and income categories, there was some overrepresentation of a working-class identification among Christian voters. In 1991 this is no longer the case; Christian League voters have a class identification which corresponds to the averages among voters at large. A constant feature found in 1983, 1987 as well as 1991 is the overrepresentation for voters who describe themselves as low-wage earners (Sänkiaho 1991, 41). What there is of survey data for Finland indicates that Christian voters in Finland are to be found somewhere in between working class and the lower bourgeoisie.

From what parties have Christian parties in Scandinavia gained votes? Unfortunately there are no data concerning, for instance, the important period immediately after the Second World War in Norway. Data for more recent periods, however, are available to a certain extent. The Norwegian Election Studies for 1973 and 1989 show, for example, that the electorate of the Christian People's Party has been highly faithful to the party. Mobility has concerned the two parties which are closest to the Christian Party in

general political terms – the Center Party and the Liberal Party. These are
the two parties which to a certain extent have lost voters to the Christian
Party. In the Finnish case, there are transition matrices for both 1979–83
and 1987-91. As for the 1983 election, the main conclusion is that the
Finnish Christian League lost votes and that the remaining voters had
already voted for the party in 1979. There is greater mobility in the 1991
election. The Christian League seems primarily to have attracted previous
non-voters but also some voters from all minor parties, including the
populist Rural Party (Risbjerg Thomsen 1990, 60–61; Berglund 1991, 338).

As to Sweden, Johansson (1985, 221–273) demonstrates that the Christian Democratic Union gained votes from other centrist parties, while at
the same time an important part of the party vote originated from newly
enfranchised voters and previous non-voters. The 1991 election again
brought about a change, as practically all parties seem to have lost votes
to the KDS. The percentage loss was greatest for the Liberals and the
Center Party. Of roughly equal importance to the Christian Democratic
Union, however, were the voters it won from the Social Democrats
(ValU91/STV). Finally, Christian voters in Denmark have normally originated from the Radical Liberal Party and to some extent from the populist
Progress Party (Risbjerg Thomsen 1990, 52–53).

A common feature for the four countries is that the Christian parties
have normally not won votes from the major parties, especially the Social
Democrats. In this respect, the 1991 Swedish election represents a certain
change. Nevertheless, the typical "loser" to the Christian parties has been
a small or medium-sized party in the political center. Fisher's thesis that
the decline of major parties has been conducive to the proliferation of
minor parties is of course true for the Christian parties as well; this decline
has made it easier for minor parties to gain an electoral foothold. Even so,
in terms of direct voter mobility, the flows between major parties and the
Christian parties have been limited.

In sum, the Christian voter in Scandinavia is primarily singled out through
his or her attitudes on questions of morality and ethics, be they related to
alcohol, sex, marriage or school. In Norway and Denmark, the Christian
party supporters have a clearer regional identity than in Finland, whereas
the Swedish party has recently managed to become genuinely nationwide
in its electoral appeal. Women and older age cohorts are overrepresented
among Christian party sympathizers, but in socio-economic or general
political terms they are not particularly different from national averages.
Typically, the Christian electorate consists of lower bourgeoisie plus some
farmers and non-industrial workers. The traditional representatives of these
groups, the centrist parties, have most clearly felt the electoral competition
from the Christian parties.

40

"Relevance" – the Christian Parties in Coalition Politics

The relevance of parties is determined by their numeric *strength* and their *utility*. Numeric strength is easy to pinpoint and measure, "utility" defies every attempt at an exact definition. The stronger a party is, the more difficult it becomes to ignore it. Being big, however, is of little avail if a party is not utile, if ideological and programmatic abysses separate it from other parties or if it in other respects represents unwelcome competition for other parties.

Nordic parliamentarism at large has drifted increasingly farther away from the classic Anglo–Saxon ideal with alternating majorities. This has in fact never been a reality in Finland. During recent decades, Finnish politics has made a virtue out of the necessity of coalitions, which has made for considerable stability in cabinet politics. The other three countries, by contrast, have moved towards increasing instability with a stronger element of minority parliamentarism and temporary coalitions in individual policy sectors and around separate issues. The process at large has increased the potential significance of minor parties as coalition partners or as allies for parliamentary oppositions (Damgaard 1990b, 176–190).

The Christian People's Party in Norway is the only one of the four parties which at no time has been a *quantité négligeable* in the parliamentary game. In the entire post-war era, the party has been one of the central actors of the divided non-socialist camp in Norway. As the prolonged social democratic reign ended in 1963, the Christian Party entered into the short-lived bourgeois minority coalition led by John Lyng. Since then, the party has participated in five out of the six bourgeois cabinets; the exception was Kåre Willoch's conservative one-party cabinet in 1981–83. In 1972–73 the Christian party leader Lars Korvald headed a bourgeois coalition formed by non-socialist opponents of EC membership after the majority of the voters had turned down full Norwegian membership in the Community (Rommetvedt 1990, 51–54).

The central factor in the arithmetic of Norwegian coalition politics has been the predominance of the left. Up until 1961, the Social Democrats commanded a majority of their own in parliament. Even after that, they have more often than not been able to count on the support of the Socialist Left Party on the extreme left. In all situations, the cooperation of the Christian Party has been a necessary, but normally not sufficient condition for a non-socialist majority cabinet. Two such cabinets have appeared: the first one led by Per Borten in 1965–71, the second led by Kåre Willoch in 1983–86.

Up until the crisis created by the EC Referendum, the distances between Norwegian parties were clear indeed: all bourgeois parties stood closer to each other than to the Social Democrats in terms of roll-call behavior in

41

parliament. Since about 1972–73, however, these distances have been blurred somewhat. Among other things, there has been a *rapprochement* between the Social Democrats and the Christian Party (Rommetvedt 1990, 88). Among non-socialist parties, European integration and regional policies are some of the important issues that have given rise to conflicts. Conservative Party stands on these issues differ widely from those of the centrist parties, particularly the Christian People's Party. Simultaneously, the emergence of the populist Progress Party has split the non-socialist front further and made the coalition puzzle even more complicated. Today, the crucial question of Norwegian policies vis-à-vis the European Community constitutes a watershed right across the non-socialist camp. The Christian People's Party policies are clearly more restrictive than those of the Conservatives and the Progress Party. Another topical issue which may develop into a deep conflict around the very core of Christian ideas is the fact that the Conservatives have signalled their readiness for a programmatic reorientation concerning the relationship between Church and State.

The relevance of the Norwegian Christian People's Party in coalition politics seems to be decreasing. Their parliamentary strength has declined somewhat since their heyday in the 1970s. At the same time, their "utility" has also been called into question due to conflicts around central political issues.

Danish coalition politics was shaken even more thoroughly as a result of the electoral protest of the early 1970s. The Danish party system has since then had a "Finnish appearance". In contradistinction to Finnish politics, however, broad coalitions bridging the divide between socialists and non-socialists have been all but absent in Denmark.[3] The power center of Danish politics has increasingly been found in parliament itself. More and more, Danish politics have been based on deals and agreements on individual issues and policy sectors reached inside parliament with varying constellations of parties supporting such deals (Damgaard 1990a, 15–17).

The entrance of the Christian People's Party into the Danish parliament in 1973 was in itself an element in the dramatic loss of political stability in the country. The party at once became a player in a highly complicated political game, where the main goal was to create temporary majorities for individual decisions. Up until 1982, the Christian People's Party actively participated in such deals with both non-socialist and Social Democratic minority cabinets. In 1982, the Conservative Party leader, Poul Schlüter, managed to form a cabinet including his own party, the Agrarian Liberals, the Center Democrats and the Christian Party. This was formally a minority cabinet, but in 1983–87 it commanded a *de facto* majority in parliament. In certain important policy areas, including defense policy, however, the cabinet must rely on "alternative majorities". The electoral success of the populist Progress Party in 1988 once again complicated the party pattern

42

further and the four-party coalition resigned (Damgaard 1990a, 23–24). The 1990 election points in the direction of a renewed Social Democratic ascendancy. Together with the increased complexity of the party pattern on the non-socialist side this may render it very difficult to achieve broad bourgeois coalitions. Consequently, it may come to limit the role of the Christian People's Party in future coalition politics as well.

Finnish parliamentarism has run counter to the development elsewhere in Scandinavia. Fractionalization of the party system has, to be sure, increased to a certain extent in Finland as well. The response, however, has been radically different from that in the neighboring countries. Instead of unstable minority parliamentarism, the past two decades have entailed cabinets based on considerable majorities in parliament. Cabinets across the socialist-non-socialist gap have been the rule rather than the exception in Finland. A major impetus behind the process leading to an overarching political consensus was the entrance of protest parties into parliament in the early 1970s. These consensual mechanisms among the major parties have naturally restricted the potential of the Finnish Christian League to exert parliamentary influence by tipping the balance in the favor of one of the blocs (Anckar 1990, 141–148).

Finnish parliamentarism displays a greater number of critical thresholds than normal majority parliamentarism. This is due to constitutional stipulations which provide a minority of one-third of the MPs with effective means of obstructing legislative work. A minor party can therefore be "pivotal" in three different ways: it can provide a cabinet with an absolute majority, it can help give it a two-thirds majority, and it can help the opposition to reach the necessary minority to defer legislation.

The Finnish Christian League has had the possibility to play a pivotal role only once during its parliamentary life. In 1979–82 Mauno Koivisto led a cabinet which was one seat short of the magic two-thirds majority in parliament. However, there was very little in the way of an effective opposition in parliament despite the fact that the parties outside the cabinet commanded the necessary minority of 67 seats. For instance, these parties did not issue one single joint declaration (Anckar 1990, 154–155). One main reason was the fear of the small non-socialist parties that such cooperation would render them the image of mere auxiliaries of the largest opposition party, the Conservatives (Anckar 1990, 156). In sum, the Christians have normally been *unable* to play a pivotal role in opposition, and when it was at least arithmetically possible they did not *wish* to play that role.

Even the entrance of the Christian League into government in 1991 goes to emphasize the supplementary role of the party in Finland. Cabinet majorities normally require the participation of at least one of the minor parties. In order not to give a minor party – normally the Swedish People's

43

Party, which is a more or less permanent cabinet participant – disproportionate influence, the larger parties frequently include two minor parties in the cabinet. These balance each other out, since one of them is, strictly speaking, superfluous. Consequently, when Esko Aho included a Christian League minister in his cabinet, a major motive was to make sure that the Swedes would toe the line. To be sure, this gave the Christians an opportunity to influence policy in the field of development aid, where they presently hold a cabinet post. Still, they are themselves well advised to toe the line in all important issues in order not to risk being ousted from government.

In the Swedish case, the Christian Democratic Union became "relevant" overnight in 1991. Before that, the party had been a *quantité négligeable* in Swedish parliamentary politics. The entrance of the KDS into the bourgeois coalition led by Carld Bildt was not, however, sufficient to give the cabinet a majority status. Bildt must rely on the support of either the Left or the controversial populist party New Democracy for parliamentary majorities. Yet the Christian Democratic Union is clearly stronger in the cabinet than its Finnish counterpart. Its parliamentary strength makes it a fairly equal partner to both the Center Party and the Liberals. Only the Conservatives clearly carry more weight in the cabinet. The three posts held by the Christians – Communication, the Interior and Development Aid – do not belong to either the most prestigious or the most peripheral ministerial posts.

The Christian Democratic Union road to parliament and cabinet was characterized by an energetic attempt to amend the profile of the party. It no longer wished to stand out as a Christian single-issue movement but as a humanist and liberal party with a pronounced interest in social welfare questions (*Nordisk kontakt* 1991:9, 84–86). In the negotiations preceding the formation of the cabinet, therefore, the party displayed great flexibility, avoiding all stands which might endanger the party's entry into cabinet politics.

In sum, the role of Christian parties in Nordic coalition politics does not constitute a clear joint pattern. The Norwegian party has at several instances in the post-war era played the role which the Swedish Christian Democratic Union assumed in 1991. At the same time, there are features in Norwegian politics today which may render the position of the Christian People's Party more difficult in the future. In Denmark the Christian People's Party carries limited parliamentary weight, but it has been able to play a role thanks to the complicated parliamentary constellations. The Finnish Christian League participates in the cabinet "at the mercy" of the larger parties; its role is clearly supplementary. Moreover, the rapid rise of the Swedish Christian Democratic Union to government position rests on one single election result. It is too early yet to judge whether this reflects a passing electoral protest or a more permanent foothold in the Swedish electorate.

44

Concluding Remarks

The Christian parties of Scandinavia emerged as parties of moral protest, and they have more or less retained this image through the years. To be a Christian party voter in the Nordic countries has meant a stand which goes beyond a conformistic church membership or an identification with general Christian values. The Christian parties have been far more "deviant" in Scandinavia than their continental counterparts have been in their political settings. Church and religion contain little political potential that might be exploited by parties in Scandinavia. The Christian parties lack the natural historical and structural preconditions on which Christian democracy farther south has thrived. The threshold created by the active stands taken by the Scandinavian parties in moral questions continues to be too high for the average voter.

The Scandinavian Christian parties have largely retained their characteristic voter profiles: overrepresentation for women and elderly persons side-by-side with highly normal distributions with respect to socio-economic groups and general political attitudes. How clear and definite the recent Swedish change may be, is uncertain at the moment.

The traditionally strongest of the four parties, the Christian People's Party in Norway, has gathered strength from the classic coincident cleavages of Norwegian politics; i.e. religious revivalism, economic structure and language make for dynamic "politics of cultural defense" outside the dominant Eastern part of the country, particularly in Western Norway. The Swedish and Danish parties have also had their geographic strongholds, but these have not been as extensive and socially dynamic as the Western and Southern peripheries in Norway.

While the core of Christian party support has always consisted of a moral protest, the parties have reached their electoral peaks thanks to more general waves of political protest. The turbulence created by the EC membership controversy in Denmark and Norway in the early 1970s paved the way for the hitherto best results of the Danish and Norwegian parties. The protest against the dominant position of President Kekkonen and against the lack of real political alternatives also largely explains the best results of the Finnish Christian League at the end of the 1970s. Similarly, it is difficult to understand the rise of the Christian Democratic Union in Sweden without reference to the general political protest in Sweden at the beginning of the 1990s.

As for coalition politics, the best days of the Norwegian and Danish parties may be over. The complex party structure which has in itself been a precondition of their "relevance" has acquired traits which make it more difficult for the Christians to play a pivotal role. Cabinet participation of the Finnish party is not necessary for the survival of the government coalition; the Christian League is in every respect supplementary in the

45

present coalition. By comparison, the Christian Democratic Union in Sweden is currently important in the parliamentary game, yet it is not able to provide the present government coalition with a necessary majority.

It would therefore be highly exaggerated to speak of a general upswing of Christian politics in Scandinavia. Quite to the contrary, three of the parties face considerable difficulties in trying to reach beyond their traditional supporters. The combination of fundamental religious homogeneity and the image of the parties as moral vigilantes is a definite disadvantage in this regard. By and large, the Danish, Finnish and Norwegian parties lead a defensive struggle against increasingly difficult odds.

Against this background, the recent success of the Christian Democratic Union in Sweden is all the more noteworthy. In connection with the 1991 campaign, it seemed as if the party had indeed managed to define a political line beyond the traditional moralist message. The general humanistic approach offered by Alf Svensson and his party appears as a new element in the Swedish political debate. Could it become a source of lasting success for the KDS?

The electoral record of the non-socialist parties in Sweden certainly calls for caution in this regard. Both the Conservatives, the Center Party and the Liberals have had considerable ups and downs during recent decades. The Environmentalist Party fell from parliament in 1991 after a rise largely similar to that of the Christian Democratic Union today. The non-socialist parties are each other's major rivals in electoral terms. In this competition, the KDS may soon find itself on the losing side. The electoral wind which blew in the favor of the party this time is no different from the relatively recent but already vanished successes of the other parties. If and when the wind turns against the Swedish Christian Democratic Union, we will suddenly be reminded of the fact that 7 percent of the vote lies merely three percentage points above the most critical of all thresholds.

ACKNOWLEDGEMENTS
Part of the data used in this publication originates from the 1973 and 1989 surveys of the *Norwegian Election Studies* program. Data in anonymized form have been made available through the *Norwegian Social Science Data Services* (NSD) in Bergen, Norway. The material was originally gathered and processed by the *Norwegian Central Bureau of Statistics*. Individual-level data on Denmark originate from the 1981 and 1988 surveys of the *Danish Election Studies* program. These were also made available through the NSD with the kind permission of the *Danish Data Archives* (DDA) in Odense, Denmark. Data and cartographic material on regional variations in Christian party support originate from the *Nordic Database for Regional Time Series* (NDRT) created and made available by the NSD. While all these institutions and their staffs deserve my warmest thanks for their valuable assistance, they bear no responsibility for the analyses and interpretations of the data in this study. The study was carried out while the author was a Visiting Research Fellow at the Department of Comparative Politics and NSD in Bergen. Special thanks are due to Jostein Ryssevik, Bjarne Öymyr, Lars

46

Holm, Dag Kiberg, Atle Alvheim and Björn Henrichsen. An earlier version of this article was published in Swedish in *Politiikka* 4/1992.

NOTES

1.   In this article, unless otherwise noted, "Scandinavia" is used to include Finland as well as Denmark, Norway and Sweden.
2.   Until 1973 the number of seats in the Norwegian parliament *Stortinget*, was 150. From 1973 to 1985 there were 155 seats, from 1985 to 1989 157 seats, and in 1989 the number was increased to 165.
3.   The exception is the 1978 coalition between the Social Democrats and the Agrarian Liberals (*Venstre*). This was also a minority cabinet.

REFERENCES

Anckar, D. 1990. "Finland: dualism och konsensus", in Damgaard, E. ed., *Parlamentarisk forandring i Norden*. Oslo: Universitetsforlaget.

Arter, D. 1980. "The Finnish Christian League: Party or "Anti-Party""?, *Scandinavian Political Studies*, 3, 143–162.

Arter, D. 1987. *Politics and Policy-Making in Finland*. Worcester: Wheatsheaf Books.

Berglund, S. 1991. "The Finnish Parliamentary Election of March 1991", *Scandinavian Political Studies*, 14, 335–342.

Damgaard, E. 1990a. "Parlamentarismens danske tilstande", in Damgaard E. ed., *Parlamentarisk forandring i Norden*. Oslo: Universitetsforlaget.

Damgaard, E. 1990b. "Parlamentarisk forandring i Norden", in Damgaard, E. ed., *Parlamentarisk forandring i Norden*. Oslo: Universitetsforlaget

Fisher, S.L. 1980. "The "Decline of Parties" Thesis and the Role of Minor Parties", in Merkl, P. ed., *Western European Party Systems*. New York: The Free Press.

Flanagan, S. & Dalton R.J. 1990. "Models of Change", in Mair, P. ed., *The West European Party System*. Oxford: Oxford University Press.

Gustafsson, G. 1985. "Utvecklingslinjer på det religiösa området i Norden – en jämförelse", in Gustafsson G. ed., Religiös förändring i Norden. Stockholm: Lieber.

Johansson, G.V. 1985. *Kristen demokrati på svenska. Studier om KDS tillkomst och utveckling 1964–1982*. Lund: CWK Gleerup.

Karvonen, L. 1981. *"Med vårt västra grannland som förebild". En undersökning av policydiffusion från Sverige till Finland*. Åbo: Åbo Akademis Förlag.

Lijphart, A. 1990. "Dimensions of Ideology in European Party Systems", in Mair, P. ed., *The West European Party System*. Oxford: Oxford University Press.

Lomeland, A.R. 1971. *Kristelig Folkeparti blir til*. Oslo: Universitetsforlaget.

Madeley, J. 1977. "Scandinavian Christian Democracy: Throwback or Portent?", *European Journal of Political Research* 5, 267–286.

Madeley, J. 1982. "Politics and the Pulpit. The Case of Protestant Europe", in Berger S. ed., *Religion in West European Politics*. London: Frank Cass.

Noponen, M. 1988. *Suomen kansanedustusjärjestelmä*. Juva: WSOY.

Nordisk kontakt 1971, 10.

Nordisk kontakt 1991, 9.

Pedersen, M. 1982. "Towards a New Typology of Party Lifespans and Minor Parties", *Scandinavian Political Studies*, 5, 1–16.

Riis, O. 1985. "Danmark", in Gustafsson, G. ed., Religiös förändring i Norden. Stockholm: Liber.

Risbjerg Thomsen, S. et al. 1990. "Assessing the Validity of the Logit Method for Ecological Inference", in Berglund S. & Thomsen S.R. eds., *Modern Political Ecological Analysis*. Åbo: Åbo Academis Forlag.

Rommetvedt, H. 1990. "Norge: Fra konsensuspreget flertallsparlamentarisme til konfliktfylt mindretallsparlamentarisme", in Damgaard E. ed., *Parlamentarisk forandring i Norden*. Oslo: Universitetsforlaget.

Rokkan, S. 1967. "Geography, Religion and Social Class: Crosscutting Cleavages in Norwegian Politics", in Lipset S.M. & Rokkan S. eds., *Party Systems and Voter Alignments: Cross-National Perspectives*. New York: The Free Press.

Sæter, O.J., ed. 1985. *Kristelig Folkepartis historie 1933–1983: Samling om verdier*. Oslo: Valo Forlag A.S.

Sundback, S. 1991. *Utträdet ur Finlands lutherska kyrka. Kyrkomedlemskapet under religionsfrihet och sekularisering*. Åbo: Åbo Akademis Förlag.

Sänkiaho, R. 1991. "Puolueiden kannattajakunnan rakenne", *Riksdagsmannavalet 1991. Statistikcentralen: Val 1991, 2*. Helsingfors, 37–45.

ValU91/STV. Unpublished electoral survey conducted by Swedish Television.

Wörlund, I. 1988. "The Election to the Swedish Riksdag 1988", *Scandinavian Political Studies*, 12, 77–83.

48

[19]

Modernity and fundamentalism: the new Christian right in America

Steve Bruce

ABSTRACT

The apparent resurgence of conservative or fundamentalist religion in various parts of the world calls into question sociological
orthodoxy about secularization. This essay uses the example of the
failure of the new Christian right (NCR) in America as an
opportunity to reconsider the relationship between religion and
modernity. In addition to assessing the career of the NCR, it argues
that there are obvious reasons why fundamentalist movements will
not succeed in establishing an imperium. Although the cognitive
threats to supernaturalistic religion of science and technology can
be readily neutralised, the problems of adapting to social, cultural
and religious pluralism cannot. In the language of church, sect, and
denomination, fundamentalism can maintain itself in a sectarian
form but given that the cultural homogeneity required for a church
no longer exists, expansion into the wider society brings pressure to
shift to a more denominational self-image.

INTRODUCTION

A number of events combine to make this an opportune moment to
review the career of the new Christian right (NCR) in America and
assess the general lessons for the study of religion and politics in
modern democracies. The Reagan presidency – for which the NCR
claims some credit – has ended. Revd Pat Robertson's attempt to shift
the movement into a higher gear by contesting the Republican party
presidential nomination has provided us with good poll data. Revd
Jerry Falwell has formally wound up Moral Majority Inc., one of the
best-known of NCR organizations. The Supreme Court has produced
a judgement which threatens to erode rights to abortion. I will briefly
sketch the origins and nature of the NCR, evaluate its impact, and
then offer some general observations about the relationship between
fundamentalism and modernity.

BJS   Volume no. 41   Issue no. 4   December 1990

THE ORGINS OF THE NCR

In explaining the rise of the NCR there are two important points. Firstly, the culture of the core constituency of the NCR – southern and 'sunbelt'[1] fundamentalists – has been increasingly threatened since the end of the Second World War. On many matters of social and moral policy, geographical and cultural peripheries have become increasing subject to the 'core' of cosmopolitan America. The sheer size, diversity of ethnic groupings, and the federal system of American government long permitted regions considerable autonomy but the recent trend is for polity and culture to become more centralized.[2] The imposition of racial desegregation policies is a good example. At the same time as it further encroached, the centre became more liberal. So fundamentalists found themselves harder pressed by a more secular and permissive culture.[3] The more prescient fundamentalists knew that electing conservative and fundamentalist councilmen in Greenville, South Carolina, had little influence where the important decisions were increasingly being made: the federal courts, the Supreme Court, the Presidency, and Congress. Ministers such as independent Baptist fundamentalist Jerry Falwell of Lynchburg, Virginia, who in the 1960s were arguing against political activism (when that meant black clergy leading civil rights marches), began to argue that the preservation of the fundamentalist enclaves (and, more grandiloquently, America) required political action.[4] They began to attract an audience who were willing to consider that the maintenance or restoration of a Christian culture required God's people to 'come out of the closet' as Dallas evangelist James Robison once memorably put it.

Like most movements, the NCR was not entirely spontaneous. At the same time as conservative pastors and lay activists such as Phyllis Schlafly were getting involved in actions such as opposing the 'equal rights for women' constitutional amendment (ERA), a number of professional conservative political activists were trying to create a new populist conservative grouping which would differ from the old eastern establishment 'conservatism' in mobilizing people around social and moral issues as well as more traditional concerns with foreign policy, the welfare state, the economy, and the regulation of business. Howard Phillips, Paul Weyrich and Richard Viguerie (the pioneer of the use of 'direct mail' to create single issue pressure groups) appreciated that fundamentalists and the audience for conservative Protestant religious television (an over-lapping but not identical constituency) would form a vital part of that new conservatism.[5]

The key figures in the mobilization of the 'new Christian right' were televangelists. James Robison of Dallas and Pat Robertson of the *700 Club* and the Christian Broadcasting Network played a part, but the most influential and consistently involved figure was Jerry Falwell,

Modernity and fundamentalism 479

whose *Old Time Gospel Hour*, computer mailing lists of supporters, and contacts with other independent fundamentalist Baptist pastors were all used to recruit support for the Moral Majority Inc. and for specific single-issue campaigns.[6]

PRESSURE GROUP POLITICS

Falwell's Moral Majority and similar organizations such as Religious Roundtable, Christian Voice, and American Coalition for Traditional Values raised money to campaign as a pressure group on a range of public policy issues (such as abortion, homosexuality, the teaching of evolution in school, the threat of 'secular humanism', minority rights legislation, and prayer in public school). The campaigns had two related purposes. There was little hope of persuading liberals to become conservatives. Instead, the aim was to mobilise conservative opinion so that legislators, judges, journalists, and educators would temper their liberalism (either out of genuine respect for the opinions of conservatives or out of fear of retribution). More particularly, the NCR tried to turn that opinion into electoral clout. Legislators who had a record of voting the 'wrong way' found themselves the targets of well-funded negative campaigns. Funds were spent on behalf of acceptable conservative candidates.

Unlike the Protestants of Ulster or South Africa whose precarious position and Calvinist 'covenant' theology (with its images of a chosen people) have resulted in a long history of sustained political involvement, American fundamentalists have tended to 'pietistic' retreat from the world.[7] Very sensibly, a lot of NCR effort went into voter registration drives and Smidt suggests that they had some success in redressing the previously low registration rate for southern fundamentalists.[8] However, the impact of this was often exaggerated because it was forgotten that voter registration is a constant 'need' of the American political system which must be met annually, and that liberals were also mobilising previously dormant populations to register. Revd Jesse Jackson was particularly successful in registering black voters.

The new rightists claimed to be bi-partisan. Viguerie once said

Conservatives should work for the day when the November contest is between a conservative Democrat and a conservative Republican. Then we can go fishing or play golf on election day knowing that it doesn't matter if a Republican or a Democrat wins. . . .[9]

In 1975 Viguerie and Weyrich tried to persuade conservative Democrat George Wallace to seek again the presidency; he declined. In the run-up to the 1980 elections, they tried to enlist ex-Democrat and Texas governor John Connally before finally throwing their weight behind Reagan. For a variety of reasons, third parties have been short-lived in America. Even if fundamentalists had been sufficiently numerous to seriously consider forming a party, the activists knew it was doomed. So the attempt to displace liberal politicians and mobilise conservative voters was accompanied by infiltration of the Republican party at local level. Although there were some successes, the better entrenched and more experienced Republican party interests soon regained control.

The NCR's electoral record was never impressive. In 1980, it claimed that its negative campaigning had been responsible for deposing four leading liberal Democrat senators but, as Lipset and Raab pointed out at the time, the swing against these four was the same, or less, than the swing against Democrats in those states where the NCR had not been active.[10] At subsequent Congressional elections little effect was claimed (except by the NCR) and only in some state legislature contests and local school board elections were there any gains which could be regarded as NCR successes.

With only at most three keen NCR supporters in the Senate, there was never any chance that the NCR would make significant progress on its legislative agenda. More significantly, Ronald Reagan, despite his willingness to make supportive noises (especially at election times) did nothing to advance NCR causes. He committed very little of his power and prestige to legislative efforts to make abortion more difficult. When a number of bills to permit prayers in public school were before the Senate (including one of his own), Reagan did nothing to press senators into consolidating the bills into one with a chance of passing.

Because many of the NCR's issues concerned the proper place of religious symbols and practices, they were often judged to involve constitutional principles concerning the free exercise of religion and the separation of church and state. Hence the federal courts became a major arena for NCR activity. The very large number of cases concerning a wide variety of issues cannot be reviewed here,[11] but they can be summarised in terms of three elements (which tended to occur sequentially). First, fundamentalists tried to acquire or maintain a public position for their religion (by having public prayer in schools judged to be constitutional, for example). Contested by liberals, these cases were all lost on the grounds that the state could not been seen to be supporting any particular religion. Second, fundamentalists argued that 'secular humanism' (a catch-all term used to describe almost anything which did not give conscious and overt support to Christianity) was itself a 'religion' and should be barred from the public arena. If they could not have their religion in schools, then that of the secular humanists should also be banned. Although some lower courts agreed, the higher appeal courts concluded that the argument was untenable and, further, that requiring children to read books which did not endorse their religion was not the same as forcing those children to abandon their beliefs and hence did not infringe their constitutional right to the 'free exercise' of their religion. The third tactic was to appeal to the courts to enforce 'fair play'. Fundamentalists tried to construct the contest as one of their perfectly plausible beliefs against some other, no more obviously plausible, set of beliefs.

Although the appeals to fair play were popular, they offered only a temporary victory because they were based on the precarious claim that fundamentalist beliefs were as plausible as the alternatives. This claim was tested in the Arkansas 'equal time' bill. With, by all accounts, very little thought to the consequences, the Arkansas legislature passed into law a bill requiring that any school teaching of Darwinian evolution be matched by teaching of 'creation science', which was offered, not as a religious belief, but as a perfectly respectable scientific account of the origins of the world and species. The American Civil Liberties Union took the bill to the courts to argue that it represented an unconstitutional state imposition of a particular religion. The creationists had to persuade the judge that someone who did not accept the Bible as authoritative would none the less find their account as compatible with both the facts and with scientific method as that of the evolutionists. They failed miserably. The bill was struck down, as was a similar bill from the Louisiana state legislature.

There are a number of significant points about the Arkansas case which can be generalised to the fate of the NCR at large. The first is that the initial fundamentalist success owed a lot to surprise and liberal neglect. Scientists had lost the habit of explaining and defending their positions, taking it for granted that their status conferred plausibility on their views. Once they realised that they had to argue their case and win over public opinion, they did it remarkably well.[12] Something similar happened with the Texas school book review process. For over a decade, Texas fundamentalists had exercised considerable influence over the content of school text books by filing objections to them in the committee which decided which school books (from lists offered by publishers) could be bought with state funds. By historical accident, the process had been designed to allow people to object to books but gave no opportunity for other groups to defend them and to argue against the objections. The Texas school market is so large that many publishers chose to drop contentious material (on Darwin, evolution, the age of the earth, sex education, gender roles, racial inequality, poverty, international relations, and the like) rather than risk losing big sales. The anti-NCR organization, People for the American Way, campaigned for, and won, a major change in the review process that broke the influence of the fundamentalists.[13]

Those commentators who initially exaggerated the influence of the NCR made the mistake of forgetting that liberals were capable of counter-attack. A great deal was written about the importance of NCR political action committees (PACS). Election funding laws introduced after the Watergate scandal to reduce the importance of big money severely curtailed the amounts that individuals could give to candidates but allowed committees to raise large sums to spend in advancing a general principle or campaigning *against* a candidate. PACs were certainly important, but the first PACs were liberal ones.

Direct-mailing technology was used by the NCR to raise large sums in small donations from a large number of 'little people'; televangelists had been using the same technology for years. But it was also used by liberals. Some NCR election campaigns were well-funded and skillfully produced but far from being impotent, liberals were equally able to deploy money and talent. People for the American Way produced a large number of extremely clever advertisements. The most memorable featured very short clips of ordinary Americans describing how they liked their eggs. An old farmer said 'I like mine easy over'. A Jewish kid said 'I like 'em boiled'. And so on. After twenty of these a voice-over simply said 'That's the American Way'. Without attacking any specific belief or value of the NCR, the advertisement had made a very strong case for diversity, tolerance, and pluralism.

In another memorable counter-strike, People For perfectly matched the resourcefulness of the NCR. In September 1986, Pat Robertson arranged to use his Christian Broadcasting satellite network to beam free to hundreds of local stations and cable systems footage of what was effectively the start of his campaign for the Republican presidential nomination. Given the under-resourced nature of local stations, they would have been happy to use the feed. People For compiled a video of clips of Robertson's utterances from his faith healing preacher period, before he re-oriented his biography to appear as a conservative businessman. This was offered to all the same stations. The result was that Robertson's material was either ignored or presented with the People For material in a balanced package.

An even more dramatic illustration of the liberal counter-attack was the failure of Robert Bork's nomination to the Supreme Court. As has already been noted, the Court is vital to many of the NCR issues and much conservative hope was vested in Reagan's opportunity to change the nature of the Court when he filled any vacancies which arose. He nominated Bork, an academic lawyer who had made a reputation as a 'movement' conservative. People For and other liberal groups ran a well-organized campaign to mobilise opposition – from women to Bork's sexism, from blacks to his racism, from Jews to his antisemitism – and it worked. For the first time, a Supreme Court nomination was rejected by the Senate on the grounds of the ideological unsuitability of the candidate. Reagan's second nomination withdrew after his history of youthful experimentation with drugs was exposed. Finally, Reagan nominated a 'moderate' conservative with a history of

uncontentious court decisions and Kennedy was accepted unanimously.

To return to the Arkansas 'equal time' case, the fundamentalists lost
because they were being asked to be judged on secular criteria.
Knowing that they could not succeed in promoting religion, they tried
to promote the same product as 'secular knowledge', and failed to
convince anyone outside their own milieu.

ALLIANCES AND MOTIVATIONAL PARADOXES

Between 70 and 80 per cent of Americans claim a religious commitment. Of these, about a third are members of Protestant denominations which are not affiliated with the ecumenical National Council
of Churches – as good a mark as any of evangelical, fundamentalist or
pentecostalist identity.[14] Conservative Protestants were numerous
enough to maintain their own sub-culture and their own institutions.
But, given that many did not share Falwell's desire for political
involvement, they could only become a 'moral majority' if they could
enlist the active support of conservative Catholics, Jews, Mormons,
Black Protestants, and secular conservatives. This failed from both
ends. It was always a threat to the motivation of fundamentalists. The
NCR asked them to get involved in politics to defend their religiously
inspired culture and then asked that, in order to do politics, they leave
behind their religion. On Sunday they believed that Catholics and
Jews were not 'saved' and the Mormons were a dangerous cult; on
Monday they had to work with Catholics, Jews, and Mormons in
defence of our 'shared Judaeo-Christian' heritage. But this separation
of religion and politics into different compartments governed by
different criteria – with religion relegated to the private home world
of leisure activity and the family – is exactly the 'secularization' of
liberal Protestantism which fundamentalists reject. Fundamentalists
cannot be pragmatic without conceding that which defines them. And
even if they could abandon their anti-semitism, racism and anti-
Catholicism, Catholics, blacks and Jews had long enough memories to
be suspicious, a posture which received frequent confirmation from
the unguarded statements of NCR leaders. In the introduction to a
pro-Zionist speech, Falwell once told a meeting: 'A few of you here
today don't like Jews. And I know why. He [sic] can make more money
accidentally than you can on purpose'.[15] The chairman of the New
York State Moral Majority said

> I love Jewish people deeply. God has given them talents He has not
> given others. They are his chosen people. Jews have a God-given
> ability to make money, almost a supernatural ability to make money
> . . . they control the media, they control this city. . . .[16]

These statements were not so much incautious as intended to be heard only by like-minded fundamentalists. Again the liberal counter-attack is relevant here. Organizations such as People For the American Way have played an important part in making sure that the discrepancies between what NCR leaders offer to their own core constituency and what they present to mainstream America are recorded and widely reported.

ROBERTSON FOR PRESIDENT

With what turns out to have been good reason, many NCR lobbyists I interviewed in 1986 were opposed to Robertson's running for President on the grounds that he would polarise opinion too drastically. However, his campaign was useful to us because it presented excellent opportunities to evaluate support for the NCR. The basic facts are these. With almost unlimited funds and with his own satellite television network (and the implied endorsement of a number of religious broadcasters), Robertson came a very poor third behind vice-president George Bush and Senate minority leader Bob Dole. Some state republican parties hold 'caucuses' where the supporters for each candidate turn up and are counted. In these contests, which measure commitment rather than breadth of support, Robertson did well because he was able to put all his troops on parade. But most states hold open primary elections, and in these Robertson performed very badly.

The reasons for his failure can be discerned from a number of data. A September 1987 poll asked respondents to rate the then six Republican candidates on a number of points.[16] As one would expect, Robertson was rated behind Bush, Dole, Jack Kemp, Pete Du Pont and Al Haig on questions relating to political experience, but one question simply asked 'Is--------------someone you can trust?'. The percentage ratings are as follows

George Bush	80
Bob Dole	73
Jack Kemp	69
Pete Du Pont	61
Al Haig	49
Pat Robertson	43

With the usual cautions about such poll data, it is still significant that a leading religious broadcaster should be regarded as less trustworthy than four professional politicians and a career soldier who was Richard Nixon's Chief of Staff! Furthermore, consider the distance between the top and bottom of the list.

A *Time* poll of southern states in February 1988 showed the nature of the problem. Only 15 per cent of southerners said they would vote for Robertson in the 'Super Tuesday' primaries. Given that the general election would see many registered Democrats splitting the ticket and voting for Democrats for local office and a Republican for the presidency, it is worth considering the details of registered Democrats and Republicans to the negative rating question 'Who would you definitely not vote for?'. With a negative rating of 72 per cent, Robertson was less popular overall than even the liberal Democratic candidates, and that in the south, the area with the greatest concentration of fundamentalists. Among likely Republican voters who described themselves as evangelicals or fundamentalists, 44 per cent preferred Bush, 30 per cent preferred Dole and only 14 per cent wanted Robertson. When asked if they were more or less likely to vote for him because of his status as a former clergyman, 42 per cent said 'less likely' and only 25 per cent said 'more likely'.[17]

Here we have a vital point. So far, I have discussed the NCR as if fundamentalists generally were in favour of the movement to mobilise politically on socio-moral issues and only structural factors or liberal opposition stopped them. Although there is economy in telling the story that way, it misrepresents the complexity of conservative Protestant views. First, not all fundamentalists hold the same views on school prayer, abortion, homosexuality, traditional gender roles and the like. Their shared religion makes them more likely to agree with each other than with liberal Protestants but they do not form a socio-moral ideological 'bloc'. Second, even when they agree about these things in principle, they disagree about how to turn principle into policy. Third, like all people, they have a wide range of other interests and concerns which often take priority over their socio-moral issues, especially when one recalls that fundamentalists do not control the setting of the political agenda, which owes a lot to geo-political and world economic movements. Fourthly, modern liberal democracy is a consequence (inadvertent perhaps) of conservative Protestantism. Although it conflicts with their desire to live in a Christian society, many conservative Protestants are genuinely committed to the principles of tolerance and individual liberty.

Although in rhetoric what distinguishes fundamentalists is their unwillingness to keep their religion separate from the rest of their lives, in practice they resolve the tension by forming separatist 'enclaves' in which an organic community is permeated by a religious worldview. Only briefly and uneasily do they act as if that enclave could be exported to the society at large.

Finally, in understanding how such social scientists as Hadden and Shupe could have been so wrong in their predictions of Pat Robertson's success, it is worth making an important point about the difference between general sentiment and support for a specific candidate or policy item.[18] In the early 1980s, much was made of the analysis of survey data which apparently showed considerable wide-spread sympathy for what were taken as 'NCR positions'. In the most extravagant claim, it was suggested that some 30 per cent of the American population was fully in agreement with the Moral Majority platform, and that 70 per cent were close to such support.[19] A detailed and convincing re-examination of that data showed that the high figures were produced by taking a very small number of questions about general attitudes to homosexuality, school prayer, abortion and the social role of women as indicative of a Moral Majority position, and then taking an inappropriately wide range of answers as supportive of the Moral Majority.[20] Instead of taking responses to general questions about sentiment, the re-analysis examined answers to specific policy questions and found very little support for the NCR. The electoral failure of NCR candidates and the response to Pat Robertson's campaign suggest that while many Americans are happy to assent to vague propositions about God, the traditional family, and the un-desirability of abortion, very few are willing to give these concerns a high priority or to support moves to make their views binding on other people.

Thus we come to the following conclusions: American funda-mentalists are not mobilizable as a 'disciplined, charging army' (to use the description of one NCR activist); there are serious obstacles to fundamentalists forming stable alliances with other conservative groups; and a widespread sympathy for socio-moral views associated with conservative Protestantism (best exemplified in Ronald Reagan himself) does not translate into active support for the new Christian right. In so far as the NCR can claim any hope for the future, it lies in the decisions likely to come from a Supreme Court to which Reagan nominated three members, and to which Bush may well be able to nominate another two. It seems likely that the Court will allow states to pass laws restricting the use of public funds for abortions but this does not necessarily mean a victory for the right. It simply means that the abortion issue will be returned to the political arena where, if some results in the November 1989 state elections are any sign, liberals will be quite capable of maintaining the status quo. The Court's recent decisions on two cases concerning the display of religious symbols in public buildings in Pittsburgh do not show any great willingness to soften its 'no nothing' line on state support for religion.[21]

FUNDAMENTALISM AND MODERNITY

I would now like to consider the relationship between funda-mentalism and modernity in a broader and more abstract way. The appearance in the 1980s of a number of 'fundamentalist' movements in various parts of the world has raised a number of questions about the relationship between traditional religious belief systems and modernity (by which I mean the vast and complex package of beliefs and structures which are normally supposed to accompany industrialization).[22] Even those commentators who objected to an assumption of secularization as an inevitable corollary of modernization usually did so on the grounds that religion was *changing* rather than disappearing. The sociologists who studied new religious movements in the later 1960s might have argued that the religious quest remained important for many people but very few suggested that we would see a shift towards a more conservative, dogmatic and supernaturalistic religion or that such a religion would acquire increasing influence in a modern democracy. The challenge of fundamentalism to previous social science orthodoxy is slightly muted by the recognition that some fundamentalist movements have been part of a deliberate reaction against the modernizing tendencies of unpopular elites: Sh'ite Islam in Iran is the most spectacular example. But the recent history of Protestant fundamentalism in America does seem to challenge the assumption that one cannot believe God actually made the world in six days, that the Bible is the inspired (and even dictated) Word of God, and that the Second Coming is imminent while living in a city making use of state of the art technology. Indeed, the challenge to the orthodoxy of the American case is dramatic because, far from being rustic survivals, American fundamentalists have made more and better use of the electronic mass media than have the liberal Protestants who defend their re-structuring of the Christian gospel on the grounds that modern man could no longer believe in miracles or the supernatural. The problem can be slightly reduced by noting that conservative Protestantism is still at its most powerful in the most rural and relatively under-developed parts of North America (although that is rapidly changing with the rise of the industrial south). But though reduced, it remains a paradox, the implications of which are worth considering.

Even before Pat Robertson's campaign or Falwell's closing of Moral Majority Inc., I argued that politicised fundamentalism in the form of the new Christian right 'will fail – in its present form already has failed – both to re-Christianize America and to prevent further displacement of the values which it supporters hold dear'.[23] Above I have given a very brief review of some of the main reasons for a conclusion very much at odds with that then being argued by others.[24] I also noted that the very limited successes which the NCR had enjoyed were bought at the cost of considerable accommodation with some of the elements of modernity which fundamentalists most abhor. Extensive cooperation with Catholics, Jews and secular conservatives is an example of the sort of compromise which was entertained. In a detailed examination of American television evangelism, I have similarly argued that, because America is a *modern* democratic society, fundamentalism is extremely unlikely to sweep all before it.[25] That conservative or 'sectarian' forms of Protestantism are more resilient to secularization than liberal or denominational forms means that fundamentalists will become an increasingly large proportion of American Protestants[26] but there are, I believe, limits to what fundamentalism can achieve in the modern world.

However, in a recent panel discussion, David Martin raised the possibility that far from supernaturalist religion being under threat, it was the liberal heritage of the Enlightenment which was both dispensable and being dispensed with.[27] I have neither the space nor the expertise to consider the extent to which a technologically advanced democracy can survive without the presuppositions of what one used to be able to call 'secular humanism' before the American new Christian right made that a synonym for evil. What I do want to do is to reflect on the limits which modernity imposes on fundamentalism.

THREATS TO FUNDAMENTALISM

One way of arguing for the precariousness of fundamentalism (or, for it is the same argument, for secularization) is to identify intellectual or cognitive challenges to specific propositions of fundamentalist belief. It was certainly the view of those who argued for the 'higher criticism' and liberal theology that the findings of modern science had made implausible many traditional Protestant beliefs. However I would suggest that the great Victorian religion and science debates, while addictive for the participants and fascinating for the historian, were of little consequence for most people. But if Bishop Samuel Wilberforce's concern over Darwin was not shared by the bulk of the population, perhaps the general assumptions filtered down through technology to alter fundamentally popular worldviews. Alternatives to religion

> may be less comprehensive . . .for their utility is restricted largely to making sense of the mundane, this-worldly experience; but this apparent disadvantage seems to be balanced by the fact that the enhanced mastery over nature, and the increased material comfort and security that have gone hand-in-hand with modernization, have guaranteed a human preoccupation with the present life and the temporal world.[28]

Technology not only redirects our attentions, but also requires and induces a consciousness which assumes a regularity and repeatability about the world which stresses technique over morality, and which places enormous stress on efficiency.[29] Although there is no single point of conflict between technological consciousness and fundamentalism (as there is between modern geology and fundamentalism), it seems reasonable to suppose the former is poor soil for the latter.

Yet American fundamentalists can be found designing and running radio stations and flying aeroplanes. To an extent, this is not as surprising as it at first sight seems. With many areas of scientific endeavour (more so with technological production) fundamentalism has no argument and merely wants to add either an additional gloss or a few specific claims. There may be an element of incompatibility in that the theoretical closure of fundamentalism discourages original and critical thought, and hence retards innovation; but this should be only a minor problem, a matter of slight professional awkwardness. A parallel would be the impact of Marxism on Soviet science. Despite being forced to hold absurd views of genetics, Soviet scientists managed to make nuclear weapons.

A bigger problem concerns specialization, professionalization, and accreditation. One of the key features of modern technological society is its high degree of specialization and the underlying assumption that there should be some body of 'professionals' who lead in this and that speciality. Fields tend to be defined by professionals. Although in many areas there is no logical reason why the specialists should be atheists or religious liberals, it is generally the case that the university education and middle class background associated with professional status is more frequently associated with liberal than with conservative religion. Claims to expertise are vetted by such professionals. When Oral Roberts University wanted professional accreditation for its medical school, it had to submit its staff, its resources, and its practices to inspection by non-fundamentalist experts and it was not allowed to offer the pentecostal belief in faith healing (the source of Roberts' initial interest in medicine) as a defence for poor facilities. That Oral Roberts himself felt the process to be humiliating is clear from his account of one of many meetings with professional educationalists

> They were in my office and they were trying to say something to me that would not offend me. They were trying to say 'You dumb faith healer! What in the world are you doing connected with a great school like this?'. That's not the way they said it but I got the point real good.[30]

But to establish that his university really was a 'great school', he had to submit to a validation process which defined as extraneous and irrelevant the religious beliefs and values of Oral Roberts University staff.

That most areas of knowledge and endeavour are defined and dominated by non-fundamentalists does not necessarily mean that success in any profession or discipline can only be achieved with the loss of faith but must be the tendency (the alternative is the separation

490 *Steve Bruce*

of work and religion into discrete compartments). Consider the example of Princeton and the first wave of religious foundation colleges and their shift to secularity, a pattern which was repeated with Southern Methodist University and the second generation, and which shows every sign of being repeated again with Wheaton College and the other large evangelical schools founded in this century. If they are being faithful to their own creed, liberal and atheist specialists will not discriminate against the fundamentalist and will judge him or her solely on rational task-related criteria, but they will insist that the religion be left to one side, be confined to the private sphere. Doubts about the ability of Oral Roberts University's law school to do this led to such delays in accreditation that it was closed.

Even in largely fundamentalist settings, specialization has similar consequences. Pat Robertson's Christian Broadcasting Network wants to employ born-again technicians and managers and punctuates the day with ceremonies which remind all concerned of the religious nature of the tasks in hand, but the selection, promotion and rewarding of staff are all done on the basis of rational, secular, task-related criteria.

To summarise, there do seem to be grounds for supposing that supernaturalistic religions will have problems in a modern industrial society. However, these should not be exaggerated. It is clearly not the case, as nineteenth and early twentieth century liberal theologians supposed, that the arrival of electricity means the departure of miracles. There are a large number of ways in which believers, individually and in collectivities, can 'interpret' the world around them so that what to an outsider seems like massive disconformation appears to the believer as further evidence of the correctness of the belief system. People do not live in 'the world'; they live in their socially constructed interpretation of the world. But while that might sound like an offer of immunity to any belief system, and assurance that any culture can survive in any context provided the carriers of that culture are sufficiently motivated to work at maintaining their belief system, it is actually a more accurate basis for identifying life-threatening ailments. The important question is not so much 'what challenges does modernity present to specific fundamentalist beliefs?' but 'what sorts of social forces enhance or inhibit the ability of any group of believers to 'socially construct' their own universe?'

SOCIAL DIFFERENTIATION AND PLURALISM

Although science, technology and rationality are important, the greatest obstacle to fundamentalist advance is pluralism. The point can be made historically by considering the two main sources of the 'denominationalism' of liberal Protestantism. The changing of actual beliefs in order to bring them more into line with what higher critics and liberal theologians thought reason and knowledge demanded was only part of liberal Protestantism. The other was the shift from holding beliefs in a dogmatic and sectarian manner to a more denominational position in which the believers could continue to maintain that their beliefs were in some sense true while also allowing that apparently quite different beliefs were also in some sense true. If one considers why such a shift occurred, one can see the problem for fundamentalism.

As an aside, I should mention the Niebuhr thesis, if only because the title of his classic examination of the attentuation of the distinctiveness of Protestant sects – *The Social Sources of Denominationalism* – reads as if it addresses precisely this question.[31] In fact, Niebuhr's work, while pointedly observant, is concerned with a process both smaller and more general than the one that concerns me. There is no doubt that the discipline of the sect produces an increased standard of living which raises the cost of asceticism and undermines it. He is also right to point to the quite different levels of commitment to be expected from the first generation which consciously creates or adopts the sect and subsequent generations who inherit it. But these are 'universals' and they are not specifically problems for fundamentalists in a modern pluralistic democracy and it is those problems which concern me.

Modernization brings pluralization in two related ways. In the first place it increases variety and choice. Pre-modern man lived in a world of *fate*. In a world of only limited technology, the one tool was accompanied by the idea of the one way

> One employs this tool, for a particular purpose and no other. One dresses in this way and in no other. A traditional society is one in which the great part of human activity is governed by such clear-cut prescriptions. Whatever else may be the problems of a traditional society, ambivalence is not one of them.[32]

Modernity *pluralizes*. Where there was one way of doing things, there are now twenty; where there was one institution, there are now forty.

This tendency interacts with the fragmentation of the society. With the advance of capitalism and the growth of the large nation-state, the organic unity of the community is fragmented and one sees the development of distinct classes with the freedom to develop their own world-view and their own variant of the dominant religion. If the society either attracts immigrants or the state expands to take-in diverse populations (for example in the case of 'Great Britain and Ireland' which, leaving aside small dissenting populations in each province, had to encompass the episcopal Church of England, the Presbyterian Church of Scotland, the episcopalians of Ireland, the Presbyterians of Ulster and the Irish Catholics), one has further diversity. The result is *religious pluralism*.

To an extent, a variety of socio-psychological defences can blunt the

492   *Steve Bruce*

challenge of diversity. If the carriers of the alternative religion are a
subordinate population, various invidious stereotypes can be used to
reduce the extent to which the new religions appear as plausible
alternatives. But once diversity appears *within* the clan or the class, the
challenge of positively defending the superiority of one's own religion
(as distinct from simply sharing with the community beliefs about how
the world is) must be met. One response is sectarian retreat. The
believers construct an enclave, a ghetto, in which their religion again
enjoys monopoly or hegemonic status. The other is the relativism
which lies at the heart of the denominational form of religion. One
learns to live with diversity by supposing that Methodism is 'true for
me' while Catholicism is 'true for him'.

But even if there were not strong socio-psychological pressures to
denominationalism (and I believe there is), there is an overwhelming
social pressure to establish religious relativism as the operating
principle for public administration. Were it the case that religious
tolerance was the product of campaigns by groups which consciously
desired that happy state of affairs, I would be less confident of this
argument because the development might be reversed by enough
people changing their minds. But toleration in most settings arose not
because dissenting groups initially desired it but because, having
failed to purify the religious establishment or to take the majority of
the people with them, dissenters were forced to argue for their own
rights as minorities and, for consistency, to argue for minority rights
per se. Established churches, unable to prevent substantial dissent and
failing miserably in attempts to coerce conformity, gradually came to
accept a reduction of their claims. To summarise an argument that I
have presented in detail elsewhere, tolerance is a necessary accommodation to religious diversity in a democracy.[33]

Of course, the claim that religious toleration is necessary applies
only to a modern universalising democracy with a considerable degree
of religious diversity. Were there a massive religious revival which
converted most Americans to the same religion, then toleration would
not be necessary. But at least part of the diversity stems from the
division of the society into a variety of class and regional groups with
differing worldviews. Although the actual composition of such groups
is constantly changing, nothing seems likely to change the fact of
division. So such a revival seems so unlikely that we need not even
consider it. A basic social requirement prevents the return of serious
religious particularism. As there is no 'society' to act independent of
the people who make it up, such a 'requirement' translates into the
willingness of enough people in powerful places to realise the
potential for conflict in allowing religious particularism to return to
the public arena. And even if the majority of active citizens forget the
lessons of the past or if, as marxists suppose, social direction comes
from the ruling class rather than from the wishes of the people, we can

still expect limits on religious particularism. Both the past behaviour of the capitalist class and an outsider's reading of their interests suggest that capitalists will not be keen to threaten the stability that guarantees profits. Although the authors of scare stories about the American new Christian right[34] are fond of listing the leaders of American capital who have given large sums to various new Christian right causes, it is the same very small number of names that appears over and over. It is also noticeable that most of the financial support goes to the least divisive, least sectarian and least political of the movements.[35] The problem with many radical assessments of capital is that they forget how single-mindedly interested in profit is capital. If there is any validity to Marx's 'opiate of the people' claim then this is religion as soporific, not as stimulant. Stirring up unnecessary antagonisms would not be part of the project of any sensible capitalist.

CONCLUSION

The purpose of this brief essay is to clarify the grounds for the general social science supposition that there are limits to the growth of fundamentalism in a modern democracy. Although other variables could have been considered, I have confined the discussion to the most obvious features of modernity: science and technology and pluralization. Perhaps because it was this which concerned the early developers of liberal Protestantism, the ideological competition from science and technology has sometimes been given too much weight in considerations of the fate of various religions. We know that people can deploy a variety of socio-psychological devices and strategies to reinterpret the world around them.

However, for such re-interpretations to be sustained and transmitted from one generation to another, they must be shared. The enduring interpretations are social not idiosyncratic constructions. Fundamentalism can endure as an enclave but it cannot be both a ghetto and an imperium. Any growth outside the enclave or any serious bid for the centre of the society requires an acceptance of diversity; that is, the loss of what makes fundamentalism distinctive. As one middle-aged fundamentalist tried to describe the general process

> In the past few years, being a Christian has become a popular thing among the young. I have mixed feelings about it. There's a lot of people genuinely becoming Christians, but it used to be so clear. If you said you were born again, people knew what you meant. Nowadays, when somebody tells me that, I'm not sure he knows what he's talking about.[36]

Initially the acceptance of religious toleration can co-exist with sectarian religion by alternation between different rhetorics – a Sunday language of sectarian certainty and 'our saving Baptist faith' and a weekday language of religious relativism and 'our shared Judeo-Christian heritage' – but there are good socio-psychological reasons for supposing that such an accommodation is stressful and short-lived. In the early period of this century, Protestant missionary activists – people with an essentially sectarian self-image – became involved in ecumenical cooperation for tactical reasons, in order to make more effective their proselytising. But the long-term result was that what had been engaged in for instrumental reasons became appreciated as worthwhile in its own right. The sectarians gradually become committed to a denominational identity. What grew from the 1910 World Missionary Conference was the World Council of Churches with its frank opposition to missionary activity.

To return to the case study with which I began, there are of course particular causes for the failure of Pat Robertson's campaign for the presidency. The sex scandals involving leading religious broadcasters Jim Bakker and Jimmy Swaggart did not help. There are also particular causes for the failure of the new Christian right more generally. However, I suggest that there are basic elements of the structure and culture of modern democratic societies which explain why the NCR or similar movements cannot go beyond being an active pressure group for the views of a minority. To return to the traditional sociological distinctions of church, sect and denomination, the church form can only flourish in a society which is either culturally homogenous or undemocratic. Once the combination of cultural pluralism and democracy makes the church form impossible, believers have a choice of the denomination or the sect. The sect – the form of fundamentalism – can survive as an enclave, as a sub-culture or as a sub-society but it cannot become a church.

(Date accepted: November 1989)

Steve Bruce
Department of Social Studies
The Queen's University of Belfast

NOTES

1. The term 'sunbelt' was introduced by Kevin Phillips in 1968 to refer to the area from 'the Charleston-Savannah-Jacksonville coastal strip to California's urban south'. Later he cited the 37th parallel. For a discussion of the social and political composition of the 'sunbelt' and the balkanization of America, see K. Phillips, *Post-Conservative America*, New York, Random House, 1982, Ch. 7.

2. As an index of increased centralization regulation, one might note that in 1976 there were 77 federal regulatory bodies and 50 of them had been created since 1960; M. Janovitz, *The Last Half-Century: Societal Change and Politics in America*, Chicago, University of Chicago Press, 1978, p. 368.

3. That is, in terms of social movement theory, I see the NCR as a movement of cultural rather than status defence. The issues are debated at length in S. Bruce, *The Rise and Fall of the New Christian Right: Conservative Protestant*

Politics in America 1978–1988, Oxford, Clarendon Press, 1988, Ch. 1.

4. F. Fitzgerald, 'A disciplined, charging army', *New Yorker*, 18 May 1981, pp. 53–97. For an excellent description of the fundamentalist world, see R. H. Balmer, *Mine Eyes Have Seen the Glory: A Journey into the Evangelical Subculture in America*, New York, Oxford University Press, 1989.

5. R. A. Viguerie, *The New Right: We're Ready to Lead*, Falls Church, VA, The Viguerie Co.; G. Peele, *Revival and Reaction: the Right in Contemporary America*, Oxford, Clarendon Press, 1984.

6. R. C. Liebman, 'Mobilizing the Moral Majority', in Liebman and Wuthnow, *The New Christian Right*, Chicago, Aldine, 1983, pp. 50–73.

7. On the role of Calvinist Presbyterianism in the politics of Ulster and South Africa, see R. Wallis and S. Bruce, *Sociological Theory, Religion and Collective Action*, Belfast, The Queen's University of Belfast, 1986, Ch. 10.

8. C. Smidt, 'Born again politics: the political behavior of evangelical Christians in the South and the non-South', in Baker, Steed and Moreland (eds.), *Religion and Politics in the South: Mass and Elite Perspectives*, New York, Praeger, 1983, pp. 27–56.

9. Viguerie, *op. cit.*, p. 89.

10. S. M. Lipset and E. Raab, 'Evangelicals and the elections', *Commentary*, vol. 71, no. 3, pp. 25–31.

11. R. S. Alley (ed.), *The Supreme Court on Church and State*, New York, Oxford University Press, 1988; T. Robbins and R. Robertson (eds), *Church and State Relations: Tensions and Transitions*, New Brunswick, Transaction Books, 1987.

12. L. Gilkey, *Creationism on Trial: Evolution and God at Little Rock*, Minneapolis, Winston Press, 1985.

13. Bruce, *op. cit.*, 1988, p. 111–14.

14. S. Bruce, *Pray TV: Televangelism in America*, London, Routledge, 1990, Ch. 1 contains details of relative sizes of denominations and theological positions. For an excellent survey of religious identification and belief as evidenced in poll data. See Gallup Organization, *Religion in America, 50 Years: 1935–1985*, Princeton, Gallup, 1985.

15. F. Conway and J. Siegelman, *Holy Terror*, New York, Doubleday, 1982, p. 168.

16. *Time*, 14 September 1987, p. 13.

17. L. I. Barrett, 'The electability test', *Time*, 29 February 1988, p. 13.

18. J. K. Hadden and A. Shupe, *Televangelism: Power and Politics on God's Frontier*, New York, Henry Holt, 1988.

19. J. H. Simpson, 'Moral issues and status politics', in Liebman and Wuthnow, *The New Christian Right*, Chicago, Aldine, 1983, pp. 188–207.

20. L. Sigelman and S. Presser, 'Measuring public support for the new Christian right: the perils of point estimation', *Public Opinion Quarterly*, vol. 52, 1988, pp. 325–37.

21. Because the Supreme Court rules only on cases that come before it (and there are many conditions which a case must meet before it reaches the Court), rather than on general principles, interpreting the mind of the Court is perilous. A number of Justices seem willing to have socio-moral issues settled by political process at state level rather than by the judicial system. Although movement in this direction is often viewed by liberals as a conservative victory, it is by no means obvious that conservatives will win if local political battle is joined instead of, as has been the case, liberals relying on court decisions to overturn conservative victories. Furthermore, it is not clear that even the conservative Justices are willing to re-open the fundamental church-state issue. In a private communication, Richard Neely, the Chief Justice of the West Virginia Supreme Court of Appeals, made the important point that, whatever their personal feelings about public endorsement of religious symbols and activities, Justices appreciate that the position taken by the Court over the last 20 years is clear and workable and that to tamper with it will bring down on their heads a mass of petty and provocative appeals.

22. The view of modernity which informs this essay is that developed by Peter L. Berger in his many works, esp. P. L. Berger, B. Berger, and H. Kellner, *The Homeless Mind: Modernization and Consciousness*, Harmondsworth, Middx, Penguin, 1974.

23. Bruce, *op. cit.*, 1988, p. 192.

24. Hadden and Shupe, *op. cit.*

25. S. Bruce, *op. cit.*, 1990.

26. W. C. Roof and W. McKinney, *American Mainline Religion: its Changing Shape and Future*, New Brunswick, Rutgers University Press, 1988.

27. British Sociological Association Sociology of Religion Study Group annual conference, Easter 1989, Twickenham.

28. A. D. Gilbert, *The Making of Post-Christian Britain*, London, Longman, 1980, p. 13.

29. Berger *et al.*, *op. cit.*

30. D. E. Harrell, *Oral Roberts: an American Life*, Bloomington, IN: Indiana University Press, 1985, p. 231.

31. H. R. Niebuhr, *The Social Sources of Denominationalism*, New York, Meridian, 1972.

32. P. L. Berger, *The Heretical Imperative*, London, Collins, 1980, p. 12.

33. S. Bruce, *A House Divided: Protestantism, Schism and Secularization*, London, Routledge, 1990.

34. J. S. Saloma III, *Ominous Politics: the New Conservative Labyrinth*, New York, Hill and Wang, 1984: Conway and Siegelman, *op. cit.*

35. Bruce, *op. cit.*, 1988, p. 51–6.

36. S. Terkel, *The Great Divide*, London, 1988, p. 214.

[20]

Cultural Conflict in American Politics: Religious Traditionalism, Postmaterialism, and U.S. Political Behavior

Geoffrey C. Layman
Vanderbilt University
Edward G. Carmines
Indiana University

Recent trends indicate that American politics is becoming more "cultural" or "value-based." However, the leading account of cultural conflict in advanced industrial democracies—Ronald Inglehart's theory of Postmaterialism—has received relatively little attention from students of American politics. The present paper argues that cultural orientations have come to exert a substantial influence on American political life; however the cultural divisions relevant for contemporary American politics are those between religious traditionalists and those rejecting traditional religiosity rather than divisions between Postmaterialists and Materialists. Using the 1980 through 1992 National Election Studies, we test the relative influence of our measure of religious traditionalism and Inglehart's value typology on the political orientations of the American populace. The analysis shows that cultural orientations significantly influence American political behavior. However, the impact of these divisions is almost always more substantial when cultural orientations are defined by religious traditionalism than when they are defined by material-postmaterial value priorities.

Ronald Inglehart's theory of Postmaterialism is the leading account of the nature of cultural conflict in advanced industrial democracies. In a series of studies, Inglehart (1971, 1977, 1981, 1990; also Inglehart and Abramson 1994 and Abramson and Inglehart 1986) has argued that over the past half-century a fundamental change has occurred in the basic value priorities of Western publics. Propelled by the remarkable affluence of the post–world war period, certain groups in Western society have begun to focus less on 'Material', economic goals and more on 'Postmaterial', noneconomic concerns.

The rise of Postmaterialism, according to Inglehart, alters the nature of political conflict in Western society. Not only do Postmaterialists emphasize new social and cultural concerns such as the environment, nuclear weapons and energy, women's rights, and issues of equality, but the rise of the Postmaterialist issue agenda tends to neutralize the class alignment predominant in Western industrial

The authors would like to thank Robert Rohrschneider for providing helpful comments and criticisms.

THE JOURNAL OF POLITICS, Vol. 59, No. 3, August 1997, Pp. 751–77
©1997 by the University of Texas Press, P.O. Box 7819, Austin, TX 78713-7819

752   Geoffrey C. Layman and Edward G. Carmines

society. Since value change results from achieving a certain level of affluence
(Inglehart 1971), the middle class is likely to adopt Postmaterialist value priorities
first and become supportive of social change on Postmaterial issues. The working
class, having achieved an adequate level of prosperity only very recently and then
only partially, will work to protect its gains and maintain the political status quo
by resisting change on these new nonmaterial concerns. The rise of Postmaterialism thus leads some members of the middle class to shift their support to
parties of the (new) Left, while some segments of the working class will move
to parties of the (new) Right. While this, to some extent, represents a reversal
of class-based political alignments, the emerging basis of political conflict is defined principally not by divisions between different social strata, but instead by
divisions between Materialists and Postmaterialists (Inglehart 1971, 1977).

Over the past two decades, some of Inglehart's predictions for Western society
have been realized in the United States. The percentage of Postmaterialists in
the American populace has increased considerably (Inglehart and Abramson
1994), class-based political cleavages have weakened (Huckfeldt and Kohfeld
1989; Ladd and Hadley 1975), and social and cultural concerns such as abortion,
homosexual rights, women's rights, and prayer in the public schools have moved
to the forefront of American politics. The struggles between those with progressive orientations on these matters and those striving to defend traditional
values have received a great deal of attention in the popular press, and attitudes
on social and cultural issues have come to play a substantial role in voting decisions in both national and state elections (Abramowitz 1995; Cook, Jelen, and
Wilcox 1994; Howell and Sims 1993). Meanwhile, the two major political parties
in the United States have become increasingly differentiated on social and cultural matters. The Democratic party, in terms of the groups that support it, the
attitudes of its activists, and the policy stances it takes in its platforms, has
become increasingly associated with cultural liberalism, while the Republican
party has become more culturally conservative by all these criteria (Baker and
Steed 1992; Green and Guth 1988; Green, Guth, and Fraser 1991; Layman 1994;
Shafer 1985; Shafer and Clagget 1995).

Despite these trends, however, Inglehart's thesis has received little attention
from students of American politics. Compared to the massive amount of research
focused on other industrial democracies, relatively little attention has been paid
to value change and its political implications in the United States. Moreover, the
modest research that exists points to the limited relevance that Material-
Postmaterial value priorities have for understanding contemporary American politics (Brown and Carmines 1995; Carmines and Layman n.d.; Huckfeldt and
Kohfeld 1989).

This paper argues that American politics *has* become more culturally based
but that Inglehart's value priorities thesis is inadequate for explaining these developments because it does not take into account the unique features of the
American political context and of cultural conflict in the United States. What
may be missing from the Postmaterialism perspective is a recognition of the

Religious Traditionalism, Postmaterialism, and U.S. Political Behavior   753

powerful role that religion and religion-based cultural differences play in con-temporary American politics. Religion traditionally has exerted a considerable influence on the political life of the United States, shaping both its political culture and its political coalitions (Wald 1992). Moreover, while religion has be-come a much less important part of politics and society in most advanced in-dustrial democracies, it continues to play an important role in the United States. Despite the nation's advanced level of economic development, Americans remain, in the aggregate, quite religious, and religious differences continue to shape American political conflict (Wald 1992). Although tensions between Christians and Jews and between Catholics and Protestants have subsided (Green and Guth 1991b; Hunter 1991), new religious divisions based on religious conservatism have emerged as politically important (Green and Guth 1991b; Hunter 1991; Wuthnow 1989).

As Inglehart would predict, young, well-educated elites whose primary focus was on nonmaterial concerns and who held progressivist orientations on these matters gained influence within some of the major institutions of American public life—the Democratic party, the national media, and the federal bureaucracy, for in-stance—in the 1960s and 1970s (Guth et al. 1988; Hunter 1983; Kirkpatrick 1976; Ladd and Hadley 1975). Inglehart posits that the principal political response to this phenomenon should come from Materialists attempting to maintain the traditional emphasis on economic growth, military security, and domestic order. However, in the United States, perhaps due to the continued strength of traditional religiosity among significant portions of the population, the primary response came from the-ologically conservative Christians (Glazer 1987; Hunter 1983, 1991; Neuhaus 1987; Reichley 1987; Wuthnow 1988). And the concern of these religious conservatives was not with the focus of these new elites on nonmaterial concerns, but rather with their thoroughgoing secularism—their rejection of traditional religiosity and its as-sociated cultural norms (Guth et al. 1988; Hunter 1983; Ladd and Hadley 1975; Wuthnow 1988)—and the public and private policies—Supreme Court decisions removing prayer from the public schools and banning state restrictions on abor-tion rights and the threatening of traditional sex roles and sexual morality by the motion picture industry, for example—that were associated with their ascendance (Glazer 1987; Guth et al. 1988; Neuhaus 1987; Reichley 1987). These policies and the threat they represented to traditional religious and moral values contrib-uted to the political mobilization of conservative evangelical and fundamentalist Christians into American politics (Guth 1983; Guth et al. 1988; Jelen 1991). Consequently, the cultural divisions between citizens who have traditional, or-thodox religious beliefs and those who tend to reject traditional religiosity in-creasingly are coming to affect American party politics at both the elite (Baker and Steed 1992; Green and Guth 1991b; Green, Guth, and Fraser 1991; Guth and Green 1986, 1989; Layman 1994) and mass levels (Kellstedt, Smidt, and Kellstedt 1991; Miller and Wattenberg 1984). It appears that the Republican party is becoming the political home of religious traditionalists while the Democratic party is becoming increasingly attractive to religious liberals and secularists. We

754   Geoffrey C. Layman and Edward G. Carmines

posit that a conception of cultural orientations based on traditional religiosity is more effective for explaining contemporary developments in American politics than is Inglehart's typology of value priorities.

Using data from the four presidential election year surveys from 1980 through 1992 of the National Election Studies (NES) conducted by the Center for Political Studies at the University of Michigan, we examine the comparative influence of religious traditionalism and Material-Postmaterial value type on American political behavior.[1] We first discuss the measurements of these variables, and then examine the relative effect of these cultural orientations on party identification, presidential vote choice, and ideological self-identification, while controlling for other politically relevant cleavages such as race, class, gender, age, region, and size of community. Next, we examine the impact of these cleavages on the political orientations of those citizens who are particularly concerned about cultural matters. Throughout these analyses, the central question we seek to answer is whether value priorities or religiosity provides a more appropriate conceptualization of cultural conflict in American politics.

The Measurement of Cultural Orientations

Value Priorities

The 1980 through 1992 NES surveys include the basic measure of value priorities employed by Inglehart in his original article (1971) and subsequently repeated in numerous surveys. In each survey, respondents were asked:

> For a nation, it is not always possible to obtain everything one might wish. . . . several different goals are listed. If you had to choose among them, which one seems most desirable to you?
>
> 1. Maintaining order in the nation.
> 2. Giving the people more say in important political decisions.
> 3. Fighting rising prices.
> 4. Protecting freedom of speech.

Respondents were then asked "Which one [goal for our nation] would be your second choice?" and were given the three remaining choices. Following Inglehart (1971), those respondents who chose both (1) and (3) are coded as Materialist

---

[1]It can be argued that the distinction between the Materialist-Postmaterialist cleavage and that based on religious traditionalism is less than clear. Postmaterialism, according to Inglehart (1971, 1981), is associated with a rejection of traditional religious values and associated cultural norms, while Materialists cling strongly to traditional religiosity. However, our argument is that religious traditionalism has a direct impact on American political behavior—in fact, a more substantial impact than value type—rather than acting indirectly through its influence on value priorities. In fact, analysis of the 1980–1992 NES surveys sheds doubt on whether there is any relationship between Material-Postmaterial value priorities and religious conservatism. The correlation between our operational indicators of these variables is $-.04$ in the 1980 NES, $-.01$ in the 1984 NES, $-.01$ in the 1988 NES, and $-.09$ in the 1992 NES. In other words, religiosity and value priorities are virtually independent of one another.

Religious Traditionalism, Postmaterialism, and U.S. Political Behavior   755

and those who chose (2) and (4) are coded as Postmaterialist. Respondents were coded as mixed if they chose any other combination of responses and provided a response to both questions.[2]

One of the chief criticisms of Inglehart's work on Postmaterialism is that the four-item indicator of value priorities is inadequate. Clarke and Dutt (1991) and Duch and Taylor (1993, 1994) raise the most serious questions about the measure's validity. They argue that respondents' choices from among the four items may reflect the nature of their economic concerns—whether they are more concerned about inflation or unemployment—rather than their underlying value priorities, and these authors show that value priorities, as measured by the four-item indicator, are highly sensitive to the effects of changes in inflation and unemployment rates.

These difficulties would seem to call for the development of a more sophisticated indicator, and, in fact, Inglehart has developed a 12-item measure of value priorities which, in addition to being less sensitive to the effects of short-run economic changes, is a more valid and reliable measure of value orientations (Inglehart 1977, 1990). Unfortunately, the NES surveys are the only studies to gauge Material-Postmaterial values over any significant period of time in the United States, and they have employed only the four-item measure. It is likely that the 12-item indicator would provide a better test than the four-item indicator of the impact of value priorities on American political behavior. However, it should be remembered that Inglehart and Abramson (1994) vigorously defend the latter. They provide evidence contradicting the claim that concern with unemployment as opposed to inflation is conducive to Postmaterialist values and argue that the four-item measure has proven to be a quite valid and reliable indicator of value priorities over a number of years and across several countries (see also Abramson and Inglehart 1995). Thus, at least according to the originator of the Postmaterialism thesis, this four-item measure should provide an effective test of the impact of Material-Postmaterial value priorities on political behavior in the United States.

Religious Traditionalism

Students of religion and politics have denoted at least four facets of religion that are relevant for understanding political behavior. One is doctrinal beliefs (Green, Guth, and Fraser 1991; Jelen 1991; Kellstedt, Smidt, and Kellstedt 1991; Miller and Wattenberg 1984; Wilcox 1986, 1990). Two of these—beliefs about the Bible and beliefs regarding the necessity of a "born-again" conversion

---

[2]In 1980, 34.2% of respondents were classified as Materialists, 56.1% as mixed, and 9.7% as Postmaterialist. In 1984, 20.8% of respondents were classified as Materialists, 63.4% as mixed, and 15.8% as Postmaterialists. In 1988, 18.5% of respondents were classified as Materialists, 64.3% as mixed, and 17.2% as Postmaterialists. In 1992, 16.3% of respondents were classified as Materialists, 65.3% as mixed, and 18.4% as Postmaterialists.

756   Geoffrey C. Layman and Edward G. Carmines

experience for attaining salvation—are used to operationalize religious doctrine.[3] Religious traditionalists have more authoritative views of the Bible and are more likely to consider themselves to be born-again Christians than are those who are more secular or religiously liberal (Jelen 1991; Kellstedt, Smidt, and Kellstedt 1991; Smidt 1983). A second religious variable with political implications is denominational affiliation. Denominational ties may influence political attitudes and behavior both through the political and social messages delivered from the pulpit (Beatty and Walter 1989; Guth et al. 1991) and through social group interaction with other parishioners (Ammerman 1987; Wald, Owen, and Hill 1988). We employ a measure of the theological conservatism of denominations (Green and Guth 1991a) which ranges from the "unchurched"—those claiming no religious affiliations—to those belonging to fundamentalist and charismatic denominations. Frequency of church or synagogue attendance and religious salience should also influence political behavior both through their independent influences and their effect on the political importance of religious beliefs and affiliations (Green, Guth, and Fraser 1991; Kellstedt, Smidt, and Kellstedt 1991; Miller and Wattenberg 1984; Smidt 1983; Wilcox 1987, 1990). Denominational ties have a greater influence on the political attitudes and behavior of frequent than infrequent attendees (Kellstedt and Green 1993; Kellstedt, Smidt, and Kellstedt 1991; Wald, Owen, and Hill 1988; Wilcox 1990), and the more salient one's religious beliefs are to one's life, the more likely one is to apply those beliefs to the political realm (Kellstedt, Smidt, and Kellstedt 1991; Wilcox 1990).

Given the fact that each of these religious variables has some effect on political behavior, it seems appropriate to use a multiple-indicator measurement of religious traditionalism. Many scholars examining the impact of religion on political behavior employ such a multiple measurement strategy (Baker and Steed 1992; Green, Guth, and Fraser 1991; Guth and Green 1987; Kellstedt, Smidt, and Kellstedt 1991; Miller and Wattenberg 1984; Wilcox 1990). A factor analysis, using principal-components extraction, of these five indicators of religion was performed for each of the NES surveys. As Table 1 shows, all five measures load strongly on a single factor in each year.[4] The religious traditionalism index for each of the NES surveys was formed by summing the products of each religious variable and its factor loading.[5]

While these religious items are strongly related statistically, it could be argued that they are less closely related conceptually. For instance, religious commitment

---

[3] The exact coding of each of these religious variables is presented in Appendix A.

[4] In 1980, that factor has an eigenvalue of 2.44 and explains 48.9% of the variance. In 1984, it has an eigenvalue of 2.45 and explains 49.2% of the variance. In 1988, it has an eigenvalue of 2.62 and explains 52.3% of the variance. In 1992, it has an eigenvalue of 2.74 and explains 54.9% of the variance. In none of those years did the eigenvalue of the second extracted factor approach 1.0, all of which strongly indicates that a single-factor solution is appropriate.

[5] The reliability coefficient (alpha) for the religious traditionalism index is .77 in 1980, .74 in 1984, .77 in 1988, and .80 in 1992.

Religious Traditionalism, Postmaterialism, and U.S. Political Behavior   757

TABLE 1

RESULTS OF PRINCIPAL COMPONENTS ANALYSIS OF RELIGIOUS
TRADITIONALISM ITEMS, 1980–1992

Variable	1980	1984	1988	1992
Religious Salience	.8031	.7834	.7959	.7978
Born-Again Experience	.6986	.6893	.7259	.7399
Church Attendance	.6966	.6667	.7210	.7378
Denominational Orthodoxy	.6057	.6748	.7114	.7490
Biblical Views	.6770	.6872	.6578	.6750

Source: American National Election Studies, 1980–1992

does not necessarily go hand-in-hand with traditional religious beliefs or affiliation with conservative denominations. There are many religious liberals who attend church regularly and for whom religion is quite salient. Accordingly, a fair amount of research has taken an approach to the measurement of religion that is different from the one we take. Rather than aggregating various religious items into an index of religious traditionalism, it examines political differences between the members of various denominational traditions, and, within these traditions, it examines the political impact of church attendance, religious salience, and doctrinal beliefs (Kellstedt and Green 1993; Kellstedt and Smidt 1993: Kellstedt et al. 1996; Miller and Shanks 1996). Thus, it is entirely possible that our measure of religious traditionalism is not ideal. However, similar measures have been used in past research (Green, Guth, and Fraser 1991; Guth and Green 1990), and the measure does have several strengths: it takes advantage of all of the religious indicators included in the NES from 1980 to 1992; its components are strongly related; and, since it is a single index, it provides a straightforward comparison to Inglehart's measure. Moreover, it seems to accomplish its fundamental purpose: distinguishing that portion of the American electorate with the most traditional religious beliefs and practices from that portion which is least committed to traditional religiosity.[6]

[6] Among the 1992 NES respondents who occupy the bottom quartile of the religious traditionalism index, large majorities pray less than once a week (65%), never read the Bible (69%), feel that religion provides no guidance in their lives (68%), hold a nonliteral interpretation of the Bible (83%), never attend religious services (87%), and do not consider themselves to be born-again Christians (100%). Among the 1992 NES respondents who occupy the top quartile of the index, large majorities pray at least once a day (85%), read the Bible a few times a week (66%), feel that religion provides a great deal of guidance in their lives (78%), believe that the Bible should be taken literally (74%), attend church once a week or more (61%), and consider themselves to be born-again Christians (93%). The most problematic component of the religious traditionalism index may be the denominational orthodoxy scale, since it involves somewhat arbitrary assignments of some religious groups. Therefore, we conducted all the analyses with that variable omitted from the index and obtained very similar results.

758   Geoffrey C. Layman and Edward G. Carmines

THE INFLUENCE OF CULTURAL ORIENTATIONS
ON AMERICAN POLITICAL BEHAVIOR

Cultural orientations should have more influence on some aspects of American political behavior than on others. Of the three types of political orientations— partisanship, presidential vote choice, and ideological self-placement—party identification is the least likely to be structured by cultural orientations. To some extent, party ties are long-term psychological identifications that are passed on from generation to generation (Campbell et al. 1960) and should thus tend to reflect cleavages such as race, class, and region that defined earlier political alignments more than the newer cultural divisions. Vote choice is determined, to a large extent, by party identification (Campbell et al. 1960; Markus and Converse 1979), but voting decisions also reflect attitudes regarding current political circumstances (Page and Jones 1984; RePass 1971). There should thus be a lingering effect of the class-based cleavages that were predominant in the New Deal era on vote choice, but voting decisions also should be influenced by the new cultural orientations. While ideological self-placement is colored, to some extent, by partisanship, it, more than vote choice, is independent of party ties and reflects current political circumstances (Inglehart and Klingemann 1976). Hence, cultural and value-based cleavages should have a strong impact on ideology.

This section examines the influence of ten social-cleavage variables—religious traditionalism, Material-Postmaterial value priorities, race (nonwhite/white), education, family income, gender (male/female), age, size of community (higher scores representing more rural areas), region (non-South/South), and union membership—on ideology, vote choice, and partisanship from 1980 to 1992. Education, income, and union membership represent different aspects of the class-based political cleavage that was predominant during the New Deal era. Race is included in the model because it has been shown to be by far the strongest sociodemographic determinant of American political behavior (Huckfeldt and Kohfeld 1989). Gender is included due to evidence of a growing gender gap both in public opinion (Conover 1988; Fite, Genest, and Wilcox 1990) and in partisanship and vote choice (Klein 1985; Wirls 1986), with women being more liberal and Democratic than men. Age has generally been assumed to be associated with political conservatism (Inglehart 1977; Nie, Verba, and Petrocik 1976). However, the relationship between age on the one hand and partisanship and voting on the other may be more complex. Not only should older citizens who came of age during the New Deal era be more likely than their younger counterparts to identify with the Democratic party, their party ties should also be stronger (Beck 1984). Meanwhile, the youngest age cohorts were the most supportive of Ronald Reagan and the Republican party during that administration (Cook, Jelen, and Wilcox 1993). Divisions between those residing in urban and rural areas and between those residing in the South and the non-South have traditionally been associated with differences in political orientations (Sundquist 1983). In addition

Religious Traditionalism, Postmaterialism, and U.S. Political Behavior 759

to their theoretical relationships with party loyalties, vote, and ideology, variables such as education, income, region, ruralism, and age are associated with either *Value Priorities, Religious Traditionalism,* or with both (Green, Guth, and Fraser 1991; Hunter 1983; Inglehart 1971). In this sense, they are included in the model in order to prevent the discovery of a spurious relationship between cultural orientations and political orientations that is in fact due to their mutual associations with these demographic variables.

In addition to these cleavage variables, each of the three models includes a control for a political factor denoted in the literature as having a particularly strong impact on that aspect of political behavior. Mother's and father's party identifications (Campbell et al. 1960)—coded so that higher scores represent greater Republicanism—are included in the partisanship model; party identification (Campbell et al. 1960) is included in the vote choice model; and affective evaluations of ideological groups (Conover and Feldman 1984)—measured as the difference between the feeling thermometer rating of conservatives and that of liberals—is included as a control in the ideological self-identification model.

Table 2 presents the results of an analysis in which party identification (ranging from strong Democrat to strong Republican) is regressed on these various social and political variables. As the table makes plain, our expectation that party identification will reflect the cleavages that defined past political alignments is realized. Variables such as family income, union membership, race, ruralism, and region have consistent and strong effects on partisanship. Parental transmission of partisanship also appears to be quite strong as both mother's and father's party identifications have effects on partisanship that are both highly significant and, as their standardized regression coefficients indicate, very strong in each of the years in which these variables were included in the NES survey. Value-based and cultural cleavages also exert significant influences on party ties. Religious traditionalism has a statistically significant effect in three of the four election years and value priorities exert a significant influence in two of the four years. As one would expect, traditional religiosity is associated with a Republican identification while Postmaterialism is more prevalent among Democrats. However, the effect of religious traditionalism is, with the exception of 1984, stronger than that of value priorities. By 1992, religious conservatism trails only race and parents' party ties in terms of the magnitude of its substantive impact on partisanship.

Table 3 shows the impact of these various cleavage variables on ideological self-placement (ranging from extremely liberal to extremely conservative) from 1980 to 1992. Not surprisingly, affective evaluations of liberals and conservatives have the strongest impact in each of the four years. While value priority does have a statistically significant influence ($p < .05$) on ideological orientations in 1988 and 1992, with Postmaterialists being more liberal than Materialists, its substantive effect is always less than that of religious traditionalism. Moreover, while demographic variables such as race, income, ruralism, and age have a significant effect on ideology in some of these years, the influence of religiosity is

TABLE 2

PARTY IDENTIFICATION AS A FUNCTION OF VARIOUS POLITICAL CLEAVAGES, 1980–1992

Independent Variables	1980	1984[a]	1988	1992
Religious Traditionalism	.10*** (.04)	.03 (.02)	.09** (.04)	.14*** (.06)
Value Priorities (Postmaterial)	.01 (.04)	-.12*** (-.42)	-.05 (-.18)	-.09*** (-.33)
Race (nonwhite/white)	.12*** (.89)	.20*** (1.29)	.16*** (.98)	.15*** (.89)
Education	.02 (.02)	.02 (.03)	.03 (.03)	.06* (.07)
Family Income	.13*** (.05)	.18*** (.06)	.08** (.03)	.11*** (.04)
Gender (female)	-.05 (-.20)	-.04 (-.17)	-.04 (-.19)	-.09*** (-.37)
Age	.005 (.0006)	-.01 (-.002)	-.05 (-.006)	-.002 (-.0002)
Ruralism	.08** (.23)	.09* (.25)	.05 (.15)	.04 (.12)
Region (non-South/South)	-.05 (-.26)	-.11** (-.51)	-.09** (-.42)	-.04 (-.19)
Union Member (Yes)	-.10** (-.50)	-.17*** (-.89)	-.11*** (-.63)	-.10*** (-.56)
Mother's Party ID (Republican)	.29*** (.63)		.22*** (.27)	.24*** (.57)
Father's Party ID (Republican)	.26*** (.59)		.24*** (.29)	.25*** (.59)
(N)	(727)	(707)	(1040)	(1222)
R^2	.38	.15	.33	.36

Source: American National Election Studies, 1980–1992

Note: Dependent variable ranges from strong Democrat to strong Republican. Entries are standardized regression coefficients; unstandardized coefficients are in parentheses.

[a]Parents' party identification was not included in the 1984 National Election Study.

*$p < .05$; **$p < .01$; ***$p < .001$

TABLE 3

IDEOLOGICAL SELF-PLACEMENT AS A FUNCTION OF VARIOUS POLITICAL CLEAVAGES, 1980–1992

Independent Variables	1980		1984		1988		1992	
Religious Traditionalism	.15***	(.04)	.07*	(.03)	.18***	(.05)	.11***	(.04)
Value Priorities (Postmaterial)	-.02	(-.05)	-.05	(-.12)	-.07*	(-.17)	-.07**	(-.17)
Race (nonwhite/white)	.001	(.005)	.04	(.19)	.06	(.24)	.002	(.01)
Education	-.03	(-.03)	.01	(.01)	.09**	(.08)	-.004	(-.003)
Family income	.07*	(.02)	.05	(.01)	.07	(.01)	-.01	(-.002)
Gender (female)	-.02	(-.06)	-.03	(-.08)	-.02	(-.07)	-.04	(-.10)
Age	-.03	(-.003)	.05	(.004)	.05	(.004)	.06**	(.005)
Ruralism	.05	(.09)	.01	(.02)	.13***	(.24)	.03	(.05)
Region (non-South/South)	-.01	(-.04)	-.03	(-.09)	-.08**	(-.26)	-.02	(-.07)
Union Member (yes)	-.01	(-.02)	-.02	(-.08)	-.04	(-.15)	.01	(.03)
Ideological Group Evaluations	.60***	(.02)	.49***	(.02)	.35***	(.01)	.58***	(.02)
(N)	(649)		(514)		(927)		(1130)	
R^2	.45		.29		.25		.43	

Source: American National Election Studies, 1980–1992.

Note: Dependent variable ranges from extremely liberal to extremely conservative. Entries are standardized regression coefficients; unstandardized coefficients are in parentheses.

*$p < .05$; **$p < .01$; ***$p < .001$

much more consistent and is substantively larger in each of the four years. Religious traditionalism appears to be strongly associated with political conservatism, while secularists and religious liberals have considerably more liberal political leanings.

It appears that cultural orientations do have a significant impact on Americans' political orientations. However, their ability to explain political behavior, at least partisanship and ideological self-identification, is greater when they are conceptualized as divisions between religious conservatives and secularists rather than as divisions between Materialists and Postmaterialists.[7]

These findings are confirmed in the results for vote choice in Table 4. Since the presidential vote is primarily a dichotomous choice in the United States, this table presents the results of a series of multivariate logit analyses in which the independent variables are the various social and political cleavages and party identification.[8] Table 4 also presents the substantive impact of each independent variable within the context of the logit model. Because the logit model is nonlinear, the effect of any explanatory variable is specific to a particular point on the probability distribution of the dependent variable. This means, in turn, that the coefficients for explanatory variables must be evaluated with respect to the dependent variable's distribution as well. Our practice is to use an estimated model to predict the variable's probability distribution while the values of one explanatory variable are manipulated and all other explanatory variables are held constant. Thus, Table 4 also shows the change in the probability of voting for the Republican candidate that results from an increase of one standard deviation in each independent variable, while all other variables are held constant, for a voter with an initial probability of .50.

Not surprisingly, party identification is the most consistent predictor of the presidential vote, being statistically significant in every presidential election from 1980 through 1992 and exerting the largest impact on the probability of voting Republican in each year. Race is the only one of the noncultural variables to have a consistent impact on the vote, reaching significance in each of these election

---

[7] Due to the nearly overwhelming impact of ideological group evaluations on ideological self-placement, we also estimated these equations without this variable. While the proportion of the variance explained by the model is considerably less, the results do not differ significantly from those presented here. Religious traditionalism has a stronger effect on ideology than any of the other variables in each year, and its impact is noticeably more substantial than that of value priorities.

[8] Given the considerable percentage of the popular vote won by a third-party candidate, Ross Perot, in 1992, a binomial logit analysis with the two-party vote as the dependent variable may not be entirely appropriate for 1992 and may produce misleading results regarding our variables of substantive interest. Thus, we also perform a multinomial logit analysis for 1992 in which the dependent variable contains three categories: George Bush, Bill Clinton, and Perot. This analysis is discussed in Appendix B and demonstrates that religious traditionalism significantly distinguished Bush voters from both Clinton voters and Perot voters in 1992, but did not significantly distinguish Clinton voters from Perot voters. Value priorities did not significantly affect the likelihood of supporting any of the candidates.

TABLE 4

LOGIT MODELS OF PRESIDENTIAL VOTE AS A FUNCTION OF VARIOUS POLITICAL CLEAVAGES, 1980–1992

Independent Variables	1980 Coeff.	1980 Change in Prob.[a]	1984 Coeff.	1984 Change in Prob.	1988 Coeff.	1988 Change in Prob.	1992 Coeff.	1992 Change in Prob.
Religious Traditionalism	-.01	-.01	.11*	.10	.04*	.06	.12***	.13
Value type (Postmaterial)	.07	.01	-.39	-.06	-.21	-.03	-.25	-.04
Race (nonwhite/white)	1.27**	.10	.96	.08	1.53***	.14	1.24***	.12
Education	-.04	.02	-.16	-.06	-.01	-.005	.01	.002
Family Income	.02	.03	.11***	.16	.04	.05	.03	.05
Gender (female)	-.32	-.04	-.20	-.03	-.06	-.01	.12	.01
Age	.0004	.002	.008	.04	.004	.02	-.001	-.004
Ruralism	.19	.04	.36	.07	-.05	-.01	.005	.001
Region (non-South/South)	-.06	-.01	.14	.02	.70**	.08	.09	.01
Union Member (yes)	-.60*	-.06	-1.24***	-.12	-.24	-.02	-.23	-.02
Party Identification	.84***	.34	.96***	.29	.90***	.37	.98***	.40
(N)	(690)		(519)		(921)		(952)	
Pseudo R²	.39		.50		.45		.51	
% cases correctly predicted	75.50		70.11		76.64		74.68	
Chi-square (DF = 11)	372.54		355.82		578.83		649.99	

Source: American National Election Studies, 1980–1992

Note: Dependent variable is coded 1 if the respondent voted for the Republican candidate, 0 if he/she voted for the Democratic candidate.

[a]Change in probability is the estimated effect of an increase of one standard deviation of each independent variable on the probability of voting for the Republican candidate for a voter with an initial probability of voting Republican of .50.

*p < .05; **p < .01; ***p < .001

764   Geoffrey C. Layman and Edward G. Carmines

years except 1984, and having a relatively strong substantive effect. It again appears that cultural orientations have come to exert a noticeable impact on American political behavior. But this appears to be true only if they are defined by religiosity and not if they are defined by Material-Postmaterial value priorities. As the table shows, religious traditionalists were significantly more likely to vote for Republican presidential nominees in 1984, 1988, and 1992, while value priorities did not affect vote choice in any of these years. In 1992, religiosity had the strongest influence on the probability of supporting George Bush of any variable in the model except partisanship.

CULTURAL-ISSUE SALIENCE AND THE POLITICAL IMPACT OF CULTURAL ORIENTATIONS

So far, our evidence indicates that cultural orientations have come to exert a political influence as strong as, if not stronger than, those of cleavages based on class, race, and other sociodemographic characteristics. However, this is more true—and often only true—when cultural orientations are defined by religiosity rather than by value priorities.[9] While these findings shed light on the nature of the cultural conflict in contemporary American politics, there may be an even better test of our hypothesis that this cultural cleavage is defined more by divisions between religious traditionalists and secularists than by divisions between Materialists and Postmaterialists.

Inglehart (1971, 1977) assumes that as social and cultural issues such as abortion, women's rights, and homosexual rights replace the traditionally dominant economic issues at the forefront of a nation's political agenda, value-based cleavages will replace class-based cleavages as the dominant political divisions in the nation. It is possible that what constrains the impact of Material-Postmaterial value priorities on American political behavior is the fact that a substantial majority of Americans continues to find other political concerns, particularly economic ones, to be more important than social and cultural matters (Abramson, Aldrich, and Rohde 1990; Himmelstein and McRae 1988; Kinder and Kiewiet

---

[9] A possible explanation for the finding that religious traditionalism has a consistently greater impact than value priorities on political behavior is that we are employing a better measure of traditional religiosity than of value priorities. We use a multiple-item measure of religious traditionalism while we employ a single indicator of value priorities which happens to be rather simplified and of potentially questionable validity. While we are unable to employ a more sophisticated indicator of value priorities, it may be possible to reduce the discrepancies in the quality of the two measures by employing only a single indicator of religion as well. Of our five items, the one that probably best captures the current religious divisions between traditionalists on the one hand and religious liberals and secularists on the other hand is view of the Bible (Hunter 1983, 1991). We performed the analyses in Tables 2 through 4 using the Biblical views variable rather than the full religious traditionalism index. While the impact of the single-item indicator of religion is not as strong as that of the full index, the results are comparable to those presented in the tables. Biblical view has a consistent effect on partisanship, ideology, and vote choice, and, with only a few exceptions, its influence is greater than that of value priorities.

Religious Traditionalism, Postmaterialism, and U.S. Political Behavior 765

1984). In other words, it may be the case that the cultural conflict in American politics is taking shape along Materialist-versus-Postmaterialist lines, but the impact of value priorities on political behavior is limited by the fact that cultural matters are not highly salient for most citizens. If this is true, then it follows that value priorities should have a particularly strong impact—in fact a stronger impact than that of traditional religiosity—on the political behavior of those citizens for whom cultural matters are quite salient. Conversely, if this is not true and American cultural conflict is defined more by religious divisions than by Materialist-Postmaterialist divisions, then religious traditionalism should have a particularly strong impact on the political behavior of those citizens for whom cultural matters are important.

In other words, an analysis of the impact of cultural orientations on the political behavior of those citizens for whom cultural matters are particularly salient should provide a strong test of the relative utility of religious traditionalism and value priorities as indicators of the cultural cleavage in contemporary American politics. The variable that plays the larger role in shaping the cultural conflict should have a greater impact on the political orientations of culturally concerned citizens. In order to identify those citizens who are particularly concerned about cultural matters, we employ the open-ended questions in the 1992 NES regarding respondents' likes and dislikes concerning the two parties and their presidential candidates, what they perceived to be the major differences between the two parties, and what they considered to be the most important problems facing the country. Respondents are classified as being concerned about cultural matters if they mentioned a cultural or moral concern at least once in their responses to these open-ended questions.[10] Since a relatively small proportion (less than one-third) of NES respondents mentioned a cultural matter in their responses to any of these questions, it is likely that those who did were particularly concerned about cultural topics.

Table 5 shows the impact of religious traditionalism, value type, and the various sociodemographic variables on the party loyalties, presidential voting decisions, and ideological self-identifications of those 1992 NES respondents who are concerned about cultural matters. As the table makes plain, the impact of religiosity on political orientations is magnified noticeably for these respondents. Not only is the impact of religious conservatism highly significant ($p < .001$) in all three equations, but its substantive impact is notably greater than for all

---

[10] More specifically, respondents were classified as being concerned about cultural matters if one of their responses to the questions about their likes and dislikes of the candidates and parties was "public morality," "abortion/birth control," "ERA/women's rights," "school prayer," or "gay rights"; or if one of their responses to the question about party differences was "abortion," "women's rights/ERA," or "homosexuality/gay rights"; or if one of their responses to the question regarding most important problems was "pro-abortion," "anti-abortion," "women's rights," "moral/religious decay," "family problems," "problems with young people" (such as "sexual attitudes" or "lack of values/discipline"), "religion too mixed up in politics/school prayer" or "homosexuality."

766

TABLE 5

PARTY IDENTIFICATION, IDEOLOGICAL SELF-PLACEMENT, AND PRESIDENTIAL VOTE (TWO-PARTY) AS A FUNCTION OF VARIOUS POLITICAL CLEAVAGES FOR THOSE WHO ARE CONCERNED ABOUT CULTURAL MATTERS

Independent Variables	Party Identification[a] Coefficient		Ideology[a] Coefficient		Presidential Vote[b] Coefficient	Change in Probability
Religious Traditionalism	.25***	(.10)	.19***	(.06)	.24***	.26
Value Priorities (Postmaterial)	-.15***	(-.59)	-.04	(-.11)	.21	.03
Race (nonwhite/white)	.08*	(.79)	-.02	(-.12)	1.26	.08
Education	.03	(.04)	-.03	(-.03)	.01	.01
Family Income	.13**	(.05)	.05	(.01)	-.001	-.01
Gender (female)	-.08*	(-.36)	-.03	(-.08)	-.21	-.02
Age	-.001	(-.0001)	.02	(.002)	.01	.04
Ruralism	.04	(.12)	.007	(.01)	-.38	-.07
Region (non-South/South)	-.04	(-.14)	-.04	(-.13)	.30	.03
Union Member (yes)	-.12**	(-.69)	-.02	(-.10)	-.24	-.004
Mother's Party Identification (Republican)	.24***	(.57)			—	—
Father's Party Identification (Republican)	.22***	(.49)			—	—
Party Identification					1.06***	.39
Ideological Group Evaluations			.63***	(.02)	—	—
(N)	(413)		(442)		(365)	
R^2 (Pseudo R^2 for Vote)	.38		.59		.58	
% Cases correctly predicted					79.92	
Chi-square (DF)					294.24 (11)	

Source: 1992 American National Election Study

[a] Entries are standardized regression coefficients; unstandardized coefficients are in parentheses.

[b] Entries are logit coefficients. Change in probability is the estimated effect of an increase of one standard deviation of each independent variable on probability of voting for Bush for a voter with an initial probability of .50.

$*p < .05;$ $**p < .01;$ $***p < .001$

Religious Traditionalism, Postmaterialism, and U.S. Political Behavior   767

respondents and is considerably stronger than that of any of the sociodemographic variables in all three models. Indeed, the effect of religious traditionalism even surpasses mother's and father's partisanship in the party identification equation and is second only to ideological group evaluations and partisanship, respectively, in the ideology and vote choice equations. At the same time, the impact of value priorities is not notably amplified. While it has a significant influence on party ties, it does not significantly affect vote choice or ideological self-placement. Moreover, its substantive impact on these political orientations is not conspicuously greater for respondents who are culturally concerned than it is for all respondents, and it pales in comparison to that of religious traditionalism. It appears, then, that when citizens are concerned about cultural matters, it is their religious orientation and not their level of Postmaterialism that plays a principal role in shaping their political behavior. Religious traditionalism appears not only to be more relevant than value priorities for contemporary American political behavior, but also to play a larger role in shaping the cultural conflict in the nation's politics.

CONCLUSION

Inglehart's value priorities thesis is the leading account of cultural conflict in advanced industrial democracies. A not-so-modest cottage industry has developed around this concept. Yet, students of American politics have paid only limited attention to Inglehart's thesis despite the fact that cultural conflict seems to be increasing in American politics. This paper has argued that Inglehart's value typology does not adequately explain developments in contemporary American politics because it does not take into account the unique features of American cultural conflict. In particular, it does not recognize the salient role that religion and religion-based cultural differences play in contemporary American politics. Our findings indicate that while Material-Postmaterial value priorities do have some impact on American political behavior, a conceptualization of cultural conflict that takes into account the contemporary divisions between religious traditionalists on the one hand and religious liberals and secularists on the other hand fares considerably better in explaining the political orientations of the citizenry as a whole and especially in structuring the political behavior of those who are particularly concerned about cultural matters.

These findings raise the question of why, given the attention devoted to Inglehart's value priorities thesis in other contexts, does the Material-Postmaterial cleavage provide relatively little help in explaining contemporary developments in American politics? One reason may be the nature of Inglehart's value-type indicator. Even if the indicator is a valid measure of value priorities, it is possible that value priorities do not provide an effective representation of a politically relevant cleavage. Scott Flanagan (1980, 1987) and James Savage (1985) both argue that Inglehart's Materialist-Postmaterialist dichotomy is overly simplistic,

768   Geoffrey C. Layman and Edward G. Carmines

as it predicts only political priorities and not the direction of political preferences. They posit that within both of Inglehart's value-type categories there are liberals and conservatives. The Postmaterialist category contains both social liberals and social conservatives; the Materialist category contains both economic conservatives and economic liberals. Flanagan and Savage argue that as value-based concerns move to the political foreground, the important cleavage is not between those who focus on "Postmaterial" concerns and those who focus on matters of economic and physical security. Instead, it is between those who hold more progressive stances on Postmaterial, value-based concerns and those who hold more traditional positions on these matters. This paper has shown that, at least with regard to the United States, Flanagan and Savage may be correct in asserting that Inglehart's Materialist and Postmaterialist groupings do not serve as effective ideological categories. A conception of cultural orientations that does differentiate between traditionalists and progressives on the cultural axis of political conflict performs better than Inglehart's value priorities variable in explaining American political behavior.

A second possibility may be that the United States' two-party system constrains the ability of new, Postmaterialist forces to find political expression for their concerns, and this reduces the impact of the Material-Postmaterial cleavage on political behavior. Inglehart notes that this value-based cleavage should have a larger political influence in multiparty systems than in two-party systems since the "existence of many parties provides a larger number of entry-points for expression of a given ideology" (1977, 258). This, however, does not seem to be a very plausible explanation for the limited effect of Material-Postmaterial divisions on American political behavior. The participatory nature of the United States' system of nominations makes it relatively easy for new groups, emphasizing new concerns, to find entry into the party system (Kirkpatrick 1976). Accordingly, activists on both the progressive and the conservative sides of the American cultural divide have had considerable success at gaining access to and influence within the Democratic and Republican parties (Green, Guth, and Fraser 1991; Kirkpatrick 1976; Rozell and Wilcox 1995; Shafer 1985).

The final and most compelling possibility is the one that this paper addresses: Material-Postmaterial value priorities have less impact on American politics because of the unique role that religion plays in the United States. While there has been some secularization among certain portions of the American population (Hunter 1983; Wuthnow 1988), the abandonment of religion has not been nearly as universal as in many other advanced industrial societies (Wald 1992). In fact, at the same time that some groups in the United States have moved toward secularism, there has been a growth in conservative Protestant congregations (Wald 1992). These simultaneous trends certainly created the potential for cultural conflict along secular-versus-traditionally religious lines, and, as the findings of this paper indicate, such a conflict has come to exert a significant influence on American politics. In other words, Inglehart's predictions of the enhanced political importance of cultural or value-based cleavages have been proven true

Religious Traditionalism, Postmaterialism, and U.S. Political Behavior 769

in the United States. However, in contrast to Inglehart's (1977, 1990) predictions and accounts of cultural politics in other advanced industrial societies, the principal political opponents of cultural progressivism have not been members of the working-class seeking to maintain the traditional emphasis on materialism. Instead, perhaps because of the continuing attachments of many Americans to traditional religiosity, they have been religious conservatives seeking to maintain the role of traditional moral values in American culture. Value-based cultural conflict has become more important in the United States; but in order to understand the nature of this conflict, it is crucial to probe its religious bases.

While this paper has shown that the religion-based cultural cleavage already has a notable influence on American politics, it also provides evidence that the political impact of this division may be even greater in the future. The impact of religious traditionalism is quite strong for those citizens who are particularly concerned about cultural matters, and, in fact, is noticeably stronger than it is for all citizens. However, only a relatively small proportion of Americans finds cultural concerns to be the most salient. This suggests that as concern about cultural issues grows, the impact of religion-based cultural conflict on American politics also will grow.

The question, then, is under which circumstances will cultural matters become more salient in the United States? The answer may lie in the behavior of political candidates and party activists. As candidates place more emphasis on cultural concerns, these issues may become more salient in the minds of voters. Since party activists exert a substantial influence on the behavior of candidates (Chappell and Keech 1986; Wright and Berkman 1986), candidates may be encouraged to devote more emphasis to these matters as activists who find cultural issues to be the most salient gain influence within the two parties. As suggested earlier, such a trend is significantly underway. The growing influence of the Christian Right in the Republican party has been well documented (Rozell and Wilcox 1995; Wilcox 1992) and secularists with liberal cultural values are growing in numbers and importance within the Democratic party (Green, Guth, and Fraser 1991; Layman 1994). If these trends continue, candidates may devote even more attention to cultural matters and voters may find these issues to be more salient. These developments may lead to further increases in the importance of religion-based cultural conflict in the United States.

APPENDIX A

CODING OF NES ITEMS USED TO FORM THE INDEX OF RELIGIOSITY

BIBLICAL VIEWS

1980–1988

1 The Bible was written by men who lived so long ago that it is worth very little today.

2 The Bible is a good book because it was written by wise men, but God had nothing to do with it.

3 The Bible was written by men inspired by God, but it contains some human errors.
4 The Bible is God's Word and all it says is true.

1992

1 The Bible is a book written by men and is not the Word of God.
2 The Bible is the Word of God but not everything in it should be taken literally, word for word.
3 The Bible is the actual Word of God and is to be taken literally, word for word.

BORN-AGAIN CHRISTIAN?

0 No
1 Yes

DENOMINATIONAL ORTHODOXY

0 Unchurched (those who never attend religious services and do not consider themselves to be part of a particular church or denomination)
1 Jews
2 Episcopalians, Congregationalists, and other liberal denominations (Episcopalian, Anglican; United Church of Christ; Congregationalist Christian; Unitarian, Universalist, Quakers (Friends))
3 Roman Catholics
4 Presbyterians, Reformed Church in America, and Lutherans (Presbyterian Church in the U.S.A., "Presbyterian," Reformed Church in America, Reformed, Evangelical Lutheran Church, Lutheran)
5 Methodists, Disciples of Christ, and Black Protestants (United Methodist Church; African Methodist Episcopal Church; Christian Methodist Episcopal Church; Methodist; Christian Church (Disciples of Christ))
6 Baptists, Mormons, and other conservatives (Seventh-day Adventist, Church of the Brethren, "Brethren," Mennonite Church, Evangelical Free Church, Brethren in Christ, Christian and Missionary Alliance, Church of the Nazarene, Free Methodist Church, Salvation Army, Wesleyan Church, Holiness, Fundamentalist Adventist, Lutheran Church—Missouri Synod, Wisconsin Evangelical Lutheran Synod, American Baptist Association, American Baptist Churches U.S.A., Southern Baptist Convention, "Baptist," The Church of Jesus Christ of Latter-day Saints)
7 Fundamentalists and charismatics (Baptist Missionary Association of America, Conservative Baptist Association of America, National Association of Free Will Baptists, Primitive Baptists, Church of God General Conference, United Zion Church, other fundamentalists, Plymouth Brethren, Pentecostal Holiness Church, other Pentecostals, Assembly of God, Church of Christ, Church of God (Anderson, IN))

Religious Traditionalism, Postmaterialism, and U.S. Political Behavior   771

CHURCH ATTENDANCE

1 Never
2 A few times a year
3 Once or twice a month
4 Almost every week
5 Every week
6 More than once a week (This category was not included in 1980 and 1984.)

RELIGIOUS SALIENCE—AMOUNT OF GUIDANCE RELIGION PROVIDES

1 None
2 Some
3 Quite a bit
4 A great deal

APPENDIX B

MULTINOMIAL LOGIT ANALYSIS OF THE 1992 PRESIDENTIAL VOTE

Given the fact that three major candidates were involved in the 1992 election, simple binomial logit analysis is not sufficient to analyze the 1992 vote. Multinomial logit is appropriate when the dependent variable takes on more than two outcomes and the outcomes have no natural ordering (Aldrich and Nelson 1984; Greene 1990). Following Greene (1990), the multinomial logit model for the 1992 vote is as follows:

$$P(y = \text{Bush}) = e^{X\beta(\text{Bush})} / [e^{X\beta(\text{Bush})} + e^{X\beta(\text{Clinton})} + e^{X\beta(\text{Perot})}]$$
$$P(y = \text{Clinton}) = e^{X\beta(\text{Clinton})} / [e^{X\beta(\text{Bush})} + e^{X\beta(\text{Clinton})} + e^{X\beta(\text{Perot})}]$$
$$P(y = \text{Perot}) = e^{X\beta(\text{Perot})} / [e^{X\beta(\text{Bush})} + e^{X\beta(\text{Clinton})} + e^{X\beta(\text{Perot})}];$$

where y is the dependent variable, *Vote Choice X* is the set of independent variables, and β represents the coefficients of these independent variables.

This model is, however, unidentified since there is more than one solution to $\beta^{(\text{Bush})}$, $\beta^{(\text{Clinton})}$, and $\beta^{(\text{Perot})}$ that leads to the same probabilities for $y = \text{Bush}$, $y = \text{Clinton}$, $y = \text{Perot}$. To identify the model, one of $\beta^{(\text{Bush})}$, $\beta^{(\text{Clinton})}$, and $\beta^{(\text{Perot})}$ has to be set to zero. If $y = \text{Bush}$ is chosen as the control group so that $\beta^{(\text{Bush})}$ equals zero and $e^{X\beta(\text{Bush})}$ equals one, the multinomial logit coefficients $\beta^{(\text{Perot})}$ and $\beta^{(\text{Clinton})}$ measure the influence of particular variables on the change in the 1992 vote relative to the $y = \text{Bush}$ group. In order to assess whether the variables of theoretical interest divided the supporters of each candidate from the supporters of each other candidate, two multinomial logit analyses were performed. In one, $y = \text{Bush}$ is the base category and in the other $y = \text{Perot}$ is the base category.[11]

---

[11] Since the multinomial logit coefficients for the Bush category when the Perot category is the base are the same, except that all signs are reversed, as those for the Perot category when the Bush category is the base, these coefficients are not presented in the table.

Table B1 presents these multinomial logit coefficients and shows that religious traditionalism significantly distinguished Bush supporters from supporters of both Clinton and Perot, with those voters who were more religious being less likely to support Clinton or Perot instead of Bush than were more secular voters, but did not significantly distinguish Clinton voters from Perot voters.

Table B1 also shows the estimated effect—in terms of the change in probability—of an increase of one standard deviation of each independent variable on the predicted probability that an individual voted for each of the three candidates while all other independent variables are held constant at their means. According to these effects, religious traditionalism had the largest substantive impact of any variable in the model except for party identification on the probability that an individual supported Bush and on the probability that an individual supported Clinton. An increase of one standard deviation in religious traditionalism is associated with an increase of .11 in the probability of supporting Bush and a decrease of .09 in the probability of supporting Clinton. However, it appears that religious traditionalism was associated strongly only with voting patterns for the two major parties' candidates. An increase in religious traditionalism is associated with only a slight decline in the probability of supporting Perot. This is not surprising given the fact that the two parties' activists have become divided increasingly along religious and secular lines (Green, Guth, and Fraser 1991; Layman 1994) and that Perot and his activists concentrated almost exclusively on economic matters in 1992. Also interesting is the fact that Postmaterialism has very little substantive impact on the probability of supporting any of the candidates.

Manuscript submitted 11 December 1995
Final manuscript received 17 June 1996

REFERENCES

Abramowitz, Alan I. 1995. "It's Abortion Stupid: Policy Voting in the 1992 Presidential Election." *Journal of Politics* 57:176–88.

Abramson, Paul R., John H. Aldrich, and David W. Rohde. 1990. *Change and Continuity in the 1988 Elections.* Washington, DC: Congressional Quarterly Press.

Abramson, Paul R., and Ronald Inglehart. 1986. "Generational Replacement and Value Change in Six West European Societies." *American Journal of Political Science* 30:1–25.

Abramson, Paul R., and Ronald Inglehart. 1995. *Value Change in Global Perspective.* Ann Arbor: University of Michigan Press.

Aldrich, John D., and Forrest D. Nelson. 1984. *Linear Probability, Logit, and Probit Models.* Newbury Park, CA: Sage.

Ammerman, Nancy. 1987. *Bible Believers.* New Brunswick: Rutgers University Press.

Baker, Tod A., and Robert P. Steed. 1992. "Party Activists, Southern Religion, and Culture Wars: An Analysis of Precinct Party Activists in Eleven Southern States." Presented at the annual meeting of the Southern Political Science Association, Atlanta.

773

TABLE B1

MULTINOMIAL LOGIT ANALYSIS OF THE 1992 PRESIDENTIAL VOTE AS A FUNCTION OF VARIOUS CLEAVAGES

Independent Variables	Bush as Base		Perot as Base[a]	Change in Probability[b]		
	Clinton	Perot	Clinton	Bush	Clinton	Perot
Religious Traditionalism	-.13***	-.10***	-.03	.11	-.09	-.03
Value Priorities (Postmaterial)	.25	.25	.04	-.03	.02	0
Race (nonwhite/white)	-1.17**	.73	-1.84***	.07	-.13	.08
Education	.02	-.12	.15*	-.01	.01	-.01
Family Income	-.03	.01	-.05**	0	-.08	.07
Gender (female)	.003	-.48**	.45***	0	0	-.02
Age	.003	-.02**	.02***	.01	.05	-.06
Ruralism	-.02	.22	-.25	-.02	-.05	.06
Region (non–South/South)	-.07	-.32	.29	.01	.01	-.03
Union Member (Yes)	.11	-.02	.02	0	.02	.02
Party Identification	-1.04***	-.46***	-.57***	.35	-.38	.02
Constant	6.89***	3.10***	3.64***			

$N = 1,174$
Pseudo $R^2 = .33$
Chi-square $= 786.81$ (DF $= 22$)

% cases correctly predicted	All voters	Bush Voters	Clinton Voters	Perot Voters
	54.37	78.74	88.92	15.53

Source: 1992 American National Election Study

[a] The coefficients for Bush with Perot as the base category are the same as those for Perot with Bush as the base category except that the signs on all of the coefficients are reversed. Significance levels are identical.

[b] Change in probability is the estimated change (using the model in which Bush is the base category) in the probability of voting for Bush/Clinton/Perot from the base probability (all independent variables at their means) after an increase of one standard deviation in the independent variable while all other independent variables are held constant at their means. The base probabilities are .25 for Bush, .54 for Clinton, and .22 for Perot.

*p < .05; **p < .01; ***p < .001

774   Geoffrey C. Layman and Edward G. Carmines

Beatty, Kathleen, and Oliver Walter. 1989. "A Group Theory of Religion and Politics: The Clergy as Group Leaders." *Western Political Quarterly* 42:29–46.

Beck, Paul Allen. 1984. "The Electoral Cycle and Patterns of American Politics." In *Controversies in Voting Behavior,* ed. Richard G. Niemi and Herbert F. Weisberg. 2d ed. Washington, DC: Congressional Quarterly.

Brown, Robert D., and Edward G. Carmines. 1995. "Materialists, Postmaterialists, and the Criteria for Political Choice in U.S. Presidential Elections." *Journal of Politics* 57:483–94.

Campbell, Angus, Philip E. Converse, Warren E. Miller, and Donald E. Stokes. 1960. *The American Voter.* Chicago: The University of Chicago Press.

Carmines, Edward G., and Geoffrey C. Layman. N.d. "Value Priorities, Partisanship, and Electoral Choice: The Neglected Case of the United States." *Political Behavior.* Forthcoming.

Chappell, Henry W. Jr., and William Keech. 1986. "Policy Motivation and Party Differences in a Dynamic Spatial Model of Party Competition." *American Political Science Review* 80:881–99.

Clarke, Harold D., and Nittish Dutt. 1991. "Measuring Value Change in Western Industrialized Societies: The Impact of Unemployment." *American Political Science Review* 85:905–20.

Conover, Pamela Johnston. 1988. "Feminists and the Gender Gap." *Journal of Politics* 50:985–1010.

Conover, Pamela Johnston, and Stanley Feldman. 1984. "The Origins and Meanings of Liberal/ Conservative Self-Identifications." In *Controversies in Voting Behavior,* ed. Richard G. Niemi and Herbert F. Weisberg. 2d ed. Washington, DC: Congressional Quarterly.

Cook, Elizabeth Adell, Ted G. Jelen, and Clyde Wilcox. 1993. "Generational Differences in Attitudes Toward Abortion." In *Understanding the New Politics of Abortion,* ed. Malcolm L. Goggin. Newbury Park, CA: Sage.

Cook, Elizabeth Adell, Ted G. Jelen, and Clyde Wilcox. 1994. "Issue Voting in Gubernatorial Elections: Abortion and Post-*Webster* Politics." *Journal of Politics* 56:187–99.

Duch, Raymond M., and Michaell A. Taylor. 1993. "Postmaterialism and the Economic Condition." *American Journal of Political Science* 37:747–79.

Duch, Raymond M., and Michaell A. Taylor. 1994. "A Reply to Abramson and Inglehart's 'Education, Security, and Postmaterialism.' " *American Journal of Political Science* 38:815–24.

Fite, David, Marc Genest, and Clyde Wilcox. 1990. "Gender Differences in Foreign Policy Attitudes: A Longitudinal Analysis." *American Politics Quarterly* 18:492–513.

Flanagan, Scott C. 1980. "Value Cleavages, Economic Cleavages, and the Japanese Voter." *American Journal of Political Science* 24:178–206.

Flanagan, Scott C. 1987. "Value Change in Industrial Societies." *American Political Science Review* 81:1289–1319.

Glazer, Nathan. 1987. "Fundamentalism: A Defensive Offensive." In *Piety and Politics: Evangelicals and Fundamentalists Confront the World,* ed. Richard John Neuhaus and Michael Cromartie. Washington, DC: Ethics and Public Policy Center.

Green, John C., and James L. Guth. 1988. "The Christian Right in the Republican Party: The Case of Pat Robertson's Supporters." *Journal of Politics* 50:150–65.

Green, John C., and James L. Guth. 1991a. "Religion, Representation, and Roll Calls." *Legislative Studies Quarterly* 16:571–84.

Green, John C., and James L. Guth. 1991b. "The Bible and the Ballot Box: The Shape of Things to Come." In *The Bible and the Ballot Box: Religion and Politics in the 1988 Election,* ed. James L. Guth and John C. Green. Boulder: Westview.

Green, John C., James L. Guth, and Cleveland R. Fraser. 1991. "Apostles and Apostates? Religion and Politics Among Party Activists." In *The Bible and the Ballot Box: Religion and Politics in the 1988 Election,* ed. James L. Guth and John C. Green. Boulder: Westview.

Greene, William H. 1990. *Econometric Analysis.* New York: Macmillan.

Guth, James L. 1983. "The New Christian Right." In *The New Christian Right: Mobilization and Legitimation,* ed. Robert C. Liebman and Robert Wuthnow. New York: Aldine.

Religious Traditionalism, Postmaterialism, and U.S. Political Behavior 775

Guth, James L., and John C. Green. 1986. "Faith and Politics: Religion and Ideology Among Political Contributors." *American Politics Quarterly* 14:186–99.

Guth, James L., and John C. Green. 1987. "The Moralizing Minority: Christian Right Support Among Political Contributors." *Social Science Quarterly* 68:598–610.

Guth, James L., and John C. Green. 1989. "God and the GOP: Religion Among GOP Activists." In *Religion and Political Behavior in the United States*, ed. Ted G. Jelen. New York: Praeger.

Guth, James L., and John C. Green. 1990. "Politics in a New Key: Religiosity and Participation among Political Activists." *Western Political Quarterly* 43:153–79.

Guth, James L., John C. Green, Corwin E. Smidt, and Margaret M. Poloma. 1991. "Pulpits and Politics: The Protestant Clergy in the 1988 Presidential Election." In *The Bible and the Ballot Box: Religion and Politics in the 1988 Election*, ed. James L. Guth and John C. Green. Boulder: Westview.

Guth, James L., Ted G. Jelen, Lyman A. Kellstedt, Corwin E. Smidt, and Kenneth D. Wald. 1988. "The Politics of Religion in America: Issues for Investigation." *American Politics Quarterly* 16: 357–97.

Himmelstein, Jerome L., and James A. McRae. 1988. "Social Conservatism, New Republicans, and the 1980 Election." *Public Opinion Quarterly* 48:592–605.

Howell, Susan, and Robert Sims. 1993. "Abortion Attitudes and the Louisiana Governor's Election." *American Politics Quarterly* 21:54–64.

Huckfeldt, Robert, and Carol Weitzel Kohfeld. 1989. *Race and the Decline of Class in American Politics.* Urbana: University of Illinois Press.

Hunter, James Davison. 1983. *American Evangelicalism: Conservative Religion and the Quandary of Modernity.* New Brunswick, NJ: Rutgers University Press.

Hunter, James Davison. 1991. *Culture Wars: The Struggle to Define America.* New York: Basic Books.

Inglehart, Ronald. 1971. "The Silent Revolution in Europe: Intergenerational Change in Post-Industrial Societies." *American Political Science Review* 65:991–1017.

Inglehart, Ronald. 1977. *The Silent Revolution: Changing Values and Political Styles Among Western Publics.* Princeton, NJ: Princeton University Press.

Inglehart, Ronald. 1981. "Post-Materialism in an Environment of Insecurity." *American Political Science Review* 75:880–900.

Inglehart, Ronald. 1990. *Culture Shift in Advanced Industrial Society.* Princeton, NJ: Princeton University Press.

Inglehart, Ronald, and Paul R. Abramson. 1994. "Economic Security and Value Change." *American Political Science Review* 88:336–54.

Inglehart, Ronald, and Hans D. Klingemann. 1976. "Party Identification, Ideological Preference and the Left-Right Dimension among Western Mass Publics." In *Party Identification and Beyond: Representations of Voting and Party Competition*, ed. Ian Budge, Ivor Crewe, and Dennis Farlie. London: Wiley.

Jelen, Ted. 1991. *The Political Mobilization of Religious Beliefs.* New York: Praeger.

Kellstedt, Lyman A., and John C. Green. 1993. "Knowing God's Many People: Denominational Preference and Political Behavior." In *Rediscovering the Religious Factor in American Politics*, ed. David C. Leege and Lyman A. Kellstedt. Armonk, NY: Sharpe.

Kellstedt, Lyman A., John C. Green, James L. Guth, and Corwin E. Smidt. 1996. "Grasping the Essentials: The Social Embodiment of Religion and Political Behavior." In *Religion and the Culture Wars: Dispatches from the Front*, ed. John C. Green, James L. Guth, Corwin E. Smidt, and Lyman A. Kellstedt. Lanham, MD: Rowman and Littlefield.

Kellstedt, Lyman A., and Corwin E. Smidt. 1993. "Doctrinal Beliefs and Political Behavior: Views of the Bible." In *Rediscovering the Religious Factor in American Politics*, ed. David C. Leege and Lyman A. Kellstedt. Armonk, NY: Sharpe.

Kellstedt, Lyman A., Corwin E. Smidt, and Paul M. Kellstedt. 1991. "Religious Tradition, Denomination, and Commitment: White Protestants and the 1988 Election." In *The Bible and the Ballot*

776   Geoffrey C. Layman and Edward G. Carmines

Box: Religion and Politics in the 1988 Election, ed. James L. Guth and John C. Green. Boulder: Westview Press.

Kinder, Donald L., and D. Roderick Kiewiet. 1979. "Economic Discontent and Political Behavior: The Role of Personal Grievances and Collective Economic Judgments in Congressional Elections." *American Journal of Political Science* 23:495–527.

Kinder, Donald R., and D. Roderick Kiewiet. 1984. "Sociotropic Politics: The American Case." In *Controversies in Voting Behavior*, ed. Richard G. Niemi and Herbert F. Weisberg. 2d ed. Washington, DC: Congressional Quarterly.

Kirkpatrick, Jeane. 1976. *The New Presidential Elite: Men and Women in National Politics*. New York: Sage.

Klein, Ethel. 1985. "The Gender Gap: Different Issues, Different Answers." *Brookings Review* 3: 33–7.

Ladd, Everett Carll Jr., with Charles D. Hadley. 1975. *Transformations of the American Party System*. New York: Norton.

Layman, Geoffrey C. 1994. "Parties and 'Culture Wars': The Cultural Division of the Parties' Elites." Presented at the annual meeting of the American Political Science Association, New York.

Markus, Gregory B., and Philip E. Converse. 1979. "A Dynamic Simultaneous Equation Model of Electoral Choice." *American Political Science Review* 73:1055–70.

Miller, Arthur H., and Martin P. Wattenberg. 1984. "Politics from the Pulpit: Religiosity and the 1980 Elections." *Public Opinion Quarterly* 48:301–17.

Miller, Warren E., and J. Merrill Shanks. 1996. *The New American Voter*. Cambridge, MA: Harvard University Press.

Neuhaus, Richard John. 1987. "What the Fundamentalists Want." In *Piety and Politics: Evangelicals and Fundamentalists Confront the World*, ed. Richard John Neuhaus and Michael Cromartie. Washington, DC: Ethics and Public Policy Center.

Nie, Norman H., Sidney Verba, and John R. Petrocik. 1976. *The Changing American Voter*. Cambridge: Harvard University Press.

Page, Benjamin I., and Calvin C. Jones. 1984. "Reciprocal Effects of Policy Preferences, Party Loyalties, and the Vote." In *Controversies in Voting Behavior*, ed. Richard G. Niemi and Herbert F. Weisberg. 2d ed. Washington, DC: Congressional Quarterly.

Reichley, A. James. 1987. "The Evangelical and Fundamentalist Revolt." In *Piety and Politics: Evangelicals and Fundamentalists Confront the World*, ed. Richard John Neuhaus and Michael Cromartie. Washington, DC: Ethics and Public Policy Center.

RePass, David E. 1971. "Issue Salience and Party Choice." *American Political Science Review* 65: 389–400.

Rozell, Mark J., and Clyde Wilcox, ed. 1995. *God at the Grass Roots: The Christian Right in the 1994 Elections*. Lanham, MD: Rowman and Littlefield.

Savage, James. 1985. "Postmaterialism of the Left and Right: Political Conflict in Industrial Societies." *Comparative Political Studies* 17:431–51.

Shafer, Byron E. 1985. "The New Cultural Politics." *Political Science and Politics* 18:221–31.

Shafer, Byron E., and William J. M. Clagget. 1995. *The Two Majorities: The Issue Context of Modern American Politics*. Baltimore: Johns Hopkins University Press.

Smidt, Corwin. 1983. "Born-Again Politics: The Political Behavior of Evangelical Christians in the South and Non-South." In *Religion and Politics in the South: Mass and Elite Perspectives*, ed. Tod A. Baker, Robert P. Steed, and Lawrence W. Moreland. New York: Praeger.

Sundquist, James L. 1983. *Dynamics of the Party System: Alignment and Realignment of Political Parties in the United States*. Washington, DC: The Brookings Institution.

Wald, Kenneth D. 1992. *Religion and Politics in the United States*. 2d ed. Washington, DC: Congressional Quarterly.

Wald, Kenneth D., Dennis E. Owen, and Samuel S. Hill Jr. 1988. "Churches as Political Communities." *American Political Science Review* 82:531–48.

Religious Traditionalism, Postmaterialism, and U.S. Political Behavior   777

Wilcox, Clyde. 1986. "Fundamentalists and Politics: An Analysis of the Effects of Differing Operational Definitions." *Journal of Politics* 48:1041–51.

Wilcox, Clyde. 1987. "Religious Orientations and Political Attitudes: Variations Within the New Christian Right." *American Politics Quarterly* 15:274–96.

Wilcox, Clyde. 1989. "Popular Support for the New Christian Right." *Social Science Journal* 26: 55–63.

Wilcox, Clyde. 1990. "Religion and Politics Among White Evangelicals: The Impact of Religious Variables on Political Attitudes." *Review of Religious Research* 32:27–42.

Wilcox, Clyde. 1992. *God's Warriors*. Baltimore: Johns Hopkins University Press.

Wirls, Daniel. 1986. "Reinterpreting the Gender Gap." *Public Opinion Quarterly* 50:316–30.

Wright, Gerald C., and Michael B. Berkman. 1986. "Candidates and Policy in United States Senate Elections." *American Political Science Review* 80:567–90.

Wuthnow, Robert. 1988. *The Restructuring of American Religion*. Princeton: Princeton University Press.

Wuthnow, Robert. 1989. *The Struggle for America's Soul: Evangelicals, Liberals, and Secularism*. Grand Rapids, MI: Wm. B. Eerdmans.

Geoffrey C. Layman is assistant professor of political science, Vanderbilt University, Nashville, TN 37235.

Edward G. Carmines is Rudy Professor of Political Science, Indiana University, Bloomington, IN 47405.

[21]

Religion, State and Society, Vol. 22, No. 1, 1994

Religion and Politics in Postcommunist Russia*

STEPHEN WHITE, IAN McALLISTER and OL'GA KRYSHTANOVSKAYA

The end of communist rule and of the USSR itself brought an end to the restrictions upon freedom of worship with which Russian religious believers had previously been obliged to contend.[1] There had certainly been significant changes in the position of believers and their churches in the late communist period. Mikhail Gorbachev, it emerged, had himself been baptised; his mother was a regular worshipper.[2] An early gesture of some importance was the return of the Danilov monastery in Moscow to the Orthodox Church; refurbished, it played a central role in the millennium of the Orthodox Church in 1988, which brought church and state more closely together than at any time in the recent past. Speaking at this time the patriarch described the communist party programme as 'highly humane' and 'close to the Christian ideal';[3] Gorbachev himself met the patriarch during the celebrations and noted that church and state shared a 'common interest' in protecting public morality.[4] In December 1989 Gorbachev had met the pope, in what was the first encounter of its kind; the following year diplomatic relations were formally established with the Holy See.[5] In 1990 the Communist Party adopted a new set of rules allowing religious believers to join its ranks. Believers, even priests, began to appear in the press and electronic media; the first religious leaders were elected to the Soviet parliament in 1989; a weekly religious newspaper was launched; and a religious presence began to establish itself in charitable and educational work.

The last months of communist rule, in 1990 and 1991, extended the liberties of believers through a series of more formal measures. The Law on Property, approved in 1990, gave the churches full rights of ownership,[6] and a Law on Freedom of Conscience and Religious Organisations, adopted later in the year, affirmed the right of believers to practise and of parents to give their children a religious upbringing. The churches, for their part, had the right to participate in public life and establish their own media outlets, although not to establish or finance their own political parties; and they had the right to establish their own schools and higher educational institutions, and to produce and sell their own literature.[7] The USSR parliament, in one of its last acts, adopted a Declaration of the Rights and Freedoms of the Individual which guaranteed freedom of religious belief and practice, including the right to evangelise and to conduct religious education.[8] The Russian parliament, meeting in November 1991, adoted a more specific set of 'rights and freedoms of the individual and citizen', and in April 1992 they were incorporated into the Russian constitution. The

*Stephen White and Ol'ga Kryshtanovskaya gratefully acknowledge the financial support of the ESRC.

74   *Stephen White* et al.

amendments made clear that the rights and freedoms of the individual were of the 'highest value' in postcommunist Russia, and that the practice or propagation of a religion was an inalienable human right.[9]

Acting within the framework of this legislation, religious groups and believers more generally had come to play a central role in Russian public life in the early 1990s. The patriarch was involved in official ceremonies of state, including the inauguration of the newly elected Russian president in July 1991.[10] There were several religious parties, including the Christian Patriotic Union (founded in 1988), the Christian Democratic Union of Russia (founded in 1989), and the People's Orthodox Movement of Russia, the Russian Christian Democratic Party and the Russian Christian Democratic Movement, all of them founded in 1990.[11] New churches and monasteries were opened; the first services took place in Kremlin cathedrals; the Orthodox Christmas became a public holiday; and the first religious broadcasts went out over state television.[12] By the early 1990s, religious believers had clearly escaped from the marginalisation and even repression of the Soviet period; yet their views were imperfectly articulated by religious parties or the church hierarchies, and there was little satisfactory information about the distribution of religiosity or its association with the policy agenda of a postcommunist system. In this paper we examine both of these issues, using two Russia-wide opinion surveys that were conducted in 1992 (for further details see the Appendix).

Religious Affiliation and Belief in Postcommunist Russia

The evidence certainly suggested that, at least in the early postcommunist years, religion and the churches were held in high public esteem. In a Russia-wide urban survey conducted in early 1992, for example, respondents were asked what feelings were evoked by the word 'Christianity'. As Table 1 shows, for 73 per cent, their response was a positive one; 24 per cent found it difficult to say; and only 3 per cent had a negative reaction. By contrast, 45 per cent were hostile to *perestroika*, 37 per cent to Marxism-Leninism and 33 per cent to socialism; a further 28 per cent were opposed to capitalism and 16 per cent to *glasnost'*. Overall, judged by the number of positive responses relative to negatives ones, Christianity ranked behind only 'freedom' and an

Table 1.   Public opinion on popular symbols[a]

		(Positive minus negative)	Positive	Undecided	Negative	Total
1	Freedom	+73	78	17	5	100
2	Indivisible Russia	+70	75	20	5	100
3	Christianity	+49	73	3	24	100
4	*Glasnost'*	+47	63	21	16	100
5	Capitalism	−3	25	47	28	100
6	Socialism	−8	25	42	33	100
7	Marxism-Leninism	−21	16	46	37	99
8	*Perestroika*	−25	21	33	46	100

[a] The question was 'We often hear the following words. What feelings do they evoke?'
  Figures may not sum to 100 due to rounding. A small number of respondents who did not answer the question are excluded.
Source: December 1992 Political Parties of Russia Survey (*n* = 1,509).

'indivisible Russia'. Positive attitudes towards Christianity, moreover, were distributed evenly across all age groups, genders and regions, and even (though less strikingly) across political persuasions. Those who still regarded themselves as communist party members were almost as favourable to Christianity as they were to socialism (53 per cent were positive, 8 per cent negative); former CPSU members — a very much larger group — were more positive still (71 per cent were favourable towards Christianity and just 5 per cent were hostile).[13]

A broadly positive pattern of responses appeared to reflect a substantial change in public attitudes in the late 1980s. Under Brezhnev, as a recent study has pointed out,[14] religion had become fashionable among intellectuals in large cities and among the creative intelligentsia more generally. But the scale of this process was small, and the polls conducted at the time 'did not show any growth of religious sentiments'. In 1988, for instance, a joint US–Soviet investigation in Moscow suggested that only about 10 per cent of the population believed in God. Between 1988 and 1990, however, the process developed 'at the speed of an avalanche'. According to surveys conducted in 1990, up to 27 per cent of Moscow's population were believers, as compared with 20 per cent who were atheists; the proportions of believers and of atheists were higher in other urban areas, but believers were also more numerous (29 per cent compared with 26 per cent of atheists). By 1991 the proportion of atheists was down in Moscow to 10 per cent, and in other cities to 14 per cent. All of this, for Filatov and Furman, was evidence of a swing of the 'religious pendulum': oriented towards atheism for a long time (from the 1930s to the 1960s), it began a 'slow and barely perceptible' movement towards religion in the 1970s, gained momentum, and 'finally assumed great speed in 1988–1990'.[15]

By 1991, according to surveys in several urban areas, religious belief was strongest among the young and the old, with 39 per cent of those aged over 60 reporting a 'belief in God'. No more than 17 per cent of any age group, however, were convinced atheists, and many more (up to 36 per cent for those aged 51–60) were at least agnostic. In the past, atheism had been inculcated by the more educated and then absorbed by workers. In the late communist years almost exactly the reverse was true: there were fewer believers among those with a higher education than among members of other educational groups, but their interest in religion was greater and they went to church more often. Levels of religiosity were especially high among the cultural intelligentsia (44 per cent believed in God), relatively high among doctors (35 per cent) and teachers (23 per cent), but lower among engineers (16 per cent). There was a certain 'symmetry' in a geographical sense as well, as Moscow and St Petersburg, where the movement towards atheism had begun in the 1920s, were now among the areas with the highest levels of reported religious belief.[16]

There was a still broader welcome to the idea that religious beliefs should play a greater role in Russian or Soviet society. In October 1991, for instance, a Russia-wide survey found that 64 per cent thought the wider diffusion of religious beliefs would be of benefit to the society, and only 6 per cent thought it would be harmful (just two years earlier only 44 per cent had favoured a greater role for religious beliefs, and 8 per cent had opposed it). In the same survey, 47 per cent thought religion could be of benefit to their own lives, with only 3 per cent taking a different view.[17] What, more generally, could religion offer a member of contemporary Russian society? For just over half (52 per cent) it was an appreciation of 'moral norms', and for another 21 per cent (including many atheists) it was an 'understanding of the meaning of life'. A further 9 per cent thought it might help to 'save souls' (there were again some atheists who shared this view); and others thought religion could help to relieve their daily

76   *Stephen White* et al.

anxieties or reconcile them to the prospect of death.[18] More generally, nearly three-quarters were strongly or very strongly of the view that they would 'like [their] life to have more of a spiritual content'.[19]

There was also a broad measure of support, in the late communist years, for a more prominent role for the church in public life. In a 1989 all-union survey, 90 per cent were in favour of the churches taking on a greater role in charitable work; 87 per cent thought the churches should be more directly involved in disaster relief; and very substantial majorities thought the churches should be involved in the conciliation of inter-ethnic disputes (77 per cent) and in the mass media (62 per cent).[20] There was general agreement, in a 1990 survey, that the church still had 'too few rights and freedoms'. There was overwhelming agreement, for a start, that religious literature should be more widely available (83 per cent), and there was substantial agreement (56 per cent in favour, 21 per cent against) that children should be able to receive a religious education provided parents had given their approval. Just over two-thirds (68 per cent) thought it was 'important' that religious leaders took part in the work of the elected soviets, and just over half (52 per cent) thought it 'essential' for religious organisations to become more prominently involved in public life, with a further 33 per cent regarding it as 'acceptable' (only 4 per cent were opposed to the proposition).[21] About half of the Soviet population, by the late 1980s, regarded themselves as religious believers; Christians were the most numerous, with about 41 per cent of the total population, followed by Muslims with 5 per cent and adherents of other faiths with 1.5 per cent. A much higher proportion (68 per cent) had themselves been christened.[22]

The position of religious belief in late communist Russia was nonethless a complex and contradictory one. Levels of identification with the Orthodox Church, for a start, were considerably higher (at 46 per cent) than the proportion of the population that reported a belief in God. There were many more who had no religious feelings or were even atheists but who believed religion made a positive contribution to national life. In a 1990 Russian survey, for example, 61 per cent of nonbelievers were sure religion was needed for national self-consciousness, 31 per cent thought it was needed for state administration, and 27 per cent for democracy.[23] There were substantial variations, as in other societies, between religious affiliation, belief in God and regular worship; and many more were ready to support a greater role for religion in the wider society than in their own lives and in those of their priests and acquaintances.[24] Asked to name the most outstanding personality that had ever lived on earth, in a survey conducted in August 1992, 13 per cent of those who identified themselves as Christians opted for Lenin; Jesus Christ himself came a poor sixth in the survey, after Peter the Great, Sakharov, Pushkin and Tolstoy, and with the same rating (2 per cent) as Stalin.[25] As for a life after death, Muscovites were more inclined to believe that it existed (44 per cent) than to take the opposite view (31 per cent); but of those that responded, 21 per cent thought they would go to heaven, 20 per cent thought they would go to hell and the remaining 59 per cent had no idea.[26]

Religious affiliations were themselves undergoing a substantial change in the late communist period. The 'religious boom', for a start, appeared to be subsiding, with a slight fall in the number of reported believers in the largest cities in which the movement of the 'spiritual pendulum' had previously been most marked.[27] There was a slight fall, similarly, in the proportion who were ready to agree that religion 'played an important part' in their life. This left levels of religiosity at a higher level than before, but lower than comparable levels in other European countries (just 46 per cent, in a 1991 survey, 'never doubted' the existence of God, compared with 87 per cent in the United States and 58 per cent in Britain[28]). There was a considerable decline, more particularly, in support for the Orthodox Church: partly in response to the reports that were emerging of its close relationship with the Soviet government and the KGB, but partly also because of a more general movement towards other religious beliefs including Catholicism or (much more commonly) towards a nondenominational identification with 'Christianity in general'.[29]

An interest in the spiritual, moreover, was by no means confined to orthodox religions.[30] The 1991 survey, already cited, suggested that an interest in the supernatural could — for the youngest age groups — exceed a belief in God or an agnostic or atheist position. Respondents of this kind were 'keenly interested' in Eastern religions, spritualism, parapsychology, UFOs and much more. Levels of belief in the paranormal were particularly high among the better educated: of those with university degrees 73 per cent believed in telepathy and 42 per cent in astrology, and for 27 per cent Oriental wisdom played an 'important part' in their lives. Only 15 per cent, by contrast, believed in God. The result was a category of people who were 'believers and nonbelievers at the same time, combining their formal membership in a Christian church with rapidly changing passions for Hasidism, the *Bhagavad Gita*, Buddhism, or anything else'. Marxism might have lost its meaning, and Orthodox Christianity had ossified, but Russia, it appeared, was 'ahead of the western world and of the whole planet' in the 'amorphous and eclectic' character of its public beliefs. In terms of politics, atheists were more likely to identify with 'socialism' than believers, agnostics or spiritualists; believers, however, were more positively disposed towards 'Marxism' and 'socialism' than agnostics or spiritualists, and they were more predisposed towards order and firm authority than all other groups. Spiritualists, by contrast, were the most likely to reject the October revolution and to support liberal reforms.[31]

Alternative ideologies, including supernatural ones, had certainly become well established by the late communist period. The main television services had begun to incorporate an 'astrological forecast' for the following day, and many newspapers — including the popular trade union daily *Trud* — contained a regular column of advice on such matters. Bookstalls in underground stations reflected the same emphases: there were Nostradamus and Madame Blavatskaya, L. Ron Hubbard and the *Bhagavad Gita*, Sigmund Freud and the Tibetan *Book of the Dead*, as well as *Emmanuelle*, the Marquis de Sade and *How to Become a Millionaire in the CIS*. A large majority (64 per cent), according to the polls, were pleased that newspapers and journals had begun to give a greater degree of attention to mysticism, unorthodox medicine, extrasensory perception and matters of this kind. More than half thought those with a special gift could foretell the future (50 per cent) and cure the sick by means of hypnosis (63 per cent) or television psychotherapy (57 per cent). There were many more believers than disbelievers in omens, telepathy, horoscopes or even flying saucers; and substantial minorities believed in witchcraft (35 per cent) or communication with the dead (11 per cent).[32] If this was a Christian society it was also one that incorporated many older and more diverse beliefs and values.

Forms of Religious Commitment

On the eve of the collapse of communism, then, three broad trends were apparent in Russian approaches to religious beliefs and practices. First, widespread religious feelings existed among the general population, and these feelings would appear to have been in evidence for some considerable time, despite the many official efforts of the state to suppress them.[33] Religious sentiments were reflected not only in a general sense of religiosity, but also in behavioural practices such as church attendance and the

78   *Stephen White* et al.

large proportion of children that were baptised. Secondly, the official churches
enjoyed considerable popular support for their role in society, again in spite of the
official policy that had − at least until the late 1980s − been adopted towards them.
Finally, as in many western societies, the 1970s and 1980s witnessed a large increase in
support for alternative religions and sects, many of them demanding a high level of
commitment from their members. Unlike the pattern in western societies, however, this
growth does not appear to have taken place at the expense of the established
religions.[34]

The international research on the sociology of religion has emphasised three major
dimensions to religious commitment, all of which have different social roots and
different consequences for social and political behaviour.[35] The first and most
obvious is religious affiliation, reflected in whether or not a person is a church
member. Membership is moulded at least in part by parental socialisation, mainly on
the maternal side,[36] and it has a variety of consequences for social and political
behaviour since people interact together within their chosen denominational groups.
The second dimension of commitment is religious behaviour or church attendance. In
contrast to affiliation, behaviour is correlated with socioeconomic status; the higher
the status, the more likely it is that the person will attend church. Like affiliation, there
are a variety of social and political consequences which stem primarily from social
interaction. Thirdly, religious belief is concerned with the fundamental tenets of
religion; although the roots of religious belief are complex, they are most often
associated with sociopersonality factors; they have few, if any, consequences for
politics.

To date, no comprehensive Russian opinion survey has been conducted which deals
with all three of these dimensions of religious commitment in detail, and the limited
inquiries that have been conducted through surveys have involved either a single
question or a small group of questions. To ascertain the extent of religious commitment in postcommunist Russia we use two national opinion surveys, conducted in
February and December 1992 respectively (for further details see the Appendix). Both
the surveys included a question on the frequency of church attendance, but only the
February survey contained a question on affiliation, and only the December survey
included a question on belief. This necessarily limits the analyses that can be undertaken, particularly with regard to the social bases and political consequences of these
dimensions; it does, however, have the advantage of enabling us to check the validity

Table 2.   Religious affiliation and religious belief in Russia[a]

	Feb. 1992		Dec. 1992
Religious affiliation[b]	51	Belief in God	44
No affiliation	21	No belief	28
Difficult to answer	28	Difficult to answer	28
Total	100	Total	100
(*n*)	(2,095)	(*n*)	(1,481)

[a] Excludes 11 respondents in February 1992 and 28 respondents in December 1992
who gave ambiguous responses or who refused to answer.
[b] Namely, Orthodox (43 per cent), believer but unaffiliated (6 per cent), Muslim (2 per cent), and
others (1 per cent).
Source: February 1992 Russian State-Market Survey (*n* = 2,106); December 1992 Political Parties
of Russia Survey (*n* = 1,509)

of the church attendance measure, asked in both surveys within the same calendar year.

The February 1992 survey indicates that just over half of the population report some form of religious affiliation (Table 2). However, this figure hides a large proportion – 28 per cent – who said that the question was 'difficult to answer'. About one in every five Russians has no religious affiliation, a level of secularisation that is broadly in line with that found in contemporary western societies.[37] The second survey shows that slightly fewer respondents, 44 per cent, believe in God; this figure is almost exactly the same as that found in a survey conducted in September 1991, already quoted, which estimated religious believers to be 41 per cent of the population.[38] Once again a significant proportion of the survey respondents found the question difficult to answer. This group is easily identifiable as those who are undecided about their belief; less easy to interpret are those who respond 'difficult to answer' to the question about affiliation, since a person must – at least in principle – be a member of a church or otherwise.

There are several possible explanations for this apparent anomaly in responses to the affiliation question. The first is the ambiguous nature of church membership, particularly in Russian circumstances. For many of the established denominations, such as the Roman Catholic Church, membership is often interpreted as having been baptised or confirmed in childhood, rather than formal membership in a local church. The Protestant churches, like the Russian Orthodox Church, adopt a more formal definition or membership involving enrolment in a local group and at least some frequency of attendance at religious ceremonies and gatherings. Given these differing definitions, it is perhaps not surprising that some respondents are confused by the concept of church membership. A second explanation is that the survey respondents interpreted the question about membership at least partially in terms of belief. The relationship between belief and affiliation in the two surveys and church attendance gives some support to this hypothesis; in each survey the 'difficult to answer' respondents are the most infrequent church attenders, whereas attendance and affiliation are less strongly correlated in Western Europe and the societies that are derived from it.[39] This suggests that Russians regard affiliation and belief as very similar concepts. This may in turn be a legacy of the communist suppression of religion; since various formal and informal sanctions existed to discourage religious

Table 3. Frequency of church attendance[a]

	Feb. 1992		Dec. 1992	
	All	Attenders only	All	Attenders only
Nonattenders	45	–	49	–
Once a week or more	1	2	1	2
Once a month or more	3	6	4	7
Few times a year	13	23	11	21
Very rarely	38	69	36	70
Total	100	100	101	100
(*n*)	(2,106)	(1,161)	(1,485)	(760)

[a] The December 1992 survey had six categories of attendance, which were aggregated as follows: once a week or more (nearly every day, several times a week); once a month or more (several times a month); few times a year (not every month); very rarely (only on certain days, difficult to answer).
Source: as for Table 2.

80   *Stephen White* et al.

involvement, affiliation was often tantamount to belief (representing a positive commitment), whereas in western pluralist societies the two are less strongly associated.[40]

Just over half of Russians attend church, according to our survey, although no more than one in five do so on an infrequent or more frequent basis. Table 3 indicates that, judged across the two surveys, those who attend church once a month or more account for no more than 5 per cent of the total population. Between 11 and 13 per cent say that they attend church several times a year, attendances that would normally coincide with major religious celebrations. Finally, just over one-third report very rare attendance, most of which would be in the form of baptism, funerals and marriages. These are levels of church attendance that are generally below those found in most western countries, and given the widespread nature of religious affiliation and belief in Russia may again reflect the consequences of the communist suppression of religious practices. The results also vary little between the two surveys, suggesting that there has been no change in levels of church attendance between the two surveys, but perhaps more importantly confirming that both surveys are reasonably accurate in the levels of attendance that they report.

The two surveys, taken together, suggest that levels of religious affiliation and belief in Russia are very similar to the levels found in western societies. Moreover, there is some evidence to indicate that many conceive of affiliation and belief in the same way. By contrast, levels of church attendance are lower than would be found in the West, particularly when levels of belief and affiliation are taken into account. The results suggest that the Soviet authorities' sustained attempt to suppress religious beliefs and practices, while they failed to eliminate those beliefs or an informal commitment to a church, did have an impact in reducing levels of church attendance – an overt and public act which is comparatively easy to monitor and control. Although these policies began to be liberalised with the accession of Gorbachev to party office in March 1985, it was not until October 1990 (as we have seen) that religious rights were guaranteed under the law.

The Social Bases and Political Consequences of Religion

The three major dimensions of religious commitment that have been identified in international studies have been shown to have distinctive roots within the societies in question. These social correlates can be traced not only to Marx, who viewed religion in terms of social class, but also to Durkheim and Weber, both on whom viewed religion as one of the fundamental bases of the prevailing social order. Religious affiliation is the easiest to categorise, since it is associated with higher social status, reflecting established social patterns of voluntary group membership. This may, of course, be complicated by the level of commitment demanded by a particular church, but in general the association has been shown to hold across a wide range of countries. Moreover, in recent years the denial of religious affiliation has been most closely associated with the young and with those who have had higher education. Participation in church attendance is usually associated with gender, age and socioeconomic status: women are more diligent attenders than men, as are older people and those in higher status positions. Finally, belief in the supernatural dimension of religion is usually associated with lower educational attainments, with women, and with older people.[41]

To evaluate the social bases of religion in Russia we use a range of variables measuring various social influences to predict affiliation, church attendance, and religious belief (Table 4). The analyses use ordinary least squares regression techniques, which control for a wide range of potentially confounding factors. The equations in Table 4 show two figures, partial regression coefficients (*bs*) and standardised regression coefficients (betas). The partial coefficients reflect the importance of a particular variable in predicting the dimension of religious commitments in question. For example, in the first equation in Table 4, the coefficient of −0.19 suggests that a man is 19 per cent less likely to report affiliation with a church than a woman, net of all the other factors controlled for in the model. The standardised coefficients show the relative weight of the variables in the particular equation. For example, in the first equation, gender (with a beta of −0.24) is about eight times more important in predicting affilation than age (with a beta of 0.03), again net of other factors.

Table 4.   The social bases of religious commitment[a]

	February 1992				December 1992			
	Affiliation		Attendance		Belief		Attendance	
	b	beta	*b*	beta	*b*	beta	*b*	beta
Background								
Gender	−0.19**	−0.24**	−0.07**	−0.15**	−0.24**	−0.29**	−0.08**	−0.14**
Age	0.00	0.03	0.01**	0.10**	−0.00	−0.01	0.00	0.06
Russian	−0.10**	−0.07**	−0.04	−0.05	−0.04	−0.03	0.00	0.00
Lives in European Russia	0.03	0.04	0.05**	0.10**	0.13**	0.15**	0.02	0.04
Socioeconomic status								
Education (elementary)								
Technical secondary	−0.07*	−0.05*	−0.08**	−0.11**	−0.12**	−0.11**	−0.05	−0.07
Technical college	−0.09**	−0.10**	−0.03	−0.06	−0.11**	−0.13**	−0.07*	−0.13*
Higher	−0.12**	−0.14**	−0.02	−0.04	−0.18**	−0.22**	−0.02	−0.03
Income	0.00	0.00	0.00	0.04	−0.00	−0.01	0.00	0.00
Living standards	0.05	0.03	0.04	0.05	0.03	0.01	0.13**	0.10**
Previous CPSU member	−0.12**	−0.11**	−0.05	−0.07*	−0.07**	−0.07**	−0.03	0.04
Constant	0.84		0.10		0.79		0.21	
Adj. *R*-squared	0.09		0.06		0.14		0.03	
(*N*)	(2,033)		(1,087)		(1,481)		(760)	

** Statistically significant at *P*<0.01, * *P*<0.05, both two-tailed.
[a] OLS regression equations predicting the probability of support for religious affiliation, church attendance, and belief in God. See Appendix Table for details of variables and scoring.

The results suggest that there is a high level of consistency in the social correlates across all three dimensions, in both surveys. The directions of the variables that are statistically significant are consistent, although their magnitudes vary. This suggests, once again, that the dimensions of commitment are less differentiated in Russia than in western societies. The predominant effects come from gender and education. As in other societies, women are significantly more likely to be religious than men; the impact varies from belief, where women are 24 per cent more likely to believe in God than men, net of other factors, to 7 and 8 per cent, respectively, for church attendance

82   *Stephen White* et al.

in the February and December surveys. These effects are larger than those found in the liberal democracies, and have been confirmed by other studies.[42] Higher educational attainments are likely to produce lower levels of commitment; for example, someone who has had higher education is 18 per cent less likely to believe in God, compared to someone with elementary education, other things being equal. Other aspects of socioeconomic status have little or no impact, with the exeception of better self-perceived living standards, which increases the probability of church attendance in the December 1992 survey.

Among the other factors that are important, ethnic Russians are less likely to have a religious affiliation than others, but this effect does not reach statistical significance for either of the other three equations. Those living in European Russia, as opposed to Asiatic Russia, are likely to attend more frequently (in the February survey) and to be religious believers. Finally, former CPSU members are less likely to be religious than nonmembers, although given the CPSU's formal policy on religion it is perhaps surprising that the effects are not larger. For example, in the first equation, former CPSU members are 12 per cent less likely to be affiliated to a church than nonmembers, an effect which is similar to attending technical college but less than half as important as gender. The only major exception to the expected patterns is age, which has no significance in three of the equations, and is significant only for church attendance in the February 1992 survey, in the expected direction. This contradicts all of the research on the sociology of religion,[43] although it is largely confirmed by other Russian survey research, which indicates that age and religion are, at best, only modestly associated.[44] The most likely explanation for this would appear to be, once again, official policies towards religion: the elderly, otherwise more likely to attend religious services, became adults at a time when practices of this kind were strongly discouraged; younger citizens, by contrast, are more likely to have experienced the relative liberalisation of the Khruschchev years and afterwards.

The Politics of Religion in Postcommunist Russia

It remains to examine the political consequences of religion in postcommunist Russia. Religion has a range of consequences for political behaviour in modern societies, partly through the historical consequences of religious divisions and cleavages that existed in earlier centuries, but partly also as a consequence of group memberships and shared beliefs and values.[45] In communist Russia, religion was forced to withdraw from any public role, although a small minority of religious activists become highly politicised as a result of their harsh treatment by the regime, particularly under Brezhnev (the churches, as institutions, were less harshly treated). In practice, however, most of those harbouring religious beliefs or values kept them to themselves, and the extent to which these beliefs influenced their political views was likely to be, at best, limited. The collapse of communism, the removal of barriers to religious expression and moves to establish more democratic institutions have all created the preconditions under which religion could have a significant role in shaping political behaviour in postcommunist Russia.

To estimate the extent to which the three dimensions of religious commitment influence political attitudes and political behaviour we examine their association with a range of political opinions, and with voting in the 1991 presidential election. Table 5 identifies nine political attitudes covering foreign affairs and defence, economic attitudes and evaluations of different political systems, and correlates these opinions with belief in God and church attendance using the December 1992 survey. The association between religion and political opinion is decidedly modest, although there are several statistically significant effects. Those who believe in God are more likely to want Russia to remain as a great power, as well as to favour a national-patriotic political system – basic nationalist goals. They are also more likely to support the principle of private property, and to be hostile to communism. Frequent church attenders are also more likely to support private property and to be anticommunist, but again the effects are noticeably weak. Whatever factors serve to shape political opinions in Russia, religion has a comparately minor role.

Table 5.   The influence of religious commitment on political attitudes (correlations)

	(Zero-order correlations)	
	Belief in God	Church attendance
Foreign affairs and defence		
Russia must be great power	0.05*	0.04
Defence capacity better	−0.04	0.02
Supports national self-determination	0.02	0.03
Economic attitudes		
Private property necessary for development	0.05*	0.05*
Gap between rich and poor normal	−0.01	0.03
Admires new rich	0.00	0.03
Evaluations of political systems		
Democracy	−0.01	0.00
Communism	−0.10*	−0.06*
National-patriotic	0.05*	0.03

* Statistically significant at $P < 0.05$ or better, two-tailed.
Source: December 1992 Political Parties of Russia Survey ($n = 1,509$).

The influence of religion on voting in the 1991 presidential election also appears to have been comparatively modest, based on respondents' recall of how they cast their ballots (Table 6). Studies of non-voting have shown that abstention is associated partly with a low sense of political efficacy, which is reflected in low levels of group membership.[46] We would therefore expect those who are affiliated with a church and are regular attenders to be less likely to have abstained in the election. This hypothesis is confirmed by the results in Table 6, though the relationships are modest; those who abstained were more likely not to have a religious affiliation (19 per cent, as against 21 per cent of voters). In the December 1992 survey, 18 per cent of non-voters attended church several times a year or more, compared with 32 per cent of voters. There are also some variations in the support given to the candidates among the religious groups. Those more likely to have attracted the support of the religious include Bakatin and Makashov, while Zhirinovsky and Ryzhkov were more likely to gain support from those with fewer religious inclinations. Once again, however, the magnitude of the effects (and to some extent their consistency across the four indicators) is decidedly modest. Yel'tsin, the winner of the election, appears to have gained no advantage or disadvantage from the religious beliefs and practices of Russian voters.

84   *Stephen White* et al.

Table 6.   Religion and the 1991 presidential election vote[a]

	(All)	Bakatin	Yel'tsin	Zhirinovsky	Makashov	Ryzhkov	Tuleyev	Did not vote
Affiliation								
Affiliation	(51)	53	52	45	61	54	57	48
No affiliation	(21)	22	20	22	23	29	20	19
Difficult to answer	(28)	25	28	33	16	17	23	33
Belief								
Believer	(44)	40	46	48	37	30	44	46
Non-believer	(28)	32	25	28	36	45	27	22
Difficult to answer	(28)	28	28	24	27	25	28	32
Attendance (February 1992)								
Once a week or more	(2)	0	2	0	0	2	0	2
Once a month or more	(6)	14	5	5	6	11	0	7
Few times a year	(23)	32	23	15	24	34	16	19
Very rarely	(69)	54	70	80	70	53	84	72
Attendance (December 1992)								
Once a week or more	(2)	3	3	0	0	3	2	0
Once a month or more	(7)	14	8	8	0	5	4	3
Few times a year	(21)	29	21	31	23	25	22	15
Very rarely	(70)	54	68	61	77	67	72	82

[a] Figures may not sum due to rounding.
Source: as for Table 2.

Conclusion

Earlier studies of the political implications of Russian religion have drawn attention to its authoritarian potential. A survey conducted in September 1991, for instance, found that believers were 'more conservative on every issue', more supportive of the existing order and of political movements at either end of the spectrum that promised to restore it, and generally 'distrustful of change'. Believers, in this survey, did not necessarily support a Marxist-Leninist social order, nor were they more positive than nonbelievers towards socialism or Lenin. They were, however, more strongly supportive of the existing social order, and they were much more favourably oriented towards two rather different symbols of stability — Stalin and the tsar. In addition, believers were less tolerant of political diversity, and more likely to agree with authoritarian solutions to social problems like the treatment of AIDS victims or the banning of 'harmful' literature; they were less favourable towards multiparty politics, and more likely to agree that changes were taking place too quickly.[47] On this basis, and given the more prominent public role that the churches have assumed and the weakness of political parties as a means of articulating a public view, Russian believers might be expected to represent a force of some importance and one that would tend to influence the society towards a greater degree of public order and ideological uniformity, if not Marxism-Leninism as such.

The surveys that we have considered in this paper, both of them comparable in scope with these earlier findings but conducted after the end of communist rule, suggest that a conclusion of this kind is premature and almost certainly misleading. The rapid increase in the proportion of society declaring a religious belief, as we have seen, had slowed down considerably in the early 1990s. By the spring of 1991 levels of religiosity had increased considerably but were still below the levels reported in Western Europe, and still more so the United States. On the evidence of our two 1992 surveys, moreover, levels of religious attendance are considerably below the levels that are typically reported in the pluralist societies of the West. And relatively high proportions are unsure of their belief, and of their religious affiliation: a response that may in part reflect the tradition of Russian Orthodoxy, based as it is upon a large and nebulous community of believers rather than a formalised pattern of individual membership, clear statements of doctrine and sometimes direct financial responsibility. Equally, it may reflect the significant increase in the numbers of 'Christians in general' without a denominational commitment.

Our findings also suggest a rather weaker association between religiosity and political beliefs and actions. For instance, we found at most a modest association between a range of political attitudes and a declared belief in God and church attendance. There were associations, but relatively weak ones, between religious beliefs and a range of broadly 'nationalist' opinions; there were again at best modest associations between religious beliefs and attitudes towards social and economic change, and towards various types of political systems. There was also a very limited association between religious belief and political affiliation, expressed in the form of the Russian presidential elections of June 1991. Believers were somewhat more likely to vote than nonbelievers, but the effects were relatively modest as compared with societies elsewhere, and religious affiliation made little direct contribution to voting choice.

It may seem surprising that religious belief does not appear to have a more direct association with public life in a postcommunist Russia in which the rights of believers, for the first time, are firmly protected by law, and religious leaders are more prominent in politics. One reason may be the absence of an established tradition of religious involvement in public affairs over the past seventy years or more, and the weakness of that tradition in the prerevolutionary period. The failure of at least some members of the hierarchy to articulate an independent and specifically Christian position after 1917, and the evidence of corruption and even KGB infiltration within its ranks, weakened the moral authority of the church leadership even further. The churches have equally had little opportunity to organise themselves as a distinctive voice in public life since it became possible to do so, and they had no organised presence in party politics that they could simply inherit after the end of communist rule (the position was very different in some of the East European countries). Finally, the particular legacy of the CPSU may have placed the churches in some difficulty. As institutions and communities of believers that were broadly supportive of the established order, the churches found themselves – in early postcommunist Russia – in the same position as a Communist Party that also supported the main features of the Soviet system, but that was at the same time a party that had sought for more than 70 years to eliminate religion from public life and one with which the churches could scarcely form a direct association. It may be some time, in these circumstances, before a distinctively Christian perspective is successfully articulated within a society that is still powerfully influenced by its recent communist and sometimes by its remoter prerevolutionary past.

86   *Stephen White* et al.

Appendix: Data and Methods

Data

The analyses rely on two opinion surveys conducted in urban areas in Russia in 1992. The 1992 *Russia Between State and Market Survey* was collected by the Public Opinion Foundation in January and February 1992. The sample was based on the urban population aged 16 years and over resident in the Russian Republic. The survey was conducted using a personal interview; the effective response rate was 82.9 per cent. The total sample size was 2,106; the analyses presented here are restricted to those aged 18 years and over ($n = 2,033$). The 1992 *Political Parties of Russia Survey* was conducted in December 1992 by the Institute of Applied Politics using a personal interview. The sample was based on the urban population aged 18 years and over resident in the Russian Republic. Neither the collectors of the data nor the sponsors are responsible for the analyses and interpretations in this article.

Methods

The analyses rely on cross-tabulation and ordinary least squares regression techniques. The latter method assumes that the relationships between the variables are linear and additive. The variables used in the analyses are scored as follows. Religious affiliation and belief are scored one if the person had an affiliation or a belief, 0.5 if they were unsure or undecided, and zero if they did not. Church attendance is scored as an ordinal variable, from a low of zero (never attends) to a high of one (attends once a week or more). All the independent variables used in Table 4 are scored as zero/one dummy variables, with the exception of age (scored in single years) and family income (hundreds of roubles per month).

Notes and References

[1] For a recent and comprehensive survey see Sabrina Petra Ramet (ed.), *Religious Policy in the Soviet Union* (Cambridge University Press, Cambridge, 1993).
[2] For Gorbachev's baptism see *Izvestiya TsK KPSS*, no. 8, 1989, p. 66; for his mother's church attendance see, for instance, Michael Bourdeaux, *Gorbachev, Glasnost and the Gospel* (Hodder and Stoughton, London, 1990), p. 24.
[3] *Izvestiya*, 9 April 1988, p. 3.
[4] *Pravda*, 30 April 1988, pp. 1–2.
[5] *ibid*, 16 March 1990, p. 6.
[6] See *Vedomosti S"ezda narodnykh deputatov SSSR i Verkhovnogo Soveta SSSR*, no. 11, 1990, art. 164.
[7] For the text see *ibid.*, no. 41, 1990, art. 813; for a discussion and translation see Giovanni Codevilla, 'Commentary on the new Soviet law on freedom of conscience and religious organisations', *Religion in Communist Lands*, vol. 19, nos. 1–2 (Summer 1991), pp. 119–45.
[8] See *Vedomosti. . .* , no. 37, 1991, art. 1083.
[9] *Gosudarstvo i pravo*, no. 4, 1992, pp. 4–8, and (for the constitutional amendments) *Vedomosti S"ezda narodnykh deputatov Rossiiskoi Federatsii i Verkhovnogo Soveta Rossiiskoi Federatsii*, no. 20, 1992, art. 1084.
[10] *Izvestiya*, 10 July 1991, p. 1.
[11] For a discussion of the establishment and objectives of these parties see V. N. Berezovsky *et al.* (eds.), *Rossiya: partii, assotsiatsii, soyuzy, kluby*, vol. 1, part 1 (RAU Press, Moscow, 1991), pp. 22–3. On the Russian Christian Democratic Movement more particularly see Richard Sakwa, 'Christian democracy in Russia', *Religion, State and Society*, vol. 20, no.

2 (1992), pp. 135–68, and the 'Documentary appendix', *ibid.*, pp. 169–200.

[12] *Pravda*, 4 February 1991, p. 6.

[13] For a more general discussion of the survey see Irina Boeva and Viacheslav Shironin, *Russians between State and Market: the Generations Compared* (Centre for the Study of Public Policy, University of Strathclyde, Glasgow, 1992).

[14] S. B. Filatov and D. E. Furman, 'Religiya i politika v massovom soznanii', *Sotsiologicheskiye issledovaniya*, no. 7, 1992, pp. 3–12.

[15] *ibid.*, p. 3.

[16] *ibid.*, pp. 3–4.

[17] *Mir mnenii i mneniya o mire*, no. 1, 1992, p. 7; for the 1989 results see *Obshchestvennoye mneniye v tsifrakh*, no. 5 (October 1989), p. 11.

[18] *Mir mnenii i mneniya o mire*, no. 1, 1992, p. 7.

[19] *RFE/RL Research Report*, vol. 1, no. 41 (16 October 1992), p. 65.

[20] *Obshchestvennoye mneniye v tsifrakh*, no. 5 (October 1989), pp. 12–13.

[21] *ibid.*, no. 12(19) (April 1990), pp. 7–9.

[22] *ibid.*, no. 2(9) (January 1990), p. 12.

[23] Filatov and Furman, 'Religiya i politika...', pp. 4–5.

[24] *Obshchestvennoye mneniye v tsifrakh*, no. 12(19) (April 1990), pp. 6–7.

[25] *Mir mnenii i mneyiya o mire*, no. 12, 1992, p. 8.

[26] *Izvestiya*, 19 October 1992, p. 3.

[27] Filatov and Furman, 'Religiya i politika...', p. 5.

[28] See *The Pulse of Europe*, *Los Angeles Times-Mirror* (Washington DC, mimeo, 1991).

[29] Filatov and Furman, 'Religiya i politika...', pp. 5–6.

[30] See Oxana Antic, 'The spread of modern cults in the USSR', in Ramet (ed.)., *Religious Policy...*, pp. 252–70.

[31] Filatov and Furman, 'Religiya i politika...', pp. 5–12.

[32] *Obshchestvennoye mneniye v tsifrakh*, no. 10, 1990, pp. 6–7.

[33] For a discussion of state religious policies in the USSR and elsewhere in the communist world see, for instance, Patrick Michel, *Politics and Religion in Eastern Europe* (Polity, Cambridge, 1991); Robert F. Millar and T. H. Rigby (eds.), *Religion and Politics in Communist States* (Australian National University, Canberra, 1986); and Ramet (ed.), *Religious Policy...*

[34] See for instance Eileen Barker, *New Religious Movements: a Practical Introduction* (HMSO, London, 1989).

[35] For reviews, see: Gerhard Lenski, *The Religious Factor* (Doubleday, New York: 1961), pp. 17–23; N. J. Demerath, *Social Class and American Protestantism* (Rand McNally, Chicago, 1965), pp. 10–14; Charles Y. Glock and Rodney Stark, *American Piety: The Nature of Religious Commitment* (University of California Press, Berkeley, 1968), pp. 16–18; and Michael Argyle and Benjamin Beit-Hallahmi, *The Social Psychology of Religion* (Routledge and Kegan Paul, London, 1975).

[36] See, for example, Ian McAllister, 'Religious change and secularization: the transmission of religious values in Australia', *Sociological Analysis*, vol. 49 (1988), pp. 249–63.

[37] See Michael Hogan, 'Australian secularists: the disavowal of religious allegiance', *Journal for the Scientific Study of Religion*, vol. 18 (1979), pp. 390–404; and McAllister, 'Religious change and secularization...'.

[38] See Mark Rhodes, 'Religious believers in Russia', *RFE/RL Research Report*, vol. 1, no. 14 (3 April 1992), pp. 60–4.

[39] See, for instance, Glock and Stark, *American Piety...*

[40] A third possible explanation might be that respondents were afraid to give a definitive response to the affiliation question in the interview. However, this would appear unlikely, since the respondents had exhibited no similar qualms on other or more sensitive questions, such as past voting behaviour, past and present CPSU membership, and income and foreign currency dealings.

[41] For reviews of these social factors see Lenski, *The Religious Factor*; Argyle and Beit-

88   *Stephen White* et al.

Hallahmi, *The Social Psychology of Religion*; Michael Hill, *A Sociology of Religion* (Heinemann, London, 1973); and Barbara Hargrove, *The Sociology of Religion* (AHM Publishing, Arlington IL, 1979), pp. 135ff.

42   For comparative data and explanations, see David de Vaus and Ian McAllister, 'Gender differences in religion: a review of the structural location theory', *American Sociological Review*, vol. 52 (1987), pp. 472–81. An assessment of the Russian evidence is provided in John Anderson, 'Out of the kitchen, out of the temple: religion, atheism and women in the Soviet Union', in Ramet, *Religious Policy...*, pp. 206–28.

43   See, for instance, Dan Blazer and Erdman Palmore, 'Religion and ageing in a longitudinal panel', *Gerontologist*, vol. 16 (1976), p. 84; C. Ray Wingrove and Jon Alston, 'A cohort analysis of church attendance, 1939–69', *Social Forces*, vol. 53 (1974), p. 330.

44   For example, a 1991 survey of residents in major cities found that 36 per cent of those aged 18–20 believed in God, compared with 39 per cent of those aged 60 or over. The range of difference was only 15 points. See Filatov and Furman, 'Religiya i politika...', p. 4, Rhodes, 'Religious believers...', shows a large age variation, although it is still only in the region of 20 percentage points (p. 62).

45   See Michael Parenti, 'Political values and religious culture: Jews, Catholics and Protestants', *Journal for the Scientific Study of Religion*, vol. 6 (1967), pp. 259–69; Guy Michelate and Michael Simon, 'Religion, class and politics', *Comparative Political Studies*, vol. 10 (1977), pp. 159–86.

46   See Raymond E. Wolfinger and Steven J. Rosenstone, *Who Votes?* (Yale University Press, New Haven CT, 1980).

47   See Rhodes, 'Religious believers in Russia'.

Part IV
Religion, Public Policy
and the Politics of Identity

[22]

On religion and public policy: Does Catholicism make a difference?

FRANCIS G. CASTLES
Public Policy Program, Australian National University, Canberra, Australia

Abstract. This paper suggests that differences in religious adherence and/or in degrees of secularization between advanced nations may be as relevant to understanding cross-national variance in a wide range of public policy outcomes as the impact of socio-economic and political factors. The *prima facie* evidence for such a thesis is demonstrated in areas as diverse as welfare expenditure, family policy and labour market policy outcomes, and is shown to have a particular salience wherever gender-related outcomes are at issue. On the basis of this evidence, it is suggested that, in policy outcome terms at least, it is possible to identify a distinctive Catholic family of nations consisting of a grouping of core Western European and Southern European countries.

Introduction

The modern social sciences have been much obsessed with an exploration of the impact of the twin revolutions marking the advent of economic and political modernity. Sociology has taken as its theme the unfolding of the processes of socio-economic transformation initiated by the industrial revolution and political science has embraced as its essence the democratic class struggle first manifested in the French Revolution. Nowhere has this obsession been more dramatically evident than in the body of research which is generally described as comparative public policy analysis. This research, which takes as its topic the variety of outcomes of state intervention in different countries, and which has been much the fastest growing branch of comparative studies in the social sciences in recent decades, is a child of both sociology and political science. In consequence, it has been an area of profound contestation, with initial hegemonic claims that only industrialization or politics mattered gradually giving way to an uneasy truce built on the basis of multivariate findings which showed that both could matter simultaneously.

Although I have been as involved as anyone in these debates on the character of the economic, social and political forces impelling public policy development in Western democracies, my intention in this paper is not to take that debate further. Rather my purpose is to suggest that the very focus on processes of economic and political modernization may have diverted our attention away from a source of differentiation of national public policy outcomes at least as important as socio-economic transformation and political

20

struggle. That source of differentiation is religious belief, and my argument is that the great divide between Catholic and Protestant Christendom, the product of revolutionary change long predating the French and industrial revolutions, remains an important factor shaping outcomes across a wide range of policy arenas, including social policy, family policy and labour market policy.

To avoid misunderstanding, I wish to make several things clear. First, I am not trying to assert that religious differences matter and socio-economic and political ones do not. The point being argued in this paper is that religion may well make a difference in addition to the already demonstrated impact of these factors.

Second, I am not seeking to elaborate a definitive theory of how religion impacts on policy. In what follows, my objective is to show a *prima facie* linkage between measures of Catholic adherence and a wide variety of policy outcomes without any detailed account of the actors involved in the policy-process or the channels through which policy outcomes are determined. Indeed, the only firm conclusion on these matters which I would venture on the basis of the analysis here is that no single account is likely to be adequate and that actors and channels are likely to be very diverse and quite possibly policy area specific. Religious beliefs may influence policy because individuals with such beliefs behave differently from those without them, because interest groups and parties may be formed to promote such beliefs, because the views of those who are influential in policy-making may be shaped by such beliefs, or even, in quasi-corporatist mode, because the state delegates to the Church the public regulation of certain spheres of social relations. Channels may involve the aggregation of individual decisions, the drafting of laws and the shaping of institutional forms – these latter, possibly, with very long-term effects, so that the impact of the religious cleavage is an historically mediated rather than a contemporary phenomenon.

Third, although I ask the question 'Does Catholicism make a difference?', I do not wish it to be thought that I am necessarily ascribing an uniquely causal role to a particular religious faith. In the context of a study more concerned with policy differences than with the character of religious beliefs, it is wise to leave such issues open. Partly, that is because, leaving the Japanese case aside, the cross-national variance associated with measures of Catholic adherence is more or less the mirror image of the strength of the combined Protestant denominations, and, to the extent that this is so, the primary role of one or the other faith in promoting diverse beliefs, doctrines and practices can only be a matter of opinion. Partly, and perhaps more fundamentally, caution as to the characterization of ultimate causes is justified by the fact that at least a part of the difference between Catholic and Protestant nations may well be attributable to a general post-war tendency to greater secularization which can be argued to have proceeded rather more rapidly in the nations where Protestantism has been strongest.[1] Moreover, secularization may take many forms, from a general decline in traditional religious beliefs to an organized challenge to a specific subset of such beliefs, such as that represented by the post-war feminist movement.[2] Given these different possibilities of interpretation, the question 'Does Catholicism make a difference?' simply becomes our shorthand for a wish to characterize the policy consequences of a cleavage in the belief structures of contemporary societies, which, whatever its present implications, clearly does owe its origins to what was once the most fundamental religious divide in Western Christendom. More definitive conclusions – both general and related to specific policy areas – will require more research and more researchers.

Finally, I do not wish it to be thought that I am claiming any degree of originality in asserting a link between religious variance and public policy outcomes. Not only has there been some theoretical speculation on the possibility of a link between types of Christian belief and the character of welfare state development in different nations (see Heidenheimer, 1983), but also, as we shall see in the next section, the idea that social security outcomes may be different in countries in which Catholicism is strong has been around for some time and is now well on the way to being an established finding. Rather the contribution I hope to make is in demonstrating the breadth of the policy impact of the religious factor. Because processes of socio-economic transformation and political struggle have been seen as fundamental, it has been too easy to dismiss the finding of a linkage between religious difference and a particular type of policy outcome as interesting, but of no wider relevance. For instance, in research I have undertaken in recent years, I have pointed to strong relationships between measures of Catholic adherence and a range of policy outcomes, including social security expenditure (Castles 1990, 1993a), educational expenditure (Castles 1989), divorce rates and divorce laws (Castles & Flood 1991), and unemployment rates (Castles & Mumford 1992). Moreover, it is apparent that policy variations in these and other areas are commonly mediated through gender-specific outcomes (for relevant data, see Norris 1987) stemming from particular conceptions of rights and family roles which are characteristic of societies in which the influence of Catholicism is strong. I no longer see these findings as fortuitous, but rather as evidence of the operation of a factor as important to the determination of the broad pattern of cross-national policy outcomes as any hitherto considered in the literature.

Rather, it now seems to me that the evidence points to the existence of what may be described as a Catholic family of nations quite distinctive in the character of its policy outcomes from other groups of Western democratic nations. The notion of a family of nations suggests the possibility that groups of nations may have common policy outcomes in consequence of shared historical and cultural attributes. Religion is but one possible basis of such commonality. Others may include the diffusion of ideas through a common language, the imposition of common institutions and laws by an imperial power and the coming together of nations for purposes of mutual protection and economic advantage in such arrangements as the European Community

22

and the European Monetary System.[3] In a recent research project, the families of nations concept has been shown to explain observed similarities in outcomes across a wide range of policy areas in English-speaking, German-speaking and Scandinavian nations (see Castles 1993b). Here, I seek to demonstrate that religious beliefs characteristic of the Catholic faith have had a major influence in shaping the policy experience of a grouping of core Western European and Southern European nations.

A Catholic world of welfare?

A good starting point for discussing the possible impact of religious belief on modern policy outcomes is to be found in Esping-Andersen's recent work on social policy development, which distinguishes diverse liberal, socialist and conservative 'worlds of welfare' on the basis of the characteristics of the policy instruments through which they deliver social policy outcomes (Esping-Andersen 1990). In this account, the liberal, socialist and conservative worlds of welfare correspond almost precisely with the English-speaking, Scandinavian and core Western European nations, with the five most conservative nations being Austria, Belgium, France, Germany and Italy, all of them in the vanguard of social security effort for much of the post-war era.

For Esping-Andersen the defining characteristics of the conservative world are the corporatism and etatism manifested by these countries' schemes of social policy provision. Corporatism betokens a high degree of status segregation in the organisation of social policy, operationally defined in terms of the substantial number of occupationally distinct social insurance schemes. Etatism denotes a strong bias in the welfare system in favour of state employees, which is demonstrated by the generosity of welfare schemes directed to this class of employee. Esping-Andersen explicitly links these features of conservative welfare systems to the teaching of the Catholic Church in the Encyclicals *Rerum Novarum* (1891) and *Quadrogesimo Anno* (1931), setting out the Church's opposition to both capitalist and socialist beliefs and advancing the principle of subsidiarity as the basis for state intervention in the field of welfare.

Later work by one of Esping-Andersen's students (van Kersbergen 1991, 1992) articulates in greater detail why we might expect to encounter a distinctive Catholic world of welfare or, rather, a world which he identifies as 'social capitalism'. First, subsidiarity directly implies a corporatist approach, since the state is not enjoined to treat all equally, but to work through existing social groups. Of such groupings, the family has doctrinal primacy, and is regarded as the fundamental unit of society in preference to the individual. Nor is equality the watchword of family life, but rather an organic unity and gender-specific division of labour under the leadership of the husband. The vital welfare issue in this conception is not one of citizenship, a concept pertaining to the individual, but of treating existing social groups according to their social worth. Second, subsidiarity involves a reluctance to hand over power to the state, and hence a preference for what is a further highly distinctive feature of Esping-Andersen's conservative type; namely, the funding of social insurance schemes through employer and employee contributions rather than through direct taxation.[4] Third, a doctrine of natural inequality reinforces the notion of status, but is counter-posed by the idea of the just wage, which leads to the belief that "benefits for adult male employees . . . ought to be characterized by a capacity to replace the family income at the level of the present status" (van Kersbergen 1992: 21). In this last feature of Catholic doctrine, it is possible to locate a potent force leading to gender-specific welfare outcomes, whilst, simultaneously, conducive to the high levels of social spending manifested in the conservative nations.

An interesting test of the robustness of the notion of a Catholic world of welfare is to see whether the concept 'travels' (Sartori 1970) to predominantly Catholic nations outside the universe of discourse on which Esping-Andersen's and van Kerbergen's conclusions are based. In a recent paper on 'Social Security in Southern Europe' (Castles 1993a), I have undertaken such a task by exploring whether the social security expenditure performance of Greece,[5] Portugal and Spain in 1960 and 1990 could be illuminated by considering these countries as members of a Catholic family of nations.

In respect of social security, the *prima facie* evidence for the attribution of a Catholic family of nations including the nations of Southern Europe is, at first sight, somewhat mixed. On the one hand, there is much in the picture of a conservative world of welfare which is redolent of the characteristics of social provision in Southern Europe. Fragmented insurance schemes catering for different social groupings on the basis of status and a strong reliance on insurance contributions are characteristic features of each of these nation's welfare systems (see OECD 1992a), and this is just as true of Greece (see Kremalis & Yfantopoulos 1992) as of the Iberian Roman Catholic nations. On the other hand, Southern European social security expenditure levels appear to be very different from those of nations of the conservative type. In 1960, Greece, Portugal and Spain were all close to the bottom of the OECD social security expenditure distribution (OECD 1992b), whereas the countries identified as conservative by Esping-Andersen and as nations of 'social capitalism' by van Kersbergen were all amongst the OECD social security leaders. By 1990, the Southern European nations had all experienced a degree of welfare catch-up and were now at or near the middle of an OECD distribution which the conservative nations still headed.

In order to test the Catholic hypothesis, it is necessary to devise an operational definition of membership of the Catholic family of nations. In the welfare state literature, the obvious candidate for such a measure is the strength of Catholic or Christian Democratic parties. This was the measure used by Wilensky (1981) in the earliest research demonstrating a linkage between Catholicism and social security expenditure effort. It is also the operational definition preferred by van Kersbergen, who uses the term 'Chris-

24

tian Democratic welfare state' as an alternative formulation for 'social capitalism' (van Kersbergen 1992).

I have always found this argument concerning the role of Christian parties unconvincing, since it denies the power of the Church in predominantly Catholic societies, such as France and Ireland, to influence politicians of all parties through its role as an elite pressure group and as a force shaping the demands of the electorate at the mass level. Clearly, too, it would be absurd to deny that the Church had a major policy-shaping role in the authoritarian conservative regimes of Southern Europe, despite those countries' lack of democratic party competition. Such a view implies, for instance, that Opus Dei had no influence on policy outcomes in Franco's Spain. My view is not that the Church is unable to exercise influence through Christian parties, but rather that, in predominantly Catholic societies where such parties do not exist, it may have avenues of influence open to it which are equally effective.

Starting from this premise, I adopt a very simple operationalization of potential[6] Catholic policy influence by counting as Catholic polities all those which have a predominantly Catholic population (75 percent or more of the population baptized into the Church – for data, see Barrett 1982) or which have experienced a major Christian Democratic presence (i.e., at a minimum, a role pivotal to majority coalition formation) in government for the entire the ten year period proceeding the expenditure point to be analysed. On this criteria, the Catholic family of nations in 1960 consisted of Germany, France, Italy, Austria, Belgium, Greece, Ireland, Luxembourg, the Netherlands, Portugal and Spain. In 1990, Germany failed to satisfy the Christian party cut-off criterion, but all the other nations specified still qualified as members of the grouping.

My test of the Catholic hypothesis consists of a simple multivariate model in which social security transfers expenditure as a percentage of GDP is seen as a function of membership of the Catholic family of nations and of real GDP per capita (data from Summers & Heston 1991), the latter variable standing as a proxy for the very considerable variation in socio-economic development between the 22 OECD nations for which we have social security data (OECD 1992a). Results for 1960 and 1990 are shown in Tables 1 and 2.

Clearly, these models are incomplete explanations of expenditure variation, but, nevertheless, they do demonstrate the very strong impact of Catholicism on social policy outcomes.[7] In 1960, Catholic nations had social security expenditure levels more than four percentage points of GDP higher than non-Catholic nations and, in 1990, the difference was a massive nine percentage points. Since estimations of the same equations excluding the three Southern European nations produce coefficients for the Catholic variable of comparable magnitude (5.02 for 1960; 8.94 for 1990), we may also reasonably conclude that these nations manifest important features in common with the core conservative countries of Western Europe.[8] In the earlier period, socio-economic modernization was co-equal in importance to the

25

Table 1. 1960 OECD transfers

Variable	Coefficient	t-statistic
Intercept	−6.16	
Catholic	4.78	4.36
Log Real GDP	14.61	4.26
Adj R^2	0.52	

Table 2. 1990 OECD transfers

Variable	Coefficient	t-statistic
Intercept	−12.21	
Catholic	9.11	4.25
Log Real GDP	21.64	2.55
Adj R^2	0.43	

religious variable; by 1990, although still statistically significant, the real GDP effect had declined appreciably.

Whilst these effects are dramatic enough, the really fascinating point arises from the contrast between the findings for the multivariate model of 1960 expenditure levels and the bivariate relationships between expenditure and Catholicism and between expenditure and real GDP for the same period. In fact, neither of these bivariate relationships is statistically significant at the 0.05 level, whereas the multivariate findings for both variables are significant at the 0.01 level. In other words, each of these variables masks the impact of the other and the very substantial impact of each can only be assessed by looking at both in conjunction. By 1990, this situation is modified. Catholicism continues to mask the impact of GDP, when looking at the bivariate relationship between real GDP and expenditure in isolation, but the reverse no longer applies, and the massive substantive impact of Catholicism on expenditure is apparent even from the simple association between the two variables.

There is enough in these findings to vindicate amply the conclusion that, in respect of social security spending at least, the notion of a Catholic world of welfare is a reality. What Esping-Andersen has argued in terms of systematic differences in the character of the instruments of social provision, and van Kersbergen (1991) has illustrated in terms of prevalent patterns of expenditure, I have further demonstrated in terms of the extent of expenditure in the widest available sample of advanced first world nations. Moreover, the existence of a masked interaction between Catholicism and real GDP makes it clear that it is necessary to take account of the religious influence on expenditure in order to comprehend other processes at work in the determination of policy outcomes. Contrary to the view of the one-time sociological orthodoxy that 'economic growth makes countries with contrast-

26

ing cultural and political traditions more alike in their strategy for constructing the floor below which no one sinks' (Wilensky 1975: 27), cultural differences, and the families of nations they define, remain the parameters that
define social security outcomes. In this area of policy at least, the impact of
religion is not just an interesting facet of a larger story, but is the vital key
to understanding the story as a whole.

Religion, rights and family policy

If the linkage between Catholicism and social security is now an established
finding of the comparative literature, the notion of a link between family
policy and religion is a commonplace of informed commentary, even if,
because comparative family policy research is in its infancy, and because
religion is an unfashionable variable, there is little in the comparative public
policy literature which bears strong witness to such a relationship. Religion
obviously ought to matter in the areas of marriage, the family, gender-related
issues generally and the rights of women in particular, if only because the
Christian churches have historically taken these issues so very seriously.
Moreover, one needs to think only of such issues as contraception, abortion,
and divorce, and the strong stance taken by the Catholic Church against law
reform in these areas in such countries as Ireland and Italy, to understand
the contemporary basis for the commonplace view.

Harking back to earlier comments concerning problems in characterizing
the nature of the causal role attributed to religious faith, there is, however,
more than a little question about how religion matters in this sphere of family
and gender-related issues. On the one hand, it is possible to argue that,
traditionally, the Protestant denominations have been as opposed to acts
interpreted as destructive of family life as has the Catholic Church and,
hence, that emergent cross-national differences coincident with the religious
cleavage must be attributable to the greater degree of secularization in those
nations in which the Protestant faith was once dominant,On the other hand,
in respect of certain gender-related rights, it seems arguable that differences
between Catholic and Protestant nations emerged appreciably before secularization, in the sense of declining religiosity, became anything like as
significant as it now is. This appears to be true, for instance, of the extension
of the female suffrage prior to 1917[9] and, still more so, of the rights of
children prior to World War II.[10] In both instances, the granting of rights
before these dates was exclusively a phenomenon of nations in which Protestantism was the dominant Christian faith.[11]

Rights are, of course, frequently legally codified, and, with only a few
exceptions (see, in particular, Kamerman & Kahn 1978), it has been the sub-
discipline of comparative law which has provided us with what research there
has been on cross-national variance in the area of family policy and the

extension of rights more generally. In this field of scholarship, the concern has been not so much with the outcomes of policy, but rather with a classification of legal systems. A traditional basis of differentiation has been between Anglo-American, Nordic and Romano-Germanic legal systems, and recent research by Glendon (1917) has shown that these distinctions remain highly relevant to both divorce and abortion legislation, with contemporary Romano-Germanic law on both issues being far more restrictive than either Anglo-American or Nordic law. Whilst the notion of families of nations may be new to the social sciences disciplines informing comparative public policy analysis, such a conception has always been to the forefront in the legal disciplines.

Clearly, Glendon's classification of types of legal system is relevant to the theme of this paper, since the divide between Romano-Germanic systems and the rest is virtually identical to the distinction between Catholic and Protestant Christendom.[12] However, from a public policy perspective, the finding is only weak evidence for the impact of religion on policy outcomes. In order firmly to establish a linkage between outcomes (the incidence of divorce or abortion) and Catholicism, it is necessary to ask, first, whether differences in the character of the law actually result in differences in outcomes and, second, whether the seeming correspondence between religious adherence and the character of the law might not be a spurious finding based on a correspondence of socio-economic modernization and religious belief.

These are issues examined in recent research I have undertaken with a colleague on the determinants of divorce rates in advanced Western nations (Castles & Flood 1991).The first and major task of that research was to use a wide range of historical and contemporary sources to establish a scale measuring the liberality of Western divorce laws both before and after the major series of divorce law reforms which took place in many of these countries in the course of the 1960s and the early 1970s. This scaling was then compared with divorce outcomes in 16 countries,[13] with the liberality of divorce law in 1960 being used as a predictor of the average incidence of divorce in the period 1961–68 and the liberality of the law in 1976 serving as a predictor of average divorce rates from 1976–83. Data for divorce rates were measured as divorces per thousand of the population and come from the United Nations Demographic Yearbook. The two major exclusions from the countries normally included in OECD policy comparisons were Japan, on grounds of non-Christian culture, and the USA. This latter country is a massive outlier, for which there exists a very substantial literature explaining exceptionally high divorce rates in terms of features unique to that country, most of them related to an equally exceptional degree of individualism that is, perhaps, a concomitant of that country's historical origins in Protestant fundamentalism (see, for instance, Rheinstein 1972; Weiss 1975; Phillips 1988). Unfortunately, in this research, Greece, Spain and Portugal had to be excluded on grounds of missing data. One must, however, presume that

28

the low divorce rates of the Southern European countries – particularly in Portugal and Spain – would serve to reinforce any findings supportive of a Catholic family of nations interpretation.

The findings suggest an extremely strong link between the liberality of the law and the incidence of divorce. For the 1961–68 divorce rate the correlation is 0.85 and for 1976–83 it is 0.91. The association between the provisions of the law and outcomes is quite clear, but does not prove the causal impact of religion. To demonstrate that, we need to show that the apparent link between legal families of nations and religious belief is not an artifact of other factors, a possibility very strongly suggested by the views of leading theorists of comparative law, such as Rheinstein (1970), who suggest that the law is ultimately a reflection of its social context and is either reinterpreted or swept away where it remains too long incongruent with that context.

Apart from Catholicism, the factors we use to account for variation in the liberality of the law include non-agricultural employment as a percentage of total employment (OECD 1992b) used as a proxy for socio-economic modernisation and female labour force participation (OECD 1992b) used as a proxy for female emancipation (for a discussion of the impact of these factors, see Phillips 1988; Price & McKenry 1988, Halem 1980).[14] In this study, where the ultimate object of concern is the incidence of divorce rather than the character of the law regulating its availability, the potential influence of Catholicism is measured as the percentage of Catholics in the population (Barrett 1982). This is, arguably, a more appropriate measure than the earlier Catholic family of nations variable for assessing the determinants of a decision – whether or not to seek legal termination of a marriage – which is made by individuals rather than by governments.[15]

Findings for the two periods are reported in Tables 3 and 4. The results for 1960 show that female labour force participation was a minor positive influence on the liberality of the law and that Catholicism had a much more substantial negative impact. Somewhat surprisingly, and totally contrary to prevalent sociological and comparative law theorizing, socio-economic modernization had no discernible impact. However, this was no longer the case in 1976, when the size of the non-agricultural labour force had as strong an impact as Catholicism and female labour force participation had ceased to be a significant predictor of divorce outcomes.

The unexpected absence of a socio-economic effect in 1960 is related to the fact that, in the period prior to the major divorce law reforms of the 1960s, the socio-economically advanced Anglo-American nations (other than the United States) had relatively low divorce rates. This finding diverges from the later strong coincidence of high divorce rates with Anglo-American and Nordic legal systems noted by Glendon (1987). It is, however, compatible with a Catholic family of nations interpretation, since the Anglo-American nations (again excepting the United States) inherited from the United Kingdom a divorce law which had its immediate origins many centuries earlier in Catholic Canon Law, prohibiting divorce on all grounds bar those of adultery

Table 3. 1960 liberal divorce law

Variable	Coefficient	t-statistic
Intercept	0.74	
Catholic	−0.02	3.89
Female labour force	0.04	2.13
Non-agricultural	0.02	0.07
Adj R^2	0.60	

Table 4. 1976 liberal divorce law

Variable	Coefficient	t-statistic
Intercept	−5.26	
Catholic	−0.02	4.37
Female labour force	−0.00	0.13
Non-agricultural	0.09	4.45
Adj R^2	0.82	

(see Kitchin 1912: 231–33; Phillips 1988: 436). As a result, in 1960, Australia, Canada (and particularly Quebec), Ireland, England and, to a lesser extent, New Zealand had as restrictive divorce laws as any then in force in Western Europe.

Indeed, the conclusion that can be derived from this study of divorce rates is very much the same as that of the research on the social security performance of the Southern European nations: that a families of nations approach is the crucial key to understanding the emerging pattern of policy outcomes in the latter half of the twentieth century. In the case of divorce, legal families of nations shaped by the historical experience of the Reformation and later the French Revolution were sufficiently strong to hold back the forces of socio-economic modernization until the 1960s. Moreover, just as was true of the trajectory of social security transformation in the post-war decades, the vast changes in post-war divorce legislation did nothing to undermine cultural divisions based on religious differences. Indeed, the substantial transformation of this period was from laws which reflected the religious cleavages of centuries past to laws which better reflected the existence of contemporary cultural divisions. Such an interpretation suggests that religion has been, and continues to be, the dominant factor impacting on policy outcomes in at least one important sphere of family policy.

Religion and the labour market

The sphere of labour market policy is, of course, the province of economics, and economics does not merely neglect the role of social factors such as

30

religion, but generally treats them as by definition irrelevant. Sociologically speaking that is absurd, for at least one major parameter of labour market behaviour, the desire to participate in gainful employment, is clearly in some measure, determined by attitudinal variables. Moreover, since those attitudinal variables are manifestly shaped by norms of behaviour concerning the domestic division of labour and appropriate codes of family life, there is every reason, given the conclusions of our previous analysis, to suspect that religious differences might play a major role.

As previously noted, the Catholic Church still seeks to uphold a distinct set of doctrines concerning the family, and those doctrines have traditionally included a belief that women's primary focus of activity should be in the home and not in the workplace. However, it is also true that the vast majority of Protestant denominations at one time emphasized a similar gender segregation, and that religiosity irrespective of denomination is frequently associated with traditional beliefs concerning the appropriate domestic division of labour. This being so, it would appear that any impact of the religious cleavage on labour market behaviour is likely, *prima facie*, to reflect a greater pace of secularization in the Protestant nations in the post-war period. In consequence, one might expect that, in recent decades, the marked discrepancy between male and female levels of labour supply, which is a feature of all advanced nations, would have become less pronounced amongst Protestant than amongst Catholic populations.

The most straight-forward explanation of the emergence of such a religiously-based difference is a simple demographic one, with an increasingly greater tendency in Protestant than in Catholic countries for older cohorts of women to return to the labour market after the birth of children.[16] Moreover, it is quite possible that such an increased propensity for women to seek employment in Protestant countries could also impact on other aspects of labour market behaviour. A higher level of labour supply induced by a decline in traditional family values might well lead to demands on politicians to expand state employment and to pressures on employers to provide jobs more suited to women's needs.

However, despite the obviousness of such hypotheses, and a broad awareness of very substantial differences in female participation between countries, there has been almost no systematic research into the determinants of cross-national variation in labour market outcomes other than unemployment. Indeed, as far as I am aware, the only major cross-national study of gendered labour markets has been undertaken by Manfred Schmidt as his contribution to the families of nations project (Schmidt 1993). His analysis confirms that the Catholic/Protestant cleavage is one of the more important factors influencing change in female labour force participation in the post-war decades.

In the context of an exploratory study such as this, it is not possible to provide an in-depth analysis of the determinants of labour market policy. Here, my intention is simply to show that a rather convincing case can be

Table 5. Catholicism and 1960 labour market outcomes

Variable	Coefficient × 75	Correlation	t-value	(cases)
Male labour force	−0.15	−0.03	0.1	(22)
Female labour force	−9.83	−0.46	2.3	(22)
Total labour force	−5.63	−0.55	2.9	(22)
Male employment	−2.55	−0.28	1.2	(18)
Female employment	−9.53	−0.47	2.1	(18)
Total employment	−6.52	−0.59	3.2	(22)
Male unemployment	1.80	0.46	2.1	(18)
Female unemployment	2.03	0.46	2.0	(18)
Unemployment	1.65	0.45	2.1	(19)

Table 6. Catholicism and 1985 labour market outcomes

Variable	Coefficient × 75	Correlation	t-value	(cases)
Male labour force	−5.10	−0.53	2.8	(22)
Female labour force	−19.58	−0.81	6.2	(22)
Total labour force	−12.52	−0.83	6.6	(22)
Male employment	−8.30	−0.58	3.0	(20)
Female employment	−21.83	−0.82	6.0	(20)
Total employment	−14.92	−0.79	5.8	(22)
Male unemployment	4.05	0.42	2.0	(20)
Female unemployment	7.65	0.65	3.7	(20)
Unemployment	5.40	0.55	2.8	(20)

made for a strong – and over time, increasingly strong – association between religion and a much wider range of labour market outcomes than that analysed in Schmidt's research. Tables 5 and 6 below report the bivariate relationships between Catholicism, measured again by the percentage of adherents in the population, and labour force participation and employment, both measured as a percentage of the population from 15 to 64, and unemployment as a percentage of the total labour force. In each case, and necessarily so in an account where the hypotheticai causal mechanism is gender-specific, the analysis is presented separately for males and females, as well as being aggregated in terms of total labour supply, employment and unemployment. All the labour force data are from (or calculated from) OECD 1992b and the data-set includes all the OECD nations other than New Zealand and Turkey. There are, however, some missing data for particular countries in respect of particular variables, with the relevant number of cases for each variable shown in parentheses in the final columns of Tables 5 and 6.

Apart from correlation coefficients, T-statistics and numbers of cases, these tables each have a column which reports unstandardized regression coefficients multiplied by 75, the cut-off percentage of Catholic adherence qualifying a country as a member of the Catholic family of nations in our earlier discussion of social security outcomes. Since a number of the Protest-

32

ant nations of Northern Europe and Japan have virtually no Catholic population, this figure may be interpreted as the percentage points difference in
labour market performance of nations at opposite extremes in terms of the
religious persuasions of their populations.

There are five immediate points to note in looking at these tables. The
first is the virtual ubiquity of the Catholic association with labour market
outcomes. Apart from male labour force participation and male employment
in 1960, in respect of every other category of outcomes at both dates, the
findings are significant at the 0.05 level or better. The second point is that,
whilst the relationships with employment and participation are negative,
those with unemployment are positive. In other words, less people work or
seek work in Catholic countries and, of those who do seek work, less find
it.

The third point is the very considerable substantive impact implied by the
figures in the first column of each table. Whatever the ultimate determin-
ant(s) of the differences in labour market performance between Scandinavia
and Japan on the one hand and Catholic Western and Southern Europe on
the other, the sheer magnitude of the differences is extraordinarily large and
the case for a distinctive Catholic family of nations very strong. The fourth
point is the very considerable increase in the substantive impact of the
Catholic variable over time, with the difference between Catholic and non-
Catholic nations in respect of each aspect of labour market performance
more than doubling between 1960 and 1985. Moreover, the relationships
between Catholicism and both participation and employment outcomes become markedly more statistically significant over time. The final point is the
gender bias revealed in the findings. In every case, the effects of the religious
cleavage are far greater for women than for men. In 1960, the significance
of the total labour force and total employment findings is solely a consequence of the inclusion of data concerning female labour market activity. In
1985, both male and female outcomes are significant, but the first column of
Table 6 shows that the substantive impact on women's participation and
employment is more than twice as great as on men's participation and employment.

These findings are quite fascinating, but can hardly be regarded as definitive. What is reported in these tables are associations which clearly warrant
much further research, but which do not, in themselves, constitute adequate
explanations of labour market behaviour and certainly do not justify the
assertion that religious differences are the only or even the main determinants
of labour market outcomes. To establish the explanatory status of differences
in religious faith or of different degrees of secularization requires that we
seek to elaborate more fully specified models of each of these aspects of
labour market behaviour and demonstrate that, even when we take into
account the numerous other factors impacting on this area, the religious
variable still retains its power to predict outcomes.

33

This is clearly beyond the brief of a paper which seeks only to present existing evidence suggestive of a link between religion and public policy outcomes. However, in concluding this section, I wish to touch on a number of obvious anomalies that emerge from the findings in Tables 5 and 6. These anomalies do not put in doubt the reality of a linkage between religion and labour market outcomes, but they do raise some questions about the nature of a causal mechanism which was conceptualized in terms of a greater and increasing propensity for women in Protestant and more secularized societies to return to the labour force after having had children.

The real problem is that the religious linkage works far too well. It accounts for the gender-related character of labour market outcomes in exactly the manner predicted – female labour supply, and hence employment, is much lower in Catholic countries and, over time, the difference between Catholic and Protestant countries increases – but it is also manifest in areas in which it is difficult to see how traditional family attitudes could be the determining factor. If the interaction between child-rearing and labour market behaviour is the mechanism of difference, why is it that males are also significantly less likely to seek work or to be employed in Catholic nations by the mid-1980s? Moreover, if the presumed impact of Catholicism is purely through the supply side of the labour market, why is unemployment higher in countries where, all other things being equal, a lesser propensity to seek work should make it lower? Finally, why is it that by the end of the period, although not at the beginning, the impact of Catholicism on female unemployment is greater than on male unemployment and that, although not shown in the figures here, women in Catholic countries tend to have higher unemployment rates than men and vice versa in Protestant countries?

Although necessarily somewhat speculatively in terms of the kind of analysis that can be deployed here, it is arguable that a major component of the answer to each of these questions lies in the diversity of labour market strategies that have characterized Catholic and Protestant nations, and, in particular, in the very different ways in which social policy and labour market policies have interacted in these nations. A number of recent studies have shown that certain nations deliberately responded to the economic crises of the 1970s and 1980s by taking steps to decrease the supply of labour and, hence, indirectly to reduce unemployment. The primary instrument of such a strategy was the use of social insurance transfer expenditures to provide a means of early retirement from the labour force and/or to subsidize job-sharing arrangements. That being so, it is scarcely surprising to discover that it was precisely that core group of Catholic nations, shown by our previous analysis to have manifested higher transfer expenditures and to have increased such expenditures very markedly over this period, which used this strategy to its fullest extent (see Esping-Andersen & Sonnberger 1989; von Rhein-Kress 1993; Schmidt 1993). In other words, the greater reduction of the male labour force and of male employment in these countries was largely

34

a function of the utilization by their governments of a policy instrument already well developed in, and much in tune with the dominant policy culture of, the Catholic family of nations.

The explanation of the higher levels of unemployment experienced in these same nations also, arguably, owes something to another aspect of the interaction of labour market and social policy strategies. In the earlier discussion of Catholic social policy doctrines conducive to higher transfers expenditure, it was noted that this preference was the reverse side of the coin of a reluctance to hand over power to the state. In the labour market, this meant that Catholic countries did not, as in Protestant Scandinavia, adopt policies of direct intervention to enhance employment levels, either by fostering the growth of public employment (usually in the area of welfare provision, so that, in effect, differences in labour market policy and in social policy amounted to the same thing) or by what has come to be called active labour market policy.[17] According to this interpretation, the higher levels of both female and male unemployment experienced in Catholic countries stem from a cultural aversion to policy initiatives that directly increase employment through state action and a preference for the more indirect route of labour supply reduction through financial (social policy) incentives to individuals.

Finally, we come to the question of why Catholicism has, in the more recent period, been associated with higher female than male unemployment. Social policy again provides part of the answer insofar as the earned social insurance entitlements on which Catholic social policy rests could only be used to retire workers early, if those workers were already in the labour force and had already accumulated substantial entitlements. In other words, the strategy of confronting the post-war crisis in employment which was utilized in the Catholic family of nations was one which only reduced unemployment amongst men, since it was, for the most part, only men who had a major stake in the existing social policy system.

Employment structure, and particularly the extent of part-time employment, is almost certainly another crucial factor helping to explain the relative levels of female and male unemployment. Part-time employment frequently offers the only viable entry route for married women to return to the labour market, and women often remain unemployed despite the existence of full-time job opportunities. Religion also appears to play a role here. Protestant countries are generally characterized by higher levels of part-time employment than Catholic countries, a difference which has tended to become greater over the past two decades (see data in OECD 1992c). This, the last of the very many major differences between Catholic and Protestant nations to be mentioned in this paper, could have a variety of causes, including possible structural adjustment problems involved in the initial shift from full-time to part-time working, the relative lack of appeal of part-time employment in the context of the earnings-related social policy systems typical of the Catholic family of nations and, possibly, stronger feminist pressures on

35

both employers and politicians to provide part-time employment in Protestant countries.

There is much in this account which is speculative, but it does make sense of a substantial number of the observed associations between Catholicism and labour market outcomes. Most particularly, it suggests that the anomalies in Tables 5 and 6 should be seen less as undermining the postulated linkage between religion and labour market outcomes and more as evidence for the variety of the mechanisms through which that linkage is established. Labour market outcomes in the Catholic family of nations differ from those in Protestant nations not merely because individual women make different choices about labour market participation, but also because both women and men confront different employment structures and social policy institutions. More complex analysis and modelling will, almost certainly, modify some aspects of the conclusions reached here, but what is undoubted is the need to undertake a program of research which does take seriously the possibility that religious beliefs may interact with other factors to shape outcomes in respect to both the supply and demand for labour.

Conclusion

In the course of this paper I have sought to demonstrate that there is a very strong *prima facie* case that religious differences are an important factor in determining contemporary public policy outcomes across a very wide range of areas and that religious doctrines, beliefs and traditions, and their crystallization in laws and social institutions, constitute the basis of a Catholic family of nations with public policies quite different from those of national groupings with other historical and cultural antecedents. Considerations of space have precluded a rehearsal of all the evidence that can be garnered from comparative research. The possibility that the character of taxation systems as much as the welfare systems they finance may reflect similar forces has been relegated to a footnote (see Note 3). The impact of Catholicism on educational expenditure, which has elsewhere (Castles 1989) been shown to have been negative in the early 1960s but transformed to a positive influence by the early 1980s, has gone undiscussed. Only the briefest mention has been made of the evidence which suggests negative relationships between the degree of Catholic adherence and both the early extension of female suffrage and the development of the rights of children.

Even so, I hope that sufficient evidence has been provided to promote debate on a facet of contemporary societies which appears to have a profound effect on how governments define the appropriate limits of state intervention, influences the character of the legislation they are willing to enact, shapes the demands individuals and groups make of government and their willingness and opportunity to participate in the economy and, to a very consider-

36

able degree, determines the character of gender-specific outcomes in Western
societies. It is, moreover, a body of evidence which helps us to comprehend
the singularity of a group or family of nations, the common features of which
have been obscured by a fascination with explaining the economic problems
of the English-speaking nations and the welfare superiority of Scandinavia.
That fascination has been an artifact of the comparative public policy discipline's obsession with the supposedly mutually exclusive duality of economic
modernization and political reformism. It is time that this duality was superseded by a recognition of the influence of religion in shaping a Catholic
family of nations.

Acknowledgements

This article was completed whilst I was a Visiting Fellow at SCASSS, the
Swedish Collegium for Advanced Studies in the Social Sciences. I would
like to record my gratitude to the Directors of SCASSS for the privileged
opportunity to undertake a period of contemplative research.

Notes

1. Reliable cross-national data on secularization processes are hard to come by. The best
   available source (Halman & Vloet 1992) provides a variety of measures of religious versus
   secular values for 16 nations for the years 1981 and 1990. These include religiosity, religious
   orthodoxy, confidence in the church, a typology of churched and unchurched people and a
   measure of Christian world views. Interestingly, none of these measures is significantly
   associated with either nominal Catholic adherence or any of the policy outcomes shown to
   be associated with such adherence in the analysis below. This suggests that these differences
   in policy outcomes are either genuinely a function of differences between religious faiths or
   that there is some other dimension of secularization, coincident with the Catholic/Protestant
   divide, to which such outcomes are attributable. Obviously, to the degree that it is possible to
   demonstrate why Protestant rather than Catholic beliefs are more susceptible to secularizing
   impulses, it would remain reasonable to attribute differences in policy outcomes to the
   ultimate impact of religious faith.
2. Reasons why Protestantism may be particularly conducive to the emergence and success of
   movements asserting female rights are rehearsed briefly in the subsequent discussion of the
   impact of religion on women's rights and family policy and addressed explicitly in footnote
   11 below.
3. Göran Therborn has made an analytical distinction between four bases of familial likeness
   "lineages, held together by descent from a common origin, separated siblings, kindred
   nations kept apart by state boundaries, or more concretely, non-state-bound social units with
   significant similarities between them, irreducible to common ancestry, (elective) affinity,
   connected by processes of diffusion, of imitation or avoidance (negative affinity), freely
   elected or established by pressure and partnerships, the unions of deliberate coordination"
   (see Therborn 1993a).
4. Although I do not explore the notion further in this paper, there are very strong reasons
   for believing that this aspect of the tax system is a key mechanism for translating Catholic
   social policy ideas into policy outcomes. Social security contributions are inherently produc-

tive of higher levels of expenditure, since (a) they confer rights to benefit and (b) are less conducive to taxpayer backlash than other forms of financing. The association between the measure of membership of the Catholic family of nations employed below and the social security contribution share of total taxation is rather strong, being more than 0.70 in the mid-1960s (the earliest date for which tax data are available) and 0.55 in 1990. Moreover, cross-national research on types of tax systems (Peters 1991; 60–64) has identified four distinctive systems, of which two are exclusively composed of countries which are members of the Catholic family of nations. On this basis, a case could almost certainly be mounted that taxation, just as much as social security expenditure, is a facet of public policy that is strongly influenced by religious factors. Finally, it is worth noting that the relationship between the social security contribution share of total taxation and social security expenditure outcomes has been confirmed in a pooled time-series analysis of the standard 18-nation OECD sample (Castles 1990).

5. Greece is, of course, an Orthodox Catholic rather than a Roman Catholic nation and, depending on the precise nature of the causal argument linking religious beliefs and particular outcomes, might be excluded from the sample on the ground of neither being influenced by Roman Catholic nor by Protestant doctrine. It should, therefore, be stressed that neither excluding Greece from the sample nor, indeed, re-scoring it as a non-Catholic nation make any major difference to the findings reported below.

6. Despite my insistence that Catholic influence may take many forms, it is important to emphasize that, ultimately, the existence of such an influence needs to be demonstrated empirically for each particular case. It could well be, for instance, that the Irish case cannot properly be subsumed as part of an argument that explicit Catholic doctrines of subsidiarity lead to higher transfer expenditure, since (a) Irish Catholicism has assumed more of a moral than a social character, (b) the shaping of the Irish social security system owes much to the legacy of English rule in the formative period of welfare formation (which is, of course, an assertion that Ireland was once a member of a quite different family of nations) and (c) that the very substantial expansion of Irish welfare expenditure since the early 1970s owes most to that country's very high levels of unemployment. In general, on the role of the Irish Catholic Church in a variety of the policy areas discussed in this paper, see Lee (1991).

7. Fuller models are to be found in the paper on Southern Europe referred to in the text (Castles 1993a), which also assesses the expenditure impact of age structure, socialist incumbency and democratization. However, nothing reported in the fuller model involves any substantial modification of our findings concerning the explanatory role of membership in the Catholic family of nations.

8. Given the relative novelty of including both Germany and the Netherlands as members of a Catholic family of nations, and the subsequent exclusion of the German case in 1990, it is worth reporting the effects of these operational decisions on the multivariate findings reported here. Excluding Germany and the Netherlands from the samples in both 1960 and 1990 does somewhat reduce the levels of explained variance, but both variables clearly remain statistically significant and the unstandardized coefficients for the Catholic dummy variable are only marginally altered. Including Germany as a member of the Catholic family of nations in 1990 also only makes the most marginal of differences, with the unstandardized coefficient declining to 8.44 from the 9.11 reported in Table 2.

9. Before 1917, the only nations to have conceded universal suffrage were New Zealand (1893), Australia (1902), Finland (1906), Norway (1913) and Denmark (1915). All other primarily Protestant nations gave women the vote before 1930, whilst a significant number of Catholic nations had to wait for female suffrage until after World War II, including France (1944), Italy (1946), Belgium (1948) and Portugal (1976). For the 22 nation OECD sample (excluding Japan and Turkey on grounds of non-Christianity), there is, according to my calculations, a statistically significant negative relationship between the date of the extension of universal suffrage and the extent of Catholic adherence circa 1900 (see Barrett, 1982). For the dates at which female suffrage was enacted in advanced Western nations and an analysis of that chronology based on factors other than religion, see Therborn (1977).

38

10. For a categorization of the historical development of the rights of children, which corresponds almost precisely with the religious cleavage of advanced Western societies, see Therborn (1993b). Therborn's own interpretation of the data stresses the special character of Lutheranism in shaping a milieu in which children's rights could mature early.
11. This is one of the few instances where it is possible to fashion an argument based on the determinative influence of Protestant rather than Catholic ideas. It follows quite naturally from the Protestant belief that all persons relate to God as individuals that all individuals (whether male or female and irrespective of age) are, in some relevant sense, equals before God. Such an argument – ultimately, if not immediately – contains a challenge to the patriarchal subordination of women and children to the authority of the husband and father.
12. If we leave out Japan of the normal OECD sample on the ground of its lack of a Christian culture, the only difference between our operationalization of the Catholic family of nations and Glendon's Romano-Germanic type is Switzerland. In fact, the evolution of Swiss divorce law over the centuries (see Castles & Flood 1991) has combined Catholic and Protestant elements with seemingly indigenous legal developments. Some countries, of course, conspicuously including Switzerland, Canada, Germany and the Netherlands, sit on the borderline between and juxtapose elements of more than one family of nations (cf. Therborn's (1993a) separated siblings variant of familial likeness).
13. The countries included are Australia, Austria, Belgium, Canada, Denmark, Finland, France, Germany, Ireland, Italy, the Netherlands, New Zealand, Norway, Sweden, Switzerland and the United Kingdom.
14. These models were empirically derived after first assessing the strength of a large number of variables suggested in the sociological literature to be associated with the incidence of divorce. Amongst these variables were GDP per capita, service sector employment, urbanization, fertility, transfer expenditures on families, marriage and early marriage rates (see Castles & Flood 1991).
15. Where the locus of a decision is individual rather than collective, variance should be manifest not merely through cross-national analysis, but also at a disaggregated micro level. In the case of divorce, a variety of national studies demonstrate that, within a given nation, Catholics are less likely than Protestants to seek the remedy of divorce and that, in some instances, divorce rates in Catholic regions of a nation are lower than in Protestant regions (see Chester 1977).
16. Charts offering country-by-country age-cohort analysis of female labour force participation clearly illustrate this demographic mechanism. Whereas female labour force participation in Protestant nations approximates to an M shape, as women of child-bearing age leave and then return to the labour force, the curve in Catholic countries does not go up again, since many women do not return to the labour force after child-bearing (see OECD 1989: 71–78).
17. Austria, perhaps because of its exceptionally strong labour movement, is at least a partial exception to this generalization, but then it is also an exception to the generalization that Catholic countries have high levels of unemployment.

References

Barrett, D. B. (ed.) (1982). *World Christian Encyclopedia: A comparative study of churches and religions in the modern world AD 1900–2000*. Nairobi: Oxford University Press.
Castles, F. G. (1989). Explaining public education expenditure in OECD nations, *European Journal of Political Research* 17: 431–448.
Castles, F. G. (1990). Australian welfare state expenditure revisited: Some implications for change, *Australian Journal of Political Science* 25(2): 251–271.
Castles, F. G. (1993a). Social security in Southern Europe. Paper given at a conference organised

39

by the Subcommittee on Southern Europe of the American Social Sciences Research Council, Bielefeld, 8–9 July.

Castles, F. G. (ed.), (1993b). *Families of nations: Patterns of public policy in Western Democracies*. Aldershot: Dartmouth.

Castles, F. G. and Flood, M. (1991). Divorce, the law and social context: Families of nations and the legal dissolution of marriage, *Acta Sociologica* 34: 279–297.

Castles, F. G. & Mumford, K. (1992). The vision of a full employment Australia, in F. Argy (ed.), *A long term economic strategy for Australia*. Sydney: CEDA.

Chester, R. (ed.) (1977). *Divorce in Europe*. Belgium: Netherlands Interuniversity Demographic Institute.

Esping-Andersen, G. & Sonnberger, H. (1989). The demographics of age in labor market management. Florence: European University Institute, Working Papers, 89/414.

Esping-Andersen, G. (1990). *The three worlds of welfare capitalism*. Cambridge: Polity Press.

Glendon, M. A. (1987). *Abortion and divorce in western law*. Cambridge, MA: Harvard University Press.

Halem, L. C. (1980). *Divorce reform: Changing legal and social perspectives*. New York: The Free Press.

Halman, L. & Vloet, A. (1992). Measuring and comparing values in 16 countries of the Western world in 1990 and 1981. Tilburg University: Institute for Social Research, mimeo.

Heidenheimer, A. J. (1983) Secularization Patterns and the Westward spread of the welfare state, 1883–1983, in R. F. Tomasson (ed.), *The Welfare State, 1883–1983*. London: JAI Press.

Kamerman, S. B. & Kahn, A. J. (eds) (1978). *Family policy: Government and families in fourteen countries*. New York: Columbia University Press.

Kitchin, S. B. (1912). *A history of divorce*. London: Chapman and Hall.

Kremalis, K. & Yfantopoulos, J. (1992). Changes in social security policy in Greece during the eighties, in B. Greve (ed.), *Social policy in Europe: Latest evolution and perspectives for the future*. Copenhagen: Danish National Institute of Social Research.

Lee, J. (1991). *The modern history of Ireland 1916–1990*. Cambridge: Cambridge University Press.

Norris, P. (1987). *Politics and sexual equality. The comparative position of women in Western democracies*. Bolder, CO: Rienner.

OECD (1989). *Employment Outlook*. Paris.

OECD (1992a). *Revenue Statistics of OECD Member Countries*. Paris.

OECD (1992b and earlier editions). *Historical Statistics*. Paris.

OECD (1992c). *Employment Outlook*. Paris.

Peters, B. G. (1991). *The politics of taxation*. Oxford: Blackwell.

Phillips, R. (1988). *Putting asunder: A history of divorce in Western society*. New York: Cambridge University Press.

Price, S. J. & McKenry, P. C. (1988). *Divorce*. Berkeley: Sage Publications.

Rheinstein, M. (1972). *Marriage stability, divorce and the law*. Chicago: Chicago University Press.

Sartori, G. (1970). Concept misformation in comparative politics, *American Political Science Review* 54: 1033–53.

Schmidt, Manfred (1993). Gendered labour force participation, in F. G. Castles (ed.), *Families of nations: Patterns of public policy in Western democracies*. Aldershot: Dartmouth.

Summers, R. & Heston, A. (1991). The Penn World Table (Mark 5): An extended set of international comparisons, 1950–1988, *Quarterly Journal of Economics* 106(2): 327–368.

Therborn, G. (1977). The rule of capital and the rise of democracy, *New Left Review* 103: 3–41.

Therborn, G. (1993a). Beyond the lonely nation state, in F. G. Castles (ed.), *Families of nations: Patterns of public policy in Western democracies*. Aldershot: Dartmouth.

Therborn, G. (1993b). The politics of childhood, in F. G. Castles (ed.), *Families of nations: Patterns of public policy in Western democracies*. Aldershot: Dartmouth.

40

United Nations (various dates). *UN Demographic Yearbook*. New York.

Van Kersbergen, K. (1991). *Social capitalism: A study of Christian democracy and the post-war settlement of the Welfare state*. Florence: European University Institute, Ph.D thesis.

Van Kersbergen, K. (1992). Catholicism and social citizenship: In search of the Christian Democratic welfare state. Paper presented to a conference on Comparative Studies of Welfare State Development, Bremen, 3–6 September.

Von Rhein-Kress (1993). Coping with economic crisis: Labour supply as a policy instrument, in F. G. Castles (ed.), *Families of nations: Patterns of public policy in Western democracies*. Aldershot: Dartmouth.

Weiss, R. S. (1975). *Marital separation*. New York: Basic Books.

Wilensky, H. (1975). *The welfare state and equality*. Berkeley: University of California Press.

Wilensky, H. (1981). Leftism, Catholicism and democratic corporatism: The role of political parties in recent welfare state development, in P. Flora and A. J. Heidenheimer (eds.), *The development of welfare states in Europe and America*. New Brunswick: Transaction Books.

Address for correspondence: Dr Francis G. Castles, Public Policy Program, Australian National University, P.O. Box 4, Canberra, ACT 2601, Australia

[23]

The Netherlands: A Passive Social Democratic Welfare State in a Christian Democratic Ruled Society

KEES VAN KERSBERGEN† AND UWE BECKER‡

ABSTRACT
The Netherlands are of considerable interest to students of comparative social policy, because christian democracy and not social democracy is the leading political force. This article analyses the history of the Dutch system of social security in terms of political forces and their power resources. In particular, it considers the reasons for the comparatively high level of social security development in the Netherlands. The various approaches which have been adopted in much current research in comparative social policy are critically discussed in the context of the Dutch experience.

INTRODUCTION

From a comparative point of view the high level of welfare state development in the Netherlands is striking and impressive. In 1982 33.3 per cent of the Gross Domestic Product (GDP) was spent on social security. By comparison the social security expenditure of the United Kingdom amounted to 23.0 per cent of GDP (*Financiële Nota*, p.99). Behind this comparatively high aggregate figure lies a welfare state about which *The Economist* wrote in 1982:

If somewhere must be found to sit out the recession, Holland must be the nicest, comfiest place to choose ... For those without jobs, Holland's de luxe, amazingly well padded welfare system soothes the pain.

Yet, according to the same observer:

Dutch thinking and debate on some aspects of social and economic policy—in particular on public finance and on the long-term effects of keeping more than a million people supported by the welfare state—is still cloudy and lacking in realism (January 30, 1982).

Indeed, the relative generosity of the Dutch system of social security can

† Department of Political Science, European University Institute, Firenze, Italy.
‡ Politieke en Sociale Fakulteit, University van Amsterdam.

be compared only with the Scandinavian social systems, which have been attracting so much attention from students of comparative social policy. The Netherlands, however, do not lend themselves to the explanations that have so far predominated in the literature. This is largely because the leading political force in the Netherlands is christian democracy rather than social democracy.

Until recently, when a period of dismantling began, the Dutch system of social security was characterised by generous social benefits (80 per cent of wages for the unemployed and up to 100 per cent in cases of sickness); highly unconditional eligibility, particularly in cases of disability; index linking of wages and social security benefits to inflation; and, most importantly, a linking of the relatively high statutory minimum wage to the minimum social benefits. House rents were kept artificially low either by subsidising the costs of construction (so-called 'social housing') or by granting subsidies to tenants. Art was heavily sponsored by the state (subsidies for small, non-profitable theatres and music halls; a special social assistance programme for 'unemployed' artists who were, in addition to their benefit, entitled to a contribution for their materials). In short, if anywhere, it was in the Netherlands that security 'from the cradle to the grave' became a reality. There is perhaps no better way of illustrating the penetration of the idea of social welfare in Dutch society than by translating the Dutch word for welfare state literally: the caring state (verzorgingsstaat). The Dutch, so to speak, are used to the fact that the state takes care of every aspect of life. In the main part of this article, however, we will confine ourselves to the central elements of income maintenance, which constitute the historical core of welfare state development.

The comparatively high rates of unemployment in the Netherlands, in particular since the second oil shock of 1979, are equally striking. In 1984, 14 per cent of the Dutch labour force was unemployed. The Netherlands now belong to the sad group of capitalist countries with mass unemployment (Belgium, Canada, Denmark, Ireland, the United Kingdom). According to Therborn (1986) mass unemployment on this scale can only be explained by the *absence* of an *institutional commitment* to full employment. Full employment as an *autonomous* policy goal has indeed gained only low significance in the Netherlands. The orientation towards industrial exports and the balance of payments has dominated social and economic policy in the post-war period. Full employment was seen as dependent on the performance of the economy.

The absence of a coherent and active labour market policy, together with the developed system of income maintenance are the reasons why the Dutch welfare state can be called a *passive* social democratic welfare state (on the concept see Schmidt 1982, pp.219ff). This passive nature of the Dutch welfare state was only clearly revealed after the economic recession of 1973. The Dutch welfare state was of course never *intended* to be passive. The adjective 'social democratic' here does not refer to the prominence of social democracy in the political system. Quite the opposite is the case, for in Dutch society christian democratic ideology and christian democratic political forces have been a dominant influence. Nevertheless, we consider this welfare state as being social democratic in character, because traditional working class and social democratic demands have to a large extent become official and normal policies of Dutch governments, irrespective of their composition.

Students of comparative social policy have great difficulty in explaining the Dutch configuration of christian democratic dominance and generous social spending. Socio-economic theories of welfare state development such as those formulated by Cutright (1965), Pryor (1968) and Wilensky (1975) stress the importance of economic development as the main cause of welfare state development. Of course, the importance of the level of economic development cannot be denied. But how are we to explain differences in the level of welfare state development between countries with similar economic conditions? These explanatory difficulties appear even greater if not only the aggregate level of welfare expenditure (as a percentage of GDP) is taken into account, but also the levels of specific welfare programmes. For example, in a direct sense the Dutch statutory minimum wage has nothing to do with social security as such.

The so-called 'politics does matter' approach, which is critically directed against economic determinism in public policy research (Cameron, 1978; Castles, 1981; 1982; Schmidt, 1982; 1983) stresses that strong unions and a high degree of organisation, a dominant electoral and governmental position of the social democratic party, a centralised political system, and an export-oriented open economy are the variables explaining high levels of welfare state development (see also Korpi, 1978; 1983; Stephens, 1979; Flora and Alber, 1981; Esping-Andersen, 1985). The Netherlands simply do not fit this explanatory scheme. They are a pre-eminently export-oriented nation and the political system is indeed highly centralised, but the labour movement is divided between religious and social democratic unions and the degree of union organisation is comparatively low (38 per cent in 1980; Therborn, 1984, p.11). In addition to this, the social democratic party is not dominant, but the christian democratic parties are.

It is also no improvement to supplement the social democracy thesis

480   *Kees Van Kersbergen and Uwe Becker*

with a christian democracy thesis (Wilensky, 1981; Schmidt, 1984, p.10). First, differences in welfare state development in such countries as the Netherlands, Belgium and West Germany would still require explanation. Second, the supposed explanatory power of the political relations in such an approach seems to fade away. For apart from Great Britain and France, every Western European country is characterised by the predominance of either social democracy or christian democracy. Moreover, not all social democratic movements in Western Europe can be that easily compared without obscuring important gradations. The same is true, of course, for christian democracy (Von Beyme, 1984, p.11). To equate christian democracy with social democracy is even more problematic. For such an approach the *particularity* of diverging roads to welfare state development is inexplicable.

As a starting point we do share the conviction that political power relations are decisive in the explanation of welfare state development. But when one wants to explain the peculiarities of the Dutch case—the generosity of welfare spending under atypical conditions—a theory is needed which leaves room for the explanation of the existence of highly developed welfare states (and their particularities) also in countries where social democracy is not the leading political force. In a brief concluding section we will return to this topic tentatively. First, however, we will describe the relevant stages in the post-war development of the Dutch welfare state while trying to identify the reasons for its generous system of social security. As far as possible we will also point to the circumstances which account for the passive character of the Dutch welfare state. This part of the analysis, however, necessarily remains somewhat restricted due to the fact that the passivity has never directly been an issue of theoretical debate nor political struggle.

POLITICS IN THE NETHERLANDS

The character and development of the Dutch welfare state cannot thoroughly be understood without taking into account one of the most striking features of the society and the political system of the Netherlands: its 'pillarisation'. 'Pillarisation' refers to the division of society into several organisational complexes which are highly isolated from one another and based on religious or ideological grounds. This pillarised society emerged at the end of the nineteenth century and reached maturity between 1920 and 1960. On the one hand it was a result of the concurrence of a catholic emancipation movement, a petty bourgeois (mainly protestant) resistance against the early industrialisation and of a general principally christian protest against the 'spirit' of the revolutions of the late eighteenth and the nineteenth centuries. On the other hand the formation of pillarisation coincided with and was determined by the struggle for universal suffrage as well as the conflicts emerging from the so-called 'social question' (that is, the social costs of early industrialisation). In the developed pillarised Dutch society, unions, the organisations of capital, political parties, occupational associations, broadcasting companies, organisations of women, sports clubs, schools, universities, hospitals, cemeteries, social welfare organisations—in sum, all social organisations—were based on one of the religions or ideologies.

There existed four pillars among which the catholic and the protestant ones were the most pronounced. The socialists as well as the liberals were not able to withdraw from this dominant form of organisation and thus formed partial pillars of their own. Perhaps it would be better to speak of three pillars (catholic, protestant and 'general'), because strictly speaking the metaphor is out of place here; liberal unions have had only marginal existence, socialist capital organisations are a contradiction in terms, and perhaps most importantly, there has never been a liberal nor a socialist equivalent to the catholic and protestant churches and schools.

As in most Western countries, socio-structural and cultural changes occurred in the Netherlands during the sixties. These changes accelerated the process of secularisation and led to the erosion of the system of pillarisation. This in turn led to a sharp decline in the electoral support of the religious parties and in particular of the Catholic Peoples Party (Katholieke Volkspartij, KVP). Moreover, after breaking ideologically with the catholic party, the catholic labour union changed its course radically in the 1960s and finally, in 1981, even merged with the socialist union. The three religious parties, too, merged and formally formed one christian democratic party (Christen-Democratisch Appel, CDA) in 1980, while electoral cooperation dated back to 1976. One striking fact of this 'de-pillarisation' is that the broadcasting associations of the various pillars themselves are no longer the most important organisations. Their place has been taken by 'general' companies. The educational system, however, is still pillarised.

Pillarisation explains the dominant social and political role of religion in post-war Holland until the sixties (and in some rural municipalities up to the present day). More importantly, major elements of the christian political ideology and the christian social theory are integral parts of the political 'discourse' of all political parties. In contradistinction to what seems to be the case in Britain, 'class struggle' for example does not exist in Dutch political vocabulary. In Holland capital and labour are 'social partners'. Moreover, in the field of social policy politicians speak of the

482   *Kees Van Kersbergen and Uwe Becker*

'weak' and the 'strong' and of the moral obligation of the 'strong' to help the 'weak'. It seems that in Dutch political culture the social security system is seen as a measure of the level of (christian) civilisation, and a fundamental attack on the right to social security of all citizens is regarded as immoral. This deep-rooted political conviction sets limits to the attempts to dismantle the social system or at least makes a far-reaching and sudden break-up questionable. The ongoing economic crisis, the financial problems of the system of social security together with the free market ideology of the christian democratic-conservative liberal government in the Netherlands since 1982, are threatening the position of the 'socially weak' more than ever before. A 'social minimum income', however, is still guaranteed, although on a much more moderate level. One typical example is that on the one hand the government is pursuing a policy of austerity with regard to social benefits, while on the other hand temporary Acts have been passed which provide for one-time benefits (eenmalige uitkering) specifically to assist the 'weak' in these difficult times.

It is almost impossible to compare Dutch christian democracy with christian democratic movements in other West European countries. Although Austria, Belgium and Switzerland can in a way be considered as pillarised societies (Steiniger, 1975; Righart, 1986) the strong religious base of pillarisation is a Dutch particularity. In particular the strength of the religious labour organisations is extremely important in this context. Until 1974 the degree of organisation of the christian (in particular the catholic) unions had been higher than the social democratic mobilisation. Finally, it is important to note that religiously inspired voting of the working class is a salient political fact in the Netherlands (Lijphart, 1968). This explains why the Labour Party (Partij van de Arbeid, PvdA) has almost never succeeded in gaining more than 30 per cent of the vote. It also accounts for the dependence of the Catholic Peoples Party on the working class vote. This means that the struggle between labour and capital, which is so important for the political history of the welfare state, principally took place within the pillars, and in particular within the catholic pillar. Hence corporatist interest intermediation became a vital condition for catholic politics in general. This 'built-in corporatism' then is a special aspect of pillarisation.

THE POLITICAL HISTORY OF THE DUTCH WELFARE STATE

It was not until the Second World War that a comprehensive statutory system of social security could develop in the Netherlands. Until that time the Dutch system of social security was characterised—as were most other Western European systems—by a mixture of voluntary and compulsory insurances and privately organised (mainly christian) poor relief funds (on this see Van Loo, 1981; Van der Valk, 1986). Between the wars, Dutch economic policy was characterised by a stubborn refusal to abandon the gold standard 'against all economic reason and just for the sake of prestige' (Klein, 1980, p.5) and by the absence of a coordinated policy to fight unemployment (see Fortuyn, 1980, p.80). In the post-war development of the Dutch welfare state three stages can be distinguished of which the first is the most crucial: foundation (1943-52); expansion (1964-75); dismantling (1982 onwards).

The foundation: the post-war consensus
The first post-war government in the Netherlands, functioning in a context largely determined by the experience of the economic crisis, war and oppression, and by the consequent severe social and economic problems, faced newly established political and social relations in the liberated country. With respect to social security, which is the core of the Dutch 'caring' state, several new and innovatory ideas and plans, supported by different groups, had come together immediately after the war and thus formed the first constellation out of which the elements of the modern welfare state arose.

During the war the Dutch government-in-exile in London established a special committee with the task of preparing the post-war direction of social policy and in particular that of the social security system. Not surprisingly the ideas as well as the motives for social security reform expressed in the so-called Van Rhijn reports (1945-46) clearly resembled Sir William Beveridge's plans for social security reform:

The community, organised in the state, is responsible for the social security and freedom from want of all citizens, on the condition that the citizens will do everything within their reach in order to provide themselves with social security and freedom from want (Commissie-Van Rhijn, 1945-46, II, p.10).

On 30 November 1946 the Economic University of Rotterdam even conferred a doctor's degree (honoris causa) on Lord Beveridge, recognising his influence on Dutch economic and social thinking at the time. The recommendations and proposals of the Van Rhijn committee were a strong impetus for the post-war political debate on social security. In spite of a consensus on the direction of the social security system in post-war Holland, a second Van Rhijn committee became necessary after the war because of severe differences of opinion regarding the organisation of the new system. The context of this debate was the permanent conflict between the religious and liberal parties on the one

484   *Kees Van Kersbergen and Uwe Becker*

hand and the social democratic party on the other. The so-called private initiative (cf. Brenton, 1982) was favoured by the christian democrats and the liberals as opposed to the active state intervention favoured by the social democrats.

Within occupied territory the Nazis had, simultaneously with the London initiatives, started to reform the system of social security as part of their strategy to 'nazify' social and political relations in the Netherlands (Asselberghs, 1982; Veldkamp, 1978). For the Dutch government in London it was hard to deny that some of the social policies pursued by the German occupier were in fact improvements. This might explain why the London government started to inform the subjugated population of the Netherlands about the intended post-war social policies at an early stage of the war, emphasising precisely those fields of social policy in which the Germans had been active (Van den Tempel, 1946).

Not all politicians and civil servants were able (or willing) to flee from the country after the German invasion. The secretary-general of the Ministry of Social Affairs, R. A. Verweij, for example, kept negotiating over social matters with the Nazis until the end of the war. He himself, as well as many of the civil servants of Social Affairs, had been deeply disappointed with the crisis management of the pre-war centre right coalition governments. Verweij is even said to have welcomed the German occupation and the resulting absence of the leading politicians because it 'freed' him from the political constraints on improving social policy in the Netherlands (Enquête, 1955, p.101).

Finally, during the war the politically divided resistance movement formulated its plans for social and political reform in post-war Holland. It is interesting to note that the resistance was able to get detailed information about social security plans of the Allied Powers and of the Dutch London government. In spite of the war and the oppression, the former organisation of labour and capital also started negotiating over the post-war organisation of labour relations in the Netherlands and over the desired social policy.

The most important socio-political measures immediately after the war were the Old Age Insurance Act of 1947 (an emergency Act; the final enactment dates from 1956) and the Unemployment Insurance Act (WW) of 1949. In addition, some other improvements were made to social security, such as better regulations in cases of sickness and disability and the introduction of children's allowances (for dates and descriptions of all laws mentioned here, see Braakman *et al.*, 1984).

The Unemployment Insurance Act of 1949 in particular must be considered as one of the cornerstones of the Dutch social system. The unemployment benefit was at the time fixed at 80 per cent of the daily wages for breadwinners, at 70 per cent for other married persons, and at 60 per cent for children still living with their parents. In 1964 the unemployment benefits were all levelled up to 80 per cent of wages. The state, the employees and the employers all paid one-third of the costs of the insurance.

The direction in which the social security system should develop was not the subject of serious political debates in the immediate post-war years, except, as mentioned before, the problem of how the system should be organised and administered. Not even unemployment insurance appears to have been a source of serious tension for the antagonistic and at the time still rather fragile relationship between capital and labour. In parliament only the communist party (10 of the 100 seats) demanded a 90 per cent unemployment benefit. None of the other parties supported this proposal. Although the employers and the liberal party feared that generous unemployment benefits would reduce work incentives and although it was known that the benefits were indeed comparatively high, the catholic-social democratic coalition government defended the unemployment insurance act by appealing to the already established 80 per cent level of benefits (Handelingen, 1948-49, bijlage 704).[1]

In general, then, social policy in these early post-war years was not the cause of severe political controversies. We would argue that the following elements can account for this:

—the political radicalisation, which even occurred among conservative political forces, and which originated in the economic crisis of the thirties, the war experience and in particular the exposure to the Nazi oppression. This radicalisation can, for example, be illustrated by pointing to the unprecedented electoral results of the Dutch communist party in 1946 and the powerful and steady position of the communist trade union (EVC), at least until the early fifties;

—the emergence of the Cold War. It is difficult to assert exactly what the effect of the Cold War has been on the scope of welfare policy in the Netherlands. We would argue, however, that the furious anticommunist attitude of the christian democratic political parties as well as that of the labour party has at least contributed to the pace of the development of the welfare state. Indeed, many a plea for social security reform was accompanied by anticommunist arguments. One intriguing example is the pamphlet that the catholic labour movement distributed at the

486   *Kees Van Kersbergen and Uwe Becker*

beginning of 1948 in all catholic churches in the Netherlands. It stated that communism would not stand a chance in the Netherlands if and only if the right social and economic conditions were present:

The communist support is due to social and economic evils of the past and in the present, which are unjust. To fight these evils by a conscious, radical, progressive reform policy based on the important encyclical letters of the Popes, is the task of every catholic worker (De Volkskrant, March 3, 1948).

The socialist union (NVV) also feared the communist movement for competitive reasons. We believe, therefore, that the post-war consensus on social policy was partly evoked by these strong anticommunist sentiments in the political context of the Cold War;
—the existence of pressing issues on the political agenda in the late forties and early fifties, in particular the problem of the de-colonisation of the Dutch East Indies. The loss of this colony might very well have stimulated the industrialisation of the somewhat backward rural economy of the Netherlands and might have contributed to the related modernisation of the society. The economic loss of the East Indies demanded—so to speak—industrialisation to secure welfare for the Dutch population. Moderating social relations and in particular the ever-smouldering conflict between capital and labour was seen as a prerequisite for the industrial policy;
—the unique character of the initially religion-based pillarisation of the society. The system of pillarisation proved to be rather enduring despite the shock of the Second World War. In spite of the relative strength of the political forces striving for the modernisation of the pre-war social and political structure (the so-called 'doorbraak' (breakthrough) movement), the old system of pillarisation gradually returned. Although the pre-war socialist party (SDAP) gained some support from other political circles and consequently changed its name, the socialist plan of forming a broad 'catch-all party' that would include all progressive forces in Dutch society only partly succeeded. The new Labour Party (PvdA) made only minimal electoral progress. It was the Catholic Peoples Party that won the first post-war elections of 1946. Its large working class support and the competition with the PvdA, however, forced the KVP to adopt a more left wing political stance in social matters. At the same time these post-war developments facilitated a workable coalition between the KVP and the PvdA;
—the result of all this was the active engagement of christian churches and in particular the catholic church and its related organisations in social matters in these first post-war years. Given the hierarchical structure of the catholic church and of the catholic pillar as well as the

drive for catholic political unity—particularly powerful at the time—one can safely assume the far-reaching influence of catholic social doctrine in the Netherlands. Bishops regularly published influential pastoral letters on social and political issues, explaining the 'natural' rights of workers and their entitlement to an income sufficient to maintain their families. The corporatist organisation of the capital-labour relationship was another repeated item of these pastoral letters, which were read by priests in every catholic church in the country. Catholic employers in particular were told to organise themselves (in catholic organisations of course) in order to perform their christian duty in the name of social justice and christian solidarity. In the words of the bishop of Haarlem who addressed a meeting of catholic employers on social issues:

The time has come to take action and the employers know this. Actions speak louder than words; the lower classes are looking forward to what employers will undertake. If the employers set an example, the result will be the strongest catholic action that I can think of. If you make sacrifices, the results will be astonishing ... I hope that the catholic employers will remain loyal to the catholic principles ... (De Volkskrant, 3 February, 1948).

The Catholic Peoples Party largely followed the progressive catholic social ideology in the first post-war years. This went so far that right wing critics both from within and outside the party started to accuse the KVP of 'degeneration' into a party for workers only. The catholic political elite had some difficulty in justifying their political course;

—the broad influence of catholic social ideology which reached further than the catholic pillar itself. In 1951 the catholic labour movement organised a mass meeting in order to commemorate the encyclical letter *Rerum Novarum* (1891) and *Quadragesimo Anno* (1931). A football stadium in Rotterdam was packed with 60,000 people who joined the celebration. Among them were ministers of the government, members of parliament and representatives of other unions and political parties. It was the socialist minister of Social Affairs who addressed the audience and praised the social philosophy of the catholic church and announced in addition the definitive old age insurance legislation;

—the relatively low participation rates of women in the labour market, resulting from the pillarisation and the christian ideology of family and the position of women. In the pre-war period, for example, several policies were pursued in order to prevent women from entering the labour market (Blok, 1978). Immediately after the war women were simply forced to leave their jobs to make room for men returning from imprisonment, forced labour camps in Germany, and the resistance. The absence of women on the labour market can partly account for the high

488   *Kees Van Kersbergen and Uwe Becker*

level of social benefits, for it made 'generous' benefits both possible and necessary as a means to maintain family income instead of an individual wage.

The social policy in the immediate post-war stage was an aspect of a more comprehensive socio-economic programme of successive coalition governments. This programme consisted of an industrialisation scheme for the predominantly rural and trading society with its traditional trading towns Rotterdam and Amsterdam. On the other hand, this social and economic programme also aimed at the restructuring of the institutional framework of labour relations in a more or less corporatist-democratic fashion (Windmuller; 1969). This component of the policy, although initiated and primarily advocated by the catholic political forces (party as well as unions), was also supported by the social democrats who had hoped to transform it into a tool of economic planning and state intervention in the economy.

The export orientation of the Dutch economy formed the core of the industrial policy. To this end a tight system of wage and price regulation was introduced in order to keep the wage level comparatively and competitively low. Both the christian and the socialist unions accepted this system of wage control mainly because of its beneficial effects on employment. Furthermore, it is plausible that the unions accepted this incomes policy in exchange for the extension of social security. The latter was supposed to compensate for the lower wage levels. Since most social benefits were linked to these comparatively modest wages, however, the apparently generous social benefits turned out to be not that generous after all. To this extent the post-war consensus could be said to have rested in part on a failure by the unions to foresee some of the implications of the measures being introduced.

The centrally guided wage and price policy was considered to be the instrument best suited to attaining the goal of export oriented industrial growth. As to full employment, the prevalent opinion was that the favourable effects on employment resulting from this policy and from complementary counter-cyclical fiscal measures would be such that no further systematic intervention would be necessary.

The prevalence of the centrally guided incomes policy in the post-war economic programmes of successive governments must also be seen against the background of the defeat of 'plan-socialist' ideas of the PvdA between 1945 and 1950. Christian democratic and conservative-liberal political forces had thwarted socialist proposals in this direction time and again. It may very well be that the impossibility of implementing 'plan-socialist' schemes gradually shifted the attention of the socialists to incomes regulation and to the politics of social security as a means of securing some central direction of the economy. The rapid success of modern Keynesian demand management and social policy (full employment, the absence of labour disputes, social security) was seen as a social democratic victory and provided the PvdA with political prestige, and fully compensated for the defeat of the 'plan-socialist' strategy (Böhl *et al.*, 1980, p.120ff). We would argue then that the political unfeasibility of 'plan-socialist' aims in the Dutch context inhibited the foundation of a more active welfare state. At the same time, however, it is questionable whether implementation of the social democratic proposals would have promoted an active capitalist welfare state. This is because a Scandinavian style reformism, which explicitly accepts state regulation of the economy as the most efficient means of production and which accordingly pursues full employment as the best form of social security, has never been present in the post-war social democratic movement of the Netherlands. Economic planning, increased economic democracy and the nationalisation of banks and industries were primarily seen as appropriate means to the traditional goal of socialism and not as elements of social policy within capitalism. A document illustrating this view is the PvdA report *The Road to Freedom: A Socialist Perspective* of 1951, which still contains far-reaching proposals to nationalise large sectors of the economy. Moreover, the pragmatic political leaders of the social democratic party were anxious to continue their participation in government and therefore directed their attention to what would be attainable in the short run: a comprehensive system of social security.

During the fifties the christian democratic and conservative-liberal criticisms of state intervention became even stronger, finally leading to the abolition of the centrally guided wage policy. The only fundamental point of agreement between social democrats and the christian democratic parties remained the extension of social security on christian democratic terms (Van Lier, 1981; Ter Heide, 1986). Proposals for socialisation or nationalisation were absent from the later programmes and plans of the social democratic movement.

In accordance with the programme of industrial growth of the first post-war governments the politics of social security were also regarded as a means to control the cyclical development of the economy, that is, as a part of a broader Keynesian inspired economic policy. The Van Rhijn committee had already expressed this point of view during the war, again highly influenced by the British example of the Beveridge Report. The key issue was, of course, the opinion that a high level of income maintenance, in particular of unemployment benefits, would stabilise total demand. Up

490   *Kees Van Kersbergen and Uwe Becker*

to 1974–75 the consensus over this ingredient of Keynesian social policy remained unbroken.

The extension: leftism of the sixties

Between 1964 and 1975 the Dutch system of social security was considerably extended. It was in this period that the system acquired its comparatively generous character. Some of the outstanding achievements of social policy of this second stage in the welfare state development were: the disability insurance for employees (WAO) and the General Disability Act (AAW); an improvement of unemployment facilities and benefits; the substitution of the old Poor Law of 1854 (sic) by the General Relief Act (ABW, social assistance, 1964). In the course of time this latter law has come to function more and more as the final safeguard of the social security system as a whole. It provides benefits for those who are not entitled to any of the other benefits. In short, this period is characterised by the growth of the social security system into an almost all-embracing safety net of income maintenance.

Perhaps the most far-reaching achievement of social policy in these years was the introduction of the statutory minimum wage in 1968 and the (since 1974 de facto) linking of the lowest social benefits to the net minimum wage. The net minimum wage and thus the minimum social benefits amounted to about 80 per cent of the net average wage (Goudswaard and De Jong, 1985). Minimum wages were in turn linked to the overall development of the wage level in the private sector and so were all cash benefits. To complete the picture, the salaries of civil servants were linked to the general wage level and the salaries of those employed in the state subsidised sector (for example, education and social work) were in turn linked to those of civil servants.

There were two central elements in the societal context of this social policy in the second half of the sixties and the early seventies: an unprecedented economic growth and a left cultural and political 'conjuncture' which gave a particularly strong impulse to the development of welfare state policies. This leftist tendency does not imply that increasing the level of welfare state development would have been possible without at least the consent of christian democratic political forces. Yet it does mean that christian democracy was part of the progressive current and therefore more or less forced to reply to the leftist challenge, the more so as the process of 'de-pillarisation' threatened to loosen the traditional bonds between the christian democratic parties and the electorate. This left political culture provided the socialist PvdA with the opportunity to seize the initiative in the field of social policy, encouraged in this by the party's left wing and by other radical democratic movements. Socio-political issues became rather popular subjects of political debates during the subsequent electoral campaigns at this stage. Undoubtedly, the exceptional growth of the economy and the absence of high unemployment figures made it easier to 'score' politically on these matters. In 1973 these events enabled the formation of the one and (so far) only Dutch government dominated by social democrats and other left wing democrats, the Den Uyl government (1973–77). With regard to social ideology these years mark the shift from the traditional Dutch family bias to the rise of individual welfare claims as the point of reference for social policy. In sum, the 'permissive society' lost sight of the fact that capitalism must generate profits in order to sustain extensive welfare claims.

The left political and ideological current of the late sixties and early seventies dragged along the unions and every political party and discredited conservative and liberal views on social and economic policy. Yet this political 'conjuncture' cannot solely account for the growth of the welfare state in this period. One other important aspect of the rapid growth of social expenditure should be mentioned here—the final break up of the centralised system of regulated wage and price policy. This system had already started to disintegrate in the late fifties, but ultimately and definitively collapsed in 1964. The effect of the incomes policy and its breakdown has been twofold. First, a regulated wage policy became accepted as the norm. This perhaps accounts for the fact that almost immediately after the collapse of the incomes policy the unions agreed with the employers' organisations on the minimum wage level in 1964. Only four years later a statutory minimum wage was introduced. Second, decontrolling the wage development of the private sector of the economy contributed to an economic boom in the late sixties, which was accompanied by a more or less intended restructuring of the Dutch economy. When wages increased, the labour-intensive industries, which until then had been taking advantage of the comparatively moderate wage level, started to modernise their means of production by investing in labour saving techniques—if they were strong enough to do so. Many of these industries (such as textiles and shipbuilding) faced bankruptcy. Takeovers of weak industries by big, strong concerns and subsequent dismissals on a large scale were the result. For the time being, however, the growth of the economy enabled many of the unemployed to find new jobs. The disability benefits (WAO), although by no means designed for this purpose, were misused by employers to get rid of their redundant personnel. Yet many 'unemployed' (actually, those who were 'socially

492   *Kees Van Kersbergen and Uwe Becker*

and economically unable to work') found here a rather generous compensation for losing their jobs. For unlike the unemployment insurances (WW and WWV) which provided a wage related benefit for a maximum of two and a half years, the disability insurance provided an 80 per cent benefit until the age of 65. The WAO illustrates the normally defensive reaction of Dutch policy makers to rising unemployment figures. In this context one should not forget that in the course of the sixties the Netherlands reached the status of a semi-OPEC country because of the exploitation of natural gas reserves. Gas revenues have contributed considerably to the government budget and have facilitated the financing of expensive social programmes.

The Den Uyl government was based on a unique although fragile political constellation. This government relied on the active support of social democrats, left wing liberals (D'66) and radical democrats (PPR) and was just tolerated by the KVP and the protestant ARP, while the christian CHU opposed the leftist coalition (Vis, 1973). In spite of the difficult parliamentary base of the Den Uyl government it was this Cabinet that introduced the above mentioned linking of the minimum social benefits to the net minimum wage. Moreover, the leftist government increased the level of the minimum wage (and thus the minimum benefits) several times and introduced a statutory minimum wage for young people. We should, however, be careful not to overestimate the socio-political influence of the labour party in this part of the history of the Dutch welfare state. Firstly, no social reform or improvement would have been possible without christian democratic participation or at least consent. Secondly, the Minister of Social Affairs under the Den Uyl government was a member of the protestant ARP and an ex-member of the christian labour movement, CNV. Thirdly, the important statutory minimum wage itself had been an achievement of a christian democratic-liberal coalition government. Finally, in 1977 the Den Uyl government fell because of one of its central reform proposals that should have given this government its progressive character.

The beginning of the Den Uyl government coincided with the outbreak of the world wide economic crisis. At the time this was by no means apparent and it took until the early eighties for the conviction to grow that the alleged cyclical and short term recession had turned out to be a structural economic crisis. The so-called politics of retrenchment which were inaugurated towards the end of 1975 have largely been unsuccessful. In the crisis the passive character of the Dutch welfare state came to the fore. There were simply no instruments and no institutional framework to respond efficiently to the rising unemployment figures.

Despite a new conservative-liberal offensive, however, the political forces defending welfare state politics (which include large sections of the christian democratic bloc) managed to throw up a dam against the hesitant and incremental politics of austerity until 1982. This year marks a turning point in the post-war development of the welfare state in the Netherlands. A new liberal policy to fight the economic crisis in the Netherlands shattered the already fragile Keynesian paradigm.

The liberal challenge
The period between 1976 and 1982 can perhaps best be described as a transition period in which a struggle took place between forces opting for the preservation of the high level of welfare state provision and those attacking the generosity and 'spend-thrift nature' of the social security system. As mentioned earlier, in this period the awareness grew that the economic recession, and above all the high rate of unemployment, were structural in character. As in Britain, the policy relevance of supply side oriented and monetarist policies appeared to increase in these years, while the expansion of the welfare state and the Keynesian policy of demand management became more and more the subject of sharp criticism. During the crisis the financial problems of the social security system became very urgent. In 1960 eight employees paid for the benefit of one inactive person. In 1983 this proportion was 2.2 to 1 (Douben, 1984, p.50). The first systematic and coherent formulation of a new economic policy strategy in the Netherlands that departed considerably from the welfare state consensus of the previous period emerged in 1982. The new coalition government of christian democrats (CDA) and conservative liberals (VVD) presented a rather ambitious programme designed to cope with the economic crisis. The contents of this programme can be summarised as follows: the seriousness of the crisis made the government feel apprehensive for the stability of society as a whole. The crisis of the market sector and especially of the export oriented industrial sector was not only perceived in terms of the world market crisis, but above all in terms of an over-regulating and over-extracting welfare state, which restricted the free flow of market forces and the profits of capital. The perceived underlying cause of the problem—a weak market sector due to the politicising activities of the welfare state—inspired the formulation of a scheme of public and social expenditure cuts and a reduction of the budget deficit. The 'permissive society' gradually made way for a historical stage in which profit-making was once again seen as the pivot of prosperity and thus welfare.

The system of social security has been drastically altered since January

494   *Kees Van Kersbergen and Uwe Becker*

1987. The unemployment facilities (WW and WWV) were replaced by the New Unemployment Act (NWW), the main difference between these acts being that the latter provides a lower benefit (70 per cent) for a shorter period of time. Moreover, after this shorter period the unemployed are only entitled to a one year benefit of 70 per cent of the net minimum wage, and after that the unemployed have to turn to social assistance (ABW). In the case of disability the benefits remain at 70 per cent until the age of 65. But one important condition was introduced: young disabled people have to undergo medical re-examination that could lead to a change in benefits. An extra allowance arrangement has been introduced to prevent benefits going below the so-called social minimum. The official definition of a social minimum is the amount of money which is sufficient for the necessities of life. The amount depends on personal circumstances, but is derived from the minimum wage. At the moment the net social minimum for a single person is 1045 guilders per month (70 per cent of the net minimum wage), for a single parent household 1345 guilders per month (90 per cent of the minimum wage) and 1490 guilders per month for couples (married or unmarried, homosexual or heterosexual). The social minimum of 1045 guilders is about £320 (March, 1987).

In contemporary debates on social policy the social minimum plays an important role. It functions as the touchstone for social policy. For the present there is no political party which dares to propose substantial cuts in the social minimum. This shows that the welfare state consensus in the Netherlands is not yet totally absent, although it has been eroded to a considerable extent.

What shifts in social and political power relations account for the break up of the post-war state consensus in the Netherlands? Firstly, we should point to the fall of the leftist political culture of the late sixties and early seventies. Secondly, Dutch voters may very well have considered the impotence of Keynesianism in the Netherlands a failure of social democracy, for in 1982 the labour party lost 5 per cent of its constituency. Thirdly, the trade unions have produced no better plan to cope with the economic crisis and to preserve the welfare state consensus. Moreover, trade union power had dramatically diminished due to internal conflicts, decreasing membership and the absence of a social democratic coalition government. Fourthly, the weakening ideological and power position of social democracy in the Netherlands provided the conservative liberals with the opportunity to gain excellent results in successive elections by using rather simple anti-socialist and anti-welfare slogans. The road to power of the new liberal (almost Thatcherite) ideology would not have been possible without christian democratic support. Until roughly 1982 a 'social fraction' of the christian democratic party, primarily inspired by the christian philosophy of social responsibility, managed to uphold a socially acceptable way out of the crisis.

In short, the power relations underlying the dismantling of the Dutch welfare state consist of the right wing of the (secularising) christian democratic party, which is developing gradually into a 'normal' conservative party, an anti-welfare state conservative liberal party, the absence of strong trade unions and the ideological impotence of the labour party.

CONCLUSION

What is the explanation of the Dutch case? In the preceding section we pointed to some of the causes of the generosity of the Dutch system of social security, namely, the post-war socio-economic circumstances, the waste of the war and the experience of the economic crisis of the 1930s. None of these factors, however, was unique to the situation in the Netherlands at the time and nor was the strengthening of left wing political forces. Yet a particularity of Holland was the pillarisation of its society and as a consequence of this the extraordinary political influence of the church and religion. This in turn favoured the predominance of a paternalist christian—in particular catholic—social doctrine of social policy. 'Caring' for 'the weak', for the victims of unemployment or sickness, therefore, has been a central political and ideological issue.

The political configuration responsible for this development consisted of a socialist and a catholic bloc, each of which absorbed one-third of the electorate. The Catholic Peoples Party had to compromise the interests of its labour support and of the strong catholic labour movement with the interests of its capitalist wing. Generous social security must be understood as such an accord in the context of the rather leftist politico-ideological climate of the immediate post-war years, which also pressed the KVP towards a position where a lasting coalition with the social democrats seemed to be inevitable or at least most plausible. To become an eligible coalition partner the social democrats in their turn had to de-radicalise their socio-economic programme. Again, a generous system of social security turned out to be a viable arrangement.

At the same time, this very arrangement between the catholics and social democrats seems to have impeded every chance at establishing a more active commitment to social welfare. As a result labour market policies have never become a central element of the Dutch welfare state.

496   *Kees Van Kersbergen and Uwe Becker*

Whether or not a stronger position for Dutch social democracy would indeed have brought about an active welfare state remains a matter for speculation. In any case, we have not found any indication that social democrats strove for the political regulation of capitalism in a more or less Scandinavian (that is, mainly Swedish) way of 'socialism in one class'. Continental reformism has always alternated between abstract programmic radicalism and pragmatic opportunism. In the Netherlands christian paternalism has for a long time played a considerable part in fostering an extraordinarily passive version of social democratic reformism. In the course of the process of de-pillarisation and deteriorating economic prospects, however, this paternalism has begun to erode and smoothed the way for restrictive welfare politics.

The Dutch experience leads us to the following observations about the theory of comparative public policy. In Western Europe the dominant pattern of the political articulation of wage earners led to the formation of social democratic or socialist forces. This historical regularity does not, however, constitute a standard from which for example christian democratic political forces would be a 'deviation'. A social democratic or socialist labour movement is not a priori to be valued higher than its christian counterparts. A christian democratic labour movement might not be revolutionary, but it need not necessarily be less reformist (and anti-capitalist) than the social democratic labour movement. A fundamental difference, however, is that in countries in which religion is a salient feature of the organisation of the labour movement, the political power relations will be structured differently from countries in which class position is the main organising principle. In the latter case we would find as an ideal type leftist forces of wage labour versus bourgeois political forces of capital. In the former case antagonistic capital-labour relations would more likely be articulated on the more narrow political domain *within* the religious party. But this does not necessarily imply that the power constellation structured in this manner would be less inclined to stimulate welfare state development or other reform politics.

Starting from the thesis that the level of welfare state development depends largely on the power of the political forces of wage labour (or, more generally, on the power of political forces oriented towards what in the marxist tradition is called 'use values' (Becker, 1986)), we would find the key to the explanation of their success or failure in the analysis of their power resources (Korpi, 1978, pp.37–44; Giddens, 1981, p.49–68). The fact that society and, in particular, state expenditures, are largely dependent upon the profitability of capitalist production, is, or must be considered as, one of the most important power resources of capital.

The Netherlands 497

Competition forces capital to maximise profits but not welfare. The very existence of developed welfare states, however, demonstrates that the power resources of capital do not necessarily prevail always and anywhere. The power resources of capital can be outweighed by those of wage labour—strength and structure of organisation, solidarity, hard-won political and social rights and even the established hegemony of an orientation towards use values (Castles (1978, p.96) confirms a social democratic variant of such a hegemony in Sweden). The Dutch case shows that christian democratic hegemony can also be a pivotal power resource of labour. In conclusion, it follows from our analysis that the study of welfare state development is much more a task of empirical research and associated theorising than of a quest for statistical correlations.

NOTES

1 In 1920 the organisation of capital and labour (the socialist as well as the christian unions) had reached a compromise over the Health Insurance Act (ZW). The employers demanded execution of this Act under civil law. The unions finally agreed on the condition that sickness benefit be 80 per cent of the daily wage. Although the Health Insurance Act could not be put into practice because of these problems of implementation, the level of benefits in general has not been subject to political controversy since the compromise (Hulsman, 1981). The tripartite financing of unemployment insurance in 1949 was also the result of compromise. In this case, however, it was the government that forced organisations of labour and capital to accept the compromise, in order to solve the conflict over who pays the premium.

REFERENCES

K. Asselberghs (1982), 'De sociale verzekering tijdens de bezetting', *Sociologisch Tijdschrift*, 9:1, 5–40.

U. Becker (1986), *Kapitalistische Dynamik und Politisches Kräftespiel. Zur Kritik des Klassentheoretischen Ansatzes*, Campus, Frankfurt.

K. von Beyme (1984), 'Do parties matter?', *Government and Opposition*, 13, 5–29.

H. de Liagre Böhl, J. Nekkers and L. Slot (eds), (1981), *Nederland Industrialiseert! Politieke en ideologiese strijd rondom het naoorlogse industrialisatiebeleid 1945–1955*, SUN, Nijmegen.

E. Blok (1978), *Loonarbeid van vrouwen in Nederland 1945–1955*, SUN, Nijmegen.

T. Braakman, M.P.C.M. van Schendelen and R. Ph. Schotten (1984), *Sociale zekerheid in Nederland*, Het Spectrum, Utrecht/Antwerpen.

M. Brenton (1982), 'Changing relationships in Dutch social services', *Journal of Social Policy*, 11:1, 59–80.

D.R. Cameron (1978), 'The expansion of the public economy: a comparative analysis', *American Political Science Review*, 72:4, 1243–1261.

F.G Castles (1978), *The Social Democratic Image of Society*, Routledge and Kegan Paul, London.

F.G. Castles (1981), 'How does politics matter? Structure and agency in the determination of public policy outcomes', *European Journal of Political Research*, 9, 119–132.

F.G. Castles (ed.) (1982), *The Impact of Parties, Politics and Policies in Democratic Capitalist Countries*, Sage Publications, Beverly Hills.

Commissie-Van Rhijn (1945/1946), *Sociale zekerheid. Rapport van de commissie, ingesteld bij Beschikking van den Minister van Sociale Zaken van 26 maart 1943, met de opdracht algemeene richtlijnen vast te stellen voor de toekomstige ontwikkeling der sociale zekerheid*, II, 's-Gravenhage.

498 *Kees Van Kersbergen and Uwe Becker*

P. Cutright (1965), 'Political structure, economic development, and national social security programs', *American Journal of Sociology*, 70, 537–550.

N.H. Douben (1984), *Sociale zekerheid, een economische benadering*, H.E. Stenfert Kroese B.V., Leiden/Antwerpen.

Enquête commissie regeringsbeleid 1940–1945 (1955), *Verslag houdende de uitkomsten van het onderzoek. Deel a en b, Leiding en voorlichting aan ambtenaren en burgers in de bezette gebieden*, Staatsdrukkerij-en uitgeverijbedrijf, 's-Gravenhage.

G. Esping-Andersen (1985), *Politics against Markets. The Social Democratic Road to Power*, Princeton University Press, Princeton, New Jersey.

P. Flora and J. Alber (1981), 'Modernization, democratization and the development of welfare states in Western Europe', in P. Flora and A.J. Heidenheimer (eds), *The Development of Welfare States in Europe and America*, Transaction Books, New Brunswick.

W.S.P. Fortuyn (1980), *Sociaal-economische politiek in Nederland 1945–1949*, Dissertation, University of Groningen.

A. Giddens (1981), *A Contemporary Critique of Historical Materialism*, Macmillan, London.

K. Goudswaard and P. de Jong (1985), 'The distributional impact of current income transfer policies in the Netherlands', *Journal of Social Policy*, 14:3, 367–383.

F.J. ter Heide (1986), *Ordening en verdeling. Besluitvorming over sociaal-economisch beleid in Nederland 1949–1958*, Kok Agora, Kampen.

T. Hulsman (1981), *Het Nederlandse sociale zekerheidsstelsel. De rol van de overheid in ontstaan, groei, krisis*, Doctoral thesis, University of Groningen.

P.W. Klein (1980), 'The foundation of Dutch prosperity', in R.T. Griffiths (ed.), *The Economy and Politics of the Netherlands Since 1945*, Martinus Nijhoff, The Hague.

W. Korpi (1978), *The Working Class in Welfare Capitalism. Work, Unions and Politics in Sweden*, Routledge and Kegan Paul, London.

W. Korpi (1983), *The Democratic Class Struggle*, Routledge and Kegan Paul, London.

Th. J.A.M. van Lier (1981), 'Op weg naar de verzorgingsstaat (1950–1960)', in J. Bank and S. Temming (eds.), *Van brede visie tot smalle marge*, Sijthoff, Alphen a/d Rhijn.

A. Lijphart (1968), *The Politics of Accommodation. Pluralism and Democracy in the Netherlands*, University of California Press, Berkeley.

L.F. van Loo (1981), '*Den Arme gegevan ...*'. *Een beschrijving van armoede, armenzorg en sociale zekerheid in Nederland, 1784–1965*, Boom, Meppel.

F. Pryor (1968), *Public Expenditure in Capitalist and Communist Nations*, Irwin, Homewood.

J.A. Righart (1986), *De katholieke zuil in Europa. Een vergelijkend onderzoek naar het ontstaan van verzuiling onder katholieken in Oostenrijk, Zwitserland, België en Nederland*, Boom, Meppel.

R. Steiniger (1975), *Polarisierung und Integration. Eine vergleichende Untersuchung der strukturellen Versäulung der Gesellschaft in den Niederlanden und in Österreich*, Verlag Anton Hain, Meisenheim am Glan.

M.G. Schmidt (1982), *Wohlfahrtsstaatliche Politik unter bürgerlichen und sozialdemokratischen Regierungen. Ein internationaler Vergleich*, Campus Verlag, Frankfurt, New York.

M.G. Schmidt (1983), 'The welfare state and the economy in periods of economic crisis. A comparative study of twenty-three OECD nations', *European Journal of Political Research*, 11, 1–19.

M.G. Schmidt (1984), 'Policy making and macroeconomic performance in periods of economic crisis. A comparative political-institutionalist view'. Paper prepared for delivery at the Project Meeting 'Future Party Government', Subgroup C Policy making, European University, Firenze.

J.D. Stephens (1979), *The Transition from Capitalism to Socialism*, Macmillan, London.

J. van den Tempel (1946), *Nederland in Londen. Ervaringen en beschouwingen*, Tjeenk Willink, Haarlem.

G. Therborn (1984), 'The prospects of labour and the transformation of advanced capitalism', *New Left Review*, 145, 5–38.

G. Therborn (1986), *Why Some People Are More Unemployed Than Others*, Verso, London.

L. Van der Valk (1986), *Van pauperzorg tot bestaanszekerheid. Een onderzoek naar de ontwikkeling van* de Armenzorg in Nederland tegen de achtergrond van de overgang naar de Algemene Bijstandswet, 1912–1965, Eburon Delft Uitgeverij, Delft.

G.J.M. Veldkamp (ed.), (1978), *Inleiding tot de sociale zekerheid en de toepassing ervan in Nederland en België, deel 1. Karakter en geschiedenis*, Kluwer, Deventer.

J.J. Vis (1973), *Kabinetsformatie 1973. De Slag om het Catshuis*, Het Spectrum, Utrecht, Antwerpen.

H.L. Wilensky (1975), *The Welfare State and Equality. Structural and Ideological Roots of Public Expenditures*, University of California Press, Berkeley.

H.L. Wilensky (1981), 'Leftism, Catholicism and democratic corporatism. The role of political parties in recent welfare state development', in P. Flora and A.J. Heidenheimer (eds), *The Development of Welfare States in Europe and America*, Transaction Books, New Brunswick.

J.P. Windmuller (1969), *Labor Relations in the Netherlands*, Cornell University Press, Ithaca.

[24]

The Basic Law versus the Basic Norm?
The Case of the Bavarian
Crucifix Order

Howard Caygill and Alan Scott

The German Constitutional Court's ruling published in August 1995 that the so-called 'Bavarian crucifix order' (*Kreuzesbefehl*) was unconstitutional stimulated widespread public debate. Subsequent events, which included threats by the Bavarian Prime Minster to ignore the ruling and a large religious demonstration led by both Catholic and Protestant bishops, suggested that the implications of the case are wider than a conflict between federal and state constitutional courts. Indeed, the judgement was thought to have ramifications not just for 'Catholic Bavaria' but for the very idea of a Christian-occidental identity within an increasingly culturally and religiously heterogeneous Germany and Europe.

The ruling raises in a particularly stark fashion questions concerning the relationship of constitutions and constitutional courts to normal politics, on the one hand, and to the specific culture within which they are embedded and whose values they may be said to embody and protect, on the other. The reunification of Germany had already produced a sharpening of cultural and value conflicts, some of which were mediated through constitutional debate. Examples include abortion, where the incompatibility between the law in (West) Germany and that in the ex-GDR had led to considerable controversy; the constitutional status of 'ethnic Germans', and asylum rights.

Under such conditions of cultural and value pluralism, appealing to the values and 'traditions' of any one community is clearly problematic. This makes an implicit or explicit appeal to the seemingly more neutral and abstract values embodied in the constitution itself an attractive alternative. The hope here would be that a minimum consensus might be reached on the basis of which less easily reconcilable differences might be bridged, the constitution acting as bridgehead. In this way pluralism seems to lend support to the Habermasian notion of 'constitutional patriotism'.[1] However, here we shall argue that the ruling on the crucifix order suggests that problems of cultural diversity and the reconciliation of conflicting beliefs are not necessarily resolved via the constitution or through an appeal to constitutional patriotism. Indeed, we suggest that such conflicts may even be exacerbated where they become the object of constitutional scrutiny. If cultural conflicts are not made more amenable to resolution through constitutional means, this prompts the

---

[1] For a recent discussion in the light of German reunification and the developments within Europe – particularly the political development of the EU – see J. Habermas, 'Citizenship and national identity: some reflections on the future of Europe', *Praxis International*, 12, 1 (1992), 1–19.

506   *The Basic Law versus the Basic Norm?*

further question as to how far claims to universality embedded in a particular
constitutional order may work to deconstitute the very cultural values which it
should protect.

What makes the case of the crucifix order such an interesting demonstration
of these broader problems of constitutional politics is the fact that the conflict
involved is not the familiar one of the confrontation between a 'minority' and a
new constitutional order or political tradition, but a conflict *within* a single
national political culture. This raises the further possibility that a constitutional
culture stands in as problematic relationship to 'its' own national culture as it
does to those that do not share 'its' political-cultural 'traditions'.

In this chapter we discuss these wider issues through an examination of the
two conflicting rulings – that of the Bavarian Constitutional Court and that
of the German Federal Constitutional Court (colloquially, the 'Karlsruher
Gerichtshof') – which lie at the legal centre of this controversy and the debate
which surrounds these judgements.

The Crucifix Affair

The *Kreuzesbefehl* which reads '*In jedem Klassenzimmer ist ein Kreuz anzu-
bringen*' [A cross is to be hung in every classroom] is contained in §13 I3 of the
Schulordnung für die Volksschulen in Bayern [School Ordinance for Primary
Schools in Bavaria], 1983. It had legal force in all Bavarian primary schools. A
case was brought against the order by a family who adhered to the anthropo-
sophic teachings of Rudolf Steiner. Their objections to the mandatory presence
of crucifixes in school classrooms were broadly twofold. First, as non-
Christians the enforced learning under a Christian symbol – '*unterm Kreuz
lernen*' – injured their right to religious freedom and to bring up their children
in accordance with their beliefs. Secondly, the symbol itself, that of a 'dying
male body' [*sterbenden männlichen Körpers*], was held by the family to have
detrimental effects upon their children. To accommodate these objections the
original large crucifix (80 × 60 cm) over the blackboard in their eldest
daughter's classroom was exchanged for a more discrete cross placed over
the door. But this compromise on the part of the school authorities in 1986 was
not in the long run thought by the family to meet their objections. Lacking the
means to avoid the dilemma by keeping their three children in Waldorf Schools,
they took their case to the Bavarian Constitutional Court. This ruled against
them in 1991. They then appealed to the Federal Constitutional Court and this
body found in their favour in 1995.

That such an explicit order concerning religious practice should have been
passed is consistent with the intentions of the authors of the Bavarian
Constitution of 1946 which, like those of other predominantly Catholic
Länder (e.g. Baden-Württemberg), attempted to give Christian culture constitutional form. For example, Article 131, which specifically addresses education
reads:

> (1) Schools should not only transmit knowledge and skills, but also build
> heart and character.
> (2) The foremost aims of education are: reverence before God, respect for
> religious conviction and for the dignity of persons, self-control, a sense of
> and joy in responsibility, readiness to help, receptivity for all that is true,

HOWARD CAYGILL AND ALAN SCOTT 507

good, and beautiful, and awareness of responsibility for nature and the environment.[2]

(3) Pupils are to be educated into the spirit of democracy, the love of their Bavarian homeland and of the German people and in accordance with reconciliation between peoples.

(4) In addition girls in particular are to be instructed in the care of infants, education of children and home economy.[3]

At the same time, like other liberal constitutions, the Bavarian Constitution recognizes rights to freedom of religious confession and practice, for example Article 107, I guarantees religious freedom (see also 107, VI: 'No-one may be forced into religious act or participation in religious practice or services or into the use of a religious oath'). Thus anyone objecting to the *Kreuzesbefehl* could point to the Bavarian Constitution itself as well as to those Articles of the Basic Law concerning religious freedom (Article 4, I), the rights of parents in determining their children's upbringing (Article 6, II), and the protection of basic rights (Article 19, IV). The tension between the cultural content of the Bavarian Constitution and its liberal universalizing form, and between the attempt to reconcile constitutionally a catholic and still (at least in 1946) predominantly rural society with the Basic Law as the embodiment of a liberal modernity was at the heart of the legal dispute over the *Kreuzesbefehl*. The rulings of the two constitutional courts lay bare these tensions, and it is to these that we now turn.

The Bavarian Constitutional Court's Ruling

The Bavarian Constitutional Courts' ruling of June 1991 against the family reads as follows:

> The placing of a crucifix or other representation of the cross in classrooms of state schools does not injure the basic right to negative religious freedom of pupils and parents who on religious or philosophical [*weltanschaulich*] grounds reject such representation.[4]

We shall abstract somewhat the grounds for this judgement from the context of their legal precedents. The Court argued that the plaintiffs could not enjoy unrestricted rights to negative religious freedom because such rights were bounded, for example by rights and duties of the *Länder* and schools to determine the pedagogic aims which were to direct children's education. In this spirit the judges noted that '... it is in fact impossible for the school to

[2] This rather contemporary final environmental thought was added as part of a fifth amendment to the Bavarian constitution in 1981. Similar amendments were added to other *Länder* constitutions around this time under the influence of the growing environmental movement.

[3] Current German *Länder* constitutions plus the Basic Law are published in C. Pestalozza (ed.), *Verfassungen der deutschen Bundesländer* (Munich, DTV, 1991). Historic constitutions (plus again the Basic Law) are published in H. Hildebrandt (ed.), *Die deutschen Verfassungen des 19. und 20. Jahrhunderts* (Paderñorn, Schöningh, 1971). A translation of the Basic Law can be found in S. E. Finer (ed.), *Five Constitutions* (London, Penguin, 1979).

[4] The full ruling is contained in *Neue Zeitschrift für Verwaltungsrecht*, (hereafter, *NZfV*), 11 (1991), 1099–1101, p. 1099.

508   *The Basic Law versus the Basic Norm?*

represent all religious/philosophical wishes and educational desires. The recognition of this must not lead the school to restrict itself to teaching in a completely value-neutral fashion or to forgo any educational aim or style of teaching where there exist differences of opinion among parents' (*NZfV*, p. 1100). Indeed they go further by arguing that such a restriction would damage the positive religious freedoms of the majority and they posit a tension between negative and positive religious freedom ('*Spannungsverhältnis zwischen negativer und positiver Religionsfreiheit*') as a further limitation on the former's sphere of validity.

However, the most remarked upon and controversial aspect of the Bavarian ruling was the judges' argument that the parents did not have the right to demand the removal of the cross because that symbol did not in and of itself carry any specific confessional baggage:

> With the representation of the cross as the icon of the suffering and Lordship of Jesus Christ ... the plaintiffs who reject such a representation are confronted with a religious worldview in which the formative power of Christian belief is affirmed. However, they are not thereby brought into a constitutionally unacceptable religious-philosophical conflict. Representations of the cross confronted in this fashion are – like the cross-confessional school prayer – not the expression of a conviction of a belief bound to a specific confession. They are an essential object of the general Christian-occidental tradition and common property of the Christian-occidental cultural circle. (*NZfV*, p. 1101)

From this they concluded that 'the mere presence of the representation of a cross demands neither an identification with the ideas or beliefs thereby embodied nor any other form of active behaviour oriented thereto'. For the sake of our later argument, the irony here is that the Bavarian Constitutional Court is ascribing a neutrality and universality to Christianity which is at least analogous to that more usually ascribed to the constitution itself. Christianity is cast as an (almost) culture-neutral backdrop against which only the other minority religions stand out:

> The problematic presented [here] is distinct from cases in which the teacher through especially determined behaviour – in particular through the wearing of attention-drawing [*auffällig*] clothing (Baghwan) – which unambiguously indicates a specific religious or philosophical conviction impermissibly impairs the basic right to negative religious freedom of pupil and parent. (*NZfV*, p. 1101)

This last quotation probably makes clear why the Bavarian Constitutional Court's ruling should have occasioned considerable amusement and disdain in Germany's liberal press. In fact the ruling rests to a considerable degree upon the putative neutrality of Christian symbolism. It is upon this basis that the judges were able to conclude that the *Kreuzesbefehl* did not entail missionary activity on the part of the school and therefore did not injure the right of negative religious freedom. It was this claim of neutrality which also attracted the attention of the German Constitutional Court in overturning the initial ruling.

HOWARD CAYGILL AND ALAN SCOTT 509

The Federal Constitutional Court's Ruling

By majority verdict the Federal Constitutional Court ruled against the Bavarian Court as follows:

> (i) The placement of a cross or crucifix in classrooms of a state compulsory school, which is not a confessional school, violates Article 4, I of the Basic Law.
> (ii) 13 I3 of the School Ordnance for Primary Schools in Bavaria is irreconcilable with Article 4, I of the Basic Law and is void.[5]

The grounds for the judgement constituted a comprehensive rebuttal of the arguments made by the Bavarian Constitutional Court and took issue with its ruling on practically every point. After criticizing the Bavarian school authorities and courts for procrastination and failing to seek with sufficient vigour an acceptable provisional solution to the conflict, the judges launched a direct attack on the legal and theological arguments used by the Bavarian Constitutional Court in supporting its decision. The core disagreements turn on (i) the interpretation of Article 4, I; (ii) the issues of the imputed neutrality of the cross as a mere symbol of occidental culture; (iii) the constitutional implications of cultural pluralism.

Regarding Article 4, I, the Karlsruher Gerichtshof judges argued that the guarantee of religious freedom means that 'the decision for or against a faith is a matter for the individual, not the state. The state must neither prescribe nor forbid a faith to the individual' (*NJW*, p. 2478). Furthermore, such a right also entails the 'freedom to avoid the cultural activities of a faith which one does not share'. But where the two rulings depart most abruptly is in the claim of the Federal Constitutional Court that Article 4, I entails a positive duty on the part of the state to guarantee this freedom of religious conviction: 'It accords to the state the duty to secure a sphere of action in which the personality within the philosophical/religious domain can develop, and to protect that sphere of activity from attack or hindrance by adherents to other religious faiths or competing religious groups' (*NJW*, p. 2478). It was this duty of the state which the judges ruled to be irreconcilable with the *Kreuzesbefehl*. Because the pupil was legally bound to attend school and therefore involuntarily exposed for extended periods to the cross, the *Kreuzesbefehl* was deemed to violate the child's right to a self-determined development of religious or philosophical conviction. This fact was thought to 'unambiguously distinguish the placement of a cross in the classroom from frequent daily encounters with religious symbols of diverse religious conviction' (*NJW*, p. 2478).[6]

The 'theological' dispute between the two constitutional courts focused upon the claim that the cross was a common object and property of Christian-occidental culture. The Federal Constitutional Court insisted against this view that 'the cross is a symbol of a particular religious conviction and not somehow merely an expression of an occidental culture partially formed by Christendom'.

---

[5] The full ruling can be found in *Neue Juristische Wochenschrift*, (hereafter, *NJW*), 38 (1995), 2477–83, p. 2477.

[6] One populist reaction to the judgement was to claim that every religious symbol from '*Wegkreuze*' (crosses and small chapels at road forks – very common in Bavaria) to the ringing of church bells would be affected by the judgement. But it is clear that the ruling is confined to cases where there is this particular combination of legal obligation, unavoidability of contact and length of exposure.

510   *The Basic Law versus the Basic Norm?*

More precisely, the Court agreed that:

> The cross belongs, as it always has, to the specific symbols of the faith of
> Christendom. It is all but its symbol of faith *per se*. It iconographizes the
> redemption of mankind from original sin through the sacrifice of Christ's
> death, and at the same time Christ's victory over Satan and death, and His
> Lordship over the world; his suffering and triumph in one ... To render the
> cross profane would be to contradict the self-understanding of Christen-
> dom and the Church [it would] as the decision criticized here does, see it
> merely as an expression of an occidental tradition or a cult sign without
> specific implications of faith. (*NJW*, p. 2479)

In what looks like intended irony, the judgement goes on to note that 'the
religious significance of the cross is clear from the context of the School
Ordinance for Primary Schools in Bavaria 13 I3'.

The third area of disagreement between the Bavarian and the Federal
constitutional courts concerns minority rights under conditions of increasing
cultural pluralism. Whereas the Federal Constitutional Court argued for a
maximalist interpretation of Article 4, I, it went for a minimalist interpretation
of legal duties of the *Länder* in the setting of pedagogic aims for schools. While
the Bavarian Constitutional Court had argued that cultural pluralism should
not inhibit the school and school authorities from inculcating children with the
religious and philosophical values of the majority (in the name of the latter's
positive religious freedom), the Federal Constitutional Court argued (in the
name of the negative religious freedom of the minority) that such pluralism
placed a duty on the school to minimize the specificity of the substantive moral/
religious values into which children were to be educated. The Federal Court
thus drew precisely the opposite conclusions from the 'tension between positive
and negative religious freedom' to those drawn by the Bavarian Court. In so
doing, it came close to arguing that precisely the thin content of Christianity
which it had maintained was not the whole content of the Christian symbol of
the cross might nevertheless legitimately provide the basis of a minimal
consensus for educational purposes:

> The affirmation of Christendom refers [here] to the formative cultural and
> educational element, not to the specific validity of faith. To Christianity as a
> cultural element belongs precisely also the idea of tolerance towards those
> who think differently. The latter's confrontation with a worldview formed
> by Christianity does not lead in such a case to a discriminatory rejection of
> non-Christian worldviews, because we are dealing here not with the trans-
> mission of faith but with the striving for the realization of an autonomous
> personality in the religious philosophical sphere in accordance with the
> fundamental principle of Article 4 of the Basic Law. (*NJW*, p. 2480)

This claim, apart from its arguably over-optimistic reading of the history of
Christianity, suggests the possibility – to which we shall return – that what we
have in these two judgements is a dispute over and within Christianity between
its broadly Catholic and its secularizing and broadly Protestant wings. Earlier
we noted the irony that the Bavarian judgement imputed to Christianity that
neutrality normally accorded to the constitution. Here we have exactly the
mirror argument with the Federal Constitutional Court ascribing to

HOWARD CAYGILL AND ALAN SCOTT 511

Christianity the fundamental principles and values embodied in the constitution. What the cross symbolized for the Bavarians, the constitution now appears to represent for the Constitutional Court! It is the constitution which now emerges as 'an essential object of the general Christian-occidental tradition and the common property of the Christian-occidental cultural circle'.

Enough has now been said to enable us to move on to the wider implications of these judgements for our understanding of constitutions and of the notions of constitutional culture and constitutional patriotism.

The Perplexities of Constitutional Culture

The case of the Bavarian Crucifix Order illustrates the problematic relationship of a constitution both to normal politics and to the community in which it is embedded. In the following discussion we examine some aspects of this relationship, and make critical observations on some lacunae in 'actually existing constitutionalism'.

What Kant described as the fallacy of 'paralogism' – taking something which could only exist within given spatio-temporal conditions, and then speaking of it as if it were free of those conditions – can be found in what may be described as vaguely 'Kelsenite' constitutionalism which identifies, proposes, or even assumes, universal basic norms to inform a constitutional order. Whatever their source – 'nature', 'human reason', the 'supreme being' or 'the ideas of scientific communism' – such *Grundnormen* profess to be universal and immune to the effects of time. If they fail to be instantiated in or sustained over time it is because of external factors. But what if the failure of a constitution is intrinsic to it, and the language of *Grundnormen* is a rhetorical means to defer this moment, and perhaps even to conceal other, political interests at play in constitutionalism?

In an essay on the *Verfassungsentwurf* – the draft constitution drawn up by the Round Table shortly before the collapse of the GDR[7] – we cited Rousseau's characteristically paradoxical and insightful statement in the *Social Contract* concerning the conditions of a successful constitutionalism: 'the social spirit, which should be created by these institutions, would have to preside over their foundation; and men should be before law what they should become by means of law'.[8] We then understood this to mean that successful constitutional politics required not only the promulgation of a constitution but also the creation of a 'constitutional culture', if we may so translate Rousseau's 'social spirit'. Thus we adjusted Rousseau's paradox to the demands of a normative constitutionalism, in which 'constitutional culture' passes for Platonic participation in bringing the universal and eternal ideas or basic norms into historical time. Indeed, many modern constitutions resolve Rousseau's paradox by building into themselves the conditions for creating a 'social spirit' or 'constitutional culture'. The 'social spirit' presiding over the 'Declaration of the Rights of Man and the Citizen' precisely looks to create itself, in others, by means of the constitution: beginning with the claim that 'ignorance, forgetfulness, or contempt of the rights of man are the sole causes of public misfortune and governmental depravity', the

[7] H. Caygill and A. Scott, 'The subject of the constitution: the debate in Germany, 1989 and after' in R. Bellamy, V. Bufacchi and D. Castiglione (eds), *Democracy and Constitutional Culture in the Union of Europe* (London, Lothian Foundation, 1995), pp. 3–20.

[8] Cf. J.-J. Rousseau (G. D. H. Cole, trans.), *Social Contract and Discourses* (London, Dent, 1973), II, vii: 'The Legislator'.

512   *The Basic Law versus the Basic Norm?*

declaration resolved to be 'perpetually present to all members of the body
social ... a constant reminder to them of their rights and duties'. Thus the body
social will be educated in, and perpetually reminded of, their duty to respect the
'social spirit' informing the Declaration of the Rights of Man and the Citizen.
Similarly, the preamble to the 1977 Soviet Constitution seeks, in the social spirit
of scientific communism, to create a communist culture in which 'to mould the
citizen of communist society'.

Before returning to the case of the crucifix order in the conclusion, we wish to
raise two questions to emerge from the attempt to create a constitutional
culture: (i) what implications for the stability of the constitution itself might the
political act of cultural de- and reconstitution have? (ii) with what exactly does a
constitution replace a pre-constitutional culture?

The Politics of Constitutional Culture

Constitutions fail when they are unable to recreate the 'social spirit' which
presided over their foundations, to create a constitutional culture or produce an
affect of what Habermas, again modernizing Rousseau's 'social spirit' has
called 'constitutional patriotism'. This all important constitutional culture is
not, strictly speaking, justiciable; it is not something within the letter of the
constitution, but is its essential supplement. What is more, the character of such
a culture is neither unequivocal nor uncontested; indeed the very promulgation
of a formal constitution may be said to destroy the social spirit which presided
over it, and which it seeks to recreate in its constitutional culture. It is in these
issues that we encounter the 'political' side of 'constitutional politics', where the
Grundnorm encounters the cases of power and violence. For 'constitutional
politics' does not stop with the implementation of a constitution, but continues
with the incessant effort of creating and recreating a constitutional culture, one
which, in the eyes of some, is intrinsically self-defeating.

The phrase 'constitutional culture' rather like the word 'constitutionalism' is
a rather neutral and innocuous term, but informing it is the ambition, in the
candid words of the Soviet Constitution, to 'mould the citizen'. Rousseau was
very clear about what this meant earlier in the passage on the legislator, where
he says, in effect, that the 'constitutional moment' involves a de- and a reconstitution of society. The projection of a pre-constitutional state of nature
makes the thought that pre-constitutional 'natural' forces have to be 'annihilated' in order to ensure that those acquired are 'the greater and more lasting'.
An important aspect of constitutional politics is, as we all know but perhaps do
not say, the deconstitution of existing social relations and their reconstitution
under the new constitutional order. Yet perhaps the work of deconstitution is
more permanent and irreversible than the hoped for reconstitution; the
'constitutional moment' may irreversibly break the mould for the new citizen.

The 'constitutional moment' then is intrinsically political, regardless of the
constitutionalist normative rhetoric of inalienability and universality, and the
causes of its success or failure are political. In order to succeed in creating a new
constitutional culture, the advocates of the new constitutional order have to be
prepared to wield force when other political tactics, such as appeals to reason
and persuasion fail. But there is an understandable tendency among advocates
of constitutional reform to pass over this aspect of constitutional politics –
namely, that constitutions are politics by other means. It is far less troubling to

regard them as concatenations of legal norms than as instruments for the deconstitution of existing patterns of government and social relations. In a sense, constitutionalism offers the luxury of engaging in normative politics without the responsibility of gaining and wielding political power.

Yet, as Carl Schmitt showed in his *Verfassungslehre* [constitutional studies],[9] if this refusal of political responsibility is consistently pursued by constitutionalists, then the constitution will fail. It will fail not because of external forces, but because it was not prepared politically to create and defend a constitutional culture. He diagnoses the malaise of the Weimar Republic in precisely these terms – showing that the advocates of the Weimar constitution were not prepared to exercise political power in creating a democratic constitutional culture. An even more striking example of such failure is posed by the failure of the GDR Round Table's *Verfassungsentwurf* [draft constitution]. The Citizens Movements such as New Forum which played a pivotal role in the 1989 Revolution were not prepared to assume the political responsibility which would have been necessary in order to implement their constitutional draft and defend the 'social spirit' of grassroots direct democracy which presided over its drafting.

Constitutional Abstraction

If the first problematic element of constitutions resides in their relationship to normal politics and to the deconstitution of pre-constitutional culture, the second resides in the no less problematic nature of the communities which they constitute, or attempt to constitute, in the process.

Recent criticism of the language or discourse of rights has accustomed us to the argument that the subject of such rights is not liberalism's abstract universal individual but rather a disguised form of a particular – male, white or European – empirical subject.[10] But there is another tradition of the critique of rights discourse which makes what appears to be the opposite claim; namely, that there is no real subject of rights whom those putative rights can or do protect. The most dramatic formulation of this argument we owe to Hannah Arendt's discussion of the 'perplexities of the Rights of Man' in *The Origins of Totalitarianism*, in which she asserts that 'the world found nothing sacred in the abstract nakedness of being human'.[11] Arendt's argument here is that the abstraction of such notions as the 'Rights of Man', 'human rights' the 'rights of the individual' etc. do not so much disguise the identity of some empirical subject as rob all empirical subjects of any social identity whatsoever. Those who are not members of any political community can make no claims, not even the claim to physical protection or to life.

Provocatively, she points out that it is the stateless who come closest to embodying the abstraction of rights subjects, but it is precisely they who are the victims of violence and arbitrary (in)justice within the modern world of nation states and whom rights are least effective in protecting:

> The Rights of Man, supposedly inalienable, proved to be unenforceable –
> even in countries whose constitutions were based upon them – whenever
> people appeared who were no longer citizens of any sovereign state.

[9] C. Schmitt, *Verfassungslehre* (Berlin, Duncker and Humboldt, 1928).
[10] C. Pateman, *The Disorder of Women* (Cambridge, Polity, 1989).
[11] H. Arendt, *The Origins of Totalitarianism* (London, Allen and Unwin, 1951), p. 299.

514   *The Basic Law versus the Basic Norm?*

And she goes on to note:

> The first loss which the rightless suffered was the loss of their homes, and
> this meant the loss of the entire social texture into which they were born
> and in which they established for themselves a distinct place in the world ...
> The second loss which the rightless suffered was the loss of government
> protection, and this did not imply just loss of legal status in their own, but
> in all countries.[12]

Underlying this criticism of liberalism is a philosophical anthropology in
which that which is 'specifically human' is held to be precisely our nature as
social beings; as members of particular human communities rather than a
'human race'. We have on such a view, no human qualities other than those we
possess by dint of the fact that we are members of particular human communities which have 'established for themselves a distinct place in the world'.
The subject of universal rights is as conceptually denuded of their cultural
heritage or 'social texture' – and hence their specifically human qualities – as
are politically the stateless victims of twentieth century totalitarianism. It is the
deprivation of their social identity which, for Arendt, is the primary and prior
tragedy of the rightless:

> The calamity of the rightless is not that they are deprived of life, liberty,
> and the pursuit of happiness, or of equality before the law and freedom of
> opinion – formulas which were designed to solve problems *within* given
> communities – but that they no longer belonged to any community what-
> soever.[13]

For these reasons Arendt sides with Edmund Burke who preferred to speak of
the 'Rights of Englishmen' rather than the 'Rights of Man', the language of
the French Revolution. By stripping subjects of a 'local habitation and a name'
the abstraction of right discourse, Arendt argues, rendered real subjects
vulnerable.

The relevance of Arendt's argument to the case in question is that it suggests
that the culture which is de-constituted may – or can – never fully be reconstituted through constitutional means with their universalizing principles and
abstracted constitutional subjects.

Conclusion

The above discussion raises the possibility that constitutions may stand in an
antagonistic relationship to the context in which they are embedded for two
reasons: first, because of the necessity of an act of cultural deconstruction in
order to create a constitutional culture; secondly, because that constitutional
culture may itself be too abstract to accommodate or sustain a substantive
normative system.

There may be two possible readings of this state of affairs: a strong reading to
the effect that constitutions are in constant danger of failure due to the strains
to which they give rise, or a weaker reading to the effect that there is a
permanent tension between the constitution and constitutional culture which

[12] Arendt, *The Origins of Totalitarianism*, pp. 293–4.
[13] Arendt, *The Origins of Totalitarianism*, p. 295.

can only be addressed imperfectly by constitutional means. We shall not adjudicate between these two readings but rather point out that on either of them: (i) the universalizing language of constitutions is problematic, and (ii) the distinction between constitutional and normal politics blurred. These points can both be made with reference to the crucifix case.

The Bavarian Constitutional Court tried to resolve the tensions between the universalizing culture of the constitution and the local culture – rather naively – by ascribing universalism to Christian values. Any such claim can be trumped by the higher universalism of constitutional culture itself. This is precisely what the Federal Constitutional Court did. But, and this is the problem which occupies those who in the words of the Bavarian Prime Minister 'would not understand' the Constitutional Court's judgement, just what substantial values can a constitution defend against the right of any real or hypothetical individual to the 'free formation of opinion'? If no such values can be constitutionally grounded, then in what is the constitution itself based? Here the problem is not merely that constitutional culture may be 'too thin' to be the basis of either public or private virtue, but that it may be incompatible with the values and virtues of any given community. This is a form of Arendt's worry about the effects of rights discourse. What we earlier described as the constitution's 'essential supplement' may not merely be incapable of incorporation into a constitution, but may be hollowed out or even deconstituted by the abstract logic of the constitution's legal formalism.

In the case we have discussed we see an attempt by a particular State constitution to mould its citizens in the spirit of Catholic Christian virtues. It then responds to a complaint against a symbolic aspect of this culture by trying to universalize it. The Federal Constitutional Court, in its turn, restores the particularity of the symbol, but in the name of provisions informed by a secular/ Protestant 'social spirit' which it seeks to impose on both the Bavarian State and civil society. Is this an example of successful constitutional politics, or rather the source of new conflicts which may not easily be contained within the framework of constitutionalism? As was widely observed, behind this conflict lies the changed religious/political composition of the new Federal Republic, which with the accession of the ex-GDR has exchanged a Catholic for a Protestant religious majority. Is this decision an imposition of an allegedly universal secular, but actually Protestant 'social spirit' on Catholic citizens, and if so what implications will it have for citizens who subscribe to either or neither religious persuasion? Should they make a tactical alliance with the Protestant universalism, or with a Catholic defence of particular religious communities against that universalism, even if that defence is itself couched in universalistic terms? These are political decisions whose stakes are not clarified by the confusing rhetoric of constitutional universalism.

With this we return to Rousseau's paradox, because a democratic constitution which has to mould its citizens – forcing them to be free – is an extremely precarious one, vulnerable to the fate of the constitutionally hypocritical cultures of the socialist democracies. In other words, the 'social spirit' produced by the constitution cannot be the same as that which presided over its foundation. The constitution deconstructs the very culture necessary for its survival, or in the words of an earlier German Constitutional Court Judge, Ernst-Wolfgang Böckenförde, already in the early 1960s 'The free secular state lives according to presuppositions that it cannot itself guarantee without

516   *The Basic Law versus the Basic Norm?*

putting its freedom into question'.[14] This has been made glaringly clear in the Constitutional Court decision which exposes the tensions which exist between a Federal and a State constitution as well as those between both and civil society. In this case the State constitution's attempt to constitute a particular constitutional culture began to deconstitute civil society, proving a source of potential civil conflict, which the Federal Constitutional Court attempted to resolve according to the Basic Law, but which in turn has generated fresh conflict.

A related aspect of the decision which was widely noted was the way in which it succeeded in politicizing the classroom wall. The absence of a symbol has become replete with significance, provoking memories of other classroom decorations which might better have been forgotten. In the GDR, it was required to adorn classroom walls with the photograph of Erich Honecker. His removal from the classroom wall was obviously political, but the space now occupied or not by a crucifix has become similarly charged. The constitution by deconstituting an existing culture has become a source of conflict, and in this case politics has invaded civil society by virtue of the constitutions very universalism that was meant to put it above the competing partial political interests.

One of the issues raised in the *Kreuzesbefehl* decision concerns the resort to conflicting arguments for the universality of particular constitutional provisions. Of course *Bundesrecht bricht Landesrecht* [Federal law overrides State – Land – law], and the Federal Constitutional Court's definition of what is universal will prevail, even though it is seen by some to be partial. Perhaps this points to a problem with constitutionalism in general, which is that it translates particular political disputes into a language of universal and eternally valid norms, which, precisely by universalizing a particular conflict risks extending it to other, previously unconcerned parties. This can be considered from two standpoints: for the constitutional believer, the constitution is successful in reconstituting social relations according to a universal and eternally valid norm; for the constitutional sceptic, this may happen on occasion, but on the whole constitutions deconstitute social relations, potentially escalating conflict by enforcing universal norms where they may be inappropriate.

We would like to end by questioning the constitutionalists' monopoly of virtue. While not rejecting constitutional politics, we would underline the intrinsically violent and destructive side of constitutionalism, its capacity to generate, escalate and proliferate social conflict through its universalizing rhetoric. This rhetoric may have been necessary in the context of the absolutist societies in which modern constitutionalism was born, but is perhaps obsolete in a pluralistic democracy. What we have in mind is a fallible constitution which does not need to resort to universal claims in order to protect particular rights, but whether such a constitutionalism is conceivable and what institutional shape it would assume or require, we remain unsure. In any case, constitutional patriotism may not be enough.

[14] Quoted in *Die Zeit*, nr. 34, 18 August 1995.

[25]

The West German Peace Movement and The Christian Churches: An Institutional Approach

Alice Holmes Cooper

Protestant participation in postwar West German peace movements has markedly outstripped Catholic participation, suggesting that age is not the only important cleavage separating participants and nonparticipants. It is argued that because churches *interpret* collective experience, they have helped shape individual attitudes and political protest across generations throughout the postwar period. In West Germany, church interpretations of fascism, World War Two, and postwar developments have offered interpretive frameworks and defined the parameters of defense issues for their members. In doing so, churches have provided or restricted ideological, as well as organizational, resources to peace protest within their midst. Similar processes are at work in institutions like parties and unions as well. Although younger generations have sometimes adopted more radical views than their elders, the interplay between generations has taken place in the context of a previous institutional framing of issues.

The West German peace movement burst onto the political scene in 1981 and held the world's attention for the next several years. Apparently emerging overnight and out of nowhere, the movement occupied the thoughts of scholars and publicists alike. Although only one among several European peace movements, the German movement was probably the most visible and the most widely discussed. Many observers focused on the significance of the peace movement for German politics. The rapid growth of the peace movement was intimately connected with the parallel rise of the Green party, which crystallized the ecology, feminist, countercultural and youth movements into the first significant challenge to the established parties since the early 1950's. The peace movement, by generating such controversy over the issue of nuclear defense, contributed significantly to the weight of "new politics" issues in German politics.

The German peace movement is a prominent example of the "new social movements" of the 1970's and 1980's, and serves as a good case study of their causes and development. This essay focuses on the origins of the German peace movement, and in particular the ways in which political and social institutions have shaped defense policy issues. This institutional shaping has crucially affected rates of participation in the peace movements of the postwar period, and is also reflected in peace movement arguments. This analysis will be presented after a brief look at the most prominent theory of new social movements.

71

According to Ronald Inglehart, material prosperity and successful
national defense undermined their own attitudinal foundations by
making the prerequisites of these conditions (*e.g.*, heavy industry
or nuclear deterrence) seem superfluous or even harmful.[1] Inglehart posits a permanent value change in Western populaces, in the
direction of what he calls "postmaterialism," through the mechanism of cohort replacement. The most important factor in this transformation are the differences between the socializing factors for successive generations. Postwar generations were much more secure
politically, economically, and militarily when growing up than their
elders, who knew instead the material deprivation of economic
depression and the destruction of life and property of World War
II. As a result, postwar generations tend not to emphasize "materialist" values of economic and national security, and are therefore
more receptive to peace movement arguments than their elders.
Within the human personality structure, satisfaction of basic needs
leads to focus on unfulfilled needs. For the young, political action
reflects new demands based on changed values.

All statistical surveys of the German peace movement do indeed
show that the young are more highly represented than the old in
two categories pertaining to the movement: actual membership or
activism, and approval or sympathy without real participation. Inglehart's theory of value change no doubt contributes to an understanding of these generational differences. A look, however, at the
Eurobarometer 17 survey (one of Inglehart's data bases for peace
movements) reveals that age does not play as big a role in support
for, or opposition to, the double-track decision as Inglehart's theory
might suggest. A higher percentage of the younger generations, it
is true, approved of the peace movement than did older generations;
of the 15–37 age category, 61–70 percent approved "strongly" or "somewhat." Of the generation which experienced World War II during
its formative years, however, 50–60 percent approved strongly or
somewhat, whereas only 20–33 percent also disapproved in any way.
This generation should have the strongest security needs, yet it
nonetheless tends to approve of a movement whose goals, according
to its critics, threaten German security.[2] While approval is somewhat higher among the young than the old, considerable continuity
of opinion across the age spectrum exists. Moreover, this has been
the case throughout the postwar period. During the controversy over
the initial stationing of nuclear weapons on German soil in the late
1950's, as many as 70 percent of West German adults, all of whom
had lived through World War II, opposed them.[3]

PEACE MOVEMENT AND THE CHURCHES 73

Considerable support for the peace movement exists across the "value" spectrum as well. While admittedly postmaterialists tend overwhelmingly to support peace movements, opposition to nuclear weapons has consistently outstripped postmaterialists as a percentage of the populace,[4] which amounted to 11.8 percent in Germany in 1982.[5] Moreover, as Anthony Messina points out, peace movement supporters do *not* take security for granted, as the postmaterialist theory assumes. Instead, "while . . . European peace groups oppose a specific . . . defense policy (*i.e.*, one dependent on the use of nuclear weapons), most do not question either the need for or the ends (*i.e.*, peace and security) of a rational defense strategy . . . CND and other antinuclear groups have long formulated alternative — and in their view, move effective — European defense strategies."[6]

Most commentary on the peace movement has followed Inglehart's lead in viewing age as the dominant determinant of movement activism. A closer look reveals, however, that age is not the only relevant cleavage separating those who participate from those who do not. Inglehart's theory neglects to explain adequately the institutional anchoring of the peace movement: Why it is so much more firmly ensconced in the Protestant than the Catholic church, or why it finds so much more support on the left than on the right? Why have the unions and the radical left played such prominent roles? Why have these institutions and groups been the mainstays of peace protest throughout the postwar period?[7]

Part of the answer lies in the fact that institutions play a major role in defining the parameters of defense issues. Arguments presented for or against missiles are not simply the result of an assessment of the military situation and the armaments or strategies necessary for defense. It is true, on the one hand, that supporters and opponents of the double-track decision include such an assessment in their arguments. Both sides, however, also argue their positions in terms of a whole host of other issues, thereby placing their views on defense (narrowly defined) in a broader moral and political context, or even substituting this context for military-related arguments altogether. Concern for arms control and detente, the question of inherited guilt from the fascist period and its consequences for German foreign policy, feminist issues, ecology, and third world problems are all examples of the secondary issues which have given the missile issue a broader context.

Institutions have played a major role in defining the missile issue in terms of these secondary issues and broader contexts. In doing so, they may provide the crucial link between mere attitude (being "for" and "against" the missiles) and actual participation. Activists in the peace movement, after all, represent only a small fraction of the West German populace which "approves" of or "sympathizes" with the movement (depending on the wording of the survey question). What separates those who are "against" the new missiles, but otherwise passive, from those who participate in the peace movement? The striking differences in actual participation in the movement according to institutional affiliation (*e.g.*, Protestant and Social Democratic participation being so much heavier than Catholic and Christian Democratic) suggest that it is perhaps these secondary issues, these broader contexts, which provide much, or perhaps most, of the stimulus for actual participation in the peace movement, shaking people out of the lethargy of merely being "against" the missiles.

This article, then, argues the importance of institutions for both the broader shaping of attitudes toward defense issues and participation in peace movements. The context of postmaterialist attitudes toward defense is not simply peace as such; peace, rather, "takes place" in the course of particular political struggles and policies, with accompanying rhetoric. These processes take place largely within institutions, including parties, churches, unions, as well as governments and other groups. Institutions help define the relevant parameters of defense issues through their interpretations of the constituent elements of war and peace, and by the way they justify their policies. In West Germany specifically, attitudes toward defense have been shaped, in part, by the way institutions interpreted the causes and consequences of fascism and World War II, and by the way they interpreted the events of the postwar period and tried to shape its course. Institutions have shaped issues for *all* generations, including both the generations which experienced the war and the postwar generations. By the way they structure defense issues, institutions provide or restrict ideological, as well as organizational, resources to peace protest.

Sidney Tarrow has arrived at similar conclusions with respect to insurgency within institutions. As he so accurately formulates the point:

> It is institutions that are most likely to provide them (protest movements) with resources — economic, organizational, ideological — to turn anger and deprivation into mobilization. The solidarities, symbolism and organization that insurgents use to attack institutions are often provided by the institutions themselves, and turned against them by those who know them best. This is why the most frequent insurgen-

cies are found within political parties, trade unions, and churches; within such institutions, traditional interpretive frames can become the basis of an insurgent group's new ideology.[8]

What Tarrow finds for insurgency originating within, and directed against, institutions also holds true for protest directed against government policy by members of various institutions. Depending on how institutions as a whole treat issues, groups can use the "traditional interpretive frames" provided by their institutions as the basis of their opposition to government policy. The lack of such interpretive frames within an institution may in turn inhibit opposition. In this way, institutions facilitate or hinder mobilization, and contribute to how people think about issues.

This article will illustrate this process with reference to the German peace movement and its relationship to the German churches.

THE PEACE MOVEMENT AND THE CHURCHES

A comparison of the German Protestant and Catholic churches provides one of the best examples of institutions' effects on peace movements. Protestants have always been more active in the peace movements of the postwar period than Catholics, in terms of statistically measured individual activism, participation by identifiably Protestant or Catholic groups, and the roles played by prominent church leaders and organizations. Compared to the German Catholic church, the Protestant church has always functioned more fully as a forum for discussion of defense and peace issues, and been more severely divided by the controversy surrounding these issues.

Survey data reveal that religious affiliation has essentially no effect on people's attitudes toward the NATO double-track decision, that is, whether they "oppose" the decision or not. Striking, however, is the effect of religious affiliation on *activism* in the peace movement. Peter Nissen found, in his analysis of a 1981 Emnid survey data, that activists in the peace movement were 70 percent Protestant, 17 percent Catholic, and 13 percent unaffiliated. In contrast, the West German population as a whole has 51 percent Protestants, 43 percent Catholics, and 5 percent unaffiliated.[9] Furthermore, the Coordinating Committee, the national umbrella organization of the peace movement, includes four Protestant but only two Catholic groups. Further evidence on this point is offered impressionistically by essays on peace movement discussion and activity within the Protestant and Catholic churches. Whether written by activists within the respective churches or by scholars, all point to various indications that Protestants are more active than Catholics. Lutz Lemhöfer, for example, notes that Catholics had no equivalent of the Protestant *Friedenswochen* of 1981 (regional week-long programs devoted to peace activities). He notes further that there were many fewer Catholic than Protestant groups which signed the official call (*Aufruf*) to the first big peace movement demonstration in 1981.[10]

Why have these differences occurred? The answer lies in a combination of doctrinal development and organizational structure. Patterns in both of these areas were established very soon after the war, and channeled future developments for decades to follow. The churches' doctrinal development on peace issues varied according to the way they interpreted the lessons of the fascist past and the results of the war, how they defined their relationship to the new West German state, and how they defined their relationship to war in general. Both official doctrine and the conflicts within each church on defense issues helped to frame the issues for church members, at least as far as their religious identity was concerned. This framing of issues probably influenced the way people of each church conceptualized defense issues, and certainly contributed to defining the range of opinions available for public discussion and political action within each church. The positions taken in the early postwar period, when so much was in flux, strongly influenced the "political opportunity structure" for groups working on these issues within each church, then and in subsequent years. Early positions opened or closed ideological space within each church with respect to future discussion, by providing or foreclosing the future option of holding each church to the standards of earlier statements.[11] The organizational structure and opportunities for lay involvement in each church further opened or constricted the space available to activist groups.

As argued above, institutions help define defense issues by placing narrow military questions in a broader context. In the case of the churches, this context has been both moral and political. Concern for detente and *Ostpolitik*, German guilt inherited from the past and its consequences for foreign policy, the relationship of West Germany to the third world and its problems, and support for conscientious objectors to military service are all issues which have become associated with the missile question. They have broadened and intensified debate, moving it beyond the confines of narrow security concerns. The extent of peace movement participation in conjunction with religious affiliation reflects the ways in which each of these

PEACE MOVEMENT AND THE CHURCHES 77

issues has been discussed in the two churches, and the degree to which a constituency has grown up around each issue among Protestants and Catholics.

This section will (more or less chronologically) trace the debate within each church in the postwar period, and show the relationship between the nature of this debate and peace movement participation by groups within each church.

THE PROTESTANT CHURCH AND THE PEACE MOVEMENT

The immediate postwar period was as important to Germany's Protestant church as it was to German Catholicism. The first five years of the postwar period (1945–1950) saw several events which set the context for later official EKD positions on peace issues,[12] and provided the basis for much of the future Protestant radicalism on these issues. In this period, the EKD accepted the Protestant share of guilt for Hitler's rise to power and the subsequent crimes of the Third Reich, redefined on this basis the Protestant church's relationship to the state, rejected war categorically as an instrument of policy, and established its concern for East Germany and the cause of German unity. These themes played major roles in the defense policy debates of the decades to come.

The church's postwar admission of its share of responsibility (because it had not resisted National Socialism more valiantly) and its redefinition of its relationship to the state had their roots in the fascist period. Hitler and National Socialism had enjoyed considerable support in both German churches, and neither church had resisted the Third Reich as fully as it might have. Both churches experienced Nazi manipulation and partial control, and persecution of those who resisted. In the Protestant church, resistance took the form of the *Bekennende Kirche* ("Confessing Church"), centered around Karl Barth, Dietrich Bonhoeffer, and Martin Niemöller, among others. During the fascist period, this group confined itself to fighting for the independence of the church from Nazi control. After the war, however, the group's leaders were instrumental in pushing the church to redefine its relationship to the state and to politics.

This redefinition took place in statements made in the context of the Protestant church's first postwar meeting in August 1945, and in the *Stuttgarter Schuldbekenntnis* ("Stuttgart confession of guilt") a few months later. These statements revealed a deep feeling of guilt and blame for the rise and crimes of the Third Reich. They laid the foundations for a doctrinal rethinking, namely the innovative admission that the church had a *political*, as well as spiritual, responsibility. The church drew two conclusions from the lessons of the Third Reich: first, the church could no longer leave the state to its own devices, under the assumption of the state's full sovereignty in the political realm; and second, the church had the duty to insure that politics stayed within the bounds of morality and were conducted in a manner consistent with general Christian principles. This meant a break with the Lutheran tradition of the "two realms" doctrine (according to which the church must leave politics to the state), and the traditional Lutheran close and uncritical relationship to the state.

The early postwar years also saw a redefinition of the EKD's relationship to war in general. The EKD issued a "Friedenswort" ("peace message") at its founding conference in Eisenach in 1948. In this statement, the EKD called on Christians to view war with other peoples as ended, even if peace was not yet at hand. Members of other nations, it noted, were brothers and sisters, and no longer enemies. Above all, Germans should not fall prey to the delusion that their problems could be solved by another war, as war leads only to hate and misery.[13]

In addition to its rejection of war in general, the EKD was concerned that the cold war not destroy the German people as a nation. East-West tensions and the gradual evolution of two German states affected the EKD in different ways from the Catholic church. The EKD by 1948 had just gone through the very difficult process of establishing its organizational unity, which had just been attained when national and international political divisions questioned it anew. Germany's traditional confessional balance made German division all the more difficult for the EKD. Nearly half of all German Protestants and many of the traditionally most important Protestant provincial churches were located on the eastern side of the European divide. It was no coincidence that many of the most passionate proponents of reunification and an accommodating policy toward Eastern Europe came from the Protestant camp.[14]

The rearmament issue of the early 1950's put all of these new developments in the EKD to the test. The rearmament debate and the discussion of nuclear weapons for the German army in the late 1950's provoked controversy so bitter that it threatened Protestant unity.

Opponents of rearmament and nuclear weapons for Germany mixed more broadly held political positions with specifically Prot-

PEACE MOVEMENT AND THE CHURCHES   79

estant themes. A fundamental antimilitarism ran through their arguments. Opponents of the government's defense policy apparently feared war itself more than any foreign enemy. The Korean War proved to them that national division was a cause of war, rather than that Communist regimes were aggressive. West German participation in a Western defense structure and nuclear weapons, these people argued, would both harden the division of Germany, and turn any East-West conflict into a German civil war. Nuclear weapons, moreover, were more likely to draw preemptive attacks than to deter aggression. To these general political arguments, Protestant opponents of rearmament and nuclear weapons added religious themes. They argued that Germany's disarmed status reflected a judgment of God and a punishment for recent crimes. A new German army contradicted true repentance for the sins of the Third Reich. They found, moreover, that the destructive capacities of nuclear weapons vastly outweighed any benefits accruing from their deterrent capability. God, they argued, gives man life to preserve it above all else, and therefore weapons of mass destruction cannot be justified with reference to some other purpose. Since such weapons indiscriminately kill civilians as well as soldiers, limiting war in the sense of a "just" war is impossible, and hence their use is injustifiable.[15]

The EKD contained supporters of Adenauer's defense policy too, who argued in power-political and military terms for defense against the Soviet Union. They denied that Christian faith required that Christians renounce force at any price or that they not defend themselves. They emphasized the need to make political decisions on the basis of political criteria, rather than turning them into questions of faith. They also charged that the EKD was overstepping its bounds and becoming too "politicized" by the strong positions taken by rearmament opponents.

After its initial pleadings against a revival or militarism in general, the EKD as a body became increasingly paralyzed by the severity of the conflict over these issues. The EKD's official positions were therefore compromises which neither fully supported nor fully opposed rearmament measures. In 1950 the EKD stated that it could not support rearmament in either East or West Germany,[16] but was subsequently accused of indirectly abetting rearmament by not opposing it more forcefully. The well-known "Heidelberg Theses" of 1959 admitted that individuals could both reject nuclear weapons and adhere to deterrence strategy on the basis of Christian faith, and thus reflected the EKD's admission that the church was deeply split over the issue. Each statement, however, reflected more clearly the arguments of the opponents than the proponents of the arms measures in question. The 1950 statement stressed the need to avoid having Germans shoot at Germans, and the 1959 statement emphasized that deterrence strategy and nuclear weapons remained acceptable only as long as no better alternative could be realized. These positions left plenty of ideological space for Protestant peace activists.

If the 1950's established the theme of German guilt and repentance as a factor in Protestant treatment of defense issues, the EKD's *Vertriebenendenkschrift* (essay on refugees driven out of the former German eastern territories after World War II) of 1965 applied these themes to the problem of West Germany's *Ostpolitik*, or its relations with Eastern Europe.[17] The essay pushed for a new foreign policy of acceptance of German division and the current German borders for the foreseeable future, and reconciliation with Eastern Europe on the basis of this acceptance. These acts, it argued, would in their turn contribute to peace and international stability, and constitute some of the building blocks of a future "peace order." In the context of *Ostpolitik*, the essay argued that accepting the consequences of the Third Reich meant stress on reconciliation and detente rather than confrontation, and peaceful (perhaps nonmilitarist) approaches to problems rather than revanchist tones. The EKD's *Ostpolitik* essay aroused a great deal of political passion. More than 250,000 copies were printed, and the essay was discussed in the press and in public fora. Both criticism and praise greeted the essay's publication, and the EKD's synod issued a statement in its defense. Although the essay deeply offended part of the populace and EKD membership, it established the EKD's commitment to *Ostpolitik*, and the value of *Ostpolitik* and reconciliation in general to the establishment of a European "peace order."

Two of the Protestant groups represented in the peace movement's Coordinating Committee reflect the spirit of the *Ostpolitik* essay. *Aktion Sühnezeichen* was founded in 1958 to do charitable work in countries which had suffered German aggression during the war, in order to show both "sign(s) of repentance" (hence the group's name) and to contribute to reconciliation with these countries through service to their postwar population. According to one of *Aktion Sühnezeichen*'s current leaders,[18] the group is motivated by a sense of German collective guilt, even on the part of postwar generations, for the deeds of the past, and by the desire to show that Germans now want to live in peace with these peoples. *Aktion Sühnezeichen*'s original founders were members of the *Bekennende Kirche* and active in the 1950's

PEACE MOVEMENT AND THE CHURCHES 81

struggles against rearmament and nuclear weapons. Supporters of *Ostpolitik* from the beginning, the group began consciousness-raising work in Germany itself in the late 1970's as detente began to decline. Via this role, *Aktion Sühnezeichen* became one of the founding groups of the peace movement.

Protestants, including clergy, also make up a large part of the membership of the *Gustav-Heinemann-Intiative* (GHI), a group dedicated to carrying on the work of Gustav Heinemann, who was active in the campaigns against rearmament and nuclear weapons in the 1950's. Although largely concerned with the subject of civil rights, the GHI enthusiastically supported detente and *Ostpolitik*. Several of the members of the GHI's executive committee are also prominent Protestants active in the peace movement, like Erhard Eppler, Helmut Gollwitzer, Heinrich Albertz and EKD Bishop Kurt Scharf.[19]

The EKD's contributions to the "guilt question" and *Ostpolitik* in the 1950's and 1960's probably represent the most original Protestant contributions to German discussion of peace issues. They are also closely linked to Protestant participation in the peace movement. Leftist stands on such issues as third world problems, religious socialism, and church support of conscientious objectors to military service, however, are also associated with Protestant groups involved in the movement. A look at EKD treatment of these issues furthers understanding of the high participation rate of Protestant groups in the peace movement. On each of these questions, religious activists were able to use organizational structures and draw on principles and positions established by earlier church positions and commitments.

Work within the world ecumenical movement brought the problems of the third world to Protestant attention, in addition to the stimulus provided by more general controversy over the Vietnam war and the discovery of the "North-South problem" by the public as a whole. Throughout the postwar period, the EKD participated in the ecumenical movement, which turned its attention to the third world early on. By the 1960's, the ecumenical movement was stressing the need to transform the world economic system, which it viewed as perpetrating "structural violence" on the less developed countries. The "theology of revolution" and the removal of restrictions from Christian participation in revolution also found wide support in the ecumenical movement during this period.[20] In 1975, the ecumenical movement called on Christians as individuals to renounce voluntarily military defense and to make this known to their governments.

82   THE REVIEW OF POLITICS

Religious socialism became a controversial topic in the EKD in the wake of the rediscovery of Marxism and its variants by the student movement as a whole. Interest in religious socialism caused concern in some parts of the church that the EKD was becoming both too politicized and drifting too far to the left. While many of those interested in the subject were students, prominent older theologians and laity have also been deeply involved. Indeed, Dorothea Sölle is a prominent example of the older generations in this area, and has been one of the Protestant luminaries in the peace movement.

The EKD was involved in the problem of conscientious objection from the birth of the West German army on. During the rearmament debate, the church strongly defended the right of individuals to conscientious objection and vowed to support and counsel them in this area. Radical groups within the church called for Germans to avail themselves of this status as a moral and political statement. The Heidelberg Theses of 1959 and the 1967 *Kirchentag* (the Protestant lay assembly) both recognized conscientious objection and military service as equally valid Christian positions, thus condoning religious pacifism. In the 1960's the church emphasized increasingly that the alternative service required of conscientious objectors could be more than a mere "substitute service"— it could actually constitute an active "service to peace" (*Friedensdienst*). This admission constituted an ideological coup for both politically and religiously motivated conscientious objectors. The student movement of 1968 led to a politicization of conscientious objection, whereafter more men objected for political reasons and fewer for purely religious reasons. This change stimulated a corresponding focus on political issues within the EKD as well.[21]

Groups like the Protestant student association, the *Evangelische Studentengemeinde* (ESG), with its chapters in the various universities, typify EKD involvement with such topics and the fairly unbroken line of radical Protestantism within the EKD in the postwar period. In the 1980's, the ESG has been a member group of the peace movement's national Coordinating Committee and a local center of activity in university cities. The ESG's history exhibits a continuity of Protestant activism throughout the postwar period. The ESG's forerunner had some pacifist leanings, and the ESG itself was associated with the *Bekennende Kirche* during the Third Reich. In the postwar period, the ESG discussed political problems in the context of biblical interpretation, and often touched on the theme of the National Socialist past and its political consequences for the present. Active in the political debates of the 1950's, in the 1960's

PEACE MOVEMENT AND THE CHURCHES   83

the ESG denounced discrimination against conscientious objectors, and continues to cooperate with C.O. associations today. Thus it is not surprising that the ESG has been open to radical politics since the 1960's. The group studied "peace research," a "leftist" alternative to traditional strategic studies, and did "antimilitarism" work. Its involvement in the ecumenical movement led to its discovery of third world problems. The ESG became caught up in the student movement of the late 1960's, which brought an interest in Marxism not previously prevalent and reinforced perceptions of the links between Christian faith and its social and political implications. Recent theological work of the ESG has centered on a rediscovery of Karl Barth, religious socialism, and third world theology. The ESG went on in the 1970's and 1980's to incorporate the themes of the "new social movements" into its work, including that of the peace movement.[22]

Another Protestant group active in the peace movement bears the name *Ohne Rüstung Leben* (ORL), ("Live without arms"). Formed in response to the 1975 call issued by the ecumenical movement, ORL members in effect espouse unilateral disarmament and radical pacifism, as they profess themselves willing to live without any military defense at all. ORL in Germany has chapters in many cities and has experienced a certain groundswell of support.[23]

The above has described the ideational component of Protestant support for the peace movement, and how the various components of peace movement argumentation came to exist within the EKD. It remains to point out how the organizational structure of the EKD favored the spread of these ideas, even when they did not enjoy majority support within the church. The EKD is actually a federation of autonomous provincial churches. Some of the more radical EKD leaders headed these provincial churches, which gave them an independent center for their activities. Protestant pastors enjoy autonomy within their own particular churches, and are not required to toe the line on policy matters. The Protestant laity also has a chance to make its many voices heard. Lay members make up half of the EKD's synod, and participate heavily in the two lay assemblies, the *Kirchentag*, and the Protestant academies. Both of these have served as important fora for political discussion and education throughout the postwar period, and have been careful to serve as a platform for the full range of Protestant opinion.[24] Their popularity was only part of both churches' weight in the immediate postwar period at a time when the populace viewed the Third Reich's collapse as a collapse of values.[25] Years later, the 1981 *Kirchentag* served as the platform for the first demonstration against the double-track decision in Germany.

While the EKD has never been united on political issues, its debates have helped frame the issues both for its members and for the broader public. Exposure to these debates has not depended on actual church attendance, although radical pastors have made their marks on some local churches. The German media has played a large role in bringing Protestant debates to the general public's attention. *Kirchentag* assemblies have consistently drawn large audiences and the media has provided extensive coverage of the events.[26] Typical of media coverage of the churches in general is the *Frankfurter Allgemeine Zeitung*'s recent reporting of the EKD Synod's position on genetic engineering.[27] Back in the 1950's the media reported on Protestant participation in peace protests as well. The various regional radio stations carried the 1949 Easter peace rally, including three members of the EKD's national leadership. The contrasting positions taken by Eugen Gerstenmaier and Heinrich Albertz at the Essen *Kirchentag* in 1950 provided arguments for rearmament supporters and opponents far beyond EKD circles. Highly visible confrontations over rearmament between Adenauer and both Martin Niemöller and Gustav Heinemann helped stir public debate as well.[28] Throughout the postwar period, some of the EKD's publications have enjoyed wide readership. The *Ostpolitik* essay, the *Vertriebenendenkschrift*, probably set a record at over 250,000 copies; the 1981 essay on peace saw a more modest volume of over 60,000 copies by the end of 1982.[29] All in all, the EKD's contribution to public discussion has been significant.

THE CATHOLIC CHURCH AND PEACE PROTEST

Catholic participation in West German foreign policy debates has differed quite markedly from Protestant participation in the postwar period on several levels. Foreign and defense policy has always divided the EKD more than the West German Catholic church, provoking much more heated intrachurch controversy and straining church unity to a much greater extent. Moreover, Protestants have provided more of the most active groups and prominent individuals throughout the postwar period. Protestants were also more active than Catholics at the level of rank and file participation at the height of the 1980's protest, according to survey evidence.[30] While Protestants have participated in peace protest throughout the postwar period, Catholic involvement was very weak up until the mid-1960's. Although stronger

PEACE MOVEMENT AND THE CHURCHES   85

since the Second Vatican Council, Catholic activity still lags behind Protestant engagement.

Why has this been the case? German Catholicism has differed from Protestantism in both doctrine and organizational structure in the postwar period. Doctrinal differences were especially apparent in Catholic treatment of the subject of German guilt and its foreign policy consequences, the Catholic church's relationship to the Adenauer government and the CDU, Catholic treatment of *Ostpolitik*, and the church's relationship to conscientious objection. The Catholic church's hierarchical structure and control of its lay associations, moreover, left much less room for opposition groups to form and act within the church. Not until the Second Vatican Council did significant changes occur, at which point Catholic thought on peace issues turned to new directions and Catholic organizational life loosened to include more heterogeneous elements.

Catholic postwar thought put much less emphasis on German guilt from World War II, along with its foreign policy implications, than did its Protestant counterparts. As with Protestants, Hitler and the Third Reich enjoyed considerable support among Catholics in the beginning, and the 1933 Concordat between the Vatican and the Third Reich reflected Catholic willingness to compromise in exchange for protection of Catholic interests. Unlike the prewar Protestant church's loss of autonomy, however, the German Catholic church resisted National Socialist attempts at penetration and organizational control of both the church itself and of parochial schools. Several Catholic bishops became famous for shielding numbers of intended victims of Nazi extermination programs. After the war, at least according to some authors, the German Catholic church evaded its share of responsibility for Hitler's assumption and consolidation of power.[31] Others have pointed to the existence of a few statements by bishops and other highly placed Catholics to the effect that Catholics were not entirely free from guilt associated with the Nazi period.[32] Be this as it may, this theme has not played a major role in Catholic foreign policy discussion as it has among Protestants.

The West German Catholic church was much more closely tied than the EKD to the Adenauer government and the CDU of the 1950's, and shared the strong anticommunism of political conservatism during this period. Indeed, the whole concept of "political Catholicism" for this period denotes the close relationship between the Catholic hierarchy and the Adenauer government, as well as the very strong Catholic voting preference for the CDU/CSU.[33] The close relationship between church and state during the 1950's and early 1960's in effect fully integrated (West) German Catholics into the (West) German state and democracy for this first time ever, while Catholic voting behavior played a stabilizing role in the early West German party system and state.[34] One component of "political Catholicism" of the period was Catholic support for Adenauer's foreign and defense policies, including rearmament, integration into Western military and economic structures, and nuclear weapons for the *Bundeswehr* in the late 1950's. In contrast to many Protestants, Catholics on the whole did not express particular concern about potential conflicts between Adenauer's policy of Western military and economic integration and his goal of German reunification through his "policy of strength." Catholics generally were not among the first to press for a change in Germany's *Ostpolitik*. This apparent lack of concern has been attributed to the traditional Rhineland and south German demographic concentration and political orientation of German Catholics, and to the corresponding lack of Catholics in East Germany and the lost territories.[35] West European integration is likewise said to have appealed more strongly to Catholics than Protestants in the 1950's because of the traditional Catholic attachment to the "Christian West" (*das christliche Abendland*) and anticommunism.[36]

Another factor in Catholic support for Adenauer's defense policy lay in papal positions of the 1950's, a time when lay obedience to church authorities was still uncontested. Although Pope Pius XII condemned offensive war as a permitted solution to international tensions and an instrument of national aspirations, he supported the right of Christian states to defend essential goods in his Christmas message of 1948. This address created a front line for Catholics against the Soviet Union and provided an important orientation. The natural law concept of war reinforced this orientation, for it also departed from friend-foe and confrontational categories. The form of the East-West conflict as a confrontation of two camps made falling back onto the doctrine of defensive war an obvious solution. Eastern European political persecution of Catholics during this period helped meld ideological and political opposition between communism and Catholicism, which was reinforced by the pope's message to the Bochum Catholic lay assembly (*Katholikentag*) of 1949, and his prohibition of Catholic's joining Communist parties.[37]

The rearmament debate of the early 1950's brought these issues to the fore. Catholic debate on the rearmament issue was conducted largely in the Catholic press. For the first few years after the war,

Catholics generally rejected any rearmament and military defense, as attention centered on social problems, and superpower conflict was not yet perceived to entail an acute military threat despite the Berlin blockade. This position prevailed for a time even after the question of rearmament was broached as an issue for West German politics, rather than merely Allied policy.

Despite this initial rejection of remilitarization, acceptance of rearmament began to grow from 1950 on, stimulated by several factors. Following the outbreak of the Korean War, perceptions of parallels between the Korean and German situation solidified into feelings of threat in the German public at large, as evidenced by both press commentary and opinion surveys.[38] The German church hierarchy drew the implications of the Korean War for its flock. A pivotal sermon by Cardinal Frings, the president of the Fulda bishops' conference, reminded people of the papal Christmas message of 1948 and stressed that it was not right to let injustice occur even if it meant war. The major organs of the Catholic press over time began to support Frings's position and rearmament, led by the *Mann in der Zeit*. As the organ closest to the bishops, this journal was influential in organized Catholicism because of its circulation to all West German dioceses and men's associations. From mid-1950 on, the Catholic press essentially approved of German participation in Western European defense, and discussion revolved around the form this participation would take. Acceptance of German rearmament was facilitated among Catholics by the proposals of the early 1950's to have German forces fully integrated into a European army, which extended support for European integration to support for military efforts in a European context. By 1952, the Catholic press more or less unanimously rejected the *ohne mich* position of the antirearmament movement. After this point, the Catholic press supported Adenauer's position on the whole, with some qualifications expressed in the nuances and timing of statements.[39]

Catholic opponents of rearmament did exist, but they did not form a wing within the church which could have opposed the church hierarchy's pressure for Catholic unity (*Geschlossenheit*) or forced a recognition of pluralism in political questions as in the EKD. A few lone individuals like Reinhold Schneider opposed rearmament for religious reasons, and other Catholic pacifists like Klara Fassbinder made their voices heard. Publicists like Walter Dirks and Eugen Kogon, centered around such journals as the *Frankfurter Hefte*, expressed political opposition to rearmament, using arguments

common to the antirearmament movement as a whole and devoid
of any peculiarly Catholic character. Thus within German Catholicism, rearmament opponents did not enjoy any broad effect, and
outside of Catholicism only insofar as other groups were already
active. Catholics constituted only a small part of the domestic opposition to rearmament, and were insufficient to change the image
of very broad Catholic support for rearmament policy. Their opposition was further limited in its effectiveness because it was primarily
politically rather than religiously motivated, and thus could not challenge Catholic doctrine on the subject.

The tight bond between the West German Catholic church and
the Adenauer government essentially continued to hold during the
controversy over nuclear weapons for the *Bundeswehr* of the late 1950's.
While there was some discussion within the church of this issue,
it did not approach the intensity or divisiveness of the Protestant
debate.[40] Opposition came solely from parts of the BDKJ (the umbrella Catholic youth organization), some publicists, and a few
"leftists," and drew the fire of established Catholicism.[41] The Catholic hierarchy and theologians largely kept out of the debate.[42] According to Heinz Hürten, if the German bishops had spoken out
against nuclear weapons, they would have found broad popular support. The fact that they remained silent on the issue spoke volumes,
and in effect amounted to support for Adenauer's policy, which was
important with respect to upcoming elections.[43]

Some prominent Catholic theologians, moreover, interpreted
papal statements to the effect that use of nuclear weapons was permissible under certain conditions.[44] On 5 May 1958, on the eve of
the Nordrhein-Westfalen *Landtag* elections of that year, seven moral
theologians published "Ein katholisches Wort zur atomaren Rüstung."
Published as a pamphlet, the "Wort" was widely distributed among
the population, and reprinted in the June edition of *Herder Korrespondenz*, a Catholic journal of wide readership.[45] According to Walter
Dirks, a leading Catholic publicist opposed to German nuclear
weapons, this statement amounted de facto to a Catholic moral and
theological justification of Adenauer's policy, as it had the character
of a theological judgment (*Gutachten*), coming from the theological
discipline which participates in the doctrinal body (*Lehramt*) of the
church.[46] According to the seven theologians' statement, the state
is required to defend law (*Recht*) and justice, and must have whatever
instruments are required to defend these goods. Although the de-
structiveness of nuclear weapons has reduced the number of instances

PEACE MOVEMENT AND THE CHURCHES   89

in which war is legitimate, defense is still justified when the moral
or physical existence of a people is attacked. Nuclear weapons do
not always escape the control of their user, the statement noted, and
thus their use is not always a sin. Although there are many other
elements which contribute to peace, in the last analysis God does
not protect those who do not protect themselves. Christian policy
must be realistic and meet the Soviet threat with appropriate means.

Catholic opponents to nuclear weapons divided into camps which
failed, however, either alone or together to become an effective force
within the church. On the one hand, there were prominent laymen
like Walter Dirks and Eugen Kogon, who opposed nuclear weapons
for the *Bundeswehr* on political grounds indistinguishable from those
held by other opponents, arguments which rested on the effect such
weapons would have on chances for German reunification or on
military-strategic reasoning. On the other hand, there were theologians who denied that nuclear weapons could be incorporated into
the doctrine of just war and thereby become permissible instruments
of defense. There was no disagreement on the definition and requirements of just war, among others, that a just war be strictly
defensive and that the instruments of defense not destroy greater
goods than their use was intended to defend. Controversy among
theologians therefore centered on the questions of whether the course
and effects of nuclear war could actually be controlled and restricted
to limited areas (a point which ultimately had to be left to natural
scientists and military strategists), and whether life under totalitarian
regimes (*i.e.* Soviet domination) was worse from a religious perspective than the physical and moral destruction caused by war itself,
and especially nuclear war. Theological opponents of nuclear weapons
answered these questions in the negative and based their opposition on these judgments.

Although Catholic opponents to nuclear weapons did exist, they
did not combine political and religious arguments in a singularly
Catholic manner which might have spurred further Catholics to opposition on the basis of their religious identity. They further did
little to dent the appearance or effect of Catholic political unity behind Adenauer's policies. The effect of such journals as Kogon and
Dirk's *Frankfurter Hefte* was quite limited, while so-called left Catholicism was more an umbrella-designation for undefined discomfort
than an effective wing really making itself felt. Thus the political
conflicts latent within German Catholicism did not condense into
effective opposition to official church policies.[47]

90   THE REVIEW OF POLITICS

Not until the papacy of John XXIII (1958–1963) and the Second
Vatican Council did Catholic thought or activity on defense issues
really begin to change. Under the new leadership, Catholic political
life changed on two fronts. New doctrine began to stress new concepts of and approaches to peace, and emphasis on democratization opened organizational avenues to dissenting Catholics.

The evolution in doctrine brought about by John XXIII and the
Second Vatican Council coincided with the end of the "Adenauer
era" on both the foreign and domestic policy fronts, which probably
increased the public's receptiveness to new ideas. While neither the
Pope John[48] nor the Vatican Council[49] condemned nuclear weapons
altogether, they both contradicted, and thereby undercut, the assumptions and inner logic of deterrence doctrine. The Council abandoned the notion of just war and shifted from a static ethic of just
war (in which nuclear weapons could play a role) to conceptualizing
deterrence as an "emergency ethic" valid only until superseded by
something better. According to Walter Dirks, the Council replaced
the idea of just war by a historical process of arriving at true peace.[50]
It further stated that the arms race and the so-called military balance neither constituted nor contributed to a secure peace. The pope
echoed these thoughts and called for disarmament and negotiations
as a means of solving conflict. He called for trust rather than military balance as the basis of peace, and stressed nonmilitary components of security, in particular development aid to poor nations.[51]
The latter increased Catholics' awareness of third world problems
dramatically at a time when they were gaining in attention generally.

John XXIII and the Second Vatican Council thus opened doctrinal space within the Catholic church for arguments and themes
of the sort that the peace movement would later use. They also opened
organizational space for the kind of opinions and groups which had
previously been labeled nonconformist. The Council in particular
introduced the principles of democratization and pluralism within
the church. While minority opinions thereafter still had difficulty
being recognized within German Catholicism, they at least had a
reference point within the church.

Nonconformist thought gained ground within German Catholicism across the board during this period. In the early 1960's, criticism grew of the church and Catholicism's behavior during the Third
Reich. Stimulated by scholarly historical research and the publication of Rolf Hochhuth's novel *Der Stellvertreter* (*The Deputy*), this criticism stimulated a rethinking of the "guilt question," resulting in a

PEACE MOVEMENT AND THE CHURCHES   91

process in some ways analogous to that set off by the Protestant *Stuttgarter Schuldbekenntnis* ("Stuttgart confession of guilt") of fifteen years earlier. Carl Amery, a prominent Catholic, extended this criticism to the close relationship of the German Catholic church to Adenauer and the CDU, contending that it constituted a "second capitulation" analogous to Catholicism's relationship to the Third Reich. The societal response which greeted his efforts revealed a certain Catholic alienation from the previous postwar course.[52]

The Second Vatican Council gave German Catholicism more opportunity to respond to the changing political climate on the subject of *Ostpolitik* as well. Catholic support for the new *Ostpolitik* of reconciliation with Eastern Europe and full acceptance of the postwar territorial status quo found expression primarily in the "Bensberger Memorandum" of 1968, published by the *Bensberger Kreis* (Bensberg Circle).[53] Its preface mentions two sources as inspirational: the Protestant 1965 *Vertriebenendenkschrift* (the "essay on refugees" mentioned above), and the Second Vatican Council's call to efforts toward a "peace order" based on truth, justice, and freedom. The Memorandum does not differ significantly in substance from the EKD's essay. Both stress the crimes perpetrated by the Third Reich in Eastern Europe, and the necessity of recognizing the permanence of current German borders as a prerequisite for a truly peaceful European order. The difference between the Protestant and Catholic *Ostpolitik* essays lay in their reception in their respective churches, and in their authorship. The Protestant essay was published in 1965 by the EKD itself. The Catholic memorandum, in contrast, was written by a group which consisted of prominent Catholics, but was formed on the initiative of the German *Pax Christi* group, and was a private Catholic "circle" rather than an official church body. Whereas the Protestant essay was approved by the *Rat der EKD*, the highest EKD council, the German Catholic bishops did not take any particular position, and noted merely the existence of plural opinions among Catholics. While some interpreted this silence as a sign of democratization within the church (since the bishops did not distance themselves from the Bensberg statement),[54] others noted that as late as 1976 German bishops had failed to support reconciliation with Eastern Europe with political means and in the political realm. They had neglected even to comment on the treaty with Poland of the early 1970's, whether due to the Catholic hierarchy's relations with the CDU, lack of internal agreement on the subject, or the church's view of its historic mission as the only stable bulwark against communism in Europe.[55] Nonetheless, Catholic opinion had revealed its diversity.

The Second Vatican Council also opened German Catholicism to a cautious recognition of conscientious objectors. The Council gave the first Catholic theological justification of conscientious objectors, stating rather reservedly that such a status "must be seen as justified."[56] The German Catholic church did not begin to deal with the problem of conscientious objection until 1968.[57] Before 1968, the church had not merely ignored the problem, but had actively defamed objectors because of the church's connection to the Adenauer government.[58] While the council brought a certain relaxation on the problem of conscientious objection, the Catholic church initially viewed it as an individual right, and took until the 1970's to see it as an equally valid political alternative to military service.[59] Whereas the EKD established an agency to advise C.O.'s as early as 1955, the Catholic church did not set up a comparable agency until 1968.[60] A survey of conscientious objectors in 1960 reflected this slowness on the Catholic church's part when it found that, although the West German populace contained Catholics and Protestants in almost equal proportions, only 23 percent of applicants for C.O. status were Catholic.[61] As late as 1981, Catholics were still underrepresented among conscientious objectors. Whereas Catholics composed 43 percent of the population as a whole, they only constituted 34 percent of those who were "unwilling to serve in the army," according to Peter Nissen's analysis of the 1981 Emnid survey. Protestants, by contrast, were slightly overrepresented, as were those without religious affiliation.[62]

Catholic discussion of security and disarmament was restricted to marginal groups in the 1950's, at a time when it threatened the very unity of the EKD. The changes of the 1960's discussed above made possible a more far-reaching Catholic discussion of these issues, and greatly facilitated Catholic participation in subsequent peace protest, as these changes gave Catholics a point of reference within the church with which to justify their actions. Even as late as the early 1980's, however, Catholic involvement in these issues was by no means as extensive as that of Protestants. As Ulrich Ruh noted in February of 1981, the EKD had been discussing these issues at synods nearly every year, and Protestants already had groups formed on the various sides of the questions; there was as yet no similar involvement by Catholics, although seeds of such a discussion were present.[63]

PEACE MOVEMENT AND THE CHURCHES   93

Discussion of the NATO double-track did in fact eventually arise in the Catholic church. Typical of the continuing preponderance of conservative Catholicism was the 1981 statement by the *Zentralkomitee der deutschen Katholiken*, the umbrella organization of all Catholic lay associations. The *Zentralkomitee*'s statement supported the double-track decision, including the stationing of new missiles if necessary. The statement argued politically, basing its support of the decision on the Soviet desire for hegemony in Europe, its military build-up in the 1970's, the positive function of nuclear weapons in deterrence, and the need to restore the military balance, including new missiles if needed.[64]

Catholic opposition to the double-track decision of the 1980's was, however, more vocal than Catholic opposition to Adenauer in the 1950's, and it was tied more closely to the official church. The Catholic groups which argued against the NATO decision reflected the influence of the Second Vatican Council. The BDKJ, the Catholic youth organization, questioned the value of additional arms, finding that they would lower rather than increase security as a general rule. The organization stressed that security policy must no longer be primarily military, but rather that peace must be pursued through a complex of structural changes, confidence-building measures and educating public attitudes.[65] The German *Pax Christi* group made similar arguments.

Originally founded to work on Franco-German reconciliation, *Pax Christi* became a major voice for alternative security ideas within the Catholic church. Next to *Pax Christi*, the Catholic *Initiative Kirche von Unten* (literally, "initiative for a church from below") is the only other Catholic group represented in the Coordinating Committee of the peace movement. The Initiative is composed of fifty-six individual groups, working on topics ranging from the socioeconomic order, to women in the church, to homosexuality. It has collectively set itself the goal of renewing the church in the sense of the Second Vatican Council, in particular in the context of grass-roots groups outside of the church hierarchy. The *Initiative* conceives of the church as partisan in the tradition of Latin American "liberation theology," and takes unambiguous positions in political, social, and economic issues, thus abjuring the notion that the church should keep to its own realm outside of politics. The *Initiative* had some of its intellectual origins in the *Bensberger Kreis*, the author of the abovementioned memorandum on *Ostpolitik*, and in the Catholic organizations which work with third world problems. The *Intiative* represents in many

94   THE REVIEW OF POLITICS

respects the "greening" of the Catholic church, including in its positions on peace and security issues.[66]

On the one hand, the *Initiative Kirche von Unten*'s presence shows
that opposition to conservative religious, social, and political policies is more active in the 1980's than it was thirty years before. On
the other hand, the political turbulence of the 1970's, while it did
not spare the German Catholic church altogether, seems nonetheless to have affected it less than the EKD did. Despite the changes
in attitude and activism spurred by Vatican II and John XXIII,
political conservatism still maintains a greater hold over German
Catholicism than Protestantism. In part as a reflection of this hold,
fewer Catholic groups are engaged in peace activities than their Protestant counterparts. The fact that the *Initiative* was not organized
until the early 1980's bears some witness to the slowness of Catholic
involvement in these themes.

CONCLUSION

The churches are by no means the only institutions which have
left their imprint on the security debates of the postwar period. The
Social Democratic party has long linked security issues to questions
of improved German-German relations (at times even reunification)
and to social and economic reform, among others. Similar processes
have taken place among political groupings outside of formal institutions. Women's groups view current security relationships as rein-
forcements of patriarchal social structures. Likewise, for the ecology-
minded, nuclear weapons represent one of the most dangerous
manifestations of the same economic growth-national security policies
they hold responsible for environmental pollution.

Such concerns show that positions on nuclear weapons have never
been a simple matter. They reflect more than mere concern over
whether such weapons are objectively dangerous or not. They also
represent more than the conditions of one's socialization. Institutional continuity in the nuclear weapons debate has helped mitigate the varying impact of socialization during war or peace. Thus
while the young tend to be more active than the old in unconven-
tional political action in the 1980's, each generation has found reasons
to oppose nuclear weapons. The existence of a sizable peace movement in the 1950's, with as much as 70 percent of the populace against
the introduction of nuclear weapons in 1958, shows that nuclear

PEACE MOVEMENT AND THE CHURCHES   95

weapons were not always popular even among those generations most traumatized by the war.

The sources of such animosity are not, of course, restricted solely to the institutional influences discussed in this essay. Instead, Germans at all times have had to face a central security dilemma: on the one hand their exposure to Soviet military power and the need for a strong deterrent; and, on the other hand, the destructive power of that very deterrent should its war-fighting capabilities ever be put to use.[67] Thus fear of the Soviet Union has generally been accompanied by a fear of the ravages of war itself, as witnessed by the drastic fall in support for nuclear weapons in response to any survey question which mentions their actual use. Along these lines, changes in the climate of superpower relations and in American foreign policy have contributed to opposition to nuclear weapons.

While not separable from the broader political context, institutions in Germany must be weighed as a critical variable in understanding the force of the postwar peace movements. Institutions like the churches have channeled and structured peace movement activism on the part of their members throughout the postwar period. In each case, the institutions in question shaped internal discussions of defense issues over time by relating them to broader concerns specific to the institution. The wide divergence in peace movement activism among social groups can only be explained by institutional influence on the security debate. This influence has cut across generations, affecting those born both before and after World War II.

NOTES

* I would like to thank Peter Hall, Anthony Messina, and Samuel K. Cohen, Jr., for their criticisms of earlier drafts.

1. Ronald Inglehart, *The Silent Revolution, Changing Values and Political Styles Among Western Publics* (Princeton: Princeton University Press, 1977).

2. Jacques-Rene Rabier, Helene Riffault, and Ronald Inglehart, *Euro-barometer 17: Energy and the Future, April 1982* (machine-readable data file), 1st ICPSR. ed., Ann Arbor, Mich., Inter-university Consortium for Political and Social Research, 1983. Cross-tabulations of age classes and approval/disapproval variables. The ranges in the percentages given above result from combining two age cohorts in the case of the younger generations (15–24 and 25–34 year olds), and two age cohorts in the case of the generation which experienced World War II (45–54 and 55–64 year olds).

3. Berthold Meyer, *Der Bürger und seine Sicherheit: Zum Verhältnis von Sicherheitsstreben und Sicherheitspolitik* (Frankfurt: Campus Verlag, 1983), pp. 270–73.

4. Anthony Messina, "Postwar Protest Movements in Britain: A Challenge to Parties," *Review of Politics* 49, 3, (Summer 1987): 413.

5. Eurobarometer 17, using weighted age samples.

96   THE REVIEW OF POLITICS

6. Messina, "Postwar Protest Movements." Scholarly consensus prevails that the young feel less threatened by the Soviet Union than the old, whether as a result of socialization during peacetime or not. Messina quite rightly points out that this does not necessarily lead to absence of feelings of threat altogether. On the contrary, the focus may shift to new sources of threat, in particular nuclear weapons.

7. For specific data on the differences in participation according to church affiliation (the only case to receive detailed attention in this article) see below.

8. Stanley Tarrow, "The Creation of New Religious Movements: Cycles, Institutions, and the Transformation of Interpretive Frames," unpublished manuscript, p. 5.

9. Peter Nissen, "Prospects for a Realignment of the West German Party System: The Impact of Oppositional Movements and the 'Green Party'" (Paper delivered at the conference entitled "When Parties Fail: Paths of Alternative Political Action," Hutchins Center for the Study of Democratic Institutions, University of California at Santa Barbara, 19–20 May 1982). Nissen does not control for class, education, age, region, or urban/rural residence when reporting these differences between Protestants and Catholics. Indirect evidence for the independent effects of religious affiliation on peace movement activism is provided, however, by a breakdown of SPD voters by religion and class between 1961 and 1972. The "vote intention" of Protestant white-collar employees rose from 41.5% in 1961 to 70.1% in 1972, while that of Catholic white-collar employees rose from 18.9% in 1961 to 42.4% in 1972. While both Protestant and Catholic white-collar employees increased their vote for the SPD, Protestant SPD voters vastly outnumbered Catholic SPD voters throughout the period. (See Hans D. Klingemann and Charles Lewis Taylor, "Partisanship, Candidates and Issues: Attitudinal Components of the Vote in West German Federal Elections," in *Elections and Parties*, ed. Hans D. Klingemann and Charles Lewis Taylor [Beverly Hills: Sage Publications, 1978], pp. 97–137, here p. 105.) This period spans the twelve years between the SPD's 1959 Godesberg Programm, which moderated the SPD's platform in an ultimately successful bid for middle-class vote, and the SPD's crowning electoral success of the postwar period in 1972. The 1972 election saw the height of the middle class's incorporation into the SPD under the auspices of Brandt's chancellorship. The most active opposition to the double-track decision in society at large, as well as within the SPD itself, came from this middle class element (particularly the youth of the "new" middle class), part of which ultimately broke rank with the SPD to swell the ranks of the Green party. Likewise, the activists of the 1950's peace protest came predominantly from the SPD.

10. Lutz Lemhöfer, "Zögernder Aufbruch aus dem Kalten Krieg: die katholische Kirche und die bundesdeutsche 'neue Friedensbewegung'" in *Die neue Friedensbewegung*, ed. Reiner Steinweg (Frankfurt: Suhrkamp Verlag, 1982), pp. 245–58.

11. To paraphrase Samuel Huntington's argument from his *American Politics and the Promise of Disharmony* (Cambridge, MA: Harvard University Press, 1981), early positions taken by the churches created or prevented the future development of an "ideals vs. institutions gap" to be used by protesters to justify their actions.

12. The *Evangelische Kirche in Deutschland* (EKD) is the official name of the postwar German Protestant church.

13. Joachim Beckmann, ed., *Kirchliches Jahrbuch für die Evangelische Kirche in Deutschland 1945–1948*, 72–75 (Gütersloh: C. Bertelesmann Verlag, 1950): 185, 186.

14. Johanna Vogel, *Kirche und Wiederbewaffnung: Die Haltung der Evangelischen Kirche in Deutschland in den Auseinandersetzungen um die Wiederbewaffnung der Bundersrepublik 1949–56* (Göttingen: Vandenhoeck und Ruprecht, 1978), p.70.

15. For the arguments of supporters and opponents of Adenauer's defense policy of the 1950's see Joachim Beckmann, ed., *Kirchliches Jahrbuch für die Evangelische Kirche in Deutschland 77–86* (Gütersloh: Gütersloher Verlagshaus Gerd Mohn, 1950–1960).

PEACE MOVEMENT AND THE CHURCHES 97

16. As the EKD Council stated, "Einer Remilitarizierung Deutschlands können wir das Wort nicht reden, weder was den Westen noch was den Osten anlangt." See *Kirchliches Jahrbuch* (1950), pp. 165–66.

17. See *Kirchliches Jahrbuch* 91 (1965) for the text and reaction to the essay.

18. In an interview in January 1985.

19. A representative of the GHI imparted much of this information in an interview in August 1984.

20. Gerta Scharffenorth, "Konflikte in der Evangelischen Kirche in Deutschland 1950 bis 1969 im Rahmen der historischen und ökumenischen Friedensdiskussion," in *Konflikte zwischen Wehrdienst und Friedensdiensten*, ed. Ulrich Duchrow and Gerta Scharffenorth (Stuttgart: Ernst Klett Verlag, 1970), pp. 17–116, here pp. 40, 41.

21. Bernd Kubbig, *Kirche und Kriegsdienstverweigerung in der BRD* (Stuttgart: Verlag W. Kohlhammer, 1974).

22. Wolfgang Wiedenmann, "Evangelische Studentengemeinde — Kirche an der Hochschule?" in *Christen in der Demokratie*, ed. Heinrich Albertz and Joachim Thomsen (Wuppertal: Peter Hammer Verlag, 1978).

23. See Pro ökumene/Ohne Rüstung Leben, eds., *Ohne Rüstung leben* (Gütersloh: Gütersloher Verlagshaus Gerd Mohn, 1983).

24. On the organization of German churches see Frederic Spotts, *The Churches and Politics in West Germany* (Middletown, CT: Wesleyan University Press, 1973).

25. Vogel, *Kirche und Wiederbewaffnung*, p. 27.

26. See, for example, the coverage of the 1987 Kirchentag in the *Frankfurter Rundschau* and the *Frankfurter Allgemeine Zeitung*, 12–20 June, 1987. The *Kirchentag* also enjoyed extensive television coverage.

27. "Gottes Liebe beginnt nicht erst mit der Geburt," *FAZ*, 3 November 1987.

28. Heinemann resigned as Adenauer's minister of the interior over the rearmament issue and formed his own party, the *Gesamtdeutsche Volkspartei*. See Vogel, *Kirche und Wiederbewaffnung*, pp. 72–142.

29. *Frieden wahren, fördern und erneuern* (Gütersloh: Gütersloher Verlagshaus Gerd Mohn, 1981).

30. Nissen, "Prospects for Realignment of the West German Party System."

31. On this point see Spotts, *Churches and Policies in West Germany*.

32. Anselm Doering-Manteuffel, *Katholizismus und Wiederbewaffnung: Die Haltung der deutschen Katholiken gegenüber der Wehrfrage 1948–1955* (Mainz: Matthias-Grünewald-Verlag, 1981), p. 42.

33. For a discussion of the ideological basis of postwar political Catholicism, see Gerhard Kraiker, *Politischer Katholizismus in der BRD: eine ideologiekritische Analyse* (Stuttgart: Verlag W. Kohlhammer, 1972).

34. Karl Forster, "Der deutsche Katholizismus in der Bundesrepublik Deutschland," in *Der soziale und politische Katholizismus: Entwicklungslinien in Deutschland 1803–1963*, ed. Anton Rauscher (München: Günter Olzog Verlag, 1981), pp. 209–264, here p. 222–32.

35. Spotts, *Churches and Politics in West Germany*, p. 241.

36. See, for example, Arnulf Baring, *Aussenpolitik in Adenauers Kanzlerdemokratie* (München: Oldenbourg Verlag, 1969), pp. 204, 205.

37. Manteuffel, *Katholizismus*, pp. 1–32.

38. Gunther Mai, *Westliche Sicherheitspolitik im Kalten Krieg: Der Korea-Krieg und die deutsche Wiederbewaffnung 1950* (Boppard am Rhein: Harald Boldt Verlag, 1977), pp. 99–108.

39. Manteuffel, *Katholizismus*, pp. 99–108.

40. Bernd Kubbig, *Kirche und Kriegsdienstverweigerung*, pp. 93–96.

41. Reinhold Lehmann, "Abrüstung, die tödliche Verschwendung" in *Kirche in der Gesellschaft: der katholische Beitrag 1978/79*, ed. Jürgen Wichmann (München: Günter Olzog Verlag, 1978), pp. 19–33, here, p. 21.

98   THE REVIEW OF POLITICS

42. Martin Honecker, "Kontroversen um den Frieden in der evangelischen Kirche und Theologie," *Politische Studien* 33, no. 261 (1982): 17–25.

43. Heinz Hürten, "Zur Haltung des deutschen Katholizismus gegenüber der Sicherheits- und Bündnispolitik der Bundesrepublik Deutschland 1948–1960," in *Katholizismus im politischen System der Bundesrepublik 1949–1963*, ed. Albrecht Langer (Paderborn: Ferdinand Schüningh, 1978), pp. 83–102, here p. 98.

44. The most prominent example of this was Gustav Gundlach, "Die Lehre Pius XII vom moderenen Krieg," published in *Stimmen der Zeit*, April 1959, and in Karl Forster, ed., *Kann der atomarer Verteidigungskrieg ein gerechter Krieg sein?* (München: Karl Zink Verlag, 1960), pp. 105–134.

45. *Herder Korrespondenz* 12, no. 9 (June 1958): 395–97.

46. Walter Dirks, "Die Gefahr der Gleichschaltung," *Frankfurter Hefte* 13, no. 6 (June 1959): 379–91.

47. Karl Forster, "Der deutsche Katholizismus," pp. 234–37.

48. In particular, his "Pacim in Terris" of April 1963.

49. In particular in "Gaudium et spes."

50. Walter Dirks, "Abschied vom 'gerechten Krieg,'" *Frankfurter Hefte* 22, 7 (July 1967): 489–96.

51. Norbert Glatzel and Ernst Josef Nagel, eds., *Frieden in Sicherheit: Zur Weiterentwicklung der katholischen Friedensethik* (Freiburg: Herder Verlag, 1981), pp. 133–41.

52. Forster, "Der deutsche Katholizismus," pp. 241–47.

53. Bensberger Kreis, *Ein Memorandum deutscher Katholiken zu den polnisch-deutschen Fragen* (Mainz: Matthias-Grünewald-Verlag, 1968).

54. Gottfried Erb, "Das 'Bensberger Memorandum'/Geschichte und erste Stellungnahmen," *Frankfurter Hefte*, 23, 4 (April 1968): 219–21.

55. Norbert Tholen, "Die Höhe des Glaubens und die Niederungen der Politik: Bishöfe schweigen zum Polenvertrag," *Frankfurter Hefte* 31, 5 (May 1976): 4, 5.

56. Scharffenorth, "Konflikte in der Evangelischen Kirche," p. 42.

57. The church, under pressure from the laity, did stand up for the individual's right to C.O. status in the 1950's rearmament debate, but only in cases where the war in question was objectively unjust, and not for conscientious objection in principle. See Manteuffel, *Katholizismus und Wiederbewaffnung*, p. 236. The qualified nature of this support was reinforced by the insistence on the part of the Catholic youth organization (BDKJ), one of the groups which pressed most strongly for the right to C.O. status, that C.O.'s should have to justify themselves before a panel, in contrast to the EKD position that the individual conscience cannot be judged by others. See Kubbig, *Kirche und Kriegsdienstverweigerung*, p. 92, on this point.

58. Kubbig, *Kirche und Kriegsdienstverweigerung*, p. 91.

59. *Ibid.*, 96–99.

60. Wolfgang von Eichborn, "Politisierung der Kriegsdienstverweigerung," in Duchrow and Scharffenorth, eds., *Konflikte zwischen Wehrdienst und Friedensdiensten*, p. 160.

61. Manteuffel, *Katholizismus*, p. 236.

62. Nissen, "Prospects for a Realignment of the West German Party System."

63. Ulrich Ruh, "Schwiergkeiten mit dem Frieden," *Herder Korrespondenz* 35, 2 (February 1981): 53–55.

64. "Zur aktuellen Friedensdiskussion. Eine Stellungnahme des Zentralkomitees der deutschen Katholiken," *Herder Korrespondenz* 35, no. 12 (December 1981): 624–30.

65. Hans-Otto Mühleisen, "Grundstrukturen der Friedensdiskussion in der katholischen Kirche," *Politische Studien* 33, no. 261 (1982): 261, here p. 44.

66. Much of this comes from an interview conducted by the author in June 1984, with one of the most active Bonn representatives of the group.

67. On this point see Leon Sigal, *Nuclear Forces in Europe* (Washington, D. C.: The Brookings Institution, 1984), p. 64.

[26]

Social Change and Moral Politics: the Irish Constitutional Referendum 1983

BRIAN GIRVIN*

University College, Cork

The dominance of the Roman Catholic Church in Ireland has been challenged by rapid socioeconomic change. To counter emerging secularist trends, anti-abortion activists pressurized the political parties to agree to hold a referendum for a constitutional amendment to ban abortion. Opposition to the referendum, and party divisions, led to the active involvement by the Catholic Church and the hierarchy in the campaign. Although the amendment was passed, the intervention of the Church has not been beneficial to it as an institution. This is the first time since the establishment of the Irish state that a significant cleavage has emerged around a religious issue. The referendum reflected a change in Irish politics—new divisions had emerged, based on age, class, religion and place of residence. This change is now having an impact on the political parties.

I. The Changing Nature of Catholic Power in Ireland

The Irish electorate decided on 7 September 1983 by a two to one majority to amend the constitution. The new clause in the constitution guaranteed the right to life of unborn children and was an explicit attempt to prevent changes in the existing anti-abortion legislation. This may not appear surprising as Ireland has been a demonstratively Catholic country for centuries and has frequently differed on moral issues from her European neighbours. However, the referendum to amend the constitution was significant because, for the first time this century, the Irish electorate had divided on an essentially religious issue. Furthermore, the campaign has demonstrated that a new political cleavage is opening up in Irish politics: that between liberal and traditional elements in the society. The divisions over the referendum reflect the broader stresses generated by two decades of industrialization. The Irish political structure has traditionally been characterized in terms of authoritarianism, conformism, and male domination. This has been sustained by a small-holding agricultural economy.[1] Under these conditions the usual political cleavages did not operate; neither class nor religion underwrote political support. Recently all these features have been challenged. As a result of industrialization, the class

---

* I acknowledge the comments of the anonymous referees. Responsibility for interpretation is mine.
    [1] R. K. Carty, *Party and Parish Pump* (Waterloo, Ontario, Wilfrid Laurier University Press, 1981), p. 22; B. Chubb, *The Government and Politics of Ireland* (Stanford, Stanford University Press, 1970).

structure has begun to resemble that of the rest of Europe, while urbanization and population growth have undermined the older social structure.[2] Although the political system has not been challenged seriously by these changes, there has been considerable tension within and between the main political parties between liberal and traditional elements. The result of the referendum would tend to lend support to the view that during industrialization in Ireland the process of liberalization and secularization has been slow. In 19th-century Europe the Industrial Revolution was accompanied by the marginalization of the churches' influence on political and moral issues. While this process has not been repeated exactly in Ireland, it is possible to discern issues which are leading in that direction. The referendum has drawn attention to cleavages based on a liberal/traditional dichotomy which had been either denied or not previously apparent.

This new liberalism should not be confused with the anti-clerical liberalism found in 19th-century continental Europe. There are anti-clericals among the liberals, but they are a minority. The majority are committed to a reform of the Church demanding greater participation, more respect for individual conscience, and less authoritarianism. The traditional goodwill towards the Church remains, but that of the liberals is contingent on an accommodation of its views. The logic, if not the intent, of the liberals is the secularization of areas once dominated by the traditional culture.[3]

This development has occurred at a time when religion has ceased to play a significant rôle in political behaviour in Europe. In some countries there is no direct correlation between religion and political behaviour, in others the relationship is there but largely passive.[4] 'Ireland', however, 'is exceptional in that the great majority of the people are not nominal but practising Catholics'.[5] In addition, anti-clericalism has played no part in political behaviour during the 20th century. Ireland's uniqueness is apparent when it is recognized that while the rest of Europe secularized its institutions and culture the Irish commitment to religion was sustained and even intensified. This was a result of the way that Irish Catholicism and political nationalism reinforced one another during the first phase of political mobilization.[6] The Irish Catholic Church, unlike some of its continental counterparts, has been a popular church. This has allowed it great flexibility in its dealings with the state and with the political parties. Moreover, the mobilization of the Irish masses was effected by concentrating on religious issues. As a result of Ireland's position as a Catholic region within the British state, religion was an important factor in political behaviour and as an

[2] D. Rottman and P. O'Connell, 'The Changing Social Structure of Ireland', in F. Litton (ed.), *Unequal Achievement* (Dublin, Institute of Public Administration, 1982), p. 71.

[3] Liam Ryan, 'The Changing Face of Irish Values', in M. Foggarty, *Irish Values and Attitudes* (Dublin, Dominican Publications, 1984), pp. 105–6. For a discussion of the traditional dimension, see J. P. O'Carroll, 'The Politics of the 1983 "Abortion Referendum Debate" in the Republic of Ireland' (unpublished paper, Department of Social Theory and Institutions, University College, Cork).

[4] G. Smith, *Politics in Western Europe* (London, Heinemann, 1980), p. 20.

[5] J. H. Whyte, 'Ireland: Politics without Social Basis', in R. Rose (ed.), *Electoral Behaviour: a Comparative Handbook* (New York, Free Press, 1974), p. 640.

[6] S. M. Lipset and S. Rokkan, 'Cleavage Structures, Party Systems, and Voter Alignments: an Introduction', in S. M. Lipset and S. Rokkan (eds), *Party Systems and Voter Alignments: Cross-National Perspectives* (New York, The Free Press, 1967), pp. 1–64.

aspect of nationalist exclusiveness. This phenomenon has been detected in other parts of Europe, and for some of the same reasons.[7] Changes in the social structure reinforced this development. After 1850 a strong Catholic middle class emerged which dominated society. This class provided the basis of the strength of nationalist politics and it was from this source that the church recruited most of its personnel. These mutually reinforcing changes made the church very influential. By 1890 its influence was so extensive that it was able to destroy the political career of Parnell.[8]

As a result of these developments, the political structure in Ireland acquired a decidely religious ethos. The church became the most powerful institution in the country: at certain times its intervention in politics determined the future direction of those politics.[9] At the same time, the church retained a certain degree of autonomy from the society. This it was able to do because of its rôle in the international church which offered the hierarchy an alternative source of legitimacy to nationalism. The two rarely came into conflict, however, but if there were a change in the unique conditions that had allowed the church to demand and receive public acceptance of its ethos there was no guarantee that the church would change. Political independence did not pose a threat to this set of circumstances. The Catholicization of the new state was achieved during the 1930s when a new constitution was enacted in 1937 reflecting, on the whole, Catholic doctrine.[10] These developments were not unpopular with the mass of the population. Catholicism gave to Ireland a sense of identity which reinforced its separateness from Britain and gave to the Irish a strong sense of self-confidence and mission in a secularizing world.[11]

The privileged position of the Catholic Church in Ireland means that while it is more than an interest group, its influence is not so strong that the state can be construed as theocratic.[12] The position of the church in Ireland might be more adequately compared to the business community in a market economy. The social environment tends to be pro-business, while governments are extremely sensitive to its demands and requirements. The legitimacy of business is rarely questioned by policy-makers, indeed even socialist governments have found it necessary to accept its special position. The acceptance of the primary rôle of business in the economy is usually unstated and governments have acknowledged this by facilitating its growth and development through legislation. So, a private association acquires an effective veto over leglislation not in its interests: in extreme cases, the withdrawal of cooperation can seriously impair the legitimacy of a government.[13] The status of the church in

[7] D. Martin, *A General Theory of Secularization* (Oxford, Basil Blackwell, 1978), p. 107.

[8] S. Clark, *Social Origins of the Irish Land War* (Princeton, N.J., Princeton University Press, 1979), pp. 107–53; E. Larkin, *The Roman Catholic Church in Ireland and the Fall of Parnell 1888–1891* (Liverpool, Liverpool University Press, 1979), pp. 191–288.

[9] Larkin, *The Roman Catholic Church in Ireland*, pp. 3–50; D. W. Miller, *Church, State and Nation in Ireland 1898–1921* (Dublin, Gill and Macmillan, 1973), pp. 391–425.

[10] J. H. Whyte, *Church and State in Modern Ireland 1923–1979* (Dublin, Gill and Macmillan, second edition, 1980), pp. 378–9; J. Blanchard, *The Church in Contemporary Ireland* (Dublin, Clonmore and Reynolds, 1963), pp. 68, 75.

[11] T. Brown, *Ireland: a Social and Cultural History 1922–1979* (Glasgow, Fontana, 1981), pp. 45–101.

[12] Whyte, *Church and State in Modern Ireland*, p. 376.

[13] C. Lindblom, *Politics and Markets* (New York, Basic Books, 1977), pp. 172–5

Ireland is not unlike this. Indeed, in certain policy areas church doctrine has been traditionally incorporated into legislation. On the one occasion when the views of the hierarchy were flouted, the minister concerned was sacked and the legislation withdrawn.[14] Whereas the business community has always had to confront countervailing tendencies, this has not been the case with the Catholic Church in Ireland as its power was uncontested for most of the 20th century. The church in Ireland excerised hegemony over the society in a way unparalleled in a democratic society. The consent of the mass of the population implied by the concept of hegemony was freely given. Although the hegemony exercised by the church was the result of a particular historical conjuncture, it has proved remarkably stable under the conditions of democratic and independent government. Such is the extent of the hegemony that most people in Ireland before the 1970s had internalized the self-image which the church offered.[15]

TABLE 1. Attitudes to Church and State.

	Agree	Undecided	Disagree
1. Church cannot be compared to any other social institution	100	—	—
2. State to be preferred to Church on hypothesis of conflict	3.5	10	86.5
3. Rome control significant	3	5	92
4. Church too much involved in politics	7.5	10.5	82
5. Church usurping rôle of state	5	15	80
6. Church harms itself by political involvement	28	13	59
7. Church should be *more involved* in state matters than it is	29	13.4	57.6
8. Greatest aid to development of patriotism	52	18	30
9. To follow Church teaching produces best citizens possible	75	14	11

Source: B. F. Biever, *Religion, Culture, and Values* (New York, Arno Press, 1976), pp. 311, 314.

That the church exercised hegemonic influence is confirmed by data derived from a survey of religious opinion carried out in 1962. Table 1 illustrates how church teaching has been internalized by the respondents and some of its political consequences.[16] The interviewer also found that the status of the state was low because it was a *human* institution. Respondents emphasized the *divine* nature of the church's authority, which meant that, in contrast to the

[14] Whyte, *Church and State in Modern Ireland*, pp. 196–238.
[15] J. Joll, *Gramsci* (Glasgow, Fontana, 1977), p. 99; A. Gramsci, *Prison Notebooks* (London, Lawrence and Wishart, 1971), pp. 12, 365–6.
[16] B. F. Biever, *Religion, culture, and values* (New York, Arno Press, 1976), pp. 311, 314.

state, the church could not make mistakes.[17] The survey found that only a few well-educated people dissented from the views of the majority, but at the time they had little influence.[18] The evidence presented here has led a number of authors to claim that Ireland is a theocratic state. (Others have rejected this view without proposing a realistic alternative.[19]) The evidence can be utilized to resolve the difficulty in another way—it is society that is theocratic, not the state. Clearly the theocratic nature of society imposes constraints on the autonomy of the state in matters affecting Catholicism. The state willingly accepted this special relationship between the church and society and this has resulted in the state appearing more clericalist than in other European societies. While the autonomy of the state might have been weak, it did, however, exist; priests, for example, were not represented in parliament or in government.

TABLE 2. Attitudes to Church Teaching.

	Agree	Don't Know	Disagree
1. Interdenominational mixed free community schools are most desirable	77.8	6.0	16.2
2. Catholic priests should be free to marry	46.7	8.8	44.5
3. Obedience to the directives of the clergy is the hallmark of the true Catholic	44.7	6.2	49.1
4. Homosexual behaviour between consenting adults should not be a crime	45.2	14.9	39.9
5. A thing is either right or wrong and none of this ambiguous woolly thinking	48.4	2.2	49.4
6. Premarital sex is always wrong	57.6	3.9	38.5
7. It is always wrong to use artificial contraceptives	31.3	5.7	63.0

M. MacGreil, *Prejudice and Tolerance in Ireland* (Dublin, College of Industrial Relations, 1977), Table 149.

The data in Table 2, based on a survey carried out in 1972, demonstrate the dramatic shift in Catholic opinion which took place between 1962 and 1972. Although Tables 1 and 2 are not directly comparable, it is clear that by 1972 more people held liberal and secular opinions. The industrialization of the 1960s had been accompanied by the reform movement in the Catholic Church internationally. Ironically it was changes in Rome which precipitated change in Ireland. The emphasis on ecumenism and freedom of conscience, although alien to Irish traditions, were quickly adopted and subsequently broke the

---

[17] Biever, *Religion, culture, and values,* pp. 304–7.
[18] Biever, *Religion, culture, and values,* pp. 509–21.
[19] Whyte, *Church and State in Modern Ireland,* pp. 365–70, for a discussion.

authoritarian mould of Irish Catholicism. Table 2 reflects these changes.[20] By the mid-1970s the hegemonic rôle of the church had been seriously questioned. Irish Catholicism had become more individualistic and diverse. Although traditional values remained strong, important sections of the society—usually the young and well-educated living in towns—proved unwilling to conform.[21] Further surveys during the 1970s confirmed these tendencies.[22] A survey undertaken by the European Values Study Group in 1981 found that a further radical shift in opinion had taken place since the mid-1970s.[23] This found that while formal participation remained high by European standards, among the young even this commitment had weakened. Previous surveys found that most respondents gave a high priority to religion in the event of it clashing with matters concerning family, employment, or leisure. By 1981 only a minority was prepared to do so; moreover, religion had ceased to be a guide to behaviour for those living in towns and particularly for those under 30. The evidence suggests that a new type of Catholic has emerged in Ireland.[24] It would appear that he/she rejects many of the traditional teachings of the church, and does not accept the authority of the church in political or moral matters. Although formally Catholic, faith no longer has the same impact on this new type, while individual conscience has become the main guide to action. In the late 1960s this growing liberalism began to come into conflict with traditional features of the Irish political culture. The political parties were slow to respond to the pressures for change on moral and associated issues. The legalization of contraception was the main focus of tension during the 1970s. Although the majority was in favour of liberalizing the laws on contraception, it proved difficult for the political parties to gain support for change from their own deputies.[25] Following a Supreme Court decision that a woman had a right to import contraceptives, the government introduced a bill to determine the position in 1974. The defeat of the bill was ensured by the negative vote of *Fianna Fail* and that of the *Taoiseach* and other government supporters. In 1979 a *Fianna Fail* administration enacted a bill to legalize the importation and sale of contraceptives. This legislation was the most conservative option available to the Minister, and it incorporated certain 'safeguards' demanded by the hierarchy. Despite the tension over contraception, the issue was resolved in 1979 without open conflict between the church and the political parties. However, by then moral issues such as adoption, divorce, and family law, among others, were beginning to cause rifts between the new liberal electorate and the more traditional electorate. This was also reflected in the political parties,

[20] M. MacGreil, *Prejudice and Tolerance in Ireland* (Dublin, College of Industrial Relations, 1977), based on Table 149, p. 411.

[21] MacGreil, *Prejudice and Tolerance in Ireland*, p. 424.

[22] M. NicGhiolla Phadraig, 'Religion in Ireland: preliminary analysis', *Social Studies*, 5 (1976), 113–64. T. F. Inglis, 'Dimensions of Irish students religiosity', *Economic and Social Review*, 11: 4 (1980), 237–56.

[23] See Fogarty, *Irish Values and Attitudes*.

[24] NicGhiolla Phadraig, 'Religion in Ireland: preliminary analysis', p. 127. Ryan, 'Faith under survey', p. 6.

[25] K. Wilson-Davis, 'Irish Attitudes to Family Planning', *Social Studies*, 3 (1974), 261–75; Whyte, *Church and State in Modern Ireland*, p. 405; B. M. E. McMahon, 'The Law Relating to Contraception in Ireland', in Desmond M. Clarke (ed.), *Morality and the Law* (Cork, Mercier Press, 1982), pp. 20–30.

where liberals and traditionalists could be found in the same party. Up to 1979 the danger of contending pressures fracturing the 'catch all' political parties had been averted. However, as the issues became more politicized, the parties would have to choose which side to support. This would be particularly important if the constitution had to be changed to effect reform, as in the case of divorce. A referendum on a moral issue would polarize opinion and irreparably damage the political parties. The importance of these issues as a basis for cleavage should not be underestimated. Irish liberalism was questioning fundamental beliefs in the community. The reticence of politicians was caused by a number of considerations. Many accepted the church's authority without question; individual conscience remained subordinate to the divine law. Others feared that support for a change in legislation on moral issues would affect their chances of re-election. Finally, governments feared both the loss of traditional votes and organized opposition from traditionally-inclined deputies. Caution appeared at first to be the most successful strategy. This, however, depended on the church remaining reasonably circumspect on these issues. The active intervention of the church would change the framework of Irish politics and deepen a cleavage based on religion. It could also lead to serious divisions within some of the political parties.

The church's response was not clear for some time, and this led some politicians to believe that the church had accepted its loss of hegemony gracefully. At first it appeared that the hierarchy might make concessions to the liberal climate of opinion. The church recognized that sections of the laity were unhappy with the authoritarian influence of the church and the statements by the hierarchy on controversial matters were circumspect, while they tried to provide a policy of adaptation. During the early 1970s, church statements implied that the state in its leglislative programme need not comply with the church's view on matters of faith and morals. The result of this would have been that the church would have reiterated its teaching on a particular issue but that sustained political opposition would not have been forthcoming if the state had legislated against the teaching. This would have led to the church withdrawing from the political sphere.[26] However the de-politicization of the Irish hierarchy did not occur. An attempt was made to grasp at a new policy but, in retrospect, it is clear that no policy change occurred. Some hesitancy was apparent up to 1975, but even before this date some of the bishops were concerned with the consequences of an accommodation with secularist forces.[27] In effect, when faced with the challenge of pluralism, the church collectively opted to reiterate its traditional authority and rights in Irish society. With its hegemony insecure, the church had to seek new methods of influencing politicians. From the early 1970s a vast array of Catholic interest groups appeared, organized and led by lay people. These groups were committed to the defence and promotion of traditional Catholic values. The mobilizing force behind these groups appears to have been the Knights of St Columbanus, an

[26] J. Cooney, 'The Bishops and Abortion', *The Irish Times*, 13 April 1983, and 'Referendum Puts Pluralism in the Balance', *The Irish Times*, 1 September 1983.

[27] J. Newman, *The State of Ireland* (Dublin, Four Courts Press, 1977), pp. 46–53, 96–8. The author is the Roman Catholic Bishop of Limerick and former Professor of Sociology at Maynooth. J. A. Murphy, 'The Church, Morality and the Law', in Clarke, *Morality and the Law*, pp. 103–14.

exclusive lay Catholic organiation.[28] This was a new departure for Irish Catholicism, as lay activism had not previously received the support of the clergy. However, under the new conditions, their emergence proved beneficial to the church. These associations, although Catholic, did not often have a formal relationship with the church. Moreover, as popularly constituted groups, they were in a good position to put pressure on politicians. Furthermore, their activism permitted the church to claim that on contentious issues their point of view had popular backing. Finally, the groups allowed the church to appear to be withdrawing from the political process, while their separateness allowed the church, if necessary, to disown them. Throughout the 1970s these groups expanded their membership and refined their organization. The contraceptive issue was a major focus of mobilization for many activists. The visit of Pope John Paul II to Ireland in 1979 made a major contribution to their organizational efforts. The Pope's advocacy of traditional Catholic doctrine, particularly his condemnation of abortion, contraception and divorce, reinforced their commitment to oppose the secularizing trends in Ireland. Following the Pope's visit, a number of these groups associated to form the Pro-Life Amendment Campaign (PLAC). The object of the new group was to agitate for a referendum to amend the constitution to prohibit abortion under any circumstances. The decision to choose abortion may appear surprising as it was illegal and the electorate was opposed to it on principle. Developments in the United States and Europe during the 1970s caused considerable concern among Catholic activists, as did the appearance of a Women's Right to Choose Group in 1980. The emergence of PLAC cannot be fully explained in these terms; it has to be placed within a process that had begun a decade earlier. The campaign was a *riposte* to the secularizing tendencies which had appeared so strong throughout the 1970s. In addition, abortion appeared to be the issue around which the maximum support for traditional values could be generated.[29]

II. The Referendum Campaign and the Dynamics of Extra-parliamentary Pressure

PLAC launched its campaign shortly before the General Election of 1981. It was an opportune moment politically in that the outcome of the election was uncertain. Due to the Irish system of voting, proportional representation with the single transferable vote, governments have usually been formed when a very limited number of *Dail* seats have changed hands. The outcome was even more unpredictable in 1981 because the constituency boundaries had been redrawn, and the major parties were led by untested leaders. Irish politics has often been characterized in brokerage terms. The local representative is usually no more than a messenger boy for his constituents, and his re-election is normally based

---

[28] E. Bolster, *The Knights of St. Columbanus* (Dublin, Gill and Macmillan, 1979).

[29] *The Irish Times*, 13 April 1983 and 1 September 1983; Fogarty, *Irish Values and Attitudes*, p. 139; D. Dooley-Clarke, 'Abortion and the Law', in Clarke, *Morality and the Law*, pp. 31–46; E. O'Reilly, 'The Current Political Objective is the Defeat of the Amendment', *Sunday Tribune,* 15 May 1983; P. Brennan, 'Abortion: Backlash and Blackmail', *Magill*, July 1983.

on the service he has rendered to his constituency.[30] PLAC extended this to the national level and sought to persuade the politicians to give a commitment to introducing amending legislation to prohibit abortion. It should be emphasized that abortion was already illegal under legislation dating from the 19th century. However, PLAC feared that the courts or the legislature would reverse this legislation. PLAC based its case on Article 40 of the Irish constitution, which guaranteed life to the citizen but not to the unborn. The campaign aimed to extend the constitutional guarantee in Article 40 to cover the time span from conception to birth. At the press conference to launch the campaign, Dr Julia Vaughan, chairman of PLAC, suggested that the anti-abortion legislation could be successfully challenged 'by interests favouring abortion, acting on the basis of a carefully-selected case'. The organizers suggested that the amendment should take the following form: 'The state recognizes the absolute right to life of every unborn child from conception and accordingly guarantees to respect and protect such right by law'. Speakers at the press conference emphasized that no distinction should be made between life before and after birth. Despite the essentially Roman Catholic nature of the support given to PLAC, the organizers believed that the non-Roman Catholic Churches would, in fact, support the amendment.[31]

Although some doubts were voiced as to the response of the non-Roman Catholic Churches to the issue, the politicians responded with alacrity. A change of government was a distinct possibility and neither of the main parties wished to jeopardize votes. The main opposition party at the time, *Fine Gael*, agreed to support the campaign adding that if necessary '... it will make an amendment referendum an issue in the coming general election'.[32] Shortly after this *Fianna Fail* agreed to promote an amendment, while the Labour Party declared itself 'unequivocally opposed to abortion'.[33] In just over two weeks PLAC had achieved their main objective: parties representing over 90 per cent of *Dail* members had acceded to their demands. There was an implied threat from PLAC that if the political parties did not promote an amendment, then a campaign would be mounted against these opponents. While this would have been a serious consideration for any politician in Ireland, it does appear that none of the main parties had considered the consequences of their commitment in May 1981, and that a mixture of piety and naïveté as well as political calculation was involved. It remained only to agree to the wording and a date for the referendum. Consequently the issue was not debated during the election campaign. Although there was a change in government, there was no change in policy. However when the new *Taoiseach*, Dr FitzGerald, was asked in January 1982 whether he was prepared to carry out his commitment on the issue, his response was a little more cautious than that of May 1981. He confirmed

[30] B. Chubb, 'Going about Persecuting Civil Servants: the Role of the Irish Parliamentary Representative', *Political Studies*, 11 (1963), 272–86; M. Bax, 'Patronage Irish Style; Irish Politicians as Brokers', *Sociologische Gids*, 17: 3 (1970), 179–91; L. Komito, 'Irish Clientalism: a Reappraisal', *The Economic and Social Review*, 15: 3 (April 1984), 173–94.

[31] *The Irish Times*, 28 April 1981.

[32] *The Irish Times*, 1 May 1981.

[33] *The Irish Times*, 15 May 1981.

that he had given a commitment to the Pro-Life Amendment Campaign that he would consult with the Attorney General and would shortly ask the government to consider whether the question of a pro-life amendment should be dealt with separately or should await the completion of the Attorney General's constitutional review.[34]

The slight shift in attitudes appears to have been due to considerations resulting from Dr FitzGerald's 'constitutional crusade'. Shortly after election, Dr FitzGerald argued forcibly in several statements for a new approach to the problem of Northern Ireland. In particular, he suggested that a review of the Irish constitution should be undertaken to ensure that the Republic became a more pluralist society. Although aimed at Northern Ireland Protestants, the impact of the constitutional crusade was felt more acutely in the Republic. However, considerations of this type had not changed FitzGerald's mind on the issue of abortion; his concern was to take the abortion issue in conjunction with a number of other issues, such as the reform of family law, divorce, and contraception. Such an approach was unpopular with PLAC, the church, and *Fianna Fail*. From the outset, PLAC stressed the singularity of the issue to the exclusion of all other questions. Given the generally traditionalist Roman Catholic composition of PLAC this should not be surprising.[35] The official *Fianna Fail* position was quite similar to that of PLAC. In the event the government of Dr FitzGerald collapsed and following an election in February 1982 *Fianna Fail* came to power, with Charles Haughey as *Taoiseach*. In March 1982, Haughey confirmed that a referendum would take place on the single issue of abortion, and therefore fulfilled *Fianna Fail's* pre-election commitment.[36]

The *Fianna Fail* party remained committed to this stance throughout the next 18 months. Its approach reflected the growing conservativeness of the party on social and moral issues, particularly under the leadership of Charles Haughey. When, at the end of 1982, a wording was formulated by *Fianna Fail*, it approximated very closely to that originally demanded by PLAC:

> The state acknowledges the right to life of the unborn and with due regard to
> the equal right of life of the mother, guarantees in its laws to protect, and as
> far as practicable, by its laws, to defend and vindicate that right.[37]

PLAC and the Roman Catholic Church welcomed this wording as did, perhaps surprisingly, *Fine Gael*. Moreover, *Fine Gael* gave a formal commitment to hold a poll in March 1983 if it were in government.[38] By December 1982 the organisers of PLAC appeared to have achieved their primary aim. At this stage the opposition to the amendment was fragmented, and *Fine Gael* had put former reservations behind.

The issue brought to light one of the major failings of the Irish political system: that pressure can be brought to bear on politicians during an election to

---

[34] *The Irish Times*, 27 January 1982.
[35] *The Irish Times*, 20 May 1982.
[36] *The Irish Times*, 24 March 1982.
[37] *The Irish Times*, 3 November 1982. There was also a widespread belief at the time that the wording was agreed with a senior cleric of the Archdiocese of Dublin.
[38] *The Irish Times*, 4 November 1982.

make concessions to interest groups. PLAC was well placed to maximize this pressure as three elections took place between June 1981 and November 1982. Garret FitzGerald, when in opposition before the June 1981 and November 1982 elections, appears to have allowed his fear of losing votes to overcome a natural liberal conscience, particularly during the last of these elections. *Fianna Fail* displayed no such ambiguity; their policies during the elections were aimed at gaining power whatever the cost. Charles Haughey promised not only a referendum, but also to build an airport at a Catholic shrine and to nationalize a number of ailing companies. Moreover, when after the February 1982 election he found himself short of an overall majority, he traded substantial state benefits for the votes of an independent socialist deputy.[39] The unstable nature of the electoral cycle from 1981 to the end of 1982, and the willingness of *Fianna Fail* to bid openly for votes in this way, increased the temptation for *Fine Gael* to give in to pressure on the specific issue of a constitutional amendment. It should be recalled that while Garret FitzGerald has been one of the leading figures in rejuvenating *Fine Gael* and giving it a liberal and modern image, some sections of his party retain strong conservative leanings, particularly where Catholic teaching is concerned. In addition, some of these deputies remain opposed to Dr FitzGerald's liberalism and to his leadership. In fairness to Dr FitzGerald there was, at this stage, no widespread opposition to the referendum: even the Protestant churches were muted in their response to the wording when it was published. Furthermore, there was a genuine concern that abortion should not be introduced into Ireland, and the amendment appeared to be the most acceptable method of ensuring this.

TABLE 3. Distribution of Second Preference Votes of Anti-abortion Activist Cork South Central, February 1982.

	Number	%	% of First Preference
Fianna Fail	764	39.8	41.8
Fine Gael	771	40.26	39.6
Labour	380	19.8	13.4

Source: *The Irish Times*, 22 February 1982.

Due to the unanimity among the political parties, the amendment did not become an issue at any of the three elections. However, there were indications of the issue's possible impact in both the February and November 1982 elections. In the former, an anti-abortion activist ran as a candidate in the largely urban constituency of Cork South Central. The candidate, Mary Kelly, received 1,929 votes although her only platform was opposition to abortion, contraception, and divorce. Although eliminated on a subsequent count, her vote was credible for an independent candidate. 1,915 of her votes were available for re-distribution and Table 3 illustrates the breakdown of second

---

[39] *Parliamentary Debates Dail Eireann*, 323: 1 (March 1982), cols. 25–28, where the terms of the agreement are recorded.

preferences by party.[40] If, as appeared likely, these electors voted for Kelly because of the issue, then their second preferences indicates their regular party allegience. It demonstrates that Labour Party loyalty was far more vulnerable when abortion was an issue than that of the other two parties. It confirms other evidence that shows conservative supporters of the Labour Party to be more conservative than the conservative supporters of other parties.[41] Moreover, it indicates that an anti-abortion candidate could secure a small but not insignificant proportion of the vote, and might, under other circumstances, affect the outcome of the election. This is even more surprising when it is recalled that abortion was not an issue at this particular election. At the November 1982 election the issue was more clear cut. Two left wing TDs, Jim Kemmy, of the Democratic Socialist Party, and Michael D. Higgins, of the Labour Party, had publicly opposed the referendum. Furthermore, the former deputy and his party had called for abortion to be available under certain very limited circumstances.[42] During the election both men complained that anti-abortion groups were counter-canvassing in their constituency. Against Kemmy, the deputy of Limerick East, there was a concerted campaign by the local media, clergy, and the Labour Party to discredit him on this issue. In both cases the tactics were successful and, as can be seen in Table 4, both candidates had a serious decline in their first preference votes between February and November 1982.[43] While other political variables may account for the loss of votes and seats, it is reasonable to assume—as the candidates themselves believed—that this organized opposition played a significant rôle in their defeat.

TABLE 4. Change in Number of First Preference Votes Received by Higgins and Kemmy 1981–1982.

	1981	February 1982	November 1982	% Change February–November
M. D. Higgins	6,226	5,718	4,449	22
J. Kemmy	4,190	6,502	4,125	36.5

Source: *The Irish Times,* 15 June 1981, 22 February 1982 and 27 November 1982.

After the November 1982 election, parties still had a commitment to the referendum. Dr FitzGerald once again formed a government, this time with a parliamentary majority, and looked set to remain in power for four or five years. The defeat of Higgins and Kemmy demonstrated how explosive the issue might become for those seen as weak on abortion issues. However, opposition to a referendum had begun to emerge and *Fine Gael* and the Labour Party proved vulnerable to this pressure. To promise a referendum under pressure

[40] *The Irish Times,* 22 February 1982.
[41] M. Gallagher, *The Irish Labour Party in Transition 1957–1982* (Dublin, Gill and Macmillan, 1982), p. 116.
[42] *The Irish Times,* 1 April 1982 and 5 June 1982.
[43] Results taken from *The Irish Times,* 15 June 1981, 22 February 1982 and 27 November 1982.

was one thing, to legislate and accept the complex political outcome was quite another. Dr FitzGerald's commitment to constitutional change to promote reconciliation between Catholics and Protestants was put in jeopardy when the main Protestant churches declared their opposition to the amendment, arguing for toleration and freedom of conscience.[44] Furthermore, the Protestant view that such an amendment would be sectarian was upheld by a leading Roman Catholic philosopher who declared that the campaign could lead to a form of 'moral imperialism'. He added that it was strange that the only exceptions permitted by PLAC were those also approved by Catholic moral teaching.[45] PLAC's reply reiterated its position coherently, but did not answer the sectarian charge satisfactorily. Its stand on the principle of no abortion under any circumstances appeared to justify the sectarian charge, as only the Roman Catholic Church had such a fixed view.[46] By January 1983 an Anti-Amendment Campaign had been launched. In addition, many members of the legal and medical professions publicly opposed the referendum. The Church of Ireland not only reiterated its position on the referendum, but suggested that there were occasions when termination of a pregnancy would be legitimate.[47] By February 1983 the pressure was having its impact. The *Fine Gael* youth group came out in opposition, while senior members of the Labour Party also declared their opposition to the referendum. The government itself was now having serious misgivings. The Attorney-General and the Director of Public Prosecutions issued statements expressing their opinions on the issue and giving reasons why the wording should be withdrawn. The Attorney General, Peter Sutherland, suggested that the wording was so ambiguous that it could lead to the introduction of abortion or, alternatively, could prohibit operations which were then permissible.[48] Following this, the Cabinet withdrew the wording and decided to introduce their own modified amendment. This differed in a number of ways from that of *Fianna Fail:* 'Nothing in this constitution shall be invoked to invalidate any provision of the law on the grounds that it prohibits abortion'.[49]

This radically changed the complexion of the issue. It had become politicized in that parliament was split between government and opposition on how to handle the question. This was a serious setback for PLAC which had worked for an all-party consensus on the issue, and, significantly, it refused to accept that such a politicization had taken place.[50] Another consequence of the change in direction was that the Catholic hierarchy began to take a more active rôle in the campaign. In a statement published in March, when the government was wavering, the bishops expressed disquiet at the difficulties then being discussed publicly. The statement went on to argue that an amendment to the constitution could be described as 'prudent anticipation', presumably as a preventative

---

[44] *The Irish Times*, 23 May 1981 and 12 June 1981.

[45] *The Irish Times*, 14 May 1982. The theologian was the Rev. Professor Brendan O'Mahony, Professor of Philosophy, University College, Cork.

[46] *The Irish Times*, 20 May 1982 and see also article in *The Irish Times*, 18 May 1982.

[47] *The Irish Times*, 3 June 1982, 26 January 1983 and 31 January 1983.

[48] *The Irish Times*, 14, 16 and 17 February 1983.

[49] *The Irish Times*, 25 March 1983.

[50] PLAC refused to participate in a television debate before the referendum because members of political parties, taking opposing positions, would be involved in the debate.

measure against the electorate or the Supreme Court.[51] Under pressure from the more conservative bishops, the hierarchy moved into a position of confrontation with the government. There was an unsuccessful attempt to negotiate a compromise wording by the government but this was vetoed by the church. According to the Minister for Justice, 'there was far more than the discussion of principles. We were discussing key phrases and specific objections.'[52] It was now evident that Dr FitzGerald had badly miscalculated. He rather naïvely believed that the hierarchy could not become involved in a new conflict on moral issues, as had occurred in the 1950s. While there was some evidence that this might be so, that evidence was not strong enough by 1983 to confidently predict the way the church would go.[53] There were divisions within the hierarchy, but the conservatives were in the dominant position. Moreover, the new wording was opposed by PLAC, *Fianna Fail* and, significantly, by a number of *Fine Gael* deputies who announced they would vote against the government alternative. This process was completed when the heirarchy declared that it found the wording unsatisfactory and suggested that, if accepted, it could lead to abortion being legalized.[54] The pressure was increased when the Archbishop of Dublin issued a pastoral letter, read in every church in the diocese, urging support for the Roman Catholic position on the amendment. The Bishop of Kerry made this explicit when he urged priests in his diocese to promote the *Fianna Fail* wording. Although the statements from the hierarchy and individual bishops were nuanced to express a general concern on the issue rather than any expressed hostility to *Fine Gael*, in effect the bishops had now become explicitly associated with *Fianna Fail* and this compounded the division already under way.[55] When the alternative wordings were debated in the *Dail* the government suffered a defeat due to the defection of a number of deputies in *Fine Gael* and the Labour Party. Although a whip had been imposed by *Fine Gael* the deputies who defied it were not disciplined. Subsequently the *Fianna Fail* wording was adopted: a small number of deputies voted against it and the majority of *Fine Gael* deputies abstained.[56]

This outcome exacerbated the latent divisions between the political parties. *Fianna Fail* urged their supporters to work for a 'yes' vote, while *Fine Gael* and Labour advocated rejection. It was these divisions which brought the church to the centre of political affairs once again. Hitherto, the hierarchy and the clergy had played a 'low-key' rôle in the campaign, believing that PLAC and the political parties could secure agreement on the issue. When this was no longer certain, a more interventionist approach was taken. The hierarchy was motivated to intervene because it feared the amendment might be rejected or the outcome might be indecisive. The declaration by the Protestant churches that they considered the campaign sectarian weakened the PLAC case considerably. Moreover, the Anti-Amendment Campaign had presented their case skilfully in the media, particularly on television, and their objections were being

[51] *The Irish Times*, 17 March 1983.
[52] *The Irish Times*, 22 April 1983 and 23 April 1983; *The Sunday Tribune*, 16 November 1983.
[53] *The Irish Times*, 13 April 1983; *The Sunday Tribune*, 16 November 1983.
[54] *The Irish Times*, 30 March 1983.
[55] *The Irish Times*, 11 April 1983 and 19 April 1983.
[56] *Parliamentary Debates Dail Eireann*, 341: 10 (27 April 1983), cols. 2002–2032, 2150–2238.

TABLE 5a. Should There Be a Referendum on Abortion?

	August 1982	February 1983	April 1983	May(1) 1983	May(2) 1983	July 1983
For	43	48	38	33	32	41
Against	41	34	43	47	53	46
Don't know	16	18	19	20	15	13

TABLE 5b. Voting Intentions if a Referendum were held.

	February 1983	May 1983	August 1983	September 1983
Yes	53	34	44	53
No	16	28	31	24
Undecided	19	20	25	14
Will not vote	12	18		9

Source: Irish Marketing Surveys and Market Research Bureau of Ireland as reported in *The Irish Times* on various dates.

taken seriously. *Fine Gael* and Labour also accepted the view that the amendment was sectarian, leading Dr FitzGerald to announce that he would advise the electorate to reject it. Therefore once opposition to the referendum became widespread, it was almost inevitable, given the traditions of the church, that a more active rôle would be played by the hierarchy. This occurred despite serious misgivings on the part of sections of the hierarchy. However, despite this the conservative wing of the church was successful in gaining support for a more aggressive rôle for the bishops.[57] Following the decision of the *Dail* to hold a referendum, there was evidence that the anti-abortion campaign was running out of steam. Table 5a shows the changing nature of public opinion on whether a referendum should take place.[58] Apparent opposition to holding a referendum is displayed in Table 5a. Table 5b outlines voting intentions *if* a referendum were held. This demonstrates that on every occasion there was a majority willing to vote in favour.[59] The opinion polls indicated that there was considerable uncertainty among the electorate concerning the proposed amendment, and that a substantial pocket of opposition had emerged. It was these factors which gave the hierarchy added justification for intervention once the original political unanimity had broken down. At the same time the church had to be careful not to alienate those who opposed the referendum, but on all

[57] *The Sunday Tribune,* 16 November 1983.

[58] Source for tables: Irish Marketing Surveys reported in *The Irish Times,* 3 June 1983 and 4 August 1983, except May (2) Market Research Bureau of Ireland, as reported in *The Irish Times,* 13 June 1983.

[59] Source: Market Research Bureau of Ireland, as reported in *The Irish Times,* 5 September 1983, except August, Irish Marketing Surveys as reported in *The Irish Times,* 4 August 1983. The September poll proved very accurate when the figures are adjusted for those undecided and those not voting.

accounts remained members of the church. This was dealt with in two ways. In the weeks before the referendum the church organized support for a 'yes' vote throughout the country. Catholics were urged to ensure a substantial majority in favour of the measure. This was supplemented by various public statements from members of the hierarchy stressing the dangers of abortion and the consequences of a defeat. These statements often emphasized that Catholics had an obligation to go out and vote on the day.[60] Shortly before the referendum, the Irish Bishops Conference issued a statement condemning abortion and calling for a 'yes' vote, but, significantly, the statement also stressed that Catholics had the right to exercise freedom of conscience, and consequently could in conscience vote 'no'.[61] The statement clearly reflected the views of a number of bishops uneasy about the way the campaign had progressed and worried about the consequences for the church after the referendum had taken place.[62] The nature of this statement was unacceptable to the conservative bishops, a number of whom issued pastoral letters just before the referendum urging a much more intransigent position.[63] The leaders of the political parties also issued statements just before the referendum. Dr FitzGerald reiterated his opposition, conceding that he had at first supported the campaign but that legal opinion had forced him to modify his position. Charles Haughey displayed no such misgivings, arguing strongly in favour of a 'yes' vote.[64] Despite the stated preferences of the party leaders, none of the main parties campaigned officially in the run up to the referendum. The campaign for and against the amendment was waged, in the main, by the two opposing interest groups—PLAC and the Anti-Amendment Campaign. However, *Fianna Fail* activists do appear to have played an important rôle in their respective constituencies in support of PLAC, while no such support was forthcoming for the Anti-Amendment Campaign from *Fine Gael*.

III. The Outcome of the Referendum

The amendment to the constitution was in fact passed by a two to one majority. However, the vote was characterized by a very high abstention rate and considerable regional differentiation. The turn-out was 54.6 per cent of the electorate: 66.45 per cent voted 'yes', while 32.87 per cent voted 'no'. However, when the vote is taken as a percentage of the electorate as a whole, the 'yes' vote accounted for 35.79 per cent, while the 'no' vote was 17.6 per cent. Under the circumstances outlined above, the high abstention rate is surprising and requires further explanation. It may be suggested that the turn-out at the referendum cannot be compared to that of a general election, or that the turn-out at the former is traditionally lower than the latter. There is some justification for this belief; a referendum in 1979 had a turn-out of only 28.6 per cent. However, it is necessary to add that a distinction must be made between referendums which are controversial and those which are not. Thus, the turn-

[60] *The Irish Times*, 1, 2, 5 September 1983.
[61] *The Irish Times*, 23 August 1983.
[62] *The Sunday Tribune*, 16 November 1983.
[63] *The Irish Times*, 2 September 1983.
[64] *The Irish Times*, 5 September 1983.

out at the 1968 referendum on proportional representation was 65.8 per cent, that at the 1972 referendum on entry to the European Community, was 70.9 per cent. On the other hand, the referendum in 1972 concerning the special position of the Catholic Church in the constitution had a turn-out of 50.7 per cent. This referendum was non-controversial because practically all interests supported it, unlike the two previously mentioned when divisions on the issues were strong. Clearly the referendum on abortion falls into the controversial category; moreover, it had a distinctly party flavour which has usually had an impact on previous referendums. In addition, for a month before the referendum the media reported the campaign extensively. Finally, the church had publicly urged Catholics to vote. The low turn-out can be explained in a number of ways. At the most trivial level, bad weather and a bus strike may have contributed to the outcome. In addition, there were those who rejected both sides of the campaign and refused to vote. More importantly, and in line with the opinion polls, the abstention rate reflected continual opposition to holding the referendum under any circumstances, but an unwillingness to vote 'no' because the individual was opposed to abortion. There was also considerable confusion concerning the issue on the part of a section of the electorate. A further group abstained because while opposing the referendum, they feared that a 'no' vote would impair the stability of society. However, on balance, it can be concluded that abstention was a protest vote. In a context where the Roman Catholic clergy used every opportunity to exhort the faithful to vote, the turn-out, if not the outcome, can only be considered a disappointment for the Church.

An alternative explanation urges that the turn-out under-estimated the 'yes' vote, because abstentions were higher in areas where one might expect a strong 'yes' vote. It can, therefore, be suggested that these voters did not feel the urgency to vote because they believed the outcome was predictable. However, if the extent of media coverage and the appeals from the clergy for a large turn-out are taken into account, this is not a full explanation. A more likely explanation is that the resistance to holding a referendum is reflected in the abstention rate and that some of the abstainers distinguished between personal opposition to abortion and the necessity of holding a referendum.[65]

Table 6 shows the regional distribution of the vote.[66] The most significant 'no' vote was returned in the Dublin area: five of its eleven constituencies actually rejected the amendment. The highest 'yes' vote was registered in the west of Ireland, where a 'yes' vote of 80 per cent was not uncommon. There were also strong regional differences. The size of the 'no' vote was determined by proximity to Dublin or the presence of a large town in a constituency. Indeed, it has been suggested that the 'no' vote was greater in urban areas, even where the constituency voted overwhelmingly in favour of the amendment.[67]

---

[65] J. Coakley, 'The Referendum and Popular Participation in the Irish Political System' (unpublished paper, European Consortium for Political Research, University of Lancaster, 1981). For the alternative view see B. M. Walsh, 'The Influence of Turnout on the Results of the Referendum to Amend the Constitution to Include a Change on the Rights of the Unborn', *The Economic and Social Review*, 15: 3 (April 1984), 227–34.

[66] *The Irish Times*, 9 September 1983.

[67] M. Gallagher, 'Where the Votes Came From', *The Irish Times*, 10 September 1983.

TABLE 6. Regional Distribution of
Vote in 1983 Referendum.

	Yes	No
Dublin	51.36	48.09
Rest of Leinster	69.14	30.10
Munster	72.05	27.21
Connacht	76.24	23.04
Ulster	81.49	17.87

Source: *The Irish Times*, 9 September
1983. Ulster signifies the three Ulster
counties in the Republic.

Of the 13 constituencies which registered a 'no' vote in excess of 40 per cent, ten of those were in Dublin, two, Kildare and Wicklow, were located in Leinster and contiguous to County Dublin, while the other, Cork South Central, was located in the second largest city. The strength of the 'yes' vote was in rural Ireland: the further west the larger the 'yes' vote. In nine constituencies the 'yes' vote was in excess of 80 per cent. Two constituencies on the western seaboard, Galway West and Limerick East, demonstrated the importance of the urban–rural cleavage. In both constituencies the 'no' vote was over 30 per cent. In contrast, their neighbouring constituencies registered a vote of approximately 80 per cent in favour. In each constituency there is an expanding urban population.[68] In addition, the left was well organized in both cities with Kemmy and Higgins playing an important rôle in the Anti-Amendment Campaign.

The further away a constituency is from Dublin in Leinster, the smaller the 'no' vote. In general, the 'no' vote was larger in east of the country than in the west, even in rural areas. The lack of uniformity in the voting figures requires one additional variable for explanation. Although the 'no' vote was high in urban areas, there were wide differences in the actual percentage. Thus in Dublin the lowest 'no' vote was in Dublin Central, 38 per cent, while that in Dun Laoghaire was 58 per cent. Moreover, the three central Dublin constituencies had a lower 'no' vote than elsewhere in Dublin city. These are settled areas of the city, with strong traditional working-class presence. They had ageing populations and were politically mobilized by *Fianna Fail* during the 1930s and the 1950s. In addition, Charles Haughey is the deputy for the Dublin North Central and *Fianna Fail* supported the campaign. The importance of the traditional working-class areas in the outcome is confirmed in the case of Cork city. The 'no' vote in Cork North Central was 35 per cent, while that of South Central was 44 per cent. The composition of the former constituency has certain similarities with that of the Dublin central constituencies: a strong *Fianna Fail* presence, an ageing population, and many working-class constituents. However, it is significant that in newly settled areas within the constituency the 'no' vote was higher than elsewhere.[69] Furthermore, this

[68] *Census of Population of Ireland 1981, Vol. I* (Dublin, Stationery Office, 1982), p. 14.
[69] Interview with member of the Cork Anti-Amendment Campaign.

BRIAN GIRVIN 79

TABLE 7. Stated Voting Intentions (excluding undecided).

	Yes %	No %	Yes Approx.	No Ratio
Overall	69	31	2	1
Community				
Urban	61	39	1.5	1
Rural	78	22	3.5	1
Sex				
Male	62	38	1.5	1
Female	75	25	3	1
Age				
18–24	69	31	2	1
25–34	58	42	1.5	1
35–49	66	34	2	1
50+	78	22	4	1
Class				
Middle	58	42	1.5	1
Working	70	30	2	1
Large farming	81	19	4	1
Other farming	91	9	10	1
Party				
Fianna Fail	80	20	4	1
Fine Gael	61	39	1.5	1
Labour	48	52	1	1
Other	42	58	1	1.4
Not stated	74	26	3	1

Source: Market Research Bureau of Ireland as reported in *The Irish Times*, 29 September 1983.

section of the working-class has had a traditionally close relationship with the clergy. The composition of the Cork South Central constituency is quite different. Politically *Fine Gael* rather than *Fianna Fail* has always been strong here. Much of it is suburban in outlook, while new satellite towns within the constituency are reflections of greater mobility. Socially, there is a wider spread of middle-class, white-collar workers and the young. These observations are in part confirmed on a national level by Table 7, which summarizes the stated voting intentions of those polled just before the referendum.[70] The ratios between 'yes' and 'no' are significant in that the urban–rural division mentioned above holds, as do differences between age, party, and class. The table demonstrates that roughly two-thirds of the working class were in favour, while nearly half the middle classes opposed the amendment. The importance of *Fianna Fail* support for the amendment is also clear, with the ratio of four to one party supporters in favour. In addition, there is a close relationship between the size of the *Fianna Fail* vote in a constituency and the size of the

[70] Source: Market Research Bureau of Ireland, as reported in *The Irish Times*, 29 September 1983.

'yes' vote. It has, in fact, been suggested that the majority of those who actually voted 'yes' were *Fianna Fail* supporters.[71]

Conclusion: The Consequences for Politics of the Referendum

A cynic might believe that there will be no consequences, and the referendum was simply an exercise in self-righteous indignation on the part of a rather smug, insular people. It is true that the Irish are fond of Irish solutions, usually ones which are so innocuous that the *status quo* remains unaffected, while those seeking reforms are conceded very little. Proponents of the amendment agreed that nothing would change if they were successful and to date nothing has. Women still travel to Britain for abortions and referral clinics still operate. Unless it is decided to prosecute women who leave the state to procure abortions—and this raises the vision of pregnancy testing facilities at points of departure—nothing will in fact change despite the 18-months' campaign.

The consequences should be sought elsewhere. The referendum reinforced the tendency for *Fianna Fail* to identify with conservative issues and *Fine Gael* and Labour to favour liberal policies. *Fianna Fail* appears to be undergoing a change: becoming less pragmatic, more doctinaire and traditionalist. At another level, the different response of the urban and rural electorate is being reflected in the attempts of the two major parties to capture and hold specific sections of the electorate: *Fine Gael* the urban and liberal vote, *Fianna Fail* the traditional and rural. The appeal of the parties has consequently been redefined and their policies modified to reflect these changes. In less than 20 years *Fine Gael*, under the pressures outlined above, has been transformed from a right-wing to a liberal-centrist party. In *Fianna Fail*, the traditionalist wing of the party has captured the pragmatic section which was dominant during the 1960s and 1970s. These divisions will be exacerbated as social, demographic, and economic pressures force the parties to identify with specific interests and policies.

These changes have also begun to affect the constitutional framework. The Irish constitution, enacted in 1937, was originally framed for a stable, Catholic, and agrarian society. After the referendum it is doubtful if it can prove an adequate instrument for the changing circumstances of the 1980s. Conservatives have invoked the constitution in a very select fashion, merely to maintain the *status quo*.[72] This is reinforced by the *Fianna Fail* policy of maintaining the constitution in its current form. These circumstances make the gradual reform of the constitution to accommodate social and economic change virtually impossible. Furthermore, the requirement that a referendum should be held before the constitution is amended or altered introduces a conservative bias to the political structure. The political parties hesitate in initiating moves for the reform of the constitution, because the outcome is uncertain and the effort often divisive and time consuming. This would mean that the constitution could be altered only if there were a reasonably large consensus in favour of the change. This consensus is unlikely to be forthcoming due to the changes which have been taking place in the parties. The referendum on abortion has accelerated a process, evident for some time: the politicization

---

[71] Gallagher, 'Where the Votes Came From'.

[72] This conservative response is not restricted to moral matters; it has relevance also for the constitutional claim on Northern Ireland and the function of private property in Ireland.

of the basic constitutional document. This politicization centres on different interpretations of the function of a constitution: whether it is a static codification or a more flexible framework open to change. The referendum reinforces the former interpretation; moreover, the resistance to change among important sections of the political élite effectively neutralizes any significant modification of the constitution in the near future.

As the character of Irish society changes there will be increased pressure on the church. The referendum was a victory for the church; it not only displayed its power, but also the result demonstrated that a considerable section of the electorate remains amenable to the church's authority. However, it was possibly a pyrrhic victory in that despite mobilizing all its resources and concentrating on a particularly emotive question, the outcome for the church was not as clear as might have been expected. The referendum confirmed what the survey data had found—that there is a growing liberal constituency in Ireland as well as a smaller committed anti-clerical movement. The irony for the church is that while it secured a specifically Catholic moral point in the referendum, its advocacy of democracy on this occasion may backfire when other issues arise. The democratic process is unpredictable; there is no certainly that the church could mobilize a majority against removing the constitutional prohibition on divorce. On this and other matters there may already be a majority in favour of change. The church will be in a predicament if it advocates majority rule when this suits its purpose, but denies its application when it does not.[73] It has shown itself unwilling to compromise, except in the most superficial way, with the secular forces in Ireland. Because of its direct involvement in the referendum, the church will find it more difficult to reconcile the two sides of modern Irish Catholicism. This is a novel situation for the hierarchy, one which it has not been successful in mediating. The divisions between liberal and conservative Catholics are likely to continue even after the referendum, as there are a number of outstanding questions which will once again divide opinion. In addition, the further secularization and liberalization of Irish society will deprive it of any but a superficial influence or power over liberal Catholics.

Political change in Ireland has been incremental rather than radical. The nature of the political system largely accounts for this. This incremental change is in strong contrast to the social, economic, and demographic changes which have transformed Irish society in 20 years. This transformation has, however, influenced the political system. Two cleavages have emerged, previously unimportant: one based on urban–rural differences, the other reflecting divisions between liberal and traditional sections of the electorate. Although these changes are not as yet explicitly reflected in the political system, they are indications that the political parties are realigning along these divisions. The referendum brought to light the incipient conflicts which resulted from change; its outcome quantified the sources of support available. Future developments should provide a more accurate assessment of the consequences for Irish politics of this issue.

[73] For a clear expression of the hierarchy's ambiguity on democracy see The Irish Episcopal Conference: Submission to New Irish Forum, 13 January 1984 as reported in *The Irish Times*, 14 January 1984. Also *New Irish Forum, Report of Proceedings, No. 12,* 9 February 1984 (Irish Episcopal Conference Delegation).

[27]

Multiculturalism and British Identity in the Wake of the Rushdie Affair

TALAL ASAD

I

IT is common knowledge that the Rushdie affair precipitated a sense of political crisis in Britain. Large numbers of Muslims publicly expressed their anger and distress at the publication of *The Satanic Verses*, demonstrated in London, petitioned Penguin Books to withdraw the book, and the government to ban it. The government rejected the call for banning and warned Muslims not to isolate themselves from the "host" society. Newspapers and television almost unanimously condemned the "fundamentalism" of Britain's Muslims. On February 14 Ayatollah Khomeini issued his shocking death sentence on Rushdie. This greatly aggravated the sense of crisis in Britain although most prominent Muslims there publicly dissociated themselves from it.[1] Ten days later Home Secretary Douglas Hurd made a speech at a gathering of Muslims emphasizing the importance of proper integration for ethnic minorities, the need to learn about British culture without abandoning one's own faith, and the necessity of refraining from

Parts of this article were read at the University of California, Davis; the University of Pennsylvania; and the anthropology departmental seminar of the New School for Social Research. I have benefited from remarks by audiences at each of these occasions. I am particularly grateful to U. Kalpagam and Rayna Rapp for their detailed comments. My greatest debt, however, is to Tanya Baker for her advice and criticism.

violence. At the beginning of July his deputy, John Patten, wrote an open letter along similar lines to "a number of leading British Muslims." Two weeks later he produced another document, entitled "On Being British," which was circulated to the news media.

I shall discuss this text in some detail below, but first I want to pose a question. Why did the British government feel the need to make such statements at this juncture? Why were these statements widely applauded by the liberal middle class, whose pronouncements both before and after the government's intervention repeatedly denounced "Muslim violence"? This was not, I would argue, because there was an unmanageable threat to "law and order" in the country. In fact no arrests or injuries had occurred as a result of the demonstrations against the book although it is true that emotional threats had been made by individuals against the author and his publishers.[2] As against this, however, it is important to bear in mind that there had been innumerable angry demonstrations through the streets of London before by antiracists, fascists, feminists, gays, "prolife" activists, trade unionists, and students. Scuffles had broken out between demonstrators and police, involving accusations and counteraccusations of violence and death threats, injuries being sustained, and arrests being made. More significantly, Britain had witnessed a number of major urban riots (in Nottingham, Nottinghill Gate, Brixton, Bristol, Birmingham, Liverpool, and so forth) in which pitched battles were fought between police and nonwhite immigrants, cars and buildings were burned, and blood was spilt—though incidentally South Asians were rarely, if ever, involved in any of these violent confrontations.[3] There has also been a steady stream of racist murders of nonwhite (mostly South Asian) immigrants and a much longer stream of violence in which nonwhites have been subjected to "attempted killing, death narrowly avoided, arson, physical assault, spitting and verbal abuse, incidents estimated to number some 70,000 each year, most of them unreported to the police or other public authority."[4] And of course supporters of the Irish Republican Army have planted bombs in London that led to death and injury. The British Government had never publicly warned the white majority against individual and collective violence, nor had they lectured Irish Catholics (or more recent immigrants) in England about the essential character of British-ness.

So what is it that leads them to make such unprecedented public pronouncements to an "ethnic minority" now? Certainly the government is not alone in feeling that a situation of unusual seriousness has developed in the country, requiring firm handling. In a leader entitled "Dangers of the Muslim campaign" (July 20, 1989), the influential British daily newspaper, *Independent*, began:

The present Government does not often forcefully represent the views of left-of-centre intellectuals....But the recent observations of John Patten, Minister of State at the Home

Office responsible for race relations, on the need for the Muslim community to integrate with British society, have broadly echoed the views of liberal opinion.

And ended, somewhat threateningly:

If Britain's more extreme Muslims ignore John Patten's advice and continue to adopt hardline positions, they are likely to turn educated, as well as popular sentiments against them.

What exactly was the danger sensed by the Tory government and "liberal opinion" in Britain? I argue that the danger is a perceived threat to a particular ideological structure, a cultural hierarchy organized around an essential *Englishness*, which defines *British* identity.[5] There are already worrying developments that threaten that identity—integration into the European community (dominated by its defeated enemy, Germany), demands of Welsh and Scottish nationalists, and the unresolvable civil war in Northern Ireland between two collective religious identities. It is too much to be confronted now by immigrants from the ex-colonies (a vanished empire) trying to politicize their alien traditions in England itself. Thus in my view the Rushdie affair in Britain should be seen primarily as yet another symptom of British, postimperial identity in crisis, and not—as most commentators have represented it—as an unhappy instance of some immigrants with difficulties in adjusting to a new and more civilized world.

II

John Patten, home minister responsible for race relations, intervened publicly in the Rushdie affair first by writing an open letter (published in *The Times* daily newspaper) addressed to "leaders and representatives" of Britain's Muslim community. Perhaps its most striking feature is its firm, paternal style. Referring to *The Satanic Verses*, he opens: "The Government understands how much hurt and anxiety that book has caused, and we also understand that insults, particularly to a deeply held faith, are not easily forgotten or forgiven." Here surely is the atavistic voice of an English colonial governor responding kindly to the injured sensibilities of his native subjects. Patten does not present himself as the spokesman of a democratically elected government rejecting the political demand of a particular body of citizens that another citizen's legal right to free speech be curtailed. He does not find it sufficient to say: "There is no law which would permit the banning of *The Satanic Verses*, and the Government will not extend any existing law to do so." Patten, who echoes the views of British liberal opinion, presents himself as the voice of a fatherly government addressing "the leaders and representatives" of an alien population that now lives under its protection.

The arrival of people from the ex-colonies to Britain since World War II, Patten assures the Muslim "leaders and representatives," has "added to Britain's wealth of culture and tradition." It would seem that this rich "culture and tradition" (both in the singular) is already in place, an essence that can be added to by foreigners precisely to the extent that there is an affinity between what they bring and what is essentially here. That is why Patten immediately goes on to pay them the compliment of describing them as potential Tories: "Many have come with values that can only be admired such as firm faith; a commitment to family life; a belief in hard work and enterprise; respect for the law and a will to succeed. To their credit, they have kept those values at the core of their life in Britain, too." Of course, he goes on, he quite understands that there are inevitable stresses and strains given the adjustments immigrants have had to make in their new environment. "No one would expect or indeed want British Muslims to lay aside their faith, traditions or heritage," he assures them (although this is precisely what many white Britons do want, at least in the measure to which they—the latter— decide is essential). But there are various things immigrant children really *must* learn "if they are to make the most of their lives and opportunities as British citizens." This includes, according to Patten, "a fluent command of English," but also "a clear understanding of British democratic processes, of its laws, the system of Government and the history that lies behind them." The remarkable thing about these demands is that they are skills and knowledge that very few white Britons can claim confidently to possess.

Stressing briefly the promise of a British society in which "equality of opportunity for all" will one day prevail, Patten then proceeds to praise those Muslims who have themselves kept within the law and publicly apologized for the bad behavior of some of their fellows. It is only after this extraordinary address at the end of the letter, that Patten explains clearly and briefly that *The Satanic Verses* cannot be banned.[6]

But this statement provoked by the Rushdie affair was clearly felt to be insufficient because two weeks later John Patten produced another in the form of a mimeographed "News Release" from the Home Office (dated 18 July 1989): "On Being British." This second pronouncement is not very long—a mere four and a half pages of double-spaced typescript. It seems at first reading to contain nothing but bland platitudes and points already made in the earlier *Times* article. Yet it was summarised and cited admiringly by the serious newspapers.[7]

The phrase "On Being British" implies that Britishness is more than a matter of paying taxes, voting, using state welfare services, and in general being subject to the laws of the country: As we shall see, it is a matter of essential sentiments and loyalties. The government feels itself obliged to explain what this essence is to immigrants (including "immigrants" who were born and schooled in Britain). Patten's disquisition does not contain any *information*, not even a clue as to where one might go to read up on one's legal rights and duties as a British citizen. Curiously, the word "state" does not appear in his text (though it is part of the author's official designation: "Home Office Minister of State"); and "government" is used only once, in passing, at the end with reference to "its considerable support for English-teaching programmes." "On Being British" urges "cultural minority communities" to aspire to a norm. The document is an implicit description of the white "cultural majority community" which supposedly sets the norm and so of what that cultural essence is.[8]

On the first page, Patten makes the point that "being British" has to do with "those things which...we have in common. Our democracy and our laws, the English language, and the history that has shaped modern Britain." At the center of this history is the idea of "freedom" —"to choose one's faith, to choose one's political allegiance, to speak and write freely, to meet, argue and demonstrate, and to play a part in shaping events." The word freedom occurs with remarkable frequency in this short text, evoking as it does so the central theme of innumerable Whig histories of England.[9] And Englishness, as every white English native knows, lies at the core of being British.

The idea of freedom appears to consist of two interconnected ideas, "tolerance" and "obligation," which are also repeated again and again in Patten's discourse. "Tolerance" requires acceptance of diversity ("There is, as I have said, plenty of room for diversity, precisely because our traditions are those of tolerance"), a diversity based on the individual's right to believe, act, and speak as he or she chooses. But rights create "obligations," above all the obligation to respect the rights of others—"respect for the safety of their property," no less than for their right to speak and write "freely."[10]

What is not immediately clear from such statements is whether "diversity" is an intrinsic feature of the British way of life or something allowed only when divergences do not contradict an essential—and therefore unchangeable—Britishness. When immigrants bring new practices, beliefs, and discourses with them to Britain, do they extend the scope of British life, or are they (conditionally) tolerated by the authentic British who are also the cultural majority?

Everyone, according to Patten's exposition of the British idea of freedom, has a "right to make a contribution," and a right to play his or her part in the mainstream. Apparently this is always an individual matter: "Our democratic system and processes not only recognise the value of the individual's right to make a contribution or to hold distinct personal views. Our system also protects and safeguards these rights...." Only the individual, so the reader is given to understand, can be the object of tolerance and the subject of obligations. And so too participation in "British life" is open only to individuals: "[P]articipation includes playing one's part in the economy, playing one's part as a neighbour, making a contribution which goes beyond one's own family or indeed community." According to Patten, an agreed cultural script defining the roles that British individuals may play is already in place.

Since "family" and "community" are the only groups mentioned in the document, the implication seems to be that groups have no place in the public sphere.[11] But as this is patently false (the public sphere is occupied by a complex array of business institutions, professional bodies, trades unions, social movements, and opinion groups representing each of these), the formulation here must be read as having the intention of discouraging "cultural minorities" from establishing themselves as corporate political actors. As far as "cultural minority" members are concerned, they must participate in Britishness (the quality that makes them part of the essential culture) as individuals.

This participation, Patten insists, does not mean assimilation, "forgetting one's cultural roots." But that is only because, and to the extent that, "being British" to which he refers presupposes a hierarchy of cultural spaces not mentioned here. Thus neither the English working class, nor the Scots, Welsh, and Northern Irish can be absorbed as collectivities into elite, metropolitan, English culture for these separate cultural spaces are necessary to Englishness as the expression of a governing norm.[12] *Individual* assimilation across these spaces has always been possible and indeed encouraged. The concept of "tolerance" relates specifically to this ideological arrangement and to the cultural script authorised by it.

What "being British" involves, says Patten again at the end of his disquisition, is what "we have in common": a framework of laws, the English language, and a history. But anyone in Britain who reads Patten knows that in practice such abstractions acquire their definition from a particular elite: (a) those who interpret and administer what counts as *English* law (the very different framework of Roman law is basic to Scotland), (b) those who speak "the Queen's English" and maintain "English literature," and (c) those who write and authorize the histories *of England* taught in schools and universities.

The life of the English governing class—its values, codes, and sensibilities— is the core of British culture. It is therefore only others who need to be warned against the treacherous lure of dual loyalties: "One cannot be British on one's own exclusive terms or on a selective basis, nor is there room for dual loyalties where those loyalties openly contradict one another." That is to say, participation in British life *does* after all require "forgetting one's cultural roots" if they cannot in some way be accomodated by Britishness. Diversity is to be tolerated only if it does not conflict with British identity to which it is necessarily external.

In nationalist vocabularies, the term "loyalty" has the useful quality of fusing two meanings: legal subjection and moral attachment. Patten employs the term in this double sense here. Thus the straightforward statement that as a British subject one is exclusively bound to the British crown when in Britain[13] is linked to the moralistic judgement that it is reprehensible to be attached to divergent identities (people, traditions) whether these are found inside the country or outside it.

Conceived as *a medium of communication*, the English language is of course a necessary part of "what we have in common," but it is not clear how in that sense it can be said to be the object of "loyalties," nor is it obvious that language conceived as *a discursive formation* (that is, as the expression of distinctive ways of acting and thinking) can be said to be something all classes and traditions found in Britain "have in common." The loyalty demanded must therefore be loyalty to a historiography that articulates a secular unity for all of Britain: "Whether our background is Pakistani, Polish, Vietnamese, or whatever, we all need to know our particular background and to cherish our own history and special traditions," says Patten. "Alongside that, however, a sound and detailed knowledge of British history and of Britain's part in world history, a feeling for what has shaped our institutions, is vital to living in, and understanding the complexities of, Britain today. It is essential to 'being British.'" It is evident that Patten assumes there is no significant contradiction between "our own history and special traditions" and an account of "Britain's part in world history" accepted by British teachers, textbook-writers, and examiners—or that if there is our "loyalties" must be given to the latter. Not surprisingly, the teaching of history in schools has become a matter of primary concern for the present government and the opposition.[14] An authorized history, so it is hoped, will express "British culture" and help develop in all children a sense of loyalty toward it. But as the educational system is not designed to make all children equally familiar with that history, the nationalist hope must be that loyalty will be given to those who speak in its name, those who draw on it to make the framework of laws that "we have in common."

A contested history might, however, raise some questions regarding Patten's easy assumption that "being British" essentially presupposes tolerance. For let us not forget that British imperial history (through which British identity was recently constructed) initiated the forcible transformation of innumerable conquered societies in the direction of British culture.

I want to stress, finally, that Patten's document is not to be described as an expression of Thatcherite, neo-liberalism. On the contrary, it draws on a much broader liberal tradition—including elements from the older, collectivist liberalism of J.S. Mill and T.H. Green.[15] What Patten seeks to articulate and defend (with the approval of a wide range of opinion outside the Conservative party) is the notion of a culture, *a common way of life*, that defines at once the substantive values of a secular British identity and the formal basis of a diversified and rationally justifiable society.

III

Let me recapitulate my main argument briefly: The political mobilization of Muslim immigrants in Britain to get *The Satanic Verses* banned produced an emotional reaction on the part of the liberal elite that was out of all proportion to what has actually happened. It also produced an unprecedented statement from a government minister about British identity directed at the Muslim minority, a statement that was warmly welcomed as representative of liberal elite opinion. I argue that these extraordinary facts require explaining and suggest that an explanation should be sought by looking for what the British liberal elite feel is being threatened. My view is that the perceived danger is neither a matter of "law-and-order" nor of "loss of freedom of speech"; it is a matter, rather, of the politicization of a religious tradition that has no place within the cultural hegemony that has defined British identity over the last century particularly as that tradition has come from a once-colonized society.

Before I proceed with a discussion of the contemporary British scene, a note on the concept of "culture" may be useful.

Raymond Williams reminded us in *Key Words* that the complex semantic structure of the word "culture" is of comparatively recent origin. He identified three interconnected senses of the noun: (1) the processes of intellectual, spiritual, and aesthetic development—a usage dating from the eighteenth century; (2) an inherited way of life whether of a particular people (as in Herder) or of humanity in general (as in Klemm and Tylor); (3) in its most familiar form, the noun indicating the activities and creations of literary and artistic endeavor.[16]

In *Culture and Society* Williams had traced the evolution of that structure in the arguments of English social critics of the nineteenth and early twentieth centuries. The distinctively modern sense of "culture," he argued, emerges with the formation of industrial liberal society. Where once culture meant the training that provided mind and soul with their intellectual and moral accomplishments, it now also means an entire way of life—the common way of life of a whole people.

The idea of culture is a general reaction to a general and major change in the conditions of our common life. *Its basic element is its effort at total qualitative assessment.* The change in *the whole form of our common life produced*, as a necessary reaction, an emphasis on attention to this whole form. Particular change will modify an habitual discipline, shift an habitual action. General change, when it has worked itself clear, drives us back on *our general designs*, which we have to learn to look at again, and as a whole. *The working-out of the idea of culture is a slow reach again for control.*[17]

This totalizing project expressed itself in the inclusion of the entire adult population into the electoral processes of parliamentary democracy but also in the growing articulation (interconnection, expression, and construction) of civil society. An inevitable consequence of this development, it should be noted, was the fact that all aspects of life (in its social as well as biological senses) were now to be politicized.

The last quarter of the nineteenth and the first half of the twentieth century witnessed the development of integrating, improving, institutions: industrial and welfare legislation, public-sector education, the arts (museums, libraries, and so forth), local (that is, municipal) government, national insurance, public hygiene and health care, trades unions, and so forth. These institutions were the outcome of initiatives by members of the upper class, as well as of pressure from militant dissenters and working-class organizations, but they should not be thought of as expressing a single, essential, social logic. They involved diverse motives and practices, and they certainly did not create "a common life" (in the sense of work and leisure, of worship and sensibility, or of commitments and aspirations) for all classes in Britian. Nevertheless the dominant political ideology of new Liberalism enabled these developments to be conceptualized in relation to a normalizing project, thus making it plausible to think of "culture" in the way Williams has traced. Although Williams does not describe these conditions in his book, which is largely concerned with the opinions of literary men and not with administrative practices, it is important to stress that they defined the political relevance of the modern sense of "culture" in Britain. For in these conditions was constructed an increasingly differentiated domain on which the "common life" of a whole people (the British nation) could be conceived in order to be rationally "recreated." Never without tensions and conflicts, and certainly not everywhere successful, the work of constructing an integrated British society (with its core culture) reveals one aspect of the modern faith in liberal reason.

But there is another aspect to the career of the modern concept of culture in Britain that Williams does not mention: the British Empire. "Empire," wrote the eminent Cambridge historian, Sir Ernest Barker, "is not only a form of government. It is also a mission of culture—and of something higher than culture."[18] In the period between the two world wars the British empire consisted of the dominions ("white" settler countries like Canada, Australia, and South Africa), the dependent colonies (including Africa and the West Indies), and India (both princely states and British India). "The problem of culture," as it was formulated in the reflective discourse of the British elite, applied only to the "nonwhite" populations and had to do with the practices of controlled reconstruction. Barker describes it initially as emerging from the clash of unequal cultures:

The cultural problem emerges from, and it has its analogies with, the biological and the economic problems. It is a problem which begins in the conflict of different social habits, different forms of political order, different worlds...of knowledge and of art: it is a problem which proceeds from conflict to contact, and, in so proceeding, rises to the level of a problem of intermixture, or at any rate co-ordination.[19]

When the culture of "a dominant stock" (who, it is assumed, must have common social habits) comes into contact with a "native culture," Barker observes, the question of contact becomes critical for the latter. It can be enriched, or it may disintegrate, with the introduction of new (that is, western) elements: Everything depends on a proper coordination (conceptual and political) of the process.

The fact of imperial rule thus renders "the problem of culture" into the British obligation to identify, study, and normalize the culture of its subject peoples (whence the importance of "the rise of sociology and anthropology,")[20] but also to help integrate them into modern (western) life in a vital and progressive manner. This obligation applies equally to India[21] and to the colonies,[22] although the native peoples in each case belong to different levels of progress.

For their part, British functionalist anthropologists of the interwar period conceptualized the problem of culture in a way that directly addressed the problem of reconstruction. What mattered for dealing rationally with "culture contact" was what actually survived of a native culture together with the new European elements absorbed by it: The totality that could be controlled, improved, and protected was the way of life that actually existed now, not the "scientifically reconstituted past" of life before European contact. "What, therefore, is relevant from the practical point of view?" Malinowski writes:

Obviously, the still surviving quota of culture and tradition observable in present-day field-work. It seems unnecessary to emphasize that only what still lives [within the new colonial polity] can give any guidance to those who have to control a living native society. Only forces of tradition actively influencing the sentiments of living men and women matter for those who have to deal with their destiny.[23]

Although the expression is not used, this might be described as an attempt to conceptualize the problem of "multiculturalism" in colonial settings. The new, diversified context of society in Africa requires the proper theoretical and practical coordination of dominant (European) and subordinate (native) cultures: equal respect for all cultures, but the realities of political power require the subordinate (less progressive) to adjust to the dominant (more progressive). "There are cultural elements which are not allowed to continue," Malinowski points out, "because they are repugnant to Whites."[24] Where its task is cultural liberation, liberal reason requires the use of force whenever persuasion (the use of reason) does not work.

Incidentally, I do not want to give the impression that I regard Malinowski's views as representative of all British anthropologists. Thus, unlike Malinowski, Radcliffe-Brown and his pupils considered the concept of culture theoretically uninteresting.[25] My concern here is to identify "culture" as part of a language of total colonial control (which should not in any case be confused with the *practices* of colonial rule, still less with the practices and discourses of the colonized). My point is that a striking feature of this language was its exclusive focus on a presently existing, directly observable, and therefore *normalizable* totality of elements—and in this respect Malinowski's writings were no different from those of Radcliffe-Brown.

What emerges from the observations by Barker and Malinowski is that the concept of culture in the distinctively modern sense of a common life and representable as such had become by the 1930s and 1940s, part of a language of controlled reconstruction—in the terrain of empire as in Britain itself—according to the dictates of liberal reason. It would be wrong, I believe, to represent this language simply as a cynical device of imperial rule[26] because a similar logic was at work both in Britain and in the empire—namely the aim of transforming (and enabling) subjects and not merely of repressing them. This is not to suggest of course that political domination in the empire was the same as in Britain. My argument is only that in both contexts the concept of culture was part of that totalizing project that Williams identified with the emergence of industrial, liberal society. The unclarity of the notion of "multiculturalism" lies precisely in the question of its compatibility with that project after the arrival of nonwhite immigrants from what was once the empire into a self-proclaimed liberal society.

IV

In the immediate postwar period, the labor shortage in Britain was met by workers imported from Poland and Italy and then from the end of the 1950s to the end of the 1960s, from ex-colonial countries—mostly the Caribbean, India, Pakistan, and Bangladesh. At first they were mainly recruited by the British to work in the London transport system, the nationalized health service, and the privately owned textile mills in the north of England. Subsequently others joined them on an individual and/or family basis. During this period, large numbers of Irish immigrants also entered the country—as indeed they had done throughout the preceeding 100 years.

It needs to be understood that the word "immigrant" has come to be identified by public opinion in contemporary Britain with non-European settlers—largely people from the Caribbean and South Asia. This is significant because the term is applied to the offspring of these immigrants even though they have been born in Britain but does not apply to white immigrants who are, according to the 1981 Census, a more numerous category than nonwhite immigrants. According to that Census, out of a total population of nearly 53 million, nonwhite immigrants (including those born in Britain) were a little more than two million and of these Muslims accounted for less than half. We are dealing here with comparatively small numbers.[27]

I want to stress that these immigrants from excolonial countries are not simply importers of "cultural difference" that they are free to synthesise and develop as they please in their new social environment. They have been inserted into very specific economic, political, and ideological conditions. Most of them live in relatively deprived innercity areas, have poorly paid jobs, are overrepresented in manufacturing industries compared with the total population, and suffer from much higher rates of unemployment—especially among the young who have been born in Britain. The everyday practices of immigrants are constrained in different ways by preexisting British institutions: Parliament, city administrations, employers, trade unions, the police, the English system of law, state schools, the welfare system, and so forth.

In his comparative study of race in the U.S. and Britain, Katznelson has given an account of how, in the early years of immigration, the British liberal elite sought to exclude the issue of race from politics.[28] After an initial brief period when the existence of *any* problem was denied, which ended with the first race riots in Nottingham and London at the end of the 1950s a new bipartisan consensus was arrived at in the form of the 1965 Race Relations Bill.

The structural arrangements announced by the political consensus White Paper, [Katznelson notes,] did not integrate the Third World immigrants into the politics of institutionalized class conflict that characterize the liberal collectivist age, but rather set up alternative political structures to deflect the politics of race from Westminster to the National Committee for Commonwealth Immigrants, and from local political arenas to voluntary liaison committees.[29]

This was, he suggests, an adaptation of colonial principles of indirect rule to the special conditions created in Britain itself. But such an arrangement, he points out, did not mean that the immigrants were now reconciled to their predicament, only that the problem of racial discrimination and resentment was cast in a form that proved virtually intractable.

According to more recent studies, however, this political exclusion does not appear to have been as effective at the time as Katznelson suggests. For example Anwar[30] describes in detail the increasingly organized involvement of nonwhites in British party politics immediately after the 1966 general elections. Because they were on the whole settled in large urban concentrations and able to generate higher levels of turnout at elections, they were able to influence electoral results in a number of marginal seats. Most nonwhite voters conformed to their socio-economic category by voting Labour, but other parties were also able to attract them. One of the most remarkable indications of this was the formation of an Anglo-West Indian Conservative Society and the more vigorous Anglo-Asian Conservative Society. The latter especially was given high priority by the Conservative central office; Thatcher is now its president and other leading Tories are among its vice-presidents. All major political parties have begun to adopt nonwhite candidates and to canvass for them. A small number of nonwhites have succeeded in being elected to Parliament, and much larger numbers have emerged at the level of local (city) government. Indeed, in 1985 the first Asian lord mayor in Britain (Labour Councillor Mohammed Ajeeb) was elected in Bradford, the city that has since gained worldwide publicity as the place where *The Satanic Verses* was publicly burned.

Katznelson's argument, regarding the nonintegration of the politics of race in Britain into an "institutionalized class conflict framework"[31] needs to be revised. Nonwhites (especially South Asians) have begun, however marginally, to make the political parties respond to their electoral power—the level at which institutionalized class conflict finds expression in Britain. But there is another, even more important, point. Precisely because the prevalant mode of dealing with nonwhite immigrants (whether through institutions like the Commission for Racial Equality or through the party system) has been in terms of race, the liberal political system has been preoccupied, as in the case of class politics, with the problem of distributive justice. "Immigrants" are represented as citizens who suffer relative deprivation, analogous to (and sometimes, as in the recently popularized notion of "the underclass," congruent with) those of class. The political problem for race as for class is how to eradicate unfair discrimination (*unequal treatment*) in civil society. The question of traditions and identities—that is, of maintaining and elaborating one's own difference—is assumed to be either already settled or something to be settled outside the sphere of national politics, for that sphere is where something called "core values" and "what we have in common" are said to be located.

In fact of course, traditions and identities are neither finally settled nor relegatable beyond the sphere of the political. The very concept of "being British," as presented by Patten and reaffirmed by liberal opinion in post-Rushdie Britain, is political. But so too are the categories that are used to describe and deal with the immigrants who are urged to identify themselves with "British culture."

V

The terms "colored" or "new Commonwealth immigrants," "blacks," "ethnic," or "cultural minorities" belong to slightly different historical phases and political contexts, but all of them serve to make a primary separation between the "host" society or "white majority" and the "immigrants," "blacks," or "cultural minorities."

In fact nonwhites relate to British society in a variety of ways. Thus although they all suffer from institutionalized racial discrimination, West Indians are in some ways "culturally" more akin to the indigenous English than are most South Asians. They are Christians (although most belong to their own churches), and at home they speak English. Their younger generation has taken a leading part in the formation of British popular culture and has excelled in British sport. When the first postwar West Indian immigrants arrived in Britain (and before they had absorbed the full brunt of British racism), they often spoke of coming to "the mother country."[32] In these respects South Asians were and still remain culturally quite unlike other black immigrants—as this statement from a study of British racism and black culture underlines: "Some inner-city whites, particularly the young, may find much in 'West Indian' culture which they can evaluate positively. If black culture appears in syncretized Afro-Caribbean forms which are relatively desirable and attractive [to whites] when contrasted to the more obviously 'alien' Asian varieties, the white racist may be faced with considerable problems."[33]

The term "black," signifying all nonwhite immigrants and their offspring (West Indian as well as South Asian), is used equally by the left and the right in Britain. While for the right it implies a racial or cultural unassimilability, for the left it underlines the experience of racial discrimination and the determination to organize politically against it through a radically reconstructed cultural identity. But South Asians have begun to argue that in using it in this way both right and left share the assumption that South Asian traditions and identities cannot become part of modern Britain.

The drawback with "black" used as a descriptive term, [one South Asian writer observed recently,] is that it defines people not in terms of their own identity but by the treatment [of them] by others; the aspirational use [of "black"], on the other hand, overcomes this deficiency but at the price of making British Asians have to define themselves in a framework historically and internationally developed by people in search of African roots."[34]

This viewpoint does not reject the call for alliances in the face of British racism, only the assumption that they must form the primary foundation for elaborating Asian identities in Britain.

The expressions "cultural—or ethnic—minorities" have also become current over the last two decades. But terms like "majority" and "minority" (which today belong to the vocabulary of electoral and parliamentary politics), when used together with the word "culture," raises an interesting ambiguity. For whereas the former relates to the principle by which public policies are made and unmade, "culture" is virtually coterminous with the social life of particular populations, including habits and beliefs conveyed across generations. One is always born into a culture, and even if one alters one's way of life later, one always belongs to cultural traditions by which one's difference is *maintained*. Belonging to an electoral majority or minority is a matter of being counted *ex post facto*. To the extent that the mutually dependent concepts of majority and minority belong to the liberal political system, they presuppose a constitutional device for *resolving* differences. To speak of cultural majorities and minorities is therefore to create ideological hybrids. It is also to make the implicit claim that members of some cultures truly belong to a particular politically defined place but those of others (minority cultures) do not—either because of recency (immigrants) or of archaicness (aborigines).

The expressions "cultural minorities" and "ethnic groups" (the former incidentally is never applied to the English upper class; the latter never to the English, Scots, Welsh, or Irish) are more than part of public political discourse. They have recently acquired the status of law.

The definition of "ethnic group" as a legal category was established in the leading case, *Mandla v Dowell Lee* (1983), which went all the way to the House of Lords. In the words of Lord Fraser:

For a group to constitute an ethnic group in the 1976 [Race Relations] Act, it must...regard itself and be regarded by others, as a distinct community by virtue of certain characteristics. Some of these characteristics are essential; others are not essential but one or more of them will commonly be found and will help to distinguish the group from the surrounding community. The conditions which appear to me to be essential are these: (1) a long shared history, of which the group is conscious as distinguishing it from other groups, and the memory of which keeps it alive; (2) a cultural tradition of its own, including family and social customs and manners, often but not necessarily associated with religious observance. In addition to those two essential characteristics the following characteristics are... relevant: (3) either a common geographical origin, or descent from a small number of common ancestors; (4) a common language, not necessarily peculiar to the group; (5) a common literature peculiar to the group; (6) a common religion different from that of neighbouring groups or from the general community surrounding it; (7) being a minority or being an oppressed or a dominant group within a larger community, for example a conquered people...and their conquerors might both be ethnic groups.[35]

Although relevant criteria logically apply to the Scots, the Welsh, and the Protestants and Catholics in Northern Ireland, the term "ethnic group" is not applied to any of them. Nor does it apply to the British royal family, of whom only one member—the reigning monarch—is the symbol of British identity and the locus of British sovereignty. The legal category "ethnic group" is in effect a device enabling English courts to normalize "ethnic customs" as exemptions from the rule[36] without, however, giving the populations concerned corporate status. There is by now a fair body of case law in this domain, but precisely because it is by definition concerned with *exceptions*, it has tended to give legal ballast to the idea of cultural *minorities*. It should be stressed, however, that the courts are concerned to ensure a single legal authority for "ethnic communities" and "the general community surrounding" them, not to promote or bring about a common life. True the customs of ethnic communities must be consistent with certain existing laws (for example, "children" may not marry and must receive a "proper education" regardless of "ethnic customs"). But consistency of ethnic customs with existing laws does not make for a single British culture in spite of the imperializing morality of the English liberal middle class.

Perhaps the crucial point about a politically established "cultural minority" is that constitutionally it cannot authorize new cultural arrangements but only request them. Furthermore the majority may bind itself to "tolerate" the permanent difference represented by a minority and even to "respect" it as an exception, but by definition the minority cannot be accorded equality. This has been the source of a disturbing political dilemma for those who would advocate multiculturalism as a general policy for dealing with the immigrant population. Does "equal respect" for cultural diversity mean the exclusion of cultural minorities from equal power?

All attempts to resolve this dilemma by insisting on some version of the distinction between public (equal access) and private (exclusive and heterogeneous) domains have failed.[37] And this is because— as two decades of studies dealing with the social workings of the modern British state have made clear—the so-called private domain is continuously structured and restructured by political, economic, and legal practices that supposedly belong to the public domain.

VI

Over the last two decades "multiculturalism" has become widely accepted as the goal for British society.[38] The main reason for this lies not in an ideological commitment to cultural diversity but in the attempt to deal with practical problems encountered in education and the social services—two major institutions of Britain's welfare state. It is here that we observe the construction of diversity as an *effect* of modern government.

It was "the problem of underachievement" by immigrant children that first led to increased attention to "institutionalized racism"—including the negative attitudes of teachers toward the ethnic background of their immigrant pupils. This resulted in a small growth of schools established outside the state sector by worried immigrant parents.[39] But many local education authorities, responding to a variety of political pressures, encouraged schools to use teaching materials from the cultural and historical background of those pupils—and in some cases even to develop black studies programs—in order to give them a positive self-image.[40] Multicultural education has subsequently attracted nonwhite critics who see in it a compensatory model based on the conception of immigrants as inherently limited and thus as a special problem for "white society." Some radical critics have even argued that multiculturalism is simply a means of "containing the black problem," and they insist (in words that Malinowski would have approved of) that "teachers should represent the present strengths rather than the past history of the black population."[41] These critics see multiculturalism as a kind of (false) consciousness and not as a modality of normalization within the modern state. In this respect they are basically in agreement with those who propose multiculturalism as the proper form of education for *all* British children[42] because both assume that learning about different ways of life at school is a way of safeguarding (or perpetuating) those differences outside school.

In the provision of social services, the notion of multiculturalism ("cultural diversity") has had a trajectory comparable to that in education. It has emerged out of a concern to engage effectively (and "equally") with a variety of immigrant communities. But social workers wanting to take the "cultural diversity" of their clients seriously have been criticized for being ineffective and worse:

The primary objection to cultural diversity as an organising principle is that it ignores the material and political realities of contemporary Britain. The difficulties faced by the black population are the result not only of migration and differences in culture and language but also of living in a society which is hostile to black people, denies them equal life chances and can expose them to enormous material and psychological pressure. The clients of social services [are] present[ed] with not only linguistic and cultural complexities, but also with the profound effects of racism. In order to offer effective help social services institutions must therefore be sensitive not only to language and culture but also the processes of racism.[43]

The main argument against multiculturalism from the radical left has been that it ignores the power of racism. This complaint is entirely justified though not always in the sense in which it is intended, namely that entrenched racist prejudices (individual and institutional) prevent the full realization of ethnic equality. For in education as in the social services, the discourse and practice of multiculturalism have been integral to the process of administrative normalization within the framework of the British state. Because fundamentally *different* traditions are described as necessarily *contradictory* (and therefore in need of regulation), state power extends itself by treating them as norms to be incorporated and coordinated.

I would argue that in insisting that the fundamental issues to be contested by immigrants can all be reduced to the problem of racism, radical critics have made it difficult to theorize from the left about difference—apart, that is, from the liberal principle of the *individual's* right to believe, act, and express him- or herself differently. For while difference is certainly a crucial issue at the level of the law's treatment of individual subjects (the bearers of rights and duties), it is also relevant to the subject's desire to have and to maintain an identity. This desire is certainly not properly addressed through the vague notion of multiculturalism according to which pupils learn about each other's cultural beliefs and customs at school and so develop "an equal respect" for these differences in the world outside. The crux of the matter lies not in the criticism that "multiculturalism" freezes cultural differences between entire communities, or that it sanctions oppressive customs. It lies in the problematic connection between learning *about* difference and learning *to become* different; and as in all learning, that connection is fraught with questions of power and authority.

VII

Recently some radical authors and cultural critics (Gilroy, of West Indian origin, and Bhabha, born in India) have argued, by drawing on a variety of postmodern currents, against multiculturalism and in favor of what they claim is a dynamic concept of British culture and identity. "Culture," Gilroy insists,

> is not a fixed and impermeable feature of social relations. Its forms change, develop, combine and are dispersed in historical processes. The syncretic cultures of black Britain exemplify this. They have been able to detach cultural practices from their origins and use them to found and extend the new patterns of metacommunication which give their community substance and collective identity.[44]

That is to say, a fluid, syncretic black culture defines the possibility of a continuously reconstructed British identity.

Bhabha takes up a similar position. *The Satanic Verses*, he thinks, has changed the vocabulary of our cultural debate:

> It has achieved this by suggesting that there is no such whole as the nation, the culture, or even the self. Such holism is a version of reality that is most often used to assert cultural or political supremacy and seeks to obliterate the relations of difference that constitute the languages of history and culture....Salman Rushdie sees the emergence of doubt, questioning and even confusion as being part of that cultural "excess" that facilitates the formation of new social identities that do not appeal to a pure and settled past, or to a unicultural present, in order to authenticate themselves. Their authority lies in the attempt to articulate emergent, hybrid forms of cultural identity.[45]

In other words, social identities *do* need to be "authenticated," but Rushdie has taught us—so Bhabha claims—that their authentication derives from our ability to continuously reinvent ourselves out of our confused cultural conditions.[46]

One can appreciate that such writers are trying to say something significant about modern Britain, but they do so in ways that do not help clarity of thought. It is of course a truism to say that everything can be shown to be ultimately connected with everything else (though surely not in the same way?), that everything changes (but certainly not at the same time or at the same rate), or that everything can be conceptually subdivided (not, however, losing thereby its conceptual unity). Yet it is also a truism that cultural units can be defined, attacked, defended, subverted, and governed. To acknowledge that cultural unities are ideological is not therefore to dismiss them as unreal. To demonstrate that elements making up a given cultural unit have diverse origins (that it is syncretic) is no proof that a unity does not exist; an account of origins tells us nothing about how the unity is structured—or how it may be "authenticated." To argue that "a culture" must be seen as a process does not exclude the possibility that it is a unified process. A unified culture is not necessarily one without contradictions; rather relations of contradiction between (cultural) elements themselves presuppose an embracing unity however temporary. In short, a particular culture may indeed not be a unified whole, but that is something to be demonstrated, not made into an essential truth about culture per se.

Let us be clear: To speak of cultural syncretism or hybrids presupposes the conceptual distinction between identifiable cultures. Of course it is misleading to think of an identifiable culture as having neutrally traceable boundaries. But if we conceive of it as always presupposing inherited narratives by which the unity of a life, of interconnected lives, is defined and redefined, the matter appears in a different light. We are back again at the concept of "the whole form of our common life" Williams historicized but this time via MacIntyre's idea of tradition.[47] For the discursive devices of inclusion/exclusion and the ways in which their effects come to be socially instituted through various traditions are always integral to the concept of "the whole form of our common life." In the sense of being the political effect of discursive traditions, "culture" *does* after all have boundaries.

I am worried by the implied suggestion that there are really no distinct traditions also for political reasons. It is a notorious tactic of dominating power to deny a distinct unity to populations it seeks to manipulate, to assume for itself the status of universal reason while attributing to others a singular contingency. The practice of disaggregating one's opponent can be maintained indefinitely even to the point of subverting his or her individuality. Since speech is the first and continuous condition of political dispute, the effectively dissolved subject cannot speak even for him- or herself let alone for a group. But his or her fragmented, indeterminate, incomplete identity can be "completed" by universal reason—or more precisely by its guardians.

To put the matter in concrete terms: How can South Asian immigrants in Britain defend and develop their *collective and historical* difference if neither their cultural traditions nor their selves can ever be identified—as aspirations to integrity? How can their religious traditions be criticized (whether by insiders or outsiders) if they cannot even be identified? But let us be clear on this matter of criticism: *no* traditional practice, in fact *no regular life*, can be identified (let alone maintained, developed, or synthesized) if it is *continually* subjected to "doubt, questioning, and even confusion." One may want to agree with those who insist that the immigrant traditions should not be maintained in British schools—that Muslims should not be allowed to have religious schools[48] although Roman Catholics and Jews have them—but that is quite a different matter from saying that there cannot be any form of continuous tradition for immigrants in Britain because of the drastic (and welcome) change to which they are being subjected.[49] It is merely an Enlightenment prejudice that counterposes "tradition" to "change" and "reason."

The demand of British Muslims to reproduce their traditions in their own schools and more generally their politicization of religious beliefs and practices (an inevitable consequence of the liberal principle of the "freedom to choose one's faith, [which is equal to the freedom] to choose one's political allegiance")[50] seems to threaten the assumptions on which British secular identity is constructed. Neither the invention of an expressive youth culture (music, dance, street fashions, and so forth) as Gilroy seems to think nor the making of hybrid cultural forms as Bhabha supposes holds any anxieties for defenders of the status quo. On the contrary, such developments are comfortably accomodated by urban consumer capitalism and by the liberal celebration of what Patten has called "the rich and diverse heritage which has added to Britain's wealth of culture and tradition."[51]

It is perhaps necessary to point out here that I am not arguing against *multiculturalism* or *syncretism* in the abstract. My concern has been to try to indicate that the specific ways in which they have been practiced in contemporary Britain has meant the reenforcement of centralized state power and the aestheticization of moral identities and that therefore neither has been seen as a potential threat to British identity. The possible politicization of religious traditions by Muslim immigrants is, however, quite a different matter: Such a development serves to question the inevitability of the nation-state, of its absolute legal demands and its totalizing cultural projects.

The Rushdie affair has helped to promote a new political discourse on "Britishness." There have been renewed calls for assimilation, the most famous of which was made by the prize-winning author Fay Weldon. "Our attempt at multi-culturalism has failed," she roundly declared.

The uni-culturalist policy of the United States *worked*, welding its new peoples, from every race, from every nation, every belief, into a whole: let the child do what it wants at home; here in the school the one flag is saluted, the one God worshipped, the one nation acknowledged.[52]

And in the general chorus about the need to teach South Asians how to be "properly British," even Roy Hattersley's statement at the height of the Rushdie affair of the *liberal* principle of multiculturalism[53] was widely denounced by excited writers and journalists[54] as a craven appeasement of dangerous forces.

Why this determination to remould South Asian immigrants in accordance with unitary principles? The assumption is that the presence of "unassimilated" immigrants constitutes a threat to "social cohesion."[55] But exactly what kind of threat is it that is feared in this context? As I argued at the beginning of this article, it cannot be the kind that is signalled by riots and other forms of collective violence. These explosions can be managed by new policing strategies that aim to anticipate, contain, and minimize physical damage. Whether the violence occurs at the bidding of a "foreign power" or not, the resources available to the British state are felt to be more than adequate to deal with the threat as the measured liberal reactions to the repeated Irish bombings in London have demonstrated. In my view the fear aroused in the Rushdie affair (and the often un-restrained language it generates among normally staid persons) has to do with a perceived threat to authority, not to power: More precisely, the fear is generated by the fact that people who do not accept the secular liberal values of the governing class are nevertheless able to use the liberal language of equal rights in rational argument against the hegemony of secular British culture and to avail themselves of liberal law for instituting their own strongly held religious tradi-tions. As one anxious liberal writer has put it: "A random and balkanised series of religious perspectives on society and its cultural diversity does not and cannot provide that core of common values which can hold society together."[56] Only a common, *secular* culture, we are to understand, defines and integrates "society"; yet it is clear that, for this writer as for others who have dealt with "what holds society together," the concern is with how a diverse population (a "multicultural population") can be effectively ruled. In that context, I would suggest what is crucial for government is not homogeneity versus difference as such but its authority to define crucial homogeneities *and* differences. The frightening thing about the Rushdie affair for the British liberal elite is the existence of political activity by a small population that seeks authority for its difference in its own historical, religious traditions.[57] And it does so in a discourse and through institutions that the liberal middle class has itself consecrated.

NOTES

1. See, for example, "Muslim leaders shun Rushdie death call," *The Guardian* 21 February 1989.

2. See Sebastian Poulter, "Cultural Pluralism and Its Limits: A Legal Perspective," in *Britain: A Plural Society*, report of a seminar organized by the Commission for Racial Equality and the Runnymede Trust, London, October 1989, p.6.

3. There were one or two minor exceptions such as Southall and Bradford where South Asian youth formed vigilante groups in self-defense.

4. Paul Gordon, "Just Another Asian Murder," *The Guardian* 20 July 1989.

5. Contrary to what is so often asserted, Britain was not an ancient, homogeneous society into which an alien presence had suddenly been introduced. The structure of British identity is a relatively new creation. In "Englishness and the National Culture," Philip Dodd has recently summarized the evidence for the thesis that "the diverse cultural histories and contemporary cultural life of these islands were organised and stabilised as a national culture" during the period from 1880 to 1920. See R. Colls and P. Dodd, eds., *Englishness: Politics and Culture 1880–1920* (London: Croom Helm, 1986), p. 21.

6. John Patten, "The Muslim Community in Britain," *The Times*, 5 July 1989.

7. For example, Michael Jones, political editor of *The Sunday Times*, in his article "Ground rules for the British way of life" enthused:

> Mr. Patten's special contribution is to explain the government's position in the context of our rights and obligations as citizens, regardless of race or creed. He lays down two guiding principles for our role in society: freedom of speech, thought and expression,

and the notion of the rule of law. It follows that if Mr Rushdie offends Muslims by his writings, it is sad but too bad.

Mr. Patten made a second, even more emphatic, attempt to explain the ground rules for being British last week. Stressing the importance of what we have in common—our democracy, our laws, our [sic] history and the English language—he declared: "We are obliged to live together and work together...one cannot decide to accept those rights in a democracy which one likes and reject the less convenient obligations that go with them." In other words, nobody is trying to force ethnic minorities to assimilate with the rest of us. But they must actively participate in our [sic] society and that means recognising and supporting those loyalties which bind this country together.

8. Fifteen years earlier Sir William Rees-Mogg, then editor of *The Times*, had identified Britishness with civilization itself: "There are people about who hate civilization because it exists, the enemies of the inner spiritual essence of our national life" (quoted in T. Nairn, *The Enchanted Glass: Britain and its Monarchy* [London: Hutchinson, 1988], p.56). The occasion was an attempt by a man (later judged to be mentally ill) to kidnap Princess Anne from her car in the middle of London.

9. "Nineteenth-century Liberalism represented English freedom as an ideal force, deep within the national character, and capable of universal dissemination as England's special gift to the world." R. Colls, "Englishness and the Political Culture," in Colls and Dodd, *Englishness*, p.30.

10. Rights of course have to be created before the obligation to respect them can arise. And it is inevitable that some rights will conflict with others. But Patten does not point out that respect for property rights (as opposed to the right to choose and follow one's faith) takes precedence over the right to speak and write freely in the British way of life. Thus the laws on patents, copyright (on music-image-text), contracts in restraint of trade, protection of trade secrets, and intellectual property—all involve restrictions on free expression in Britain. Unlike other restrictions such as those relating to blasphemy or incitement to hatred that arise because of undesirable *consequences* that free speech has, these are property rights that consist precisely of limiting free expression. It is not that free expression has undesirable social effects and must therefore be curbed, it is that one's rights (properties) are nothing other than the limitation of free expression by others. The structure of British life is unthinkable without these limitations in a sense that is not true for the laws forbidding blasphemy or incitement to hatred.

11. Although it must be said that "public sphere" is not an expression used by Patten, his use of the expression "being British" has an important point of contact with what Habermas has described as the public sphere: that sphere which mediates between the state and civil society, in which reasonable citizens engage in rational discourse as equals. See Jürgen Habermas, *The Structural Transformation of the Public Sphere* (Cambridge, Mass.: MIT Press, 1989).

12. As T.S. Eliot pointed out in *Notes towards the Definition of Culture*, (London: Faber and Faber, 1962), "Chapter III, Unity and Diversity: The Region."

13. This qualification is necessary because the United Kingdom, unlike many countries, accepts the principle of dual nationality.

14. See M. Kettle, "Thatcher Prefers Learning by Rote," *Manchester Guardian Weekly*, 15 April 1990.

15. Synthesized in L.T. Hobhouse's classic *Liberalism* (New York: Oxford University Press, 1964).

16. R.Williams, *Key Words: a vocabulary of culture and society*, rev. ed. (London: Fontana, 1983), p.90.

17. R. Williams, *Culture and Society; 1780–1950* (Harmondsworth, Eng.: Penguin Books, 1961), p. 285 (emphases added).

18. Sir Ernest Barker, *Ideas and Ideals of the British Empire* (Cambridge, Eng.: Cambridge University Press, 1941), p. 20.

19. Ibid., p. 31.

20. Ibid., p. 32.

21. Ibid., pp. 113–114:

A century ago, when English became the language of education (after Lord William Bentinck had stated, in 1835, that "the great object of the British Government ought to be the promotion of European literature and science among the natives of India"), trade and government, the two previous links, began to pass into a contact of culture which made a firmer and far subtler link. In this new but now century-old process of culture contact, the old culture of India has drawn on the culture of the West: it has absorbed Western ideas of nationalism and constitutionalism: it has begun to fuse into a new amalgam with Western culture—an amalgam which has still to settle the nature of its own further development and (more important still) the nature of the contribution it can make to the general progress of man. A great responsibility is laid upon Great Britain, the partner with India in the making of this amalgam—as great, and even greater, is laid upon India herself—for the settling of that future and the making of that contribution."

22. Ibid., pp. 161–162:

[The British] have sought, with a growing sense of the trust imposed upon them, to introduce among the native peoples of their colonial empire a culture which is without compulsion, and a faith which acts by persuasion....When the British Government declares that "it is the mission of Great Britain to work continuously for the training and education of the African towards a higher intellectual, moral and economic level," it is not using idle words.

23. B. Malinowski, "Introductory Essay: The Anthropology of Changing African Cultures" in *Methods of Study of Culture Contact in Africa*, International African Institute Memorandum XV (London: Oxford University Press, 1938), p. 31.

24. Ibid., p. 28.

25. For Radcliffe-Brown the central theoretical concept was "social structure," which he believed was directly observable:

We do not observe a "culture," since that word denotes, not any concrete reality, but an abstraction, and as it is commonly used a vague abstraction. But direct observation does reveal to us that...human beings are connected by a complex network of social relations. I use the term "social structure" to denote this network of actually existing relations.

A.R. Radcliffe-Brown, *Structure and Function in Primitive Society* (London: Cohen and West, 1952), p. 192. The above quotation comes from an essay first published in 1940.

26. See G. Viswanathan's illuminating monograph on literary study and British rule in India, *Masks of Conquest* (New York: Columbia Unversity Press, 1989).

27. Compare this with Europe where the overwhelming majority of nonwhite immigrants are Muslims. Here too anti-Muslim sentiments have recently become disturbingly prominent—as in *l'affaire des foulardes Islamiques* in France.

28. I. Katznelson, *Black Men, White Cities* (London: Oxford University Press, 1973), p. 125.

29. Ibid., p. 150.

30. Muhammad Anwar, *Race and Politics* (London: Tavistock, 1986).

31. Katznelson, *Black Men, White Cities*, p. 185.

32. This was often echoed in government rhetoric of the time. For example, in 1954 Henry Hopkinson, Tory minister of state for the colonies, observed: "[I]n a world in which restriction on personal movement and immigration have increased we can still take pride in the fact that a man can say *civis Brittanicus sum* whatever his colour may be, and we take pride in the fact that he wants to and can come to the mother country." *Hansard*, 5 November 1954, Col. 827.

33. Paul Gilroy, *There Ain't No Black in the Union Jack* (London: Hutchinson, 1987), p. 231. This argument seems to me a little careless: There is surely no inconsistency in racists finding the arts (even the bodies) of those they consider "racially inferior" to be attractive?

34. T. Madood, "'Black,' racial equality and Asian identity," *New Community*, 14, no.3 (Spring 1988).

35. Quoted in S. Poulter, *English Law and Ethnic Minority Customs* (London: Butterworths, 1986), pp. 185–186. The particular concern of *Mandla v Dowell Lee* was to determine whether Sikhs were an ethnic group and protected as such against discrimination under the provisions of the 1976 Race Relations Act.

36. For example:

> Marriage ceremonies must generally be conducted in the presence of either an officiating clergyman of the Church of England or a registrar or an "authorised person" (usually a minister of the religious group concerned). In most instances it is a criminal offence knowingly and wilfully to celebrate a marriage outside the hours of 8 a.m. to 6 p.m. though a marriage solemnised outside these hours will nevertheless remain valid. Marriages in a register office or registered building must be solemnised with open doors, i.e. the public must not be excluded if they wish to attend, and the bride and groom must attend in person and exchange their vows using a standard form of words....From all these regulations concerning solemnisation two select groups are exempt. These are Quakers and "persons professing the Jewish religion."...Their ceremonies may take place at any hour of the day or night, need not be in any particular building (and may even be celebrated in a private home or garden) and do not require the presence of any state official. They are merely required to follow the usages of the Society of Friends or the usages of the Jews, as the case may be. (Ibid., p. 34.)

37. For example John Rex, a prominent British sociologist specializing in "race relations," argues like many others in Britain today, that the construction of a *democratic* multicultural society requires a distinction between a "public domain," equally accessible to all citizens, and "private domains" in which religious and familial distinctions can be cultivated. See J. Rex, "The concept of a multi-cultural society," *New Community*, 14, no. 1/2 (Autumn, 1987).

38. See *Education for All: The Report of the Committee of Enquiry into the Education of Children from Ethnic Minority Groups*, The Swann Report (London: HMSO, 1985).

39. In the case of Muslims there were also religious motives for setting up such separate schools.

40. In an analysis of recent examination results from London schools, Parekh concludes that "racism cannot account for the differences and we need to look at their economic

and cultural backgrounds." Bhikhu Parekh, "Educational achievement and ethnic minority children," *Perspectives in Education* 5, no. 1 (1985): 35.

41. R. Carr-Hill and H. Chadha-Boreham, "Education," in *Britain's Black Population*, A. Bhat, R. Carr-Hill, S. Ohri, eds. (Aldershot, Eng.: Gower, 1988), p. 153. For a more extended criticism of multicultural education from a Marxist perspective, see M. Sarup, *The Politics of Multiracial Education* (London: Routledge and Kegan Paul, 1986).

42. See J.M. Halstead, *Education, Justice and Cultural Diversity* (London: Falmer Press, 1988).

43. P. Roys, "Social Services," in *Britain's Black Population*, Bhat, Carr-Hill, Ohri, eds., p. 221.

44. Paul Gilroy, *There Ain't No Black in the Union Jack*, pp. 217, 219.

45. Homi Bhabha, "Down among the writers," *The New Statesman and Society*, 28 July 1989.

46. It is not clear from Bhabha's argument whether he thinks that because any given version of the cultural past is contestable, it isn't worth contesting. For it is not "the past" that is pure or impure, settled or unsettled, but only representations of it, and such representations are always part of the present and always subject to future revision. But if versions of the past are seen only as aesthetic resources for inventing new narratives, such contestation is pointless.

47. See Alisdair MacIntyre *After Virtue* (London: Duckworth, 1981)—especially "Chapter 15: The virtues, the unity of a human life and the concept of a tradition."

48. The British school system consists of a "maintained sector" (state schools) and an "independent sector" (private schools). All private schools must be registered and inspected for suitability of buildings and educational provisions in order to operate. If independent schools fulfill certain requirements, they may obtain voluntary maintained status, that is, they will be largely financed by the state although retaining an independent character. At present there are large numbers of voluntary aided religious schools: Roman Catholic (by far the largest single group), Church of England, Jewish, and Methodist; there are no Muslim schools in this category. See Jean Coussins, "Voluntary maintained religious schools: A draft policy paper," Commission for Racial Equality, London, July 1989. Muslim attempts to acquire voluntary aided status for their schools have been meeting with strong resistance. See D. Caute, "Labour's satanic verses," *New Statesman and Society*, 5 May 1989.

49. In February 1989 a group of prominent westernized Asians in London (academics, authors, journalists, and actors) met to issue a statement in support of Rushdie entitled "Beyond fundamentalism and liberalism" written by Bhabha and published in the *New Statesman and Society*, 3 March 1989. It is not immediately clear why they felt themselves called upon to comment *as Asians* (not as Muslims, for there were non-Muslims among them, or as immigrants, for there were no West Indians among them), but anyway they were quite persuaded that "[w]here once we could believe in the comforts and continuities of Tradition, today we must face the responsibilities of cultural Translation," and they evidently expected that Britain's immigrant Muslims would take due note and order their lives accordingly.

50. Patten, "On Being British."

51. Patten, "The Muslim Community in Britain."

52. Fay Weldon, *Sacred Cows* (London: Chatto and Windus, 1989), p. 32.

53. Roy Hattersley in *The Independent*, Friday 21 July 1989:

The principle is clear enough. Salman Rushdie's rights as an author are absolute and ought to be inalienable. A free society does not ban books. Nor does it allow writers and publishers to be blackmailed and intimidated. The death threats are intolerable whether they are seriously meant or the rhetoric of hysteria....Every group within our society must obey the law. But support for that principle is not the same as insisting that "they" must behave like "us." The doctrine of assimilation is arrogant and patronising....In a free society the Muslim community must be allowed to do what it likes to do as long as the choice it makes is not damaging to the community as a whole.

54. For example, the liberal journalist Edward Pearce:

The Hattersley faction of the Labour party has taken up a position at once illiberal, repressive and abjectly deferential to a bunch of Islamic clergy firmly planted in the 15th century....The problem of Mr. Hattersley and certain allies is that they sit for bits of Birmingham, Bradford and Leicester where the imams can cut up nasty at election time. Low politics is low politics, contemptible but understandable. In Mr. Hattersley's case matters go further. Behind sanctimoniousness lies power worship. Part sycophant, part bully, he seeks fearfully to accomodate the imams and respect their power....Mr. Hattersley, who does his cringing with panache, says that deference to the imams should extend to curtailing publication. (*The Sunday Times*, 23 July 1989.)

This vituperative language is highly unusual for a "serious" liberal newspaper talking about a right-of-center Labour politician. Even Enoch Powell did not provoke such emotional outbursts from the same source for his racist speeches. What, one is led to wonder, is the cause of this intemperateness on the part of what is, and knows itself to be, the majority opinion?

55. Thus the final seminar in a series organized by the Commission for Racial Equality in London in the wake of the Rushdie affair was devoted to "the kind of society Britain needs to evolve into if it is to reconcile the demands of social cohesion and national integration with proper respect for cultural diversity and autonomy." (Bhikhu Parekh, "Introduction", *Britain: A Plural Society*, report of a seminar.

56. James Lynch, "Cultural Pluralism, Structural Pluralism and the United Kingdom" in *Britain: A Plural Society*, report of a seminar, p. 33.

57. The Muslims in Britain are not homogeneous in terms of class, language, or sect, nor do they have a single body to represent them like the Jewish Board of Guardians. Apart from important doctrinal disagreements concerning clerical authority between Sunnis (the great majority in Britain) and Shi'is (not all of whom belong to the Ithna 'Ashari sect that prevails in Iran), the de facto authority of religious leaders among British Muslims is very variable. But none of this affects my main argument, which has to do with liberal constructions and anxieties.

Politics & Society 18, no. 4 (1990): 455–480.

[28]

Paradigms, power, and identity:
Rediscovering Orthodoxy and regionalizing Europe

ELIZABETH H. PRODROMOU
Department of Politics, Centre of International Studies, Princeton University, USA

Abstract. In an effort to explain, to predict and to manage the ways in which organized religion affects patterns of public contestation at the state and regional levels in post-Cold War Europe, social scientists and policymakers have formulated a cultural map that divides Europe into two spaces incompatible by virtue of their historical experiences: one space is 'modern', 'civilized', Western Christian; the other space is 'anti-modern', 'uncivilized', Eastern Christian. This paper proposes that a specific 'orthodox' version of Eastern Orthodox Christianity has gained ascendance in Euro-American academic and policy discussions, in order to provide a cultural argumentation that supports political-economic and military power objectives in post-Cold War Europe. The paper claims that the 'orthodox' version of Orthodoxy is theoretically inaccurate and methodologically unsound, but is rooted in intellectual efforts to salvage a neo-modernization paradigm as well as in Orientalist tendencies in Modern Greek and Central European identity debates. An alternative to the 'orthodox' conception of Orthodoxy is presented, along with suggestions for how to analyze and to manage the potential synergy between efforts at consolidating liberal democracies in European societies with an Eastern Christian tradition emphasizing personal freedom and human relationality.

Introduction

Since the conclusion of the Cold War and the ratification of the Maastricht Treaty on European Union, the project of remaking Europe has become equated with institutionalizing democracy and market economies and with safeguarding NATO and West European Union security interests.[1] Within this broader political-economic and security context, scholars and policymakers have undertaken to construct a specific, 'orthodox' idea of Eastern Orthodox Christianity, whose definitive features are the religion's supposed incompatibility with democracy and modernity. The main argument of this article is that the significance of the emergent 'orthodox' idea of Orthodoxy lies in its use as the primary marker for remapping the New European Order into alternative cultural spaces: 'the civilized Europe of the modern West'; and 'the Other European civilization of the non-West'. This article also argues that the new European map rests on a hierarchy of power prioritizing the Europe of the West over the Other Europe of the non-West, a hierarchy that poses interesting operational questions about the possible integration of the various regions of Europe into a single whole. By elucidating the links between the invention

126

and transmission of a particular idea of Eastern Orthodox Christianity, on the one hand, and the policy agenda of reconstituting the political-economic and geo-strategic boundaries of late-modern Europe, on the other, the article helps to illustrate the dynamic interplay between knowledge and power.

To explore the above two arguments, I organize the article as follows. In the first part, I develop the claim about the construction of an 'orthodox' conception of Eastern Orthodox Christianity, by introducing several emblematic treatments that illustrate the formulation of Orthodoxy which has gained credence in the context of larger discussions about Europeanness in the Maastricht and post-Cold War political order. The pieces which I reference are selected from a mixed author pool comprised of academics, policymakers and journalists. The eclecticism of the choices is meant to demonstrate the broad consistency in patterns of language and imagery used to formulate what I refer to as the 'orthodox' version of Orthodoxy – 'orthodox' in that this version has become the ascendent interpretation of the Eastern Orthodox religion in the Euro-American political and academic communities. In the second part of the article, I will suggest two possible explanations for the resonance of this 'orthodox' conception of Eastern Orthodox Christianity: first, the 'orthodox' idea of Orthodoxy is functionally useful in supporting the intellectual assumptions and policy aims of the neo-modernization paradigm; and second, the formation of an 'orthodox' idea of Orthodoxy reinforces a larger Orientalist argumentation by which Modern Greek and Central European identities can be constructed for cultural and regional purposes.

A parenthesis on methodology is in order before I turn to the above arguments. Throughout the article, I will rely heavily on quotations and citations from a range of academic and policy contexts. I believe that the only way to demonstrate and, ultimately, to critique how Orthodoxy is being rediscovered and invented in the post-Cold War era, is to allow the discussants to speak in their own voices.

Eastern Orthodox Christianity: Some notes on a forgotten religion

There is a basic logic not only in the fact that academic and policy discussions of Eastern Orthodox Christianity have largely been catalyzed by the post-Cold War projects of security integration, liberal democratization and marketization in Europe, but in the fact that such discussions reflect a process of intellectual rediscovery as well as invention. The end of the Cold War lifted the curtain on millions of Eastern Orthodox Christians and on an attendant religious institutional structure which had almost completely fallen out of the intellectual and political consciousness of the Euro-American social sciences since the Ottoman conquest of Constantinople in the late fifteenth century. A review of the academic titles dealing with nearly any aspect of twentieth century European development reveals that the study of Eastern Christianity and social transformation had been virtually abandoned to historians and theologians. The only notable exceptions to this trend were a short list of East European area studies works which, by virtue of their largely historical and descriptive approach, reinforced the conventional intellectual wisdom that Orthodoxy's relevance to twentieth century Europoan development lay either in its links to pre-communist nationalisms or to the homogenizing nationalities policies of totalitarian and ethno-chauvanist regimes. The predominance of this conventional wisdom is reflected in the fact that Euro-American studies on the contemporary politics of Greece largely ignored the relevance of Eastern Christianity as anything other than a mechanism used to reinforce anti-communist ideology and aggressive nationalism.[2]

Because the literal rediscovery of Eastern Christianity by social scientists and public policymakers occurred within the above context, the emergent post-Cold War conception of Orthodoxy has been constructed out of, or invented from, a deficit of social science scholarship. The process of inventing an 'orthodox' version of Orthodoxy therefore has ignored the defining features of the Eastern Orthodox religion which, in fact, are most relevant to a meaningful grasp of the doctrinal and institutional history of that faith as well as to the constructive management of Eastern Orthodox Christianity as a factor in consolidating pluralist democratic regimes across the European Continent.

The intellectual limitations and policy misapplications reflected in the 'orthodox' conception of Orthodoxy can be most fully appreciated by setting the rediscovered version of the religion against a sketch of Eastern Orthodox Christianity's defining features. In short, an introductory profile – a larger theoretical treatment far exceeds the space limitations of this paper – of Eastern Orthodox Christianity *qua* religion will offer a stark contrast to the 'orthodox' version being propounded in Euro-American academic and policy domains.

Eastern Orthodox Christianity is a religious tradition whose genesis lies in the origin of Christianity itself and which claims direct, unbroken continuity with the original dogma and teachings of the one Holy, Catholic (universal) and Apostolic Church established by Christ and embodied in that same unified Church prior to what is known as the Great Schism of 1054.[3] The Great Schism formally split Christianity into separate, antagonistic theological and institutional entities, corresponding jurisdictionally at that time to the Latin Western and Byzantine Eastern regions of the Roman Empire, and existing to the present in what eventually came to be the Western (Roman Catholic and Protestant) Churches, on the one hand, and the Eastern Orthodox Church, on the other.

The central feature of Eastern Orthodox Christianity is its claim to stand as a way of life[4] where there is a '... profound and direct internal relationship between dogma and [praxis], i.e. the unity of faith and life'.[5] Eastern Orthodoxy offers a rich anthropology of personhood,[6] which assumes that, without that way of life which priorizes freedom, relationality, dynamism and distinctness, the ontological reality of personhood is unattainable. Moreover, Orthodox ecclesiological discourse views the Church as the only institutional modality through which the fullness of personhood can be actualized; indeed,

128

the Church is conceived of as '... not simply an institution ... [but as] a "mode of existence", *a way of being*'.[7]

The above synopsis of Eastern Orthodox Christianity's defining features makes clear the striking contrasts to Catholic and Protestant Christianity, both of which denominations were indelibly marked by the impact of Scholasticism and, likewise, were differentiated since the early sixth century from most of what came to be the Orthodox historical experience. Any attempt to arrive at an understanding of how Eastern Orthodox Christianity affects the political and cultural realities of contemporary Europe, much less to posit claims about the 'European' features of a Church grounded in principles of freedom and relationality, must take seriously Weber's well-known dictum about understanding each religion on its own terms. The Weberian *caveat*, therefore, would require the use of an analytical lexicon faithful to Eastern Orthodox theology rather than one adapted from Western Christianity, as well as a careful examination of those political factors that help to explain the Orthodox Church's historical performance under non-democratic regimes. As the remainder of this article will show, the scholars and policymakers who have articulated the 'orthodox' version of Orthodoxy have paid short shrift to Weber's methodological legacy, and therefore have invented a religious marker of non-European Otherness whose fundamental substantive flaws illustrate the considerations of power politics which drive such an intellectual project.

The rediscovery and invention of an idea

Without a doubt the most explicit and by now widely cited articulation of the 'orthodox' interpretation of Orthodoxy was advanced by political scientist Samuel Huntington. In two articles published during 1993 in *Foreign Affairs*, Huntington presented what he called '... the best simple map of the post-Cold War world'[8] in the form of the civilizational paradigm. In the Hobbesian post-Cold War world posited by Huntington, the major faultlines of conflict will be across civilizations. Huntington loosely defines a civilization either as 'a cultural entity'[9] or as differentiated by 'history, language, culture, tradition and, most important, religion'.[10] The world is divided into eight civilizations (including the Western, Slavic-Orthodox and Islamic),[11] but the driving force of international relations in the New World Order will be the clash between 'the West and non-Western civilizations'.[12]

The civilizational paradigm is loaded with conceptual inconsistencies,[13] but what is of interest with regard to the idea of Orthodoxy is the categorical nature of Huntington's claims about Eastern Christian civilization in the New European Order. Huntington posits that

> [a]s the ideological division of Europe has disappeared [with the end of the Cold War], the cultural division of Europe between Western Christianity, on the one hand, and Orthodox Christianity ..., on the other, has reemerged. The most significant dividing line in Europe ... may well be

the eastern boundary of Western Christianity in the year 1500. . . . In the Balkans this line, of course, coincides with the historic boundary between the Hapsburg and Ottoman empires. The peoples to the north and west of this line are Protestant or Catholic; they . . . may look forward to . . . the consolidation of democratic political systems. The peoples to the east and south of this line are Orthodox . . . ; they historically belonged to the Ottoman or Tsarist empires and were only lightly touched by the shaping events in the rest of Europe; . . . they seem much less likely to develop stable democratic political systems.[14]

Huntington concludes that absolutized, totalized 'Western ideas of individualism, . . . human rights, equality, . . . democracy, . . . the separation of church and state, . . . have little resonance in . . . Islamic . . . or Orthodox cultures',[15] and suggests that Europe's decades-long division by the Iron Curtain of ideology may be replaced by the Velvet Curtain of religion.[16]

The above language leaves no doubt about the idea of Orthodoxy constructed in Huntington's Europe of civilizations. Eastern Orthodox Christianity is incompatible with democracy and all other qualitative and structural features deemed the hallmarks of Western civilization. Likewise, insofar as the West and modernity are synonymous, Orthodoxy's non-Westernness suggests that societies shaped by the Orthodox religion are not modern. The idea of Orthodoxy as incompatible with Western civilization, defined as synonymous with modernity and democracy, leads to a cultural map of Europe on the eve of the twenty-first century that recalls the map of medieval Western Christendom.

It is precisely in its political message that the civilizational paradigm is most important as a standard for a particular idea of Orthodoxy and as a functional mechanism for building a regional Other Europe. The political instrumentalism of the 'orthodox' idea of Orthodoxy emerges quite clearly in Robert Kaplan's *Balkan Ghosts*. Kaplan's shoddy attention to accuracies of historical detail and at-times outright racism prevent the classification of *Balkan Ghosts* as serious scholarship. However, the fact that *Balkan Ghosts* now enjoys paperback printing and a place on undergraduate reading lists in several prominent American universities, speaks to the book's wide crossover readership in the academy and the general public, and suggests a formative influence in the construction of an 'orthodox' version of Orthodoxy.

Kaplan uses a very deliberate argumentation to reinforce an essentialist vision of Eastern Orthodox Christianity as a cultural marker that drives an insurmountable wedge between two ontologically incompatible Europes. Specifically, Kaplan identifies Eastern Orthodox Christianity with an Oriental Otherness associated with Byzantine, Ottoman and, to a lesser extent, Russian historical experiences. Kaplan formulates Orthodoxy in the context of his exploration of the Balkans, a region he terms 'the original Third World'[17] where

130

... the battle between Communism and capitalism is merely one dimension of a struggle that pits Catholicism against Orthodoxy, Rome against Constantinople, the legacy of Hapsburg Austria-Hungary against that of Ottoman Turkey – in other words, West against East, the ultimate historical and cultural conflict.[18]

Kaplan locates Eastern Orthodoxy in a space outside the European West. He implicitly agrees with Croatian and Slovenian views of '[t]he Serbs ... as ... Eastern Orthodox and, therefore, as much a part of the hated East as the Muslim Turks'.[19] Similarly, politics in Greece under the 1980s PASOK (Panhellenic Socialist Movement) governments of Prime Minister Andreas Papandreou was the logical result of 'just how close to the Balkans and to the Middle East Greece really [is]'.[20]

Kaplan embeds his version of Eastern Orthodoxy in a message of historical determinism, with his conclusion that the post-Cold War reconfiguration of Europe into incompatible regions reflects the natural evolution of Balkan politics which 'perfectly mirrors the process of history and is thus ... predictable'.[21] The fall of the Berlin Wall meant that

[t]he Cold War and the false division of Europe were over. A different, more historically grounded division of Europe was about to open up ... Instead of democratic Western Europe and a Communist Eastern Europe, there would now be Europe and the Balkans ... It struck ... [Kaplan] just how far away from ... Western Europe, in both time and space, the Balkans were.[22]

Despite the stylistic differences between Huntington's civilizational paradigm and Kaplan's Balkan travelogue, the substantive convergence in their invention of a particular idea of Orthodoxy central to remapping Europe into alternative regions is unmistakable. Also unmistakable is the growing hegemony of this 'orthodox' version of Orthodoxy. It is important to recognize that the rediscovery and invention of Orthodoxy has not been restricted to the domains of the academy and popular culture. Indeed, a kaleidoscopic review of the US and Western European print media speaks directly to the links between identity building and region building in the New European Order.

Even before the fall of the Berlin Wall, a *New York Times* editorial prophesied that Yugoslavia's 'Roman Catholic republics ..., the country's most advanced and politically enlightened region', were likely to face 'bullying ... [from the] ... Orthodox Christian republics'.[23] A few short months later the *Washington Post* posited about the Balkans that 'the authoritarian traditions of the dominant Orthodox Church have helped fashion intense nationalism but have not fostered participatory democracy'.[24] The *New York Times* has agreed, with references to the 'industrious Roman Catholic Slavs ... [whose culture] was shaped by centuries spent under Austrian rule ... [whereas] ... 'southern Yugoslavia, where the religion is either Muslim or Eastern Orthodox, ... [is] ... a foreign country, strange and threatening'.[25]

The American press has expanded the religious distinctions initially limited to the former Yugoslavia, to include broader differences between '[t]he populations of Czechoslovakia and Hungary [which] are either Roman Catholic or Protestant, ... [while] Romanians and Bulgarians are for the most part Eastern Orthodox – a more conservative religion that historically has acted as the servant rather than the rival of the state'.[26] Meanwhile, François Mitterand explained to the French and German press that the inability of the European Union to help stop the civil war in former Yugoslavia was partially due to the intractability of 'ancestral hatreds' in 'Tribal Europe' as a whole, that is the Balkans.[27] No less an authority on Russian history and international security policy than Zbigniew Brzezinski wrote in the *New York Times* that Russia's 'distinctive Eurasian identity' justifiably produces security fears from 'the insecure Central Europeans'.[28] He expanded this argument in a discussion in *Foreign Affairs* about Russian neo-imperialist designs in Europe, concluding with the recommendation for a new Euro-Atlantic security system whose borders are '... the Petrine Europe of the Holy Roman Empire'.[29]

I do not intend to overstate the existence of a continuous, monolithic formulation of Orthodoxy in the print media, since press coverage remains irregular and, above all, driven by the whims of a fickle reading public. Yet, the enormous importance of the mass media in both inventing and shaping political and cultural images on a global scale is unquestionable, and the aforementioned media citations reflect the emergence of a coherent standard of Eastern Orthodox Christianity that has been constructed for intellectual, policy and popular reference: Orthodoxy is identified with authoritarianism, reactionary and conservative nationalism, and in general, all political and cultural tendencies incompatible with modern, Western, pluralist democracy; the Orthodox Church is viewed as the institutional repository and promoter of traits incompatible with Western civilization.[30]

To sum up, the 'orthodox' idea of Eastern Orthodox Christianity is presented as the determinant factor in a larger set of mutually exclusive identities, which are used in turn for the purposes of building alternative European regions with unequal real and symbolic measures of power. These two large regional hierarchies of Europe, which are the European West and an Other Europe, are comprised of sub-regions: for example, the European West includes the European Union and that group of countries increasingly referred to as Central Europe (Poland, Hungary, the Czech Republic, the Slovak Republic, the Republic of Slovenia and the Republic of Croatia) – despite their membership in the European Union, the literature on Central European identity largely includes Germany and Austria under the rubric of Central Europe. The Other Europe includes the Southeastern European cases, usually referred to as the Balkans (Bulgaria, Rumania, Albania, the Former Yugoslav Republic of Macedonia and the rump Yugoslavia), as well as the Russian Federation. Parenthetically, since the primary marker of distinction between these two Europes is religious, the regional designation of Greece becomes

132

problematic for reasons for which will become clearer in the remainder of this article.

In search of a new paradigm: The neo-modernization response

What explains the growing hegemony of the Orthodox religious designation as both discursive mechanism and policy tool in the New European Order? I will suggest two inter-related explanations for the resonance of the 'orthodox' version of Orthodoxy. The first explanation begins with the paradigm crisis characterizing the social sciences since the end of the Cold War.[31] The paradigm crisis is the result of the fact that the modernization thesis, whose assumptions had shaped post-WWII international relations, was of little use either in explaining or in managing the collective problems plaguing Europe in the past half-decade. These problems originated in the cultural confusion over the meaning of Europe, since the coincidence of state socialism's demise and Maastricht's ratification produced for the first time since Yalta the possibility of integrating a multiplicity of regions into a Greater Europe. Paradoxically, European political leaders, particularly those in the European Union, as well as American policymakers, were not prepared to confront a reality which had remained, for nearly half a century, a matter of academic speculation. Therefore, the recent theorizing about Orthodoxy must be at least partly understood as academics' efforts to impose new rules of the game and new arbiters of power on European inter-state relations.[32]

The specific form in which Orthodoxy has been rediscovered and invented is based on an argumentation whose logic supports the rehabilitation of modernization theory. Huntington, one of the main architects of modernization theory in its original incarnation, has used the civilizational paradigm to repackage two key aspects of the original theory: first, the equation of the West with modernity and democracy, and second, a culturally determined, unilinear conception of development. The critical nature of the idea of Orthodoxy for neo-modernization theory is in the linkage between definitions of Westernness, modernity and democracy, on the one hand, and assumptions about the immutability of religion, on the other. The result is that Orthodoxy is used to produce a more rigid intellectual and political formulation of the paths to and representations of modernity.

The works of representative theorists in the neo-modernization school are useful in illustrating how the idea of Orthodoxy rehabilitates modernization theory. Huntington recasts the dichotomy of traditional and modern in terms of Protestant-Catholic Christianity and Slavic-Orthodox Christianity, respectively. Insofar as Western economic and military power are the product of a political and cultural mix alien to non-Western civilizations, and insofar as religion as '*the* central force that motivates and mobilizes people',[33] at best is mutable over centuries of prolonged conflict and at worst 'is a given that cannot be changed',[34] modernizing societies part of the Orthodox civilization face

133

the unsavoury possibility of condemnation to permanent political-economic and military backwardness.

Anthropologist Ernest Gellner echoes the claims about permanently divided modern and non-modern regions of Europe. He explains the ethnic, religious and nationalist conflicts which have erupted in former state socialist Europe as the logical outcome of the process of belated development; the sometimes violent completion of nation-state building is the final stage in a process of modernization already completed in Western Europe by the close of the nineteenth century. An optimistic reading of Gellner's thesis suggests that Orthodoxy, while an antipode to civic nationalism, inevitably will be assimilated, albeit through brutal ethno-religious conflicts, into modern democratic polities. Yet, because Gellner designates religion as a primordial form of identity, Orthodoxy emerges as intrinsically and permanently incompatible with modernity defined in terms of the Western European model of the nation-state.[35]

Sociologist George Schopflin's recent writings on the post-communist condition of East-Central Europe lead to an even more pessimistic reading of the regionalizing impacts of Orthodoxy.[36] He argues that the patterns which have emerged in Europe's former communist bloc constitute a *sui generis* developmental condition called post-communism. Schopflin equates modernization and 'non-dysfunctional' development with Westernization, and forecasts that the post-communist 'Central European countries (Poland, the Czech lands, Hungary, Slovenia) have a reasonably good chance in the long run of moving towards ... rejoining Europe'.[37] In contrast, because Schopflin equates modernity with Westernness, and because he argues that the Byzantine-Ottoman-Russian imperial experiences prevented the Eastern Christian societies of Russia and the Balkans from sharing in the hallmarks of Westernness,[38] Schopflin implies an interpretation of historical progress that offers no way out of the condition of backwardness in Orthodox Russia and South-eastern Europe.

Reflecting a straightforward theoretical instrumentalism, neo-modernization arguments construct a particular version of Eastern Orthodox Christianity that adds a cultural dimension to the original modernization thesis. The cultural dimension makes Orthodoxy a crucial variable for resolving the paradigm and policy crises facing post-Cold War Europe, by basically producing an argument that perpetuates the pre-Cold War *status quo* in both intellectual and power terms. The primordial obduracy of Orthodoxy means that the cognitive, evaluative and behavioural patterns of Orthodox societies are indefinitely non-modern, irrational and unstable.[39] This line of argument provides the intellectual basis for political decisions whereby a threatened non-Orthodox West would be justified in restricting membership in the new European political-economic and security architectures to promising modernizers of the Protestant-Catholic persuasion.

134

Orientalizing Orthodoxy: The case of modern Greek identity

The second explanation for the rapid and virtually unchallenged coalescence of the 'orthodox' version of Orthodoxy lies in the consistency of this idea with a broader Orientalist argumentation, according to which cultural and regional identities can be constructed for the purposes of remaking Europe's political map. I will use two sets of literatures, the one on Modern Greek identity and the other on Central European identity, to illustrate this claim about the Orientalist nature of the idea of Orthodoxy. The review of both literatures will be necessarily stylistic, given the space constraints imposed by a journal article, and will move from the discussions of identity in general to the specific place of Orthodoxy in Modern Greek and Central European identity. In each case, I will show that the term Orientalism applies to the idea of Orthodoxy in the following respects.[40] First, in intellectual terms, the formulation of a mainstream view of Eastern Orthodox Christianity in Euro-American academic and policy discussions has been achieved through the deliberate and repeated identification of the religious tradition with language, imagery and political-cultural characteristics associated with the space of the Greater Orient, defined as the Near and Middle Eastern Islamic world, Russia and Asia. Second, in operational terms, the identification of Eastern Orthodox Christianity with a Greater Oriental space has designated Oriental-Orthodox Europe as a constituting Other against which a new Occidental European political-economic, cultural and security architecture can be built.

The literature on Modern Greek identity has been preoccupied with a single problematic,[41] namely the meaning of Greekness in the historical period coincident with the modern era beginning with the establishment of the nation-state. Over the course of the last two centuries, the outlines of the continuing debate over the meaning of Modern Greek identity have been formulated according to, and largely trapped between, two dichotomous imaginaries: on the one hand, the Greek nation-state has been invented as the modern West's incarnation of an idealized classical Hellas, while on the other hand and to a far lesser extent, the Greek nation-state has been expressed as the modern representation of the Eastern Roman Empire that was fundamentally, Byzantine, Orthodox, and eventually, Ottoman imprinted.

The origins of these two identity archetypes lie in Western Europe's own process of reimagining, inaugurated with the Renaissance and unexpectedly reopened since the main international events of the last five years. Indeed, it is crucial to recognize the formative impact of international politics[42] in setting the broad parameters for discussions about the meaning of Greekness for the past two centuries. Whether with regard to the formation of a Greek nation-state independent from the Ottoman Empire, the irredentist programme of the 'Great Idea' for expanding the boundaries of the nation-state, or the defense of the nation-state according to the ideological framework of anti-communism, Greek intellectual and political elites have recognized that the cultural question of identity building is linked to the political project of region building. But by deliberately adapting images of Greekness to Western European and American perceptions, Greek scholar-practitioners have been forced to reject nearly fifteen hundred years of post-classical Greek history. In short, the Westernist formulation of Modern Greek identity came to be situated within the larger Western intellectual tradition that Said described as Orientalism. Modern Greek identity and the interpretation of the Orthodox dimensions of Greekness are informed by and constrained by their association with a non-European, Oriental Other.

For example, the predominant Western European interpretation of the Byzantine Empire viewed the period as the rupture of Greek ties with the West and the start of a long decline culminating in, according to the inimitable words of Austrian historian J.P. Fallmerayer, the '... miscegenation... directly linked with [the] moral and cultural decay [of Hellenism]'[43] under the Ottoman Empire. German historian Karl Dieterich portrayed the Greek nation-state as the outcome of a '... battle between Asia and Europe ... [which had resulted] in the victory of Europe, [a moment] when all traces of Byzantium have disappeared from the character of the Greek people'.[44] This interpretation meant that the security of the Europeanness of Modern Greek identity depended on purging the residue of '... alien despotism, [associated] ... with [Byzantium and] the decaying Ottoman Empire,'[45] and decisively separating Greece from that Asian Oriental space '... beyond the pale of civilization ... [that is] "enlightened Europe"'.[46]

Once Greek elites themselves accepted the designation of the Byzantine and Ottoman periods in the Greek historical experience as representative of the Oriental, non-European aspects of Modern Greek identity, those intellectuals and politicians who tried to legitimize these parts of the historical experience were trapped in the language and imagery — and attendant power assumptions — established by the Orientalist template. For example, Constantine Paparigopoulos' seminal argument that Modern Greek identity is a culturally continuous experience stretching from classical to Byzantine through Ottoman times to the present, was largely penned in response to Fallmerayer's claims, and so engaged in a discussion that utilized — albeit for purposes of rejection — Orientalist terminology. Moreover, the irredentist nationalism encapsulated under the 'Great Idea' of reincorporating all Greek Orthodox populations under Ottoman rule into a Greater Greece was articulated in terms that posited Greekness against the uncivilized Ottoman Turkish brutes repeatedly referenced in the crudest of Western European Orientalist scholarship.

The collapse of the non-Westernist vision with the defeat of the Greek army in the 1922 Asia Minor campaign, while signalling the ascendance of the Westernist vision of Greekness, paradoxically reinforced the dichotomization of Greek identity in an Orientalizing paralysis. Symbolically, the political failure of the alternative identity conception meant the internalization of all Orientalist condescensions associated with the now discredited and disproved Byzantine dream. Practically, Greece was forced to accept Western European

136

tutelage as the best means of protection against the real threat of the Turkish nation-state created in 1923,[47] which came to be represented by Orientalists as a modern Oriental Other. Moreover, the absorption of Greece's Oriental (that is, Anatolian) refugees coincided with the ideological rooting of communism in Greece, a development whose ultimate result was the reconceptualization of Modern Greek identity in ideological, political-economic and strategic terms derfined by the Cold War.

Greece's role as a small state in the international system constituted the parameters within which Modern Greek identity was again recast in the dichotomies of Western versus non-Western, as the bipolar system meant that ideology, economics and military security were the benchmarks for identity designation. While Greece was firmly embedded as the client member in the political-economic and security architecture of the totalized West, the country's own developmental trajectory was continually held up against the industrialized members of the Western alliance as a reminder of the deficiencies between all that Greece had spawned but had supposedly failed to reactualize.

It is within the context of Greece's role in the New European Order that both Greek and non-Greek scholars have most consistently identified Orthodoxy with a set of supposedly Oriental (that is, Middle Eastern, Islamic, Slavic-Russian) characteristics that call into question Greece's membership in the civilized *Europa Occidens*, and which threaten to relegate Greece to an opaque symbolic and political space that is neither of nor separate from the European West. The Orientalization of the Orthodox dimensions of Greekness is actually rooted as far back as the seventeenth century, when Western European travelogues, diplomatic texts, and scholarly works began to reflect on the origins of a Western civilization designated as distinct from all other civilizations. The contemporary reinvention of Orthodoxy resonates with these earlier Orientalist interpretations, that referred to the '[Orthodox] Christian subjects of the Ottoman Empire'[48] as 'dirty and illiterate and grasping',[49] and as people marked by '... the debasement of their character'[50] due to their endorsement of a religious tradition which 'represents man as a criminal and God as a tyrant'.[51] Enlightenment intellectuals and politicians lamented the fact that 'the [Orthodox] Christian Slavs ... of the Ottoman Empire',[52] while 'beginning to work out their redemption from barbarism – or, if you prefer it, beginning to contract the disease of ... Western civilisation',[53] were such that the 'in the hands of the Greeks and Russians [the region in question] ... would hardly be livable'.[54]

The most compelling evocation of these earlier Orientalist interpretations, with their cultural and political differentiation of Europe into regional antagonists, is the 1993 re-release of the Carnegie Endowment's 1914 inquiry into the Balkan Wars.[55] In the new introduction to the reissued report, legendary historian George Kennan casts Orthodoxy in terms identified with a non-Western, Greater Oriental space, and explains conflict in the Balkans as

137

historicatly determined by the immutability of the non-European, Orthodox element. Kennan observes that

> ... In the period of these [First and Second] Balkan wars, the Croats, as the only Roman Catholic people, were still, with very minor exceptions, living in areas belong to, or under occupation of, the Austro-Hungarian Empire. They were not, therefore, directly involved in these two Balkan wars; and so the Eastern Orthodox-Roman Catholic religious antagonisms that were to play so unfortunate a role in later years were not at that time prominently involved ... [S]o it remains today ... [that the] ... Balkan wars [then and now draw] ... on deeper traits of character inherited, presumably, from a distant tribal past.[56]

According to Kennan, the antagonism between the Western and Eastern Christian communities in the Balkans is rooted in the Byzantine, Ottoman, and Turkish essences of the latter. He notes that

> [t]he roots [of the current Balkan problem] ... reach back, clearly, not only into the centuries of Turkish domination but also into the Byzantine penetration of the Balkans even before that time. ... [E]vents of the ... thirty years of communist power ... prolonged it. ... [D]evelopments of those earlier ages, not only those of the Turkish domination but of earlier ones as well, had the effect of thrusting into the southeastern reaches of the European continent a salient of non-European civilization that has continued to the present day to preserve many of its non-European characteristics.[57]

Native scholars working on Modern Greek identity have legitimized the historical determinism and political-cultural oppositional structure embedded in the Carnegie report's explicit reference to Oriental Orthodoxy.[58] The renewed[59] Orientalization of Orthodoxy in the Modern Greek identity discourse has been particularly acute in the post-1974 period, with '... the return to Greece ... of a critical mass of intellectuals and academics representing the first generation of Greeks systematically trained in the social sciences in major European and American institutions'.[60] Whether from a neo-modernization, neo-marxist, or post-structuralist perspective, these scholars (as well as Greek scholars remaining in the Anglo-American diaspora space) have analyzed Greece's agenda of political democratization, economic modernization and cultural pluralization in language that reinforces the Oriental Otherness of Eastern Orthodox Christianity. For example, despite Greece's successful consolidation of democracy, social scientists refer to 'the atrophy of civil society [due to] Orthodoxy and the communitarian nationalism which flows from it'.[61] Similarly, critics charge that controversies in Greece related to freedom of religious conscience are the result of an Orthodox Christian worldview[62] incompatible with European norms. The handful of analyses of Greece's post-1974 political culture have pointed to the contradictions between the country's Westernist

138

and non-Westernist tendencies, where the latter are identified with the 'formidable confining conditions' to modernization and democratization posed by a sultanistic heritage identified principally with all post-Ottoman societies, but also grounded in a 'long-term heritage'[63] that links both '... the long Byzantine (Church, law) and Ottoman (state) heritages'.[64] More specifically, the '... significance of Orthodoxy for the development of ... [the sultantistic] cultural tradition ... ',[65] is emphasized, thereby reinforcing the identification of Byzantine Orthodox and Ottoman Islamic elements in contemporary Greek culture. Moreover, even the most discerning cultural analyses undertake extensive discussions of an '... Orthodox *Weltanschauung*'[66] marked by '... a profound antipathy towards cultural and political structures identified with the Catholic Church and, more generally, "the West" ... ',[67] such that abbreviated observations about the intellectual and political reasons for the 'misguided identification of Greek with Eastern Orthodox'[68] are not explored with regard to the implications for Greece's contemporary historiography and democratization project.

On the other hand, the insidiousness of the Orientalist approach to the Orthodox dimensions of Greek culture is reflected in the fact that reactions against the Westernist interpretation of Modern Greek identity have been monopolized by scholars who describe Orthodoxy, conversely, in terms which totalize both the Catholic-Protestant West and the Islamic East. Whether in reference to the Orthodox clergy's support for 'the liberation of the [Orthodox] Christians from the tyranny of the [Muslim] Turks',[69] or in condemning 'the West ... [for spawning] ... the capitalist or Marxist systems, ... two forms of unscrupulous barbarism',[70] the Orientalization of Orthodoxy by virtue of its location in a dichotomizing West versus East discussion has made its way into the wider spectrum of discussions of Modern Greek identity. So taken as a whole, Orthdoxy becomes the fulcrum for in-betweeness and for Greece's Euro-Oriental Otherness from the West.

To sum up, the result of the Orientalizing discussions about Orthodoxy has been to locate contemporary Greece (and by extension, its neighbouring Orthodox societies) in a cultural topos which is, in the words of an interwar Swedish traveller,

> ... elusive of definition – the body of the East, but without its spirit, ... a traitorous deserter from itself ... ; it is an artificial trumpery ... which has deliberately broken with its past and renounced its ancient heritage ... [Its people are a] type ... psychologically and socially, truly a 'wavering form', a composite of Easterner and Westerner ... [T]hese creatures are homeless; they are no longer Orientals nor yet Europeans. They have not freed themselves from the vices of the East nor acquired ... the virtues of the West.[71]

That Orientalization of Modern Greek identity reinforces the intellectual assumptions and political prescriptions of the neo-modernization thesis. Euro-

pean Union cohorts decry Greece's economic performance as evidence that
the country is 'a new kind of decaying Ottoman Empire',[72] and speak of
Greece as a country which, '... from being one of us since the [Cold] War,
has become one of them [the Balkans]. With the collapse of the Soviet empire
in eastern and Central Europe, Greece's usefulness [to the West] ... has
disappeared'.[73] In short, as a designator for a constellation of cultural features associated with the Greater Orient of Byzantium, Islam, the Ottoman
Empire and Turkey, the Orthodox dimensions of Modern Greek identity provide the intellectual artifice by which the European West can constitute its
totalized Self in cultural terms. Moreover, insofar as the Orientalist approach
constructs Orthodoxy as an interminable problem for the modernization of
Greece and its neighbours – as Kennan observes, '[e]ighty years of tremendous change in the remainder of Europe ... have done little to alter the essence
of the problem this geographic region [the Balkans] presents for Europe[74] –
the religious designation provides the European West with a functional legitimacy for building regional architectures that exclude the supposedly hostile,
congenitally unstable non-European, Orthodox Other.

Expanding the Orient and distancing Orthodoxy: Central Europe exits

The second significant literature that Orientalizes Orthodoxy in a manner
consistent with neo-modernization claims is the work on Central European
identity. The discussion about whether or not 'Central Europe exists' has a
long geneology dating back to Metternich's time,[75] but has been reinvigo-
rated as a subtext to the larger current discussion about the cultural meaning
of and spatial boundaries for Europeanness. The Central European identity
discussion has involved deliberate cultural and political engineering whereby,
intellectuals in particular but policymakers as well, have capitalized on the
fluidity of the current historical conjuncture to relocate Central Europe within
the symbolic and political space of the European West.[76]
    There is no doubt amongst scholar-practitioners participating in the current
discourse that Central Europe does indeed exist. Self-designated members of
the region include Austria, Germany, the Czech Republic, the Republic of Slo-
vakia, Hungary, Poland, the Baltic Republics and the Republic of Slovenia;
it is testimony to the combined intellectual capabilities and political acu-
men of the scholar-practitioners in these countries that the self-designation is
increasingly accepted by their European Union and American cohort in politics and the academy.[77] The aim of Central European scholar-practitioners is
to show how Central Europe exists, and they accomplish this aim by elaborating certain paradigmatic themes[78] related to identity and dependent on the
Orientalization of Orthodoxy.
    The first noteworthy theme relevant to the Orientalization of Orthodoxy
concerns the emphasis on culture as the primary variable for identity. Central European intellectuals have reinvented their region's identity, through an

140

historical interpretation of culture that culminates in a distinctive civilizational profile of *Europa Occidens*. This Europe is shaped by the widely cited
experiences of Western Christendom, the Renaissance, the Reformation and
Counter-Reformation, the Enlightenment and the Euro-American ideological
and security arrangements built to defend against the former Soviet bloc.
Central European identity is constructed in terms of its commonalities with
this civilizational profile of the European West.

Most importantly with regard to religion, the cultural argument repeatedly
references the fact that '[t]he common cradle of Western and Central European culture is Western Christianity'.[79] The Western, 'universal church' is
cited as 'the dominant integrative institution' in the formation of a shared
Western-Central European culture. Catholic-Protestant Christianity is credited with a congruity between internal and external behaviours which are
rational, functional, rule-based, and pluralist and which are explicitly posited
as behavioural characteristics 'much less important in Orthodoxy'.[80]

The logic of the religious element in this larger cultural argumentation leads
to the following conclusion: that the Orthodox populations of Europe had and,
given the temporal language, continue to have, no experience with 'the ideas
of liberalism, pluralism, modern democracy, socialism and the defence of
the human individual, all of which constitute the shared reality of the West
at the present time'.[80] In short, Central European intellectuals use Western
Christianity to locate their regional culture within the symbolic boundaries of
Europe as a whole, and therefore, *de facto*, cast Eastern Orthodox Christianity
as a symbolic Other to this Europe.

How is this generalized cultural Otherness of Orthodoxy Orientalized by
Central European identity debates? Central European intellectuals draw on
the crude Orientalist opposition between barbarian and civilized regional
identities which undergirds the historiography on Modern Greek identity.
However, by using a carefully constructed organic imagery to articulate the
ontology of civilized *Europa Occidens*, Central European intellectuals go
beyond the cultural argument and posit a geo-political and strategic rationale
for the reattachment of Central Europe to its natural regional Self.[82]

The aforementioned organic imagery has critical implications for the idea of
Orthodoxy. Because Western and Central European cultures, rooted in Western Christendom, share an essence that is innate and not subject to change,
Orthodoxy becomes the marker for a cultural matrix that can never acquire
the features of Europeanness; Orthodoxy is a permanent, organic stigma of
non-Europeanness. In the words of Schopflin, the culture of Central Europe
is marked by '... the enracination of ... [Western values that have made]
... these lands a part of Western Christianity and ... [have] located Central
Europe firmly in association with the West'.[83] The political boundaries of the
New Europe begin to assume a sense of inflexibility and friend-foe delineation
in light of the fact that cultural Otherness of Orthodoxy is cast as 'immanent,
as well as ineradicable'.[84]

The exclusivist formulation of Europe's political regions is reinforced by the second noteworthy theme that Orientalizes Orthodoxy in Central European identity debates. Specifically, the literature on Central European identity conceptualizes Russia as the primary constituting Other, as well as a historically continuous cultural and security threat,[85] to the regions of Central and Western Europe. The external boundaries of Europe are set against a totalized Russia constructed in terms of a Greater Oriental space, which is Asian (Tartar-Mongol) and Islamic. Orthodoxy is then Orientalized through its identification with this totalized, Greater Oriental Russia.

The presentation of Russia as the representative of a Greater Orient is based on an historical sweep covering nearly a millenium. The Polish writer Georgy Konrad makes reference to Russia's Greater Oriental history, in his lament that '... Central Europe's historical misfortune [was] that it was unable to become independent after the collapse of the Eastern, Tartar-Turkish hegemony ... and that it once again came under Eastern hegemony, this time of the Soviet-Russian type'.[86] By defining the Russian '... [O]ther ... [as not] simply confined in time to the Soviet political system, [but instead as] "eternal Russia"'.[87] Central Europeans establish the historical framework for an eternal Russian identity whose Oriental traits range from the Principality of Muscovy up through the Tsarist and Soviet Empires and through the present Russian Federation.[88]

Orthodoxy is implicitly associated with the timeless opaqueness of Russia's Oriental ontology. For example, Russia is distinguished from Europe[89] by its '... quite specific history anchored in the Byzantine world',[90] by the 'real cultural division and different values between Europe and Byzantium',[91] and by its links, in general with '... the Eastern empires (Russian and Ottoman); in other words, Orthodoxy is part of a Greater Orient of Byzantium, Russia, Asia and Ottoman Islam'.[92] Similarly, the association of Orthodoxy with the non-European Oriental space of Russia and Islam emerges in Central European treatments of the Balkans. As Jeno Szucs notes, both the Russian (and Ottoman) presence in South-Eastern Europe[93] forced that region to 'secede from the European structure'[94] along with the gradual decline of Byzantium by the end of the Middle Ages. Here again, the implicit message is the claim that the Byzantine, Russian and Ottoman Empires severed the Balkans from the organic map of Europe; of course, the religious traditions of these three Empires are Orthodoxy and Islam.

Once having identified eternal Russia with a Greater Oriental space whose non-Europeanness is Orthodox and Islamic in cultural terms, the Central European literature explains how the admitted similarities between Russian and European historical experiences were overwhelmed under the historically continuous dilution by the aforementioned Oriental influences. The result of such analysis is to designate Russia, in Milan Kundera's words, as '... a singular civilization, an *other* civilization ... [and] totalitarian Russian civilization ... [as] ... the radical negation of the modern West'.[95] Mihaly Vajda echoes this view, arguing that '... Russians are incapable of tolerating

142

another civilization, another form of life'.[96] Yet another work contrasting the Central European and Russian intelligentsia concludes that '... the vast difference between Russia and the West ... [is] ... large enough to denote Russia as *another* civilization'.[97]

The Greater Oriental Otherness of Russian civilization provides the basis on which Central Europeans build their arguments for regional integration into the European West. Because Russian civilization is identified with a Greater Orient historically hostile to an essentialized Western civilization, Central Europeans argue that rapid integration of their region into the European Union, the West European Union and NATO is the only logical means of protecting all the regions of Europe's organic whole. Orthodoxy, as a component of the hostile, Greater Oriental Otherness of Russia, is instrumental as a part of the region building argument of the Central European identity debates. The link between identity building and region building is explicitly made in the comments by a former Polish Minister of Foreign Affairs, who explained that the expansion of the security architecture of

> ... the stable nucleus of the countries of the European Communities, the Western European Union and the North Atlantic Alliance ... [should include] ... the three countries [of Hungary, Poland and Czechoslovakia] ... [so that] ... the hard core of Europe will comprise a bigger territory.[98]

To sum up, the literature on Central European identity constructs regional identity in cultural terms which are then explicitly used to make an argument for new political-economic and security arrangements in the European Order. The relevance for the idea of Orthodoxy lies in the fact that the region is implicitly and explicitly separated from the Western Christian civilization of *Europa Occidens*, as well as in the fact that Orthodoxy is associated to an essentialized Russian Other represented by a Greater Oriental space. Orthodoxy is thereby Orientalized and marginalized, in both cultural and political terms, from the regional members of the New European Order. Insofar as Orthodoxy is linked to designations of underdevelopment, backwardness and permanent threat vis-à-vis civilized Europe, the Central European identity literature thereby reinforces neo-modernization theory's primordialist assumptions about the religious dimensions of culture. This literature also therefore underscores the hierarchies of power implicit in how the neomodernization paradigm interprets Orthodoxy with regard to remapping Europe's regions.

Conclusion: Revising the 'orthodox' conception of Orthodoxy and integrating Europe

It should be clear from this article that the 'orthodox' conception of Orthodoxy, which has gained widespread acceptance in the Euro-American academic and policy discussions, diverges dramatically from my introductory profile of Eastern Orthodoxy Christianity as a religion conceived as a way

143

of life prioritizing personal freedom and relationality. Insofar as this article assumes that the 'orthodox' conception of Orthodoxy is theoretically inaccurate and methodologically unsound with respect to the alternative referent, the main conclusion of this article is that, taken as a whole, the neo-modernization arguments and the literatures on Modern Greek and Central European identities, constitute an intellectual corpus with potentially negative implications for the project of integrating the multiple regions of post-Cold War Europe into a unified supra-regional whole.

With respect to the above conclusion, the article underscores the need to consider the implications of the dynamic process of mutual reinforcement between constructed knowledge about Eastern Orthodox Christianity, on the one hand, and balance of power decisions regarding the expansion of Europe's geo-strategic and political-economic architectures, on the other. In normative terms, this article therefore takes issue with the scholarly and journalistic representation of Orthodoxy found in 'orthodox' treatments; in practical terms, this article concludes that the language and policies of exclusion which already have resulted from the 'orthodox' version of Orthodoxy bode negatively for the successful longterm democratization and marketization of Southeastern Europe and Russia, and therefore, contribute to longterm problems of political-economic stability for Europe as a whole. To paraphrase the former Deputy Commander in Chief, US European Command in Bosnia, whether academics or policymakers in the USA and the European Union, 'we must see Eastern Orthodoxy as it is, or as it may be, not as ... [we] ... wish it to be. We must separate reality from image'.[99]

What concrete measures may be taken to provide a more discerning and, in my view, more constructive interpretation of Eastern Orthodox Christianity and its potential impacts on the overall European projects of democratization and marketization? Three specific research agendas come to mind, each of which could enrich the social science literature on Eastern Orthodox Christianity and social change, and therefore, which could broaden the range of policy choices for supporting democratic consolidation and market pluralization in European societies with an Orthodox religious tradition.

A thumbnail sketch of each research agenda follows. First and foremost, social science research on Eastern Orthodox Christianity and social change must respect the Weberian dictum of studying every religion on its own terms. Academic and policy studies must utilize language and concepts specific to and embedded in Eastern Orthodox Christianity itself, as the basis for introducing Orthodoxy to the plethora of debates over the meaning of modernity, the possibilities for public religions in the modern world and the religious dimensions of civic versus ethnic models of nation. Serious research on the question of the potential compatibilities between Orthodoxy and democracy, therefore, must begin with an understanding of: how the Orthodox way of life relates to the public-private divide; how Orthodox ontological formulations of the person as an hypostatic event of freedom and relationality compare to liberal democratic conceptions of the individual; and finally, how Orthodox

144

conceptions of sources of authority and of the meaning of community compare to classical conceptions of democracy which prioritize normative over
procedural requirements.

Second, any social science research on Orthodoxy must pay far greater
attention than heretofore to comparative empirical analysis of church-state
relations in countries with an Eastern Orthodox Christian tradition. The discipline of political science, in particular, has neglected such empirical analyses,
and rigourous comparative studies of the longterm historical trajectory of
church-state relations in Southeastern European and Russia are limited in
number. Church-state analyses must focus on: the non-monolithic character
of ecclesiastical structures, where the triadic relationship amongst hierarchy-
clergy-laity tells, in most countries, a rich institutional story of organizational power struggles and macro-political transformation; the interactions
between changes in the supra-national versus national ecclesiastical structure, as evidenced in the recent example of calls by the current Ecumenical
Patriarch at Constantinople for reforms in local (national) Orthodox churches
in post-totalitarian societies; and, the impacts on state legitimacy attendant to
constitutional dis-establishment of Orthodox churches.

Finally, social science research framed in terms of the cultural and political
separation of Europe into incompatible and, according to more doomsay-
ing accounts, mutually hostile Catholic-Protestant versus Eastern Orthodox
spaces, must take a hard look at the history of Great Power politics. In short,
the current religious and cultural differences between those parts of Europe
roughly correlating with Western and Eastern Christendom cannot be grasped
without studying: the process of transmission of Enlightenment ideas beyond
their original Western European context, to those regions of Europe deemed,
according to the 'orthodox' version of Orthodoxy, hostile to Enlightenment
culture; and, the metamorphosis of Enlightenment ideas according to local
religious conditions and political circumstances, on the one hand, and regional
power alignments, on the other.

To sum up, current social science research and, even more so, contemporary
policy discussions, almost uniformly ignore the historical fact that the national
models and state structures which emerged in Europe's Orthodox regions were
significantly constrained by the conjunctural victory of conservative ideology
and balance-of-power politics which marked Restoration Europe in the mid-
late nineteenth century. Indeed, academics and policymakers would do well to
recognize that the admittedly strong challenges to democratic consolidation
in Europe's Orthodox regions—namely, Southeastern Europe and Russia—are
as much the legacy of Great Power interventions in local political outcomes
as of Eastern Orthodox Christianity's *weltanschauung*. In this regard, as
a country with an overwhelmingly Orthodox history and a longterm geo-
strategic importance in Great Power politics, Greece presents an example of
successful democratic consolidation well worth additional study. The general
point remains, however, that academics and policymakers concerned with
integration and stability in Europe, must analyze the role of Eastern Orthodox

145

Christianity in processes of democratization and marketization at the local level within the larger international context of Great Power politics in the post-Cold War era.

Acknowledgments

Elizabeth Prodromou is resident at Princeton University, where she is a Visiting Lecturer in the Politics Department and a MacArthur Fellow and Alexander Papamarkou Fellow at the Center of International Studies. She would like to thank Nikiforos Diamandouros, Richard Falk, Dimitris Keridis, Eva Konstantellou, Vassilis Lambropoulos and Artemis Leontis for their criticisms and comments on earlier versions of this paper. Portions of an earlier version of this article were presented in 1995, at the Center of Ethnological Studies in Granada, Spain, and the City University of New York, and in 1996 at the Center for European Studies at Harvard University.

Notes

1. An explicit statement of the priority of promoting democracy across Europe, tempered by the broader contingencies of American security and economic considerations, was offered by Morton Halperin, currently the Clinton Administration's National Security Council member directing the administration programme for 'Promoting Democracy Abroad'. In remarks at the Woodrow Wilson School at Princeton University, Halporin outlined the administration's definition of democracy, the mechanisms for operationalizing this definition abroad, the range of responses for responding to challenges to democracy-building in former state socialist Europe, and the prioritization of democracy versus security versus economic stability. Particularly interesting was Halperin's 'regional priorities checklist' for democracy, whereby Russia and East-Central Europe led the list of regions where democracy promotion is key for the administration; according to the criteria used by applied by Halperin, South-eastern Europe was not mentioned on the remainder of a list that included Latin America, Asia, Africa and the Islamic world. See Halperin (1994).
2. The dearth of social science and humanities scholarship on Eastern Orthodox Christianity and social change is best contextualized within the larger tendency in approaches to the study of 'modern' Greece, that is the Greek nation-state experience as distinct from the classical and Byzantine period, and reflects what Margaret Alexiou has analyzed as '. . . the marginalization of the Greek-speaking world (both modern and Byzantine) by those western scholars whose histories of 'European' thought, literature and popular culture from the Middle Ages to the present day consistently exclude Greece from the most cursory consideration, despite the richness and relevance of the material available'. See Alexiou (1986: 5).
3. The theological and historical literature on the Great Schism is enormous. For an excellent summary understandable to the non-specialist, see Ware (1983). A more comprehensive historical account is provided by Runciman (1955).
4. An excellent concise summary of the notion of Eastern Orthodox Christianity as a way of life which unifies the doctrinal and the practical, the intellectual and the experimental, dimensions of the faith is provided by Yannaras (1992: 44–47).
5. Guiltsis (1990: 56).

146

6. By far the fullest and most formative English-language formulations of the Eastern Orthodox anthropology of personhood are found in Yannaras (1984) and Zizioulas (1985).

7. Zizioulas (1985: 15).

8. Huntington (1993b).

9. Huntington (1993b: 23).

10. Huntington (1993b: 25). On the same page, Huntington states that the power of civilizations as organizers for the global system lie in the fact that they are '... the highest cultural grouping of people and the broadest level of cultural identity ... short of that which distinguishes humans from other species'.

11. The other civilizations cited by Huntington are the Confucian, Japanese, Hindu, Latin American and 'possibly', the African. See Huntington (1993b).

12. Huntington (1993b: 23).

13. Some of the most immediate – and representative – responses to the civilizational paradigm were published in *Foreign Affairs*, by Ajami (1993), Bartley (1993), Binyan (1993), Kirkpatrick (1993) and Kishore Mahbubani (1993). Other comments relevant to the issues raised by Huntington include, in the same issue of *Foreign Affairs*, articles by Asmus, Kugler & Larrabee (1993) and Harries (1993). The conference at Princeton University, held from 5–7 May 1995, was entitled 'Clash of and dialogue across cultures and civilizations'; the participants undertook an interdisciplinary examination of the major propositions in Huntington's paradigm, and took a critical approach to the theoretical and methodological formulation of his argument.

14. Huntington (1993b: 29–30).

15. Huntington (1993b: 40–41).

16. Huntington (1993b: 30–31).

17. Kaplan (1993: xxiii).

18. Kaplan (1993: 7).

19. Kaplan (1993: 25).

20. Kaplan (1993: 259).

21. Kaplan (1993: 8).

22. Kaplan (1993: 48).

23. *The New York Times* (4 April 1989).

24. *Washington Post* (9 February 1990).

25. *The New York Times* (6 April 1990).

26. *The New York Times* (17 June 1990).

27. Mitterand's references to the Balkans and to those parts of Europe outside the boundaries of the European Union were cited by French sociologist Jacques Rupnik in a lecture entitled 'The Bosnian crisis: A European perspective' (1994) at the Woodrow Wilson School of Public and International Affairs at Princeton University. See also *Le Monde* (10 July 1992; 9 March 1993).

28. *The New York Times* (28 December 1994).

29. See Brzezinski (1995).

30. It is not my intention to apologize for the Eastern Orthodox Church's real and apparent failures to engage in a constant battle against non-democratic forms of government – whether in the form of authoritarian or totalitarian regimes – in Cold War Europe. Nor am I ignoring the historical factors which shed light on cross-national variations in the cultural and institutional impacts of differing religious traditions in Europe. While extensive attempts to understand the institutional and cultural role of Eastern Orthodox Christianity in the process of democratization exceed the limit of this article, it bears mentioning that discerning analyses which seek to disaggregate the Eastern Orthodox Church in order to determine its varied impacts on processes of regime change are nearly non-existent.

31. For an excellent discussion of the processes by which social scientists have, or conversely, have not been willing to shift their paradigms in the face of changing empirical realities, see Janos (1986).

32. Indeed, the paradigm and policy crises have been met with a spate of proposed models for remaking the New World Order, with the civilizational paradigm competing with, amongst other proposals, Ernest Gellner's modelling on ethnicity, nationalism and religion, Brzezinski's two-track expansion programme for the Euro-Atlantic security system, and Richard Haas' augmented realism model for American foreign policy. Against the aforementioned backdrop, the production and transmission of a standard interpretation of Orthodoxy represents an interesting case in the sociology of knowledge. Gellner's work on ethnicity and religion is widely known and voluminous. In response to the end of the Cold War and the emergence of religious, ethnic and nationalist conflicts across European societies, Gellner has proposed theories on the links between ethnicity, religion and conflict in former Soviet territories and on the durability of Islamic fundamentalism worldwide. On the former, see Gellner (1990). On the latter, see Gellner (1992b). Based on his overview remarks in an article in the *New York Times* (28 December 1994), Brzezinski (1995) elaborates a fuller conception of a two-track expansion of the Euro-Atlantic security system.
33. Huntington (1993a: 192).
34. Huntington (1993b: 27).
35. For the most complete statement of his theory of nationalism, see Gellner (1983). Recent works on the questions of religion, ethnicity and nationalism in Europe's former state socialist societies include Gellner (1990, 1991, 1992a, 1993).
36. My arguments with regard to Schopflin's work draw on his articles. See Schopflin (1990 and 1994).
37. Schopflin (1994: 137–139).
38. He defines Westernness as the result of 'feudalism, medieval Christian universalism, the Renaissance, the Reformation and Counter-Reformation and the Enlightenment'. See Schopflin (1990: 61).
39. Neo-modernization scholars tend to write about democracy and economic development in terms of a '... moralizing dismissal of nationalist values, attitudes and practices as pre-modern and unenlightened. See Offe (1993: 1).
40. Taken together, the literatures on Modern Greek and Central European identity contribute to a version of Orthodoxy that meets the original Saidian definition of Orientalism: namely, there occurs the formulation of an Orthodox cultural and regional space in Europe, against which the region of the European West 'makes statements, authorizes views, describes, restructures and [over which it thereby also] rules'. I am paraphrasing Said's definition of Orientalism. See Said (1978: 3).
41. The problematic of Modern Greek identity is embodied in the designation itself, since the qualifying adjective 'Modern' points to the central issue at hand, namely how to articulate and then to institutionalize a cohesive expression of Greekness in the post-classical, post-Byzantine and post-Ottoman historical period. An excellent synoptic commentary on the intellectual and practical implications of the qualifying adjective is offered in Alexiou's 'Modern Greek Studies. For useful summaries of the contours of the debates over modern Greek identity as well as over the definition of Modern Greek Studies, see the collections on these topics in the *Journal of Modern Greek Studies*, Vol. 7, No. 1 (May 1989) and Vol. 8, No. 1 (May 1990), as well as the ongoing discussions about Modern Greek Studies in the Greek weekly newspaper *To Vima*, dating from early 1993 to the present.
42. The major international parameters which impinged on the form and substance of debates over Modern Greek identity include the protracted dismemberment of the Ottoman Empire, the establishment of the Turkish nation-state and the rise of fascim and communism culminating in the Cold War.
43. In terms of Greek historiography and popular imagination, Jakob Phillip von Fallmerayer is the most widely reviled exponent of the thesis about the genetic discontinuity between modern and ancient Greeks. See Alexiou's discussion (1986: 9) of Fallmerayer for the quote. For Fallmerayer's thesis in its various incarnations, see Fallmerayer (1945: 1830, 1836).

148

44. This quote by the late nineteenth-early twentieth century German library historian Karl Dietrich is found in Jusdanis (1987: 5).

45. Kitromilides (1994: 57).

46. Kitromilides (1994: 57). As one scholar of Modern Greek Studies has aptly summarized, '[t]he tilt toward Europe necessitated the cleansing of all oriental 'blemishes' accumulated over four hundred years . . . [and] put the Greeks at the vanguard of the struggle between Orient and Occident, between "barbarians" and "civilization"'. See Jusdanis (1991: 31).

47. Perhaps one of the most profoundly complex psychological results of the military defeat of 1922 was the fact not only that the subsequent absorption of approximately one-and-a-half million refugees from Asia Minor into Greece literally forced the country to internalize those human elements of the nation arriving from the now lost Oriental portion of the national psyche, but that the ensuing political-economic problems aggravated by the refugee absorption provided a catalyst for the next phase of dichotomization in Modern Greek identity according to Western versus non-Western prototypes.

48. West (1969: 1095).

49. West (1969: 1095).

50. Gibbon (1993: 33).

51. Gibbon (1993: 37).

52. West (1969: 1095).

53. Shaw (1975, Vol. 1: 490).

54. J.B.S. Morritt of Rokeby, *A grand tour*, p. 245, quobd in Todorova (1994b: 466).

55. The official title of the document was the *Report of the International Commission to inquire into the causes and conduct of the Balkan Wars* (1914). The re-released document is entitled *The other Balkan War: A 1913 Carnegie endowment inquiry in retrospect with a new introduction and reflections on the present conflict* by George Kennan (1993).

56. *The other Balkan War* (1993: 11). The tone of the original report, which devoted several chapters to '. . . the excesses, and particularly the atrocities, that marked the hostilities . . . [as] . . . abundant evidences of violations not only of international law but of the minimum dictates of common humanity', was reiterated in the recent reissue, with an introduction whose intellectual and policy authority would seem to be confirmed by the legendary status of Kennan. *The other Balkan War* (1993: 8).

57. *The other Balkan War* (1993: 12–13).

58. *The other Balkan War* (1993: 22).

59. For references to this language, see Clogg (1969, 1976). The basic reason for the anticlericalism of leading protagonists of the Greek war of independence and early statemakers lay in the cooptation of portions of the Orthodox hierarchy (along with other political and cultural elite strata) by the Ottoman state, but the antagonism towards Orthodoxy also lay in the anti-Westernism of an ecclesiastical hieruchy which recalled the thirteenth century sacking of Constantinople by Roman Catholic Crusaders and which likewise rejected the Enlightenment interpretation of religion and modernity as incompatible. As far back as the early nineteenth century, anti-clerical Greek statemakers such as Adamantios Korais condemned the superstitious and ignorant Orthodox clergy and railed against the ecclesiastical satraps who had complied with the Ottoman regime.

60. Diamandouros & Spourdalakis (1991: 379).

61. Lipovats (1993: 46).

62. Pollis (1987, 1992).

63. Diamandouros (1991: 10). A fuller characterization of the 'long-term heritage' of Balkan regimes as (post)-sultantistic is found in Diamandouros (1994: 9–11), which is the final version of the former text.

64. See Diamandouros (manuscript version, 1993: 13).

65. Diamandouros (manuscript version, 1993: 16).

66. Diamandouros (manuscript version, 1993: 17).

67. Diamandouros (manuscript version, 1993: 17–18). The full elaboration of his points about the impacts on the cultural contradictions, process of state-building, and democratization

project in modern Greek history, due to the links between Ottoman rule, Orthodox *weltanschauung* and sultantistic rule, are found in Diamandouros (manuscript version, 1993: 12–25).

68. I paraphrase a quote in Diamandouros (manuscript version, 1993: 19).
69. Pringos (1931: 852), quoted in Jusdanis (1991: 23).
70. Yannaras (1983: 113), quoted in Konstantellou (1991: 8).
71. Ehrenpreis (1928), translated by Huebsch. I am grateful to Maria Todorova for introducing this source, as well as for her suggesting the richness of travel accounts treating the Balkans and the Levant during the eighteenth and nineteenth centuries as a source of Western European attitudes toward other regions in Europe and the Near East. For other representative accounts and references dealing with the travels of Western Europeans to Greece, Southeastern Europe and the Near East, see Angelomatis-Tsougarakis (1990), Beck (1987), Blount (1636), Jenkyns (1980), Leake (1814; Vol. IV, 1935) and West (1941).
72. Quote from an anonymous author in an article entitled 'Europe's Trojan horse', *The Sunday Telegraph* (27 March 1994).
73. Paraphrase from Adam Nicolson, 'A fall from cultural grace', *The Spectator* (12 November 1993).
74. *The other Balkans Wars* (1993: 12–13).
75. The origins of the Central European question lie in the geostrategic and territorial problematic of Germany's role in Europe during the first half of the twentieth century and were codified in the widely known work of Friedrich Naumann. See Naumann (1915). For a useful introduction to the idea of *Mitteleuropa* as part of the problematic of Germany's role in Europe during the first half of the twentieth century, see Judt (1990) and Mere (1955). The Cold War effectively terminated the problematic over German expansion, and references to the opaque region known as Central Europe loosely and, quite arbitrarily, came to mean the Alpine and Czechoslovakian regions, the Western and Eastern regions of Germany and the Benelux countries; this constellation excludes Poland, Hungary, Italy and Yugoslavia. Reflecting the arbitrariness of the designation, Central Europe is often referred to according to the aforementioned designation, plus Hungary and the former Habsburg portions of Yugoslavia. Yet another analyst has designated Central Europe as that region encompassing Austria, Hungary, Czechoslovakia, Poland, Romania, Yugoslavia and Italy. See Mutton (1961: vii–viii).
76. Aware of the fact that the symbolic disappearance of Central Europe during tho Cold War was a function of *realpolitik*, Central European intellectuals and policymakers have responded to what Ash (1989: 191) has called the European Union's 'semantic trick . . . [of] arrogating to itself the unqualified title, "Europe" '.
77. For a short but telling illustration of the hegemony of the designation of Central Europe in US policy circles, see William Safire's article, 'Hello Central', in *The New York Times* (14 March 1995).
78. The Central European identity literature is marked by a striking theoretical and methodological diversity, but the grand narrative in the most recent round of writings was set out mainly by former dissidents. Notable examples are Vaclav Havel and Adam Michnik, who now engage in the politics of Central Europe, evidence of the cross-fertilization between the domains of knowledge and power. The diversity of the works on Central European identity prompted Schopflin & Wood (1989: 2) to observe that '. . . it has . . . become all but impossible to digest them [the writings on Central Europe] completely'. The main impetus for the revitalization of the debates on Central European identity came with the publication of three pieces in the early 1980s by Jeno Szucs, Czeslow Milosz and Milan Kundera, that is a Hungarian, Polish and Czechoslovakian writer, respectively; likewise, the English translation of works by Vaclav Havel, George Konrad and Adam Michnik, Czech, Hungarian and Polish scholar-dissidents, respectively, have been equally powerful in communicating to the American academy and popular audience the idea of Central Europe. The first troika of authors, however, launched the rediscovery of

150

Central Europe prior to the formal resolutions of 1989, as an inquiry into alternatives to the obvious crisis of state socialist regimes, and their works were presciently preoccupied with reconceptualizing the idea of Central Europe in cultural terms oriented toward the European West and away from an Oriental East represented by Russia (inclusive of the historical incarnations of the Russian Empire, thc Soviet Union and the Russian Federation). The translations of the second troika, as well as their involvement in consolidating democratic regimes in their respective national contexts, have sustained in the international public mind the idea of Central Europe. The relevant pieces for each author are the following: Szucs (1983), Milosz (1983) and Kundera (1984).

79. Duray (1989: 98).
80. Schopflin (1989: 13). Religion is also used to link Central European culture with Western democracy. For example, Duray (1989: 98) notes that the experiences of 'the Reformation and Protestantism ... [were] innovatory movements [that] did not give rise to new antagonistic churches and sects – as in the case of other religions – but led instead to a process of democratization'.
81. Duray (1989: 98).
82. Examples of the organic language used by Central Europeans in setting out ontologically incompatible regions of Europe are numerous. For example, Kundera speaks of the Cold War as a period in which the West, by abandoning Central Europe to Soviet Russia, '... had lost part of its own heritage and that it had been thereby impoverished'. See Kundera (1984). Others speak of the European West's Cold War abandonment of Central Europe as '... the amputation of a very part of its [the West's] flesh. ...' See Kis (1987: 6). With the end of the Cold War, the organic vision of Europe has become a staple in the Central European vocabulary on identity and in the politics of region-building. Branislav Lichardus (1995), Slovak Ambassador to the United States, has stated that 'the un-natural division of Europe had ended with the fall of the Iron Curtain, since Central Europe naturally belongs to the West. ... The enlargement of the European Union through integration of Central Europe is a correction of a previously un-natural situation'.
83. Schopflin (1989: 20).
84. Schopflin (1989: 12).
85. The rationale for the construction of Russia as Central Europe's constituting Other can not be fully understood without recognizing the oftentimes overlooked psychological dimensions of what is also a cultural and political project. In light of Kundera's widely held view that Yalta represented the willing choice of Western Europe to allow the kidnapping of Central Europe from its natural place in the Western European political space (a conviction reiterated throughout the majority of the Central European identity literature), the decision of intellectuals and policymakers from the region to formulate Russia as a hostile Other whose ontology is irreconcilable with the West represents an effort to take out an insurance policy that will guarantee against *Europa Occidens* ever making the sort of regionalizing choices of the Cold War past.
86. Konrad (1984), translation by Allen, quotod in Ash (1989: 194).
87. Neumann (1993: 359).
88. The designation of eternal Russia as part of a larger space that is Byzantine and Ottoman obviously suggests that Russia's non-European essence is Oriental, a characterization most explicit in the repeated references to the Asian, thereforo Oriental, roots of Russian identity in the Mongol and Tartar-Turkish experiences. For references to the Asian threads in the Russian historical experience, see Seton-Watson (1989). For references to Russian-language sources dealing with this issue, see the book review article by Hudson (1994).
89. In describing the religion dimensions of Russian culture, in contrast to that of Central-Western Europe, Schopflin (1989: 10) emphasizes that '... the Tsar of Russia or any Asiatic ruler' did not submit to the separation of religious and secular powers which

occurred with the '... kingship and papacy; the Orthodox tradition in Tsarist Russia is thereby associated with what is Asiatic and non-European'.

90. See Matejka (1990: 131).
91. This reference to the characterization of the difference between European Byzantine culture is part of a larger argument regarding the threat of Russia to the new European order, as discussed by Prizel (1994), with the quote and an account of the lecture is found in Todorova (1994a: 51–52).
92. Agh (1991: 85). Likewise, in arguing that Central-Western European political values of '... sincerity, openness, [and] honesty' are weakly rooted '... in Byzantium and Muscovy, where the Byzantine tradition was reinforced by the influence of Islam', Agh (1991: 13) associates both Orthodox Byzantium and Muscovy to the Islamic Orient. Ash's metaphor of Ottomanization to describe how Central Europe was able to break away from the Soviet imperial centre, namely through a process of *emancipation in decay* due to the empire's '... relative backwardness in relation to ... Western Europe'. The paraphrasing and direct quote are taken from Ash (*The uses of adversity*: 253–254). A fuller discussion of the Ottomanization metaphor with regard to the Soviet Union and the Central European emancipation therefrom is found in Ash (252–255). Ash (254) points out, in a balanced manner, that his emphasis that Ottomanization as a means for understanding the Soviet Union ... is not a detailed historical analogy, just a crude metaphor, "good enough for government work" as ... they say in the State Department'.
93. Szucs (1983: 134).
94. Szucs (1983: 134).
95. Kundera's remark is quoted in Neumann (1993: 359).
96. Vajda (1989: 173).
97. Mellor (1989: 167).
98. Skubiszewski (1992), quoted in Neumann (1989: 366). Vajda (1989: 175) also exhorts that 'we East-Central Europeans must do something to safeguard the possibility of remaining Europeans — if Europeans we wish to remain', and concludes with a warning not to '... annoy the beast [Russia] on our borders ... [in any way that might] increase its feelings of inferiority ... [and make it] ... more aggressive than it has been'.
99. The paraphrase is from Boyd (1995: 23).

References

Agh, A. (1991). After the revolution: A return to Europe, in K.E. Birnbaum, J.B. Binter & S.K. Badzik (eds.), *Towards a future European peace order?* London.

Ash, T.G. (1990). *The uses of adversity: Essays on the fate of Central Europe.* New York: Vintage Books.

Ash, T.G. (1989). Does Central Europe exist?, in G. Schopflin & N. Wood (eds.), *In search of Central Europe.* Totowa, New Jersey.

Ajami, F. (1993). The Summoning, *Foreign Affairs* 72(4): 2–9.

Alexiou, M. (1986). Modern Greek studies in the West: Between the classics and the Orient, *Journal of Modern Greek Studies* 4(1): 3–15.

Angelomatis-Tsougarakis, H. (1990). *The eve of the Greek revival: British travellers' perceptions of early nineteenth-century Greece.* London: Routledge.

Asmus, R.D., Kugler, R.L. & Larrabee, F.S. (1993). Building a new NATO, *Foreign Affairs* 72(4): 28–40.

Baker, D. (ed.) (1976). *Ecclesiastical history*, Vol. 13. Oxford: Basil Blackwell.

Bartley, R.L. (1993). The case for optimism, *Foreign Affairs* 72(4): 15–18.

Beck, B.H. (1987). *From the rising of the sun: English images of the Ottoman Empire to 1715.* New York: Peter Lange.

152

Binyan, L. (1993). Civilization grafting, *Foreign Affairs* 72(4): 19–21.

Blount, H. (1936). *A voyage into the Levant. A Freife relation of a journey, lately performed by Master H.B. Genlemena, from England by the war of Venice, into Dalmatia, Slavonia, Bosnah, Hungary, Macedonia, Thesaaly, Thrace, Rhodes and Egypt, unto Gran Cairo: With particular observations concerning the moderne condition of the Turkes, and other people under that Empire*. London: Andrew Crooke.

Boyd, C.G. (1995). Making peace with the guilty: The truth about Bosnia, *Foreign Affairs* 74(5): 22–38.

Brzezinski, Z. (1995). A plan for Europe, *Foreign Affairs* 74(1): 26–42.

Carnegie Endowment for Intercourse and Education (1914). *Report of the International Commission to Inquire into the Causes and Conduct of the Balkan Wars*. Washington, DC.

Carnegie Endowment for International Peace (1993). *The other Balkan War: A 1913 Carnegie endowment inquiry in retrospect with a new introduction and reflections on the present conflict by George Kennan*. Washington, DC.

Clogg, R. (1969). The *Dhidaskalia Patriki* (1793) [The fatherly teaching]: An orthodox reaction to French revolutionary propaganda, *Middle East Studies* 5: 87–117.

Clogg, R. (1976). Anticlericalism in pre-Independence Greece, c. 1750–1821, in D. Baker (ed.), *Ecclesiastical history*, Vol. 13. Oxford: Basil Blackwell.

Diamandouros, P.N. (1991). Prospects for democracy in Southeastern Europe: Comparative and theoretical perspectives. Unpublished manuscript. University of Athens.

Diamandouros, P.N. (1993). *Cultural dualism and political change in postauthoritarian Greece*. Madrid: Instituto Juan March de Estudios e Investigaciones.

Diamandouros, P.N. (1994). Prospects for democracy in the Balkans: Comparative and theoretical perspectives, in F.S. Larrabee (ed.), *The volatile powder keg: Balkan security after the Cold War*. Washington, DC: The American University Press.

Diamandouros, P.N. & Spourdalakis, M. (1991). Political science in Greece, *European Journal of Political Research* 20(3–4): 375–387.

Duray, M. (1989). The Europan ideal: Reality or wishful thinking in Eastern Central Europe?, in G. Schopflin & N. Wood (eds.), *In search of Central Europe*. New York: Polity Press.

Ehrenpreis, M. (1928). *The soul of the East: Experience and reflections*, Alfhild Huebsch (trans.). New York: Viking Press.

Fallmerayer, J.P. (1830, 1836). *Geschichte der Halbinsel Morea wahrend des Mittelalters*, 2 vols. Stuttgart & Tobingen: J.G. Cotta.

Fallmerayer, J.P. (1945). *Fragmente aus dem Orient*, II. Stuttgart & Tubingen: J.G. Cotta.

Gellner, E. (1983). *Nations and Nationalism*. Oxford: Basil Blackwell.

Gellner, E. (1990). Ethnicity and faith in Eastern Europe, *Daedalus* 119(1): 279–294.

Gellner, E. (1991). Nationalism and politics in Eastern Europe, *New Left Review*, No. 189.

Gellner, E. (1992a). Nationalism reconsidered and E.H. Carr, *Review of International Studies* 18(4): 285–294.

Gellner, E. (1992b). *Postmodernism, reason and religion*. London: Routledge.

Gellner, E. (1993). Homeland of the unrevolution, *Daedalus* 122(3): 141–154.

Gibbon, E. (1993). *The decline and fall of the Roman Empire*, Vol. 4. New York: Alfred A. Knopf.

Guiltsis, V. (1990). An ethical approach to justice and peace, in G. Limouris (ed.), *Justice, peace and the integrity of creation: Insights from Orthodoxy*. Geneva: World Council of Churches Publication.

Halperin, M. (1994). Promoting democracy abroad: An administration perspective. Unpublished manuscript/lecture. Princeton University, Woodrow Wilson School of Public and International Affairs.

Harries, O. (1993). The collapse of the West, *Foreign Affairs* 72(4): 41–53.

Hudson, G.E. (1994). Russia's search for identity in the post-Cold War world, *Mershon International Studies Review* No. 38: 235–240.

Huntington, S.P. (1993a). If not civilizations, what? Paradigms of the post-Cold War world, *Foreign Affairs* 72(5): 186–194.

Huntington, S.P. (1993b). The clash of civilizations?, *Foreign Affairs* 72(3): 22–49.

Janos, A. (1986). *Politics and paradigms: Changing theories of change in social science.* Stanford, CA: Stanford University Press.

Jenkyns, R. (1980). *The Victorians and ancient Greece.* Cambridge, MA: Harvard University Press.

Judt, T. (1990). The rediscovery of Central Europe, *Daedalus* 199(1): 23–55.

Jusdanis, G. (1987). East is East – West is West: It's a matter of Greek literary history, *Journal of Modern Greek Studies* 5(7): 1–14.

Jusdanis, G. (1991). *Belated modernity and aesthetic culture: Inventing national literature.* Minneapolis, MN: University of Minnesota Press.

Kaplan, R. (1993). *Balkan ghosts: A journey through history.* New York: St. Martin's Press.

Kirkpatrick, J. (1993). The modernizing imperative, *Foreign Affairs* 72(4): 22–27.

Kis, D. (1987). Themes d'Europe Centrale, *La Nouvelle Alternative*, Vol. 8.

Kitromilides, P. (1994). *Enlightenment, nationalism, orthodoxy: Studies in the culture and political thought of South-Eastern Europe.* London: Ashgate Publishing Company.

Konrad, G. (1984). *Antipolitics: An essay,* R.E. Allen (trans.), New York: Harcourt Brace Jovanovich.

Konstantellou, E. (1991). Returning to the 'Lost Center': *Critical perspectives on the neo-orthodox challenge to Eurocentrism.* Unpublished manuscript/lecture. Harvard University.

Kundera, M. (1984). A kidnapped west or a culture bows out, *Granta*, No. 11: 95–118.

Leake, W.M. (1814a). *Researches in Greece.* London: John Booth.

Leake, W.M. (1814b). *Travels in Northern Greece,* IV. London: Jay Rodwell.

Lichardus, B. (1995). Central Europe between integration and regionalization. Unpublished manuscript/lecture. Princeton University, Woodrow Wilson School of Public and International Affairs.

Limouris, G. (ed.) (1990). Orthodox perspectives on creation, in G. Limouris (ed.), *Justice, peace and the integrity of creation: Insights from orthodoxy.* Geneva: World Council of Churches Publication.

Lipovats, Th. (1993). *Orthodoxos Christianismos kai Ethnikismos: Duo Ptyhes tis Sygchronis Ellinikis Politikis Koultouras* [Orthodox Christianity and nationalism: Two sources of contemporary Greek political culture], *Elliniki Epitheorisi Politikis Epistimis* 2(3–4): 31–47.

Mahmubani, K. (1993). The dangers of decadence, *Foreign Affairs* 72(4): 10–14.

Matejka, L. (1990). Milan Kundera's Central Europe, *Cross Currents* 9.

Mellor, J. (1989). Is the Russian intelligentsia European? (A reply to Simecka), in G. Schopflin & N. Wood (eds.), *In search of Central Europe.* New York: Polity Press.

Mere, H.C. (1955). *Mitteleuropa in German thought and action.* The Hague: Martinus Nijhoff.

Milosz, C. (1983). *The witness of poetry.* Cambridge, MA: Harvard University Press.

Mutton, A.F.A. (1961). *Central Europe: A regional and human geography.* London, UK: Longmans.

Naumann, F. (1915). *Mitteleuropa.* Berlin: Georg Reimer.

Neumann, I.B. (1993). Russia as Central Europe's constituting other, *European Journal of Political Research* 7(2): 349–369.

Offe, C. (1993). Ethnic politics in European transitions, *Papers on East European Constitution Building* 1/93: 1–41.

Pollis, A. (1987). The state, the law and human rights in modern Greece, *Human Rights Quarterly* 10: 587–614.

Pollis, A. (1992). Greek national identity: Religious minorities, rights and European norms, *Journal of Modern Greek Studies* 10: 171–195.

Pringos, I. (1931). *To Chroniko tou Amsterdam* [The Amsterdam Chronicle], *Nea Estia* 10: 846–853.

Prizel, I. (1994). Poland between East and West: A false dichotomy? Unpublished manuscript/lecture. Woodrow Wilson Center.

154

Runciman, S. (1955). *The Eastern schism: A study of the Papacy and the Eastern Churches during the XIth and XIIth centuries.* Oxford: Oxford University Press.

Rupnik, J. (1994). The Bosnian crisis: A European Perspective. Unpublished manuscript/lecture. Princeton, NJ: Princeton University.

Said, E. (1978). *Orientalism.* New York: Pantheon Books.

Schopflin, G. (1989). Central Europe: Definitions old and new, in G. Schopflin & N. Wood (eds.), *In search of Central Europe.* New York: Polity Press.

Schopflin, G. (1990). The political traditions of Eastern Europe, *Daedalus* 119(1): 55–90.

Schopflin, G. (1994). Postcommunism: The problems of democratic construction, *Daedalus* 123(3): 127–142.

Schopflin, G. & Wood, N. (eds.) (1989). *In search of Central Europe.* New York: Polity Press.

Schopflin, G. & Wood, N. (1989). Introduction, in G. Schopflin & N. Wood (eds.), *In search of Central Europe.* New York: Polity Press.

Seton-Watson, H. (1989). What is Europe, Where is Europe? From mystique to politique, in G. Schopflin & N. Wood (eds.), *In search of Central Europe.* New York: Polity Press.

Shaw, G.B. (1975). *Collected plays with their prefaces,* Vol. 1. New York: Dodd, Mead and Company.

Simecka, M. (1989). Which way back to Europe? (A reply to Mihaly Vajda), in G. Schopflin & N. Wood (eds.), *In search of Central Europe.* New York: Polity Press.

Skubiszewski, K. (1992). The challenge to Western policy of change in Eastern Europe. Unpublished manuscript/lecture. Oxford University, All Souls College.

Szucs, J. (1983). The three historical regions of Europe: An outline, in *Acta Historica Academiae Scientiarum Hungaricae* 29(2–4): 131–184.

Todorova, M. (1994a). Hierarchies of Eastern Europe: East Central Europe versus the Balkans. Unpublished manuscript/paper. Philadelphia, PA.

Todorova, M. (1994b). The Balkans: From discovery to invention, *Slavic Review* 53(2): 453–482.

Vajda, M. (1989). Who excluded Russia from Europe? (A reply to Simecka), in G. Schopflin & N. Wood (eds.), *In search of Central Europe.* New York: Polity Press.

Ware, T. (1983). *The Orthodox Church.* Middlesex, UK: Penguin Books.

West, R. (1969). *Black lamb and grey falcon.* New York: Penguin Books.

Yannaras, C. (1984). *The freedom morality.* Crestwood, NY: St. Vladimir's Seminary Press.

Yannaras, C. (1992). *Orthodoxia kai Dysi stin Neoteri Ellada* [Orthodoxy and the West in modern Greece]. Athens, Greece: Domos Publishing.

Zizioulas, J.D. (1985). *Being as communion: Studies in personhood and the church.* Crestwood, NY: St. Vladimir's Seminary Press.

Address for correspondence: Elizabeth Prodromou, Center of International Studies, Princeton University, Bendheim Hall, Princeton, NJ 08544–1022 USA
Phone: (609) 2582179; Fax: (609) 2583988

Name Index